HOME, SCHOOL, AND COMMUNITY RELATIONS

Join us on the web at

EarlyChildEd.delmar.com

HOME, SCHOOL, AND COMMUNITY

RELATIONS

SIXTH EDITION

Carol Gestwicki

THOMSON
—★—
DELMAR LEARNING

Australia   Canada   Mexico   Singapore   Spain   United Kingdom   United States

THOMSON

DELMAR LEARNING

Home, School, and Community Relations, Sixth Edition
Carol Gestwicki

Vice President, Career Education SBU Dawn Gerrain	**Director of Production** Wendy A. Troeger	**Director of Marketing** Wendy E. Mapstone
Director of Learning Solutions Sherry Dickinson	**Production Manager** J.P. Henkel	**Channel Manager** Kristin McNary
Managing Editor Robert L. Serenka, Jr.	**Production Editor** Rebecca Goldthwaite	**Marketing Assistant** Scott Chrysler
Acquisitions Editor Martine Edwards		**Cover & Text Design** TDB Publishing Services
Editorial Assistant Stephanie Kelly		

Library of Congress Cataloging-in-Publication Data

Gestwicki, Carol, 1940–
  Home, school, and community relations / Carol Gestwicki. — 6th ed.
      p. cm.
  Includes bibliographical references and index.
    ISBN-13: 978-1-4180-2974-6 (alk. paper)
    ISBN-10: 1-4180-2974-2 (alk. paper)
  1. Home and school—United States.
  2. Parent-teacher relationships—United States.   I. Title.
  LC225.3.G47 2006
  371.19'2—dc22
                                    2006011904

NOTICE TO THE READER

CONTENTS

SECTION I
Introduction to Families

"It's a note from my parents, my former parents, my step-grandmother, and my dad's live-in."

SECTION II
Teacher–Family Partnerships
in Early Education

SECTION III
Methods for Developing Partnerships

*"Excellent communication skills.
Poor choice of words."*

SECTION IV
Making a Partnership Work

FOREWORD

Once upon a time, not much more than a hundred years ago, the United States was predominantly a rural culture. A book purporting to be a "guide to working with families" would have been an anachronism. The farm family was then a self-contained economic and social unit, the heart of human groupings. With children numerous and desired, the family often included grandparents, sometimes uncles, aunts, and cousins. It was a communal center with parents at the hub, responsible for vocational training, education both religious and secular, discipline, and recreation.

Teachers were a rarity. Perhaps during a few short winter months one would be hired to teach a roomful of multi-aged children. She, or he, would make his or her home with one of the farm families. When spring and planting time came, school would be out. The relationship between parents and teachers was not a particular concern. Though the physical hardships of those days were considerable, a certain simplicity and security for children existed. Firm boundaries of existence and few choices for the individual led to a kind of tidiness in living. How-to volumes were extraneous.

Today the world, the family, and the community are topsy-turvy different. The changes that have occurred in a century are profound. The family has been turned inside-out: single-parent homes; step-children of second and even third marriages often blended together; women working outside the home; children bearing children; isolated urban nuclear families; urban life with its noise, crowded housing developments, traffic. All of this contrasts with the simplicity of the rural era. There is now a very definite need for guidelines to help us cope with this flux.

Child care is now less the responsibility of the parents and more that of the teacher, the professional child care provider, the after-school counselor, as ever-increasing numbers of young children and babies are being cared for outside the home. School-age children return to empty homes, and child care centers are facing the need for establishing "sick care" facilities. Though parents remain the most important persons in a child's life, it is certainly true that a child may easily spend most of his or her time with other adults.

The teacher today, or the student training to be a child care provider, is preparing for a profession quite unlike that of the rural one-room teacher. It is a complicated, ever-changing world out there for teachers and parents. Their relationship—the positioning of their several turfs, division of responsibility, defining the home ground upon which they both stand—provides a unique human relations challenge.

For this reason the appearance of a sixth edition of this book by Carol Gestwicki, *Home, School, and Community Relations*, is most welcome. It is a lively text (I have used previous editions in teaching a community college course, "Working with Parents") that argues effectively for the value and necessity of a partnership between parents and teachers. It is too often the easy way out for them to assume adversarial roles in this hurried age of pressured parents with too little time, and teachers in low-paying positions responsible for too many children.

This book makes clear that an adversarial relationship between families and teachers is not in the best interest of the children, the adults, or the community. The text is packed with creative suggestions for working cooperatively that will be satisfying to both teachers and families, as well as promoting the child's healthy development. Research has shown that a parent's level of involvement in a child's center or school is a major factor in a child's well-being. Though Ms. Gestwicki is aware of the hurdles that contemporary society places in the path of teachers, families, and children, her outlook maintains a positive stance; with determination and goodwill the confusions of this uncharted territory may be overcome.

This edition includes a section on the value of political awareness and child advocacy. The author discusses ways parents and teachers can combine forces to make a difference. In a country that appears less concerned about children and families than most other industrialized nations, this chapter is of signal importance.

In keeping with the current emphasis on discovery and age-appropriate learning for children, this book might be called a "hands on" text for teachers. In addition to the very specific descriptions of real schools with photographs of children, teachers, and families, the book includes a vivid assortment of case studies of families and teachers, juxtaposing a variety of lifestyles and attitudes, a rich view of our heterogeneous culture.

As a teacher, I know from experience that it is impossible to isolate "teaching" from families. We cannot—we must not—teach in a vacuum, but we must recognize, relate to, and attempt to understand the child's family. This book is a great help in doing that.

Sue Spayth Riley

NAEYC Ethics Commission
and author of
How to Generate Values in Young Children

PREFACE

It is not unusual in my classes for teachers and students preparing to become teachers to hear the statement, "I do just fine with the children; it's the parents who . . . (you could fill in the blank)

- Make me crazy.
- I can't stand.
- I could do without.
- Make me think about quitting."

As more families and teachers share the care of young children, it becomes obvious that disruptive tensions are more common than rare. Learning the skills of communicating effectively with parents about matters both routine and emotionally charged has become an important part of a teacher's preparation. In fact, the standards set by NAEYC for college programs that prepare early childhood teachers require that teachers become skillful in building family and community relationships.

In addition, attention is increasingly focused in our society today on the stress experienced by the contemporary family. Television specials and politicians have found it appropriate to speak out about the dilemmas of working parents, caught between choices of unaffordable or inadequate child care, and stretched between home and work responsibilities. Schools feel inadequate to the task of filling in the gaps in children's lives created by families under stress. Efforts are being made in both public and private sectors to offer some external support to alleviate family stresses, as the understanding dawns that family breakdown is responsible for many of the ills plaguing the community at large. Conversely, it may also be stated that the breakdown of the community, with escalating incidences of drug use, violence, unemployment, and economic hardships for families, may contribute to many of the ills that plague families. Teachers as part of the community must participate in the initiatives of family support that are becoming more numerous.

This sixth edition of the text continues to stress the specific attitudes, philosophies, and practical techniques that teachers in any setting can find useful in building relationships with families. The underlying philosophy of the book is that those relationships are crucial in providing appropriate experiences for children.

This book is intended for you—as a student, a new or experienced teacher, or any professional working with families of children in public and private schools and kindergartens, early childhood programs, family child care homes, and other settings. Someone suggested that this new edition should add specific materials for pre-K and elementary school teachers, as well as those working in out-of-school programs for children. Although examples and new materials have been added to clarify the applicability of the material, my response is that the principles of partnership and communication with families remain constant whether you are a teacher who is concerned about relationships with families of kindergarten students, fourth grade students, or toddlers in a child care setting. If you read an example in the book that seems relevant to younger (or older) children, ask yourself how the ideas would apply in your particular situation. Good professional communication practices are the same, even though the content may differ.

The philosophy and practical techniques discussed in this textbook are appropriate for use no matter where you work with children and their families. Examples of elementary and pre-K teachers added to this edition help make this clear, as well as information about the No Child Left Behind legislation that affects public schools and all families with children. Indeed, this important piece of legislation has far-reaching effects on every community and citizen.

■■■ ORGANIZATION AND CONTENT

Section I is designed to introduce students to the experience of parenting. Chapter 1 introduces the subject by taking a close look at what life is like for two families, reminding students of the need to prepare to work respectfully with families of diverse backgrounds and experiences and with unique needs. Chapter 2 considers families in our modern world and the factors that shape their lives. Chapter 3 describes the various roles of parents in bringing up children and creating families.

Section II explores the subject of teacher–parent partnerships in early education. Chapter 4 examines the various models and motivations for family involvement. Chapter 5 identifies benefits for children, parents, and teachers when parents and teachers work in partnership. Chapter 6 considers potential barriers to teacher–parent relationships. Chapter 7 describes the attitudes and conditions that create the foundations for successful partnerships.

Section III moves the student into a discussion of the various techniques that teachers can use to involve families in the educational process. Chapter 8 describes the orientation process for children and parents to begin the process of exchanging information and supporting one another during the separation experience. Chapter 9 introduces a number of informal communication methods, including newsletters, bulletin boards, and other personal methods. Chapter 10 outlines the planning and conducting of effective parent–teacher conferences. Chapter 11 discusses the process of making home visits to families, as well as the home-based education programs that exist nationwide. Chapter 12 focuses on including families in their children's classrooms in a variety of ways. Chapter 13 considers parent education. Chapter 14 describes ways that parents and teachers can collaborate to affect community policy and action on family and children's issues as we recognize the need to support families' efforts. It also discusses current legislation that affects families and schools.

Section IV moves to discussion of working with families with specific needs and issues. Chapter 15 examines ways to welcome and include all families, no matter how richly diverse their language, culture, race, religion, or family structure. Chapter 16 considers working with families in particular circumstances: Families experiencing separation and divorce, families with infants, families with children who have special needs, families who have experienced abuse and neglect, and adoptive families are discussed in particular. Chapter 17 identifies strategies for teachers who face particularly troublesome attitudes and situations. Chapter 18 describes several different early education programs that have found their own ways to involve and include parents.

Each chapter begins with clearly defined learning objectives. Specific examples and dialogues from teachers and parents, who may be quite like those encountered by students, make ideas and suggestions real, as in the previous editions. The exercises for students listed at chapter end and in the instructor's guide are designed to help students grapple actively with the concepts. Bibliographies of suggested readings can help students examine the issues further.

■■■■ NEW ADDITIONS

Included in this sixth edition is a strong focus on local and national community efforts and organizations to remind teachers that they have responsibilities to work with, and in support of, families beyond the walls of the schools or centers in which they work with young children. The federal No Child Left Behind legislation has implications for families and for teachers, as well as larger implications for schools and communities. This legislation and its significance to teacher–family concerns are addressed in Chapters 4 and 14. There is an expanded discussion of the many components that constitute parent involvement, as well as a look at the history of parent involvement in this country. Also expanded are lists of books to use with children related to particular family situations. Throughout the book students will encounter an extended understanding of the importance of working respectfully with families of very diverse backgrounds and beliefs. Included in this edition are descriptions of programs that work effectively to celebrate diversity and draw in diverse families.

Also presented are specific techniques teachers can use to be sure of conveying an attitude of welcoming acceptance to every family. Discussions of dealing with common problems that arise between teachers and parents, including the current issues of testing young children for "readiness" and changes in parenting concerns, have been expanded. Additional aspects of various models of parent education are included. Chapter 2 has been updated to include the latest demographic information about modern families. There are updates on current legislative and corporate initiatives focused on the family and its needs, and updated mandates from professional and community organizations that increasingly demand that teachers no longer focus on the child and avoid the parent. Updated references and suggestions for further reading will be helpful to students who wish to go beyond the text.

Working with families will always be one of the more challenging tasks for early educators. Students are encouraged to realize that this is not a separate role, but one that is integrated into the concept of working with the whole child—and one for which they need to prepare fully.

Several features have been incorporated in this sixth edition to further your understanding of fundamental concepts and their application in contemporary early education settings. These include the following.

Reflections for Journal Entries

This feature is intended to encourage you to consider your personal attitudes and experiences related to the concepts discussed in each chapter. Thought-provoking questions are included to promote your individual reflection and class discussion.

Case Studies

Case studies are included in each chapter to encourage the application of particular concepts to classroom practice and teacher experience. Questions may be used for individual thought and group discussion. In addition, most chapters include realistic scenarios of interaction and attitudes of teachers and parents.

Helpful Web Sites

This feature recognizes the important role that technology plays in today's world in expanding resources for learning. Web addresses included at the end of each chapter will allow readers to further explore topics and organizations discussed in the text.

NOTE: *The author and Delmar Learning affirm that the Web site URLs referenced in this book are accurate at the time of printing. However, due to the fluid nature of the Internet, we cannot guarantee their accuracy for the life of this edition.*

Online Companion

The Online Companion to accompany the sixth edition of *Home, School, and Community Relations: A Guide to Working with Families* provides supplemental material that applies the content presented in each chapter of the text. Special features of the Online Companion include frequently asked questions; chapter outlines to be used as study guides; scenarios that both encourage large and small group discussions and provoke new thoughts and ideas; and chapter resources, including chapter summaries, interactive questions, Web links, and Web activities. In addition, forms from the text are available for download.

Pedagogy

Pedagogy is designed to facilitate student mastery:

1. Key words and terms are listed alphabetically at the beginning of each chapter, are printed in **bold type** where they first appear in the chapter, and are defined in the margins and again in the glossary at the back of the book. Reinforcement and cross-referencing enhance comprehension.

2. Objectives appear at the beginning of each chapter to help you focus on key concepts within the chapter.

3. Bulleted lists alert you to specific examples.

4. Real-life photographs taken at various centers and schools illustrate aspects of working with children and families.

5. Boxes illustrate and highlight important concepts.

6. A summary concludes each chapter and is followed by
   - Student activities for further study, which may be used for in-class or out-of-class assignments.
   - A case study.
   - Review questions.
   - Suggestions for further reading.
   - References.
   - Helpful Web sites.

7. An appendix includes additional information about organizations and agencies discussed throughout the book.

8. A comprehensive glossary and index conclude the text with reader-friendly cross-references.

Ancillaries

Instructor's Manual

The Instructor's Manual includes discussion topics and suggestions for classroom presentation and activities, ideas for assignments, multimedia resources, answers to chapter-end questions, and a test bank.

Computerized Test Bank

The computerized test bank contains multiple-choice, true/false, short answer, essay, and completion questions for each chapter. Course instructors can use the computerized test bank software to create sample quizzes for students. Refer to the CTB User's Guide for more information about how to create and post quizzes to your school's Internet or intranet server. Students may also access sample quizzes in the Online Companion at www.earlychilded. delmar.com.

Web Tutor

The Web Tutor to accompany *Home, School, and Community Relations*, Sixth Edition, allows you to take learning beyond the classroom. This online course-ware is designed to complement the text and benefits students by enabling them to better manage their time, prepare for exams, organize their notes, and more.

Special features include chapter learning objectives, online course preparation, study sheets, glossary, discussion topics, frequently asked questions, online class notes, online chapter quizzes, and Web links related to chapter content. Printing features allow students to print their own customized study guides.

A benefit for instructors as well as students, the Web Tutor allows online discussion with the instructor and other class members, real-time chat to enable virtual office hours and encourage collaborative learning environments, a calendar of syllabus information for easy reference, e-mail connections to facilitate communication among classmates and between students and instructors, and customization tools that help educators tailor their courses to fit their needs by adding or changing content. The Web Tutor allows you to extend your reach beyond the classroom and is available on either the WebCT or Blackboard platform.

Professional Enhancement Text

A new supplement to accompany this text is the *Home, School, and Community Relations* booklet for students. This resource, which is part of the Thomson Delmar Learning's Early Childhood Education Professional Enhancement series, focuses on key topics of interest to future early childhood directors, teachers, and caregivers. Students may keep this informational supplement and use it for years to come in their early childhood education practices.

ABOUT THE AUTHOR

Carol Gestwicki was an instructor in the early childhood education program at Central Piedmont Community College in Charlotte, North Carolina, for over 30 years. Her teaching responsibilities have included supervising students in classroom situations as they work with families. Earlier in her career she worked with children and families in a variety of community agencies and schools in Toronto, New York, New Jersey, and Namibia (South West Africa).

She received her M.A. from Drew University. She has been an active member of NAEYC for many years, including making numerous presentations at state and national conferences. She has been a Fellow in the Early Childhood Leadership Development Project at the University of North Carolina at Chapel Hill, and she has been associated with the T.E.A.C.H. Model/Mentor program.

Her other publications include more than two dozen articles about child development and family issues, and scripts and design for 14 audiovisual instructional programs. The author has three other books on topics in early education published by Delmar Learning: *Developmentally Appropriate Practice: Curriculum and Development in Early Education,* Third Edition (2006); *Essentials of Early Education* (1997); and *Authentic Childhood: Exploring Reggio Emilia in the Classroom* (2002). Currently she writes a regular column for *Growing Child* and is an early childhood consultant with Teaching Strategies, Inc.

ACKNOWLEDGMENTS

Students and colleagues in Charlotte and throughout North Carolina have been enormously helpful in the continuing discussion of working to support children and their families. I would especially like to mention members of the North Carolina Community College Childhood Educators, who shared with me their own feedback and that of their students; and Sue Riley, who has been an inspiration in her classroom interaction with children and their families, as well as adult students. I am grateful to Barbara Pimento of George Brown College in Toronto, Ontario, for her insightful comments and helpful materials about the Canadian perspective. I am especially grateful to Connie Glass and Becky Landrum, fine teachers who also take great photos and were generous in allowing me to use them, Thanks also to Mike Meyers of CPCC, who found resources to pay for the use of a cartoon. I am grateful to the directors and staff of Lakewood Preschool Cooperative, Gorham House Preschool, Family Resource Center, and the Lincoln Nursery School. I am also grateful to Sean, my computer guru at Computer Discovery in Norway, Maine, who saved me many times while I was working on this manuscript.

I appreciate the helpful comments of the reviewers:

Alice D. Beyrent, M.Ed.
Hesser College, NH

Jill M. Boeck, M.Ed.
Villa Maria College, NY

Sylvia J. Brooks, Ed.D.
University of Delaware, DE

J. Christine Catalani, M.Ed.
San Antonio College, TX

Susan Davies, M.S.
Ivy Tech Community College, IN

Dede Dunst, M.Ed.
Mitchell Community College, NC

Regina Fontana, Ed.S.
Seminole Community College, FL

Jennifer M. Johnson, M.Ed.
Vance–Granville Community College, NC

Leanna Manna, M.A.
Villa Maria College, NY

Linda Hall Richey, Ph.D.
Middle Tennessee State University, TN

Jeanne Thomas, M.A.
West Valley College, CA

Lyn Tysdal, M.A.
Tysdal and Associates, SD

And as always, I appreciate the support of my husband, sons, and their families, who continue to teach me the importance and complexity of family.

"It's a note from my parents, my former parents, my step-grandmother, and my dad's live-in."

SECTION I
INTRODUCTION TO FAMILIES

Unless you have already experienced parenthood, it may be difficult for you to appreciate fully the enormity of the emotions and roles that parents experience and that affect their ability to function as parents. Even if you are a parent, the diverse cultures, communities, and circumstances that influence families in modern America make individual lives unique; one parenting experience and one family will be quite unlike another.

Effective teachers work to understand empathetically the lives of the families with whom they work. This first section will further this understanding. Chapter 1 begins with stories of two families, encouraging teachers to understand families' lives with empathy. Chapter 2 examines the social circumstances that affect modern families. Chapter 3 looks at the phenomenon of parenting itself, considering the separate roles of a parent and common emotional responses.

CHAPTER 1

A Day with Two Families: Diversity of Experience

OBJECTIVES

After reading this chapter, you should be able to

1. List several external factors causing stress in the families portrayed.
2. List several emotional responses evidenced in the parents portrayed.
3. Identify types of diversity that may be found in typical communities.
4. Understand that teachers have an obligation to understand family life and how family life impacts teaching.

The most important beginning place for teachers learning how to work effectively with families is to become sensitive to the needs and pressures of every family. This requires an authentic appreciation of the strengths and problems inherent in each situation. The experiences and families teachers encounter may be difficult to understand or even accept. Teachers are unlikely to find another family that exactly duplicates the families with which they are most familiar, in which they grew up. Families are created by the ideas, emotions, and experiences of unique individuals. Their living places, their foods and family traditions, and their styles of communicating and living together are familiar and comfortable to those within the family and to no one else. Even families who share the same cultural, linguistic, or religious traditions will not be alike because of the unique inner and outer views of the individuals involved. And in contemporary society, with the myriad cultures and lifestyles that live side by side, interacting within the same schools, workplaces, and communities, it is vital that this assumption and celebration of uniqueness be made explicit.

The differences in families create divisions with teachers when those differences are seen as frightening, threatening, and mysterious. When they are seen as interesting and enriching to society in general and to the lives they touch in particular, differences are to be valued. When individuals come together to form relationships and communicate in the spirit of openness that is vital for effective family–teacher partnerships, a first step is to attempt to understand the other and to convey an attitude of respect and acceptance. Both understanding and acceptance are products of knowledge. In this chapter an examination of the hypothetical lives of two of the fictitious families we will meet throughout the book may help to heighten awareness of the demands and stresses in the lives of families and of the individuality of each family's life. The more sensitivity that teachers can develop to the complex lives of different families, the more likely they can approach them with true empathy.

As a teacher working daily with children, it is important always to be mindful of the importance of the family from which they come. Families are unique in the circumstances of their lives, but they are related by the common roles and experiences of parenthood. No one who is just an onlooker to the living drama of any family can come close to appreciating the thousands of details, interactions, and emotional nuances that compose a family's experience. Researchers (or teachers) frequently do not have the opportunity to record the actions of family members as they live their daily lives, but it is probably only through such methods that the individual threads of the family fabric can be perceived and appreciated. Children and their families may face enormous individual and social pressures, which may not be perceived or understood by teachers. This is why teachers must become as familiar as possible with the story of each family. This has nothing to do with being intrusive; rather, it helps a teacher become as professionally helpful as possible. Appreciating the contribution of each family is a good starting place to consider how to build effective partnerships with them. Here is a closer look at two of our fictitious families as they move through a day.

THE LAWRENCE FAMILY

When the alarm went off at 6 a.m., no one moved. Fannie stayed quite still, hoping Otis would remember it was his morning to get the children up and start the dressing and breakfast process. She felt so tired, she couldn't get up yet anyway, she told herself, stifling the guilty reminder that it was 11 the night before when Otis got home from his class, and he must be pretty tired too. But this past month she'd seemed to be completely exhausted at the start of each day. She wondered how she would get through the next three months and thought again that it might be a mistake to work right up until the birth, but that was the only way she could get three months off afterward. In her head she reviewed the whole decision, but there appeared to be no other way out. Their income looked fine on paper, but when you subtracted the $950 a month that Otis sent for the boys—and it would soon be more now that Danny had to get braces—there just wasn't any extra for her to take additional unpaid leave.

She groaned, but Otis still didn't move. In a burst of exasperation she maneuvered out of bed and banged the bathroom door louder than was necessary. Otis stretched and turned over, feeling guilty about Fannie, but also telling himself he needed the extra rest after the late night at class and the late night he would have tonight at work. He'd get up in just a few minutes and help Fannie get the kids ready.

Fannie laid out breakfast things and went back up to wake the children. Pete was tired and hard to get moving, so she practically had to dress him; and Kim was impatient to get her hair done. By the time they were eating breakfast, Fannie looked at the clock and realized she'd have to skip hers and dress quickly, or she'd be late again. In the still-darkened bedroom she fumbled for clothes and shoes, then went into the bathroom to shower quickly and dress.

She returned to the kitchen to find the TV blaring and the table a mess of cereal and milk. "Kim, when I leave you in charge, I don't expect you to let Pete watch TV. Just look at this mess. Turn that off and at least put the milk in the fridge and get your teeth brushed, and Petey, see if you can't tie your shoes to help Mama out today."

Kim said, "Mama, I want a lunch packed. It's that dumb fried chicken for lunch at school today, and I hate it."

"Kim! I told you before, I have to fix lunches at night. I don't have the time. We've got to leave right now, so don't start that." Kim's lip trembled, and Fannie turned away abruptly. She did not have time for one of Kim's scenes now; besides, she was getting pretty sick of them, as often as Kim was doing this. Last night she'd spent an hour whining that she didn't have any friends in her class and she hated Miss Johnston. This wasn't like Kim, Fannie thought distractedly. She'd always been a happy child.

Otis appeared in the kitchen just in time to see Kim burst into tears. "Hey, what's the matter here?" he asked cheerily. Fannie glared at him, as Kim sobbed that Mama wouldn't make her a lunch and she couldn't eat the lunch at school. "Oh won't she—" Otis began teasingly, but Fannie snapped quickly, "Just be quiet, Otis, I haven't had one second this morning. I haven't even had time for breakfast, so if she wants a lunch, you'd have to make it, but we have to leave right now!"

Otis handed some change to Kim and said, "Well, at least you can eat some ice cream, OK? Now leave your Mama alone." He patted Fannie's shoulder apologetically. "Slow down, babe. You'll make it. You shouldn't be skipping breakfast. Have a good day. Come on, Petey, hurry up, your Mom's in a hurry. Don't forget I work late tonight, Fannie. See you by 10. Try to be awake," he joked, patting her again.

"Fat chance," muttered Fannie and hustled the children to the car, Kim still sniffling loudly. As she drove along, Fannie thought to herself that sometimes she wondered why they'd gotten married. With work and the college classes Otis was never home in the evenings. Instantly she stifled the thought and wished she'd at least given him a hug. He did work hard, and goodness knows this was a good marriage, better than the too-young one with Kim and Pete's father that had left her a single mother for two years before she had met Otis, also recently divorced.

She dropped Kim off at her school with a determined smile. Kim walked off sullenly, and Fannie tried not to mind. She noticed that there was no one else entering the door along with Kim. It was early, she knew, but she had to drop Kim off, then Pete, and still arrive at her own school by 7:45 a.m. She just wouldn't have felt right leaving Kim to wait for the bus, but this was one of the things Kim complained about—all the other kids got to ride the bus. She made a mental note to try to see Kim's teacher soon and ask her whether Kim was justified in saying she had no friends. Perhaps she could arrange for a girl to come with Kim after school—on a day when her own schedule allowed Kim to skip going to after-school child care. Anyway, she'd have to ask Miss Johnston if Kim being dropped off early created a problem; she was a little afraid to do that because the teacher was a young, single woman who probably wouldn't understand hectic morning schedules. Heaven knows it would be worse next year because Pete's school did not offer care for infants; that would mean three stops before 7:45 a.m. She'd been tempted to move Pete to another school, but decided he'd already had a lot of changes to adjust to in his young life, and the baby would be yet another one. Better she should be inconvenienced and leave him in the school where he was already comfortable. She sighed and then realized they were at Pete's school. Thank goodness he'd been quiet, unusual for him.

"Oh, no," she whispered as they passed the classroom bulletin board with its reminder that the school needed toothpaste. "I forgot again." Fannie helped Pete take off his jacket and smiled toward a teacher who approached her.

"Oh, Mrs. Lawrence, I see Pete's got one of his cars again. We really can't let the children bring their own toys; it creates such problems. Please take it with you."

Confused, Fannie looked down and realized Pete was clutching a tiny car in his hand. She started to explain to the teacher that she hadn't realized he'd brought it and fell silent as she realized that made her sound like a pretty careless mother. Pete grabbed his hand away, and Fannie looked for help from the teacher, who looked away. Fannie realized she would have to take the car away. She thought a nasty thought about the teacher and pried the car out of Pete's fingers. Pete burst into tears, and Fannie's stomach tightened. She gave him a quick hug and muttered a few words in his ear, looked appealingly at the teacher—who now seemed even more annoyed—and quickly dashed down the hall. She felt like crying herself as she listened to

Pete's wails and thought about what a horrible morning it had been for all of them. She was so preoccupied with thinking about the kids' reactions and making resolutions for a tranquil evening that she walked right past another parent, who called hello after her. Sheepishly she waved back and then hurried on, her face hot with embarrassment.

The trip to her own school was punctuated by stoplights and blocked lanes, and she found herself almost running from her parked car, aware that several busloads of children had already arrived.

The day went fairly smoothly for Fannie, although with 28 third graders to look after, plus her turn at playground duty, she was very tired by the time the final bell rang. A parent who came to pick up her child wanted to talk about the new reading program, but Fannie had to cut her off to get to the weekly faculty meeting on time. As she hurried down the hall, she reminded herself to make an appointment with Kim's teacher so she wouldn't start off by annoying the teacher. The faculty meeting dragged on, and Fannie found herself glancing repeatedly at her watch, estimating how long it would take to pick up Kim and get her to her dancing class.

At last the meeting ended, and she rushed out to her car, noticing with longing the group of young women who stayed back, chatting and planning to go out for a drink.

Her heart lifted when she saw Kim playing happily with another girl at the after-school child care where the bus dropped her each afternoon. The college student in charge of the group apologized for not having remembered that it was Kim's dancing class day and having her already changed. Fannie swallowed her irritation, but it became more difficult to control as Kim dawdled with her friend to the point where Fannie had to brusquely order her to leave and hurry up and change. Kim began to whine, but she stopped when she saw the look on her mother's face.

Fannie tried to relax and make pleasant conversation about Kim's day as they drove to the dancing class. Kim chattered happily about her new friend at child care and asked if she could come to their house to play one afternoon. Fannie promised, thinking uneasily of the logistics problems of rides and permission that might entail. She dropped Kim at the door, promising to try to be back in time to watch the last few minutes of the class. Checking her watch, she tried to organize her errands to fit them into the hour time slot—drop off the dry cleaning, cash a check at the bank, pick up a few groceries, and get to the post office for stamps before it closed. That would cut it pretty close for picking up Pete, and she hated his day to be so long, but she knew from experience it was worse to drag a tired child with her. Trying to ignore her own fatigue, she hurried on.

Pete looked up hopefully as she walked into his room at the child care center, and she realized with a pang he'd probably been doing that as each parent entered the room for the previous half hour. His teacher said he'd had a good day after the upsetting beginning. Fannie was annoyed that she'd brought that up again. She just wished this young woman could understand that it was bad enough having to rush Pete in the morning, let alone strip him of all his favorite things for the day.

There was an accident holding up traffic on the road back to the dancing studio, and by the time they got there Kim was waiting in the parking lot with the dancing teacher, who looked in a hurry to leave. Kim's face was stormy as she accused Fannie, "You promised." Fannie tried to explain but felt both helpless and angry before the 8-year-old's indignation. Impulsively, changing the mood and giving in to her own fatigue, she suggested supper at McDonald's.

Amidst the kids' squeals of glee, she thought glumly about the nutritional consequences and decided she wouldn't ask them what they'd eaten for lunch. Some mother, she thought, conjuring up an image of her own mother's plentiful dinner table. And what's more, there'd be nothing to keep warm for Otis. Well, maybe she would fix him a nice omelet if he wasn't too late.

The kids were cheerful and chatty over hamburgers, so Fannie relaxed and enjoyed their stories. "We're doing OK," she told herself. "They're really fine."

It was after 7 when they got home. Fannie put Pete in the bathtub and started Kim on her reading homework in the bathroom to watch him so Fannie could unpack the groceries and put a load of laundry in. At least Otis had had the time to clean up the breakfast mess; that was more than she could have stood, 12 hours later!

She read Pete a bedtime story and then tucked him in. He was tired and settled in quickly. Fannie looked back at him tenderly. He was growing so quickly; pretty soon he wouldn't be the baby anymore. For the thousandth time she wondered how he'd feel when the new baby arrived.

Kim wanted to watch some television, but Fannie reminded her to first find her clothes for the morning and decide if she wanted a lunch, which she did. Making the sandwiches, Fannie thought, "Maybe tomorrow will be a better day." At bedtime Kim asked her to be sure to give Daddy a kiss for her. Fannie wished again that Otis could be home more at night, so they could feel like a real family. She knew what Otis would say if she brought it up again. "The classes are important if I'm ever going to be able to stop selling cars at night. It's only a couple more years. And in the meantime selling cars is giving us a good living." He was right, of course, but the kids practically never saw him. For that matter, it was tough on all of them.

Fannie folded the laundry, washed her hair, spread out her clothes for the morning, and lay down on the bed to read the morning paper. Within 10 minutes she had fallen asleep. When Otis came in at 10:00 p.m., she was still asleep. He sighed, turned out the light, and went to see if there were any leftovers in the kitchen.

THE ASHLEY FAMILY

Sylvia Ashley got up quickly when the alarm went off at 6:00 a.m. She had washed out Terrence's shirt the night before and wanted to iron it before it was time for him to get up. Anyway, she liked having time in the early morning, when the building was still quiet. The rest of the day there was hardly a moment when someone wasn't yelling or throwing something. She turned on the kitchen light cautiously, knowing the roaches would scurry away from the sink.

She ironed carefully. She felt bad that Terrence had to wear the same clothes over and over, but at least he was always clean and tidy. She hoped the teacher would notice that and not treat him badly. The way some people treated people without money—she hated it for herself, and she didn't want her kids to grow up thinking they weren't as good as everyone else just because they lived in subsidized housing and were in a single-parent family.

She sighed, remembering she had to go back to the social services office today to talk to the social worker. She dreaded that, but because their check had been reduced two months before, she simply hadn't been able to make it on the lower amount. Last week she had to borrow three dollars from her neighbor across the hall to get some macaroni and milk for the kids' supper, and she knew she couldn't do that again—the woman barely spoke to her anyway. Because she was entering that job training program she knew she'd have to get herself a new pair of shoes. Ricky's sneakers had a hole right through the toe, too.

She unplugged the iron and glanced at the clock. Time to get the boys up. They were cheerful and chattered away, Terrence helping Ricky get dressed. Ricky ate a bowl of cereal; Terrence drank a glass of milk to have something in his stomach until he got to school. He preferred to have breakfast at home, and she'd always let him until things got so tight. Because he was eligible for the free breakfast at school, it made a little place she could save.

She dressed quickly and then cleaned up the kitchen. Terrence was ready at the door, hair neatly combed, when she got there. He grumbled a bit every day about his mother and little brother having to go with him to school, but she didn't like the idea of him walking alone six blocks through this neighborhood.

Ricky struggled to keep up. They waved to Terrence from the street as he climbed the school stairs by himself. Sylvia worried about him—he never mentioned a friend, and after school she and Ricky walked him home, and then he played with Ricky. She knew he needed friends his own age, but she kept him in the apartment unless she could go to the playground with them. She'd seen and heard plenty of fights and wildness from some of the kids in their building, and she knew some of them were already in trouble with the police. She was going to keep her boys free of that. Terrence was a good student, a smart boy—he would grow up differently than those other kids.

She and Ricky waited at the bus stop for the bus that would take them downtown to the square where they could transfer to the one that would take them out to the social services building. She barely heard Ricky talking away and pointing out cars and asking questions as they rode along and as she rehearsed what she had to say.

The waiting room was full; she found one chair and held Ricky on her lap for a while until he got wiggly. Then she let him sit on the floor beside her. She kept listening for the woman to call her name, knowing that Ricky was getting restless. He asked her for something to eat as he watched a man eating crackers he'd bought from the vending machine. Sylvia didn't want to waste 50 cents on that and wished she'd remembered to bring something for him. Fortunately they called her name just then, and Ricky was distracted by moving into the small office.

At least this social worker was better than the last one, who'd positively glared every time Ricky moved. Sylvia had been furious underneath—this woman had to know there was no money for baby-sitters and that nobody could help them out, but it wouldn't have done to let that anger show.

By the end of the discussion, Sylvia felt very depressed. She hated the questions about whether she'd heard from either of the boys' fathers; she always wanted to say she was thankful she hadn't and wouldn't take a penny from either of them anyway. Now that she was going into the job training program, Ricky's child care would be paid for until after she was working full-time.

Sylvia worried about whether her wages would be enough to support all of them when she was no longer receiving assistance and whether the children's medical expenses would be covered, but she understood the changes in the welfare system and was hopeful about what her work could mean for her small family.

Then maybe she'd be able to make enough to get them into a little apartment somewhere nicer, and she'd have some friends from work, and Terrence could have friends to play with, and things would be better. She had to do it. Her kids deserved more.

Ricky was tired and cranky as they waited for the bus home. He started to cry, and she shook him a little—not very hard, but she just couldn't stand to listen to it right now or have the bus driver stare at her when she got on with a crying child.

He fell asleep on the bus and she pulled him against her shoulder, knowing he'd wake up when they had to transfer. Poor thing, it had been a long morning for him. Neither of them said much as they rode the last bus and walked home for lunch. Ricky finished his soup, and she put him in bed for a nap. She sat thinking about Ricky starting in child care and about herself starting in the training program. She hoped she could do it. It had been a long time since she'd been in school, and then she didn't have kids and everything else to worry about. She worried about how it would be for Ricky; he'd never been away from her at all. The social worker had told her that the school was a good one, but that didn't reassure her that Ricky would not get upset.

She glanced at the clock; in a few more minutes she'd have to wake up Ricky to go get Terrence. The poor thing was so worn out she'd like to let him sleep, but there was nobody to ask to stay with him. She worried briefly about Terrence, who would have to come home and be by himself for a couple of hours until she finished her class, picked up Ricky, and arrived home. She'd already lost sleep worrying about that, but there was nothing else to be done. She'd warn him about answering the door, not using the stove, and everything else she could think of, and then just hope he'd stay in the apartment, safely, by himself.

Terrence was quiet coming home. In the apartment he unfolded a note and handed it to her. It was a reminder that parents needed to send two dollars the next day to pay for a ticket to a play at the children's theater next week. Sylvia avoided Terrence's eyes as she said that she couldn't send the money, so he could stay home from school the day of the play. Terrence said nothing.

She gathered the laundry and her wallet and keys, then took the boys with her down to the basement laundry room. The children sat arguing. When another woman came in, Sylvia snapped at the kids to be quiet, and they sat glumly until she asked Terrence to help her match the socks. Back upstairs, the boys watched cartoons while she made hamburgers for supper. After supper Terrence did his homework at the kitchen table, and Ricky sat beside him and colored in a coloring book. She put them in the bath together while she tidied the kitchen. After the children watched some more TV, she put them in bed and sat by herself in the living room, on the couch where she'd sleep. There was nothing she wanted to see on TV, but she left it on to keep her company. After an hour or so, she turned out the light and went to sleep.

■■ ■ IMPLICATIONS FOR TEACHERS

It is a good idea to try to comprehend the lives of the families with whom you will work. Perhaps this has been a useful consciousness-raising exercise for you. It is often too easy for teachers to be critical of parents who pick up their children late, forget the rules about bringing toys from home or signing reading records, or seem unwilling to cooperate with field trip plans. Seeing only one perspective is a common problem that disrupts relationships and communication.

When looked at more closely, both of these families have unique living circumstances and experiences, but in both there is a common thread of stress with the various roles and responsibilities, the isolation that comes from concentrating on children's care, and the deeply felt concerns for the children's lives. They are alike in that, as with every other family you will encounter, they have both strengths and needs.

You, the teacher, may or may not be a parent. If you are, then you have had daily experiences from a parent's perspective and do not need further convincing of the astonishing task of blending and fulfilling these various roles. Separately and on the printed page, they appear demanding; when experienced together in the context of daily life, they can be staggering. But even so, it is not unusual for teachers to use their own experiences as a standard against which to measure all other families: "If I could do it as a single parent, why can't she do a better job?" This is dangerous because each individual is unique.

For those of you who are not parents, recollections of your parents' lives during your childhood may be faint and will not do justice to the enormity of life's demands. Even acquaintance with the parents of children in your classroom probably does not fully expose you to the extent of the demands on them. An active imagination will help you best here. On a sheet of paper, jot down any facts you know of several families' lives—the family members' ages, jobs or schools, hobbies and interests, and special family circumstances.

Now mentally take yourself through a sample of their days—and nights. (Parenting does not have a neatly prescribed limit on working hours!) Remember to include the details of daily life such as doctors' visits, haircuts, and trips to the library and bank, as well as the unforeseen emergencies that pop up—the car breaking down, the baby-sitter getting sick, the additional assignment at work.

Choose a cross section of families to contemplate; remember that the socioeconomic circumstances of any family may add additional strains, whether they are the daily struggles of a poverty-level family or the demands on an upwardly mobile professional family. If you're doing this right, you will likely soon be shaking your head and growing tired in your imagination.

This might be a useful exercise to repeat whenever you find yourself making judgments or complaining about families. It is virtually impossible for a teacher to work effectively with classroom families until she is able to empathize with them. Remember, this is only an attempt to mentally understand possible situations; no outsider can fully appreciate what really goes on in any one family. Every family truly stands alone in its uniqueness.

◼◼◼ DIVERSITY

In recent years teachers have been urged to ensure that the children in their classrooms are supported in developing multicultural understanding and appreciation of the many differences and similarities that exist among people. Indeed, developmentally appropriate practice depends in part on teachers' responsiveness to their "knowledge of the social and cultural contexts in which children live to ensure that learning experiences are meaningful, relevant, and respectful for the participating children and their families" (NAEYC, in Bredekamp & Copple, 1997). Culturally responsive teachers create an environment where children feel comfortable in exploring the differences that occur naturally among themselves and their families, or among families to whom they may be introduced through stories, pictures, dolls, or classroom visitors. A crucial element in such an environment is a teacher who has taken the time to identify personal biases and has the courage to go beyond bias to reach for real understanding and appreciation of differences. Biases are mostly the result of fear, ignorance, and misinformation. It is vital that teachers make the effort to become comfortable and informed about the kinds of life experiences, values, and behaviors of diverse cultural groups and develop nonjudgmental dispositions toward working with the **diversity** of individual families.

Culture is a comprehensive term that includes the various understandings, traditions, and guidance of the groups to which we all belong. "Culture influences both behavior and the psychological processes on which it rests. Culture forms the prism through which members of a group see the world and create shared meanings" (Bowman in Burgess, 1993). This includes the cultures of family; ethnic, linguistic, and racial groups; religious groups; gender and sex role identifications; and geographical and community orientations.

In Chapter 15 we will explore in more detail ways that teachers can incorporate classroom practices that indicate the welcoming of each unique family and the valuing of the contributions their culture can make for rich classroom experiences and positive dialogue. Welcoming each family lays the groundwork for the development of positive identity formation and self-esteem for children and for respectful communication with their parents. But in the context of this chapter's appreciation of unique family orientations, it is important that teachers see they must take the initiative in attempting to understand the cultural backgrounds and circumstances of the families with whom they work (see Figure 1-1). The information to do this may come from published accounts written by members of particular cultural backgrounds.

Published accounts, as in the case of imaginary accounts of the daily lives of families found in this chapter, may be less than perfect sources of understanding. But they can certainly heighten teacher awareness of cultural patterns of behavior and communication styles that might otherwise be misinterpreted or even offensive.

FIGURE 1-1 Teachers must go beyond their own cultural experiences to try to understand the backgrounds and circumstances of all families with whom they work.

Teachers preparing to work with the diverse cultures represented in America or Canada today should become familiar with literature about working with at least the following cultural groups: African American, Native American or indigenous people, various Hispanic cultures, various Asian cultures, new immigrant families, interracial and biracial families, gay and lesbian families, and inner-city, homeless, single-parent, teenaged, and migrant families. In addition, the populations of particular schools or centers may reflect unique characteristics related to their geography, parents' occupations, or class composition. Such reading will at least begin to open the doors of understanding that will increase within relationships with members of the particular cultures; each family will still have its own specific interpretation of its own culture. The extensive list of resources in the Suggestions for Further Reading section should be a helpful starting place. Teachers are also cautioned that learning about other cultures is not for the purpose of further separating groups into subjects to be studied, but to bring people closer together through increased understanding and respect. As Janet Gonzalez-Mena warns in *Multicultural Issues in Child Care* (2000), "cultural labels are necessarily generalizations." Teachers must always remember that the best source of information about any individual family comes from the relationship with the family itself. And only as families perceive a genuine spirit of welcome and acceptance conveyed by a teacher will they become willing to share information about themselves.

REFLECTIONS FOR JOURNAL ENTRIES

How would you rate the experiences you have had so far in your life in experiencing the diversity that exists in America? Have you been fairly removed from individuals with different experiences, or have you had some encounters?

If you have been removed, reflect on the circumstances that have created this isolation. If you have encountered diverse lifestyles and values, what was your response? What does this imply about what you will have to concentrate on in your professional development?

SUMMARY

No one can truly understand all the emotional implications of parenthood: Each parent has a particular set of needs, experiences, and motivations. Nevertheless, it is important to realize the potential strains of daily life that come with family life so that teachers do not unwittingly ignore or exacerbate strong emotional responses or add to family stress. Understanding something of the framework within which members of various cultural groups operate is important for teachers as a beginning place to appreciating the family's unique perspective. As teachers learn about the families of the children in their classrooms and their own responses to them, they have begun the process of respect and acceptance that will lay the foundation for successful communication and partnerships.

STUDENT ACTIVITIES FOR FURTHER STUDY

1. Consider a family you know. Create an imaginary day in their life, similar to the stories you just read. Work with a partner, brainstorming to stimulate your thinking. Share your account with the class.

2. Invite a parent of a young child to join your class discussion. Ask him or her to come prepared to present a sample diary of the family's daily life.

3. Read an account of a family or cultural group that might increase your understanding of various cultures or segments of society. For ideas, refer to the Suggestions for Further Reading. Then small groups of students could create a day in the life of a particular family, such as a newly immigrated Asian family, a Latino family, a family with two mothers, and so forth.

4. Read the children's book *On the Day I Was Born* by Debbi Chocolate (Scholastic Press, 1995). Discuss with your classmates the specific ways that your family celebrates the birth of a new baby. How do the celebrations you hear about differ from the customs in the book? How are the family's emotional responses like the emotional responses you hear described by your classmates? Write a brief summary of the differences and similarities among various family experiences.

5. With your classmates, generate a list of questions that would help you conduct a respectful interview with a person from another cultural or religious background. For example, you might want to formulate some questions that ask about family customs and holidays; religious observances; the roles played by family members; how discipline was approached within the family; and so on. Conduct the interview and then share some of your learning with your classmates. You may find the person to interview among your classmates, among the faculty at your college, in your neighborhood, or in one of your community institutions.

CASE STUDY

This chapter is about the case studies of two families. Now that you have finished reading the case studies, consider these questions to further your understanding:

1. Identify the distinct emotions felt by Fannie Lawrence. What situations caused these emotions?

2. Identify the distinct emotions felt by Sylvia Ashley. What situations caused these emotions?

3. Identify some sources of stress for the children in the Lawrence family.

   Identify some sources of stress for the children in the Ashley family. What effect did the children's stress have on the parents?

4. In addition to the stress felt by the children, what are some other causes of stress for each mother?

1. List several external factors causing stress in the families portrayed.

2. List several emotional responses evidenced in the parents portrayed.

3. Describe why it is important for teachers to understand family life.

SUGGESTIONS FOR FURTHER READING

A selected annotated bibliography on black families. Washington, DC: U.S. Government Printing Office, Publ. no. 78-30140.

Barrera, R. M. (1993, March). Retrato de my familia: A portrait of my Hispanic family. *Child Care Information Exchange,* 31–34.

Bernard, J., Lefebvre, M., Chud, G., & Lange, R. (1995). *Paths to equity: Cultural, linguistic, and racial diversity in Canadian early childhood education.* Toronto: York Lanes.

Bowman, B. (1994). The challenge of diversity. *Phi Delta Kappan, 76* (3), 218–225.

Buirski, N. (1994). *Earth angels: Migrant children in America.* San Francisco: Pomegranate Books.

Chavez, L. (1991). *Out of the barrio: Toward a new politics of Hispanic assimilation.* New York: Basic.

Chavkin, N. F. (Ed.). (1993). *Families and schools in a pluralistic society* [most minority groups]. Albany, NY: State University of New York Press.

Clay, J. W. (1990). Working with lesbian and gay parents and their children. *Young Children, 45*(3), 31–35.

Corbett, S. (1993). A complicated bias [gay and lesbian families]. *Young Children, 48*(3), 29–31.

DeJong, L. (2003). Using Erikson to work more effectively with teenage parents. *Young Children, 58*(2), 87–95.

de Leon Stantz, M. (1996). Profile of the Hispanic child. In S. Torres (Ed.), *Hispanic voices: Hispanic health educators speak out.* New York: NLN Press.

Deparle, J. (2004). *American dream: Three women, ten kids, and a nation's drive to end welfare.* New York: Viking Books.

Diaz Soto, L. (1997). *Language, culture, and power.* Albany, NY: State University of New York Press.

Duarte, G., & Rafanello, D. (2001). The migrant child: A special place in the field. *Young Children, 56*(2), 26–34.

Ehrenreich, B. (2002). *Nickled and dimed: On (not) getting by in America.* New York: Owl Books.

Espinosa, L. (1995, May). Hispanic parent involvement in early childhood programs. *ERIC Digest,* EDO-PS-95-3.

Feng, J. (1994, June). Asian-American children: What teachers should know. *ERIC Digest,* EDO-PS-94-4.

First, J., & Carrera, J. (1988). *New voices: Immigrant students in U.S. public schools.* Boston: National Coalition of Advocates for Students.

Fu, V. (1993, March). Children of Asian cultures. *Child Care Information Exchange,* 49–51.

Garcia, E. (1995). Educating Mexican-American students: Past treatments and recent developments in theory, research, policy, and practice. In J. Banks & C. Banks (Eds.), *Handbook of research on multicultural education.* New York: Macmillan.

———. (1997). The education of Hispanics in early childhood: Of roots and wings. *Young Children, 52*(3), 5–14.

Gonzalez, G. (1991). Hispanics in the past two decades, Latinos in the next two: Hindsight and foresight. In M. Solomayor (Ed.), *Empowering Hispanic families: A critical issue for the 90s.* Milwaukee: Family Service America.

Hale, J. (1991). The transmission of cultural values to young African American children. *Young Children, 46*(6), 7–15.

Hale-Benson, J. (1986). *Black children: Their roots, culture and learning styles* (rev. ed.). Baltimore: Johns Hopkins University Press.

Hare, J., & Koepke, L. A. (1990, Winter). Susanne and her two mothers. *Day Care and Early Education,* 20–21.

Hidalgo, N. (1992). *I saw Puerto Rico once: A review of the literature on Puerto Rican families in the U.S.* Boston: Center on Families, Communities, Schools, and Children's Learning.

Hildebrand, V., Phenice, L., Gray, M., & Hines, R. (1999). *Knowing and serving diverse families* (2nd ed. [most cultural groups]). Englewood Cliffs, NJ: Prentice Hall.

Huntsinger, C., et al. (2000). Understanding cultural contexts foster sensitive care giving of Chinese American children. *Young Children, 55*(6), 7–15.

Joshi, A. (2005). Understanding Asian Indian families: Facilitating meaningful home–school relations. *Young Children, 60*(3), 75–79.

Klein, H. A. (1995, March). Urban Appalachian children in northern schools: A study in diversity. *Young Children, 50*(3), 10–16.

Kotlowitz, A. (1991). *There are no children here: The story of two boys growing up in the other America* [inner city]. New York: Doubleday.

Kozol, J. (1988). *Rachel and her children* [studies of homeless families]. New York: Crown Publishers.

———. (1998). *Amazing Grace* [inner city]. New York: Crown Publishers.

———. (2001). *Ordinary resurrections: Children in the years of hope.* New York: Perennial.

Lee, F. Y. (1995). Asian parents as partners. *Young Children, 50*(3), 4–9.

Linehanst, M. (1992). The children who are homeless: Educational strategies for school personnel. *Phi Delta Kappan, 74*(1), 61–66.

Liontos, L. (1992). *At-risk families and schools: Becoming partners.* Eugene, OR: ERIC Clearinghouse on Educational Management, ED 342–055.

Lipper, J. (2004). *Growing up fast* [teenaged mothers]. New York: Picador.

Locust, C. (1992). Wounding the spirit: Discrimination and traditional American Indian belief systems. *Harvard Educational Review, 58*(3), 315–330.

Lundgren, D., & J. Morrison. (2003). Involving Spanish-speaking families in early education programs. *Young Children, 58*(3), 88–95.

Lynch, E., & Hanson, M. (1992). *Developing cross-cultural competence: A guide for working with young children and their families.* Baltimore, MD: Paul H. Brooks.

Martinez, E. (1999). Mexican American/Chicano families: Parenting as diverse as the families themselves. In H. McAdoo (Ed.), *Family Ethnicity* (2nd ed., pp. 121—134). Thousand Oaks, CA: Sage.

McCormick, L., & Holden, R. (1992). Homeless children: A special challenge. *Young Children, 47*(6), 61–67.

Morrison, J., & Rodgers, L. (1996). Being responsive to the needs of children from dual heritage backgrounds. *Young Children, 52*(1), 29–32.

Pang, V. (1990). Asian-American children: A diverse population. *Educational Forum, 55*(1).

Polakow, V. (1993). *Lives on the edge: Single mothers and their children in the other America.* Chicago: University of Chicago Press.

Russell, C. (1998). *Racial and ethnic diversity: Asians, blacks, Hispanics, Native Americans, and whites* (2nd ed.). New York: Strategist.

Sample, W. (1993, March). The American Indian child. *Child Care Information Exchange,* 39–40.

Schultz, S. B., & Casper, V. (1992). *Tentative trust: Enhancing connections between gay and lesbian parents and the school.* New York: Bank Street College of Education.

Sheehan, S. (1994). *Life for me ain't been no crystal stair* [inner city and foster families]. New York: Pantheon.

Shen, W., & Mo, W. (1990). *Reaching out to their cultures: Building communication with Asian-American families.* ERIC 351–435.

Shipler, D. (2004). *The working poor: Invisible in America.* New York: Knopf.

Siu, S. (1992). How do family and community characteristics affect children's educational achievement? The Chinese-American experience. *Equity and Choice, 8*(2).

———. (1992). *Toward an understanding of Chinese-American educational achievement: a literature review.* Boston: Center on Families, Communities, Schools, and Children's Learning, Report #2.

———. (1994). *Taking no chances: Profile of a Chinese-American family's support for school success.* Boston, MA: Wheelock College.

Walker-Dalhouse, D., & Dalhouse, A. D. (2001). Parent–school relations: Communicating more effectively with African American parents. *Young Children, 56*(4), 75–80.

Wardle, F. (1993, March). Interracial families and biracial children. *Childcare Information Exchange,* 45–48.

Washington, V., & Andrews, J. D. (Eds.). (1998). *Children of 2010.* Washington, DC: NAEYC.

Wellhousen, K. (1993). Children from nontraditional families: A lesson in acceptance. *Childhood Education.* Annual Theme Issue, 287–288.

Wickens, E. (1993). Penny's question: I will have a child in my class with two moms—what do you know about this? *Young Children, 48*(3), 25–28.

Zuniga, R. (1992). Latino families. In E. Lynch & M. Janson (Eds.), *Developing cross-cultural competence.* Baltimore, MD: Paul H. Brooks.

REFERENCES

Bredekamp, S., & Copple, C. (Eds). (1997). *Developmentally appropriate practice in early childhood programs* (rev. ed.). Washington, DC: NAEYC.

Burgess, R. (1993, March). African American children. *Child Care Information Exchange,* 35–38.

Chocolate, D. (1995). *On the Day I Was Born.* New York: Scholastic Press.

Gonzales-Mena, J. (2000). *Multicultural issues in child care* (3rd ed.). Mountain View, CA: Mayfield Publishing Co.

HELPFUL WEB SITES

http://www.naeyc.org
> This site contains the NAEYC position statement "Responding to linguistic and cultural diversity, recommendations for effective early childhood education." Adopted Nov. 1995.

http://www.fmhi.usf.edu
> This site provides information for working with diverse families.

http://www.nbcdi.org
> National Black Child Development Institute. NBCDI initiates positive change for the health, welfare, and educational needs of all African American children.

http://www.clas.uiuc.edu
> Culturally and Linguistically Appropriate Services. The CLAS Institute identifies, evaluates, and promotes effective and appropriate early intervention practices and preschool practices that are sensitive and respectful to children and families from culturally and linguistically diverse backgrounds.

Additional resources for this chapter can be found on the Online Companion to accompany this text at www.earlychilded.delmar.com. This supplemental material includes frequently asked questions; chapter outlines to be used as study guides; scenarios that both encourage large and small group discussions and provoke new thoughts and ideas; and chapter resources, including chapter summaries, interactive questions, Web links, and Web activities. In addition, forms from the text are available for download.

CHAPTER 2
Families Today

OBJECTIVES

After reading this chapter, you should be able to

1 Define family and consider several characteristics of families.

2 Describe seven characteristics of contemporary life that influence the nature of modern families.

KEY TERMS
demographics
dysfunctional
extended family
nuclear family
TANF

For a teacher of young children, one very important role is communicating with families. Throughout a teaching career, working with families is an inseparable part of the teacher's life. Although many teachers might prefer to concentrate only on the children who enter the classroom each day, children live in the context of their families, and their families are the most important influence on their development. Teachers must understand those family contexts and respect their individuality while drawing them into the child's educational world.

The families with whom a teacher works may not resemble the teacher's own and may be quite unlike each other in their structure, family lifestyle and values, and relationships. As America grows increasingly diverse, teachers need to prepare themselves to recognize, appreciate, and work with such diversity. Although the media report that the family is a fatally wounded institution in today's world, in truth the more traditional forms of the family are diminishing while other forms are rising.

In this chapter we begin to consider some of the reasons for the diversity and change in family appearance that are apparent in most American classrooms.

■■■ WHAT DEFINES A FAMILY?

The family is the most adaptable of human institutions, able to modify its characteristics to meet those of the society in which it lives. Certainly the family has adapted to much in recent decades: industrialization, urbanization, a consumer-oriented economy, wars and terrorist attacks, changes in traditional religious and moral codes, and changes in all relationships basic to family life, between male and female, young and old. Moving into this new century, these changes have been occurring in every corner of the world, although our primary concern here is the American family.

In a special edition titled "The Twenty-First Century Family," the weekly magazine *Newsweek* stated,

> The American family does not exist. Rather, we are creating many American families, of diverse styles and shapes. In unprecedented numbers, our families are unalike: We have fathers working while mothers keep house; fathers and mothers working away from home; single parents; second marriages bringing children together from unrelated backgrounds; childless couples; unmarried couples, with and without children; gay and lesbian parents. We are living through a period of historic change in American family life. (1990)

This list can be made even more comprehensive when you consider the families you might meet within any classroom or community: single-father families and single-mother families, who may be never married, widowed, or divorced; adoptive families; grandparents functioning as parents in the absence of the intermediate generation; surrogate-mother families; foster families; and families of mixed racial heritage, either biological or adoptive.

Consider the complexity in families by the categories of fathers suggested recently by the president of the National Fatherhood Initiative: Beyond the major subtypes of dads familiar through most of our history—in-home, married dads, widowed dads, and stepdads—today we add biological, in-home cohabiting dads; nonresident divorced fathers; nonresident unwed fathers; joint physical custody dads; stay-at-home dads; single head of household dads; and cohabiting, nonbiologically related "father figures." Such lists may make us feel uncomfortable in their distance from our values or ideals, or comforted by the realization that our families are not the only ones that seem not to fit the perfect image of 1950s families in *Father Knows Best* or *Ozzie and Harriet* seen on late night television reruns.

About those 1950s families, Stephanie Coontz points out that the family forms and values of the 1950s were actually a result of "*experimentation* with the possibilities of a new kind of family, not the expression of some longstanding tradition" (Coontz, 1997). At the end of the 1940s, the divorce rate that had been rising since the 1890s dropped sharply, the age of marriage fell to a 100-year low, and the birthrate took off to create what is known as the Baby Boom generation. Women who had worked during the Depression and World War II quit their jobs as soon as they became pregnant, and the timing and spacing of childbearing became compressed. The result was that women became more economically dependent on marriage, contrasting with trends in the opposite direction since the early 20th century. Family life and gender roles became much more settled during this brief decade than they had been 20 years earlier or would be 20 years later. As the organization of family life changed, so too did values. Driven by the spread of suburbs and automobiles, along with the destruction of older ethnic neighborhoods in many cities, came "the emphasis on putting all one's emotional eggs in the small basket of the immediate **nuclear family**" (Coontz, 1997). Yet even then everyone knew that such shows as *Donna Reed, Ozzie and Harriet, Leave It to Beaver,* and *Father Knows Best,* familiar to today's grandparents, were not the way families really were. "People didn't watch those shows to see their own lives reflected back at them. They watched them to see how families were *supposed* to live" (Coontz, 1997). So our nostalgia for the fictitious family portrayed from those times may just get in the way of our acceptance of the way families are today. But one thing seems clear: There is no way to find simple unanimity in any discussion of *family.* "All (these forms) are now recognized, if not fully accepted, as ways to put together a family" (Elkind, 1994).

The word *family* has always meant many things to many people. What comes to mind when you think of the traditional family? In an earlier book, *The Way We Never Were: American Families and the Nostalgia Trap* (1992), Coontz reminds us that this answer has changed depending on the era and its particular myths. Despite the obvious fact that the phrase *the American family* does not describe one reality, it is used sweepingly. What most creators of television commercials seem to think it means is a usually white, middle-class, monogamous, father-at-work, mother-and-children-at-home family, living in a suburban one-family house, nicely filled with an array of appliances, a minivan or SUV in the driveway, and probably a dog in the yard. Such a description excludes the vast majority of American families, according to the last census (which does not enumerate dogs or minivans but found only 7% of households conforming to the classic family headed by a working husband with a wife and two children at home). The comment was made recently that, whereas most families used to have 2.6 children, now many children have 2.6 parents.

The entire Western world has experienced similar changes in family life since the mid-1960s. Politicians and preachers have issued warnings about declines in family values, which they seem to equate with changing family structure. Others have suggested that it is time for a more inclusive interpretation of this term, saying that *family values* means valuing families, no matter what their form.

If you are a student in Canada, you will note that similar sociological changes affect Canadian families. For recent data on Canadian families, see *Profiling Canada's Families III*, by R. Suave of the Vanier Institute of the Family, 2004, or that organization's Web site (http://www.vifamily.ca). Rather than suggest that the family is under siege, it is more accurate to suggest that it is this mythical form of family that does not widely exist and that our image of family may need to be broadened to accept diversity. It may be more important to concentrate on what families do rather than what they look like. Family may be more about content than about form (see Figure 2-1).

(a)

(b)

(c)

(d)

FIGURE 2-1 Families come in all shapes and sizes. (Continues)

(e)

(f)

(g)

FIGURE 2-1 Continued

"Ideal" Family Images

What image comes to your mind when you see the word *family*? People's mental images vary greatly, based in large part on their individual life experiences.

Try an experiment now as you think about family. On a piece of paper draw stick figures to represent the members of the family you first knew as a young child; who represented family to you then? Then do the same to represent the family you lived in as a teenager. Had your family changed? Was anyone added or removed? What were the reasons for any changes?

Now draw the family in which you presently live. Who is there? What does this say about the changes in your life? And if, as an adult, you have lived in numerous family structures, represent them as well.

Now for one last picture. Imagine that you could design the ideal family for yourself. What would it look like?

Sorting through your pictures may generate some thinking about family. One prediction is that most of the ideal pictures include a father, mother, and two children (probably a boy first and then a girl!). Usually the ideal family includes these members, no matter what the actual composition of the families in which individuals have participated or presently live. Often there are dissimilarities; reality for some ranges from growing up with one parent to having two stepfathers or a large number of siblings, being an only child, or having grandparents or others in the home. All of these real experiences are often passed over in favor of the ideal two-parent, two-child home. Some create more elaborate fantasy families and specify that the mother be a full-time homemaker—this from women themselves preparing for a career. The only women whose ideal family approximates the reality in which they now live are usually women who married and had children before becoming students—unless the marriage was disrupted by divorce. Then their ideal family includes another partner.

For many, the image of an ideal family is influenced less by real experiences than by subtle cultural messages that have bombarded us since childhood.

The Vanier Institute reports that 86% of high school students surveyed, including 78% of the teens whose own parents had not stayed together, expect a lifelong marriage. From magazine advertisements to children's books, and even more pervasively from television shows, the attractive vision of husband, wife, and children beams at us. What has been called the "Leave It to Beaver syndrome" has given several viewing generations, including those who are now our leaders and legislators, a clear yardstick against which to measure desirable family characteristics and measure guilt and negative feelings when the reality does not match the ideal.

Interestingly, students surveyed are aware that their ideal image is just that and are also aware of the societal influences that helped produce it.

FAMILY IMAGES

1. **Draw the family you lived in as a child.**

2. **Draw the family you lived in as a teenager.**

3. **Draw the family in which you presently live.**

4. **Draw the ideal family you would design for yourself.**

5. **Share your pictures with two other classmates.**

6. **Considering all the pictures, what statements can you make about family and the influences that have created your sense of ideal?**

But they may be less aware of how insidiously this subliminal image can influence their encounters with real families. If an ideal, lurking unknowingly in the teacher's value system, is considered the "good," a negative evaluation can be made of any family that does not measure up to this standard. The problem with assessing this nuclear family model as the "good" is that it may prevent us from considering alternative family structures as equally valid.

One way to become aware of your prejudices is to list the names of the families in your classroom (or neighborhood). Mark a check beside each family you would like to be friends with or those you think are doing a good job. Mark an "X" beside those families you feel most comfortable with and those you have contact with frequently. How many of these families look somewhat like your ideal family or the family you grew up in? In doing this exercise, it is important not to make value judgments about which are the "right kind of families" but merely examine your initial reactions based on prior experiences. It is too easy for a teacher to feel more affinity and comfort with a family that approaches her or his ideal than with one that is clearly outside the teacher's individual frame of reference.

It is important for a teacher to consider these ideas actively. Recording thoughts about families in a notebook is a good starting place. Throughout this textbook you will find suggestions titled Reflections for Journal Entries. Thinking in a journal offers teachers opportunities to reflect actively on the attitudes and experiences that will shape practice and to ask questions that will help them decide on future actions. Watch for the journal entry after you read about the varieties of families teachers may encounter. Reflecting about ideals does not mean that teachers have to give up either their images or ideals. But teachers should notice when these ideas become limiting factors in relationships with the variety of parents they will encounter.

Samples of Diverse Family Structures

If personal images of family cannot convey a complex enough picture, perhaps brief descriptions of families you might meet and work with will help. We will meet these families now to begin to consider the diversity in structure that corresponds to the differing values, customs, and lifestyles that have evolved in our world. These same families will help us later when we consider different relationships and techniques in teacher–parent communication.

A. Bob and Jane Weaver have been married 5 years. They married the day after Jane graduated from high school. Sandra, blond and blue-eyed just like her parents, was born before their first anniversary. Bob and Jane live in an apartment down the street from her parents, around the block from her married sister. Jane has not worked outside the home much during their marriage. They are hoping to have another child next year. A second pregnancy ended in stillbirth last year. Bob earns $39,750 on the production line at a furniture factory. Jane started working part-time this year to help save for a down payment for a first home purchase. Her mother cares for Sandra while Jane works. Her income of $750.00 a month after taxes would not go far if she had to pay for child care.

B. Sylvia Ashley, 29, lives alone with her sons Terrence, 9 and Ricky, 3. Her marriage to Ricky's father ended in divorce before Ricky's birth; she was not married to Terrence's father, who was in one of her classes in college before she dropped out during the first semester. She has had no contact with her parents since before Terrence's birth. Although she lives in a subsidized housing apartment, she rarely has contact with her neighbors; hers is the only white family living in the area. Before Ricky was born she worked in a department store. Since then her income has come from **TANF** funds and food stamp payments, as well as the subsidized housing. She is now beginning a job training program, hoping to follow through with her plan to become a nurse's aide. Ricky has been home with Sylvia, but he will enter a child care program when his mother begins the job training program.

C. Otis and Fannie Lawrence have each been married before. Otis has two sons from his first marriage—14 and 10—who visit one weekend each month and for about six weeks each summer. Fannie's 7-year-old daughter, Kim, and 4-year-old son, Pete, see their father, who has moved out of state, only once or twice a year, and have called Otis "Daddy" since their mother married him three years ago. Fannie is six months pregnant, and they have recently moved into an attractive new four-bedroom house, knowing even that will be too small when the boys visit. Fannie teaches third grade and will take a three-month maternity leave after the baby is born; she is on the waiting list at four centers for infant care. Otis sells new cars and is finishing up a business degree at night. Kim goes to an after-school child care program that costs $95.00 a week. Pete is in a private child care center, operated by a national chain, that costs $145.00 each week. The Lawrence family income is $98,000 annually. The Lawrence family is African American.

D. Salvatore and Teresa Rodriquez have lived in this country for 6 years. Occasionally one of their relatives comes to stay with them, but the rest of the family has stayed in Mexico. Right now Sal's 20-year-old brother Joseph is here taking an auto mechanics course; he plans to be married later this year and will probably stay in the same town. Teresa misses her mother, who has not seen their two children since they were babies. Sylvia is 7 and has cerebral palsy; she attends a developmental kindergarten that has an excellent staff for the physiotherapy and speech therapy that she needs. Tony is 4. Teresa works part-time in a bakery. Her husband works the second shift on the maintenance crew at the bus depot so he can be home with the children while she is at work. This is necessary because Sylvia needs so much extra care. They rent a six-room house, which they chose for the safe neighborhood and large garden.

E. Mary Howard is 16 and has always lived with her parents in a predominantly middle-class neighborhood of African American families. Her grandmother has had a stroke and now lives with them, too. When Mary's daughter, Cynthia, was born last year, her mother cared for the baby so Mary could finish the 10th grade. Cynthia is now in a church-operated child care center because Mary's mother needed to go back to work to cover increased family expenses. Mary still hopes she might someday marry Cynthia's father, who is starting college this year. He comes to see her and the baby every week or so. Mary is also wondering if she will go on to train in computer programming after she finishes high school, as she had planned, or if she should just get a job so she can help her mother more with Cynthia and with their expenses.

F. Susan Henderson celebrated her 39th birthday in the hospital the day after giving birth to Lucy. Her husband, Ed, is 40. After 13 years of marriage, they've found adding a child both joyful and shocking. Lucy was very much a planned child. Susan felt well enough established in her career as an architect to be able to work from her home for a year or so. Ed's career as an investment counselor has also demanded a lot of his attention. Some of their friends are still wavering over the decision to begin a family. Ed and Susan are quite definite that this one child will be all they'll have time for. Money is not the issue in their decision; their combined income last year was well over $200,000. Susan's major complaint since being at home with the baby is that the condominium where they live has few families with children, and none of them are preschoolers. She has signed up for a Mother's Morning Out program for infants one day a week and has a nanny who comes to their home each day so she can work.

G. Sam (2) and Lisa (4) Butler see both of their parents a lot—they just never see them together. Bill and Joan separated almost two years ago, and their divorce is about to become final. One of the provisions calls for joint physical custody of their two preschoolers. What this means right now is spending three nights one week with one parent and four with the other. The schedule gets complicated sometimes because Bill travels on business, but so far the adults have been able to work it out. The children seem to enjoy going from Dad's apartment to Mom in the house they've always lived in, but on the days they carry their suitcases to the child care center for the midweek switchover, they need lots of reassurance about who's picking them up. Joan worries about how this arrangement will work as the children get older. Both the children attend a child development center run by the local community college. Joan is already concerned about finding good after-school care for Lisa when she starts school in the fall, and she knows that it will further complicate things to have to make two pickup stops after work. She works as a secretary for the phone company and needs to take some computer courses this fall, but she doesn't know how she can fit them in and the kids, too—let alone find time to date a new man she's met.

H. Ginny Parker and Sara Leeper adopted a 1-year-old Korean girl four years ago. They have been together in a committed relationship for six years, and they live a fairly quiet life, visiting with Sara's family, who lives in the same town, as well as a few friends, including another family they met at an adoptive parents' support group. Anna is in a prekindergarten classroom in an early childhood program at a church in their neighborhood. Sara is a nurse on the second shift at the hospital. Ginny works for a travel agency downtown. When asked if they are worried about their daughter growing up without a relationship with an adult male, Ginny responds that Anna has a grandfather and uncle to whom she is close, and that they are more concerned about helping her come to know something of her native culture.

I. Justin Martin, age 5, lives with his grandparents. His grandfather retired this year after working for the city as a horticulturalist for 30 years. His grandmother has never worked outside the home, having raised five children of her own. Justin is the child of their youngest daughter. She left high school after his birth and has drifted from one minimum-wage job to another. On several occasions she left Justin alone rather than find a child care arrangement for him, and she was reported for neglect by neighbors in her apartment building. His grandparents felt they could provide a better home environment for him, so they petitioned the court for his custody. Neither Justin nor his grandparents have much contact with his mother—she did not come over to the house for his last birthday, and she sent some money for Christmas. Justin is in a public school kindergarten. His grandfather takes him to school. His grandmother is quite homebound with arthritis and often finds a lively 5-year-old exhausting.

J. Nguyen Van Son has worked very hard since he came to this country with his uncle 12 years ago. After graduating from high school near the top of his class, he completed a mechanical drafting course at a technical college. He has a good job working for a manufacturing company. His wife, Dang Van Binh, an old family friend, came from Vietnam only 6 years ago, and they were married soon after. Her English is still not good, so she takes evening classes. Their 3-year-old son Nguyen Thi Hoang goes to a half-day preschool program because his father is eager for him to become comfortable speaking English with other children. Their baby daughter, Le Thi Tuyet, is at home with her mother. On weekends the family spends time with other Vietnamese families, eager for companionship and preserving their memories of Vietnam.

K. Richard Stein and Roberta Howell have lived together for 18 months. Richard's 5-year-old son, Joshua, lives with them. Roberta has decided she wants no children; she and Richard have no plans for marriage at this time. Roberta works long hours as a department store buyer. Richard writes for the local newspaper. On the one or two evenings a week that neither of them can get away from work, Joshua is picked up from a neighborhood family child care home by a college student that Richard met at the paper. Several times this arrangement has fallen through, and Joshua has had to stay late with his caregiver, who does not like this because she cares for Joshua and five other preschoolers from 7:00 a.m. until 6:00 p.m. each day.

L. Ted Sawyer winces when a member of his basketball team calls him "Mr. Mom." He doesn't like the name; but he admits it is often difficult for others to understand why he is the primary caregiver in his family while his wife Jana works for a large corporation for which she travels, often being gone for most of the workweek. Ted cares for their first grader Jacob and their toddler daughter Emma. Between getting Jacob to school and watching out for his active daughter, Ted rarely has time for part-time plumbing jobs, the work he did before the children were born. He has already decided that he will likely not return to full-time employment until both children are in high school because both he and his wife believe that one parent should be available as much as possible during children's early years. Jana is happy and very successful in her work, providing for a comfortable lifestyle, although she misses being home with the family and talks with the children on the telephone every night.

In this sample, as in any other you might draw from a cross section in any school, the family some call "traditional," with a father who works to earn the living and a mother whose work is rearing the children and caring for the home, is a distinct minority in the variety of structures. Figure 2-2 indicates how family structure and children's living arrangements have changed over the past two decades.

In addition, the last census indicated the diversity and continuing change in patterns of living situations. The percentage increase in single-father homes has far outpaced other living arrangements, rising 62% in 10 years and now being 1 household in 45. Nevertheless, women heading a single-parent household increased 25%, so that now 6 of 10 children under the age of 18 are living in such a household. Couples who live together without marriage now account for 5% of all households (up from 3% in 1990), and homes with married couples have decreased 3% in the same period, to 52%. Only a quarter of households consist of a married couple with one or more children at home. And fully one quarter of the nation's households are people living alone (http://www.census.gov).

Canadian figures show similar changes in family structures. At the last census, Canadian families were composed of married couples with children, 45%; married with no children, 29%; common-law (cohabiting) couples with children, 5%; common-law couples with no children, 6%; single-parent families with children, 15% (83% of these female-headed) (Vanier, 2004).

	1980	2000
Total U.S. Population		
Two-parent families (biological, adoptive, or stepfamilies, married or unmarried)	77%	68%
With mother only	18%	23%
With father only	2%	4%
With other adults, no parent in home	4%	4%

	1990	2000
White Children		
Two-parent families	81%	77%
Mother only	15%	16%
Father only	3%	4%
No parent (other adults)	2%	3%
Black Children		
Two-parent families	36%	35%
Mother only	51%	52%
Father only	3%	4%
No parent (other adults)	8%	10%
Hispanic Children		
Two-parent families	67%	63%
Mother only	22%	27%
Father only	3%	5%
No parent (other adults)	3%	5%

FIGURE 2-2 Family structures and children's living arrangements have changed over the past two decades. Statistics from http://www.childstats.gov/ac2000/pop5a.

How do we define *family?* The Census Bureau definition of "two or more people related through blood, marriage, or adoption who share a common residence" seems too narrow to include all the dynamics of these sample families. *Webster's Tenth New Collegiate Dictionary* suggests a broader interpretation and no fewer than 22 definitions that seem more applicable when considering these sample families: "a group of people united by certain convictions or common characteristics" or "a group of individuals living under one roof and usually under one head." Perhaps the most inclusive definition of a family is "a small group of intimate, transacting, and interdependent persons who share values, goals, resources, and other responsibilities for decisions; have a commitment to one another over time; and accept the responsibility of bringing up children." Or simply, from the definition in a survey by the Massachusetts Mutual Life Insurance Company, "a group of people who love and care for each other" (Roberts, 1993). The organization Family Support America says that "family is a group of people who take responsibility for each other's well-being, and defining the family is up to the family itself." What about the idea that *family* is "not only persons related by blood, marriage, or adoption, but also sets of interdependent but independent persons who share some common goals, resources, and a commitment to each other over time" (Hildebrand et al., 1999)? Mary Pipher (1996) adds these thoughts:

> Family is a collection of people who pool resources and help each other over the long haul. Families love one another even when that requires sacrifice. Family means that if you disagree, you still stay together . . . all members can belong regardless of merit. Everyone is included regardless of health, likability, or prestige . . . families come through when they must . . . From my point of view the issue isn't biology. Rather the issues are commitment and inclusiveness.

> **CONSIDER THE TRUTH OF THIS STATEMENT**
>
> **A family is like no other family, like some other families, and like all other families.**

REFLECTIONS FOR JOURNAL ENTRIES

Think about the families just described. Are there any families with whom you would be uncomfortable? What is causing this discomfort? How would you work with this family, given the discomfort? Which families seem closest to you in values?

How do you define *family*? The Vanier Institute of the Family points out that families

- Provide for physical maintenance and care of family members.
- Add new members.
- Socialize children.
- Exercise social control over their members.
- Produce, consume, and distribute goods and services.
- Provide love and affective nurturance (Vanier, 2000).

No matter how we define it, family is important to us (see Figure 2-3).

Families may include more than just parents and children. Mary Howard's family includes her parents, grandmother, and child, and the Rodriquezes have Uncle Joseph. The extension of the nuclear family is more for affection and support than for the self-sufficient economic unit the traditional **extended family** created. Families may include people not related by blood and hereditary bonds. The Parker–Leeper and Stein–Howell households include parents and children and others whose relationship is based on choice, not law. New relatives, such as those acquired in a stepfamily like the Lawrences, may be added. Families may omit a generation, such as Justin Martin and his grandparents.

> We may be related by birth or adoption or invitation.
> We may belong to the same race or we may be of different races.
> We may look like each other or different from each other.
> The important thing is, we belong to each other.
> We care for each other.
> We agree, disagree, love, fight, work together.
> We belong to each other.

FIGURE 2-3 Family defined as caring.

TOP 10 TRENDS IN MODERN FAMILIES

The Vanier Institute reports these trends:

1. Fewer couples are getting legally married.

2. More couples are breaking up.

3. Families are getting smaller.

4. Children experience more transitions as parents change their marital status.

5. Adults are generally satisfied with life.

6. Family violence is underreported.

7. Multiple-earner families are now the norm.

8. Women still do most of the juggling involved in balancing work and home.

9. Inequality is worsening.

10. The future will have more aging families. (from Sauve, 2004)

In Justin Martin's case, as with increasing numbers of children, he is being raised by grandparents in the absence of his own parents. Aunts, grandparents, and other family members, as well as thousands of foster parents who are not related to children by blood, are all some of the adults who head modern families.

Families may be composed of more people than those present in a household at any one time. The Butler joint custody arrangements and the "blended" Lawrence family are examples of separated family structures.

Families change. Their composition is dynamic, not static. It is assumed that Uncle Joseph will form his own household when he and his fiancée marry; Mary Howard hopes to marry and establish her own household. The Butler family may be added to when the parents remarry, as both say they'd like to.

The Weavers hope to add another baby. Change occurs as family members grow and develop. Family members are continually adjusting to shifts within the family dynamics that challenge earlier positions (see Figure 2-4).

Ackerman, K. *By the Dawn's Early Light.* (mom works the night shift)

Adoff, A. *Black Is Brown Is Tan.* (interracial family)

Aylette, J. *Families: A Celebration of Diversity, Commitment, and Love.* (photos and descriptions of all kinds of families)

Bauer, C. *My Mom Travels a Lot.*

Baum, L. *One More Time.* (child going between mom's house and dad's house)

Blain, M. *The Terrible Thing That Happened at Our House.* (mom takes a job)

Blomquist, G., & Blomquist, F. *Zachary's New Home: A Story for Foster and Adopted Children.*

Bosch, S. *Jenny Lives with Eric and Martin.* (two fathers)

Boyd, L. *Sam Is My Half-Brother.*

Brownstone, C. *All Kinds of Mothers.* (mothers who work both in and out of home)

Bunting, E. *Fly Away Home.* (homeless child and father)

—— *Can You Be This, Old Badger* (living with grandparent)

Cowen-Fletcher, J. *Mama Zooms.* (mother in a wheelchair)

Crews, D. *Bigmama's.* (extended family)

Drescher, J. *Your Family, My Family.* (different shapes and sizes)

Eichler, M. *Martin's Father.* (nurturing single father)

Eisenberg, P. *You're My Nikki.* (new working mother)

Falwell, C. *Feast for 10.* (large family)

Galloway, P. *Good Times, Bad Times—Mummy and Me.* (working single mother)

—— *Jennifer Has Two Daddies.* (child alternates weeks with her mom and stepdad and her father)

Hayes, M., & Witherell, J. *My Daddy Is in Prison.*

Hickman, M. *Robert Lives with his Grandparents.*

Hines, A. *Daddy Makes the Best Spaghetti.*

Jenness, A. *Families.*

Kroll, V. *Wood–Hoopoe Willie.* (African American family)

Kuklin, S. *How My Family Lives in America.* (real stories of different ethnic backgrounds)

Lasker, J. *Mothers Can Do Anything.* (many jobs mothers do)

Loewen, I. *My Mom Is So Unusual.* (contemporary American Indian)

Maslac, H. *Finding a Job for Daddy.* (unemployed father)

Merriam, E. *Mommies at Work.* (in and out of home work)

Moore, E. *Grandma's House.* (spending the summer with an active, nontraditional grandmother)

FIGURE 2-4 Good books to read with children to celebrate family diversity. (continues)

Newman, L. *Gloria Goes to Gay Pride.*

Pelligrini, N. *Families Are Different.*

Quinlan, P. *My Dad Takes Care of Me.* (unemployed father at home)

Rotner, S., & Kelly, S. *Lots of Moms.*

Schlein, M. *The Way Mothers Are.*

Schwartz, A. *Oma and Bobo.* (mother, grandmother, and child)

Simon, N. *All Kinds of Families.*

Skutch, R. *Who's in a Family?*

Soto, G. *Too Many Tamales.* (Mexican American family)

Spelman, C. *After Charlotte's Mom Died.* (single father)

Stinson, K. *Mom and Dad Don't Live Together Any More.* (divorce)

Tax, M. *Families.* (variety of families)

Valentine, J. *One Dad, Two Dads, Brown Dad, Blue Dads.*

Vigna, J. *My Two Uncles.*

Wickens, E. *Anna Day and the O-Ring.* (two mothers)

Wild, M. *Space Travelers.* (homeless)

Willhoite, M. *Daddy's Roommate.* (divorced parent, gay father)

Williams, V. *A Chair for My Mother.* (families, generations of urban working–class family)

See also list of books about divorced families, stepfamilies, and adoptive families in Chapter 16.

FIGURE 2-4 Continued

More recently, some of the changes occur because the "nuclear family is reeling from several decades in an economic and social atom smasher. Spouses, siblings, and generations were separated at dizzying speeds" (Roberts, 1993). It is time to look at some of those changes.

DEMOGRAPHICS OF MODERN FAMILIES

Is it harder or easier to be a parent today than it was a generation or two ago? There is no question that today's families are functioning under different conditions than their grandparents or even parents did. Changes in family forms and functions are not necessarily bad or worrisome—unless one insists on clinging to the past, maintaining the exclusive rightness of bygone ways. Almost all the changes discussed in this chapter have had some positive and negative impacts on today's families.

Some recent trends in contemporary life influencing the nature of families include these:

- Marital instability and rising numbers of unmarried mothers.
- Changes in role behavior.
- Mobility and urbanization.
- Decreasing family size.

"Our family is very secure, except for the possibility of death, illness, unemployment, separation or divorce."

FIGURE 2-5 Families are vulnerable to many external pressures.
Courtesy Johns Hopkins University Press.

- Increased rate of social change.
- Development of a child-centered society.
- Stress in modern living.

Each of these will be discussed in this chapter (see Figure 2-5).

Marital Instability and Unmarried Mothers

Statistics tell us part of the story. Since 1900 the divorce rate has increased nearly 700%. It is estimated that about 50% of marriages begun today will end in divorce (37% in Canada). Sixty percent of second marriages will collapse. According to Census Bureau predictions, it is likely that nearly half of all children born in this decade will spend a significant part of their childhood in single-parent homes. "Over the whole postindustrial West, fewer than two-thirds of parents who are legally married when their first child is born remain together until their youngest child leaves school" (Leach, 1994).

Between 1970 and 1990 the proportion of children growing up in single-parent families more than doubled, to over one in four. The majority of these single-parent families are created by divorce. But divorced parents—70–80%—often remarry. One child in five lives in a stepfamily or blended family (Coontz, 1997). One prediction is that one-third of all children born in the past decade will be a stepchild before age 18. In many areas children living with two biological parents are a distinct minority.

In addition, some of the single-parent families are the result of a rising birthrate among unmarried women. Although births to unmarried women leveled off somewhat in the 1990s, the rate is still approximately one-third of all births each year, compared with just over 3% of births in 1940. What is interesting is that the birthrate to teenaged mothers has dropped 2% since 1997 and an impressive 18% since 1991, when the rate peaked.

Now fewer than one-third of infants are born to teenaged mothers, falling from half 20 years earlier. Even so, in some hospitals in poor urban areas, well over half of the women giving birth are single teenagers. The over-all decrease is likely the result of widespread public and private education efforts focusing on responsible behavior and abstinence, as well as the long economic expansion of the 1990s that increased economic opportunity for all, leading many young women to value education and postpone pregnancy (Halpern, Fernandez, & Clark, 2000). Figure 2-6 indicates that the majority of single women who become mothers today are older (see Figure 2-7).

Mothers head the majority of single-parent families. Many unmarried fathers take both financial and psychological responsibility in supporting their children and their mothers, but some mother-headed homes do so without the fathers' support. Although there is no question that many single parents do a remarkable job of parenting capably, additional difficulties can face a single-parent family. A growing body of social and scientific data indicates that children in families disrupted by divorce and birth outside of marriage often do worse than children in intact families in several respects. They are two to three times as likely as children in two-parent families to have emotional and behavioral problems, more likely to drop out of high school, get pregnant as teenagers, abuse drugs, and get in trouble with the law. They are also at much

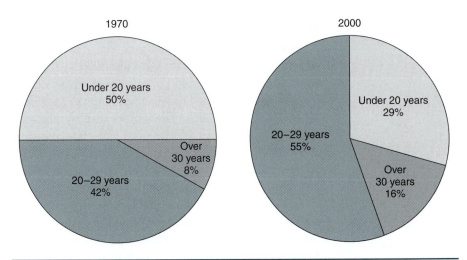

FIGURE 2-6 The majority of single women who become mothers today are older.

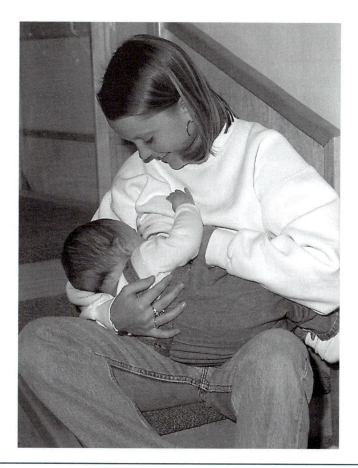

FIGURE 2-7 The birthrate among adolescent girls is declining.

higher risk for physical or sexual abuse (Whitehead, 1993). Yet single-parent families are as diverse as any other. When all things are equal—when a single mother has a job that pays a decent wage, is basically contented with her life, and is not overly stressed—there are no major behavioral differences between children raised by single parents and those raised by two (Kennedy & King, 1994). In Chapter 16 we will consider the effects of divorce on children of various ages and the differing effects on boys and girls. But for purposes of considering demographics and families, here we note that family structure may be linked to children's well-being. In the absence of one parent, families often have less social and human capital to draw upon.

Poverty

The term *single parent* does not fully convey the reality that mothers head most of these families. Just under 20% of all American children (18%) lived in female-headed families in 2000, a figure that actually has declined in recent years; fewer than 4% of all children live with their fathers alone, although this

MYTHS AND MISCONCEPTIONS

MYTH Families of the past didn't have problems like those of families today.

REALITY Desertion, child abuse, spousal battery, and alcohol and drug abuse have always troubled significant numbers of families.

MYTH A return to traditional family values and gender roles would save many marriages and protect children.

REALITY Many problems exist not because we have changed too much but because we haven't changed enough, such as the failure of men to share household and child care providing a source of overload for working mothers—a major source of conflict.

MYTH The 1950s male breadwinner style of family has always been the traditional form of family in America.

REALITY Not until the 1920s did the majority of children come from homes where the husband worked and the mother was a full-time homemaker.

MYTH The sexual revolution of the 1960s caused the rise in unwed motherhood.

REALITY The sharpest increase in unwed motherhood was between 1940 and 1958, when the number tripled. The rate leveled off between 1960 and 1975, then doubled between 1975 and 1992 and is again leveling off and declining.

MYTH Children of divorced and unwed mothers are almost sure to fail.

REALITY It's how a family acts that really counts, not its makeup. The number of times the family eats dinner together is a better guide to how they'll turn out than the number of parents at the dinner table.

MYTH The collapse of the traditional family is the main source of American social and economic problems.

REALITY Most poverty in America is caused by changes in wage and job structure, not in families.

Adapted from http://www.contemporaryfamilies.org/education.htm.

figure is an increase of 25% over the previous census, perhaps indicating changes in the way custody is granted to parents and more social acceptance of single fathering.

Poverty affects about 17% of all children, or one in six—a figure that is down from its peak in 1993 but still makes the United States a shocking leader in the percentage of poor children among the 21 most affluent nations in the world. But poverty disproportionately affects children who live in single-parent households.

Who Are America's Poor Children?	
Poor children are	17% of total of children
White poor children	13% of total
Black poor children	33% of total
Hispanic poor children	30%
Asian poor children	11%
Living with single mothers	57%
Living with single fathers	6%
Living with both parents	10%
Living with grandparents	27%
Living with neither parent	32%
Living in central city	25%
Living in suburbs	11%
Living in rural areas	20%

FIGURE 2-8 America's poor children are everywhere.

Children under 6 who are living with single mothers are five times more likely to be poor than children who live in two-parent households. Children living with single fathers are two and a half times more likely to live below the poverty line. Figure 2-8 indicates how poverty among children is divided by specific factors. Research indicates that three factors indicate particular risk for poverty. These factors are

- Single parenthood.

- Low educational attainment.

- Part-time or no employment.

In the current economic climate these factors may intertwine and make it very difficult for single-parent families to escape poverty. Surprisingly, about two-thirds of poor young children live in families in which a parent is employed.

Single-parent families created by divorce may precipitously plunge children into poverty. In the years following divorce, living standards for ex-wives and their children drop by an average of 30%, while those for the men involved rise 8%. Only half of all families with an absent parent have child support orders; of these families, only half receive the full amount ordered. About a quarter receive partial payment, and a quarter receive nothing. Despite successful efforts in some states to enforce such legal obligations, a majority of fathers' scheduled payments are still in arrears.

Child support accounts for only 15% of the total income of single-parent families. Financial stress is a major complaint of divorced women. Many single-parent families are not able to provide adequate support services they need, such as child care while a mother works, or recreation or other social relief for a parent.

Poverty in the United States is increasingly linked to family structure. This is the first decade in the nation's history in which a majority of all poor families are headed by women, in what has been called the *feminization of poverty*. In female-headed families the poverty rate is over 40%; in families headed by a parent under age 30, this rate is even higher. African American and Latino families are disproportionately represented among poor and single mother–headed households. More than 500,000 of these poor children are homeless. Children and families are the fastest-growing group among the homeless population, now representing about 40% of all homeless.

The welfare reform law enacted in 1996 changed the federal government support system available to poor families. States now receive a fixed grant for income support and work programs, based on an earlier level of spending. Stringent requirements in most states say that services or cash assistance received by any family may not add up to a total of five years over a lifetime for any reason; some states allow shorter periods. Although attention has been given to the subsequent drop in welfare caseloads across the nation (over 57% since 1996), many people fail to recognize that adults working at minimum-wage jobs, even full-time and year-round, earn only 82% of the current poverty level for a family of three. Moving families out of poverty and not just off the TANF rolls requires providing education, training, and work experience.

Other cuts in social spending have included drastic reductions in the food stamp program. Food stamp benefits have been reduced about 20%, with nearly two-thirds of the reductions borne by families with children. As the 21st century began, it appeared that government safety nets for poor families had been torn away. Families that are particularly affected by this are single-parent families, especially those headed by young parents.

Stress

A family that began with two parents and shifts to single-parent status will undoubtedly experience increased stress for some time, if not permanently.

Adjustments will have to be made by all family members to the changed living patterns that include

- The loss of a relationship, regardless of how negative
- A move and new job or school arrangements.
- Other changes necessitated by the constraints of a more limited budget.
- Less contact with one parent.
- Changed behaviors in both parents.

We'll talk more about this stress in Chapter 16.

Although custody arrangements now often include joint physical custody for both parents, and more divorcing fathers are granted custody than previously, the majority of single-parent families created by divorce are headed by women. A mother in a single-parent family is under the additional strain of adding the father role to her parental responsibilities. Not only do many divorcing fathers abandon their children financially, they also do so emotionally; half of all divorced fathers do not see their children. In one study of children living in female-headed households, 40% of the children had not seen their fathers at all during the previous year. Of the remaining 60%, only a fifth sleep overnight once a month in their fathers' homes; even fewer see their fathers at least once a week (Louv, 1995–96). The mother may easily overload herself while trying to compensate for her concern induced by social attitudes that a single-parent family is a pathological family. The mixed data in this area are scarcely reassuring, and real or feared changes in children's behavior can add appreciably to a parent's burden at this time. Social attitudes toward divorce may have undergone a shift toward acceptance, but attitudes toward what some have unfortunately called a "broken family" still leave many single parents with an additional burden of guilt.

If a single-parent family is merged to create a new blended family, additional stress may be created. A new family may begin with financial problems created when one income must support more than one family, with emotional burdens created by the multiplicity of possible new relationships, as well as the striving to create an "instant" family, warm and close, to make up for the earlier pain and banish the "ugly stepparent" fears. Unfortunately these burdens may be too heavy: Up to 60% of blended family marriages end in divorce within four years. This means that many children may experience divorce, remarriage, and all of the attendant stresses two or three times before they become adults. Chapter 16 will examine in depth the results of stress on all members of these families.

Never-wed single-parent families also may face stress in the form of a possible lack of cultural, social, or economic support for the family.

Changes in Role Behavior

In the reruns of old television series from the 1960s and early 1970s, Beaver Cleaver's mom was home baking cookies, and Aunt Bea raised Opie while Andy worked to support the family. Today, however, most moms, in both television sitcoms and real life, are working outside their homes. Fewer mothers are playing the traditional role of homemaker, and more than ever are also working outside the home. Current census figures indicate that the majority of women in the workforce are mothers of children living at home. To put this in perspective, in 1900 only 1 wife in 20 was in the labor force, but by 1950 the ratio was 1 out of 5, and now it is about 3 out of 5. In 1940 8.6% of mothers with children under age 18 worked; now over half of children under age 1— 65% of preschool children and 75% of 6- to 13-year-olds—have mothers who work outside the home. Canada reports that in 7 out of 10 families, both parents work outside the home. But labor statistics show that more mothers are now staying home when they have a choice. According to the last census, the number of working mothers has declined for the first time since 1976. Demographers note that many mothers who are members of the so-called Generation X, now in their 20s and 30s, are looking for a sense of realistic balance, wanting to be both good workers and good mothers (Howe, Strauss, & Matson, 2000). Howe sees these mothers at the cutting edge of a generation that is "very protective of family life."

Women's Roles

Statistics alone cannot describe all that has occurred since the 1960s with the redefinition of women's roles. Since the publication of *The Feminine Mystique* (Friedan, 1963), women the world over have urged each other to find equality in their relationships with men and in their places in the community and at work. This has not been an easy change for anyone involved. For women it has meant adding new roles while often retaining much of the responsibility for household maintenance and child rearing. If a woman tries to combine all the roles she saw her mother play at home with her new work roles, she is in danger of falling into the "Superwoman" syndrome, with exhaustion and stress spilling over into all aspects of her life. Four out of every 10 women "often" or "very often" report feeling "used up" at the end of the workday. Working mothers are more likely to get sick than their husbands. Although women have cut back their household work from about 30 hours a week two decades ago to 20 hours a week today, their working husbands have not made up the difference, increasing their household work only from 5 to 10 hours, according to some sources (Coontz, 1997).

Coontz refers to mothers working outside the home as the "revival of women's roles as co-provider," noting that earlier in this century, women's employment was the most viable means for family economic advancement. Today women work so they can contribute to the necessities for their families as well as the items considered important for a rising family living standard. But it is more than a dollars-and-cents issue. Many women would not give up the satisfaction of work even if money were not an issue (although the number who would choose to stay home is increasing). Mothers working outside the home are likely here to stay. But this creates complexity in blending real and mythical issues about social roles.

One difficulty for many adult women is that a change in social thinking about women's rights and roles occurred after their early impressions had been formed by examples set by their own mothers and their youthful fantasies of what their lives would be like as grownup women. The female role they had learned was to nurture and care for others in their small home world; but current values urge them to care for themselves, to expand into the world. In confusion, many women have attempted to fit into the traditional pattern while expanding chaotically in all directions. Fortunately, now two generations later, many women are working out new patterns that better suit them and their situations.

FIGURE 2-9 Over half of all preschoolers have mothers working outside the home.

There is hope that children raised by women working outside the home will integrate several facets of female behavior into their sex role perceptions with less difficulty (see Figure 2-9).

Work is not the only aspect of women's lives to be reconsidered. The language of the women's movement in the 1960s and 1970s spoke of women as one of society's minorities, without equality at home or outside the home. Issues of sexuality and reproduction, of sex role stereotypes and limitations were discussed nationwide. Some real changes were effected, and consciousness was raised. The increase in marital instability may be partly attributable to this questioning of traditional relationships, and the women's movement may have been a major influence on the nature of families and society in years to come. Whether or not women and men agree with the push toward equality, it is virtually impossible for anyone in the country to remain untouched by the debate and its repercussions on lifestyles. But change comes through turmoil, and this environment of changing relationships and role behaviors has pushed women and men in the family into less comfortable territory.

One point should be added to this discussion of women's roles. Women may play the role of mother in a two-parent family, a single-parent family, or a stepfamily. Whereas the stresses of mothering in a single-parent family have been noted earlier, the parenting role of these women is more like the mother in a two-parent family than is the role of a woman who is a stepparent. It takes much time and effort for stepmothers to become effective in their parenting role; indeed their function will usually be different in the family unless the biological mother is deceased or completely out of contact with the family. Stepparents are developing their own responses to this unique role.

Men's Roles

Men's family roles are on similarly challenging new ground. Not only are they asked to share positions and power in the workplace with women, but at home more is expected of them than was expected of their fathers. They may still not be carrying their equal share of household chores, but the days of hiding guilt-free behind the newspaper until dinner is on the table are gone. Gone also are the models of paternal behavior they knew as children. But, after all, this is what happened to their fathers before them. Grandfather's role in the family was to exert authoritarian control, but after World War II a father's major role with his children became that of playmate. As fathers received more leisure time due to changing work patterns, and as the expert advice to parents continued to change from stern rigidity to concern with children feeling loved and happy, fathers became someone with whom their children could have fun.

Today's father plays with his child, but he also takes his turn sitting in the pediatrician's office, cooking dinner, supervising homework, and carpooling. Frequently he is involved before his child's birth—attending childbirth classes with his wife to learn how to coach her through prepared childbirth (see Figure 2-10). But is this involvement as pervasive as some articles in women's magazines portray?

The answer appears to be increasingly yes in families where mothers are "work-committed"—that is, who work full-time and share financial decisions. In these families men are beginning to shrink the labor gap in the household and are becoming more involved with their children. A recent Census Bureau report says that men are now the primary caregivers in one out of every five dual-earner households with preschool children. This suggests that many more men have significant child care responsibilities than is usually thought.

Certainly the pressure for men to become more involved with household and child care responsibilities has come from women, especially those with growing economic power. "The fact that so many mothers now bring home the bacon gives them more say about who cleans up after eating it" (Holcomb, 1996/97). But fathers themselves are frequently looking for a new lifestyle, one that allows them to be more involved with their families. Trying to find a balance between job and family responsibilities creates new stress for some fathers today (Levine & Pittinsky, 1998).

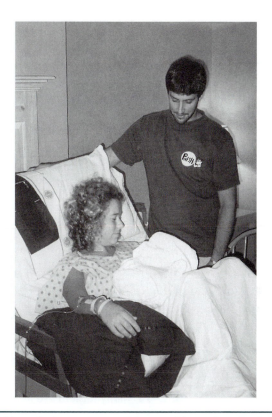

FIGURE 2-10 Many fathers now participate with mothers in their infants' birth.

Although increased participation is occurring in many households, the primary responsibility for both house and child care remains the mother's, perhaps due to the constraints of role behavior norms for men and women and the signals sent by society that moms are the parents who really count while dads are in minor roles. One writer (Helms, 2000) offers the example of a school secretary trying to get in touch with the mother of a sick child. When asked by a coworker whether she had already called the father, she said she didn't like to interrupt him. The implication is that mom's work is more easily interruptible and it is her job really (an additional source of stress for working mothers), but also that dad is either less caring or less capable of handling the emergency, rather than equally competent and caring as mom. Such implicit messages weaken men's attempts to be fully involved parents.

Certainly there are not a lot of models of highly participant fathers, and the few fathers who do participate equally as parents receive little recognition and support, at least in their perceptions. In a study by the National Institute of Mental Health about why so few fathers took parental leaves when their babies were born, over 60% said that their supervisors would not like it, and more than 40% said they thought their coworkers would view it negatively (Coontz, 1997). Many men who try to take time off to attend a teacher

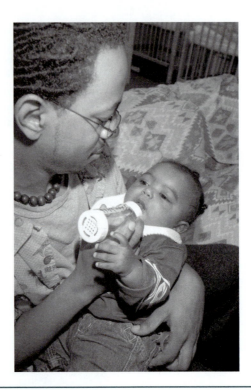

FIGURE 2-11 Many fathers are more involved in parenting today.

conference or school play get the impression that the boss and coworkers see them as slackers and expect the mothers—working or not—to handle such matters.

Some research projects also show that men who attempt to take on more family responsibilities get increased negative feedback from grandparents and even from wives. The legacy of the model of male as breadwinner and female as caregiver may create stress for men trying to find new roles. But it is probably fair to say that today's father is often called upon to share with his wife all aspects of the children's care, to display many of the nurturant behaviors previously associated only with mothers (see Figure 2-11.) Indeed, one phenomenon that occurs in many communities is fathers becoming stay-at-home parents while their wives work outside the home, with these fathers assuming the full responsibility for the household and care of children that was previously thought to be the woman's role. To define what it means to be a man, major shifts in thinking are required. However men feel about it—and most fathers are pleased with their new roles—the change in women's roles in contemporary society has changed their own. Figure 2-12 shows fathers' changed roles in the household. The Fatherhood Project at the Families and Work Institute in New York City studies current trends in fathers' roles and provides a national guide to services for and about fathers. Chapter 3 will look more at

	Fathers in 1975	Fathers in 2000
Present at birth	27%	91%
Primary caregiver when mother works	12%	20%
Time spent with child/day	2.5 hours	4.0 hours
Time spent on housework/week	4.5 hours	10 hours

FIGURE 2-12 The number of fathers participating in the household has increased since 1975.

recent research on the absolute importance of fathers' involvement with their children's lives.

It should also be noted that agreement about the desirability of this sharing of father and mother roles is not universal. A strong conservative orientation is currently advocating a return of "paternalism"—fathers being the strong voice in running the family and women returning to the home for primary responsibility in child rearing. It will be interesting to follow this trend in our culture.

Certainly some shifts in thinking have occurred, though many more may be required. The doctor who advised so many parents in earlier generations, the late Dr. Benjamin Spock, offers an example of those changes. In 1946, in his first edition of *Baby and Child Care,* he was quite definite that it made no sense for mothers to work and hire someone else to care for their children. By 1976 he had changed his position to the idea that both parents had an equal right to a career and an equal obligation to share in the care of their children. Slowly society has been pushed to alter its expectations regarding the roles of family members, and individuals are caught between trying to balance the external realities and demands and the internal psychological conflict caused by attempting a new social pattern.

The jury is still out on what impact the different patterns of family roles and parenting have on family members. Certainly there are more opportunities for personal growth with alternatives from which to choose freely. Children have a more democratic family model as an increasing number of fathers take on the loving and nurturing aspects of parenthood, and an increasing number of mothers take on leadership roles outside as well as inside the home. Changes in roles have opened doors for everyone, men and women alike.

Mobility and Urbanization

With increasing industrialization and employment patterns, many workers and their families move frequently in the search for new and better jobs. The average American moves 14 times in a lifetime. According to the latest census, more than 16% of American families had moved during the previous year (http://www.census.gov).

What does this mean to contemporary families? When earlier families worked together on economic production in the home and family farm, parents were much more available to their children. The shift to urban occupations enabled many families to improve their economic status. Recent changes in the structuring of business and industry have made family job security more fragile, and families have had to move where jobs dictate. This increased geographical mobility has brought less sense of community and more isolation. It probably means that the nuclear family—the parents and their children—are far removed from the physical presence of others who may have acted as sources of support in earlier times.

A new mother coming home from the hospital with her new baby may know little about how to care physically for the infant, let alone how to deal with the anxiety that arises about 3:00 a.m. Her only support is her husband, who may be as ignorant and anxious as she. In a bygone day her mother, mother-in-law, aunts, cousins, sisters, and neighbors who had known her since she was a baby may have surrounded her.

As time goes by, the young couple needs baby-sitters to be able to shop in peace or have some recreation time away from the child, someone to care for the sick child when the parents have to work, someone to delight along with them in the child's success at school or commiserate and calm them when the child begins to throw temper tantrums, use bathroom talk, have learning problems, or anything else that may come as a shock to a first-time parent. Increasingly parents have to turn to others to fill functions that could have been performed by the extended family were they not so far away (see Figure 2-13). For example, they might hire the neighbor's teenaged daughter to look after the baby so they can have an evening out, or they might decide they can't afford the expense or the anxiety and just stay home instead.

FIGURE 2-13 Many nuclear families are so far from grandparents and other family that children have to show on the map where they occasionally visit.

The isolation caused by moving far from traditional sources of support causes stress for today's parents. Parents are totally responsible for everything, creating an ambivalent situation in their home and family. In one sense the nuclear family so created has a special sense of solidarity that separates this unit from the surrounding community; its members feel more in common with one another than with anyone outside the family. Although this may produce some warm feelings, a cold feeling of isolation may also be present. "In our nuclear family culture, each new generation searches for its own values, even if it is a lonely search. Without the last generation as a backup, young families can feel anxious and anchorless" (Brazelton, 1989).

Part of this isolation is self-induced. American families, taught to value independence, feel that seeking help beyond the family circle is an admission of failure. Today, without the traditional backup system, this lingering myth further isolates families.

Rearing children in an urban setting offers its own problems for parents in addition to isolation. While the diversity of cultural, religious, and racial backgrounds offers richness and variety in today's world, it can also be a potential source of conflict as children are exposed to such a pluralistic society. And cities continue to offer the main environment for child rearing. Cities grew nearly twice as fast as other communities in the past decade, with that growth bringing problems of pollution, crime, and stress for families. Lest this be misinterpreted as a condemnation of cities, it should be recalled that our cities have become the major repositories for current culture and knowledge. Moreover, the events of September 11, 2001, showed how the inhabitants of cities, as well as any small town, can come together powerfully to support one another in times of crisis.

Family Size Decreasing

A family household, according to the Census Bureau, is two or more persons related by blood, marriage, or adoption. Current statistics indicate the average family has shrunk over the years, from 4.76 in 1900 to 3.67 in 1940 to just 2.6 currently, in both Canada and the United States, with the exception of Hispanic and Asian households, which have increased to over 3.5. (Figures are from the U.S. Census Bureau current population reports, from Statistical Abstract/US, 2000, and the Vanier Institute.) This decrease is due to fewer children under age 18 in each household—from 1.34 in 1970 to fewer than 1 now. There are numerous reasons for this.

A major reason is delayed marriage and childbearing with increased standards of education and career expectations. As recently as 1975, 63% of women between the ages of 20 and 24 were married; by the 2000 census this figure had shrunk dramatically to 27%. Currently the median age for American men marrying is 26.8 years, and for women it is 25.1; in Canada men's median age at marriage is 30, and women's is 27 (figures from 2000 Census and Vanier Institute).

This later age for marriage of contemporary women is higher than the previous historical peak in 1890, and approaches the highest age ever recorded for Western Europe, where marriage has always taken place later than anywhere else in the world (Coontz, 1997).

Besides the need for prolonged education and career expectations, other reasons for decreasing family size include these:

- The economic burden of raising children in times of inflation with no corresponding asset of children's economic contribution to the family unit.
- Changing attitudes about women's roles in the home and workplace.
- Increased expectations for the family living standards and material wants.
- The move from rural to urban environments.

There are also more single-child families. In practical terms this means that it is possible to become a parent without ever having touched a small baby or having had any share of responsibility for caring for younger brothers and sisters, leaving today's parents anxious and confused in their new roles. The earlier form of a larger family offered its members more experience as they grew up with other children (see Figure 2-14).

FIGURE 2-14 Many families now have only one child.

Another factor contributing to the decrease in family size is the increasing absence of adults other than parents living in the home. In the 1920s more than 50% of American households had at least one other adult living in the home—grandparents, aunts, or uncles. It was common for young families to begin married life living with their own parents. By the 1950s this had decreased to 10%; today probably only 3–4% of homes have another adult. If families include grandparents today, they are likely to be single-parent families that have moved into the grandparents' home for economic and social support—clearly a role reversal of the old pattern of living with extended family, when younger families were helping maintain the older generation.

Or grandparents may have included their grandchildren in their families, but the children's parents are not present, as is the case for 5.5% of American children. In addition, if there are adults in the household, they may well be adult children of the householder. More than half of the young men between ages 18 and 25 were living in their parents' homes in the last census. This may well reflect the delaying of marriage and tight economic times.

The Census Bureau notes the phenomenon of a marked increase in the number of people living alone, both people older than 55 and people in their 20s. In the past, these would have been members of an extended family household. This implies that the smaller nuclear family is without the additional supportive resources of time, money, and companionship that other adults in the household could offer.

It is somewhat difficult to get an accurate reading on family composition today. When reading the results of the latest census (Bianchi & Casper, 2000), we can see that families and their composition are really too complex for simple classification or counting. For example, families that are counted as being headed by a single father often include a female adult who is likely functioning in many ways as the other parent. And of those classified as unmarried cohabiting partners, two-fifths are also likely to include children.

Again, the most important aspect of considering demographics is to realize how much change families are undergoing.

Increased Rate of Social Change

Parents in a relatively static society encounter less difficulty than those in a society where social change occurs rapidly and drastically, as in the United States and Canada for the past three decades and more. A generation gap develops when adults play increasingly complex roles in a world their own parents could not prepare them for and when parents try to help their own children face a world they cannot yet imagine. It is not a comfortable world where parents can simply produce children like themselves, but a new world where parents are unsure about their best move—a world of challenge and potential, but also of stress for today's fathers and mothers.

HOW WE LIVE AND HOW WE USED TO LIVE

	1970	2000
Traditional families—married couples, including stepfamilies, with children under 18	40%	25%
Married couples, no children—never had or grown	30%	28%
Women living alone—young, widowed, divorced	12%	15%
Men living alone	6%	11%
Single mother, children under 18	5%	8%
Single mother, grown children	4%	5%
Single father, children under 18	1%	2%
Roommates—unmarried heterosexual or homosexual	2%	5%

They themselves grew up in the world of yesterday, a world that is now largely dead, and they internalized that world; they rear their children in the world of today, a world they only partially understand and only partly accept; but they are trying to prepare their children for the world of tomorrow, a world that nobody yet understands (LeMasters & DeFrain, 1983).

The rate of change is dizzying as upheaval occurs in every major institution in society. Major discontinuities in relationships among people develop, as changing values, laws, and norms of behavior result in a different way of life.

Beginning with the civil rights movement, the women's movement, the Vietnam war, and the turmoil from groups opposing and supporting it, society has continued to be beleaguered by anxieties:

- Disillusionment with government leaders with questionable practices or moral beliefs.

- Worry about the educational system.

- Turmoil in the world overseas and at home.

- Fears of terrorist attacks at home as well as abroad.

- Worry about keeping children safe at school and in the community.

- Concerns about environmental deterioration.

- Fears about drugs invading our lives.

- Concerns about diseases without cures becoming epidemic.

- Worry about what inflation, debt, and pollution mean to the future.

An endless succession of new ideas and images has bombarded us during recent decades. Closer to home, the structure and appearance of the family,

FIGURE 2-15 Many grandparents are now raising their grandchildren.

the roles family members play, attitudes toward sexual activity, contraception, abortion—all are different now than they once were. There are new life span events, created by the need to respond to increased longevity and the psychosocial identity adjustments within ever more complex family arrangements. Just imagine the mental adjustments that have to be made by a grandparent raising her own grandchild in the absence of parents. The 2000 U.S. Census showed that more than 2.4 million grandparents have their grandchildren living with them, being responsible for the children's basic needs (see Figure 2-15). Past census counts found grandchildren living with grandparents, but the 2000 census was the first to ask about the grandparents' role in caring for grandchildren, indicating this dramatic shift in responsibility (AARP, 2002). Playing the dual roles of parent and grandparent is something for which there is no model, perhaps promoting role conflict and additional family stress.

This makes parents unsure of themselves, and they worry about almost everything that touches their lives and their children's. They worry about whether they're too permissive or expecting too much in a changing world; they worry about the influence of television and violence and the quality of education; and most of all they worry because they are making decisions alone—they are reluctant to seek advice from others.

The customs of the work world make this lack of certainty doubly hard for many parents to deal with.

> All parents worry about making mistakes. . . . One reason it can be difficult for successful working parents to adjust to child rearing is that the culture of the workplace is often one of perfectionism and dependable rewards. In raising a family, on the other hand, rewards are rarely dependable . . . (Brazelton, 1989).

Parents are not the only ones unsure in a world that has changed so quickly. The society that surrounds them is equally confused. In a recent Gallup poll Americans supported seemingly contradictory family values. Eighty-seven percent reported they held "old-fashioned values about family and marriage," and 68% believed that "too many children are being raised in day care centers today." At the same time, 66% rejected the idea that "women should return to their traditional roles in society," and 64% also rejected the idea that "it's more important for a wife to help her husband's career than to have one herself." Clearly change has happened too quickly for some of our values and beliefs to catch up. Families are caught in the dilemma of rapid change in very real ways. Most jobs are still designed as if there were a home-maker to provide support for a working husband, and many institutional practices assume that all children live with two biological parents. Social structure has changed rapidly; changes in social and personal values and feelings lag behind.

Child-Centered Society

More than one expert has pointed out how the child's role in the family and in society has evolved over the centuries, particularly in current times in the Western world. In earlier times a child was measured harshly by the yardstick of the adult world and restricted to fit into it.

> As early as 1820, maternal associations were formed in the larger cities that addressed the Calvinist idea of "breaking children's wills." Editorial space in newspapers and magazines occasionally was devoted to discussions of techniques that would result in children's submission to the authority of the mother (Bigner, 2001).

In the late 1920s parents were still given restrictive advice, as evidenced by this excerpt from the writing of J. B. Watson: "There is a sensible way of treating children. Treat them as though they were young adults. . . . Never hug and kiss them, never let them sit in your lap" (Bigner, 2001).

But in modern America, a child is the darling of his or her world (see Figure 2-16). Whole industries have sprung up to cater to children's wishes—toys, children's television, designer clothing, and breakfast cereals. The efforts

FIGURE 2-16 Increasingly we are a child-centered society.

of psychologists and other researchers are directed more toward telling parents what they should and should not be doing to nurture their children. A large part of current research and thinking concerning child development now is available in forms both popular and technical. Bookstores have many shelves of books of advice to parents, often suggesting conflicting views of a variety of experts (Hull, 2003). Parenting magazines and Web sites abound.

Parent education classes are available in almost every community. Anyone who has taught a parent education class has heard two frequent reactions from the parents involved. One is to marvel that parents in earlier times did an acceptable job of parenting without possessing this knowledge: "My mother raised five kids, and we all turned out pretty well, and she never even heard of Erikson or Piaget!" The other reaction is from the parent who concentrates, with guilt, on what she or he has already done or missed the chance to do. "If only I'd known this five years ago." Whether parents decide on their own that they could have done a better job, or whether the society around them does, the result is that parents come out the "bad guys" in a culture that centers on the child.

It should also be noted, ironically, that alarming figures suggest our rhetoric may be more child-centered than our practices. Children's Defense Fund (2004) notes that the United States—first among industrialized countries in gross domestic product, the number of millionaires and billionaires, health and military technology, military exports and defense spending—is 14th in efforts to lift children out of poverty, 16th in rates of low birth weight births, 18th in the percentage of children in poverty, 23rd in infant mortality, and last in protecting our children against gun violence. One in five of all American children was born to a mother who did not finish high school; one in eight of all American children has no health insurance; one in six is born to a mother who did not receive prenatal care in the first three months of pregnancy; and one in three is behind a year or more in school. These facts make us question the genuineness of our so-called child-centered society.

Stress in Modern Living

A generation ago it seemed that shorter workweeks due to modern technology would make life easier for many families. Unfortunately, that dream was never realized. Today adults are working harder than ever. According to a recent study, the average workweek jumped from under 41 hours in 1973 to nearly 47 hours today, with many professional and higher-level jobs demanding 50 or more hours each week. A *Wall Street Journal* study found that almost all top executives were working 10 or more hours a day, and nearly one in five was working 12 or more hours. As parents feel overloaded at work, their emotional well-being suffers (Galinsky et al., 2001; Brownfield, 2001). It is no wonder that there seems to be so much stress on the family and individuals when the adults are spending so much time competing to keep their jobs in a time of employment insecurity. Much of this stress is related to economic changes: declines in real wages, demands for a more highly skilled and educated work-force, increasing technology creating competition for jobs, and an increased cost of raising children. Parents may not have real choices about the time spent in work and apart from family.

Obviously the fallout affects both adults and children under such conditions. "It seems clear that overload, exhaustion, and strain do not make for good parenting, and yet these qualities are part and parcel of mainstream American life now that there are so many dual-worker and single-parent households" (Hewlett, 1991). Hewlett refers to the "parental time deficit" and claims that parents are devoting much more time to earning a living and much less time to their children than they did a generation ago. This is not purely an American phenomenon. The Vanier Institute reports that nearly half of the respondents in a Canadian survey said they felt stressed by the demands of their professional, family, and marital lives (Sauve, 2004; Daly, 2000) (see Figure 2-17).

The UCLA Center on Everyday Lives of Families has spent the past four years observing families to examine the intersection between family life and work. Finding that parents and children live apart at least five days a week, reuniting only for a few hours at night, the researchers suggest that the nonstop pace seems to erode families from within, with playtime, conversation, and intimacy falling by the wayside. Most families have no unstructured time (News-Press, 2005). In her study of how children perceive their parents' negotiation of work and family life, Galinsky (1999) found that the quantity of time mothers and fathers have with children matters a great deal. When children spend more time with their parents on both workdays and nonworkdays, they see their parents as putting their family first. Nevertheless, many children mention that the time they spend with their parents feels rushed and hectic, and they comment on the lack of focus from many parents, indicating

"Mom!"

FIGURE 2-17 With so many responsibilities and so much stress, it is not surprising that parents may get a little confused.

that families today need to find ways of getting out from under the stress to make changes that will benefit all.

In fact, in recent years modern parents not only are increasing their time at the workplace, but also have greater demands on their nonworking time. There is increased pressure from society for individuals to fulfill self-centered goals. Finding and fulfilling oneself are acceptable and necessary activities that demand time. The highly organized community offers more choices and demands more participation for both adults and children. Someone recently commented that most modern children are being brought up by appliances and in moving vehicles; this does seem an apt image for the on-the-go style of modern families. Those who point out the extremely busy life of the suburban child, moving from swimming lessons to Boy Scouts to doctors' appointments to activities organized with friends, fail to also mention that behind this busy child are parents who make all the arrangements and drive the child around! A parent who works full-time at a job has only begun to fill the expected responsibilities at the end of the working day.

"Mom!"

For many families in lower socioeconomic circumstances, stress may be caused not by fulfilling responsibilities to children's social lives, but by carrying a heavy workload to provide necessities of daily life for their children. Often parents are working more than one job, working odd shifts, and keeping appointments with community agencies for needed support, so they have little time for either their children or themselves. Such a schedule brings burdens to all.

Chapter 3 looks more carefully at the various roles a parent plays; at this point it is important to realize that a contemporary parent's day is filled with more demands and expectations than there are hours. Societal attitudes and lack of support may add stress to some family structures. David Elkind points out that the nuclear family kinship structure may be the least stressful in current society, but only insofar as the family is emotionally healthy and financially secure (Elkind, 1995).

The real stress in all this is that parenting, when done properly, takes much more time and energy than almost anything else. "Well-developing children dramatically limit personal freedom and seriously interfere with the pursuit of an ambitious career" (Hewlett, 1991). As long as modern parents are pulled in so many directions, stress will accompany the family. Urie Bronfenbrenner stated this well in his report to the White House Conference on Children:

> In today's world parents find themselves at the mercy of a society which imposes pressures and priorities that allow neither time nor place for meaningful activities and relations between children and adults, which downgrade the role of parents and the functions of parenthood, and which prevent the parent from doing things he wants to do. (1974)

In a more recent statement (1991) he said, "The hectic pace of modern life poses a threat to our children second only to poverty and unemployment."

■■■ WHY STUDY SOCIOLOGICAL TRENDS?

Beginning teachers may wonder why the conditions in society that currently affect families are a topic that deserves their attention. In fact, it is vital to effective relationships with families to understand the conditions and circumstances in which they grow. It is too easy for teachers to set up a kind of oppositional stance, an "us against them" mentality—to judge parents as somehow not measuring up to some sort of ideal standard of what parents are "supposed to do." But when the larger picture of changes in our entire society is considered, it becomes clear that all of us are caught up in and affected by the trends that change the face and functioning of families. Rather than judging families against some artificial standard, or perhaps the way we never were, it is vital that teachers be able to recognize the forces that influence the thinking of us all. Empathy and the compassion needed to work with people very different from ourselves are the result of seeing contemporary families against the backdrop of the real world in which we now live (see Figure 2-18).

Two student teachers were once heard describing their common experience in "both coming from **dysfunctional** families." When pressed for elaboration, they clarified that they had both been raised by single parents, one as a result of divorce, the other as a result of a parent's death. So influenced were they by the dominant social images of typical families that they confused form with function; because their families did not resemble the usual image, they labeled them dysfunctional. In actual fact, both of their families had functioned well to raise the children with caring, protection, and helpful communication.

Studying sociological trends may keep other teachers from making the error of confusing the form of a family with its ability to carry out its functions. It is important for teachers to focus not on family composition but rather on family disposition, such as beliefs, values, and behaviors.

A family functions successfully when it supports and nurtures its members so that everyone's needs are met. Members of a successful family feel emotional and social attachment to one another. They understand the importance of both independence and interdependence. They know how to communicate effectively, to resolve conflicts, and to cope with problems that can't be solved. They know how to provide a secure and protective environment in the home. They provide a safe base for family members to grow and develop, expecting the best from each other (Gonzalez-Mena, 2005).

Dysfunctional families, on the other hand, are those where something has gone wrong so that all family members' needs are not met. Combinations of personal, psychological, and environmental factors may produce homes that do not support healthy growth and relationships. Dysfunctional families may include those that have

- *Deficient parents.* Here children are hurt more by omission than by commission. The emotional needs of the parents tend to take precedence over those of their children, and children often have to become their parents' caretakers.

- *Controlling parents.* These parents fail to allow children to assume responsibilities appropriate for their age and continue dominating their lives.

21 Key Facts about American Children

3 in 5	preschoolers have mothers in the labor force.
2 in 5	preschoolers eligible for Head Start do not participate in the program.
1 in 2	will live in a single-parent family at some point in childhood.
1 in 3	is born to unmarried parents.
1 in 3	will be poor at some point in childhood.
1 in 3	is behind a year or more in school.
1 in 4	lives with only one parent.
1 in 5	is born to a mother who did not graduate from high school.
1 in 5	was born poor.
1 in 5	children under 3 is poor now.
1 in 6	is born to a mother who did not receive prenatal care in the first three months of pregnancy.
1 in 7	children eligible for federal child care assistance through the Child Care and Development Block Grant receives it.
1 in 7	never graduates from high school.
1 in 8	has no health insurance.
1 in 8	lives in a family receiving food stamps.
1 in 9	is born to a teenaged mother.
1 in 12	has a disability.
1 in 13	was born at low birth weight.
1 in 13	will be arrested at least once before age 17.
1 in 14	lives at less than half the poverty level.
1 in 35	lives with grandparents but neither parent.
1 in 60	sees their parent divorce in any year.
1 in 83	will be in state or federal prison before age 20.
1 in 146	will die before their first birthday.
1 in 1,339	will be killed by firearms before age 20.

FIGURE 2-18 Teachers need to understand the facts of the real world in which we now live.

Used with permission of the Children's Defense Fund. All rights reserved.

- *Addicted parents.* Parents addicted to drugs or alcohol provide a chaotic and unpredictable environment for their children.

- *Abusive parents.* When parents abuse their children physically, emotionally, and sexually, the parent–child relationship is disrupted and dysfunctional.

We will talk more about working with these last two kinds of dysfunctional families in Chapter 16.

REFLECTIONS FOR JOURNAL ENTRIES

What do you think is the most important function of family? What do you think families need most to be able to fulfill this function? How can communities best support families? How can an individual teacher support families to fulfill their functions?

WHAT DO STRONG FAMILIES HAVE IN COMMON?

Strong families

- Work for the well-being or defend the unity and continuity of the family.
- Support each other.
- Respect each family member's uniqueness and difference.
- Spend time together to build family cohesion.
- Delegate responsibility.
- Allow children to make mistakes and face consequences.
- Have a spiritual dimension.
- Contribute to the well-being of their neighborhoods, city, country, and world.

From Strong & Devault, 1995.

METAPHORS FOR FAMILY

If the family were a container, it would be a nest, an enduring nest, loosely woven, expansive, and open.

If the family were a fruit, it would be an orange, a circle of sections held together but separable—each segment distinct.

If the family were a boat, it would be a canoe that makes no progress unless everybody paddles.

If the family were a sport, it would be baseball: a long, slow, non-violent game that is never over till the last out.

If the family were a building, it would be an old, but solid, structure that contains human history and appeals to those who see the carved moldings under all the plaster, the wide plank floors under the linoleum, the possibilities.

L. C. Pogebrin in Schlesinger, 1998.

SUMMARY

The new demographics mean that the American family and the growing-up experiences of many of our nation's children have been drastically altered. Condensing all aspects of contemporary life, there are benefits as well as disadvantages for parents. The trend toward mobility that has enforced isolation for many American families has at the same time brought an increased number of opportunities for employment, prosperity, and personal growth. The trend toward marital instability has brought stress and pain for many adults and children, to be sure; in many cases divorce has also brought the opportunity to find less discordant ways to live. It is not the purpose here to evaluate sociological trends; rather, it is important only to stimulate the teachers who will be working closely with modern families to consider the influences in the world that impinge on those families and mold their shape and direction, sometimes without their agreement.

Modern families are beset by difficulties related to new social patterns that have evolved from without, and by the psychological pressures from within that arise when individuals' life experiences differ from the models they have learned.

Parenting is already a complex task, and within the context of modern American culture, the challenge of parenting is heightened.

STUDENT ACTIVITIES FOR FURTHER STUDY

1. Do your own ministudies to consider the nature of social influences on contemporary families.

   a. Involve a group of parents of your acquaintance in an informal discussion. What are the differences between theirs and their parents' experiences as parents? Which cultural conditions discussed in the text do you find in their comments?

   b. With parents who are willing to discuss their lifestyles, try to learn family patterns of sex role participation—who shops, cleans, cooks, cares for children, and takes them to the doctor, to the library, or for haircuts?

   c. Ask several parents of your acquaintance where they were born and raised, and where their extended families now live. How do your findings agree or disagree with the text discussion of mobility?

   d. Note the family structure of children in any classroom. Figure out the percentage of traditional two-parent families, families with two working parents, single parents, stepparents, or other arrangements. What about family size? Are there additional family members in the household? How do your findings compare with the text discussions of marital instability, changing roles of women, and family size?

2. Interview three generations of a family: your grandparents, your parents, and yourself or your spouse, or others who would be of those

generations. Ask questions that will give you insights regarding their views and concerns about family structure and changes, number of times they have moved, issues of balancing work and family time, who was in charge, and the joys and challenges of family life at each stage. Share some of these insights with your classmates.

3. In class discussion, consider some of the causes of divorce and other changes in family patterns.

4. In small groups, discuss the following questions:

   a. Would you rather be a parent today than in 1960? Why or why not?

   b. Would you plan to stay at home with children, work, or do both if you were a parent?

   c. What do you consider some of the biggest challenges families face today?

CASE STUDY

Reread the stories of the 12 fictional families described in this chapter. Concentrate on two families in particular as you answer these questions:

1. How do these families illustrate the concept that contemporary families are under stress? Identify the sources of stress in each family.

2. How do these families illustrate the concept that family structure takes many forms? Identify the types of families you are looking at.

3. How do these families illustrate concepts about changing male and female roles?

4. Name any other social changes discussed in this chapter that are illustrated by the two families you chose.

REVIEW QUESTIONS

1. Define *family*.

2. Describe two characteristics of a family.

3. List seven characteristics of modern life that influence the nature of modern families.

SUGGESTIONS FOR FURTHER READING

Benkou, L. (1994). *Reinventing the family.* New York: Crown Publishers, Inc.

Birckmayer, J., Cohen, J., Jensen, I., and Variano, D. (2005). Kyle lives with his Granny—where are his mommy and daddy? Supporting grandparents who raise grandchildren. *Young Children, 60*(3), 100–104.

Blankenhorn, D. (1995). *Fatherless America: Confronting our most urgent social problems.* New York: Basic Books.

Brooks, A. A. (1990, April). Educating the children of fast-track parents. *Phi Delta Kappan, 71*(8), 612–615.

Chow, E., Wilkinson, D., & Zinn,. B. (1996). *Common bonds, different voices.* Newbury Park, CA: Sage.

Christian, L. G. (2006). "Understanding families: Applying family systems theory to early childhood practice." *Young Children, 61(1), 12-20.*

Coleman, M. (1991). Planning for the changing nature of family life in schools for young children. *Young Children, 46*(4), 15–20.

Danitz, T. (2001). "The voices of America's families." *U.S. Society and Values, 6*(1), electronic journal of the Department of State. Available online at http://www.usinfo.state.gov. Search in the journals for this article.

Fields, J., & Smith, K. (1998). Poverty, family structure, and child well-being: Indicators from the SIPP. *US Census Bureau.* Search for this article online at http://www.census.gov.

Gore, A. & T. (2002). *Joined at the heart: The transformations of the American family.* New York: Henry Holt and Co.

Hernandez, D. (1997/98). Changing demographics: Past and future demands for early childhood programs. In K. Paciorek & J. Munro (Eds.). *Annual editions early childhood education 1997/98.* Guilford, CT: Dushkin.

Musick, J. (1995). *Young, poor, and pregnant: The psychology of teenage motherhood.* New Haven, CT: Yale University Press.

Nunez, R., & Collignon, K. (1997, Oct.). Creating a community of learning for homeless children. *Educational Leadership,* 56–60.

Procidano, M. E., & Fisher, C. B. (Eds.). (1992). *Contemporary families: A handbook for school professionals.* New York: Teachers College Press.

Reed, S., & Sautter, R. C. (1990, June). Children of poverty: The status of 12 million young Americans. *Phi Delta Kappan, Special Report, K1–K12.*

Roberts, P. (1996, May/June). Fathers' time. *Psychology Today,* 48–55.

Scherer, M. (1996). On our changing family values: A conversation with David Elkind. *Educational Leadership, 53*(7), 4–9.

Shames, S., Kozol, J., & Edelman, M. W. (1991). *Outside the dream: Child poverty in America.* New York: Aperture.

Smith, A., Dannison L., & Vach-Hasse, T. (1998, Fall). When "Grandma" is "Mom": What today's teachers need to know." *Childhood Education, 75*(1), 12–16.

REFERENCES

AARP. (2002). U.S. begins to track grandparent caregivers. *AARP Bulletin, 43*(7), 2.

Bianchi, S. M, & Casper, L. M. (2000). American families. *Population Bulletin, 55*(4). Available online at http://www.prb.org.

Bigner, J. J. (2001). *Parent–child relations: An introduction to parenting* (6th ed.). New York: Macmillan.

Brazelton, T. B. (1989). *Families: Crisis and caring.* Reading, MA: Addison-Wesley.

Bronfenbrenner, U. (1974). The roots of alienation. In N. B. Talbot (Ed.), *Raising children in modern America: Problems and prospective solutions.* Boston: Little, Brown and Co.

———. (1991, March 29). Rush-hour children: An interview with Urie Bronfenbrenner. *Charlotte Observer.*

Brownfield, E. (2001). *The time crunch.* New York: Families and Work Institute.

Children's Defense Fund. (2004). *The state of America's children. Yearbook 2004.* Washington, D.C: Author.

Coontz, S. (1992). *The way we never were: American families and the nostalgia trap.* New York: Basic Books.

———. (1997). *The way we really are: Coming to terms with America's changing families.* New York: Basic Books.

Daly, K. (2000). It keeps getting faster: Changing patterns of time in families. *Vanier Institute of the Family.* Available online at http://www.vifamily.ca.

Elkind, D. (1994). *Ties that stress: The new family imbalance.* Cambridge, MA: Harvard University Press.

———. (1995, Sept.). School and family in the postmodern world. *Phi Delta Kappan,* 8–14.

Friedan, B. (1963). *The feminine mystique.* New York: Norton.

Galinsky, E. (1999). *Ask the children: What America's children really think about working parents.* New York: Morrow.

———, Kim, S., & Bond, J. (2001). *Feeling overworked: When work becomes too much.* New York: Families and Work Institute.

Gonzalez-Mena, J. (2005). *The child in the family and the community* (3rd ed.). Upper Saddle River, NJ: Prentice-Hall.

Helms, A. D. (2000, Feb. 1). Why can't we see Dad as the go-to guy? *Charlotte Observer.*

Halpern, A., Fernandez, L., & Clark, R. (2000). "Snapshots of American families.

Children's environment and behavior. *Families Worldwide.* Retrieved Feb. 23, 2006 online at http://www.fww.org.

Hewlett, S. A. (1991). *When the bough breaks: The cost of neglecting our children.* New York: Harper Collins Publishers.

Hildebrand, V., Phenice, L., Gray, M., Hines, R., Bubolz, M., & Sontag, M. (1999). *Knowing and serving diverse families* (2nd ed.). Englewood Cliffs, NJ: Merrill.

Holcomb, B. (1996/97). How families are changing . . . for the better! In K. Paciorek & J. Munro (Eds.). *Annual editions early childhood education 1996/97.* Guilford, CT: Dushkin.

Howe, N., Strauss, W., & Matson, R. (2000). *Millennials rising: The next great generation.* New York: Vintage.

Hull, A. (2003). *Raising America: Experts, parents, and a century of advice.* New York: Knopf.

Kennedy, M., & King, J. (1994). *The single-parent family living happily in a changing world.* New York: Crown Publishers.

Leach, P. (1994). *Children first: What our society must do—and is not doing—for our children today.* New York: Knopf.

LeMasters, E. E., & DeFrain, J. (1983). *Parents in contemporary America: A sympathetic view* (4th ed.). Homewood, IL: The Dorsey Press.

Levine, J., & Pittinsky, T. (1998). *Working fathers: New strategies for balancing work and family.* Reading, MA: Addison-Wesley.

Louv, R., (1995/96). The crisis of the absent father. In K. Paciorek & J. Munro (Eds.). *Annual editions early childhood education 1995/96.* Guilford, CT: Dushkin.

News-Press. (2005, March 20). American family like ships passing in dark.

Newsweek. (1990, Winter). The twenty-first century family. *Newsweek Special Edition.*

Pipher, M. (1996). *The shelter of each other: Rebuilding our families.* New York: G. P. Putnam's Sons.

Roberts, S. (1993). *Who we are: A portrait of America based on the latest U.S. census.* New York: Random House.

Sauve, R. (2004). *Profiling Canada's families* III. Ottawa, Ontario: Vanier Institute of the Family.

Schlesinger, B. (1998). Strengths in families: Accentuating the positive. *Vanier Institute of the Family.* Available online at *http://www.vifamily.ca.*

Spock, B. (1946). *Baby and child care.* New York: Dutton.

——— (1976). *Baby and child care* (rev. ed.). New York: Dutton.

Strong, B., & Devault, B. (1995). *The marriage and family experience* (6th ed.). New York: West Publishing Co.

U.S. Census Bureau. Search for current population reports and Statistical Abstract 2000 at http://www2.census.gov/census_2000.

Whitehead, B. D. (1993, April). Dan Quayle was right. *The Atlantic Monthly, 271*(4), 47–84.

HELPFUL WEB SITES

http://www.familysupportamerica.org

Family Support America, formerly Family Resource Coalition of America, promotes family support as the nationally recognized movement to strengthen and support families.

http://www.contemporaryfamilies.org

Council on Contemporary Families (CCF) is a nonprofit organization dedicated to enhancing the national conversation about what contemporary families need and how these needs can best be met.

http://www.census.gov

The U.S. Census Bureau Web site provides information and statistics about states and population groups.

http://www.childstats.gov

This Web site offers easy access to federal and state statistics and reports on children and their families, including population and family characteristics, economic security, health, behavior and social environment, and education.

http://www.childtrends.org

Child Trends is dedicated to improving the lives of children by conducting research and providing science-based information to improve the decisions, programs, and policies that affect children.

http://www.nationalpartnership.org

The National Partnership for Women & Families is a nonprofit, nonpartisan organization that uses public education and advocacy to promote fairness in the workplace, quality health care, and policies that help women and men meet the dual demands of work and family.

http://www.childrensdefense.org

The mission of the Children's Defense Fund is to Leave No Child Behind® and to ensure every child a healthy start, a head start, a fair start, a safe start, and a moral start in life and successful passage to adulthood with the help of caring families and communities.

http://www.childrennow.org

Children Now is a research and action organization dedicated to ensuring that children grow up in economically secure families where parents can go to work confident that their children are supported by quality health coverage, a positive media environment, a good early education, and safe, enriching activities to do after school.

http://www.futureofchildren.org

The primary purpose of The Future of Children is to promote effective policies and programs for children by providing policy makers, service providers, and the media with timely, objective information based on the best available research.

http://www.vifamily.ca

The Web site of the Vanier Institute of the Family in Canada provides information on important issues and trends critical to the well-being and healthy functioning of Canadian families.

http://www.gu.org

The Web site for Generations United, the national center on grandparents and other relatives raising children.

http://ncfr.com

The Web site for the National Council on Family Relations provides a forum for family researchers, educators, and practitioners to develop and disseminate knowledge about the family and family relationships.

http://www.ncfy.com

The National Clearinghouse on Families and Youth is sponsored by the U.S. Department of Health and Human Services, Administration for Children and Families. The Web site provides links to information to help support young people and their families.

Additional resources for this chapter can be found on the Online Companion to accompany this text at www.earlychilded.delmar.com. This supplemental material includes frequently asked questions; chapter outlines to be used as study guides; scenarios that both encourage large and small group discussions and provoke new thoughts and ideas; and chapter resources, including chapter summaries, interactive questions, Web links, and Web activities. In addition, forms from the text are available for download.

CHAPTER 3
Parenting

OBJECTIVES
After reading this chapter, you should be able to

1. Discuss seven roles that parents play and the implications for teachers.
2. Describe seven emotional responses of parents and the implications for teachers.

In Chapter 2 we considered the sociocultural context of modern parenting in this country. Parenting has never been a simple task, no matter what the societal conditions. Taking on the responsibilities of parenting involves adjusting to numerous roles and profound emotional responses that are quite often unexpected in the midst of adulthood. No one is ever quite prepared for parenthood and the resultant adjustments in relationships, lifestyle, and responsibilities that require major reorientations and adaptations. Unfortunately, our society does little initially to assist parents through these changes and as they continue to fill complex roles with their developing children. As teachers working with parents who are in the midst of these major adjustments, it is important to understand and recognize the nature of parenting responsibilities in order to support parents optimally. It is also crucial to recognize the deep emotional responses to parenthood that necessarily impact relationships with others. In this chapter we consider both roles and emotional responses of parents.

Teachers working with families may become frustrated by the parents' apparent inability to focus their attention fully on matters regarding the children. It is sometimes difficult for teachers to remember that parenting involves many complex behaviors and roles and that parents may be preoccupied with matters beyond this one particular child in a particular classroom situation. It is important that teachers continually try to remain aware of the complexity of parents' lives to avoid making assumptions that parents are not truly interested in their children's welfare.

Consider the following situation; does the teacher sound at all familiar?

Jane Briscoe is becoming impatient. As she describes it to her director, "These parents, I don't get it. I'm trying to take time to talk with them, and that's tough, believe me, with everything else I've got to do. But some of them just don't seem interested. Mrs. Lawrence, the other day, kept looking at the clock when I was talking. And Mary Howard this morning—she looked as if she wasn't even listening to me. I've tried, but if they don't care about their own kids, what am I supposed to do?" The director, Mrs. Forbes, is sympathetic. She knows Jane's frustration arises partly from her concern for the children, as well as from the human reaction of wanting response when initiating communication. But she realizes also that Jane is seeing only one perspective and needs to remind herself of how life may seem from the parents' point of view to increase both her compassion and effectiveness. A teacher who assumes parents aren't interested decreases her effort; a teacher who recognizes the multiple pulls on the time and attention of a parent keeps trying.

"I know that's frustrating for you, Jane, when you're trying hard. There's no one easy answer, I'm sure. Sometimes I try to imagine what life must be like for some of our parents, all the things that could be on their minds when they walk in here. There's your Mrs. Lawrence—she has all the concerns of her work with 28 third graders on her mind this Monday morning, as well as her own two. And I happen to know her two stepsons visited this past weekend, and that always makes it difficult—both crowded and hectic. And she's been looking tired now that her pregnancy's further along. Must be a lot to think about, trying to get both her children and his children used to the idea of a new baby. Her husband works long hours, too—must be hard to find time to relax together, let alone finish up all the chores in that new house."

Jane looked thoughtful. "You're right, you know. And I guess if I think about it, I can figure out some things that might keep

(continues)

(continued)

Mary Howard's attention from being completely on me. It's exam time at the high school, and I know she's trying to do well in case she decides to go on to college. And she is still a high school kid, mother or not—I sure remember the million-and-one problems my friends and I had, from figuring out how to get enough money to buy the latest fashions to how to get along with our parents. It must really be hard for her to be living with her parents, still an adolescent, as well as a young mother who needs our help in looking after her own child. There just wouldn't be room for rebellion, would there? I wonder if she gets excluded at school because of her baby. Keeping the baby must have been a big decision for her to make, and she's still so unsure of what's ahead for her." Jane broke off and smiled ruefully. "I guess I've been spending too much time being annoyed with the parents, and too little trying to get inside their skin to see life from their perspective. Thanks, Mrs. Forbes."

Mrs. Forbes smiled as Jane went out, thinking that the young teacher would be all right; she had made the first big step in working effectively with parents. She had begun to try to understand the experience of parenting, including the many roles a parent plays and the emotional responses of parenting.

ROLES PARENTS PLAY

Although the teacher was thinking about two mothers, it should be noted that changes in social attitudes have encouraged people to think of **androgynous** adult roles—those that are shared by men and women and have similar functions. While recognizing that fathers and mothers likely relate and interact differently with their children because of the differences in their natures and their past experiences, many parents no longer separate aspects of parenting and family living into male and female tasks. This text, following that model, will examine these roles and briefly consider the implications for teachers. There are seven of these roles, and although they can be discussed as separate entities, each of the roles overlaps and influences the others.

The Parent as Nurturer

The **nurturing** role encompasses all the affectionate care, attention, and protection that young children need to grow and thrive. This implies caring for the physical needs of children both before and after birth, but perhaps the greatest need for healthy development is emotional support and caring. Being a nurturer is the parent's primary role in providing a psychological environment of warm, emotional interaction in which the child can thrive (see Figure 3-1). Nurturing involves most of the family's developmental tasks, as listed in Figure 3-2. Researchers have found important correlations between warm and responsive parenting in infancy, including close physical contact between

FIGURE 3-1 An important parental role is to provide warm, emotional nurturing.

FAMILY DEVELOPMENTAL TASKS

- Physical maintenance—shelter, food, clothing, health care, safety.
- Allocation of resources—meeting family needs, authority, affection.
- Division of labor—earning income, managing household, caring for family members.
- Socialization of family members—learning acceptable behavior, standards for moral behavior.
- Maintaining order within family system—communication and interaction.
- Reproduction, rearing, and release of family members.
- Inclusion of family members in larger society—community activities.
- Maintaining motivation and morale—satisfying individual needs for acceptance, sense of family loyalty.

—*From Duvall*

FIGURE 3-2 Nurturing involves most of the family's developmental tasks.

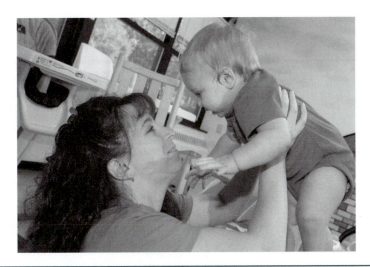

FIGURE 3-3 Warm, responsive parenting in infancy leads to secure attachments.

parent and baby and attention to needs, and the development of **attachment**, defined as the strong, affectional, mutual tie formed in the two years following birth and enduring over time (see Figure 3-3). Attachment is felt to be critical to optimum development in every other aspect of development: (1) physical growth and development; (2) interest in and interaction with peers and other adults; (3) cognitive and problem-solving skills, including curiosity and interest in the world; and (4) language development. Older, school-aged children with whom teachers work are still the product of the quality of that earlier attachment. The basis for differences in behavior and development related to attachment may be that the attachment relationship offers the child a secure base from which to venture forth to explore the world and learn how to interact.

Ainsworth reports that by toddlerhood, children's responses in observed "strange situations" indicate that attachment is already formed. Indeed, variations in parents' nurturing behaviors determine the kind of attachment the child will have with the parent. Some children show secure attachment behaviors. These include easy separation from mother to explore nearby toys, while periodically touching base with mother; friendly behavior toward a stranger when mother is present; probably crying when mother leaves, but usually resuming play; somewhat friendly to a stranger after the initial distress; warm greeting to returning mother. Babies become securely attached when their parents give them responsive feedback, including attention to the baby's signals, interpreting the signals correctly, and giving appropriate feedback promptly enough so the child feels her communication caused the response. Responsive parents also show sensitivity to the baby's activity, not interfering or intruding.

Anxious attachments in babies may be either anxious–ambivalent or anxious–avoidant. The anxious–ambivalent baby shows resistance to the mother as well as clinginess. This child usually is wary of leaving mother to explore toys and also wary of new people. When mother leaves, the child becomes very upset, will not be comforted, and completely rejects a stranger's offer to play. But when the mother returns, the child reacts ambivalently, both seeking comfort and rejecting it, sometimes appearing to be angry with the parent.

The anxious–avoidant pattern of attachment is evident when the child seems not to particularly care if either mother or stranger is present, leaving both easily to play. No distress or disruption of play is shown when the mother leaves, and the child interacts unemotionally with a stranger. When the mother returns, the child avoids reunion contact with her. Parents of anxiously attached babies respond differently to their babies. They either ignore the baby's cues or respond inappropriately, continuing to play with a tired baby who wants to stop, or holding the baby too tightly and ignoring his efforts to squirm free. Some parents avoid physical contact with their babies, and others express little emotional warmth that radiates to the baby. Other parents show no pattern of consistent responsiveness to their children, either through enforced long periods of separation or through their own emotional difficulties (Ainsworth's work, reported in Karen, 1990).

Two of the most recognized names among Americans working with young children and their families are Dr. T. Berry Brazelton and Dr. Stanley Greenspan. In a joint work, *The Irreducible Needs of Children: What Every Child Must Have to Grow, Learn, and Flourish* (2000), the authors underline the vital importance of consistent, caring relationships in the early years to foster the emotional interaction that is the most critical primary foundation for social and intellectual growth. Brazelton points out that emotional learning comes first through warm interaction, and cognitive learning follows (Brazelton & Greenspan, 2001). The ongoing nurturing work of parents continues throughout the child's years of development, leading to growth in all areas. His work in developing the **Touchpoints model**, a model developed to support families at key points of disruption during their children's development (see the appendix to this chapter for more information), helps teachers, caregivers, and other professionals learn how to support families in developing their nurturing roles.

Recent research on brain development corroborates the connection between emotional nurturing and the actual physical development of the brain in the earliest months and years. It has been noted that the parts of the brain that process emotions grow and mature relatively early in a child and are very sensitive to parental feedback and handling. Many experts on child development are convinced that children raised without sufficient affection, attachment, and attention "suffer an abnormal process of synapse formation and pruning, leaving them without normal circuitry in emotional brain regions, and without a normal range of emotional responses or control" (Diamond & Hopson, 1998). There is a growing body of research confirming that parents' attitudes and actions are central to children's emotional adjustment to learning at home and at school. Thus the actual **dendritic** growth (the branching process of neurons, or brain cells) in the cortex of the brain occurs in response to environmental stimulation of young children. These stimuli include

- A steady source of positive emotional support.
- A nutritious diet with enough protein, vitamins, and minerals.
- Stimuli for all senses.
- An atmosphere free of undue pressure and stress.
- A degree of pleasurable interaction.
- A series of novel challenges.
- Social interaction for significant percentages of time.
- Active participation and promoting of exploration (Diamond & Hopson, 1998).

So the indivisible link of parental nurturing and brain growth and development confirms decades of research.

In recent years there have been concerns about whether full-time child care placements in the infant's first year will disturb the attachment relationship between parent and child. As early as 1986, Jay Belsky suggested that infants under 1 year who spent more than 20 hours in child care formed weaker attachments to their mothers than those whose mothers cared for them full-time, noting that his findings were likely related to the uneven quality of infant child care in America. Alison Clarke-Stewart (1989) found less alarming evidence in her research. Some findings of a comprehensive study of families and child care were released in 1996 by the National Institutes of Health: the result of following 1,300 families since 1991. The results showed that children's attachment to their mothers is not affected by whether they are in child care, the age at which they enter child care, or the number of hours

---

THE SEVEN IRREDUCIBLE NEEDS OF CHILDREN

1. **The need for ongoing nurturing relationships.**
2. **The need for physical protection, safety, and regulation.**
3. **The need for experiences tailored to individual differences.**
4. **The need for developmentally appropriate experiences.**
5. **The need for limit setting, structure, and expectations.**
6. **The need for stable, supportive communities and cultural continuity.**
7. **Protecting the future: commitment of rich, developed nations to children in less developed parts of the world.**

—*From Brazelton, T., & Greenspan, S., 2000*

they spend there. This research will continue to follow the children, but the evidence at that point seemed to suggest that the earlier concerns were not well founded (Coontz, 1997; NICHD, 1997).

Then in April 2001 Jay Belsky again created an uproar when he made a report to the Society for Research in Child Development. Belsky is one of more than 30 researchers conducting the National Institute of Child Health and Human Development (NICHD) Study of Early Child Care (NICHD, 1997). In an interview with CBS News, Belsky said, "There is a constant dose–response relationship between time in care and problem behaviors, especially those involving aggression and behavior." The resultant media coverage fueled public concern over healthy development of children in child care. Subsequent comments by other researchers involved in the study (Caldwell, 2001) remind us that the researchers have been concerned with family variables, child care variables, and child characteristics, and that the study is ongoing. Regarding attachment, the general finding is that "not one of the major child care variables—age of entry, type of care, amount of care—*in and of itself* is associated with lack of secure attachment. The most powerful predictor was *maternal sensitivity*" (Caldwell, 2001). The discussion will no doubt continue as each side interprets the evidence in particular situations. It is important for all adults who care for young children to realize the importance of early emotional nurturing and to support parents in whatever life circumstances they do their parenting (see Figure 3-4). As caregivers understand the critical importance of parents

FIGURE 3-4 Experts disagree about whether full-time child care during infancy may create less secure attachments.

and children forming attachment bonds, they will recognize that one of their own roles is to support the development of attachment.

Teachers should be aware that children can develop different kinds of attachment to key adults in their lives. For example, 2-year-old Enrico might have developed an anxious attachment with his mother, perhaps due in part to his mother's two lengthy hospitalizations and ill health during much of his infancy. However, when Enrico is observed with his grandmother, a warm woman sensitive and responsive to his needs and personality, Enrico appears securely attached.

For years such nurturance has been equated with "mothering." Little research was done on fathering until the last two decades. In fact, earlier social scientists felt impelled to explain the necessity for adding the father role to the family, implying that providing physical and economic protection was a less important function and excluding him from the nurturing role. Recent research indicates that earlier myths about the nature of fathering are not presently true, if they ever were.

The consensus of research findings is that fathers do not differ significantly from mothers in being interested in infants and children; they become involved with their offspring if encouraged to do so; they are as nurturant as mothers toward children (see Figure 3-5); and they may engage less frequently in active caregiving but are competent in carrying out the activities they perform (Bigner, 2001).

Fathers are not only competent but also absolutely crucial, according to other findings. Research is showing that the involvement of fathers with their children has important influences at every stage of child development (Turbiville, Umbarger, & Guthrie, 2000; Rohner, 1998). At six months of age, babies with actively involved fathers score higher on the Bailey test of mental and motor development; in the preschool years, children with involved fathers show greater ability to take initiative and direct themselves and a sense of competence; father involvement in children's school life increases the chances that a child will excel by as much as 42 percent; father involvement in adolescence reduces risks of juvenile delinquency, teen pregnancy, and drug use, while increasing the amount of education completed (Levine & Pittinsky, 1998). And in a 26-year study of empathy that tracked young children into adulthood, paternal involvement was the single strongest parent-related factor in adult empathy (Loux, 1993).

One study on the importance of fathers, reported in 1998, finds that the more time fathers spend with their children and the more supportive their relationship is, the fewer childhood behavior problems there are. Evidence shows that children also benefit when divorced fathers without custody stay close, and has found beneficial links with stepfathers who are positively involved as well. A 1997 U. S. Department of Education study reconfirms the important role fathers play in the school achievement of their children. The research focused on the involvement of fathers in school programs of children in grades 6 through 12.

(a)

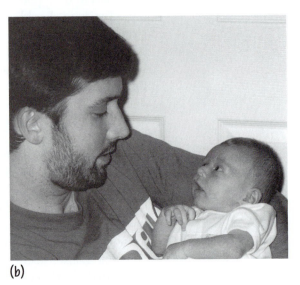
(b)

(c)

FIGURE 3-5 Fathers may be as nurturing as mothers toward children.

The study found that children from two-parent homes whose fathers participated in school activities were more likely to receive As on assignments, participate in extracurricular activities, and enjoy school. Although the report recognized the importance of mothers to the social and emotional adjustment of the child, father involvement may be more important for academic achievement (U.S. Department of Education, 1997). A 2000 report from the Department of Education (National Center for Education Statistics, 2001) suggested that when fathers get involved in their children's education, they demonstrate to their children that male adults can take responsibility, help to establish appropriate conduct, and provide a daily example of the importance of achievement and productivity.

There is no question that there are currently three faces of fatherhood: those who are virtually nonexistent in their children's lives, having disappeared in what Blankenhorn calls the "culture of fatherlessness" (Blankenhorn, 1995); those who come and go, much as busy working fathers often have; and those who have become involved in their children's lives in areas in which their own fathers were excluded or chose not to enter.

Some of the more recent involvement of fathers is certainly due to societal shifts over recent decades, not least of which are the numbers of women working outside the home and changes in the definitions of social roles (Parke, 1996; Holcomb, 1996–97). This may be best exemplified by changes beginning in the early 1970s in practices related to pregnancy and childbirth that permitted and encouraged fathers to become more involved from the beginning. This contributed significantly to changing fathers' perceptions of their own role in the family. Several studies conclude that the father's participation at birth helps the mother assume her role; the birth itself may be a strong stimulus for nurturant behaviors from both fathers and mothers, as well as a time for attitude formation (Bigner, 2001). When fathers assist in the delivery room, they go on to change diapers, be involved with toilet learning, drive car pools, and supervise homework. Children may be strongly attached to both fathers and mothers.

Most findings concur that the parenting role most crucial for a child's optimum development is the nurturing role. It is within the context of family that children learn about intimate and personal relationships. This is probably one of the most demanding roles a parent plays; it includes the myriad prompt responses to an infant's needs at any hour of the day or night during the long period of infant helplessness and the frequent setting aside of adult needs in favor of growing children's requirements and demands.

The need for nurturing in its various forms does not diminish as young children become older; parents are still the people children look to for comfort, security, and approval. Parents with several children may have differing demands placed on them at the same time—the infant crying to be picked up, the preschooler fearful of being left, the school-aged child needing comfort after an encounter with peers (see Figure 3-6). It is no wonder that many parents feel "burned out" from time to time, so depleted by filling the nurturing needs of their children that they have little time or energy to meet some of their own needs.

FIGURE 3-6 Parents with several children may have differing demands at the same time.

REFLECTIONS FOR JOURNAL ENTRIES

One of the things teachers have to recognize is that they likely have some images and feelings related to the nurturing role that could get in the way of full acceptance of parents. Consider how you feel about men as nurturers: Are you as comfortable seeing fathers in the nurturing role as mothers? Consider how you feel about mothers who leave their small children in the care of others. Do you worry about their children's attachment?

Implications for the Teacher

- Teachers can help by understanding the importance of the parents' nurturing role and the many demands this places on both mothers and fathers. Emotional support from sources outside the family allows parents to devote more energy to nurturing.

- Teachers can supplement the nurturing role without violating the parent–child bond.

- Teachers who are familiar with behaviors in children associated with both secure and insecure attachments can be alert to situations that indicate trouble and can help parents learn about the specific nurturing responses that are related to developing secure attachment.

- Caregivers of infants can promote particular classroom practices to enhance attachment (see Chapter 16).

- Teachers of children of all ages can encourage involvement and nurturing activities that include both fathers and mothers, as well as any other key adults in children's lives.

- Teachers can also be sensitive to broadening activities to be sure they include stepparents, grandparents, and all other nurturing people in the family, excluding no family structure of any child.

The Parent in Adult Relationships

Parents are people first, and there is evidence that those who are fulfilled and contented as individuals are better able to function effectively as parents than those who are disappointed in their personal lives. It is evident that the support one parent gives to the other facilitates the development of the parenting role as well as optimizing conditions for nurturing the child. Although the primary adult relationship may be with a marriage partner or cohabiting adult, the adult's life may be crisscrossed with a network of adult relationships—parents, friends, and former spouses. In fact, many parents are also help arrange for their own parents' health or living conditions and must make complicated arrangements with former spouses to share custody and negotiate financial matters. The relationship with one's child is an extremely important relationship, but it begins in the context of relationships with other adults.

Before an individual becomes a parent, there is first a relationship with another adult. One of the demands on a parent is to foster the continuance of that relationship or of another that has replaced the original relationship.

One of the long-standing myths surrounding parenthood is that children give meaning to a marriage, improve the relationship between a couple, help a troubled relationship, and actually prevent divorce. In fact, the addition of parenthood roles to a marriage introduces a time of abrupt transition. Many researchers report this as a time of some degree of crisis. The severity of the crisis may depend on the degree of a couple's preparation for parenthood and marriage, the degree of commitment to the parenthood role, and patterns of communication. One long-term study followed over 250 couples from the last three months of pregnancy through the third year with their first child. The study concurred that stress is inevitable, but the quality of marriage that couples experienced before parenthood is the determining factor in whether the

FIGURE 3-7 The demands of children may interfere with adults being able to pay close attention to adult relationships.

addition of a child disrupted the relationship between husband and wife. The best marriages stayed the best, and the worst stayed the worst. Whether or not the transition is a time of severe crisis, a couple is unquestionably going to have to reorganize their relationship and interactions; changes will occur in a marriage with an altered lifestyle and the addition of new role images and behaviors associated with parenthood (see Figure 3-7).

These changes are linked to a decrease in marital satisfaction. Studies report a U-shaped pattern in the degree of satisfaction, declining from after the birth of a child and as children grow older, then gradually increasing as children are raised and begin to lead independent lives. One reason offered for this decline in satisfaction is role strain. This occurs when

- There are incompatible expectations for a person holding several roles at the same time—recall the earlier discussion of the Superwoman syndrome.
- The demands of one social role are in conflict simultaneously with those of another social role—imagine a candlelit dinner disrupted by the baby's cries.
- Strong demands for performance are placed on all social roles—that Superwoman image again!

It is difficult for spouses to pay close attention to the needs of their adult relationship while caring for the needs of their developing children.

All of these studies support the idea that using children as a means to improve a marriage is a mistake. The parent as a nurturer of children may discover that the parent as an adult in a relationship may neglect and be neglected. A 2005 Op Ed article in the *New York Times* suggests that "attachment parenting," with the family bed and long-term breast-feeding, has erased the distinction between married life and family life to the detriment of family happiness. Although the divorce rate has gone down, the percentage of couples saying they are in less-than-happy marriages has gone up (Warner, 2005).

Actually, the probability of divorce is doubled when couples have children during their first year of marriage; evidently many couples are too unsettled to face parenthood before they can work out some of the marital behaviors. However, if children do not improve a marriage, their presence may serve to cement it together a little longer. The median duration of marriages among childless couples before divorce is about four years; couples with several children stay together about 14 years (Bigner, 2001).

Although there is statistical evidence that children stabilize marriages for at least a while, this is not the same as improving them. Some married couples have their worst disagreements over their actions as parents!

Implications for the Teacher

- Teachers should relate to parents as interesting adults in their own right, not just in the role of parent. For example, knowing that a father is training for an upcoming marathon, a teacher might give him an article she read about diet to improve muscle. Another teacher, aware that a grandfather who raises his grandson alone has an extensive collection of baseball cards, can invite him to participate in the neighborhood hobby show.

- When opportunities arise in conversation, teachers can convey acceptance, approval, and encouragement of parents' efforts to enhance their marriages, to engage in hobbies, and to pursue personal and social enrichment.

- It is easy for teachers to be critical when parents do not seem to be devoting all their time and attention to their children, but it is important to remember that a significant gift that parents can give their children is a stable home and the model of caring relationships.

The Parent as an Individual

Americans have come to value the development of the individual person. We are now aware that this personal development is a lifelong process. Parents concerned with nurturing their children's development are also encountering growth in their own lives.

From the turbulent analysis of social values in the 1960s and 1970s, through the more introspective consideration of personal values and lifestyles of more recent years, parents expect their lives to continue to develop and change. It is relevant for teachers to consider how Erikson's theory examines the psychosocial tasks of adulthood that must be resolved. Many young parents are preoccupied with issues of identity. Erikson speaks of this as the fifth stage, beginning in adolescence. With the prolonging of education and financial dependence on parents, and with the confusing multiplicity of roles, careers, and lifestyles to select from, many identity issues are still being actively worked on in young adulthood. One measure of this may be the postponing of marriage, perhaps seen as an entry step into the adult world, a sign that a young person has settled some issues and is ready to embark on adult life. The events of marriage and parenthood cause many young parents to reexamine identity issues as they take on two roles symbolic of adult life. It is not just real-life events that have to be assimilated into an individual's self-concept, but also expectations and attitudes from within the individual and from society that set the standards used to measure the new view of self. There are several problems here. One is that most of today's parents grew up with daily facts of life and social role expectations that are radically different from those of the present.

It is difficult to let go of those early perceptions of the way life is supposed to be. When a woman's own mother was always waiting for her in the kitchen after school and had dinner cooked when her father came home from work at 6 o'clock, it is difficult for her to have to call her daughter daily, knowing her child has gone home to an empty house and will be alone for another two hours, sometimes beginning the supper preparations until her divorced mother comes home from work. Somehow, despite the changed circumstances, perceptions of what *should* be happening have not changed. Many parents struggle with feeling less than successful because of their patterns of life.

Many mothers find their self-esteem being attacked, whether they have chosen to fill the traditional role of homemaker or have joined the majority of mothers working outside the home. "In the national conversation we have been having in this country about work and family life, having a working mother alternates between being seen as being either good OR bad for the children" (Galinsky, 2000).

WHAT MAKES A GOOD PARENT?

In Galinsky's survey, eight critical parenting skills emerged. These are

- **Making the child feel important and loved.**
- **Responding to the child's cues and clues.**
- **Accepting the child for who she or he is, but expecting success.**
- **Promoting strong values.**
- **Using constructive discipline.**

(continues)

(continued)

- **Providing routines and rituals to make life predictable and create positive neural patterns in developing brains.**

- **Being involved in the child's education.**

- **Being there for the child.**

—*From Ask the Children: What America's children really think about working parents (1999).*

In what Galinsky refers to as the "mommy wars," at-home mothers feel they are being dismissed and devalued, and they resent having to "pick up the slack" as classroom volunteers or emergency child care for mothers who have chosen to work. Their working counterparts feel the stress of having to succeed on two fronts. The media continue to indict working mothers subtly for increasing family stress and sacrificing their children for materialism and success, now that they have added to their traditional roles. Working mothers are themselves caught in conflict and ambivalence. A majority of working mothers and fathers feel that it's bad for the family for mothers to be at work. When mothers return to work, they do so in a climate of subtle societal disapproval. And some of the criticism is directed back and forth between working mothers and stay-at-home mothers, each resenting the others' choice and judging their performance and contribution (Hattery, 2000). (See Figure 3-8.)

Actually, a major finding of Galinsky's recent study on work and family life (1999) is that there is no difference in the assessments of children with employed mothers and those of children with mothers at home. What matters most is how children are being parented, rather than whether their parents are working outside the home. A current phenomenon is that women's and mothers' groups are finding common ground on issues that span women's concerns as both parents and family breadwinners (Shellenbarger, 2005).

In the "Ask the Children" study, Galinsky found that certain job factors created better mental attitudes in parents and gave them more energy for their interactions with their children. These factors were

- Having reasonably demanding jobs.

- Having jobs that permit parents to focus on their work.

- Having meaningful, challenging jobs that provided opportunities for learning and job autonomy.

- Having workplace environments with good interpersonal and supportive relationships, where parents don't feel they have to choose between job and parenting.

FIGURE 3-8 Many mothers are challenged by combining the roles of mother and career.

A father's task of assimilating his new role into his identity is no easier. Although more recently he is gaining attention as part of the family, for many years he has been considered nonessential to the functioning of the family.

The Fatherhood Project at the Families and Work Institute in New York City now provides a national guide to services for and about fathers. The sad part is that even when men are truly motivated to share parenting responsibilities in an essential way, society does not make it easy. Most employers find it easier to consider working mothers' family needs rather than those of working fathers (see Figure 3-9). Men who ask for flexibility or other privileges in their employment conditions to accommodate family needs are often seen as less serious about their careers.

After identity, Erikson's next task of adulthood coincides with the stage of establishing family life until early middle age. The previous attainment of a sense of personal identity and engagement in productive work leads to a new interpersonal dimension of intimacy at one extreme and isolation at the other. By this Erikson means the ability to share with and care about another person

FIGURE 3-9 Contemporary fathers have new roles to fit into their identity.

without fear of losing oneself in the process. Family relationships are based on this kind of interdependency. Parents are called on to share their world freely with their children and each other in caring relationships. It seems obvious from our earlier discussions about identity and nurturing that these tasks actually occur simultaneously.

Older parents may have added the dimension of Erikson's seventh stage, in middle age, when the task may be to work from a sense of what Erikson calls "generativity," rather than negative self-absorption and stagnation. Generativity involves the adult's concern with others moving beyond the immediate family to active striving to make the world a better place for future generations (see Figure 3-10). Parents with this perspective may become involved beyond the narrower focus on their own children and jobs, working for issues that may improve prospects for other families, schools, and communities. (A brief discussion of Erikson's theory is found in Elkind, 1970.)

Issues of identity are never closed. As life circumstances change, a reexamination of roles and relationships and the resulting implications for an individual is necessary. A person's identity as a parent is not fixed either. As children

FIGURE 3-10 Many adults are concerned with issues beyond the immediate family.

move through successive stages of development, parents are presented with new challenges. Skills and behaviors that served well with an infant, for example, must be abandoned in favor of new strategies to live compatibly with a toddler or a school-aged child and then an adolescent. Parents' feelings of competence may fluctuate as their ability to adapt to the changing child fluctuates.

Traditional family stage theories used in recent decades describe family life in stages usually marked by children's ages. The best known of these was the eight-stage model outlined by Duvall and Hill (1948). Those stages were

1. Married couples (no children).

2. Childbearing families (oldest child aged birth to 30 months).

3. Families with preschool children (oldest child aged 21.2 months to 6 years).

4. Families with school-aged children (oldest child 6 to 13 years).

5. Families with teenagers (oldest child aged 13 to 20 years).

6. Families launching young adults (this stage begins when the oldest child leaves home and ends when the youngest child leaves home).

7. Middle-aged parents (this stage begins with an "empty nest" and ends at the start of retirement).

8. Aging family members (this stage begins with spouses' retirement and ends at their deaths).

There are some obvious problems using this common and traditional stage theory. One is that this theory best fits the traditional family, with assumptions about what constituted the tasks of the family at a particular stage. Considering the diverse family forms in contemporary society, it is difficult to apply the stage theory, especially if families are going through stages out of order or repeating stages dues to remarriage. Nevertheless, stage theory allows us to quickly convey the particular concerns of the people living within a particular family. For instance, when mentioning "the family with infants and toddlers," it is safe to assume we all understand at least some of the issues of that family.

Ellen Galinsky's more recent theory looks at family life from the parent's perspective, outlining a six-stage model to describe parent development (Galinsky, 1987). The six stages of parenthood include

1. The image-making stage, of the prenatal period.
2. The nurturing stage, for the first two years, a period of attachment and questioning.
3. The authority stage, when the child is between 2 and 4–5 years, and the parents decide what kind of authority to be.
4. The interpretive stage, from the child's preschool years to the approach of adolescence, where parents are interpreting the world to their children.
5. The interdependent stage, during the teen years, where parents form new relationships with "almost-adult" children.
6. The departure stage, when children leave home and parents evaluate the whole of their parenting experience.

Implications for the Teacher

- Parents need additional support from teachers as they develop parenting skills to match the changing needs of their developing children.
- Recognition of their skills and positive feedback helps parents develop a positive sense of themselves as parents.
- Teachers can form relationships that allow them to learn from parents and not have to rely on theories of parenthood.
- Teachers will be challenged to work with parents at many different ages and stages of adult development.
- Parents of all ages are struggling with issues of parental identity. Very young parents may be struggling with issues of personal identity; others are focused on forging relationships of intimacy; still others can look beyond their own families with concern for society at large. Teachers need to learn as much as they can about adult development to understand and accept individual responses.

The Parent as Worker

The stage in the life cycle when parenting usually occurs is a time of concern with being productive. Most adults find their means to this goal in one or both of the two channels of parenting and work. However, the two are often in competition with each other as parents try to balance work and family life and try to do both well. [In fact, Galinsky suggests that we eliminate the word *balance* from this discussion because it implies that when one side (work or home life) is up, the other is down, as when using a scale. Rather, *navigating* conveys the concept of process, working through to clear goals in both areas (Galinsky, 2000)].

About two-thirds of mothers with children under age 6 are currently employed outside the home; nearly 80 percent of mothers of school-age children are working. This is an increase of more than 10 percent over the previous decade, with the sharpest increase being for married women in two-parent families with children under age 6. There are several reasons for this increase in the number of working mothers:

- Increased costs in rearing children and living expenses.
- An expanded economy with the creation of new job opportunities.
- Earlier completion of families so that women are younger when their children start school.
- Reduced amount of time needed for housework.
- Better education of women.
- Expectations of a better lifestyle.
- Changes in basic attitudes toward roles, with new social perspectives.

Economic reasons are dominant for most women: 35 percent more families would be below the poverty line if both parents did not work.

Despite the fact that a majority of mothers are working outside the home along with fathers, much in our society indicates we are still operating on two related assumptions—that it is the natural role of men to work as providers and that it is equally natural for women to take care of children. One measure of this is that there are no national statistics kept on the number of working fathers, though careful note is made of the number of working mothers. With similar bias, studies are done on how mothers' working affects children; no such research is done when fathers work. Although such attitudes may annoy many women in the workplace, their effect is more than mere bother; the attitudes frequently translate into equally outmoded working hours and conditions that are neither helpful nor supportive to a parent both working and carrying out home responsibilities.

The majority of these parents have an inflexible working schedule of around 40 hours per week. Only a small but growing percentage of employees have flextime schedules, according to Department of Labor statistics, despite the fact that when working mothers are polled, flexible work schedules are the benefit they most desire (Bailey and Ulman, 2005). The U.S. government as an employer does set an example here. Over 40 percent of government agencies allow their employees to flexibly schedule their hours.

The option of job sharing, eminently suited to many parents who would like to decrease the demands of their working life, is still available to only a handful. A tiny fraction of adults are able to work from their homes. This number is growing regularly now that technology allows some work to be done from home. But many parents are in jobs that require travel away from home. Worse yet, many American workers are asked to change their jobs and move often, disrupting family arrangements.

Perhaps the place where we see most clearly how the roles of parent and worker may come into conflict is when the parents are involved in the birth or adoption of a new child into the family. At a time when the family unit is most under the stress of change and new roles, many parents find their employers are not able to give them the time to adapt and adjust.

Just contrast the difference in the policies regarding maternity and paternity leave in the United States and other countries. At this most crucial and stressful period of a young family's lives, structures are rarely in place in the United States to support the parents' leaving the workplace temporarily to have time with their new child. In a recent study (Kamerman, 2000), 98 percent of 130 countries offered paid maternity leave to mothers; countries that offer paid leave are as diverse as Iraq, Spain, Brazil, Russia, Libya, Mexico, and France. See Figure 3-11 for the amounts and length of time currently available in selected countries. Of the remaining 2 percent, the United States was one of only three countries (along with Ethiopia and Australia) that had no such government-supported system for providing paid leave, with 12 weeks of unpaid leave available to many workers under the Family Medical Leave Act. Some private employers offer paid maternity leave to a small percentage of their female employees.

Although it is a relatively new phenomenon, paid paternity leave is currently being added to employee benefits for fathers in a number of countries. Such paid leave is supported by specific government social services funds.

Government—Funded Maternity Leave in Selected Countries	
Canada:	25 weeks, 55% of gross pay paid, plus 2 weeks unpaid
Chile:	18 weeks, 100% paid
China:	15 weeks, 100% paid (if wife 24 or older, husband and wife are each allotted 15 additional days of time)
France:	16 weeks, 100% paid, plus until child is 3 at flat rate*
Germany:	14 weeks, 100% paid, plus 2 years at flat rate
Italy:	20 weeks, 80% paid, plus 6 months 30% paid
Japan:	14 weeks, 60% paid, plus 1 year unpaid
Norway:	52 weeks, 80% paid, plus 2 years at flat rate
Russia:	28 weeks, 100% paid, plus up to 18 months at minimum wage
U.K.:	26 weeks, flat rate
U.S.:	12 weeks, unpaid

Flat rate means that all parents who qualify receive the same modest amount during this extended time period. About 80% of families qualify, based on income.

FIGURE 3-11 Government-funded maternity leave in selected countries.

Government—Funded Paternity Leave in Selected Countries	
France:	2 weeks, 80% of gross pay
Finland:	3 weeks, 100% paid
Iceland:	13 weeks, 80% paid
Malaysia:	2 weeks, 100% paid
Philippines:	1 week, 100% paid (for first 4 deliveries)
Sweden:	30 days, 80% paid
U.K.:	2 weeks, flat rate
U.S.:	12 weeks, unpaid

FIGURE 3-12 Government-funded paternity leave in selected countries.

Prime Minister Tony Blair of Great Britain and Prime Minister Paavo Lipponen of Finland were two of the fathers in the news who recently took advantage of the paternity leave policies in their countries to spend time bonding with their new infants. Probably one of the most liberal parental leave policies is that of Sweden, where parents are eligible for 360 days' leave at 80 percent of their normal salary. The decision about which parent will take the leave is largely left up to the father and mother, although the father is expected to take a minimum of 30 days, and the family may also elect a further period of 90 days' leave at a lesser rate. See Figure 3-12 for a listing of policies in some of the countries that have created systems to allow employers to support fathers at the birth or adoption of a child.

The Family Medical Leave Act offers the only possibility for unpaid leave for American fathers, although some private employers allow paid leave. Since the passage of the Family and Medical Leave Act in 1993, parents working for businesses with at least 50 employees are eligible to take an unpaid protected leave of up to 12 weeks for circumstances in the family that require their attention, such as the birth or adoption of a baby or illness of a child or parent. Unfortunately, economic realities prohibit many families from being able to take unpaid leave. A recent study reported that the act has not increased leave taking by new fathers at all, and it has increased new mothers' leaves only slightly. It seems likely that parents are unable to take substantially more unpaid leave when a new child is born, even when they are given the right to do so (Han and Waldfogel, 2003). Financial pressures limit employee use of unpaid leave. In the United States, California is the only state to have enacted a paid-leave law for maternity or paternity leaves, for which only certain workers are eligible. Only 20 states and the District of Columbia have laws that give some female employees the right to job-protected maternity leaves.

What do these employment facts mean to parents? In practical terms, parents as workers spend the majority of their waking hours going to or from work, working, or being tired from working. Their young children, who are likely to be awake during these same hours, are of necessity cared for by someone else during the parents' workday. Their older school-age children are probably in school during many of the same hours, but before and after school, the long vacations, and other days off all necessitate making arrangements for child care or leaving the children unsupervised. Numerous special events will be hard for parents to either fit in or miss—the kindergarten field trip, the fifth grade band concert, the mothers' breakfast at the preschool. Employers know that they can expect an increased absentee rate for mothers of preschoolers during the winter months when colds and other infections run rampant. Parents who feel they cannot spare another day off are faced with the dilemma of leaving a sick child at school (pretending the child isn't sick because most schools will not accept sick children) or facing the employer's wrath. Pulled between the displeasure of the employer and the caregiver, and the needs and schedule of the child, parents may feel resentful, exhausted, guilty, and inadequate to all the tasks. And this stress does not go unnoticed by children. In Galinsky's study, she found that about two-thirds of children worry about their parents. They worry because they feel their parents are tired and stressed.

No matter what changes have occurred in the relationship of men and women and in their child-rearing participation, it is still true that in most families the "psychological" parent—the one who takes primary responsibility for the children's well-being—is the mother. This means that most women never leave for work with a clear sense of division between home and office; the concerns of home and family remain with them through the working day, and when working mothers return home they have less free time than their husbands (Goodnow & Bowes, 1994; Hochschild, 1989).

> Only women who have tried to cope with both roles—mother and working woman—can understand the constant sensation of tension and fragmentation, the overwhelming complexity of living in constant uncertainty. And the sense of responsibility is enormous. Their double roles cause costly divisions for most working women, who find difficulty freeing up energy for the workplace while worrying about adequate child care (Kamerman, 1980).

No wonder it is more common to speak of stress in working mothers than in working fathers, though many women keep their stress a private matter rather than let anyone think they are not equal to these new tasks. The good news is that "in dual-earner couples, women are no longer alone in working a second shift. The bad news is that everyone is working very long hours. . . . Nobody is doing much time in the easy chair" (Levine & Pittinsky, 1998).

Considering work–family conflict as only a women's issue ignores the pressures on today's fathers. The conflict between work and family responsibilities is an issue that goes beyond gender (Rapoport et al., 2001). Employers who see the worker as more than one-dimensional and provide for family needs in some measure are often rewarded by increased productivity and loyalty from workers relieved of some of their dilemma. Companies that provide on-site child care have found there is less absenteeism, and employees

	Employed	Nonemployed
How mothers spend their time		
Total free time	28	41
With children	27	32
Sleeping	53	58
Watching TV	10	16
Housework	16	24
How mothers feel about family life (percent)		
Always feel rushed	51	26
Get a great deal of satisfaction	85	77

FIGURE 3-13 How mothers spend their time (hours per week).

stay longer in their jobs. Generally, even as conditions improve (Galinsky, 2002), American parents find that work frequently conflicts with parenting demands, and they must deal with the life shaped by their work schedules.

Rather than see such data as completely negative regarding working mothers, we should note that a recent study found that employed mothers are generally more satisfied with their family lives than mothers who don't work outside the home (Cherlin and Krishnamurthy, 2004) As seen in Figure 3-13, working mothers get less sleep, watch less TV, spend less time with their children, and generally have less free time than at-home mothers. But they clearly protect their family time; employed mothers spend only 5 hours fewer a week with their children. Yet the percentage saying they got a "great deal" or "a very great deal" of satisfaction from their family lives is somewhat higher for mothers who work than for those who don't. Perhaps a busy life that combines employment and child rearing is also a fulfilling one.

Implications for the Teacher

- Teachers can support community and business attempts to alleviate stress for working parents by providing care for sick children or personnel policies that support families' attempts to care responsibly for their children.
- Teachers can try to schedule events for parents at times that may best fit into their working schedules—conferences during after-work hours, programs during lunch hour, and so on.
- When teachers and schools keep open visitation policies, parents feel able to come for lunch, story time, or any other times they are free to volunteer.
- Teachers can encourage parents to learn techniques for managing stress and share ideas for homecoming rituals to allow them to smooth the transition from home to work.

The Parent as Consumer

With inflation rates that increase every year, the real buying power of modern families continues to decline. Economic survival with the multiple material demands and expectations of our time has been a major factor in establishing the two-working-parents family structure.

A good deal of the family income is devoted to rearing children. Children at one time considered to be an economic asset—more available workers in a rural, self-sufficient family—must now be considered economic liabilities. Recent statistics show it costs between $160,000 and $237,000—depending on the family's income—to raise a child born in 2000; and that's just for basic household expenses from birth through age 17. Figures break down to about $12,500 per year when children are between birth and age 2, peaking at more than $13,800 for children between ages 15 and 17. This is an increase of more than 20% since 1960. (The estimates include providing for basics of food, shelter, clothing, transportation, and medical care plus an annual inflation rate.) College demands many more thousands of dollars for tuition and expenses, with annual increases far outstripping the inflation rate. Note also that these estimates cover only the basics—no piano lessons or summer camp. A 2000 estimate is that miscellaneous expenditures for things like entertainment, reading material, VCRs, lessons, and summer camp might add up to $18,510 for a family with income between $38,000 and $64,000. How much of the family budget goes to raising the children to age 18? Probably as much as 30% for one child, 40–45% for two, and 50% for three. (U.S. Department of Agriculture, 2000).

When both parents work outside the home, a large proportion of income pays for child care. After housing and food, child care is one of the most significant expenses in many working families' budgets, particularly for low-income families. Although there are variations by region or city or type of care, the annual cost of care for one child ranges between $4,100 and $10,000, with the average over $5,700 per preschooler; costs for infant care are much higher, as Figure 3-14 indicates (Children's Defense Fund, 2005). While the average family spends about 10% of its yearly income on child care, low- income families spend 25 to 35% of their incomes on such care. Affordable care should be no more than 20% of a family's income (Bergmann and Helburn, 2002). A study by the Urban Institute found that three out of five low-income families do not receive any help with child care expenses. Among those who do get help, one-fifth receive government assistance, and fewer than 1% get help from an employer. In some cases mothers find that nearly all their additional family income is spent on child care plus the purchases necessitated by employment—additional clothing, transportation, and food while away from home. In this case continuing employment is probably either for maintaining career continuity or for personal fulfillment.

Costs of child care in many European countries are paid for by government support, with families sometimes making a small contribution. In

City	Infant (12-month-old)	Preschooler (4-year-old)
Boston	$12,300	$7,900
Minneapolis	9,400	6,700
Seattle	8,800	6,100
Hartford, CT	7,200	5,700
Wake County, NC (including Raleigh)	5,800	5,000
Denver	5,100	4,600
Tucson, AZ	5,100	4,100

FIGURE 3-14 Representative average annual child care fees at programs in selected cities.

Sweden and Denmark nearly half of all children under age 3 are in full-day, publicly supported child care; about 85% of 3- to 5-year-olds are in full-time, publicly supported child care. In France and Belgium nearly 100% of pre-school children are in high-quality *ecoles maternelles,* mostly paid for by public funds. Italy has similar public expenditure for high-quality preschool child care. The U.S. government supplements costs of child care only for poor parents; the number of children getting government help is only about 2 million. The U.S. Department of Defense subsidizes child care for military dependents. Middle-class families receive a maximum tax credit of $1,000 annually. The U.S. rate of spending for children is about $200 annually for each child under 15 in the country. Comparable annual expenditures per child are 5 times that in France and 10 times in Sweden and Denmark. Without government support, families have to shoulder the full cost of child care and are often forced to choose lower-quality, more affordable alternatives. A recent proposal suggests that the federal government should institute a system of copayments for child care that parents choose to expand coverage to 17 million more children, helping the United States catch up with policies in European countries (Bergmann & Helburn, 2002). But in times of strained budgets and economic downturn, this may be merely a dream.

Parents are caught in a child care "trilemma." Even when their children enter the school system, it is usually necessary to pay for some kind of after-school care until parents return home from work. In too many communities parents on tight budgets are allowing dangerous latchkey arrangements for their school-aged children to stay at home alone and unsupervised. It is not a question of whether parents should work; they are working, and the income figures quoted illustrate why they need to work. Nor is it an issue of whether child care is good or bad for children; many studies support the idea that good care is good and bad care is bad for them. The real trilemma for society is how to balance quality care for children, decent and fair living wages for child care staff, and affordability for parents. Child care professionals are still providing an unseen consumer subsidy by earning low salaries and few benefits. The result of this involuntary financial assistance to working parents is that child care workers have high rates of job turnover, more than one-third every year—thereby lowering quality (Cost, Quality, and Outcomes Study, 1995).

All sides of the consumer trilemma need urgent attention. It has become obvious that the solution to the problem will have to come from sources beyond the triangle. Although a few employers are beginning to see the need to supplement employee payments for quality child care, and the government still considers various tax assistance plans, parents are caught paying too much while child care workers are earning far too little (see Figure 3-15).

It is no wonder that many parents feel they are on a financial treadmill. A major concern stated by most parents is money; a leader in the causes of marital friction is arguing about money. The parent in the role of consumer is stretched thin; when the economic health of the nation is shaky so that many parents lose jobs temporarily or permanently, the family may be thrown into crisis.

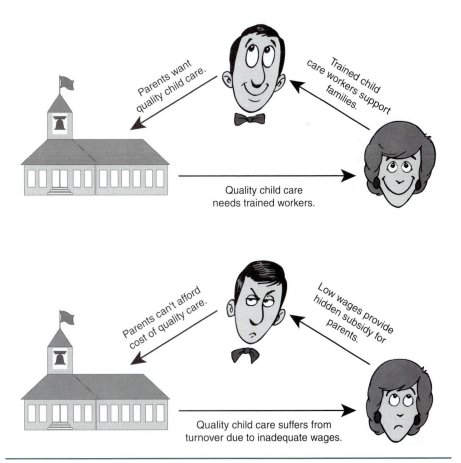

FIGURE 3-15 The child care trilemma.

Implications for the Teacher

- Because child care is an expensive item in the average family budget, parents often feel pressed to be sure they are receiving their money's worth. This may help the teacher understand the demands they make for nutritious foods and clean diapers, and the annoyance they express for missing mittens or damaged clothing. Teachers need to be sympathetic to the financial pressures on parents.

- It is in the best interests of parents, teachers, and children for both parents and teachers to support each others' efforts to gain financial relief through support of community or government plans to subsidize the cost of quality child care.

The Parent as Community Member

With the increasing complexity of modern life, a growing number of family functions have been taken over by community institutions and organizations: education by the school system; recreation and entertainment by the Y and other clubs, as well as the church, which has often expanded its purely religious function. There are as many organizations as there are interests in any given community. The community itself has become more highly structured as groups of people coming together have dictated more rules, legislation, and decision making, both public and private. But institutions and organizations do not run themselves; there are many demands on community members for their time as volunteers and for their money and other supportive efforts. Parents are asked to support the organizations that benefit their children as well as themselves.

It would not be unusual to find a week where families are asked to bake cupcakes for the PTA carnival, spend an hour staffing a booth at the carnival, driving children to and from the church junior choir practice, assisting children in magazine sales to aid the Y in getting new uniforms for the basketball team, coaching the team, making telephone calls to remind others about a local environmental group meeting, and soliciting funds door-to-door on behalf of a local branch of a national charity—as well as turning down several requests to participate in similar ways for other organizations (see Figure 3-16). For some parents who must work several jobs to make ends meet, there is enormous pressure to still find time to involve themselves and their children in the community, or else be seen as not participating fully within the community. The wider the age range of the children, the broader and more fragmenting are the demands on parents. Most parents today face constant tension between outside demands on time and energy and the amount available for personal and family needs.

As community members, parents may not only give but also receive help from the social network of community organizations. If families do not isolate themselves from the larger community, they receive assistance and provide

FIGURE 3-16 Parents may have community responsibilities, such as coaching.

models for children of interacting within a broad base of support. Learning about and utilizing community resources is an important role for parents.

It is also important for parents to realize that their actions within the community can help shape opinion and policies on issues of importance to both teachers and families. Parents need communities that care for children and families and that make children a high priority. As advocates in their own communities, families speak out on behalf of their children and themselves, as well as on behalf of all children and families. No one has as much interest in their children as do parents; therefore, they have a right and obligation to stand up for their children. Parents who advocate within their communities for children's and families' rights stay informed about children's issues and involved in their educational institutions, talk to legislators and vote, speak out in the workplace for family benefits and supports, and support improved working conditions for those who care for their children. Through such active advocacy they can have a powerful influence in the community. An expanded discussion of parents' roles in the community is found in Chapter 14.

Implications for the Teacher

- Any requests for parent participation add another thing to make time for. Teachers must realize this and be sure the idea is worth what it will cost the parent in time and pressure.

- Schedule activities with consideration of other regularly scheduled community events that involve parents or siblings.

- Teachers must guard against assuming that parents are too busy to become involved and so never make the effort or invitation. Parents have the right to make the decisions about how they spend their time, not to have these decisions made for them arbitrarily.

- It is vital for teachers and parents to build alliances for mutual education on common issues and for support in trying to reach common goals within the community.

The Parent as Educator

Perhaps the role for which parents feel most unprepared is the role of educator, used here to mean guiding and stimulating the child's development and teaching the skills and knowledge that children need to eventually become effective adults in society. Yet families teach their children from the time they are babies and continue to teach them what they consider important.

They teach first responses, personal hygiene habits, safety rules, and how to be friendly and polite. And schools expect parents to teach certain skills to children before they enter school, and then offer support, encouragement, and opportunities to practice as children continue their education. As other institutions take over many of the family's educative functions, the primary task of parents is (1) the socialization of their children to the values held by the family, as well as (2) assisting and monitoring children's development as learners and providing preparation for schooling. Recent brain development research confirms that interaction and stimulation in the earliest months and years are critical for optimum brain development (Shore, 1997; Diamond & Hopson, 1998); therefore, it is even more critical that parents perceive the importance of their roles as educators.

Socialization of Children

There are two primary reasons why education toward socialization is such a difficult task for parents. The first was alluded to in Chapter 2. In today's rapidly changing world, it is difficult for a parent to be sure what life will be like even in the near future. Childhood experiences of today's parents were quite different from what they see their children experiencing; their memories of what their own parents did will probably not serve them well in their present situations.

The second reason why parents often find the role of educating their own children overwhelming is that the only on- or off-the-job training most receive is through having been parented themselves. Children learn through living with parents most of the basic information they will ever get for their future role as parents. Adults tend to parent as they were parented, and this pattern will likely be inadequate in the changing world (see Figure 3-17). At least half of children who were abused by their parents become abusive

FIGURE 3-17 Children learn to parent by watching their own parents.

parents themselves, although evidence also shows that education of at-risk parents provides a key for stopping such vicious cycles. But early experiences certainly have the potential to repeat themselves. Studies indicate that the characteristics, values, beliefs, and, most important, the practices of our own parents have the greatest influence on our child rearing.

It seems ironic that our society has become skillful at imparting technical knowledge and education to prepare workers for a career but has made little headway in similarly devising methods to prepare young people for the tasks of parenthood. Most parenting skills are learned by trial and error on the job, giving rise to the not-so-funny old joke about parents wanting to trade in their firstborn because that was the one they learned on! No wonder many parents find the enormous task of parenthood without preparation overwhelming.

Parents who seek training (from childbirth classes on) often feel pressure to become "textbook" parents, fearing that they will make mistakes or not be able to follow the experts' instructions. This can be overwhelming as well.

It is important that teachers become aware of positive parenting models and practices to be able to assist parents in their growth as effective parents. The discussion of parent education in Chapter 13 includes a list of books about parenting issues and effective parenting skills. Although these skills cannot necessarily be acquired by reading a book, this can nevertheless be an important starting place. The models of parenting that many parents and teachers have experienced may often be the only sources for learning, unless adults deliberately seek additional information. While there are as many styles of parenting as there are humans, many psychologists refer to two extremes and a middle ground; most parents likely fall somewhere along a continuum between the descriptions. Teachers should realize that parenting style has absolute significance for healthy or unhealthy development of children.

One style that has been defined is the **authoritarian** parent. This parent requires complete obedience to authority and seems to feel that it is essential to hold very tight reins to control children. Such a parent retains all the power in the parent–child relationship, maintaining rigid rules and punishing when the rules are broken. Children are not given information or choices that would help them learn how to manage their own behavior. Anger and harshness may color the communication between parent and child. Unfortunately, the results of this extreme in parenting style are often fear of the parent, little development of the child's ability to control his or her own behavior, and diminished self-esteem. This style of parenting has been used all over the world for generations and may be effective in societies that experience little change, where there is one way to do things. However, it may be a mismatch for a rapidly changing society that values change and innovation.

At the other extreme is the parent who is overly **permissive** with the child, failing to provide clear and firm guidance about appropriate behavior. Whether because of lack of experience and understanding about children's needs, little self-confidence, or attention directed elsewhere in their lives, these parents simply allow their children inappropriate amounts of power to regulate their own lives long before the children are capable of doing so. Many teachers today express concern that modern parents err in being too permissive, with the result that their children are unfamiliar with limits and discipline. This creates unhappy situations for children, who give evidence of craving some limits. They are unable to develop self-control when anything goes, and they suffer diminished self-esteem because no one seems to care enough about them to provide necessary parenting. Children raised with permissive parenting may have trouble fitting in with the expectations of others in school, the community, or the workforce.

Happier situations for children result when parents exercise **authoritative, sometimes also called assertive/democratic**, and warm relationships, recognizing children's needs for guidance and direction while understanding and accepting the slow process of children's learning about the world. These parents are more likely to explain reasons for behavior and teach more appropriate behaviors than to punish for the inevitable mistakes growing children make. These children get lots of practice with decision making and are guided to see the consequences of their choices. These parents help children slowly assume more and more control over their lives as they become able, supporting the children with firm but loving evidence that parents are in control but available to help children learn. There is pleasure in such

FIGURE 3-18 Continuum of parenting styles.

parent–child relationships for everyone as parents perceive their children's gradual growth and children see their own expanding abilities. Warm, assertive, and authoritative parents are usually somewhat knowledgeable about children's development, as well as secure enough in their adult lives to be able to share power as children need their worlds to expand. This style of parenting seems appropriate in a society where change is constant and choices must be made, with no one right way to do things. (For further discussion of parenting styles, see Brooks, 2000, and Moore, 1996.) For a comparison of parenting styles, see Figure 3-18.

Preparation for Schooling

The issue of assisting children's development as learners and providing preparation for schooling has as many facets as there are opinions about appropriate early childhood education. Basically there are two broad viewpoints.

One represents the idea that early childhood is a time for allowing children to learn and develop through play, exploration, and child-initiated discovery. These proponents advocate home and school environments that provide varieties of open-ended materials with opportunities to manipulate, create, and learn with the whole self—body and mind—in direct encounters with materials, activities, and people. The idea is that through play a child learns best to understand the world, others, and her or his own capacities; this preparation lays the foundation for the more formal academic learning of later childhood. Many teachers and parents strongly believe that young children should be allowed their childhoods and that anything else is "miseducation" (Elkind, 1987).

> The "voice of the hurrier" (Gross, 1963) has been heard in the land for many years but has now become strident. It is imperative that we listen to our own voices telling us that young children need time to grow, time to learn about the social world, time to explore their own ideas through the use of materials and through play, time to become lovers of books through being read to, time to become productive young members, time to develop self-confidence through success—time (Balaban, 1990). (See Figure 3-19.)

(a)

(b)

(c)

(d)

FIGURE 3-19 Children need time to learn about friends (a), time to become lovers of books (b), and time to explore their own ideas through the use of materials (c) and through vigorous play (d).

Guidelines for developmentally appropriate curricula for children at birth through age 8 as defined by the National Association for the Education of Young Children (NAEYC) (Bredekamp & Copple, 1997) support this viewpoint.

REFLECTIONS FOR JOURNAL ENTRIES

Reflect on the parenting style your parents used. What is the parenting style you use, or would like to use, with your own children?

The major alternative viewpoint is that the sooner adults begin to "teach" young children the skills, concepts, and tasks necessary for academic success, the greater the likelihood of achieving that success. Some parents and teachers, concerned by reports of declining reading and SAT scores and just about everything else that has been tested in recent years, believe that school skills should be taught earlier and more intensely. The emphasis on accountability and end-of-grade tests legislated by the No Child Left Behind Act only exacerbates adult concern to start academic learning as soon as possible. Commercial interests, eager to capitalize on parents' desire to give their children an early start in learning, have been quick to manufacture endless numbers of products guaranteed to help children become "baby Einsteins." Proponents of teaching earlier also point to the abilities of some young children to learn to read at unprecedented early ages, to manipulate computer games, to play tiny Suzuki violins, or to speak foreign languages. The curriculum from the upper grades has increasingly been pushed down to the lower grades and kindergarten so that academic expectations have risen.

But people with the other viewpoint are concerned about the effects on children and families when developmentally inappropriate demands are made on young children. A major danger is that with the increase in *teaching* young children, there is a need for testing, which is "essentially a method for labeling these 60-month-old fledglings as failures or passers. The extreme to which this can go was reported in a *New York Times* article. The headline read 'On Flunking Kindergarten'" (Balaban, 1990).

The entire assessment process has serious implications for children, parents, and early childhood education professionals. Born from the prevailing trend to evaluate children's progress as a measure of school and program accountability, standardized tests are now frequently used to test children's readiness to move on from or even enter a particular program. Actually, the increased reliance on test scores for school placement points to the bigger problem of schools offering developmentally inappropriate curricula in kindergarten and primary grades, and therefore expecting young children to enter kindergarten "ready" with the skills that once were learned there. Parents become caught in the dilemma of knowing that their children are chronologically eligible for school but being told the children have not passed the "readiness test." NAEYC urges parents, teachers, and administrators to make decisions about children's readiness based on multiple sources of

FIGURE 3-20 When a teacher watches children at play, she may get more accurate information than from standardized tests.

information, including parents' and teachers' observations, and never on the basis of a single test score (NAEYC in Bredekamp & Copple, 1997). Educators continue to support the need for a consensus among the educational community and families to support only practices that are beneficial to young children (NAECS/SDE, 2001). (See Figure 3-20.)

The concern about advancing children's learning pervades the schools as well as the preschools. The testing mandated by No Child Left Behind makes all adults nervous about how their children and schools will perform.

The issue of what is developmentally appropriate practice in preschool and school experiences for children and how children may be considered "ready" for them may well become a major issue of concern for both parents and teachers as we move further into this century.

Implications for the Teacher

- Parents are often eager to talk with other parents, as well as with education experts, to share experiences and concerns, to discover they are not alone in their anxieties, and to be supported by others who can identify with their positions.

- Parents need all the information, help, and emotional support they can get as they work toward competence in their parental roles.

- Teachers need to become knowledgeable about the effects of various parenting styles and interaction in order to support parental learning.

- Parents and teachers must engage in active discussion of developmentally appropriate curricula for young children and must support each other in attempts to protect children from anxieties about standardized tests.

■■■ PARENTHOOD AS AN EMOTIONAL EXPERIENCE

People arrive at parenthood via a number of routes. For some it is a carefully thought-out and planned venture, an anticipated and joyful happening. For others, it is an unthought-of consequence in an adult relationship, an event possibly dreaded and resented.

Having children means very different things to different people. There may be one or more possible motivations at work when people decide to become parents or adjust to the concept after the fact. These motivations include

1. Validation of adult status and social identity.
2. Expansion of self—a continuance of the family.
3. Achievement of moral value—contributing something or sacrificing in parenthood.
4. Increasing sources of affection and loving ties.
5. Stimulation, novelty, fun.
6. Achievement, competence, creativity.
7. Power and influence over another.
8. Social comparison and competition.
9. Economic utility.

It is worth noting that some of our cherished beliefs, including ideas from this list of motivations, are myths that are part of the mystique surrounding parenthood. Raising children is not always fun, nor are all children cute or necessarily appreciative and loving toward their parents much of the time. Not all married couples should necessarily have children, nor are all childless married couples unhappy. (Despite the fact that many adults today consider having children to be an option—which increasing numbers are choosing not to exercise—there is still considerable pressure on women particularly to consider parenthood an essential experience of adult life. The increasing number of women who give birth to their first child when approaching 40 is testimony to the inner pressure of what has been called the "biological clock," as well as cultural attitudes.)

Some of the assumptions people make when deciding to become parents are removed from the reality they will discover. No matter what their motivation was to have children, there are common realities for all parents.

Irrevocability

There is no turning back. From the time of birth on, parents discover that the responsibility for the care and support of this human being will be entirely theirs for a period of approximately 20 years or longer. Even when other institutions are available to share the task, as in education, the ultimate responsibility rests with the parents. This responsibility may be willingly and joyfully undertaken, but it is always there, 24 hours a day, seven days a week, constantly to be reckoned with. As one writer put it, "We can have ex-spouses and ex-jobs, but not ex-children" (Rossi, 1968). This is a staggering thought for a parent who, when faced with the reality of the developing child's needs, may feel unequal to the task. However, it's too late—the child is here and the parenting must go on. But the feeling of total responsibility often causes parents to worry considerably about matters both large and small. Anxiety seems to be an inevitable part of being a parent: anxiety about both the child's welfare and the adequacy of the parents' efforts. The increasing complexity of the modern world has given parents new causes for concern and even fear as they think about protecting their children. Paradoxically, whatever mistakes parents make and however burdened they feel, most find it difficult to hand the job over to anyone else.

Implications for the Teacher

- Teachers can indicate understanding and empathy for the parents' position. Many parents feel greatly burdened by the demands and responsibilities of parenthood and alone in their concerns. They will respond positively to someone who cares about their position, someone with whom they can talk freely.

- Teachers can help by indicating willingness to support them and their children in ways parents decide are helpful for their families.

- Teachers can help parents be realistic about dangers requiring protection and the current desire to overprotect or smother children.

Restriction, Isolation, and Fatigue

One of the more dramatic changes in becoming a parent is the near total restriction on activity that comes with caring for a totally dependent being. Instead of acting spontaneously, a parent must make elaborate plans to leave the child even briefly. (There are periods in a child's early development when it is difficult to go into the bathroom alone.) And when the child is accompanying the parent, there are myriad preparations to make and paraphernalia to drag along. It is no wonder that many parents restrict their activity, preferring not to bother with it all.

Along with this restriction in activity comes the isolation in which many parents live. Separated from extended family and by the physical housing of the modern city, hampered by the difficulty of finding free time for social arrangements, further restricted by the expenses of the child, and psychologically isolated in coming to grips with situations and emotions, many parents feel alone. Preoccupied with the care of a small child and the experience of parenthood, many parents even become isolated from each other, suffering a loss of the intimacy they knew when they were just a couple. Many parents are reluctant to admit they need help because becoming a parent is supposed to be a measure of adult status.

Most young parents, especially mothers, complain of fatigue. From early morning until late at night they are responding to the needs of others—children, spouse, employer, and as many more as can be squeezed into the schedule. When mothers are asked what they want most, the common response is "time by myself." For most this is an impossible dream.

Implications for the Teacher

- Teachers need to take care not to make it seem as if they are adding still heavier demands on the parent; parents will protect themselves and avoid such teachers.

- Teachers can realize that parents do not have excess time to waste. Activities they are involved in need to be both meaningful and streamlined.

- Teachers can provide opportunities for parents to meet other parents for mutual support and socialization to help them feel less isolated as they discover common experiences (see Figure 3-21).

Dealing with Parenting Myths and Images

Despite the fantasies promoted by magazine advertisements and movies, many parents do not always feel love for their children. Humans operate beyond the level of instinct, and much parenting behavior and response, including love, comes after time, experience, repeated contact, and learning. Many parents feel ambivalent about their children some of the time, with feelings ranging from exasperation to resentment, with anger occasionally overshadowing feelings of love.

(a)

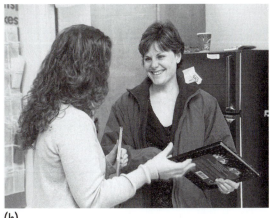

(b)

FIGURE 3-21 Parents are often eager to talk with other parents. (continues)

(c)

(d)

FIGURE 3-21 Continued

Because parents labor to some extent under the delusions of the "perfect parent," many do not consciously admit these less-than-positive feelings about their children to themselves or anyone else. They are left concerned about their "unnaturalness" and perhaps feel a little guilty.

Implications for the Teacher

- Teachers can subtly educate parents to try to remove some of the myths and images under which many parents labor.
- Teachers can comment on the real and positive things they see parents doing with their children.
- Teachers can empathize, displaying understanding that children can be exasperating and frustrating, even for the most caring adult.

Guilt

It is astonishing how frequently today's parents refer to guilt. Many factors precipitate this feeling:

- The ideal parent imaged in the various media.
- The changes in lifestyles and role behaviors, which mean that many parents live quite differently than their parents did.

THE GUILT TRAP

Working mothers feel guilt when

- Leaving a crying child with a substitute caregiver.
- Being apart from child for long hours.
- Being short-tempered at the end of a tiring day.
- Feeling inadequate at mothering.
- Not receiving supportive attitudes from others.
- Struggling with the decision of whether to work.

At-home mothers feel guilt when

- Worrying that children may become too dependent.
- Considering the extras that additional income could provide.
- Feeling that society expects more than "just a housewife."
- Feeling tired of being restricted to home and children.
- Knowing that their spouses bear the financial burdens.
- Realizing that their children are not perfect despite full-time mothering.

- The prevalent feeling that parents should produce children who will do better than they have done.
- The social attitude that "there are no bad children, only bad parents."

The parent most susceptible to guilt is the mother, probably because she realizes society views her as the most powerful parent. It does not matter whether she has chosen to work outside the home: Both employed and stay-at-home mothers are equally susceptible. The working mother may feel guilt because she is breaking a known pattern and is aware of the mixed reviews coming in from researchers and society. "We live with a deep-seated view that a woman's role is in the home. She should be there for her children, so the theory goes, and both she and they will suffer if she's not" (Brazelton, 1989). This is a strong message to fight against for most mothers (see Figure 3-22). Probably a good portion of the Supermom phenomenon is fed by this guilt, pushing her to make sure her child misses no right or privilege. Much of today's materialism and marketing frenzies feed off this emotion of guilt. If the child has been deprived of time and interaction, at least he or she can have the latest item advertised.

FIGURE 3-22 It is hard for a parent to leave a crying child.

The mother who is at home with her child is not immune from exhaustion or frustration and less-than-perfect maternal behavior. Against the image of the ideal parent, which is impossible to match in reality, mothers do not stand a chance; but they are left with the guilt that comes from not measuring up.

Implications for the Teacher

- Teachers do well to remember that guilt may lie below the surface in many conversations and encounters with parents. Such awareness helps the teacher consciously weigh actions and words, ensuring that nothing on the teacher's part increases any sense of inadequacy that parents may feel.

- Teachers should affirm the child and parent with small appreciative comments as often as possible, especially because teachers may sometimes have to increase the guilt load by sharing something worrisome about the child.

Satisfaction

Despite the obvious negative aspects of total responsibility and restriction, most parents find much to rejoice in. There is great satisfaction in watching children grow and develop, especially when one has played a large part in nurturing that growth. For many parents the achievements and characteristics of their children give feedback to be incorporated into the parents' own self-esteem; to some extent the degree to which the child does well (or badly) reflects how well the parents feel they are doing. Most parents feel no one else can know their children as well as they do and care for them quite as well.

Another source of parental satisfaction is the affectionate mutual attachment that forms between adult and child. It is a very positive feeling to know you are the most important person in the world to another. Because it is so important, many parents fear any event or person that could be conceived of as disruptive to that relationship. Many parents experience jealousy or resentment when others become important in the loved child's life, although frequently these emotions are disguised or not even recognized by the parent.

Implications for the Teacher

- Teachers need to respect the closeness of the parent–child bond. Ensure that classroom attitudes and practices nurture and preserve attachment.

- Teachers can be aware that jealousy may lie behind some of their encounters with parents so that no actions on their part increase feelings of competition.

- Teachers should learn to present comments in ways that avoid personal evaluation and reaction. Parents frequently react defensively if they feel their children (and therefore their parenting skills) are criticized.

- Teachers can offer tangible and reassuring evidence that the child is cared for adequately by the supplemental caregiver—and at the same time, reassurance that the child still needs the parent!

Uncertainty

Each child has a unique response to the world; no matter how well-read a parent is on child development and parenting skills, it is often a different matter putting principles into practice in specific situations with a specific child! As children change, parents must also, so parenting techniques that worked well at one point must be discarded and new ones learned. Often what worked with one child's personality has no effect on a sibling. Usually parents do not feel totally confident that they are performing their tasks correctly. With the changes within the family and the surrounding culture (discussed earlier in Chapter 2), today's parents are doing the job without role models, clear directions, or firm approval from society. No wonder most parents often feel unsure of the situation. Societal values imply that responsible adults know what they are doing. Parents feel they should not be uncertain.

> There is a near-universal bias in our society toward the idea that there is only one right way to do something, while all others are wrong. And if we follow this right way, achieving our goal is a fairly simple process (Bettelheim, 1987).

Because every parent feels deep inside that child rearing is not quite so simple, real feelings of uncertainty trigger an unproductive cycle of feeling unsuccessful against this false societal standard.

Implications for the Teacher

- Parents need someone who understands the uncertainties involved in the situation. They do not need people who believe there is only one right answer in child rearing or who convey the impression that they are totally certain of their own actions at all times.

- Teachers are helpful when they convey the impression of looking for answers together.

- Teachers are supportive when they do not immediately assign blame for children's difficulties to parenting.

Real Concern and Caring for Children

However it may appear to an outsider, most parents love and care for their children. In fact, most parents care passionately with a feeling that is "highly personalized, that comes with a history and a future" (Gonzalez-Mena, 2005). Parenting is about these strong connections with children, a continuity over time. Parents want the best for their children, whether this means physical care, education, or future plans. They care, and they care deeply (see Figure 3-23). Teachers must believe in and value that parental caring using their passion to bring parents into partnership.

FIGURE 3-23 Parents care deeply about their children.

TOUCHPOINT ASSUMPTIONS ABOUT PARENTS

- **The parent is the expert on his or her child.**
- **All parents have strengths.**
- **All parents want to do well by their children.**
- **All parents have something critical to share at each developmental stage.**
- **All parents have ambivalent feelings.**
- **Parenting is a process built on trial and error.**

—*Brazelton, 1998*

Implications for the Teacher

- Teachers must understand that parents genuinely care and are concerned for their children. Even when parental behavior strikes them as indifferent or uncaring, they must believe that caring exists. Many factors may cause behaviors that convey negative impressions. (Some of these will be discussed in Chapters 6 and 17.)

REFLECTIONS FOR JOURNAL ENTRIES

Consider the statement that parents care deeply. What experiences have you had that cause you to agree or disagree with this idea? How will this idea influence you as you work with families?

SUMMARY

In the area of interpersonal relationships and communications, most breakdowns occur because of insensitivity to the other's position and feelings. There is no question that teachers bring their own needs and emotional responses to the encounter, and these must be reckoned with; but an awareness of the possible roles and emotional responses that accompany parenthood will help teachers to work with parents.

Several distinct roles make up a parent's life. These include the parent as

1. Nurturer.
2. Part of adult relationships.
3. An individual.
4. Worker.
5. Consumer.
6. Community member.
7. Educator.

Despite the fact that every parenting experience is unique to the individual, several common emotional responses have implications for the teacher working with parents. Most parents experience

1. Irrevocability of parenthood, accompanied by anxiety.
2. Restrictions, isolation, fatigue.
3. Dealing with parenting myths and images.
4. Guilt.
5. Satisfaction related to self-esteem.
6. Uncertainty.
7. Real concern for their child.

STUDENT ACTIVITIES FOR FURTHER STUDY

1. Read a personal account written by a parent. Here are some suggestions:

Buchanan, A. (2003). *Mother shock: Loving every (other) minute of it.* Emeryville, CA: Seal Press.

Black, K. (2005). *Mothering without a map: The search for the good mother within.* New York: Penguin reprint.

Coll, C., Surrey, J., & Weingarten, K. (Eds.). (1998). *Mothering against the odds: Diverse voices of contemporary mothers.* New York: Guilford Press.

Greenberg, M. (1985). *The birth of a father.* New York: Avon.

Greene, B. (1985). *Good morning merry sunshine: A father's journal of his child's first year.* Boston: G. K. Hall.

Halliday, A. (2002).*The big rumpus: A mother's tale from the trenches.* Emeryville, CA: Seal Press.

Jackson, M. (1994). *The mother zone: Love, sex, and laundry in the modern family.* New York: Henry Holt.

Kelly, M., & Parsons, E. (1992). *The mother's almanac* (rev. ed.). New York: Doubleday.

Kline, C. (1998). *Child of mine: Original essays on becoming a mother.* El Dorado, AR: Delta.

Krasnow, I. (1997). *Surrendering to motherhood: Losing your mind, finding your soul.* New York: Hyperion.

Lamott, A. (1994). *Operating instructions: A journal of my son's first year.* New York: Ballantine.

Mead-Ferro, M. (2004). *Confessions of a slacker mom.* Philadelphia: Da Capo Lifelong.

Pitts, L. (1999). *Becoming Dad: Black men and the journey to fatherhood.* Atlanta: Longstreet.

Warner, J. (2005). *Perfect madness: Motherhood in the age of anxiety.* New York: Riverhead.

2. Talk with several parents. Choose parents whose children include infants, toddlers, preschoolers, and school-aged children, if possible.

Talk with at least one father. Discuss their reactions to parenthood: adjustments, negative aspects, positive aspects, and changes in adult relationships and lifestyle. Share your findings with your classmates. Try to identify which of Galinsky's stages of parenthood these parents are in.

3. Talk with a professional in an agency that works to support and educate parents. What are some major concerns, difficulties, and needs of parents that he or she reports?

4. In small groups, brainstorm additional practical ways for classroom teachers to support parents in the seven different roles of parents as defined in this chapter.

5. Interview your own parents if possible. Ask them to describe their satisfactions from parenting and what they were most proud of in being your parents.

CASE STUDY

Allison Smith is a single mother of a 4-year-old and an 18-month-old. She works as a secretary at the local electric company. She is also active in her church, working with the youth choir and teaching Sunday school. Her children attend a child care center run by the church. When her children visit her ex-husband every other weekend, Allison goes to visit her parents, who are elderly and increasingly frail. Recently she has begun to date a man whom she met at work, who also has two young children. She hopes to begin taking classes next year at the local community college so she can work toward her lifelong dream of becoming a nurse.

1. What roles do you see, or can you guess, that Allison plays as a parent?

2. Knowing what you know about Allison's life, what emotional responses might you imagine?

3. Knowing what you know about Allison's responsibilities, what challenges can you identify to bringing Allison into partnership with her child care teachers?

4. In what ways is Allison's life the same as every parent's? Different from some other parents?

REVIEW QUESTIONS

1. List seven roles that parents play.

2. Discuss the implications of these roles for a teacher working with parents.

3. List seven emotional responses of parents.

4. Discuss the implications of these emotional responses for teachers.

SUGGESTIONS FOR FURTHER READING

Brazelton, B. (1989). *Families: Crisis and caring.* New York: Ballantine Books.

Bronfenbrenner, U. (1984). The parent–child relationship and our changing society. In E. L. Arnold (Ed.), *Parents, children, and change.* Lexington, MA: Lexington Books.

Cowan, C., & Cowan, P. (1992). *When partners become parents: The big life change for couples.* New York: Basic Books.

Crittenden, A. (2002). *The price of motherhood: Why the most important job in the world is still the least valued.* New York: Owl Books.

Cryer, D., & Burchinal, M. (1997). Parents as child care consumers. *Early Childhood Research Quarterly, 12,* 35–38.

Hamner, T., & Turner, P. (2001). *Parenting in contemporary society* (4th ed.). Englewood Cliffs, NJ: Prentice Hall.

Hewlett, S. A., & West, C. (1998). *The war against parents: What we can do for America's beleaguered moms and dads.* Boston: Houghton Mifflin Co.

Hochschild, A. (2001). *The time bind: When work becomes home and home becomes work.* New York: Owl Books.

Holcomb, B. (1998). *Not guilty! The good news for working mothers.* New York: Touchstone.

Jackson, M. (1994). *The mother zone: Love, sex, and laundry in the modern family.* New York: Henry Holt.

Meyer, D. (1995). *Uncommon fathers.* Bethesda, MD: Woodbine House.

Peri, C., et al. (Eds.). (2000). *Mothers who think: Tales of real-life parenthood.* New York: Washington Square Press.

Schwartz, J. D. (1993). *The mother puzzle: A new generation reckons with motherhood.* New York: Simon and Schuster.

Sullivan, S. A. (1992). *The father's almanac* (rev. ed.). New York: Doubleday.

Unell, B., & Wyckoff, J. (2000). *The eight seasons of parenthood: How the stages of parenting constantly reshape our adult identities.* New York: Time Books.

Williams, J. (2001). *Unbending gender: Why family and work conflict and what to do about it.* New York: Oxford University Press.

REFERENCES

Bailey, M., & Ulman, B. (2005). *Trillion dollar moms: Marketing to a new generation of mothers.* Chicago: Dearborn Trade Books.

Balaban, N. (1990, March). Statement to the Montgomery County Council. *Young Children, 45*(3), 12–16.

Belsky, J. (1986). Infant day care: A cause for concern? *Zero to Three: Bulletin of the National Center for Clinical Infant Programs.*

Bergmann, B., & Helburn, S. (2002). *America's child care problem: The way out.* New York: Palgrave MacMillan Ltd.

Bettelheim, B. (1987). *A good enough parent: A book on child-rearing.* New York: Knopf.

Bigner, J. J. (2001). *Parent–child relations: An introduction to parenting* (6th ed.). New York: Prentice-Hall.

Blankenhorn, D. (1995). *Fatherless America: Confronting our most urgent social problems.* New York: Basic Books.

Brazelton, T. B. (1989, October 10). Working parents. *Newsweek,* 66–70.

———. (1994). *Touchpoints: Your child's emotional and behavioral development.* Cambridge, MA: Perseus Publishing.

———. (1998). How to help parents of young children. *Clinical Child Psychology and Psychiatry, 3*(3), 481–483.

Brazelton, T. B., & Greenspan, S. (2000). *The irreducible needs of children: What every child must have to grow, learn, and flourish.* Cambridge, MA: Perseus.

———. (2001). The irreducible needs of children: An interview with T. Berry Brazelton, M.D., and Stanley I. Greenspan, M.D. *Young Children, 56*(2), 6–14.

Brazelton, T. B., & Sparrow, J. (2001). *Touchpoints 3–5: Your child's emotional and behavioral development.* Cambridge, MA: Perseus Publishing.

Bredekamp, S., & Copple, C. (Eds.). (1997). *Developmentally appropriate practice in early childhood programs* (rev. ed.). Washington, DC: NAEYC.

Brooks, J. (2000). *Parenting* (3rd ed.). New York: McGraw-Hill.

Caldwell, B. (2001). Déjà vu all over again: A researcher explains the NICHD study. *Young Children, 56*(4), 58–59.

Cherlin, A., & Krishnamurthy, P. (2004, May 9). What works for Mom. *New York Times.*

Children's Defense Fund. (2005) *State of America's children 2005.* Washington, DC: author.

Clarke-Stewart, A. (1989). Infant day care: Maligned or malignant? *American Psychologist, 44,* 268–269.

Coontz, S. (1997). *The way we really are: Coming to terms with America's changing families.* New York: Basic Books.

Cost, Quality, and Outcomes Study Team. (1995). Cost, quality, and child outcomes in child care centers: Key findings and recommendations. *Young Children, 50*(4), 40–50.

Diamond, M., & Hopson, J. (1998). *Magic trees of the mind.* New York: Dutton Press.

Duvall, E. and Hill, K. (1948). *When You Marry.* New York: Association Press.

Elkind, D. (1970, April 5). Erik Erikson's eight ages of man. *New York Times Magazine,* 15–22.

———. (1987). *Miseducation: Preschoolers at risk.* New York: Knopf.

Galinsky, E. (1987). *The six stages of parenthood.* Reading, MA: Addison-Wesley.

———. (1994). Families and work: The importance of the quality of the work environment. In S. Kagan & B. Weissbourd (Eds.). *Putting families first.* San Francisco: Jossey-Bass.

———. (1999). *Ask the children: What America's children really think about working parents.* New York: Morrow.

———. (2000). Finding from *Ask the Children* with implications for early childhood professionals. *Young Children, 55*(3), 64–68.

————. (2002). *Navigating work and family: Hands on advice for working parents.* New York: Families and Work Institute.

Gonzalez-Mena, J. (2005). *The young child in the family and the community* (4th ed.). New York: Prentice-Hall..

Goodnow, J., & Bowes, J. (1994). *Men, women, and household work.* New York: Oxford University Press.

Han, W. J., & Waldfogel, J. (2003). Parental leave: The impact of recent legislation on parents' leave taking. *Demography, 40*(1), 191–200.

Hattery, A. (2000). *Women, work, and family: Balancing and weaving.* Thousand Oaks, CA: Sage Publications.

Hochschild, A. (1989). *The second shift: Working parents and the revolution at home.* New York: Viking.

Holcomb, B. (1996/97). How families are changing . . . for the better! In K. Paciorek & J. Munro (Eds.). *Annual editions early childhood education.*, Guilford, CT: Dushkin.

Kamerman, S. B. (1980). *Parenting in an unresponsive society: Managing work and family life.* New York: The Free Press.

————. (2000). From maternity to parenting policies: Women's health, employment, and child and family well-being. *Journal of the American Medical Women's Association, 55*(2).

Karen, R. (1990, February). Becoming attached. *The Atlantic Monthly,* 35–70.

Levine, J., & Pittinsky, T. (1998). *Working fathers: New strategies for balancing work and family.* Reading, MA: Addison-Wesley.

Loux, R. (1993). *Father love: What we need, what we seek, what we must create.* New York: Pocket Books.

Moore, S. (1996). The role of parents in the development of peer group competence. *ERIC Digest.*

NAECS/SDE. (2001). *Still* unacceptable trends in kindergarten entry and placement: A position statement developed by the National Association of Early Childhood Specialists in State Departments of Education. *Young Children, 56*(5), 59–62.

NIHCD Early Child Care Research Network. (1997). The effects of infant child care on infant–mother attachment security: Results of the NIHCD study of early child care. *Child Development, 68*(5), 860–879.

National Center for Education Statistics. (2001). *Measuring father involvement in young children's lives.* Washington, DC: Department of Education.

Parke, R. (1996). *The developing child: Fatherhood.* Cambridge, MA: Harvard University Press.

Rapoport, R., Bailyn, L., Fletcher, J., & Pruitt, B. (2001). *Beyond work—Family.* San Francisco: Jossey-Bass.

Rohner, R. (1998, October). Father love and child development: History and current evidence. *Current Directions in Psychological Science,* 157–161.

Rossi, A. (1968). Transition to parenthood. *Journal of Marriage and the Family, 30,* 26–39.

Shellenbarger, S. (2005, February 18). Both sides in 'Mommy War' search for peace. *Wall Street Journal.*

Shore, R. (1997). *Rethinking the brain: New insights into early development.* New York: Families and Work Institute.

Turbiville, V., Umbarger, G., & Guthrie, A. (2000). Father involvement in programs for young children. *Young Children,* 55(4), 74–79.

U.S. Department of Education. (1997). *Fathers' involvement in their children's schools.* Available online at http://nces.ed.gov/pubsearch.

Warner, J. (2005, February 14). I love them, I love him not. *New York Times,* A23.

HELPFUL WEB SITES

http://www.parentsunite.org

The National Parenting Association believes that helping parents helps kids. The organization, founded by author–activist Sylvia Ann Hewlett to give parents a greater voice in the public arena, is trying to build a parents' movement to unite mothers and fathers across the country. Working together, the association believes that parents can create a society that values parenting, benefits children, and strengthens America.

http://www.familiesandwork.org

The Families and Work Institute is a nonprofit center for research, providing data to inform decision making on changing the workplace, changing families, and changing communities.

http://www.npin.org

The National Parent Information Network, sponsored by ERIC, offers access to research and information about the process of parenting and family involvement in education.

http://www.tnpc.com

The Web site of the National Parenting Center provides information for parents from renowned child-rearing authorities.

Additional resources for this chapter can be found on the Online Companion to accompany this text at www.earlychilded.delmar.com. This supplemental material includes frequently asked questions; chapter outlines to be used as study guides; scenarios that both encourage large and small group discussions and provoke new thoughts and ideas; and chapter resources, including chapter summaries, interactive questions, Web links, and Web activities. In addition, forms from the text are available for download.

APPENDIX: TOUCHPOINTS MODEL

The Touchpoints model, developed by Dr. T. Berry Brazelton, is a system designed to help professionals form alliances with parents in providing a nurturing environment for children. The focus is on helping providers to think preventively and to value parents' ethnic, religious, and lifestyle attributes. Professionals using the ideas and principles of the Touchpoints model can offer the necessary information and modeling for parents to understand and enhance their young children's development, thus helping the whole family system succeed.

Touchpoints are periods during the first years of life during which children's spurts in development disrupt the family system. Brazelton refers to the Touchpoints as a map of child development that can be identified and anticipated by both parents and professionals. He has identified 13 touchpoints in the first 3 years, beginning in pregnancy, and then in the first 3 years of life. The touchpoints are centered around caregiving themes such as feeding and discipline rather than traditional milestones. As the child negotiates these times, families need awareness of the touchpoints and strategies for dealing with them. This will help reduce negative patterns and problems.

Professionals can use the touchpoints as a frame of reference in their work with families during the early years. Anticipatory guidance in the Touchpoints model is not just delivering advice, but having a dialogue with a focus on the common interest in the child, sharing discussion about how parents feel and would react in the face of new challenges. Sharing touchpoints helps parents feel more confident in themselves, in their children, and in the process of development.

Here are the guiding principles of the Touchpoints model:

- Value and understand the relationship between you and the parent.
- Use the behavior of the child as your language.
- Value passion wherever you find it.
- Focus on the parent–child relationship.
- Look for opportunities to support mastery.
- Recognize what you bring to the interaction.
- Be willing to discuss matters that go beyond your traditional role.

The Touchpoint parent assumptions are listed on page 115. Touchpoint assumptions about practitioners are these:

- Each practitioner is the expert within the context of his or her practice setting.
- Practitioners want to be competent.

- Practitioners need support and respect of the kind we are asking them to give parents.

- Practitioners need to reflect on their contribution to parent–provider interactions.

Training in the Touchpoints model is offered at many sites around the country. For more information, contact Touchpoints Project, Children's Hospital, Boston, 1295 Boylston St., Suite 320, Boston, MA 02215 (617) 355–6947, http://www.touchpoints.org. For other useful sources see Brazelton, 1994, and Brazelton and Sparrow, 2001.

"*Did Momma's little angel stretch his potential today?*"

SECTION II

TEACHER–FAMILY PARTNERSHIPS IN EARLY EDUCATION

Now that we have completed our initial study of parenting in modern America, it is time to consider the importance of creating teacher–family partnerships. Because this is a task undertaken with the teacher's initiative, it is crucial that teachers understand why teacher–family partnerships are a necessary part of the educator's role. In Chapter 4 we consider the various facets and motivations of family involvement teachers may encounter. Chapter 5 discusses the benefits for children, families, and teachers when parents and teachers work together. Chapter 6 addresses the various barriers that may prevent the development of optimal working relationships. Chapter 7 identifies the attitudes and practices that form the foundation for healthy partnerships. You will meet teachers and parents who demonstrate through their dialogue and comments the spectrum of experience that teachers may meet.

CHAPTER 4

What Is Family Involvement?

KEY TERMS
deficit model
empowerment
family-centered
intervention
mandate

When the term *parent* or *family involvement* is used, different individuals may think of very different activities and characteristics that define the involvement of parents in education programs and schools. There is no uniform requirement or philosophy that can be applied to working with families; indeed, many programs seem to feel this is the least important aspect of their function, paying only perfunctory attention to parents, while others work hard to include parents in as many aspects of their programs as they can. In this chapter we will explore the various motivations that impel schools and centers to bring parents into the educational process for their children, as well as the models of programs that you might find defined as family involvement.

■■■ PERSPECTIVES ON FAMILY INVOLVEMENT

Jane Briscoe again. "You know, I'm really confused. At a meeting I went to recently, the subject of parent involvement came up. After several people discussed what they thought about parent involvement, I realized I have been using that term differently than most of them. One of them implied that parent involvement was parents meeting together and making the decisions in a program. Another spoke as if parent involvement meant parents working as aides in the classroom. Somebody else mentioned the early intervention programs in which parents are being taught more about their children so they can expand the ways they help their own children develop. And I've been thinking parent involvement is when I try to let parents know as much as I can about what's going on in their children's classroom lives."

Small wonder that Jane is confused. In program descriptions, research, and conversational usage among teachers, the term *parent involvement* is used to describe all of these patterns of parent participation in early childhood education.

> "Parent involvement" is an all-purpose term used to describe all manner of parent–program interaction: policy making, parent education, fund-raising, volunteering time, and even the simple exchange of information of various sorts with staff. Under a general goal of continuity of care, the desired end involved may be better parenting, better child care and schools, or both. The parent involvement continuum runs from an expectation of parent control to complete subservience of parents to professionals. Parents may be cast in a variety of roles from experts (on their own children) to students, thus putting staff in positions ranging from servants to savants (Pettygrove & Greenman, 1984).

As this statement implies, there is no single model of parent involvement. Schools and programs have chosen to address the issue of parent involvement in a variety of ways, ranging from a low level to a high level of parent involvement.

Schools and programs with a low level of parent involvement allow parents to take part in activities that do not challenge the expertise of a teacher or the decision-making power of the school. Activities such as newsletters, parent meetings, or individual parent conferences tend to keep parents at a distance, learning secondhand about their children's life at school. Schools with a high level of parent involvement provide opportunities for parents to make their presence known, particularly in the educational setting, by parent visits, observations, or visits to volunteer assistance of many kinds; here parents are perceived as a source of help (see Figure 4-1). The highest levels of parent involvement occur in schools that believe both teachers and parents have expertise, and both parents and the school have decision-making rights.

FIGURE 4-1 Parents may assist teachers with special events or with routine tasks in the classroom.

Communicating via many channels, parents have the power to make decisions concerning the education of their children.

Four categories of parent involvement have been identified by the Home and School Institute in Washington, D.C. (Boone & Barclay, 1995). These categories include *home–school communication,* using strategies such as newsletters, telephone calls, informal notes, and conferences; *parent education,* using methods such as parent workshops, home visits, written materials, libraries, and videotapes; *public relations,* having the goal of providing consistent, positive contact with the school and its programs; and *volunteerism,* soliciting support for children, school activities, or the administration with tasks performed at school, home, or in the workplace.

Joyce Epstein, a leader in parent–teacher–school research, identifies six types of parent involvement and finds that successful programs generally incorporate all six. Many schools are now following this model. Here are the six types of involvement:

- *Parenting:* Here schools help families with parenting and child-rearing skills, child development knowledge, and creating home conditions that support children at each grade level. Reciprocally, schools have to learn to understand families.

- *Communicating:* The school involves parents by communicating about school programs and student progress through effective two-way channels that may include memos, notices, conferences, newsletters, phone calls, and electronic messages.

- *Volunteering:* Schools work to improve recruiting, training, and schedules to involve families as volunteers and as audiences to support students and school programs.

- *Learning at home:* Schools involve families with the children in learning activities at home, including homework and other curriculum-related activities.

- *Decision making:* Schools include families as participants in school decisions and governance through PTA, advisory councils, committees, and other leadership opportunities.

- *Collaborating with the community:* Schools coordinate services and resources for families and the school with businesses, agencies and other groups. Schools also provide services to the community (Epstein et al., 1997; Epstein, 2000).

You will read more about how one early education program uses the Epstein model to frame family involvement activities in Chapter 18.

■■■ A BRIEF HISTORY OF FAMILY INVOLVEMENT

An interest in the involvement of parents in early childhood education is not new. Parents were involved in some of the first preschool education movements in America in the earliest decades of this century. For middle-class parents, parent cooperative nursery schools blossomed throughout the 1920s, 1930s, 1940s, reached a peak around 1960, and continue today to a lesser degree. (See an account of one such program in Chapter 18.) Often appearing in middle-class enclaves such as university or suburban towns, these schools welcome parents, primarily traditional stay-at-home mothers, who often undergo some training. The parents frequently take the position of paraprofessional in the preschool classroom, assisting a trained, paid, professional teacher. Such close involvement in their children's classroom lives offers opportunities for parents to enrich the lives of their children and themselves.

Parent cooperatives usually provide opportunities to participate in the life of the school, from defining the philosophy and practices to contributing to the care and maintenance of the facility. The belief is that parents know what they want for themselves and their children and therefore should be involved in the school. (The parent cooperative model has been used more recently even in child care facilities for parents employed full-time. The contributions of parents decrease budget costs for such items as cleaning, accounting, purchasing, and laundry, as well as strengthening the ties between parent and school.) Many of today's charter schools work from the parent cooperative model, with parents involved in the initial philosophy and design of the school and in its organization and management.

Parents from lower socioeconomic backgrounds were involved in the nursery schools and child care centers set up by the government to supply children's nutritional and health care needs in families disrupted by the Depression (Works Progress Administration, or WPA, centers). Later, in World War II, the Lanham Act Child Care Centers funded by the government, as well as private employer-sponsored centers, offered child care for parents working in the war effort. Even with the demands of those stressful times, and coming from backgrounds of cultural and ethnic diversity, these parent groups were extremely responsive to parent educators associated with the centers to provide support for parental self-development and learning.

It was another 20 years or so before the field of early childhood education expanded again, and with this expansion came renewed interest in efforts to work with parents. Programs for the disadvantaged, including Head Start and other **intervention** programs, appeared in the 1960s and 1970s. Parents were involved in most of these programs (see Figure 4-2). Rodd (1998) refers to the kinds of parent involvement that developed in the intervention programs as taking "a compensatory approach to parental involvement in which **deficit models** of family life were responded to with the provision of interventionist strategies" (Rodd, 1998). Here the early childhood educators

Unity

I dreamt I stood in a studio and I watched two sculptors there
The clay they used was a young child's mind
And they fashioned it with care
One was a teacher—the tools he used
Were books, music, and art
The other, a parent, worked with a guiding hand
And a gentle loving heart
Day after day, the teacher toiled with touch
That was deft and sure
While the parent labored by his side and when at last, their task was done
They were proud of what they had wrought
For the things they had molded into a child
Could neither be sold nor bought
And each agreed they would have failed
If each had worked alone
For behind the teacher stood the school
And behind the parent, the home.

—*Anonymous*

FIGURE 4-2 Working together.

perceived themselves as knowledgeable and parents as lacking the knowledge and skills to create optimal family environments for raising their children. The unfortunate result of working with a deficit model perspective is that the professionals involved did not see the parents as capable of being allies. The professionals were clearly in control, in an uneasy tolerance of the families.

Shortly after, changes in the structure of American society brought increasing numbers of women into the out-of-home workforce. With the growing need for child care for families with infants and very young children, attention was again focused on finding ways for parents and teachers to negotiate answers to the questions of who has the power, and for what?

Although day care has been around for a long time to help social workers deal with families in a state of crisis, this new form of child care used by nearly all American families is puzzling to many adults who did not grow up in such programs and therefore have no clear models of what it is like or how children's experiences should be shared with parents. This creates unresolved tensions about just how parental interests and needs should be accommodated: How much weight should be given to parental ideas, based on their commitment to their own children? How much weight should be given to the judgment of the professional staff, based on professional training? Where are the boundaries?

The hesitancy is there, along with confusion about what counts as parent involvement. The early childhood professional stance in the 1970s, according to Rodd, was to improve communication with parents, believing that "parental involvement was a matter of communication and contact" (Rodd, 1998). Then the philosophy of communication gave way to the philosophy of accountability in the 1980s. Here parents were perceived as "consumers of a service who possessed rights and responsibilities that early childhood professionals were obliged to meet." Throughout all of this parents were informed or consulted, but there was little partnership or collaboration. Currently the early childhood education field is in the process of trying to clarify its professional responsibilities toward families and define appropriate and helpful practices. Rodd suggests that a philosophy of partnership gained momentum in the 1990s as early childhood education professionals recognize that they have "both shared and complementary goals with the parents who are associated with their centers" (see Figure 4-3). There is a recognition that both parents and teachers are experts related to children and families, each bringing different types of expertise. In the partnership approach, cooperative activity is stressed over joint activity, and parents may decide the level of involvement that is compatible with their lives and commitments.

Many factors are driving recommendations for partnerships between families and schools: a concern for parental rights and parental **empowerment**, and for program responsiveness to family values and cultural tradition (Powell, 1998); ecological considerations of children and families that see the supportive nature of other systems for the child and family (Bronfenbrenner & Morris, 1998); and attention and imperatives from school systems and government agencies, with a view to supporting the educational process. The

FIGURE 4-3 Parents have been involved in many intervention programs.

discussion will surely continue throughout the professional lives of those who read this text.

> There is no consensus in the field about the operational meaning of partnership and similar labels, and hence there is the potential for enormous variation in the way similar or identical labels are put into operation (Powell, 1989).

The attempts to involve families in elementary schools and higher have been based on abundant research over long periods that continues to link parent involvement with student performance in any number of areas, including test scores, attentiveness, homework completion, reading ability, and other academic achievements (Henderson & Berla, 1994). Every reform effort and educational interventions list and much recent governmental legislation have all been focused on parent involvement as an important ingredient for success of schools (Finn, 1998).

The most recent legislation that links parents with the educational process is the No Child Left Behind Act, signed into law in 2002. This federal legislation and its implications for families and parent involvement will be discussed in more detail later in this chapter.

Enabling, Strengthening

Just as there are more than one philosophy and model of parent involvement, there are also more than one set of circumstances that motivate the involvement. At least three separate forces have brought home and school together.

One influence on parent involvement has been the research on education and child development that underscores the interdependence of parent, child, and community agencies in providing for optimal development of children. Examples of this include the research on cognitive and social development related to parental interaction and style and involvement with programs, especially the intervention programs.

A second set of motives is through force of **mandate**, enunciated by various laws and funding arrangements, that parents play a part in the education of their children. Examples of mandated parent involvement include Head Start; Title I and Chapter I funding; the Education for all Handicapped Children Act (PL 94–142) and Amendments (PL 99–451), now reauthorized as the Individuals with Disabilities Act (IDEA: PL 101–576 and 108-446); Goals 2000: Educate America Act of 1994; and NCLB (No Child Left Behind).

A third influence is community concern and efforts, encouraging parental involvement as a means of both improving the schools and strengthening the family, thus eliminating some problems of concern to the community. Examples here include the collaborative approaches to family support and education that have developed nationwide. All of these motivations suggest larger issues than the token bake-cookies-and-go-on-field-trips approach to working with parents.

Today many American teachers working with young children are not working in programs that have mandates to include parents in a specific way. But the rising numbers of private for-profit child care programs, including child care franchises and family child care homes, and nonprofit child care programs, added to the more traditional nursery school programs, place many early childhood teachers on the front lines of contact between home and school, hopefully establishing a pattern that will continue through the school years. Many other teachers are working in classrooms in school systems or in after-school child care programs, where legislation and mandates for accreditation and funding ask for partnerships with families. Many of these teachers are convinced that joining together in partnership with families may help them find better ways to create a supportive environment for the developing children in their care.

Therefore, this text will offer a brief overview of the motives behind the various forms of parent involvement and point to some of the program patterns and the research done on these.

■■■ RESEARCH ON CHILD DEVELOPMENT AS MOTIVATION TO INCLUDE PARENTS

A lasting result of the intervention programs begun in the 1960s and 1970s is a body of research that describes the effects of various kinds of interaction and environmental influences on the development of young children. Such data impel many educators to press for increased parent involvement. Studies suggest that the early years are of utmost importance in setting learning patterns for children and families. More recent brain research emphasizes the crucial

FIGURE 4-4 Attachment correlates with curiosity, language, and many other aspects of development.

importance of the early years in developing the brain after birth and in providing stimulation for learning. It is almost impossible to overemphasize the importance of parenting in relation to learning language and other foundations for later learning.

Attachment, the strong, mutual, parent–child bond that forms during the first two years of life, is correlated with virtually every aspect of development: physical thriving; the exploration, curiosity, and problem solving that are foundations for cognitive skills; the appearance of language and communication skills; and emotional security and social comfort (see Figure 4-4). But beyond the overall well-being that comes with that warm parental relationship, studies confirm the assumption that specific factors in the parents' (particularly mothers') style have important and lasting impacts on children's learning styles, cognitive growth, and educational achievements. For example, it has been noted that many mothers from lower socioeconomic backgrounds, when working with their young children on a particular task, focus most on getting the job done, with little attention to giving verbal directions, helping develop problem-solving skills, or giving positive feedback. It is not surprising, then, that their young children come to the academic environment less prepared for its learning style and interaction with a middle-class teacher who expects children to be able to follow her verbal directions and solve problems independently.

But such deficits have solutions. A long-term investigation by Hart and Risley (1995) investigated how home experiences influenced children's development. Verbal interactions between parents and children were studied by analyzing one-hour tape recordings from about age 10 months to 36 months. Forty-two families were included in the study and were divided into families from professional backgrounds, working-class backgrounds, and families on welfare. Although all the children started to speak at about the same time, their vocabulary, as measured by the number of different words used, varied significantly. By age 3 the children from the professional families had an average vocabulary of 1,100 words; the average vocabulary for children from working-class backgrounds was 750 words, whereas the vocabulary of children from the welfare backgrounds was just around 500 words. The children heard very different amounts of language: The children from professional backgrounds heard an average of 2,153 words per hour, while the other two groups heard 1,251 and 618 per hour, respectively. In addition, the study found that the most positive parenting practices included specific ways of talking:

- Lots of "just talking," using a wide vocabulary.
- High rates of verbal approval and few prohibitions.
- High information content in the speech.
- Giving children choices and asking children about things.
- Listening to children and responding to their communication.

There were positive correlations between verbal abilities and intellectual development as the children were followed to age 9 or 10. Perhaps most strikingly, the researchers later found that low-income parents who were trained in parenting skills could change their methods of communication, resulting in children's attainments equal to the national average. These researchers concluded that the quality of parenting and communication is the key factor that determines cognitive abilities and accounts for achievement— certainly a finding that should have implications for teachers and families.

Educational intervention programs are deliberately designed to improve children's first learning opportunities by stimulating changes within key elements of their early learning environment, including changes in parental behavior. Those who design programs for young children and families often act on the belief that intervention directed at parents is as necessary as intervention directed at the child. Many programs give parents knowledge about child development, techniques for interacting with their children, advice on health and nutrition, and self-improvement options such as assistance with employment, education, or housing. The Head Start program is the longest-lasting of all early intervention programs, having started in the mid-1960s as part of President Johnson's War on Poverty. Early studies specific to Head Start suggested an excessive optimism in its evaluation of gains in children's cognitive development, nevertheless affirming that parental involvement was positively related to children's test scores, academic achievement, and self-concept, as well as to parental feelings of success and involvement in community activities (Midco, 1972). Other studies offer more optimistic findings about the long-term effects on school performance, confidence, and self-image up to 15 years after children participated in the preschool program (Collins & Deloria, 1983). However, the effectiveness of Head Start has continued to be questioned due to inconsistencies in various studies (Schweinhart & Weikart, 1986).

The most recent study, *Head Start Children's Entry into Public School: A Report on the National Head Start/Public School Transition Demonstration*

Study (Ramey et al., 2000) finds strong support for the conclusion that Head Start children typically enter school "ready to learn" and that they can achieve academically at national norms. It goes on to state, "This study clearly refutes the longstanding view of a 'fadeout' effect of benefits for Head Start Children." But perhaps most important, parent involvement emerged as a critical factor in children's retention of IQ gains. The gains also extended to other siblings if the parents were involved. And mothers themselves showed gains in confidence and self-concept, with assumed positive spillover effects for their children. In the recent study one finding was that many Head Start families steadily declined in their need for public assistance programs, indicating the increased self-sufficiency that results from gains in self-confidence and self-concept. The full impact of a program on children, families, and communities cannot be assessed on the basis of children's scores alone (Bronfenbrenner, 1976).

Another measure of national confidence in Head Start and its effects on families was the establishment of Early Head Start in the mid-1990s. Framed as a child development program with comprehensive two-generation services, these programs may begin working with families before a child is born and focus on enhancing children's development and supporting the family as the primary educators of their children during the critical first three years of life. The program is designed to produce outcomes in four domains:

1. Child development, including health, resilience, and social, language, and cognitive development.

2. Family development, including parenting and relationships with children, home environment and healthy family functioning, parent involvement, and economic self-sufficiency.

3. Staff development, including professional development and relationships with parents.

4. Community development, including enhanced child care quality, community collaboration, and integration of services to support families with young children.

An early report of 17 programs participating in the National Early Head Start Research and Evaluation Project (2000) found that some of these programs were operating as center-based programs, some as home-based programs, and others as a combination of the two (see Figure 4-5).

Other well-known center-based intervention programs include the Perry Preschool Project begun in Ypsilanti, Michigan, in the early 1960s. In addition to children attending high-quality early childhood programs for two-and-a-half hours five days a week, teachers visited parents in their homes for 90 minutes every week. In this rare long-term study, researchers followed 123 children from the preschool program through their 40th birthdays as of the latest report (Schweinhart et al., 2005). Participants did very well in a number of measures of social and educational achievement; they received less remedial education, graduated from high school, and went on to jobs or more

FIGURE 4-5 Head Start is an example of both an intervention program and one where family involvement is mandated.

education at twice the rate of children who did not attend the preschool programs. In addition, they had fewer arrests, fewer teenage pregnancies, and less welfare dependence or other behavior that creates problems for families and the community at large. As adults they were more likely to be married, own homes, and hold stable jobs.

Early Head Start and some intervention efforts also have home-based programs, offering the child and family direct services in their own homes. Studies indicate that test scores not only improve over time with this method but are maintained for several years after the intervention has been discontinued. Effects may be found even in younger children within the family who were directly involved; this shows the impact of the new skills learned by the parents. The continuing importance of the Head Start program is indicated by the efforts to expand the program through congressional funding even in times of government budget cuts.

In Head Start and most other intervention programs, parent participation is now considered a necessary component. The Head Start policy manual states that involvement of parents is essential:

> Many of the benefits of Head Start are rooted in "change." These changes must take place in the family itself, in the community, and in the attitudes of people and institutions that have an impact on both. (*U.S. Dept. of HHS.,* 1998)

In the intervention programs, the emphasis for family involvement is on

- Parents as learners, increasing parental knowledge about children and their needs, and ways that child development can be nurtured and supported.

- Parents as teachers, working with professionals in the classroom and in the home to enhance and extend the professionals' efforts.

The model is for parent education so that families and children can orient themselves successfully toward school. This approach assumes that the educational system is sound, that success in it is desired by a family although they may not know how to achieve it, and that offering chances for new knowledge and attitudes to parents is the key to that success. Some research indicates that the involvement of parents in a program over time is a critical factor in the gains made by children.

Numerous studies also indicate that additional factors related to later school success may be indirectly influenced by parents' involvement in their children's programs. There are documented gains in reading for children whose parents are encouraged to help with reading activities at home (Eldridge, 2001). Children whose parents are involved have more positive attitudes about school, improved attendance, and better homework habits than do children whose parents are less involved (Epstein, 2000; see Figure 4-6). Indeed, literally hundreds of studies suggest the value of involving parents in their children's

FIGURE 4-6 As parents get involved in their children's education, children's attitudes and school achievement reflect positive gains.

schools and doing so as early as possible (Henderson & Berla, 1994; Hoover-Dempsey, Bassler, & Burow, 1995; Ho & Willms, 1996). For a full listing of some of this research, see the North Central Regional Laboratory (NCREL) Web site address at the end of this chapter. It seems evident that parental interest is positively associated with children's academic achievements.

The value the home places on school learning is related to differences in academic performance. In fact, it has been found that home attitudes and factors affect the positive outcome of children's schooling twice as much as do socioeconomic factors, and the single most important factor is the self-esteem of the parent.

There are some obvious ways parental self-esteem is enhanced by involvement in their children's programs. The schools seek parents out to include them as an essential part of their children's education. Improved interaction skills help parents feel more effective with their children and more effective in the parenting role. Parents perceive their own role as important.

Experience in leadership skills and decision making, along with fulfilling social interaction with other adults, all add to parents' positive self-image (see Figure 4-7). Head Start evaluations report that mothers who participated claim fewer psychological problems, greater feelings of mastery, and more satisfaction with their present life situations at the end of the program. Surely spillover effects for children could be anticipated from such positive feelings in parents.

Research that suggests benefits to the development of children and their parents from parental involvement offers powerful motivation to many programs to work toward parent participation. School systems and government agencies believe so strongly in the importance of involving families in their children's education that they develop policies and strategies to facilitate that involvement (Funkhouser & Gonzales, 1997; also available online at

FIGURE 4-7 Experience in decision making may help parents' own self-esteem.

http://www.ed.gov/pubs/FamInvolve/title.html). Read about Lakewood Preschool Cooperative, an intervention program that involves parent participation, in Chapter 18.

■ ■ ■ MANDATED PARENT INVOLVEMENT

When the powers that control funding mandate family involvement as a program requirement, there is no longer any debate about whether to have parent participation. Several legislative efforts have included parent participation as part of the required structure in agencies and actions providing services to children. In addition, recent policies and practice guidelines have proclaimed specific directions for programs to follow in relation to families, sometimes in order to win accreditation or professional status. Several examples of mandated parent involvement will be discussed next.

Head Start

We have already mentioned Head Start as an example of the research linking family involvement with children's school success. From the beginning, Head Start was required to have "maximum feasible participation" of the families served. In its policy manual Head Start has specified performance standards for four areas of parent involvement:

1. Decision making about direction and operation of the program via membership on the Policy Council.

2. Participation in classrooms as volunteers, with the possibility of moving up a career ladder as paid employees.

3. Parent activities planned by the parents themselves.

4. Working with their own children, along with the center staff.

The rationale for parent involvement is stated thus: "If Head Start children are to reach their fullest potential, there must be an opportunity for Head Start parents to influence the character of programs affecting the development of their children" (*U.S. Dept. of HHS.*, 1998). Parents are given a concrete means of doing something for their children. The major role of decision maker is emphasized to offer parents opportunities to become competent in running the program. Parents set the standards for the hiring of professional staff, often interviewing and selecting staff. They also participate in decisions on budgetary matters. Parent decision makers influence the agency to become sensitive to the culture and needs of the families served.

Title I

More recent federal initiatives authorize funds as part of Chapter I of Title I (of PL 100–297). Called Even Start, the family-centered education program funds local efforts to improve the educational opportunities for the nation's children and adults by integrating early childhood education and adult education for parents into a unified **family-centered** literacy program. The mandate calls for

- Plans to build on existing community resources to create new ranges of services that include identification and recruitment of eligible children.
- Screening and preparing parents and children for the program.
- Establishing instructional programs to promote adult literacy.
- Training parents to support the education and growth of their children.
- Preparing children for success in regular schools.
- Providing special training for staff to develop skills to work with parents and children.
- Integrating instructional services through home-based programs where possible (see Figure 4-8).

Each program funded by Title I funds must have a plan to involve families. Sample activities and services for families that may be funded by Title I include things like

- Family literacy activities.
- Parent meetings and training activities.
- Transportation and child care so parents can come to school activities or volunteer in classrooms.

FIGURE 4-8 Parents involved in their children's classrooms learn new skills.

- Parent resource centers.
- Materials that parents can use to work with their children at home.

An example of the mandated involvement for parents can be seen in a Parent/School Partnership agreement signed by parents whose children were participating in a prekindergarten program funded by Title I resources. In this agreement parents agree to

1. Make sure my child attends school regularly.
2. Make arrangements for my child before and after school. Arrange for an adult to wait with/for my child at the bus stop in the morning and in the afternoon.
3. Keep immunizations/physicals up to date and handle any medical needs that arise.
4. Attend the orientation session for parents.
5. Attend conferences requested by my child's teacher and be available for contact on a regular basis with staff. (This may involve home visits, telephone conferences, or school/worksite conferences.)
6. Participate in at least four parent/child/staff events during the year.
7. Read with my child and sign the reading log as required.
8. Participate with my child in regular at-home activities designed to promote literacy learning as requested by my child's teacher.
9. Attend a minimum of five hours of family–school partnership workshops offered by the school.
10. Complete and return progress reports so that there is open, ongoing communication between the teacher and myself.

Parents are informed that failure to fulfill these requirements may mean their child cannot remain in the program.

Education of Children with Disabilities

Parent involvement in plans to provide services for children with special needs was mandated first by PL 94–142, the Education of All Handicapped Children Act of 1975. This law requires parents' participation in planning with professionals to develop an individualized education program (IEP) for their children.

Parents can initiate a hearing if they do not agree with the child's diagnosis, placement, or IEP. The 1986 Education of the Handicapped Act Amendments and all later reauthorizations and amendments added services for infants and toddlers and required a focus on the family for delivery of services. Parents or guardians are included in a multidisciplinary team that develops an individualized family service plan (IFSP), including a statement of the family's strengths and needs in maximizing the development of the infant or toddler with disabilities. These provisions are continued in the reauthorization of the Individuals with Disabilities Act in 1990 and the Amendments of 1997. The reauthorization of the Individuals with Disabilities Educational Improvement Act of 2004 (PL108-446) included provisions to align special education with the NCLB legislation, such as requiring parents to monitor whether the IEP was in line with state standards for achievement. Families are required to be involved with all aspects of planning for the education of their children with special needs.

Child Care and Development Block Grants

The Child Care and Development Block Grants, finally funded by the Congress in 1990 and known as the ABC bill during lobbying for its passage, are a historic, freestanding, federal child care program—the first ever—culminating almost 20 years of efforts following President Nixon's veto of child care legislation in 1971. The legislation lays the foundation for a national system of safe and affordable child care. Many provisions of CCDBG highlight the importance of parental choice and involvement. The bill preserves the rights of parents in the system by stating that nothing in the bill should be applied to "infringe upon or usurp the moral and legal rights and responsibilities of parents." Parents are given the right to help set child care standards and policies on national, state, and local levels. The legislature sets minimum national standards, including parent involvement, to help parents measure and improve program quality. It is stated that providers of care must ensure unlimited parental access to their children during the day. The bill also funds resource and referral programs to educate parents and the public about child care options and choices, licensing and regulatory requirements, and complaint procedures. Each state must maintain a list of substantiated parental complaints and make it available on request. These CCDBG provisions recognize the importance of including parents in child care systems.

Early Childhood Environment Rating Scale

A tool that is widely used in the United States, and indeed in programs around the world, is the Early Childhood Environment Rating Scale, now in a revised edition (Harms, Clifford, & Cryer, 1998). Program administrators, credentialing evaluators, and teachers wanting to identify areas of strength and need for improvement in an early childhood program use the 43 items of the rating scale. One of the items, number 38, is focused on provisions for parents.

The specific indicators identified under this item delineate practices that may be rated from inadequate to excellent. Many programs must get at least a good rating to gain a higher standard of licensing or certification. The descriptors that suggest quality are described in Figure 4-9.

Goals 2000

In 1990 the first national educational goals were formulated as a result of an Education Summit Conference called by President George Bush and passed into law under President Bill Clinton as *Goals 2000: Educate America Act of 1994.*

	Inadequate		Minimal		Good		Excellent	
	1	**2**	**3**	**4**	**5**	**6**	**7**	

PARENTS AND STAFF

38. Provisions for parents

Inadequate (1)	Minimal (3)	Good (5)	Excellent (7)
1.1. No information concerning program given to parents in writing.	3.1 Parents given administrative information about program in writing (fees, hours of service, health rules for, attendance).	5.1 Parents urged to observe in child's group prior to enrollment. 5.2 Parents made aware of philosophy and approaches practiced (parent handbook, discipline policy, descriptions of activities).	7.1 Parents asked for an evaluation of the program annually (parent questionnaires, group evaluation meeting).
1.2 Parents discouraged from observing or being involved in children's program.	3.2 Some sharing of child-related information between parents and staff (informal communication; parent conferences only upon request; some parenting materials).	5.3 Much sharing of child-related information between parents and staff (frequent informal communication; periodic conferences for all children; parent meetings, newsletters, parenting information available).	7.2 Parents referred to other professionals when needed (for special parenting help, for health concerns about child).
	3.3 Some possibilities for parents and family members to be involved in children's program.	5.4 Variety of alternatives used to encourage family involvement in children's program (bring birthday treat, eat lunch with child, attend family potluck).	7.3 Parents involved in decision-making roles in program along with staff (parent representatives on board).
	3.4 Interactions between family members and staff are generally respectful and positive.		

Questions

(1.1, 3.1) Is any written information about the program given to parents? What is included in this information?

(1.2, 3.3, 5.4) Are there any ways that parents can be involved in their child's classroom? Please give some examples.

(3.2, 5.3) Do you and the parents ever share information about the children? How is this done?

(3.4) What is your relationship with the parents usually like?

(5.1) Are parents able to visit the class before their child is enrolled? How is this handled?

(7.1) Do parents take part in evaluating the program? How is this done? About how often?

(7.2) What do you do when parents seem to be having difficulties? Do you refer them to other professionals for help?

(7.3) Do parents take part in making decisions about the program? How is this handled?

FIGURE 4–9 Descriptors that suggest the signs of parent involvement in quality programs.

Goal one states, "By the year 2000, all children in America will start school ready to learn." Parents are specifically mentioned in one of the three objectives to meet this first goal: "Every parent in the United States will be a child's first teacher and devote time each day helping his or her preschool child learn. Every parent will have access to the training and support parents need." The last of the eight goals states, "Every school will promote partnerships that will increase parental involvement and participation in promoting the social, emotional, and academic growth of children." The objectives of this goal are that

1. Every state will develop policies to help local schools and local education agencies establish programs for increasing partnerships that respond to the varying needs of parents and the home, including parents of children who are disadvantaged or bilingual, or parents of children with disabilities.

2. Every school will actively engage parents and families in a partnership that supports the academic work of children at home and shared educational decision making at school.

3. Parents and families will help to ensure that schools are adequately supported and will hold schools and teachers to high standards of accountability.

The National School Readiness Task Force has made numerous recommendations so that "caring communities" can create vehicles to support the families of young children as they prepare children for educational success, including parent involvement in development programs for children and family support programs (NASBE, 1991).

No Child Left Behind (NCLB) Legislation

The Elementary and Secondary Education Act, commonly known as No Child Left Behind, was signed into law in 2002 (PL 107-10) and has far-reaching effects on educational systems, schools, classrooms, and the children served. There are four main goals behind the law:

- Stronger accountability for results measured by student achievement test scores, with corrective actions to be taken as needed.

- More freedom for state and communities to use federal education funds.

- Encouraging the use of proven education methods to improve student learning and achievement.

- More choices for parents.

Teachers should be familiar with all provisions of the law, but we will focus on the choices and opportunities for families mandated by the law.

Parents of children in low-performing schools have new options for making changes for their children. In schools that do not meet state standards for

FIGURE 4-10 NCLB provides additional services for students in schools that fail to meet state standards.

at least two consecutive years, parents may transfer their children to better-performing public schools, including charter schools, within their district, with transportation provided by the district. Students from low-income families that fail to meet state standards for at least three years are eligible to receive supplemental educational services, such as free tutoring, after-school services, and summer school. Parents can also choose another public school if the school their child attends is unsafe (see Figure 4-10).

Schools are required to give parents annual report cards that show how well students in each school performed on required standardized tests, broken out by race, gender, disability, and the like, so parents can clearly see how well their schools are performing. In addition, parents must be given an annual report about how teacher qualifications at the school meet the law's requirements.

In addition to these family rights, the law makes clear statements about requirements for parent involvement. The requirements include

- A written parent involvement policy that has included parents in creating and evaluating the policy.

- Involvement of parents in planning, evaluating, and improving the various programs for parents.

- Giving parents understandable descriptions and explanations of the curricula and forms of academic assessments used to measure student progress.

- Offering a flexible number of meetings for parents at various times, and using funds to provide transportation, child care, and home visits to facilitate parent attendance.

- Emphasizing the importance of communication, including (a minimum of) annual parent–teacher conferences in each elementary school, frequent reports to parents about children's progress, reasonable access to staff, and opportunities to volunteer, participate, and observe in their children's classrooms.

- Building the capacity for parent involvement, including providing assistance to understand curriculum content and offer materials and training to help parents work with their children, such as with literacy training and technology.

- Educating teachers on how to reach out to, communicate with, and work with parents as equal partners, building ties between parents and the schools.

- Training parents to enhance the involvement of other parents.

- Sharing responsibilities between home and school for high student achievement.

- Coordinating parent involvement activities with Head Start, Reading First, Early Reading First, Parents as Teachers, HIPPY (Home Instruction for Parents of Preschool Youngsters), and public preschools to encourage parents to participate more fully.

- Establishing parental information and resource centers.

Parental information and resource centers (PIRC) are to assist parents of children identified for improvement under Title I. These school-based and school-linked centers are designated to help implement effective parental involvement policies, programs, and activities that will improve children's academic success. Another purpose is to develop and strengthen partnerships among parents (including parents of children from birth through age 5), teachers, and their children's schools and programs. Fifty percent of the funds designated for PIRC are to serve areas with a high concentration of low-income families; of the funds, a minimum of 30% is to be used to establish, expand, or operate early childhood parent education programs. (See the information about the PIRC program at the Web site http://www.pirc.org, at the end of this chapter.)

With these provisions and requirements, the act is sending clear messages to schools about the necessity of family involvement programs in all schools. It is important for teachers to understand the requirements of the law and help interpret them to families. Many people hope that this is the beginning of a new era of home and school communication and partnership.

Two resources could be particularly useful to teachers trying to help families understand the implications of NCLB for themselves and their children. A fact sheet, titled *Facts and Terms Every Parent Should Know*, is available to download and print from the Department of Education Web site; see the reference at the end of this chapter. A booklet, *A Practical Guide for Talking with Your Community about No Child Left Behind and Schools in Need of*

Improvement, is available from the Learning First Alliance; see the information about this Web site at the end of this chapter.

Recommendations of Professional Organizations

Beyond these legislative mandates, clear statements issued from several professional organizations point toward inclusion and involvement of parents in schools for young children as a measure of a quality program.

NAEYC Accreditation

The National Association for the Education of Young Children has developed standards to accredit high-quality programs for young children. The NAEYC governing board approved revised accreditation performance criteria in 2005. Among the program standards, partnerships with families are included as a necessary component. Program Standard 7 says, "The program establishes and maintains collaborative relationships with each child's family to foster children's development in all settings. These relationships are sensitive to family composition, language, and culture."

Rationale Young children's learning and development are integrally connected to their families. Consequently, to support and promote children's optimal learning and development, programs need to recognize the primacy of children's families; establish relationships with families based on mutual trust and respect; support and involve families in their children's educational growth; and invite families to fully participate in the program (NAEYC, 2005).

The following specifics are drawn from the performance criteria in the section related to families (NAEYC 2005, Accreditation Criteria, pp. 13–15):

- New and existing program staff develop skills and knowledge to work effectively with diverse families as a part of orientation and ongoing staff development.

- Program staff use a variety of formal and informal strategies (including conversations) to become acquainted with and learn from families about their family structure; their preferred child-rearing practices; and their socioeconomic, linguistic, racial, religious, and cultural backgrounds.

- Program staff actively use information about families to adapt the environment, curriculum, and teaching methods to the families they serve.

- To better understand the cultural backgrounds of children, families, and the community, program staff (as a part of program activities or as individuals) participate in community cultural events . . . geared to children and their families.

- Program staff provide support and information to family members legally responsible for the care and well-being of a child.

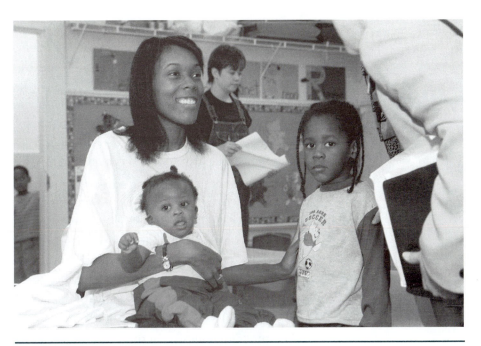

FIGURE 4-11 Program staff foster strong reciprocal relationships from the first contact with families.

- Program staff establish intentional practices from the first contact with families designed to foster strong reciprocal relationships and maintain them over time (see Figure 4-11).

- Program staff ensure that all families—regardless of family structure; socioeconomic, racial, religious, and cultural backgrounds; gender; abilities; or preferred language—are included in all aspects of the program, including volunteer opportunities. These opportunities consider families' interests and skills and the needs of the program staff.

- Program staff engage with families to learn from their knowledge of their children's interests, approaches to learning, and the children's developmental needs and to learn about their concerns and goals for their children. This information is incorporated into ongoing classroom planning.

- Program staff use a variety of formal and informal methods to communicate with families about the program philosophy and curriculum objectives, including educational goals and effective strategies that can be used by families to promote their children's learning. They implement a variety of methods, such as new family orientations, small group meetings, individual conversations, and written questionnaires, for getting input from families about curriculum activities throughout the year.

- The program works with families on shared caregiving issues, including routine separations, special needs, the food being served and consumed, and daily care issues.

- Families may visit any area of the facility at any time during the program's regular hours of operation as specified by the procedures of the facility.

- The program facilitates opportunities for families to meet each other on a formal and informal basis, work together on projects to support the program, and learn from and provide support for each other.

- The program's governing or advisory groups include families as members and active participants in the program. Family members are mentored into leadership roles by staff or other families in the program.

- Program staff and families work together to plan events. Families' schedules and availability are considered as part of this planning.

- Program staff use a variety of mechanisms, such as family conferences or home visits, to promote dialogue with families. Program staff ask adults to translate or interpret communication as needed.

- The program compiles and provides information about the program to families in a language the family can understand. This information includes program policies and operating procedures.

- Program staff inform families about the program's systems for formally and informally assessing children's progress. This includes the purposes of assessment, procedures for gaining family input and information, the timing of assessments, the way assessment results or information will be shared with families, and ways the program will use the information.

- When program staff suspect that a child has a developmental delay or other special need, this possibility is communicated to families in a sensitive, supportive, and confidential manner, with documentation and explanation for the concern, suggested next steps, and information about resources for assessment.

- Program staff encourage families to regularly contribute to decisions about goals for their children and plans for activities and services.

- Program staff encourage families to raise concerns and work collaboratively with them to find mutually satisfying solutions that staff then incorporate into classroom practice.

- Program staff encourage and support families to make the primary decisions about services that their children need, and they encourage families to advocate to obtain needed services.

- Program staff use a variety of techniques to negotiate difficulties that arise in their interactions with family members. Program staff make arrangements to use these techniques in a language the family can understand.

- Program staff provide families with information about programs and services from other organizations. Staff support and encourage families' efforts to negotiate health, mental health, assessment, and educational services for their children.

- Program staff use established linkages with other early education programs and local elementary schools to help families prepare for and manage their children's transitions between programs, including special education programs. Staff provide information to families that can assist them in communicating with other programs.

- To help families with their transitions to other programs or schools, staff provide basic general information on enrollment procedures and practices, visiting opportunities, and program options.

- Prior to sharing information with other relevant providers, agencies, or other programs, staff obtain written consent from the family.

Code of Ethics

The Code of Ethical Conduct and Statement of Commitment, approved by NAEYC's Governing Board in 1989 and revised in 2005, includes a section of ethical responsibilities to families, articulating 9 ideals and 15 specific principles governing actions. The ideals are

1. To be familiar with the knowledge base related to working effectively with families and to stay informed through continuing education and training.

2. To develop relationships of mutual trust and create partnerships with the families served.

3. To welcome all family members and encourage them to participate in the program (see Figure 4-12).

4. To listen to families, acknowledge and build on their strengths and competencies, and learn from families as we support them in their task of nurturing children.

5. To respect the dignity and preferences of each family and to make an effort to learn about its structure, culture, language, customs, and beliefs.

6. To acknowledge families' child-rearing values and their right to make decisions for their children.

7. To share information about children's education and development with families and to help them understand and appreciate the current knowledge base of the early childhood education profession.

8. To help family members enhance their understanding of their children and support the continuing development of their skills as parents.

9. To participate in building support networks for families by giving them opportunities to interact with program staff, other families, community resources, and professional services (NAEYC, 2005, Code of Ethical Conduct and Statement of Commitment, Rev.).

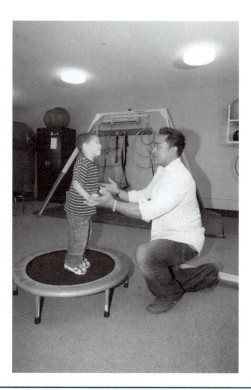

FIGURE 4-12 One of the ideals of the revised code of ethics is to welcome all family members and encourage them to participate in their children's school.

The 15 principles that are enunciated in this section of the code of ethics are useful in helping teachers determine appropriate professional actions when they face dilemmas in serving families:

P-2.1   We shall not deny family members access to their children's classroom or program setting unless access is denied by court order or other legal restriction.

P-2.2   We shall inform families of program philosophy, policies, curriculum, assessment system, and personnel qualifications, and explain why we teach as we do—which should be in accordance with our ethical responsibilities to children.

P-2.3   We shall inform families of and, when appropriate, involve them in policy decisions.

P-2.4   We shall involve the family in significant decisions about their child.

P-2.5   We shall make every effort to communicate effectively with all families in a language that they understand. We shall use community resources for translation and interpretation when we do not have sufficient resources in our own programs.

P-2.6 As families share information with us about their children and families, we shall consider this information to plan and implement the program.

P-2.7 We shall inform families about the nature and purpose of the program's child assessments and how data about their children will be used.

P-2.8 We shall treat child assessment information confidentially and share this information only when there is a legitimate need for it.

P-2.9 We shall inform families of injuries and incidents involving their children, of risks such as exposures to communicable diseases that might result in infection, and of occurrences that might result in emotional stress.

P-2.10 Families shall be fully informed about any proposed research projects involving their children and shall have the opportunity to give or withhold consent without penalty. We shall not permit or participate in research that could in any way hinder the education, development, or well-being of children.

P-2.11 We shall not engage in or support exploitation of families. We shall not use our relationship with a family for private advantage or personal gain or enter relationships with family members that might impair our effectiveness in working with their children.

P-2.12 We shall develop written policies for the protection of confidentiality and the disclosure of children's records. These policy documents shall be made available to all program personnel and families. Disclosure of children's records beyond family members, program personnel, and consultants having an obligation of confidentiality shall require familial consent (except in cases of abuse or neglect).

P-2.13 We shall maintain confidentiality and shall respect the family's right to privacy, refraining from disclosure of confidential information and intrusion into family life. However, when we have reason to believe that a child's welfare is at risk, it is permissible to share confidential information with agencies, as well as with individuals who have legal responsibility for intervening in the child's interest.

P-2.14 In cases where family members are in conflict with one another, we shall work openly, sharing our observations of the child, to help all parties involved make informed decisions. We shall refrain from becoming an advocate for one party.

P-2.15 We shall be familiar with and appropriately refer families to community resources and professional support services. After a referral has been made, we shall follow up to ensure that services have been appropriately provided.

NAEYC Position Statement on Developmentally Appropriate Practice

The revised NAEYC Position Statement on Developmentally Appropriate Practice (Bredekamp & Copple, 1997) makes explicit the professional commitment to

- Appreciating and supporting the close ties between the child and family.
- Recognizing that children are best understood in the context of family, culture, and society.
- Respecting the dignity, worth, and uniqueness of each individual (child, family member, and colleague).

These are the statements most directly related to working with families and their cultures, customs, and beliefs.

Of the five sections in the NAEYC position statement on roles of the teacher, one deals specifically with "establishing reciprocal relationships with families." Pointing out the "complexity of the partnership between teachers and parents that is a fundamental element of good practice," the guidelines suggest at least the following:

1. Reciprocal relationships between teachers and families require mutual respect, cooperation, shared responsibility, and negotiation of conflicts toward achievement of shared goals.

2. Early childhood teachers should work in collaborative partnerships with families, establishing and maintaining regular, frequent, two-way communication with children's parents.

3. Parents should be welcome in the program and to participate in decisions about their children's care and education. Parents should be allowed to observe and participate and serve in decision-making roles in the program.

4. Teachers should acknowledge parents' choices and goals for children and respond with sensitivity and respect to parents' preferences and concern without abdicating professional responsibility to children.

5. Teachers and parents should share their knowledge of the child and understanding of children's development and learning as part of day-to-day communication and planned conferences. Teachers must support families in ways that maximally promote family decision-making capabilities and competence.

6. To ensure more accurate and compete information, each program should involve families in assessing and planning for individual children.

7. The program should link families with a range of services based on identified resources, priorities, and concerns.

8. Teachers, parents, programs, social services, health agencies, and consultants who may have educational responsibility for the child at different times should, with family participation, share developmental information about children as they pass from one level or program to another (Bredekamp & Copple, 1997).

NAEYC Standards for Professional Preparation

In 2001 NAEYC published core standards for initial teacher licensure programs, followed in 2003 by similar core standards for associate degree preparation of teachers. Of the five standards, the second is *Building Family and Community Relationships.* This requires education to enhance experiences so that students

- Know about, understand, and value the importance and complex characteristics of children's families and communities (see Figure 4-13).

- Use this understanding to create respectful, reciprocal relationships that support and empower families and to involve all families in their children's development and learning.

Specific opportunities to learn these concepts are suggested in the standards, along with ways that students may demonstrate their growth within their college programs.

FIGURE 4-13 The standards for teacher education mean that all students will gain experiences in interacting with families.

These standards mean that students enrolled in college early childhood education programs accredited by NAEYC will be involved in learning about families during their professional preparation.

NASBE Report

The report *Right from the Start,* issued in 1991 by the Early Childhood Task Force of the National Association of State Boards of Education, focuses attention on involving parents in the school system from the beginning. One recommendation is for elementary schools to establish early childhood components that will involve parents as essential partners in their children's education, recognizing them as primary influences in children's lives:

> Only through a sincere respect for the parental role can teachers begin to see parents as a source of support for their work and will some parents overcome the suspicion and resistance to approaching educators they may have developed from their own school experiences (NASBE, 1991).

NASBE recommendations for programs serving children in preschool through third grade include the following:

- Promote an environment in which parents are valued as the primary influences in their children's lives and are essential partners in the education of their children.
- Recognize that self-esteem of parents is integral to the development of their children and should be enhanced by the parents' positive interaction with the school.
- Include parents in decision making about their own children and about the overall early childhood program.
- Ensure opportunities and access for parents to observe and volunteer in the classroom.
- Promote exchange of information and ideas between parents and teachers that will benefit the children.
- Provide a gradual and supportive transition process from home to school for children entering school for the first time (NASBE, 1991).

National Parent–Teachers Association Standards for Parent/Family Involvement

In a statement published in 1997, the National Parent–Teachers Association published six national standards seen as essential for any school or program involving parents. These are

- Regular, two-way, meaningful communication between home and school.
- Promotion and support of parenting skills.

- Active parent participation in student learning.

- Parents as welcome volunteer partners in schools.

- Parents as full partners in school decisions that affect children and families.

- Outreach to the community for resources to strengthen schools (PTA, 1997).

It has long been recognized in American society that parents have the primary responsibility for deciding what is in their children's best interest. Public policy now seems concerned with safeguarding family authority in the "education, nurture, and supervision of their children." The increasing official attention to policies involving family matters may lead to more specific mandates regarding parent involvement.

■■ ■ COMMUNITY CONCERN FOR FAMILY SUPPORT

The changing demographics of American society that have created changes in the lives of families have focused attention on parents' needs. Families who today may be more isolated, more stressed, and perhaps poorer than ever before need all the help they can get. As communities count the costs of inadequate parenting and family stress in the numbers of teenage pregnancies, school dropout rates, drug addictions and other illnesses, crime rates, and other antisocial disruptions, there is powerful motivation for schools, social agencies, legislatures, businesses, and other concerned community organizations to mobilize and combine efforts for family support. The family is seen as a complex and dynamic system that sits at the hub of, and is influenced by, other complex systems such as schools, the workplace, the health system, the human services system, and government at every level. Schools are concerned about the lack of quality preparation for children prior to entering formal education, especially in families not proficient with English, and they recognize that schools and communities cannot do it alone (Lueder, 1998).

Family resource and support programs have appeared all over the country, offering services to parents that may include parenting education, adult education and job training, emotional support, and varieties of child care services. Teachers, psychologists, social workers, other professionals, or other parents run the programs. The difference between the intervention models of the 1960s and 1970s and this more recent family resource movement is that the intervention programs see the child as the unit for intervention, whereas family resource and support programs see the entire family as the unit for intervention.

The focus is not on intervention as a means of solving a deficit problem, but as a developmental service needed by all families, regardless of socioeconomic or cultural background, to support them to optimum functioning, particularly at key points in the family life cycle when stresses, crises, and change are the norm. The approach is prevention, not treatment. Not all families need exactly the same kinds of support, so family resource and support programs are individualized, flexible, and adaptive. Collaborative efforts between community agencies offering health, welfare, social services, and education meet the family's comprehensive needs.

State-Funded Family Support Programs

Examples of state-funded family support initiatives include Minnesota's Early Childhood Family Education program, begun in 1975. Operated by local school districts, this program offers a variety of approaches to enhance the competence of parents in nurturing the development of their children: child development classes, home visits, parent discussion groups, developmental preschool activities, newsletters, drop-in centers, toy and book lending, and special services for special populations (such as single parents or southeast Asian immigrant families).

The Parents as Teachers program in Missouri, also operated through school systems since 1985, offers information and guidance during the third trimester before birth until the child's third birthday via home visits and individual parent conferences each month, monthly group meetings with other parents, use of a parent resource center at the schools, and periodic screenings for the children.

Kentucky's Parent Child Education program, funded through school districts since 1986, strives to improve the educational future for parents and children by offering GED tutoring for mothers, a preschool program based on the High/Scope developmental model for 3- and 4-year-olds, joint parent–child activities, and support groups in self-esteem and competence for mothers. Also since 1986, both Connecticut and Maryland have run statewide systems of parent support centers that provide a number of parent education and support services.

Individual Community Efforts

Individual cities and communities have also developed various kinds of programs that offer support and education to parents of young children, including efforts to involve families in early childhood programs. New York City has Giant Step, a program offering health and educational services to 4-year-old children, with a family social worker in each classroom. Family Focus, in the Chicago area, operates a number of drop-in centers in a cross section of ethnic and socioeconomic neighborhoods. Parents may choose from various educational and support offerings, while other children are cared for in quality preschool programs. AVANCE Family Support and Education Program in San Antonio, Texas, has offered a parent support program to Mexican American families with very young children since 1973. The founder of AVANCE hoped that by teaching parents how to communicate better and motivate their children during the formative years, the high school dropout rate could be cut and the cycle of poverty broken. AVANCE tries to create strong families by providing intensive parent education classes, social support, adult basic and higher education, quality early childhood education, personal development, and community empowerment.

REFLECTIONS FOR JOURNAL ENTRIES

As you read this chapter, are you finding your own definition of family involvement expanding? What has your definition been until now? What new ideas are you adding to your definition?

The Los Angeles Unified School District offers hundreds of parenting and family life education courses. This started as child observation and discussion classes in 1928, attracting primarily middle-class parents. The program has expanded to meet the special needs of many groups of parents—infants and toddlers, adolescents, fathers, working parents, parents who have been ordered by the courts to seek parent education, and all socioeconomic classes. Through a multidisciplinary educational process, parents are given a variety of learning opportunities designed to enhance the parents' competence and the children's growth and development. One typical pattern is for parents and children to come to centers once a week, with some time spent in parent–child activities. Seminars for working parents are offered in the workplace. Because California state law mandates parent education classes, there is no registration fee for parent education classes offered through adult and occupational education.

Other similar programs are springing up in communities all over the country. The Family Resource Coalition of America is a national grassroots organization of over 2,000 community programs that offer information, education, advice, and support to families. The purpose of the coalition is to offer information, models of programs, and funding for communities who want to begin their own family resource and support effort. (For more information, contact Family Resource Coalition of America at 20 North Wacker Drive, Suite 1100, Chicago, IL 60606, or the Web address at the end of this chapter.) A comprehensive listing of family support centers nationally can be found at http://www.familysupportamerica.org. For sources that describe a number of family resource and support programs in detail, see *America's Family Support Programs,* and *Programs to Strengthen Families,* and look in the Suggestions for Further Reading section at the end of this chapter.

In addition to offering parents psychological support and knowledge necessary to help them understand their children's development and needs, family resource and support programs have set a model for parents and professionals working together as equals, each respecting, valuing, and supporting the contribution of the other. Such a stance makes a school one of the agencies offering a constellation of services to the family. The school's most important role is to confirm the importance of child rearing and the parent's role in it and not to be a substitute for the family or another source of threat to the unit. The program that shares in child-rearing endeavors with parents

FIGURE 4-14 Schools and early childhood programs can function as a new form of extended family.

may act as a reconstituted form of the extended family, offering parents support and avoiding the isolation of child rearing (see Figure 4-14).

Support for families as extended family just may be the newest role for educational institutions to incorporate. The first change in the form of the home and family occurred when the Industrial Revolution removed work from the home to the factory. John Dewey, an influential educator at the beginning of the twentieth century, responded by putting into the school the occupations of the earlier home so that children could still experience the world of work. The second transformation of the way home and family function has occurred in recent decades, as parents have been removed from the home to the world of work. Some people suggest that this requires schools to assume the moral imperative of becoming homes for children and their families, responding to their needs (Martin, 1992). Empowering parents keeps the locus of family power within the family, where it needs to be. As communities focus attention and collaborative efforts to support the family through various programs, the momentum will develop for schools to become increasingly responsive to the needs of families and inclusive of their strengths and resources.

There can be no doubt that the education of a child is of great importance, and this predisposes the parent to being concerned and getting involved. School, which by its very nature is an environment for exchange and involvement, cannot ignore this predisposition. The participation of parents is therefore, by its very nature, one of the fundamental premises of the educational experience, if the school views it as essential and not as an accessory or an option (Spaggiari, 1998, p. 110).

The traditional method of conveying the image of teacher–parent partnerships was as a triangle with a corner for each of the protagonists: teacher, parent, and child (see Figure 4-15). This design seems inadequate in the sense of a true collaborative partnership, where teachers and parents come together to center their attention on the developing child, as in Figure 4-16. Here there is no sense of rivalry or separation, but a united, focused, child-centered effort.

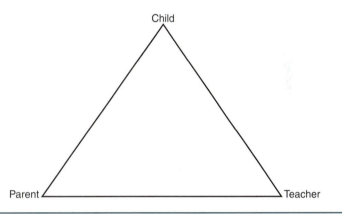

FIGURE 4-15 Old model of family involvement.

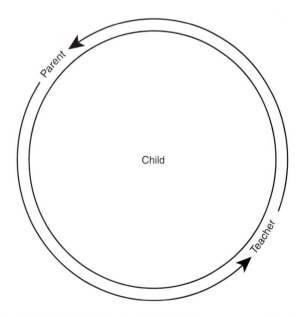

FIGURE 4-16 New model of family involvement.

SUMMARY

There are three main reasons to consider ways to involve families in their children's care and education:

1. Research on family involvement as an optimal factor in child development and learning.

2. Mandates from government and professional associations.

3. Community concern and collaboration for family support programs.

STUDENT ACTIVITIES FOR FURTHER STUDY

1. Find out if your community has a parent cooperative-style preschool program. If so, visit and discover what aspects parents are involved in.

2. Interview several teachers. Find out
   a. How they define parent or family involvement.
   b. What activities and strategies they use to involve families.
   c. How much time each week or month they would estimate they spend working with parents.
   d. Their opinion of the value of parent involvement considering the time involved.

3. Talk to several parents who have children in schools or programs. Find out what they want in terms of their own involvement with the programs and teachers and what they have actually experienced.

4. Find out if there is a Head Start or Title I preschool program in your community. If there is, visit and discover how parents are involved in the program.

5. Call your local United Way office or any information and referral service in your community. Ask what family support and resource organizations exist in your community. Contact those agencies to learn what services they offer for families.

6. Discover if your community has any schools for young children that have received accreditation from NAEYC. If so, visit to learn how parents have been involved in each of the program criteria listed in this chapter. Discuss your findings with classmates.

CASE STUDY

Betty Young works in a prekindergarten program in a child care program that has been exploring becoming accredited by NAEYC. Until now her communication method with families has been to give out a brief daily report, filling in the blanks. Parents are invited to come for lunch on their children's birthdays.

1. According to the accreditation standards discussed in this chapter, what are some additional methods of involving families that she will need to consider?

2. How are these methods also supported by other NAEYC position statements discussed in this chapter, such as the code of ethics and the statement on developmentally appropriate practice?

3. Are these changes mandatory or just what Betty chooses to use to improve her classroom?

REVIEW QUESTIONS

1. Describe three motivations for parent involvement.
2. For each type of parent involvement, explain the underlying ideas.

SUGGESTIONS FOR FURTHER READING

Burns, R. (1993). *Parents and schools: From visitors to partners.* Washington, DC: National Education Association.

Clifford, R. (1997). Partnerships with families. *Young Children, 52*(3), 2.

Coleman, M., & Churchill, S. (1997). Challenges to family involvement. *Childhood Education, 73*(3), 144–148.

Comer, J., & Haynes, M. (1991). Parent involvement in schools: An ecological approach. *Elementary School Journal, 1,* 271–278.

DeCarvalho, M. (2001). *Rethinking family–school relations: A critique of parental involvement in schooling.* Mahwah, NJ: Lawrence Erlbaum Associates.

Focus on the first 60 months, available from the National Governors Assoc., Hall of the States, 444 North Capital St., Washington, DC 20001.

Goetz, K. (Ed.). (1992). *Programs to strengthen families: a resource guide* (3rd ed.). Chicago: Family Resource Coalition.

Goldberg, S. (1997). *Parent involvement begins at birth: Collaboration between parents and teachers of children in the early years.* Needham Heights, MA: Allyn & Bacon.

Hoover-Dempsey, K., & Sandler, H. (1997). Why do parents become involved in their children's education? *Review of Educational Research, 67,* 3–42.

Kagan, S. (1994). Families and children: Who is responsible? *Childhood Education, 71*(1), 4–80.

Kagan, S. L., Rowell, D. R., Weissbourd, B. T., & Zigler, E. F. (Eds.). (1987). *America's family support programs: Perspectives and prospects.* New Haven: Yale University Press.

Knitzer, J., & Cauthen, N. (2000). Innovative strategies support children and families coping with welfare change. *Young Children, 55*(1), 49–51.

McBride, S. (1999). Family-centered practices. *Young Children, 54*(3), 62–68.

Patrikakou, E., Weissberg, R., Redding, S., & Walberg, H. (2005). *School–family partnerships for children's success.* New York: Teachers College Press.

Programs to strengthen families. Yale University Bush Center on Child Development and Social Policy. Available from Family Resource Coalition, 20 N. Wacker Dr., Suite 1100, Chicago, IL 60606.

Reynolds, A., Miedel, W., & Mann, E. (2000). Innovation in early intervention for children in families with low incomes—Lessons from the Chicago Child–Parent Centers. *Young Children, 55*(2), 84–88.

Rioux, J., & Berla, N. (1993). *Innovations in parent and family involvement.* Princeton, NJ: Eye on Education.

Rosenthal, D., & Sawyers, J. (1996). Building successful home/school partnerships: strategies for parent support and involvement. *Childhood Education, 72*(4), 194–200.

Schorr, L. (1997). *Common purpose: Strengthening families and neighborhoods to rebuild America.* New York: Doubleday.

Schorr, L. B., with Schorr, D. (1988). *Within our reach: Breaking the cycle of disadvantage.* New York: Doubleday.

Swick, K. (1991). *Teacher–parent partnerships to enhance school success in early childhood education.* Washington, DC: National Education Association.

Swick, K., & Graves, S. B. (1993). *Empowering at-risk families during the early childhood years.* Washington, DC: NAEYC.

Weissbourd, B., & Kagan, S. (1994). *Putting families first: America's family support movement and the challenge of change.* San Francisco: Jossey-Bass.

Workman, S., & Gage, J. (1997). Family–school partnerships: A family strengths approach. *Young Children, 52*(4), 10–14.

REFERENCES

Boone, E., & Barclay, K. (1995). *Building a three-way partnership: Linking school, families, and community.* New York: Scholastic.

Bredekamp, S., & Copple, C. (1997). *Developmentally appropriate practice in early childhood programs* (rev. ed.). Washington, DC: NAEYC.

Bronfenbrenner, U. (1976). *Is early intervention effective? A report on longitudinal evaluations of preschool programs.* U.S. Dept. of Health, Education and Welfare, Office of Child Development. Washington, DC: U.S. Govt. Printing Office.

Bronfenbrenner, U., & Morris, P. (1998). The ecology of developmental processes. In R. Lerner (Ed.), *Handbook of child psychology. Vol. 1. Theoretical models of human development.* New York: Wiley.

Cicerelli, V., et al. (1969). *The impact of Head Start. An evaluation of the effects of Head Start on children's cognitive and affective development.* Westinghouse Learning Corporation and Ohio University. Washington, DC: Government Printing Office.

Collins, R. C., & Deloria, D. (1983). Head Start research: A new chapter. *Children Today, 12*(4), 15–20.

Consortium for Longitudinal Studies. (1983). *As the twig is bent: Lasting effects of preschool programs.* Hillsdale, NJ: Lawrence Erlbaum.

Eldridge, D. (2001). Parent involvement: It's worth the effort. *Young Children, 56*(4), 65–69.

Epstein, J. (2000). *School and family partnerships: Preparing educators and improving schools.* Boulder, CO: Westview.

Epstein, J., Coates, L., Salinas, K., Sanders, M., & Simon, B. (1997). *School, family, and community partnerships: Your handbook for action.* Thousand Oaks, CA: Corwin.

Finn, J. (1998, May). Parental engagement that makes a difference. *Educational Leadership,* 20–24.

Funkhouser, J., & Gonzales, M. (1997). *Family involvement in children's education: Successful local approaches, an idea book.* Office of Educational Research and Improvement, U.S. Department of Education. Washington, DC: GPO.

Harms, T., Clifford. R., & Cryer, D. (1998). *Early childhood environment rating scale* (rev. ed.). New York: Teachers College Press.

Hart, B., & Risley, T. (1995). *Meaningful differences in everyday parenting and intellectual development in young American children.* Baltimore: Paul H. Brookes.

Henderson, A., & Berla, N. (Eds.). (1994). *A new generation of evidence: The family is critical to student achievement. A report from the National Committee for Citizens in Education.* Washington, DC: Center for Law and Education.

Hess, R. D., et al. (1971). Parent involvement. In E. Grotberg (Ed.), *Day care: Resources for decisions.* Washington, DC: Day Care and Child Development Committee of America.

Ho, E., & Willms, J. (1996). Effects of parental involvement on eighth-grade achievement. *Sociology of Education, 69*(2), 126–141.

Hoover-Dempsey, K., Bassler, O., & Burow, R. (1995). Parents' reported involvement in students' homework: Strategies and practices. *The Elementary School Journal, 95*(5), 435–450.

Lazar & Darlington. (1979). Consortium for Longitudinal Studies. *Lasting effects after preschool: Summary report.* Washington, DC: U.S. Dept. of Health, Education and Welfare.

Lueder, D. (1998). *Creating partnerships with parents: An educator's guide.* Lancaster, PA: Technomic Publishing.

Mann, A. J., Harrell, A. V., & Hunt, M. J. A review of Head Start research since 1969. In B. Brown (Ed.) *Found: Long-tem gains from early intervention.* Boulder, CO: Westview Press.

Martin, J. (1992). *The schoolhome: Rethinking schools for changing families.* Cambridge, MA: Harvard University Press.

Midco. (1972). *Perspectives on parent participation in Head Start: An analysis and critique.* Washington, DC: Project Head Start.

NAEYC. (2001 and 2003). *Standards for Professional Preparation.* Available online at http://www.naeyc.org.

———. (2005). *Accreditation criteria and procedures of the National Association for the Education of Young Children.* Washington, DC: Author. Available online at http://www.naeyc.org.

———. (2005). *Code of ethical conduct and statement of commitment (rev. ed.).* Available online at http://www.naeyc.org.

NASBE. (1991). *Right from the start: The report of the NASBE task force on early childhood education.* Alexandria, VA: NASBE.

————. (1991). *Caring communities: Supporting young children and their families.* The Report of the National Task Force on School Readiness. Alexandria, VA: Author.

Paulsell, D., et al. (2000). *Leading the way: Characteristics and early experiences of selected early Head Start programs.* Executive Summary, Vols. I, II, III. Princeton, NJ: Mathematica Policy Research.

Pettygrove, W. B., & Greenman, J. T. (1984). The adult world of day care. In J. T. Greenman & R. W. Fuqua (Eds.), *Making day care better: Training, evaluation and the process of change.* New York: Teachers College Press.

Powell, D. (1998). Reweaving parents into the fabric of early childhood programs. *Young Children, 53*(5), 60–67.

Powell, D. R. (1989). *Families and early childhood programs.* Washington, DC: NAEYC.

PTA. (1997). *Building successful partnerships: A guide for developing parent and family involvement programs.* Chicago, IL: National PTA.

Ramey, S., et al. (2000). *Head Start children's entry into public school: A report on the National Head Start/Public School Transition Demonstration Study.* Washington, DC: Head Start Bureau.

Rhodes, M., Enz, B. and LaCount, M. (2006). Leave no parent behind: Three proven strategies. *Young Children, 61*(1), 50–51.

Rodd, J. (1998). *Leadership in early childhood: The pathway to professionalism* (2nd ed.). New York: Teachers' College Press.

Schweinhart, L., & Weikart, D. (1997, spring/summer). Child-initiated learning in preschool—Prevention that works. *High/Scope Resource, 16*(20), 1, 9–11.

Schweinhart, L. J., & Weikart, D. P. (1986). What do we know so far? A review of the Head Start synthesis project. *Young Children, 41*(2) 49–55.

————. (1993). Changed lives, significant benefits: The High/Scope Perry preschool project to date. *High/Scope Resource, 12*(30), 1, 10–14.

Schweinhart, L., et al. (2005). *Lifetime effects: The High/Scope Perry Preschool Study through age 40.* Ypsilanti MI: High/Scope Press.

Spaggiari, S. (1998). The community–teacher partnership in the governance of schools: An interview with Lella Gandini. In *The hundred languages of children: The Reggio Emilia approach—Advanced reflections* (2nd ed.). Norwood, NJ: Ablex Publishing.

Upshur, C. (1988). Measuring parent outcomes in family program evaluation. In H. Weiss & F. Jacobs (Eds.) *Evaluating Family Programs.* New York: Aldine de Gruyter.

U.S. Dept. of HHS. (1998). *Head Start policy manual.* Washington, DC: Author.

HELPFUL WEB SITES

http://www.ed.gov

Find information about the No Child Left Behind legislation at the Department of Education's Web site. Also search here to find *Family involvement in children's education: Successful local approaches, an idea book* (Funkhouser & Gonzales, 1997). This idea book is offered to stimulate thinking and discussion about how schools can help overcome barriers to family involvement in their children's education—regardless of family circumstances or student performance.

http://www.ncrel.org

The Web Site for the North Central Regional Educational Laboratory is one of ten regional laboratories funded by the United States Department of Education to provide high quality research-based resources to educators and policy makers.

www.pirc-info.net

This is a website that provides information about parent information and resource centers, funded by the Department of Education for parents to find out more about NCLB legislation.

http://www.acf.dhhs.gov/programs/hsb

The Head Start Bureau's official Web site. Search here for the report on ongoing research for Head Start: "Building their futures: How Early Head Start programs are enhancing the lives of infants and toddlers in low-income families."

http://www.projectappleseed.org

Search here for the checklist for Epstein's six standards of parental involvement.

http://www.learningfirst.org

The Learning First Alliance is a partnership of eleven education associations dedicated to strengthening public schools.

http://www.pta.org

The National PTA's Web site has information on the national standards for parent/family involvement programs.

http://www.familysupportamerica.org

This is the Web site of the Family Resource Coalition, the nation's clearing house in family support issues.

http://www.naeyc.org

Site of the National Association for the Education of Young Children. Here you can find the revised accreditation standards, the code of ethics, and the position statement on developmentally appropriate practice.

Additional resources for this chapter can be found on the Online Companion to accompany this text at www.earlychilded.delmar.com. This supplemental material includes frequently asked questions; chapter outlines to be used as study guides; scenarios that both encourage large and small group discussions and provoke new thoughts and ideas; and chapter resources, including chapter summaries, interactive questions, Web links, and Web activities. In addition, forms from the text are available for download.

CHAPTER 5

Benefits of Teacher–Family Partnerships for Children, Parents, and Teachers

OBJECTIVES
After reading this chapter, you should be able to

1 List three benefits for children when parents and teachers work together constructively.

2 List three benefits for families when parents and teachers work together constructively.

3 List three benefits for teachers when parents and teachers work together constructively.

The education and care of a group of children are serious responsibilities for any teacher in any program or setting, requiring enormous amounts of time and energy. The prospect of adding to this already heavy load by taking time to find ways of communicating and working with families may be daunting. Why would any teacher want to add this role? The answer lies in the profound benefits for children, for parents, and for teachers themselves. Without the establishment of a positive working relationship with families, much of what teachers would like to do does not get done, or does not get done as well as it could. Everyone in a productive relationship gains and grows. This chapter explores the benefits of establishing a positive working relationship with families.

Teachers have to see for themselves that the effort of working with families really supports and enhances everything else they do. Whether you have already had experiences in a classroom or are preparing for them, it is vital for you to become convinced that the work in creating and maintaining partnerships with parents will have long-lasting effects and is indeed inseparable from all other teaching roles.

As the previous chapter pointed out, *parent involvement* has a variety of meanings and motivations. Variations in the attitudes and emotional responses to these concepts by teachers who are primarily responsible for creating the atmosphere and leading activities may help or hinder such endeavors.

Listen to several teachers in various schools and programs; we'll see them again later in various activities with families.

You've already met Jane Briscoe. Jane is 27 years old, single, and has been teaching 4-year-olds in a demonstration preschool in a college town since she graduated from the child and family development program at State College five years ago. She describes herself as an extrovert, the oldest of a family of four girls. She believes wholeheartedly in working as a partner with parents. She complains that many of her parents seem too busy to spend much time in the classroom, but she keeps on trying.

Anne Morgan is 35, a divorced mother of a 10-year-old daughter and an 8-year-old son. She has been working at the child care program since her divorce four years ago. Before that her only teaching experience had been student teaching. Anne is often heard criticizing some of the behaviors of parents at the center, who seem to her to be less than conscientious about their parental duties. She does not encourage or invite parents to be involved in her classroom, though she is always polite when she sees them. When a parent with a problem called her at home in the evening, she complained bitterly to her director about the infringement on her private time.

This is John Reynolds's first year of teaching kindergarten. He's had to endure a lot of kidding from friends because they feel it's an unusual career choice for an African American man who played football in college. He's hoping salaries in the field will increase so he can stay in the work that he finds so satisfying. He is deeply involved with the children, conscientious about observing them and making individual plans to fit in with their developmental needs and interests. However, he feels uncomfortable in his contacts with parents, feeling that they are always watching him. He is unsure how much he should tell them about some of his concerns for the children. One parent asked for a conference next week, and he's afraid this means she wants to criticize. He and his wife expect their first child this year, and he's hoping that may help some of the parents accept him as competent. It's not so much that anyone has openly questioned his competence with the children, but he's sure that's what they think.

Connie Martinez is enjoying teaching in a primary school in a small town, which she chose because of the good master's program at the university nearby. She is working hard to finish her degree at night and says that although she believes in parent involvement, she just doesn't have any extra time beyond her planning and preparing the curriculum for the children and preparing them for the end-of-grade testing. She has never told anyone, but she really thinks too many of the parents are letting the school expect teachers to do it all for their children, and she doesn't believe this taking on of the parents' role should be encouraged. Last week a mother brought in her child, who had just come from the doctor's office, and asked if the teacher could give the first dose of the prescribed eardrops because she had to get right back to work. Connie was annoyed with this example of parents shifting their responsibilities to the teacher. When asked if she believes in parent involvement, she says she's too busy to spend much time with parents.

MiLan Ha came to America as a 6-year-old. When she graduated from high school, she was second in her class. After a year of college she took a job in a preschool and has received some training in workshops. MiLan is a talented artist and encourages creative art with her children. She is a quiet young woman with no close friends on the staff. She lives at home with her parents, an uncle, two nieces, and a younger brother. She dreads the conferences and meetings that are scheduled at her preschool and uses the excuse that her English is not good. In fact, her English is excellent; she is just extremely uncomfortable in social encounters. When parents enter her room, she smiles and quickly turns to the children. The parents feel she is a good teacher but are also uncomfortable with her.

Dorothy Scott has been teaching second grade in a private school for 13 years. She took five years off when her own son was a preschooler. She has quite definite ideas about child rearing and feels most parents don't handle things with their children as well as they should. She believes it's important to hold conferences and meetings to tell parents what they should be doing and doesn't mind spending extra time to do these things, though she finds it discouraging when parents don't attend or disregard her advice. Some of the parents have asked the director privately if it is necessary for their children to be in Mrs. Scott's room, but, unaware of this, she states proudly that she has never had a parent complain.

Jennifer Griffin was hired as an assistant teacher this year after graduating from high school last spring. She is not sure what she wants to do and felt this would be a job she could do while she was making up her mind. She was rather surprised to have to attend some orientation training and scheduled workshops: She believed her experience in baby-sitting would be enough background for the job. She enjoys the children but finds herself somewhat puzzled by the guidance policies, so she allows her head teacher to handle most of the problems that arise or questions from parents. Because she stays late, it's up to her to respond to parents' questions about their children's day. At this busy time of day, she usually says that she's just an assistant and wasn't there all day. Her major complaint is the few parents who are frequently late in picking up their children. She's told another teacher that she may really blow up at one particular mother the next time it happens.

Jeannie Sweeney runs a family child care center in her home for six toddlers and preschoolers, including her own 3-year-old. She started the business seven years ago when her first child was born so she could have some income while still caring for her own children. Her earlier job experience has been in retail sales. Although she forms close relationships with most of the parents for whose children she cares, she has had several frustrating experiences lately with one family who have rather different child-rearing values from her own. Despite her request in the parent handbook that children not bring violent toys to school, this child continues to bring action figures that are associated with a television show that Jeannie considers too violent. The parents, when approached, laugh and say Jeannie is taking it too seriously. Jeannie is considering asking them to find other child care because she feels this is undermining her approach to teaching the children.

Eight different teachers have eight different experiences and attitudes that clearly determine the responses and relationships each would offer to parents.

Let's go back and listen to Anne Morgan again. She seems quite definite about her position:

> Look, I'm not their parent, I'm their teacher. There's a lot of difference between the two. All I can do is work with the children for the eight hours or so they're at the school and in after school. After that they're the parents' responsibility. Goodness knows some of those parents could use some help—some of the things they say and do! I do get annoyed when I work so hard with a child and then see the parent come right in and undo everything I've tried to do. But it's really not my business, I guess. Let them do their job and I'll do mine.

Anne Morgan apparently has decided that there is no purpose in establishing a working partnership between herself and her children's families. Chapter 6 looks at her attitudes as barriers to the relationship, but first let's examine the areas Anne is overlooking: the benefits to children, parents, and teachers as the adults learn to communicate and cooperate.

■ ■ ■ BENEFITS FOR CHILDREN

Security in a New Environment

In their early years children are dependent on the key adults in their lives to foster first a sense of security and then feelings of self-worth. Children develop a sense of trust in the people and world around them as they perceive a predictable and consistent response from their caregivers. Parents are, of course, of primary importance here. An attachment is made to specific people that an infant associates with comfort and warm sensory contact; the attachment is a long-lasting, emotional, learned response. It is this attachment in a parent–child relationship that forms the basis for a child to trust or not trust the environment.

Most researchers conclude that this parent–child attachment is crucial for the development of a healthy personality. The presence of the mother or other primary caregiver to whom a child is attached serves as a secure base from which to move out and respond to other aspects of the environment. Preferably, when a child moves into the school world, the first important attachment provides a base of security that can be extended to other adults (see Figure 5-1). This task is made easier if the child's familiar, trusted adults are comfortable with the new adults. Contrast the effects, for example, on these two young children:

> Susan's mother feels nervous around the new teacher. She feels that the teacher is looking critically at some of the things she does, and she does not seem like a friendly person. As a result, she spends little time talking to her, hurrying in and out of the classroom when picking Susan up. She's made some negative

FIGURE 5-1 Children can move more easily into new situations from the secure base of those first important attachments with family.

comments to Susan's father at home about the classroom situation. Susan's teacher is perturbed by this avoidance behavior and feels both annoyed and uncomfortable when Susan's mother darts in and out. Susan, puzzled but aware of the strain between the adults, does not allow herself to relax and feel secure in her new classroom world.

Jenny's parents, on the other hand, looked long and hard before they found a preschool that seemed to match their beliefs about child rearing. They took the time to talk with the teacher at length; they discovered that they shared some leisure interests. Both parents and teacher now feel comfortable and trusting as they share conversations daily. Jenny seems to feel that her circle of loved and trusted adults has widened; she moves easily back and forth from home to school.

A young child's anxiety in a new school experience may be lessened if there is not an abrupt division between home and school. Children thrive when they feel continuity between family and teachers that can be present only when the adults have reached out in an effort to understand and respect each other (see Figure 5-2). (And, not incidentally, the child is also offered positive examples of cooperation and social skills in communication.) Just as a teacher's first task in relating to a child is to build a sense of trust and mutual

FIGURE 5-2 Children feel more secure when their parents appear comfortable with their teachers.

respect, the same task is important in working with families. It is not realistic to expect to like all parents. However, it is essential and possible for teachers to respect all parents for their caring and efforts and their central position in their children's lives. In most cases parents care deeply about their children. This belief should be the basis for all teacher interaction.

> The participation and active involvement of the parent in the school is perceived and appreciated by the child, who can derive from it a sense of security besides seeing it as a model and incentive for his or her own personal growth. (Spaggiari, 1998, p. 110)

Many teachers of school-aged children believe that children at later periods of development do not have the same need for their parents in the school setting in order to build their confidence. However, all the research proves over and over again that when families are involved, not only is children's performance enhanced, but also they have more positive attitudes about school (Epstein et al., 1997).

Sense of Self-Worth

Children also gain feelings of self-worth if they perceive that their families are valued and respected by others. A child's sense of who she is relates closely to the sense of who her parents are. If her parents receive positive feedback, she also feels worthwhile and valued. On the other hand, if a child observes a

FIGURE 5-3 The welcome and acceptance of his parents are especially valuable for the minority child.

teacher ignoring her parents or treating them with obvious disdain, her own self-esteem suffers.

> Jenny beams when her teacher comes over to greet her father in the morning and asks how the weekend camping trip went. In her eyes, her teacher and father are friends, and this means her father is somebody special in her teacher's classroom. This makes Jenny feel she has been treated in a special way and is therefore valued.

The presence of families and their welcoming acceptance by a teacher are especially valuable in affirming for children of ethnic and cultural minorities a sense of value for and integration of their own culture in the classroom world (see Figure 5-3). The teacher who makes the effort to learn even a greeting word or two in the language of minority families demonstrates such acceptance.

Many teachers still cling to stereotypical expectations that parents from minority or low-income families will not become involved in communication with teachers. However, when they reach out positively and sincerely to all families, they usually discover that their assumptions were wrong: Families want success for their children and will work to support that success. In fact, recent studies indicate that the school success of African American children is directly related to their parents' values and expectations, as well as the active participation and emotional availability of their parents (Murphy, 2003). As teachers draw families into the educational process, minority children benefit in both self-esteem and academic success. We'll talk more in Chapter 15 about classroom practices that convey inclusiveness and welcome to all families.

Knowledgeable and Consistent Responses

Another benefit for children in a constructive parent–teacher partnership is the increased ability of all adults to guide and nurture a child's development knowledgeably, creating "seamless care" with fewer mistakes and less confusion or tension between home and school (Baker and Manfredi-Petitt, 2004).

Parents and teachers who can comfortably share personal observations and insights, general knowledge and ideas, and specific incidents and reactions expose each other to a wealth of information that may help them provide the most appropriate response for each child. Such an exchange of information surely benefits the child. As families and teachers plan together, they identify and reconcile their understandings of children's needs and their goals for children (Murphy, 1997).

> Last month Jenny missed her daddy very much when he was out of town on a long business trip. At home she became clinging and demanding of her mother. Miss Briscoe noticed lots of crying at school and easy frustration with everyday tasks. At first she was puzzled by the sudden change, but when Jenny's mother shared her description of the behavior at home and the temporary change in the family pattern, she was able to help Jenny talk openly about her concern for her daddy. She read a story at group time about a daddy who sometimes had to go away; Jenny took it off the shelf almost daily to read it by herself. How lucky for Jenny that her teacher knew and didn't simply respond to the new crying as an undesirable behavior by either ignoring or punishing it.

In some cases teachers and families may work together to provide consistent responses, feeling it may help children's learning if all adults respond to specific behaviors in the same way. For example, when Roger's response to frustration is to whine, his parents and teachers have agreed they will ignore the whining and redirect his attention to something else. This approach seems to be helping him decrease the whining.

Many of the gains for children resulting when parents and teachers cooperate, share information, and expand their skills are measurable (see Figure 5-4). Research reveals that children gain in academic skills, positive self-concept, and verbal intelligence when extensive family participation with teachers is required (Henderson & Berla, 1994).

The three benefits to children when parents and teachers work together are

1. Increased security in the new school environment.

2. Increased feelings of self-worth.

3. Increased number of helpful responses and appropriate learning experiences.

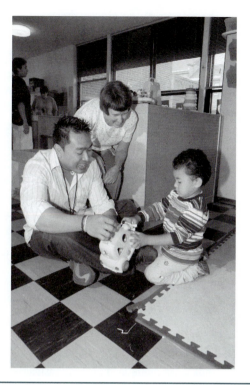

FIGURE 5-4 When teachers and parents share information, the child benefits.

BENEFITS FOR PARENTS

What do parents gain from developing a working relationship with their children's teachers?

Feelings of Support for Parenting

An immediate benefit is the feeling of support in carrying out the responsibilities of parenthood. As discussed earlier, the changing nature of contemporary life means that many parents are removed from the natural supports of family and roots, traditions, and models when they begin the usually unprepared-for task of parenting. The many questions and uncertainties that occur in everyday activities often make parenting lonely, worrisome, and indeed overwhelming.

Lisbeth Schorr writes of our longstanding cultural commitment to "rugged individualism," a belief that each family should be able to care for its own without outside help. This almost mythical belief in the self-sufficient strength of individual families "has made the United States the only industrialized country in the world without universal preschools, paid parental leave, and income support for families with young children" (Schorr, 1997). And the same unrealistic ideal of self-sufficiency that has impacted our national policies for family support and early childhood education has left many parents reluctant to reach out to others for the emotional or cognitive supports that

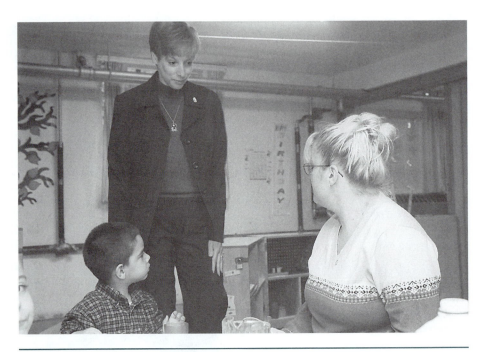

FIGURE 5-5 A parent–teacher relationship can give parents the feeling of being not quite alone in their responsibilities.

are so essential to optimal functioning as a parent. In reality, parents can never be totally independent; they need others to watch their children while they work or go to the store, or just to talk to, to make the job of parenting seem less overwhelming. They also need others with specialized expertise to educate their children.

Having an adult who cares about their children, to share both the good and the not-so-good times of day-to-day life, is extremely helpful in alleviating anxieties. It has been noted that after mothers have a chance to express their feelings and concerns to others willing to listen with an empathetic ear, they often exhibit more patience with their children, listen more carefully to them, and are more responsive to their needs than before the opportunity to unburden themselves. A parent–teacher relationship can offer much needed support to parents (see Figure 5-5). In this way it has been suggested that the child care program and its personnel can function as a new kind of extended family, part of the constellation of community support that each family needs—what Bronfenbrenner has referred to as a **microsystem** in the **ecology** of human development (Bronfenbrenner, 1979). You will read more about Bronfenbrenner's ideas in Chapter 14. An educator in Reggio Emilia, Italy, where family participation is a hallmark of the excellent programs, expresses it this way: "Families cannot be left to themselves. They need a network of shared responsibility and solidarity that is of benefit and support to them" (Spaggiari, 1998). The mother who wrote the note to the teacher about

February 20

Dear Katie and Sue,

I am concerned about Jeremy's safety at school.

He says he got the bump on his nose by being bitten by a fish while swimming at school.

When you take him swimming (in Myers Park, he says) please be sure he stays away from the sharks.

Thanks,
Jessica

FIGURE 5-6 This mother clearly enjoys a comfortable relationship with the teachers, so she can share her young son's imaginative story.
Thanks to Katie Donovan at Open Door School for sharing this and granting permission to print.

her child's active imagination (see Figure 5-6) clearly felt part of a supportive relationship and knew she could share her amusement with the teacher and it would be appreciated. This kind of supportive relationship allows parents to function optimally with their children.

Knowledge and Skills

In addition, teachers provide a background of information and skill from their expertise and experience in dealing with a variety of children, as well as a model for positive guidance techniques. There is no question that families possess firsthand knowledge about their children, but frequently the experience of living with them is their only opportunity to learn about child development.

Many parents never have the opportunity to learn relevant developmental information and often misunderstand the nature of developing children (Lally, Lerner, & Lurie-Hurvitz, 2001). They may be unaware of appropriate nurturance at each phase, as evidenced by the current tendency of many parents to push their "hurried children" into early academics, assuming that "sooner is better" rather than understanding that young children are not ready for such learning. When teachers share their knowledge of child development, they help parents respond more appropriately to their children's developmental needs.

Teachers have specific education in the principles of child development and are trained in effective guidance techniques. When parents converse with teachers and watch and listen to teachers working with children, they can expand their knowledge and ideas and become more effective as parents (see Figure 5-7). They learn informally, comfortably, through the conversation of a relationship. This learning does not threaten parents' self-esteem if the teacher is careful to create a relationship of equals, rather than teaching from the lofty pinnacle of old-style professionalism. Parents can learn in an atmosphere of feeling trust and being relaxed.

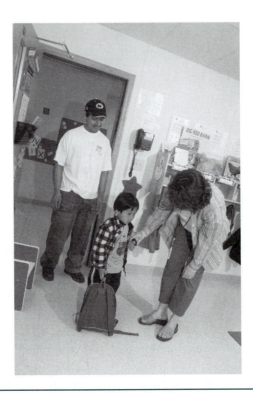

FIGURE 5-7 Parents learn new skills by watching and listening to teachers communicating with children.

"You know," says Jenny's mother, "I sure am glad to have you tell me most 4-year-olds tend to get a little out of bounds; when she began to spit last month, I was horrified. Jenny's the first 4-year-old I've ever known. My sister's family lives in California, so I never had a chance to see much of her children at that age. It makes it a little easier to live with Jenny to know that it's not just her or to think we've done something wrong. And it's also been helpful to watch you dealing with some of that behavior in the classroom. It would never have occurred to me to be so calm and suggest she go into the bathroom to spit."

Enhancing Parental Self-Esteem

It is essential that parental self-esteem develop in a positive way. Parents who believe in themselves are far better able to develop and use appropriate parenting skills; parents who feel self-confident are far better able to provide their children with a secure environment and foster positive feelings of self in their children. Thus nurturing parental self-esteem contributes to optimum parental functioning. Gilda Ferguson, the director of Family Focus in Chicago's North Lawndale neighborhood, has said, "We nurture parents so they can nurture their children" (Schorr, 1997).

FIGURE 5-8 All parents enjoy feeling that they are part of their child's school world.

The most important predictor of children's school success is related to positive parental self-esteem. Studies indicate that there is a definite impact on the development of feelings of competence and self-esteem in parents involved in their children's schools (Epstein, 2000; see Figure 5-8). Empowered parents function at their best.

Perhaps one reason for the increase in parental self-esteem is that parents can get specific positive feedback on their functioning as a parent—feedback that is especially meaningful because it comes from an "expert" in child development.

"You know," says Miss Briscoe, "I admire the way you talked with Jenny this morning. You were sensitive to her feelings, but also quite definite that you had to go. That approach helped her see where the limit was."

Teachers are powerful people: In many cases they are the first people outside the family to see children and their parents on an ongoing basis, so their approval is important to parents.

A positive feeling of parental self-esteem is also nurtured when parents feel they are a vital part of their child's school world as well as home world. Teachers who help parents feel included in the education process contribute to feelings of competence in parents. Parents feel they are in control, sure that their children are getting the kind of education and care they want, rather than feeling that control is elsewhere and they are powerless to provide what their child needs. This feeling of being necessary and included is helpful for all parents—especially fathers, who often feel cut off by our culture, unimportant to the overall needs of the child (Berger, 1998).

"You know, Miss Peters," Jenny's father said at a recent conference, "I'm very glad you suggested I'd be welcome to come and spend some time any afternoon I can get off work a little early. I really like knowing who the kids are that Jenny talks about at home—just to see what part of her day here is like. It's important to me not to feel as though I have nothing to do with part of her life."

The three ways that parents benefit from positive teacher–parent relationships are

1. Feelings of support in the difficult task of parenting.

2. Knowledge and skills gained by parents to help them in child rearing.

3. Enhanced parental self-esteem from receiving positive feedback on their parenting actions and feeling an important part of their child's life away from home.

BENEFITS FOR TEACHERS

What about teachers, whose efforts to develop a positive working relationship may be the greatest? Are there benefits to justify such efforts? Again, the answer is *yes*.

Anyone who has worked in a classroom is aware of the uniqueness of each child's personality and needs. Teachers have learned much that is applicable about the general characteristics of children at particular ages, stages, and grade levels; but to be effective with each child, additional information is needed. Each child comes to the classroom with a history—years of reactions, experiences, and characteristic styles of behaving that are unique. Each family

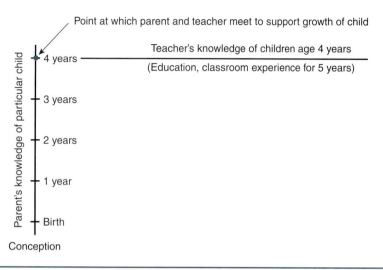

FIGURE 5-9 Teachers' knowledge is horizontal; parents' is vertical. Where these two points intersect, parents and teachers can strengthen each other's effects.

has its own dreams and expectations for its children, its own patterns of behavior and values related to the specific cultural or ethnic ethos from which it comes, its own structure, relationships, and needs. Teachers need to know all this and learn it early in their associations with children and families. With this specialized knowledge, parents are in a position to assist teachers in working with their children. One way of describing the difference in the kinds of knowledge that parents and teachers have of children is that parents' knowledge is vertical, having developed longitudinally through the child's life; teachers' knowledge is horizontal, encompassing much about a particular age group or grade level. At the point where these two lines intersect, teachers and parents can support each other in a partnership of knowledge (see Figure 5-9). To leave untapped such a resource would reduce teachers' abilities to work to optimal capacity with each child. Teachers who build effective communication with families are less likely to be frustrated while working with the many unknowns in children and are more likely to meet realistic goals for each child and support each family in reaching their own particular goals.

At the same conference Miss Peters commented how helpful it has been for her to know, before Jenny's entrance to the classroom, that she was a quiet child who normally took a long time to warm up in a new situation. "Otherwise I'd have been concerned. But that helped me give her lots of time and support and not to expect too much talking until she was comfortable. I was also glad to know she especially liked puzzles—that way I could plan something special for her during those first days."

In addition, when teachers are open to learning from families, there is much knowledge about the practical aspects of living with children that can be learned. Not only can this help a teacher who has not had the firsthand experience of parenthood, but also it may increase the teacher's store of ideas to pass along to other parents.

"You know, I got some really good mealtime tips from one of my parents. Let me share them with you. In fact, the ideas would likely be helpful to everyone—I'll include them in my next newsletter.

Positive Feedback Increases Confidence

Teachers' self-confidence will grow as positive feedback is received from others regarding their job performance. To have their efforts valued and respected, as demonstrated by parents' positive responses and desire to cooperate, is an important contribution to teachers' sense of professional well-being (see Figure 5-10).

There is no question that teachers have frustrating and negative experiences as they work with families; there is no such thing as 100% success in complex endeavors involving human personalities, needs, and other foibles. But for teachers who honestly and warmly try to reach out to parents, there is enough success for them to realize that their efforts are effective and appreciated. And

FIGURE 5-10 Teachers benefit when they see that their efforts are valued and respected.

when frictions arise, as they inevitably will, teachers who have formed relationships with families will be better able to resolve differences.

The reaching out may be difficult, especially for teachers who are not very comfortable in social situations. In fact, one effect of enhanced teacher self-confidence is that personal social skills may develop and expand. Teachers' personal growth is often a by-product of their experiences with parents that garner positive feedback for them.

Parents involved in schools and centers learn so much about the functioning of teachers that they often become advocates for teachers, urging communities and institutions to establish working policies and personnel conditions that benefit teachers and allow them to do their best for children.

> "For all you do, that's what they pay you? I think that should be brought up with the board."
>
> "I'm writing a letter to the editor. This community needs to get behind the efforts to make good preschool education available to all who need it. It's too important."

REFLECTIONS FOR JOURNAL ENTRIES

In your personal or professional life to date, either as a parent or as a teacher, consider some of the experiences you've had that confirm any of the benefits for children, families, or teachers discussed in this chapter. What has been helpful to you or to children involved?

It is evident that the advocacy efforts of teachers to support quality for children's schools and programs can be greatly strengthened when parents recognize the benefits of good early education and join in supporting teachers' efforts. Recent authors on early childhood leadership and advocacy recognize the importance of strengthening partnership and collaborative efforts with parents (see Blank, Crompton, and Whitebook in Kagan & Bowman, 1997).

It is interesting to note that, through partnership, both teachers and parents may have some of their personal emotional needs satisfied on the subject of competence. "Education is a very human partnership. It depends for its strength, to a great degree, on how teachers and parents feel about each other and what they do to meet each other's needs" (Preece & Cowden, 1993).

Parental Resources for Enriched Learning Experiences

Teachers have only the resources of one person, with individual limitations on time, energy, knowledge, creativity, experiences, and other resources. Families may offer additional resources in all these commodities, as well as others

FIGURE 5-11 More one-to-one attention to children can be available when parents spend time in the classroom.

(see Figure 5-11). To hear again a view from Reggio Emilia: "The contribution of ideas, expectations, and abilities offered by families to the schools help the teachers to perceive the link with families as something that enriches rather than interferes. . . . Even with the best-prepared teachers and in the richest situations, there are areas that can only be realized through sharing and interactive choices" (Spaggiari, 1998, p. 111). The learning experiences teachers can offer children in the classroom are multiplied and enhanced by parents who feel invited and included in the educational process. Parents learn a good deal about interacting with their own children and often "teach" very well. Parents as a classroom resource will be discussed further in Chapter 12.

Families who are included in the educational process will also continue learning experiences with their children at home, strengthening teachers' efforts. A review of research on the importance of involving parents in the education of their children strongly suggests that the effectiveness of teachers and their programs is reinforced and increased by an active involvement of the families of children (see Chapter 4). One reason for this is that parents can reinforce the teachers' learning activities by conversations and activities in the home if they are fully aware of what is happening in the school.

The three benefits for teachers of working with parents are

1. Increased knowledge, which enables teachers to be more effective with each child.

2. Positive feedback, which increases their own feelings of competence in their profession, and advocacy of their interests.

3. Parental resources to supplement and reinforce their own efforts in providing an enlarged world of learning.

The best way for teachers to have an impact, especially a long-lasting one, on the children in their care is to work to strengthen and meet the needs of the whole family. The partnership between teachers and families benefits them both, but most of all it benefits the children for whom they both care.

> Beyond any question, when you work closely with parents you pay a price. You adjust to the other fellow's ideas, sometimes going faster and sometimes going at a slower pace than you desire. But there are rewards in working together that isolation could never bring. Teachers do gain. Parents gain. And children are the real winners. (Hymes, 1975)

Because it is the children that bring families and teachers together, the benefits for children alone should be motivation enough to work to create effective partnerships. Nevertheless, all of the adults involved will also become more effective at what they do.

SUMMARY

Because there are benefits for all—teachers, parents, and children—it should also be stated that it is difficult to discover any disadvantages to forming a healthy sense of working together. Why, then, are more teachers and parents not involved in constructive partnerships? The answer, as we discuss in the next chapter, may lie in examining attitudes and behaviors on both sides that act as barriers to effective teacher–parent relationships.

STUDENT ACTIVITIES FOR FURTHER STUDY

1. Choose one of the teachers described in this chapter. How are you like this teacher? Is there anything you want to change in yourself regarding your attitudes about parent involvement?

2. Talk with a teacher about what he feels he has gained and learned from his working relationships with parents. Compare your findings with the benefits to teachers discussed in the chapter.

3. Ask a teacher to think of one specific child in her class. What are some things she has learned about that child that could have been learned only through the parents?

4. Talk with a parent whose child has been in a classroom for any age this year. What are some of the things the parent feels he or she has gained from the teacher?

5. Ask both teachers and parents for examples of situations regarding children where adults have been able to work as partners, coordinating plans and information.

6. Do a study of a group of parents in your school. Compile a list of potential resources these parents offer the school and your teaching efforts.

CASE STUDY

Maria Gonzalez is a first-year Head Start teacher. She is enjoying her work and is particularly challenged by one of the families in her classroom. The Martinez family consists of a young single mother, Rosa; a charming 4-year-old who is very shy, Diego; and an elderly grandmother who speaks no English.

1. How might Rosa, the mother, benefit from her daily conversations with Maria?

2. What are some of the things Diego learns as he watches his mother and teacher talk together each day?

3. How might Maria benefit as a teacher by her close communication with this family?

4. Do you see any potential benefits of teacher–family partnership for anyone else in the family?

REVIEW QUESTIONS

1. List three benefits for children when parents and teachers work together as partners.

2. List three benefits for parents when parents and teachers work together as partners.

3. List three benefits for teachers when parents and teachers work together as partners.

SUGGESTIONS FOR FURTHER READING

Baker, A., & Manfredi/Petitt, L. (1998). *Circle of love: Relationships between parents, providers, and children in family child care.* St. Paul, MN: Redleaf Press.

Briggs, N. (1997). Working with families of young children: Our history and our future goals. In J. Isenberg & M. Jalongo, (Eds.). *Major trends and issues in early childhood education: Challenges, controversies, and insights.* New York: Teachers College Press.

Coleman, M. (1997, July). Families and schools: In search of common ground. *Young Children, 52*(5), 14–21.

Eldridge, D. (2001). Parent involvement: It's worth the effort. *Young Children, 56*(4), 65–69.

Gage, J., & Workman, S. (1994). Creating family support systems: In Head Start and beyond. *Young Children, 50*(1), 74–77.

Greenberg, P. (1989). Parents as partners in young children's development and education: A new American fad? Why does it matter? *Young Children, 44*(4), 61–75.

Hannon, J. (2000). Learning to like Matthew. *Young Children,* 55(6), 24–28.

Lawrence-Lightfoot, S. (2003). *The essential conversation: What parents and teachers can learn from each other.* New York: Random House.

Powell, D. (1998). Research in review. Reweaving parents into the fabric of early childhood programs. *Young Children,* 53(5), 60–67.

Rockwell, R., Andre, L., & Hawley, M. (1996). *Parents and teachers as partners.* Fort Worth TX: Harcourt Brace.

Stone, J. G. (1987). *Teacher–parent relationships.* Washington DC: NAEYC.

See also the entire issue of 1998 *Childhood Education,* International Focus Issue, *74*(6) (dealing with international perspectives on school–family–community partnerships).

REFERENCES

Baker, A., & L. Manfredi/Petitt. (2004). *Relationships, the heart of quality care: Creating community among adults in early care settings.* Washington, DC: NAEYC.

Berger, E. (1998). Don't shut fathers out. *Early Childhood Education Journal* 25(1), 57–61.

Blank, H. (1997). Advocacy leadership. In S. Kagan & B. Bowman (Eds.), *Leadership in early care and education.* Washington, DC: NAEYC.

Bronfenbrenner, U. (1979). *The ecology of human development: Experiments by nature and design.* Cambridge, MA: Harvard University Press.

Crompton, D. (1997). Community leadership. In S. Kagan & B. Bowman (Eds.), *Leadership in early care and education.* Washington, DC: NAEYC.

Epstein, J. (2000). *School and family partnerships: Preparing educators and improving schools.* Boulder, CO: Westview.

Epstein, J., Coates, L., Salinas, K. C., Sanders, M., & Simon, B. (1997). *School, family, and community partnerships: Your handbook for action.* Thousand Oaks, CA: Corwin.

Henderson, A., & Berla, N. (Eds.). (1994). *A new generation of evidence: The family is critical to student achievement. A report from the National Committee for Citizens in Education.* Washington, DC: Center for Law and Education.

Hymes, J. L. (1975). *Effective home school relations* (rev. ed.). Carmel, CA: Hacienda Press.

Lally, J. R., Lerner, C., & Lurie-Hurvitz, E. (2001). National survey reveals gaps in the public's and parents' knowledge about early childhood development. *Young Children,* 56(2), 49–53.

Murphy, D. (1997). Parent and teacher plan for the child. *Young Children,* 52(4), 32–36.

Murphy, J. (2003). Case studies in African American school success and parenting behaviors. *Young Children,* 58(6), 85–89.

Preece, A., & Cowden, D. (1993). *Young writers in the making: Sharing the process with parents.* Portsmouth, NH: Heinemann.

Schorr, L. (1997). *Common purpose: Strengthening families and neighborhoods to rebuild America.* New York: Doubleday.

Spaggiari, S. (1998). The community–teacher partnership in the governance of the schools. An interview with Lella Gandini. In C. Edwards, L. Gandini, &

G. Forman, (Eds.), *The hundred languages of children: The Reggio Emilia approach—advanced reflections* (2nd ed.). Greenwich, CT: Ablex Publishing.

Whitebook, M. (1997). Who's missing at the table? Leadership opportunities and barriers for teachers and providers. In S. Kagan & B. Bowman (Eds.), *Leadership in early care and education.* Washington, DC: NAEYC.

HELPFUL WEB SITES

http://www.ncpie.org

National Coalition for Parent Involvement in Education (NCPIE) is a coalition of major education, community, public service, and advocacy organizations working to create meaningful family–school partnerships in every school in America.

http://www.education-world.com

The Parent Involvement Education Web site. Read about *practical* ways in which schools are involving parents. Learn about parent involvement strategies that are working for others—and that could work for you.

http://www.par-inst.com

The mission of the Parent Institute is to encourage parent involvement in the education of their children. The Parent Institute publishes a variety of materials including newsletters, booklets, brochures, and videos.

http://www.ncrel.org

This Web site for parent involvement offers literature reviews and database links. The North Central Regional Educational Laboratory (NCREL) is a nonprofit organization dedicated to helping schools and the students they serve to reach their full potential.

Additional resources for this chapter can be found on the Online Companion to accompany this text at www.earlychilded.delmar.com. This supplemental material includes frequently asked questions; chapter outlines to be used as study guides; scenarios that both encourage large and small group discussions and provoke new thoughts and ideas; and chapter resources, including chapter summaries, interactive questions, Web links, and Web activities. In addition, forms from the text are available for download.

CHAPTER 6

Potential Barriers to Teacher–Family Partnerships

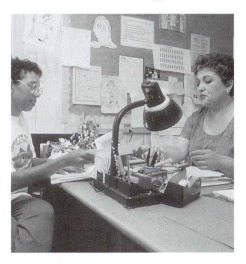

KEY TERMS
affect
gatekeeping
partiality
rationality
spontaneity
turf

Although we can agree on the benefits for children, parents, and teachers discussed in the last chapter, we can also agree that some of the attitudes conveyed by the teachers you met in that chapter are not uncommon among teachers working with young children. The complexity of human relationships fosters particular attitudes and behaviors in teachers and parents that may act as obstacles to communicating openly and comfortably and establishing working relationships. This does not mean that these negative responses are valid reasons for abandoning attempts to create partnerships; rather, these potential barriers must be recognized, examined, and understood by teachers, on whom rests the burden for trying to remove as many barriers as possible. As teachers consider the attitudes and emotions that act to distance psychologically, and some of the institutional practices that create physical separateness, they can also discover new ways they can bridge those gaps.

There will always be some barriers and some failures to topple those barriers. This chapter is intended to raise teacher awareness and to continue to erase some of the obstacles.

WHY ARE THERE BARRIERS?

Chapter 5 explored the potential for families and teachers to offer each other strength, support, and knowledge as they work together for children's benefit. But why sometimes does the relationship never get off the ground? Some of the families and teachers introduced earlier may help demonstrate the reasons.

John Reynolds is quite ready to admit it: He's frankly terrified of the prospect of his contacts with parents in his first year of kindergarten teaching:

> "Look, I'm just feeling my way with the kids this year. I'm sure those parents are wondering what's going on, and I'm not comfortable with them asking many questions. And I don't even have any kids of my own, to draw on that experience. I'm sure they wouldn't even listen to me. What's more, some of these parents are well-established in their own professions—I'm not even sure how to talk to them."

Connie Martinez shares his negative feelings about the parent involvement philosophy, but for different reasons:

> "Enough time goes into running a good classroom for young children without asking teachers to spend even more time on trying to do things for parents. And if you ask me, the whole idea is wrong, anyway. Parents today are pushing their responsibilities off on someone else, always asking the government or somebody to do more for them. Many of my parents live in public housing and get their child care subsidized already. It's just wrong; the more you do for them, the more they'll let you do. How will they learn to do a good job with their own kids that way, if we're helping them every step of the way? My parents raised six children without any preschool teacher working along with them."

Dorothy Scott shares her pessimism:

> "I've been working with children for 13 years now, and believe me, the majority of parents just don't seem to care. I've knocked myself out planning meetings to teach them the things they ought to know, and most of them never show up. You tell them what they should do, and they keep on doing things the same old ways. It can be pretty frustrating, let me tell you."

MiLan Ha won't say much about her feelings:

> "I really wish I could just work with my children without anyone suggesting I should also be working with the parents. When

parents begin to talk to me, I just freeze up and can't think of anything to say. With the children I'm fine."

These teachers are expressing strong attitudes that will clearly influence any interactions they have with families. But some of the parents have equally potent viewpoints. Sara Leeper says, "That teacher can hardly stand to talk to me. You can see her disapproval written all over her face. I'd like to know who she thinks she is, passing judgment on me. I'm a good mother."

Jane Weaver is very uncomfortable around the teacher, but for different reasons. "She just knows so much. I never went to college, and sometimes I don't quite understand some of the words she uses when she talks about what she's trying to accomplish with the children. I'm afraid I'd show my ignorance if I said anything. And she's such an expert—she always knows what to do with those children. She makes me feel—dumb."

Mary Howard explains her biggest problem with the teacher: "I feel like a nuisance. I mean, she's always so busy I hate to bother her to ask her anything. I feel like I'm butting in, and that makes me feel kind of bad. Cynthia's with her all day long and sometimes I just feel left out."

These comments exemplify some of the attitudes that we will explore. Consider these ideas and emotions in light of your experiences; think of parents and teachers you have observed. Have you heard comments or seen behaviors that convey discomfort or negative attitudes about working with one another? Many of these reactions are natural human reactions that constitute a problem only when they are unrecognized interferences between parent and teacher. Simply becoming aware of some of these will help.

When considering family–teacher communication, remember that the initiative must come, in most cases, from a teacher. Because this communication takes place in school, a teacher's home territory, it gives the teacher the advantage of her own environment, and with this advantage comes the burden of responsibility.

A teacher is responsible for creating an atmosphere open to dialogue. She must recognize not only the experiences and feelings of parents that might stand between them, but also analyze her own attitudes and behaviors so that she does nothing to exacerbate parents' discomfort.

In one sense parents and teachers can be described as natural adversaries—not because of the dynamics of any individual relationship but because of the nature of the relationship that emerges from the roles defined by the social structure of society. Parents and teachers generally have different perspectives on how to approach and view a child, a difference that evolves from their social and cultural roles. Our culture defines parents as ultimately responsible for their children's well-being. Because of their attachment, parents tend to be protective and highly emotionally invested in their children. Their perspective is quite focused on the individual, and they have particular expectations, goals, and intense feelings for their children. Teachers are given the cultural role of rational guide; their perspective can be described as more universal, concerned about children in the context of broad goals of socialization and education (Lightfoot, 1978). A teacher can be affectionate and still able to regard a child with objectivity not possible for a parent, what Katz calls a "detached concern" (Katz, 1995). Katz distinguishes between parenting and teaching in seven dimensions.

Role Dimension 1: Scope of Functions Parents must play every role related to the care and development of their children, from trips to the dentist and barbershop to making decisions about dance lessons or vacation plans to deciding whether the budget can stretch enough to afford a new pair of shoes. It is their responsibility to make sure that the child is physically healthy and well nourished, emotionally secure, socially happy, stimulated, and responded to cognitively and reading at grade level, and that tomorrow's laundry has been folded! Teachers are concerned about the child's more limited classroom life.

Role Dimension 2: Intensity of Affect Parents are highly emotional regarding everything that concerns their children, both positive and negative. Teachers are only mildly emotional about the same children because they are less dependent on children in the classroom meeting their emotional needs; children meet many of their parents' psychological needs. Gonzalez-Mena suggests that the passionate feeling of parenthood is highly personalized and "comes with a history and a future" (Gonzalez-Mena, 2005); this sense of long-term connection creates intense interactions when parents discuss their children.

Role Dimension 3: Attachment Parents are deeply involved in the mutual attachment that endures over time and is essential to the child's development. Teachers care sincerely about children, but they do not form deep attachments because they know their relationship is temporary. Parenting is a long-term relationship.

Role Dimension 4: Rationality Parents are supposed to be quite "crazy" about their children; children thrive when they bask in unconditional love. This may mean that parents cannot move away from their subjective response to matters about their children and become completely objective, the optimal condition for making factual assessments. In contrast, because of their emotional distance, teachers can be deliberate and objective in their analysis of a child's strengths and needs.

Role Dimension 5: Spontaneity Because of attachment and related emotions, parents will often act by emotional reaction in unpremeditated ways. Teachers are more likely to be able to keep cooler heads and can plan and speak with more objectivity.

Role Dimension 6: Partiality   Parents are most likely biased on their child's behalf. When teachers complain that some parents seem to believe there is only one child in the classroom, this is a reflection of the parents' partiality.

Teachers, however, are expected to show no favoritism or partial treatment toward any particular child.

Role Dimension 7: Scope of Responsibility   Parents are responsible for and responsive to the needs and lives of their individual children. Teachers are responsible for the needs of a whole group of children. Looked at this way, it is not surprising that parents and teachers frequently approach the same issue from different perspectives. Look back again at the cartoon on page 124 and appreciate it as you think about Katz's distinctions.

Today, more than ever, parents and teachers run into difficulty because so many very young children are being cared for by other adults, causing an overlapping of parents' and teachers' spheres of influence. Much of what caregivers of children in the first three years or so do for them are things also done by parents when they are present; in effect, early childhood caregivers and educators are sharing in parenting, creating what Stamp and Groves call a *third institution* (Stamp & Groves, 1994). The culture has not yet moved to define clearly the roles within this new context, nor can they *be* easily defined or separated, thus creating an ambiguous situation with unclear boundaries (see Figure 6-1; Johnston, 1990). In addition, many parents feel somewhat conflicted about leaving their young children in the care of "strangers" for most of the day, clouding their communication with caregivers.

The issue is further complicated by the fact that it is important that young children become attached to adults who care for them during so many of their waking hours in their parents' absence. But attachment is a mutual process. When two or more adults are attached to the same child, they frequently engage in **gatekeeping**, a phenomenon described by Dr. T. Berry Brazelton as a subtle attempt to undermine the position of the other adult in relation to the loved child. Gatekeeping is a sign that strong bonds are forming with the child, and although it can be stressful, it is also a good sign (Brazelton & Sparrow, 2002). It is no wonder that the ambiguous roles and responsibilities, complicated by emotional responses of competition, lead to an uncomfortable mistrust of the other that is usually not admitted or discussed. An acceptance of the differences and, perhaps, conflicts in the relationship of parents and teachers should not also imply an acceptance of distancing, mistrust, and hostility as inevitable. These responses result from a lack of communication and from mistaking differences for complete alienation.

Although teachers in elementary schools have more clear-cut roles than do teachers working with younger children in child care situations, there has long been a tradition of professional separation and formality when dealing with families. Indeed, powerful influences always affect parents and teachers

FIGURE 6-1 Early childhood caregivers are sharing in parenting, creating an ambiguous situation with unclear boundaries.

as they develop working relationships. It is important to remember that when people come together, they do so as individuals whose personalities, past experiences, present needs, and situations all determine their perceptions and reactions. "Humans of all ages get caught in a powerful web spun of two strong threads: the way they were treated in the past and the way the present bears down on them" (Hymes, 1974). Teachers need to examine sensitively the words and behaviors that pass between parents and themselves; to do so requires self-esteem and a sense of competence, or teachers will be reluctant to undergo so searching an examination.

This is not to suggest that professional attention and skill can simply remove the difficulties in something as complex as teacher–parent relations, or that it would even be desirable to be able to reduce the complexity to following simple formulas. With experience, teachers will come to realize that this complexity adds both challenge and richness to the process of professional and personal growth. Loris Malaguzzi, the founder of the early childhood programs in Reggio Emilia (noted for their strong family involvement, among other things) spoke of the value of creative conflict and dissonance.

> Family participation requires many things, but most of all it
> demands of teachers a multitude of adjustments. Teachers must
> possess a habit of questioning their certainties, a growth of
> sensitivity, awareness, and availability, the assuming of a critical
> style of research and continually updated knowledge of children,
> an enriched understanding of parental roles, and skills to talk,
> listen, and learn from parents. . . . Such relationships are and
> *should* be complicated (Malaguzzi, 1998, p. 69).

Many of the barriers to effective parent–teacher relationships can be caused by specific factors. These include

- The essential differences between teaching and parenting (already discussed).
- The question of maneuvering over **turf**.
- The issue of trust.
- Differences in expertise (adapted from File, 2001).

Some of these barriers may be erected by teacher behaviors and attitudes, and others by parents. Other more external barriers may be caused by larger circumstances of the school structure or community. Consider the list of barriers suggested by teachers in Figure 6-2; Figure 6-3 shows barriers that parents have identified. In the following discussion we will consider in more detail all of these obstacles to creating comfortable and effective partnerships. The issue is not to assign blame, but rather to find ways of maneuvering around these barriers.

Why Are Teachers Reluctant to Involve Parents?

- It takes too much time and organization.
- Parents may become too dominant in the classroom.
- Parents may not agree with teachers' methods.
- Teachers feel intimidated by parents' presence.
- Teachers are unsure of parents' expectations.
- Teachers are afraid of parent scrutiny.
- Teachers lack confidence.
- Teachers want to retain their authority, power, and control.
- Parents have unrealistic perceptions of their children.
- Lack of administrative support.
- Lack of communication skills.
- Lack of classroom space.
- Lack of knowledge about how to involve parents.
- Teachers are unwilling to admit they need help.
- Teachers just don't want to deal with parents.

FIGURE 6-2 Teacher identification of circumstances that create barriers.

**Barriers to Participation
Identified by Parents**

When asked why they did not participate in their children's school settings, parents identified these barriers:

Not enough time	89%
Feel have nothing to contribute	32%
Don't understand or know how to be involved	32%
Lack of child care	28%
Feel intimidated	25%
Not available during time scheduled	18%
Language and cultural differences	15%
Lack of transportation	11%
Don't feel welcome	9%
Other barriers	21%

FIGURE 6-3 Barriers to participation identified by parents.

DIFFERENCES BETWEEN TEACHING AND PARENTING

One of the most noticeable differences between teaching and parenting (refer back to discussion on pages 194 and 195) is that parents' responsibilities are seen as "diffuse and limitless" and teachers' as "specific and limited." This means that parents feel responsibility for everything they do related to their children and the outcomes of the children's behavior or performance. Fairly or unfairly, parents are placed squarely on the hook for these outcomes, even when they occur in the classroom. Thus parents often feel that they are in the position of having to defend themselves and their parenting actions. Parents generally feel vulnerable. There is a strong desire in most people to preserve their self-image; anything perceived as a threat to an individual's self-image serves as a barrier because an individual tends to avoid the source of the threat.

Being vulnerable makes parents sensitive to implied (or interpreted) criticism. Aware of the cultural myths and facts that place the burden for children's success and positive functioning squarely on parents' shoulders, most parents dread any indication that they are not doing a good job. With many parents uncertain that what they are doing is "right," yet feeling they must prove it is right in order to be accepted as capable parents, defensiveness against any suggestion of change often results. If a teacher gives the impression of evaluating parents' efforts, it may be easier to avoid that teacher or be defensive rather than hear the results of the evaluation. Hearing teachers speak of imperfections in their own children may seem like implied criticism of the parents.

Jane Weaver admits, "When I saw the teacher watching me scold Sandra the other day, I felt as nervous as a kid myself. You could tell by the look on her face she didn't like it. Well, I don't care—she doesn't have to live with her and I do. What does she know about children, anyway—she never had any of her own 24 hours a day."

Regardless of their personal outlook and how they view their parenting performance, most parents find it difficult to seek outside help, even under serious circumstances. It is incorporated into the self-image of most American parents that they should work things out for themselves as a sign of personal strength, achievement of adult status, and parenting success. Therefore, for many parents, reaching out to share responsibilities with teachers is contrary to their self-image. For some parents raising children is a private affair, and many parents feel that they know their children best and don't need teachers meddling in their matters.

Because of their strong attachment, many parents see their children as extensions of themselves; to comment negatively on one is like commenting negatively on the other. Teachers need to remember Katz's observation that it is not possible for parents to deal with information about their children from a rational and objective perspective. Their responses are emotional and intense.

> "It really bothers me when the teacher says Sandra is shy. I've always been pretty quiet myself, and it just hurts to hear her say that."

When children go to school, both parents and children are facing their first big test: "How will he—and therefore we—do?" Parents have made a heavy emotional investment in their children and may avoid a teacher as a source of possible hurt and criticism (see Figure 6-4).

Even though teachers do not have the weight of complete responsibility on them, they also can be vulnerable to criticism, or what they interpret as criticism. As John Reynolds expressed it, these teachers would rather avoid parents as a source of possible criticism. This is particularly true of young teachers who fear that their position may not be accepted because of a lack of teaching experience or because they have not experienced parenthood first-hand. Teachers unsure of their own abilities fear any negative feedback that may confirm their inner doubts, dreading parents' discovery of their mistakes or inadequacies. They put invisible "Do Not Enter" signs on their classroom doors to tell parents that their presence and opinions are not welcome.

A consequence of feeling vulnerable is that people become defensive. "Defensiveness is an equal opportunity pitfall for both professionals and families" (File, 2001, p. 72). When parents become defensive, they can become belligerent and hostile in their attacks on a teacher's skills and knowledge. When teachers feel defensive, they may hide their concerns behind a "professional" mask.

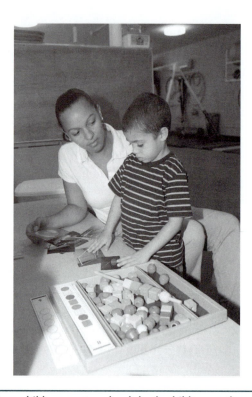

FIGURE 6-4 When children go to school, both children and parents are facing their first big test, wondering how the children will do.

A defensive teacher may depend too heavily on the image of the professional person who knows the answers and is all-important in the task of caring for children. This exaggeration of professional behavior intimidates parents and keeps them at a distance, which may be a teacher's unrecognized goal. Such a teacher has a hard time acknowledging the importance of parents' contributions or the right of parents to be involved. When one's sense of being in control is shaky, it is difficult to share power.

> "After all, I've been trained to do this. I frankly don't see why parents who haven't should be able to plan policies, make suggestions, or interfere with what I do in my classroom."

Rodd points out that the types of relationships established with families and the level of family involvement appear to be determined by the stage of professional development the teacher has reached.

> At earlier stages of career development and professional maturity, relationships with parents are more likely to be authoritarian and paternalistic, token in nature and from a deficit perspective—that is, where parents, even those who are considerably older than the

staff member, are not thought to possess the knowledge and skills necessary for bringing up their children (Rodd, 1998).

Exhibiting the aloofness of false professionalism or unwillingness to recognize and respect parents' significant role masks a teacher's defensive position and uncertainties that the teacher hopes will go unchallenged.

Parents perceiving a teacher's self-imposed distance of excessive professionalism withdraw behind fear and resentment:

> "I'd like to ask her some questions, but she never seems to have time. The other day she frowned and suggested I make an appointment to talk with her. Why does she make it such a big deal?"

It is hard to communicate comfortably across this distinctly cold gap. Parents are reluctant to spend energy in a situation where they feel they are not needed or wanted:

> "Who's she trying to kid? She really thinks she does a better job with them anyway—why does she even bother to ask parents to come in?"

> Jennifer Griffin says, "I hate having parents watch me—it's worse than the director coming in. They ask so many questions— it's as if they're just trying to find something I've done wrong."

■■■ MANEUVERING OVER TURF

Power is an interesting issue. Individuals can work to exert power *over* others, or they can work and communicate in such a way that they *share* power with others. Parents feel they should have power to participate in decisions and practices that involve their children. After all, in their homes and in their child rearing they have the power and are ultimately the ones with the responsibilities, the ones who have to answer for the final product.

Unfortunately, in most schools and programs teachers work on their own turf, the classrooms where they have the power. Families obviously feel less secure and comfortable in the school setting than in their own familiar home settings. So the issue becomes whether teachers genuinely want to share the power, which will involve finding ways to make family members feel a basic sense of equality and mutual contribution (see Figure 6-5).

Teachers who get caught up in this issue of power develop "territoriality"— resentment of having parents invade their turf—and try to draw lines that prevent fearful encounters with parents. "This exclusion works to conceal the teacher's work from parental scrutiny and protect professional authority in the classroom, thus maintaining the teacher's dominant position over parents in the educational hierarchy" (Gorham & Nason, 1997). Another possible reaction of

FIGURE 6-5 Both parents and teachers can get caught up in maneuvering over turf.

parents faced with a teacher's excessive professionalism and turf protection is to become aggressive in trying to bridge the gap, further alienating or frightening a teacher by demonstrating "pushy" behaviors:

> "There's no way I'm going to let these parents come into my classroom. Mrs. Randall called the other day and insisted she wanted to come sing some holiday songs with the children. Next she'll be telling me what to plan. Give them a little power and they'll take over!"

When teachers spend energy on protecting their turf, they may also protect their professional self-esteem by blaming others when they feel their efforts are not producing the desired outcomes:

> Dorothy Scott again: "Well, I'm certainly not going to bother planning another open house. Fifteen children in my room, and five parents show up. It's a big waste of my time."

Working with parents is an ongoing process; it takes time and effort to build a relationship, and that relationship is only the beginning. Teachers looking for immediate results from their efforts will be disappointed. If teachers are not prepared to accept the idea that this is an ongoing process and expect immediate evidence of effectiveness, they might be tempted to abandon all attempts rather than leave themselves open to a sense of failure.

Certainly people dislike feeling unsuccessful in their efforts, and teachers who define family involvement only by numbers present at any single event may protect themselves in the future by withdrawing, rather than feel their time and effort are not yielding the results they want. As teachers recognize that building relationships is a process that occurs over time, and that different parents will respond in different ways, and some not perceptibly at the present moment, they can avoid setting themselves up for a sense of failure.

■■■ THE ISSUE OF TRUST

Teachers spend a lot of time discussing trust in programs and schools. They are well aware that establishing trust with children is a first step to developing supportive learning relationships. They also recognize that establishing families' trust in their program is critical to families' confidence in the school. But a separate issue is related to teachers' abilities to trust families, to give up the common teacher stance of negative judgments about family capabilities.

One reason for this is that teachers often find themselves working with families whose experiences and viewpoints may be very different from their own. The majority of teachers are middle-class and have experienced little beyond middle-class lifestyles, value systems, and ways of thinking. Teachers encountering parents from a variety of backgrounds, experiences, and viewpoints may fall into the all-too-human tendency to stereotype people, their conditions, and their actions. A major barrier found in many situations is "racism, or behavior that is not intentionally racist but has a racist effect" (Boone & Barclay, 1995). Other common types of discrimination are based on differences in sex or sexual orientation, social class, education, marital status, economic status, or language. Even without deep prejudices or bigotry, assumptions made on the basis of stereotypes create barriers that preclude true openness to individuals and their actual personalities, needs, and wishes. It is sometimes easier to criticize and avoid than to try to understand and empathize. Barriers may rise in as many directions as there are classes, cultures, and circumstances. When these barriers exist, they may appear as negative behavior, indifference to the other, or stereotypical assumptions:

> Connie Martinez talks about some of her families. "Well, of course, the Butlers are college-educated and pretty well off, so I expect them to do a good job with their children. They really don't need much advice from me." (The Butlers are inexperienced and uneducated in child development and guidance, and they are shaken by the breakup of their marriage. They hunger for advice and support.) "Sylvia Ashley's just off welfare, so I don't suppose she'll make the effort to come to a parent conference." (Sylvia Ashley has never missed an opportunity to talk with any teacher who offered it.)

It is easy for teachers to selectively attend to information that is consistent with their beliefs and self-concepts and to screen out, ignore, or criticize people or beliefs that differ from their own. It is also easy for teachers to become convinced that others should and would do things differently if they only had the same knowledge the teachers have.

It has been noted recently, for example, that many teachers fall into the trap of stereotyping the behavior of men in low-income and high-risk backgrounds as absenting themselves from child rearing (McBride & Rane, 1996). If teachers ignore the strengths these father figures can bring to the parenting situation and fail to try to involve them in the early childhood education program, a valuable resource is neglected that could have positive impacts on children's development.

It is important that teachers realize that it is neither moral nor ethical to bring people into the educational setting who may not be treated with respect and understanding when they get there (Boone & Barclay, 1995). Trust includes both acceptance of others and putting aside one's own viewpoints as absolutes.

> Ignoring all the good parenting Sara Leeper and Ginny Parker do, Connie continues to complain, "I really don't see why they let them adopt a child. I certainly wouldn't have, if I'd been making the decision. What kind of environment can lesbians offer a child?"
>
> "And speaking of environments, Joshua's father lives with his girlfriend. I've heard Joshua refer to her that way: 'My dad's girlfriend.' Now what does that teach a child?"

Teachers who disapprove of family lifestyles, or approach parents with a patronizing attitude because they are of lower socioeconomic status, communicate a feeling of superiority, which is not helpful in forming relationships as equals. Parents, in turn, may avoid contact with teachers whose manner or appearance, communication style, and expectations are uncomfortably different from their own.

> "That teacher, I don't know, she talks too good," explains Mr. Rodriguez.
>
> "You know," says Mary Howard, "just because I'm black, she talks to me like I live in a ghetto or something."
>
> Nguyen Van Son is angry. "She's never tried to find out how our children live at home, what we want. I don't want my children losing everything from our culture, and if you ask me, she's ignoring the fact that we have a culture!"

In many schools and programs, invisible (but not imaginary) lines exist based on race and class that prevent effective interaction. Often there are real differences in backgrounds between teachers and parents. Such distinctions can be less divisive when teachers are careful to behave in ways that diminish the importance of the differences and make an effort to get to know parents as individuals, not as members of a particular ethnic group or social class. Trust works two ways; parents trust that they and their children will be accepted and treated with respect, and teachers come to trust that parent viewpoints and experiences are valid. Genuine respect results when teachers make the effort to learn more about diversity, as we will discuss further in Chapter 15.

■■■ DIFFERENCES IN EXPERTISE

Very much related to the issue of trust is the topic of expertise. In the early childhood education profession, practitioners are increasingly called on to develop their professional knowledge base. As the profession has developed standards of developmentally appropriate practice, teachers have increasingly become oriented toward a vocabulary and tradition of a common body of expert knowledge. Although this has been a positive step toward increasing professionalism, in some cases it has also had the effect of distancing teachers from families. Partnerships require teachers to see parents as having expertise about their own children and families. Yet it is sometimes difficult for teachers to value that expertise because it seems so much less standard than their own professional knowledge. However, family knowledge must be recognized genuinely, or the barrier of expert relating to novice will be erected (see Figure 6-6).

The role of expert is one that may interfere with comfortable communication, but teachers and parents also have unique responses and strong reactions to the very role of the other. Parents have their own childhood histories of encounters with teachers and learning experiences. Some of these may be positive, causing the parent to automatically consider a teacher a friend. But for many parents, painful memories of past school experiences cause

FIGURE 6-6 New mothers may feel intimidated by the obvious knowledge of the professional.

unconscious responses to a teacher as someone to fear, someone who will dis-approve, correct, or "fail" the parent (and child). With such an underlying assumption, messages from a teacher may be interpreted more negatively than the sender intended. Some parents, particularly in lower socioeconomic classes, have had numerous encounters with case workers, social workers, and other figures in authority. A parent who has a history of dehumanizing or dis-illusioning experiences with professional people may already have erected barriers in the form of negative expectations.

Teachers, on the other hand, need to realize how their unconscious reactions to parents are influenced by their relationships with their own par-ents. A teacher who has unresolved hostilities with her own parents may have trouble relating comfortably to others who bear the label "parent." A teacher's experiences that have shaped his values about family life may conflict with the reality of parents with whom he works. For example, a teacher who feels that mothers really should be at home may not be able to relate sympathetically to a working mother. People alienated by unconscious emotional responses can never really hear or speak to each other clearly.

When teachers dominate as experts, they often create negative emo-tional responses in parents. One of these is that parents may fear antagonizing teachers by their questions or comments, with the anxiety that a teacher could single out their child for reprisals when they are absent:

> "I'd like to tell his teacher that I don't like the way she lets the children do such messy art activities, but if she gets mad she'll just take it out on Ricky when I'm not around. I'd better not."

A majority of all parents, and even more minority parents, report that they are never sure how well their children will be treated when they leave them in a classroom. With such feelings of uncertainty, it is not surprising that parents fear that speaking out might have a negative effect. (Interestingly enough, recent information shows that teachers do not carry their disapproval of parents into dislike or avoidance of their children. If anything, they seem to compensate for that dislike by paying extra attention to these children.)

Another emotional response created by the separation between teachers and parents is the fear that teachers will replace parents in their children's af-fections. Attachment is a mutual process, and the affectionate relationship with their children satisfies many emotional needs of parents. Despite research that shows that additional attachments do not undermine the primary parental re-lationship (Baker and Manfredi/Petitt, 2004), many parents fear this loss and are inhibited from forming relationships with teachers because of their feelings of jealousy and competition with teachers for their children's regard:

> "I'll tell you, it makes you wonder. She comes in to give the teacher a good morning hug, and not so much as a goodbye kiss for her own mother, who's going to be gone all day. I get pretty sick of hearing Miss Ha this and Miss Ha that at home all

weekend, I can tell you. How do you think I feel when she cries at the end of the day and just doesn't want to go home?"

There are often ambivalent emotions here: A mother wants her child to be independent and happy away from her but resents the perception that a teacher is taking over in the child's regard. Feeling that she is losing her child to other people may threaten the mother's own identity.

Teachers themselves are not immune from competing for children's affections, especially if their own emotional needs are not being met in their lives beyond the classroom. A warm, affectionate bond with each child is important; but when a teacher finds herself thinking that she "can do a much better job with him than his own mother" or "would like to take the child home with me; he'd be better off," she has slipped into the dangerous territory of identifying with a child so completely that she sees him only as a child she loves in the classroom, not as a member of the more important world of his family. Parents are the most important people in their children's lives and need to be supported as such. A teacher who begins to confuse her role with being a "substitute" for parents, or a "savior" of children in less-than-perfect situations, engenders fear and suspicion. A teacher who needs to feel more important to a child than his parents may find it too easy to blame the parents for the child's shortcomings and convey such an attitude in her choice of words (see Figure 6-7).

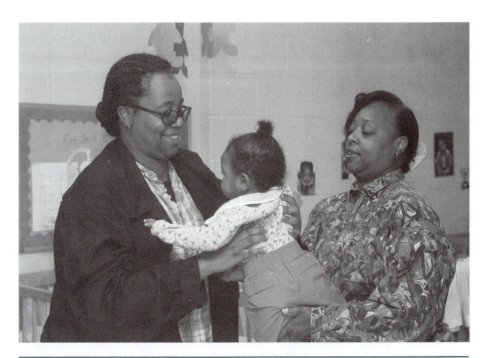

FIGURE 6-7 Teachers must be aware of competing with parents for the child's affection.

"The way you're reacting each time Pete has a temper tantrum is
really causing him to have more outbursts.

Teachers need to realize that emotions of jealousy and fear of loss are
hidden factors limiting much of what is truly said and heard. If teachers ignore
the likely presence of these emotions, they may unwittingly fan such sparks
into destructive flames:

"Oh, she was just fine, Mrs. Weaver. She played as happily as can
be all day and never asked for you once. You don't need to worry
about her missing you.

This may be intended as reassurance, but it will simply confirm the mother's
worst fears. Most parents believe that no one else can do the job for their children as well as they can, and teachers who help parents feel they are not being
displaced from this important position prevent barriers from being raised
between them:

"She went to sleep well at naptime today. That was a good idea
you had to bring her blanket from home. I know she misses you
especially then, and it helps to have that blanket as connection
for her.

The word *guilt* creeps into many conversations when contemporary parents have a chance to talk freely. The many demands on parents, along with an
unrealistic image of perfection and a feeling of not doing what should be
done, result in feelings of guilt. This emotion may operate as a hidden barrier;
parents feeling inadequate to the task may avoid all possible reminders of this,
including the person doing things for their children that parents feel
they should be doing, who seems so very expert in her performance (see
Figure 6-8). They may also react unreasonably when receiving unfavorable
communication about their children's behavior or abilities. Resentment can
creep into the relationship from both teacher and parent.

REFLECTIONS FOR JOURNAL ENTRIES

*This is a difficult area for teachers to consider, but real honesty can
help a teacher identify some of the emotions and attitudes that have
been barriers to forming effective partnerships with families. Take
some time to think about your own perspectives. Can you identify with
some of the issues and emotions that have been discussed so far in this
chapter? Write about some of the experiences and examples that come
to mind. Continue to think about this subject. Self-awareness will help
you move past some of these barriers.*

FIGURE 6-8 When children show fondness for their teachers, some parents may feel guilt and resentment.

Early childhood teachers have extremely demanding jobs that use enormous amounts of energy, creativity, and emotion for long hours each day. In most cases preschool teachers are paid much lower salaries and receive fewer benefits than their counterparts in schools for older children. They are accorded less professional status and recognition, even when they have completed the same number of years of training. Though elementary or after-school teachers may be more highly paid, they too often feel as if their contributions to children's lives go unrecognized by families and the community. Therefore, it is easy for teachers to feel the community in general, and parents in particular, take advantage of them.

"I don't see why they can't pick their kids up on time—don't they know I have other things to do in my life?"

"Do you realize she had today off and went and played tennis and brought him to my classroom just like any other day?"

"Look at her dressed like that. I'll bet she spends more on her clothes in a month than I get paid in six months!"

Parents have their own reasons for resenting teachers. It hurts to be removed from their children's lives. The TANF legislation that changed how welfare funds are distributed to lower-income families has meant that many parents have had to leave very young children in the care of others in order to support their families. This is just one way in which the political decisions of the country impact families and their relationships with schools. No wonder parents feel resentful in such a situation over which they have no control.

When it appears that teachers are making decisions and setting rules that exclude parents from classrooms and communication, parents are left with little recourse but can seethe with resentment toward those teachers. It is also a genuine cause of resentment when parents disagree with some of the decisions made about their children's care and education but feel powerless to influence the teacher or program (Delpit, 1995).

In most families where both parents work, child care arrangements are the most critical components for the smooth running of the entire enterprise. This places parents in the ambiguous position of recognizing how important a teacher is to their way of life but at the same time resenting having a person outside the family play such a necessary role. Contradictory, to be sure, but enforced dependence often breeds not gratitude, but resentment.

Parents and teachers who resent each other will be unable to communicate clearly. Thus it can be seen that the emotions of guilt, jealousy, and resentment may impede the process of open communication, becoming barriers that keep them from sharing their expertise.

Personal Factors

Some teachers explain their lack of communication with parents as caused by their own personalities or their discomfort in social situations. These factors require special efforts on the part of teachers, and they should not be accepted as justification for failure to take the initiative in reaching out to parents.

> Milan Ha knows that she doesn't have nearly as much contact
> with parents as many of the teachers in her center, but she says
> she can't help it. She says it shouldn't make a difference because
> she works so well with the children, but she does wonder what she
> might do to help the situation.

Teachers aware of their introverted personalities need to find ways of pushing their own efforts: perhaps setting specific goals, such as talking to a certain number of parents each day, or approaching a parent they have never talked with much, or saying one sentence beyond "Hello, how are you?" Teachers having difficulty getting started may need to plan their comments to parents. (Thinking of one thing each child has done or been interested in may be a good place to start.) It may help to share feelings of discomfort with coworkers and be encouraged by their support. Some initial success in getting to know a few parents makes subsequent encounters a little easier. Students who have the opportunity to practice communication in classes and field experiences will find that communicating becomes easier with experience.

Teachers need to remind themselves frequently that part of a teacher's responsibility is to work with families as well as children, and that parents, because of a lack of familiarity with a school situation, may be far more uncomfortable than the teachers themselves. As the leader in a classroom, teachers are automatically placed in the role of hostess. Just as a hostess does not allow guests to flounder, unspoken to and uncomfortable, in her own living room, so a teacher must take the initiative to converse with parents. It is also important for teachers to keep reminding themselves that personality and social comfort may also affect parent responses.

Too often teachers interpret quiet parents or those who do not readily engage in conversation as having "attitudes" or thinking themselves too good for communication with the teacher. Personal factors may work from both perspectives. Awareness will help; pushing oneself a bit will help; a little success will help. Personality and social discomfort must not be allowed to interfere with the communication process (see Figure 6-9).

FIGURE 6-9 Teachers must push themselves past social discomfort to communicate with families.

■■■ BARRIERS CAUSED BY EXTERNAL FACTORS

As well as internal feelings and experiences, the external circumstances in which teachers and parents find themselves may act as barriers. Recall that both teachers' and parents' list of barriers to partnership included several external factors.

Time

Both parents and teachers are undoubtedly under time constraints. If school philosophies and administrative actions do not support working with families, teachers may not receive either the staffing arrangements or the compensatory time that is needed to respond with flexibility to families' lifestyles and working patterns. When staffing arrangements have full-time caregivers of young children arriving after and leaving before parents arrive, part-time floaters may greet parents at pickup or drop-off times, putting a strain on families who need information and the temporary caregivers who don't have it. Parents never have enough time for the demands of their lives, but they will find the time for parent involvement if they feel it is really important.

There are ways to maneuver around time as a barrier (see Chapters 9, 10, and 12 for ideas that do not take large amounts of time) if working together is perceived as important to parents and teachers. It is more productive to consider time as a real problem and search for creative solutions than to interpret the other's lack of availability as a lack of concern for the child.

"Busy-ness"

Another external factor that may function as a barrier is a teacher's appearance of always being busy. This may result from the realities of caring for the needs of a group of children or from an unconscious desire to keep parents at a distance.

Whatever the reason, the perception that a teacher has too much to do to be bothered by a parent keeps many parents from more than the briefest greeting. If teachers try consciously to dispel this impression of being too busy to talk, there are things that can be done. At the beginning of the day, preparations for classroom activities can be made before the children arrive or by another staff member, leaving a teacher available to talk. Teachers need to plan, and have ready for use, activities that children may begin by themselves that require little supervision: puzzles on the table, dried beans and cups to fill in a basin, or several lumps of clay waiting in the art area (see Figure 6-10). When children begin to play, parents and teachers will be free to talk. A classroom should be arranged so that when parents enter they have easy access to a teacher. Staffing arrangements and physical locations at the end of the day should provide enough teachers to care for children so that some are free to talk with parents.

FIGURE 6-10 Having open-ended materials ready for children to begin play allows time for parents and teachers to talk.

Planning and attention to details convey the message that teachers are there for parents.

Old Ideas of Parent Involvement

The changes in family structure and living patterns over the past several decades demand changes in the timing, content, and form of family involvement, activities, and expectations. Teachers or schools that continue to offer nothing more than the traditional forms and times for meetings, conferences, and the like—what Swap calls *institutionalized rituals,* which are so obviously unsupportive of good relationships (Swap, 1993)—fail to recognize the current needs of families.

Examples of institutionalized rituals are parent–teacher conferences scheduled at 10:30 a.m., on the teacher's break, or meetings held every first Tuesday at 6:30 p.m. Sometimes the old ideas are adhered to as an unconscious punitive attitude toward parents deviating from traditional lifestyles—such as mothers who work instead of being available to come in for that conference at 10:30 in the morning. Administrators and teachers must be aware that their own values and the weight of traditional practices may contribute to any reluctance to change forms of parents' involvement. Schools and programs must examine their practices for evidence of outdated concepts of parent involvement and family needs.

Powell points out that program practices must be "in tune with widespread demographic changes, especially the characteristics and circumstances of families being served. . . . One size does not fit all" (Powell, 1998). When schools bring families into the planning process, they can articulate the changes that need to be made to accommodate family realities.

Administrative Policies

Some school and program policies discourage or forbid contact and discussion between parents and staff other than supervisory personnel, perhaps on the grounds that unprofessional contacts may take place. The major difficulties here are that parents are denied the opportunity to build a relationship with a child's primary caregivers and that the designated supervisory personnel are often not available in the early morning or late afternoon when parents need to talk. Such policies effectively deter any meaningful parent involvement. In addition, families have likely shared information about their children with the administrator who conducts initial interviews, and this information may not reach the teachers who would benefit from it. If the family establishes a relationship with an administrator only, they may not invest in a relationship with the child's actual caregiver (Baker and Manfredi/Petitt, 2004).

Another administrative policy that undermines formation of teacher–parent relationships is staffing patterns with multiple caregivers or frequent changes in personnel. Although administrators often justify such conditions as necessary for children and staff to learn to be flexible and to meet staffing needs, frequent changes do not facilitate formation of authentic relationships. Administrative staffing policies that provide only a bare minimum of staff available at arrival and departure times also work against forming effective relationships. Parents quickly recognize that harried teachers are not available for communication (see Figure 6-11). When the administration provides training and practice for teachers to learn how to form relationships with parents, lack of knowledge of how to work with adults is removed as a barrier. When administrative philosophy and policies support family involvement, and parents are given clear guidelines for ways they can communicate with staff, parents know what is expected of them and do not retreat because of confusion, anger, or frustration.

All of these external factors can be solved with concrete changes in the physical and social environment if they are identified as the cause of some barriers. Indeed, these are the easiest barriers to remove, needing only creative thought and perhaps a little money!

Personal Problems

From the families' side, the pressure from personal problems can act as a barrier to the parent–teacher relationship. As much as parents care about their children and how they are functioning in the classroom setting, too many concerns about other life matters may require parents' primary attention. Such a parent should neither be condemned for indifference nor ignored because of absence, but shown continued support and understanding from a teacher concerning the demands on parents. As teachers take responsibility to link families with appropriate community agencies, problems may be eased.

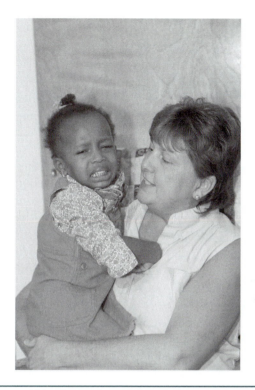

FIGURE 6-11 It would be fairly obvious to any observing parent that this caregiver has too much on her hands to be free to talk.

This barrier for parents can be removed with community support and empowerment of attitudes. Jesse Jackson is credited with saying,

> Parents must make room in their hearts and then in their house and then in their schedule for their children. No poor parent is too poor to do that, and no middle-class parent is too busy.

 ## REFLECTIONS FOR JOURNAL ENTRIES

Can you think of an example of an institutionalized ritual that needs to be changed in a school with which you are familiar? Why does it persist? What change can you think of that would remove barriers to family participation?

In the same way, no teacher who believes in the importance of working as a partner with parents will find the problems so immovable as to abandon all attempts.

It is interesting to realize that teacher attitude about family involvement seems to be a key factor in success. Several researchers have noted that most teachers surveyed said that they were stronger supporters of family involvement than were the parents; however, surveys of the parents involved contradicted this perception (Boone & Barclay, 1995). In addition, many teachers tend to blame parents for their low level of involvement, even when other teachers in the same building successfully involve parents in their children's education. It is vital that teachers consider the importance of their own attitudes.

SUMMARY

The key to removing many of the barriers to parent–teacher relationships is a teacher's mind-set. When teachers believe that there is value in working with families, they will find the time and energy to commit themselves to identifying and dealing with potential barriers. These barriers "include the intense feelings, ego involvements, deeply held attitudes and values, past histories, and current concerns" (Chilman, 1974) that parents and teachers bring to the process of communication. It is an interesting reminder that each group sees the main obstacle in the other: Teachers note parents' unwillingness, and parents note teachers' distant behavior. Rather than blaming others, it is more productive to examine personal attitudes and behaviors. The barriers can be broken by "a bit more relaxation, a bit more empathy, a bit more recognition of the many complex factors that shape life for all of us" (Chilman, 1974).

STUDENT ACTIVITIES FOR FURTHER STUDY

1. As you work in your classroom or practicum placement, keep a journal of your experiences and encounters in working with parents. Use the journal to be honest about your emotional responses. How does your awareness compare with some of the emotional responses discussed in this chapter?

2. Examine your own biases. Is there a style or kind of family with which you would be less comfortable working than with others? Discuss this idea in small groups.

3. Wherever possible, observe teachers and parents talking together. What nonverbal signs of comfort and discomfort do you see?

4. Talk with several teachers. Ask them to recall negative experiences in working with families. Afterward, try to analyze which of the barriers discussed in the text might have been at work.

5. Talk with several parents whose children are involved in preschool programs or elementary schools. Do they recall negative experiences in relationships with teachers? Try to analyze which of the barriers discussed in the text may have been present.

CASE STUDY

Catherine Green has just begun to teach second grade in a private school. This is her first teaching experience after graduation. Her preservice education included several courses on communication with children, child guidance, and curriculum and planning methods. However, the only course she had related to working with families was a course on modern families, which was interesting but quite theoretical. During her interview she was told that family involvement was an important part of her teaching role. She is a little unsure what her principal meant by "family involvement." She hopes that occasional conferences will be enough; the idea of inviting parents to come into the classroom is intimidating. Several parents have asked her how long she has been teaching, so she is afraid they don't think she has enough experience.

Today in the teachers' lounge she heard several teachers complaining about the open house they are required to attend next week and another teacher telling her coworker that she was just fed up with the Osmonds, who had been late twice this week already to pick up their child. They also commented to her that she was going to get the Osmond child next year, and good luck! She saw the Osmonds in the hall; the mother looked stressed, and the father appeared to be from another culture.

1. Identify the potential barriers to Catherine's partnerships with families.

2. If Catherine is to overcome these barriers, what are some ideas and behaviors for her to consider?

3. What factors in Catherine's environment may be influencing her attitudes?

4. Imagine life from the Osmonds' perspective. What implicit messages might they be picking up from teachers that could act as barriers to their relationships in the school?

REVIEW QUESTIONS

1. Identify four factors affecting parents and teachers that may act as barriers to the development of effective relationships.

2. Describe four emotional responses that may impair the communication process.

3. List four external factors that may act as barriers.

SUGGESTIONS FOR FURTHER READING

Allen, L. (1997). Do you resent and stonewall parents?—Matthew's line. *Young Children, 52*(4), 72–74.

Coleman, M., & Churchill, S. (1997). Challenges to family involvement. *Childhood Education, 73*(1), 144–148.

Davies, D. (1997). Crossing boundaries: How to create successful partnerships with families and communities. *Early Childhood Education Journal, 25*(10), 73–77.

Doner, K. (1996). My teacher hates me. *Working Mother, 19*(9), 46–48.

Galinsky, E. (1988). Parents and teacher–caregivers: Sources of tension, sources of support. *Young Children, 43*(3), 4–12.

Greenman, J. (1998, November/December). Parent partnerships: What they don't teach you can hurt. *Child Care Information Exchange,* 78–82.

Grossman, S. (1999). Examining the origins of our beliefs about parents. *Childhood Education, 76*(1), 24–27.

Katz, L., Aldman, A., Reese, D., & Clark, A. M. (1996, November). Preventing and resolving parent–teacher differences. *ERIC Digest,* EDO-PS-96-12.

Kimball, G. (1998). *21st century families: Blueprints to create family-friendly workplaces, schools, and communities.* Chico, CA: Equality Press.

Lombardi, J. (2002). *Time to care: Redesigning child care to promote education, support families, and build communities.* Philadelphia, PA: Temple University Press.

McBride, S. (1999). Research in review. Family-centered practices. *Young Children, 54*(3), 62–68.

St. John, E., et al. (1997). *Families in schools: A chorus of voices in restructuring.* Portsmouth, NH: Heinemann.

Willis, Scott. (1995). When parents object to classroom practice. *Education Update 37*(1), 1, 6, 8.

REFERENCES

Baker, A., & Manfredi/Petitt, L. (2004). *Relationship, the heart of quality care: Creating community among adults in early care settings.* Washington, DC: NAEYC.

Boone, E., & Barclay, K. (1995). *Building a three-way partnership: Linking school, families, and community.* New York: Scholastic Leadership Policy Research.

Brazelton, T. B., & Sparrow, J. (2002). *Touchpoints three to six: Your child's emotional and behavioral development.* Cambridge, MA: Perseus.

Chilman, C. S. (1974). Some angles on parent–teacher learning. *Childhood Education, 51*(12), 119–125.

Delpit, L. (1995). *Other peoples' children: Cultural conflict in the classroom.* New York: The New Press.

File, N. (2001). Family–professional partnerships: Practice that matches philosophy. *Young Children, 56*(4), 70–74.

Gonzalez-Mena, J. (2005). *The child in the family and the community* (4th ed.). Upper Saddle River, NJ: Prentice-Hall.

Gorham, P., & Nason, P. (1997). Why make teachers' work more visible to parents? *Young Children, 52*(5), 22–26.

Hymes, J. (1974). *Effective home–school relations.* Sierra Madre: Southern California Assoc. for the Education of Young Children.

Johnston, J. (1990). *The new American family and the school.* Columbus, OH: National Middle School Association.

Katz, L. (1995). Mothering and teaching—some significant distinctions. In L. Katz (Ed.), *Talks with teachers of young children: A collection.* Norwood, NJ: Ablex Publishing.

Lightfoot, S. L. (1978). *World apart: Relationships between families and schools.* New York: Basic Books.

Malaguzzi, L. (1998). History, ideas, and basic-philosophy interview with Lella Gandini. In C. Edwards, L. Gandini, & G. Forman (Eds.), *The hundred* languages of children: The Reggio Emilia approach to early childhood education.* Norwood, NJ: Ablex Publishing.

McBride, B., & Rane, T. (1996, October). Father/male involvement in early childhood programs. *ERIC Digest.*

Powell, D. (1998). Reweaving parents into the fabric of early childhood programs. *Young Children, 53*(5), 60–67.

Rodd, J. (1998). *Leadership in early childhood: The path to professionalism* (2nd ed.). New York: Teachers College Press.

Stamp, L., & Groves, M. (1994). Strengthening the ethic of care: Planning and supporting family involvement. *Dimensions of Early Childhood, 22*(2), 5–9.

Swap, S. M. (1993). *Developing home–school partnerships: From concepts to practice.* New York: Teachers College Press.

HELPFUL WEB SITES

http://www.nea.org
> National Education Association There are many resources here regarding parent–teacher relationships.

http://www.ldac-taac.ca
> Learning Disability Association of Canada.This site is a good resouce of information on parent–teacher relationships.

Additional resources for this chapter can be found on the Online Companion to accompany this text at www.earlychilded.delmar.com. This supplemental material includes frequently asked questions; chapter outlines to be used as study guides; scenarios that both encourage large and small group discussions and provoke new thoughts and ideas; and chapter resources, including chapter summaries, interactive questions, Web links, and Web activities. In addition, forms from the text are available for download.

CHAPTER 7

Foundations of a Successful Partnership

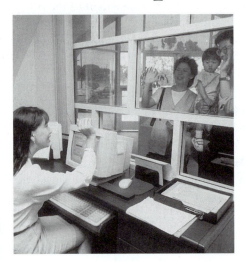

OBJECTIVES

After reading this chapter, you should be able to

1 Discuss six attitudes or ideas of teachers that are conducive to forming a partnership with families.

2 Discuss concrete actions that are necessary in laying the foundation for a parent–teacher partnership.

KEY TERMS
authentic
code of ethics
collaborative
cultural mores
empathize
expertise
professionalism

When administrators and teachers in early childhood schools and programs have decided that reaching out to include families is an important part of their mission, they have taken a first step toward creating partnerships. Having made that decision, they can then design the policies and practices to work with families. Every program, responsive to what it knows about its particular population of families, will necessarily create methods of working with families that are unique; thus many programs may look quite unlike each other in their approaches and still work well in their own situations. Therefore, it would be impractical and not very helpful for this text to set down one specific plan of action for working with families.

But certain common elements can be found in any program that has some success in reaching families. Some of these include attitudes of the staff involved. Others include the factors that support teacher efforts. By exploring these common elements, we will be able to determine the essential ingredients of successful partnerships.

In this chapter we will explore some of the attitudes, behaviors, and other factors that facilitate the formation of a productive partnership between families and teachers.

TEACHER IDEAS AND ATTITUDES

Jane Briscoe has become convinced that there are enough good reasons to merit really trying to form partnerships with parents. "Where do I start?" she wonders.

Because a teacher acts as initiator in forming the partnership, the starting place lies in an examination of some essential teacher ideas and attitudes.

Concept of Professionalism

Basic to the formation of a parent–teacher partnership is a teacher's concept of **professionalism** and the professional teaching role. One traditional characteristic of professionals is keeping a certain distance between themselves and their clients to allow more objective professional judgments, emotional protection from too many client demands, and enhanced status. But this separateness precludes an uninhibited social exchange between client and professional. With the traditional definition of the professional, teachers see their relationships with families as a one-way process of informing parents and attempting to influence them. In such a relationship families are passive clients, receiving services, depending on the experts' opinion, in need of direction, and quite peripheral to the process of decision making. Such a concept implies that there is a deficit that the professional is trying to rectify, an idea that effectively makes shared understandings and responsibilities impossible. Inherent also in this stance is the idea that authority and power must rest with the professional: power over another. A partnership can develop only when teachers create a different mental concept of their role. When early childhood programs value relationship-based care, they understand "professionalism" in a new way, following a model that fosters caring connections between adults (Baker and Manfred/Petitt, 2004).

Teachers who can accept the partnership concept consider parents to be active members in making and implementing decisions regarding their children and capable of making major contributions. These teachers share responsibility and power, believing that both teachers and families have strengths and equivalent, though different, expertise. Such a belief implies reciprocity in a relationship, with parents contributing, as well as receiving, information and services. Families are viewed not as a problem but as part of a solution to common puzzles; power is shared.

FIGURE 7-1 Teachers who believe in partnership can share responsibility.

"Partnership models call for a move away from previous conceptualizations that portray people as in need of our expertise and educational efforts" (File, 2001). The belief in partnership is a prerequisite to everything else. It requires teachers to define their professionalism in a new way, to see themselves as leaders of an educational team, using their special skills and knowledge to enlist the help of parents, expecting to exchange information with them, consider their opinions, and learn from them. "The touchstones of the new practice are new professional skills, new professional norms, new power relationships, and a new mind-set about what it means to be a professional" (Schorr, 1997; see Figure 7-1). It is a challenging idea for teachers to understand that having **expertise** is not necessarily the same thing as providing all the answers and advice to those who have not learned the same body of knowledge as the professional. Sometimes a more appropriate use of teacher expertise involves helping families find their own solutions to the challenges regarding their children. Families have their own expertise, being the ones who best understand the goals and values they prize for their children, their own traditions, their community and cultural norms. This expertise must be drawn upon to create truly developmentally appropriate schools and programs. Teacher skills in identifying and drawing out that parental expertise are part of these new professional skills.

A partnership can be both exciting and anxiety producing because teachers who function as partners with parents are frequently in a position where so much is untried and without guidelines. "The new practitioners' **collaborative** stance involves a willingness on occasion to be uncertain about what to do" (Schorr, 1997). But as partners, teachers trust the parents are capable of growth; and in demonstrating this belief, they grow themselves. In a partnership children, parents, and teachers grow and learn as they are drawn together by the same objective: what is best for the children. There is strength as professionals help create a sense of community.

Sense of Self

Teachers who are most able to move into a collaborative partnership with families have a strong sense of self. They have learned to be in touch with and can effectively communicate their feelings. They are aware of their own strengths, weaknesses, concerns, and values; sure of their positions, they are not easily manipulated or threatened, nor do they try to manipulate others through fear. Because they respect themselves, they treat others with equal dignity, relate as one individual to another, and avoid stereotyping. They are **authentic** to themselves.

Teachers must consciously clarify their values to understand themselves. Jersild suggests that the crucial question to consider is "What, in my existence as a person, in my relations with others, in my work as a teacher, is of real concern to me, perhaps of ultimate concern to me?" (Jersild, 1955). Bowman renews the call for teachers to become reflective practitioners (Schon, 1987), "to reflect upon themselves with the same intensity that is given to the study of others" (Bowman, 1995). When teachers find themselves in professional contexts that are not especially supportive of forming partnerships with families, their personal qualities and ability to reflect may allow them to break through barriers in relationships. As teachers identify their values, they also make opportunities for parents to consider and specify their own values. In a parent–teacher partnership it is important for both to know themselves and each other, and to know also the areas of agreement and disagreement in their value systems. It is not necessary or desirable for teachers and parents to attempt to convince the other of the rightness of their beliefs. What is desirable is for both to feel comfortable expressing their viewpoints.

As teachers believe in themselves and their abilities to create partnerships with families, they demonstrate a perception of self-efficacy. *Self-efficacy*, defined as an individual's perception of personal competence, will determine how much time will be spent on an activity, how much time will be spent when obstacles are met, and how resilient the individual will be when faced with adversity (Vartuli, 2005). "High teacher self-efficacy relates significantly to increased levels of family involvement in conferences, volunteering, and home tutoring. Teachers with high self-efficacy are more likely to invite families to become involved in the classroom." (Vartuli, 2005, p. 78).

Humility

Another attitude of teachers related both to the concept of partnership and to the new definition of professionalism is *humility*—the ability to wait, be silent, and listen. Teachers who do not make impossible demands on themselves do not expect to immediately understand each question or to have an instant response.

This is not just a pose of hesitancy, but an ability to trust the outcome of the process of communication between individuals that is acquired only when teachers are able to dispense with some professional pretensions and keep truly

FIGURE 7-2 The attitude and behaviors of approachability suggest real partnership.

open minds. This may be called *approachability;* it is demonstrated by behaviors that suggest, "We're all in this together—help me out—what do you think?" (see Figure 7-2). Teachers with humility are able to step outside standard frames of reference and find creative, novel ways to work with families because they are not limited by believing only the traditional methods will work. This allows teachers to take the nondefensive "why not" approach to parent requests, as advocated by Jim Greenman (Greenman, 1993). In this approach parent requests are recognized as legitimate ideas to mull over, rather than eliciting knee-jerk responses that "we just can't do that" or "our policies state" or even an automatic yes. Hesitancy and humility result in thoughtful practices and increased trust from families that teachers are professionals who support empowerment and genuine partnership. The attitude of humility also allows teachers to keep on trying when some attempts to work with families have failed, to move "into new areas not because we know they're going to succeed, but because the element of success might be proportionate to the element of risk" (Fredericks, 1989). The increased feelings of comfort resulting from continual contact with parents may help a teacher to relax and not rush the process.

Compassion

Teachers who can work in a partnership display compassion for themselves and for others. As they attempt to understand parents, they try to realize not just what they are thinking, but also what they may be feeling (see Figure 7-3). Such sensitivity is a first step toward the development of genuine mutual respect.

The ability to **empathize**, to truly try to understand the perspective and emotional responses of another, is a valuable ability for teachers working with families whose life experiences and motivations are often different from their

"Some parents have a hard time letting go."

FIGURE 7-3 When teachers attempt to understand parents' feelings, they are better able to build partnerships.
Used by permission of Keith Larson.

own. Being able to take the perspective of another means, for example, recognizing that there are emotional reasons why parents refuse to leave promptly after saying good-bye to their child, or get upset when their children get dirty, or always criticize the school, or any one of many things that irritate teachers who do not attempt to recognize the family's perspective. Empathy, by its nature, necessitates loosening the boundaries that teachers sometimes create around themselves.

There is no question that teachers will encounter families whose socioeconomic backgrounds, life experiences, values, and **cultural mores** are quite removed from theirs. Differences are guaranteed. While classrooms today reflect the diversity of the larger society, "the composition of the teaching force is becoming more Caucasian and more female" (National Center for Educational Statistics, 1999, in Walker-Dalhouse & Dalhouse, 2001). So most teachers must consciously reach out in genuine attempts to understand life from the point of view of diverse families, a perspective that they recognize is different from their own. At the same time teachers must be mindful that *difference* is not synonymous with *deficit*; it is not the goal to encourage each family to adopt the values of the dominant culture. Compassionate understanding means learning about the other in a spirit of openness and acceptance. Chapter 15 will continue the discussion on specifics of teachers working with diversity and how understanding and acceptance help both teachers and families.

One thing teachers can do is educate themselves about some of the general differences they may find in members of a certain class or ethnic group. For example, studies on differing expectations of lower- and middle-class mothers for their children's behavior and educational achievements, or on styles of family interaction in a particular cultural ethos, are helpful in preparing teachers to recognize the variations in child rearing they will encounter. A useful resource for getting started on raising consciousness about differences that could separate teachers and parent is *Multicultural Issues in Child Care* by Janet Gonzalez-Mena (2000). She reminds us that when teachers meet someone who obviously doesn't move in the same cultural framework that they do, they're jarred. An attempt to understand the ideas of parenting inherent in another's culture will lead to a more compassionate approach. Moreover, just as teachers would not depend solely on textbook descriptions of typical 3-year-old characteristics in teaching their preschoolers, they won't depend on such general knowledge to guide them in understanding parents. As teachers take time to build relationships, to question their own beliefs and biases, to ask more, and to assume less, they open the door so that families feel comfortable in revealing themselves. Families communicate who they are, in particular, to help teachers understand the specific knowledge that will best support that family. And understanding the facts of another's experience is still worlds apart from genuinely attempting to understand what experiences mean to them emotionally. Compassionate teachers attend sensitively to the unique reactions of each parent, no matter what the background.

Something should be added to this consideration of teacher compassion. It is often tempting for teachers to become overwhelmed by the complex needs and situations of some families and fall into the "Oh, isn't it awful" syndrome. These teachers can become too emotionally involved to retain helpful perspectives and move into trying to "fix" things for families. Compassion means the ability to understand that families may need the support and understanding of others while they learn to determine their own needs and seek their own solutions.

Respect for Others

Teachers who move into partnerships with families express a genuine respect for parents, for their position as the most important people in their children's lives, and for their accomplishments in child rearing. They respect the experiences, knowledge, and expertise that each participant brings to the situation. In so doing they validate parents and themselves, finding areas of strength rather than of weakness. They also respect the rights of individual parents to define their own needs for the education and care of their children.

They convey this respect by treating families with dignity as individuals, listening to their needs, questions, and requests. It is too easy for teachers to begin to treat parents as "they" or "the parents," "not as a collection of individuals" (Greenman, 1993). When teachers create a "they," Greenman goes on to say, they usually use the annoying behavior of the least agreeable families to complain about with distant condescension. Leaving behind the "they" and coming to know and respect individual parents and families is a helpful stance for teachers striving for partnership. Teachers must try to find ways to meet the individual needs of parents. They may not always agree, but they still can convey the attitude that it is all right to disagree and that they can still work together.

One teacher describes this attitude as the need to take people seriously:

> Whatever comment or criticism or suggestion a person comes up with, I must assume that it carries that person's individual and cultural perspective and deserves my respect. For example, a parent might say, "If she swears at adults, I want you to smack her face." Then I'd say, "It sounds like you really want her to learn to respect adults. I agree—that's important to me, too. I don't hit children, so maybe we can figure out something we can both agree on." And then we talk. I have to take the lead in finding common ground. (Hoffman, 1997).

The respect becomes mutual as families are encouraged to learn more about the teachers' and school's philosophy. (see Figure 7-4).

FIGURE 7-4 Respect is shown in taking people seriously.

Trustworthiness

Teachers often discuss the concept of being trustworthy for families, so that parents can build a sense of confidence in the choice they have made for their children's education and in those who are caring for their children in their absence. Building trust takes time and effort and is at the heart of comfortable, open communication. It is vital that teachers realize their behaviors can assist in this endeavor or detract from families' ability to trust.

First teachers must consider trust building as a two-way street (File, 2001). The section on families in the NAEYC **code of ethics** describes the first ideal as "to develop relationships of mutual trust with families we serve." As well as program commitment to being trustworthy *to* families, there must be a commitment to establish teachers' sense of trust *in* families. This means that teachers must assume that families generally know what is best for their children, rather than thinking that if they just knew better—as the professional does—they would do things differently. It means setting aside the typical professional mistrust of families and sometimes also setting aside individual strong ideas. It means finding common ground instead of turning differences into battlegrounds, and trusting that parents really care for their children with love that goes beyond our professional concern and commitment.

Trustworthiness also implies complete teacher respect of families' rights to maintain their privacy. Often teachers complain that parents don't tell them what is happening at home, implying that this information is the teacher's right in order to work more effectively with the child in question. In fact, teachers do not need to know all the details of a family's personal life to understand a child; generally it is sufficient to know that a child is under some unusual stress to respond supportively. It is most likely that families do not share specifics of their personal lives precisely because teachers are not careful to indicate to families their complete respect for parents' rights to control what information they choose to share, as well as the confidential way such information would be treated. As teachers gather in the lounge for breaks or in staff meetings for discussion, it is too easy to reveal information casually that ought to be kept purely confidential, between teacher and family, or even to gossip about assumptions rather than facts. Teachers should realize that they are professionally bound to keep information that families have revealed as completely confidential, revealing information to others who need to know only after first gaining permission from the family. Except when the situation involves abuse or neglect, families deserve the right to trustworthy privacy.

Again, the code of ethics defines this principle for teachers:

P.2.9 We shall maintain confidentiality and shall respect the family's right to privacy, refraining from disclosure of confidential information and intrusion into family life. However, when we are concerned about a child's welfare, it is permissible to reveal confidential information to agencies and individuals who may be able to act in the child's interest.

When teachers understand this ethical boundary, they carefully convey to both families and colleagues their adherence to confidentiality. Additionally, teachers should understand that they could be legally liable if evidence of breach of confidentiality were given. When teachers indicate that their relationship is governed by confidence, they often find that parents trust them with information more freely.

To summarize, teachers trying to move into a partnership with parents must work toward the following ideas and attitudes:

1. New image of professional role as partnership.

2. Strong sense of self.

3. Humility.

4. Compassion.

5. Respect for others.

6. Trustworthiness.

■■■ EXTERNAL FACTORS

There are four elements in a partnership between home and school (Swap, in Lueder, 1998):

- Creating two-way communications.

- Enhancing learning at home and at school.

- Providing mutual support.

- Making joint decisions.

All of these can be supported by several other concrete, external factors.

Administrative Support Systems

Support systems are necessary for teachers striving to work with parents. Administrative support and leadership set the tone and atmosphere for a family involvement program. Support for family involvement needs to permeate the program from the top down; without wholehearted administrative belief in the importance of working with families, it will be difficult to convey to parents that their participation is a necessary part of the whole. Support may come in the form of

- A clearly stated philosophy in a parent handbook that values and welcomes the contributions of parents in the educational process.

- Training of staff so they will be knowledgeable in techniques of working with adults.

- Assistance, motivation, and appreciation of staff efforts.

FIGURE 7-5 Administrative support helps teachers create partnerships with families.

- Providing fair compensatory time and staffing arrangements to support efforts.
- Coordinating plans and strategies that emphasize family involvement throughout a school or program.

Such support sanctions and gives power to teachers' efforts (see Figure 7-5).

It is important for administrators to realize that teachers need assistance and support to develop communication skills for working with families. "Without providing teachers with strategies and techniques for working with parents, schools will not move beyond the rhetoric about the need and importance of home–school partnerships to the practice of making them happen" (Brand, 1996). It is sobering to learn from the study *Training for Parent Partnerships: Much More Should be Done* that a majority of states do not require teachers or administrators to study parent involvement or to develop skills in promoting parent involvement (*Young Children*, March 1995). However, recently published standards for degree programs declare that the skills for building family and community relationships are a required part of a college program of study (NAEYC, 2001, 2003). Support and education to develop skills are vital components.

It is possible for teachers to create an atmosphere of partnership and involvement on their own; but when the administration of a school supports and recognizes those efforts, they are far more productive. In some instances the administration actively discourages contact between teachers and families. If teachers choose to remain in such situations, their only recourse may be to work toward convincing the administration of the need to change its stance through (1) the positive experiences and proofs offered by research on the effectiveness of family involvement (see the references at the end of Chapter 4 for such data), (2) using community support and advocacy efforts (such as the NAEYC position statements on family involvement in quality early childhood programs), (3) legislative movements (such as the requirements written into the NCLB legislation for family involvement), and (4) enlisting the efforts of parents to press for their own involvement. It can also be useful to point out to administrators that there are advantages from a commercial viewpoint because working closely with families may improve retention rates! (See this viewpoint expressed in Meservey, 1989.)

Even with administrative support, working with a cross section of families with individual needs, responses, and demands on teachers' time and energy can be stressful. Teachers can benefit from personal support systems, including colleagues and supervisors, that offer the opportunity to recognize and vent feelings of frustration or strain and gain new ideas and perspectives. When teachers are part of working groups that encourage them to try new activities or experiment with new methods for communicating with families, they are more likely to take risks.

Communication Time

One of the most crucial components in the foundation of a parent–teacher partnership is time for teachers and parents to communicate freely together. Communication time with families may be made available by a flexibility in teachers' time options that fits parents' schedules, such as offering evening conferences, prearranged phone conversations, weekend home visits, and early morning coffee discussions. To have this flexibility, teachers should have their "after hours" work compensated. When teachers are allowed compensatory time, this is a tangible indication of administrative support for their efforts. Additional staff members or staggered coverage may be required to cover this compensatory time, as well as to free teachers to talk with parents at the times communication takes place—when children are dropped off and picked up. Because the frequency of casual communication has a direct bearing on the quality of a teacher–parent relationship, it is worthwhile to set up patterns in staffing arrangements and classroom planning and a variety of opportunities that allow teachers the freedom to talk (see Figure 7-6).

Teachers and schools can become advocates for businesses and employers to allow working parents the time to attend conferences and school functions. In some communities the Chamber of Commerce has clearly stated that employers should support any efforts of parents to become involved in their children's education. Such a stance helps ease the problem of parent unavailability. Time may be an expensive commodity, but it is

FIGURE 7-6 Teachers can find time to talk with parents when staffing patterns provide enough staff to watch children while others can be free to talk.

worthwhile to the effort of forming parent–teacher partnerships. The efforts made by various communities to involve employers in partnerships to bring parents into schools can be viewed by visiting the NCREL Web site listed at the end of the chapter.

Variety in Family Involvement

Another factor facilitating parent–teacher partnerships is to offer a variety of forms of family involvement and communication. Ames (1995) found that parental involvement increased as communication from the classroom was continual and varied. A program reflects its understanding and responsiveness to the various needs of families by allowing parents to choose when, where, and how to participate. Flexibility in timing increases the variety. You will recall from Chapter 4 that families may be involved in a continuum of methods ranging from low involvement to high involvement. Offering a variety of ways of being involved in a school allows families to participate at a level that meets their current needs. A program ready to meet individual needs, concerns, and interests indicates respect for parents and their value within the program.

Someone within each program must take the time to find out what parents need and want, as well as what they have to offer and are willing to share (see Resource Files, Chapter 12, and Surveys, Chapter 13), and evaluate the effectiveness of various methods of involvement. Asking parents for their evaluative feedback on particular plans, and using suggestion boxes or other formats to encourage parent ideas about the program facets that would be helpful to them, persuades parents to see the school as responsive to their needs. Such variety in family involvement opportunities allows parents to accept what is useful and reject what does not match their needs.

Epstein (1995) suggests a framework of six types of involvement for parents, including parenting, communicating, volunteering, supporting learning at home, decision making, and collaborating with the community. Her emphasis also is on considering the challenges to teachers for facilitating each of the kinds of involvement and in redefining the practices available for parents. This is a reminder to provide variety not only in forms of involvement but also in practices responsive to parents' circumstances.

Information

For a constructive parent–teacher partnership, clear understanding and knowledge of what is expected or possible in any program are required. Parents who clearly understand their responsibilities and obligations in a school are more comfortable. Routine encounters such as conferences and home visits will not generate apprehension if parents are familiar with the procedures and their role in them.

Many schools offer this information to families in the form of a parent handbook, which is discussed as a parent receives orientation information and may be referred to later. Administrators and teachers understand that much that is presented orally may later be forgotten, so the reinforcement of written material is essential (see Figure 7-7). A parent handbook should define the general philosophy and services of a program as well as the specific philosophy concerning family involvement, so parents understand both the work of a school and how they can be involved. Information is needed regarding a program's policies that concern parents, such as admission requirements, the daily schedule, hours and fees, attendance policies, late pickup policies, health and safety regulations, and children's celebrations. Care must be taken to examine the center's policies to ensure that they match the realities of today's families (Copeland & McCreedy, 1997). Many handbooks include general information on the developmental characteristics of children and ways parents can help nurture development.

A handbook should also describe the methods that teaching staff use in the classroom and in reporting a child's progress, lists of supplies parents may need, and ways parents may be (or are obliged to be) involved in a center's activities. Some well-chosen examples illustrating parent roles can be added. Other information might include dates of scheduled meetings; names and phone numbers of parent advisory committee members; and facilities for parents in the school, such as bulletin boards or a parent lounge. Clear statements about when the school can help parents are useful. It is important that both

FIGURE 7-7 Parent handbooks must be written to meet parents' reading and language abilities.

limitations and choices for parents be explicit, as well as clear mechanisms for families who wish to raise concerns. It is also important, in the handbook as well as in personal communication, to convey the absolute confidentiality of all communication between families and staff.

> We welcome parents to enlarge the children's world by sharing an interest (job-related or hobby) or ethnic or religious traditions. Last year two parents helped us learn a Hanukkah song. Another parent helped us prepare a simple Vietnamese dish. A truck driver father brought his truck to school, and the mother of a new baby let us look at the baby—toes and all! Please come—what experience can you bring us? At the last parent work night, some of our handy parents fixed three broken tricycles and two limbless dolls. And some of our less handy parents helped us organize the housekeeping area. Please come on the next scheduled night.

In order not to miss important information when developing a parent handbook, it is helpful to ask families whose children are presently in the school what they would like to have been told before their children started, and to ask teachers what they would like to tell parents. The handbook needs to be concise, attractive, on a basic reading level, and clearly organized. It must be translated into every language represented by the school's population. Much of the information will be reinforced later in newsletters and personal conversation, but it is helpful initially to answer all possible questions for parents, to help them feel comfortable in the new relationship without the concern that there may be surprises forthcoming. A parent handbook is also a concrete example of administrative support for parent involvement.

See Figure 7-8 for evidence of parents wanting information, contact, and specifics about how they can help. Figure 7-9 lists the seven elements common in successful family involvement programs.

What Parents Want to Know

Parents Want to Belong
  —I want to belong.
  —Welcome me to the school; don't shut me out.
  —Invite me to school; take the initiative.
  —Tell me how I can participate in school activities.
  —I would like to be a member of an advisory council or parent involvement committee.

Parents Want Teacher Contact
  —I would like my children's teachers to call me.
  —Because I work, I need evening teacher conferences.
  —Let me know what my children are studying.
  —I want to meet the teachers at least once a month.
  —Keep communications clear, brief, simple, not overly technical.
  —Contact me about good news, too, not only about problems.

Parents Want Information
  —Tell me the philosophy of the school, the channels of authority, and the general goals of each subject studied.
  —Tell me the best time to call the teachers, the names of the staff, and their telephone numbers.
  —Send me a weekly or monthly newsletter that lists school events, community resources, and enrichment programs.
  —I would appreciate parent education workshops.

Parents Want to Help
  —Give me ideas about how to complement what my children are learning in school.
  —What are your expectations of my children?
  —What can I do to help?

Parents Want Teachers to Love Their Children
  —Do something to make my children feel good about themselves.
  —Remind yourselves that you are an important influence in children's lives.
  —If I complain about something, don't "take it out" on my children.
  —Avoid stereotyping children and families.
  —Care about my children.

FIGURE 7-8 Responses to informal surveys expressing what parents would like to say to teachers and their needs for specific information.

Seven Elements Common to Successful Family Involvement Programs

1. Written policies and a statement that identifies parent involvement as vital.

2. Administrative support in the form of funds, space and equipment, and personnel.

3. Training for staff and parents.

4. Partnership approach—joint planning and goal setting, a sense of ownership.

5. Two-way communication.

6. Networking with other programs to share information and resources.

7. Evaluation of effectiveness of parent involvement efforts.

FIGURE 7-9 Seven elements common to successful family involvement programs.

Family-Friendly Environments

School and program staff should take the time to look around the building with the perspective of a rushed parent or a tired grandmother. Does the environment suggest that families are part of the school and should linger for conversation, or does it suggest a coldly efficient institution where families are not meant to stay? The example of the excellent schools and infant–toddler centers in Reggio Emilia in Italy is instructive here. Each school is created with a central piazza or meeting area, with comfortable seating for adults, and interesting things for both adults and children to look at. With plants, attractive and intriguing displays of children's work, and photos, the environment welcomes families for relaxed greeting and transition times with children and teachers, exchange of information, and mutual enjoyment. When there are pictures and words posted about children, their families, and the teachers who work in the school, the implicit message is one of welcome and the importance of all participants. When children's classrooms have areas with couches or stuffed chairs, plants, and soft lighting, tired parents may linger for conversation and opportunities to watch the goings-on.

An interesting suggestion from Margie Carter (1999) is to delay the barrage of required paperwork and forms to be completed when families enroll in the center. Instead, she suggests first offering simple pages to fill out as a family, to become part of a classroom family book. With photos, children's drawings, writing, or dictated words, the child's page might include his or her name and birthday and things like

- What I look like.

- Something I love to do.

- How I got my name.
- What makes me happy.

The family page could include spaces for

- Who's in our family.
- Something special about each person in our family.
- Something we like about where we live.
- A favorite family dish.
- A favorite story we tell in our family.

These pages could be added to the classroom family book, kept close to the couch or wherever families relax in the classroom. Such a method includes families from the start, creates a feeling of community, and sends nonverbal positive messages to children and their families of welcome and acceptance of all.

Communication Skills

Teachers attempting to create constructive partnerships with families need to develop their communication skills. Many teachers are fortunate to have opportunities to speak with parents frequently. However, frequency of communication does not guarantee increased understanding or improved relationships. Unless teachers are aware of different styles and purposes of communication, of how to communicate verbally and nonverbally, to listen and convey attentive caring, and to interpret messages from parents, miscommunication can create real barriers to a partnership (see Figure 7-10).

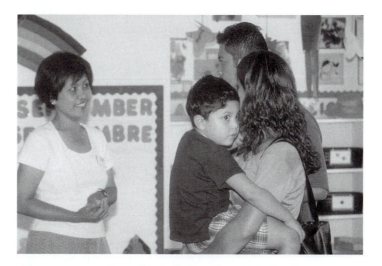

FIGURE 7-10 A teacher's communication style is important in establishing a comfortable relationship.

Some communication styles are almost certain to produce defensiveness: ordering, warning, blaming, advising, extensive questioning, and lecturing. Effective teachers learn to avoid these ways of talking. In addition, teachers should practice skills of listening and interpreting, of reading the behaviors in others that indicate how communication is causing them to feel.

Four basic communication styles have been identified, each carrying its own amount of risk and value in sharing information (Flake-Hobson & Swick, 1979):

REFLECTIONS FOR JOURNAL ENTRIES

If you are working or doing student teaching in a school or center, consider which of these external factors seem to be present to support the work of teachers with families. Can you also identify external factors that could be improved? What could be a starting step in moving toward improving these?

Style I

The superficial style ("What a pretty dress you've made!") uses informal small talk to get to know others on an information basis. There is little risk involved, but little beyond "ice-breaking" is accomplished in a relationship.

Style II

The command style ("Why are you not firmer about bedtime?") is riskier because the authoritative tone that can be used effectively in some group situations often creates defensive reactions in an individual, providing little personal or factual information.

Style III

The intellectual style ("Research studies indicate that the style of maternal interaction is definitely correlated with cognitive abilities and educational achievement.") is used to convey objective information and is therefore low-risk, though excessive use of this style can create the barrier of too impersonal a relationship.

Style IV

The caring style ("I am concerned about Ramon. He frequently seems lonely. I wonder if his language understanding is keeping him apart.") openly shares personal information. The caring style requires the use of four sets of skills: listening, sharing self-information, establishing shared meaning through clarifying information received and sent, and making a conscious commitment to care for the self and others that requires the individual to risk self in relationships (Flake-Hobson & Swick, 1979).

Schon (1987) distinguishes two models of interpersonal communication, based on different governing values. Model I values are designed to "achieve the objective as *I* see it." The communication strategies used here are based on assumptions such as "Interpersonal interactions are win–lose games" and "Be rational," in the sense of using cool reason to persuade others, to exercise control over the other. Such a stance decreases effective communication.

Instead Schon advocates using Model II, with assumptions that aim to create a world in which people can exchange valid information, even about difficult or sensitive concerns. Model II permits joint control of communication and public sharing of internal dilemmas. Some of the advice offered by Schon to those who would open their communication toward Model II includes these ideas:

- Do not try to be complete or perfect.
- Do not hesitate to correct what you say after you've thought about it.
- After stating a position, invite others to correct or challenge it.
- Respond to the meanings that you gather from what the other says and expresses through nonverbal language.
- Don't feel compelled to have an answer—leave the subject open.

Lee Canter, who has developed a program on communication skills for teachers (Techniques for Positive Parent Relationships) suggests that teachers who can communicate their concern for a child will be most effective in eliciting family support (Canter, 1989). He suggests also that teachers use assertive communication skills that do not apologize, minimize, or belittle the teachers' abilities and concerns.

With experience, teachers will discover that some words convey different meanings to some families, and they will become more precise in their statements and descriptions. Teachers recognizing the social and cultural experiences of their listeners make adaptations accordingly and strive for unambiguous, descriptive words with no emotionally loaded connotations. They avoid professional jargon that may alienate or intimidate—words like *cognitive, fine motor, affective*. They paraphrase a parent's statements and their own interpretations—"What I hear you saying is"—to elicit genuine feedback from the parents to verify their understanding. They focus on parents' statements or questions to clarify their primary issues—"I'm confused about . . ."; "Could you explain that problem again, please?" They use verbal reinforcers—"I see," "Yes," "Mm," or the parent's name—to show they are listening and following what a parent has to say. They practice listening at least 50 percent of the time in discussion or conferences with parents. They realize that open-ended attempts to obtain more information—"Let's talk about that," "I'm wondering about . . ."—are more effective than "who," "what," "how," and "when" questions that may threaten the parent. They summarize for parents the ideas discussed.

Teachers need to remember that the verbal message they send accounts for only a small fraction of communication between people. Mehrabian claims that facial expressions have the greatest impact on the receiver (55 % of the message) and that the impact of voice tone is next (38 % of the message), leaving only 7 % delivered by words alone. What's more, in situations in which the sender's facial expression is inconsistent with the words (such as when a teacher says "I'm glad you could come for this conference," but her face shows apprehension or indifference), the facial expression will prevail and determine the impact of the total message (Mehrabian, 1981).

Eye contact plays an important role in opening or closing channels of communication. Looking at the partner in communication conveys the physical impression of listening, or of seeking feedback, or desire for the other's speech. Looking away may indicate a desire to avoid contact or hide some aspect of inner feelings, or an attempt to process difficult ideas. (Although this generalization about eye contact may often be true, keep in mind that cultural factors affect the amount of eye contact offered in communication.)

Because of the intensity of the emotional bond between parents and their children, teachers may notice that tears are often close to the surface in both fathers and mothers when the conversation touches important issues, including very positive issues. Many parents are uncomfortable with this display of emotion and look away to hide the tears. Teachers sensitive to the amount of eye contact offered by parents may be able to perceive when their communication is too painful or too difficult and can alter the message accordingly. Teachers who realize how closely their own eye contact conveys evidence of listening and acceptance can make conscious attempts to improve this aspect of communication.

Other nonverbal communication for teachers to monitor in themselves and others that may produce effects of distance and discomfort include leaning toward (or away from) the other person; body language that conveys aggressive or closed stances; tone of voice similar to the other person; occasional head-nodding to indicate attention and approval; occasional gestures; smiles; and speech errors or higher speech rates that can indicate anxiety and uncertainty. Even a teacher's style of dress may send a message that could help or hurt the development of rapport.

Such nonverbal cues are sometimes missed if the receiver is inexperienced, temporarily not paying attention, preoccupied with his own internal messages, or from another culture where cues may have different meanings. People are likely to base their response to messages on their perception of the source rather than on the message content. Therefore, a prerequisite for effective communication is to relate to one another as individuals and avoid stereotyping. (For further exploration of communication techniques the student is encouraged to refer to Gamble & Gamble, 1996, and Samovar & Porter, 1995).

Here is a final word to all teachers who are anxious to start developing family–teacher partnerships. Family–teacher relationships, as we have seen, are complex things, uniting two sets of internal experiences, needs, and responses with two sets of external circumstances. Teachers who expect total success will be disappointed if they measure complete success as full participation by every parent. Parents have unique responses to family involvement opportunities; some families are reached in one way, others in another. And some may be reached at another time, after one teacher's efforts have long seemed to bear no result. So the measure of success lies not in the numbers responding to any initiative, but in the quality of interaction; not in total agreement, but in continuing dialogue. Teachers will discover they are in long-term relationships with families. When children are in a school for a number of years, family members and teachers may learn to recognize each other informally before a child is actually in a particular teacher's classroom and maintain ties of friendship after a child moves on to the next classroom. Such extended contact allows the growth of comfort and communication, as well as the acceptance of ideas. The teacher realizing this is less likely to become frustrated and abandon all attempts.

SUMMARY

Concrete steps can be taken and skills can be developed to help lay foundations for parent–teacher partnerships:

1. Administrative support to provide collaborative philosophy and tangible assistance with staffing arrangements and time provisions; emotional support systems for teachers.

2. Time, created by allowing teachers to interact with parents at crucial points in the workday and compensating them for offering flexible options for parent involvement beyond normal working hours.

3. A variety of forms of family involvement, allowing parents to select where, when, and how to participate.

4. Clear explanations of policies, expectations, and openness to welcome families into the educational program.

5. Family-friendly environments.

6. Developing and practicing effective communication skills.

For teachers like Jane Briscoe, who want to create partnerships with families, these are some starting places. A variety of techniques to involve parents will be explored in Section III.

STUDENT ACTIVITIES FOR FURTHER STUDY

1. Contact several schools in your community. Ask for copies of handbooks or printed materials for families. Examine the material to discover any stated or implied philosophies of working (or not working) with families.

2. With your classmates, work on creating a parent handbook that clearly conveys information parents want to know and the attitude of welcoming

families into specific participations. (Each student might take on a segment after the necessary information and format have been decided.)

3. With your classmates, generate a list of words such as those discussed on page 239 that might convey different meanings depending on the cultural or environmental experiences of the receiver.

4. Imagine you are a teacher beginning employment at a school or early childhood program. What kinds of guidance, support, and training do you feel you need to become comfortable and capable in areas of working with families? How might you go about getting this assistance? What could you ask for from a supervisor? What questions might you ask a more experienced colleague?

5. When possible, observe a teacher you feel works well with families. What personality characteristics and behaviors do you see? What do you notice regarding the teacher's nonverbal communication?

CASE STUDY

Tom Bradford is a second-year teacher in first grade. As he reflected on his experiences in working with families during his first year, he felt dissatisfied. Some parents responded to his overtures to communicate regularly with him via e-mail, and others never responded to any phone call or newsletter that he sent. The number of absences at PTA meetings had puzzled him. Some parents had not even come to the required parent–teacher conference in January. He'd like to establish better communication with his families this year and wonders if he'll have a better group of parents to work with. His colleague—the other first grade teacher—seemed to have better success than he did.

1. What personal attitudes should Tom consider to create the atmosphere of welcoming communication with families?

2. What questions might he ask the other first grade teacher to learn how she achieved her greater success in building relationships?

3. What techniques or strategies might help Tom set the tone for forming partnerships?

4. What might Tom discuss with his supervisor in terms of necessary supports for his work with families?

REVIEW QUESTIONS

1. Identify three out of six attitudes of teachers conducive to forming a partnership with families.

2. List six external factors important in laying the foundations for partnerships with families.

SUGGESTIONS FOR FURTHER READING

Bloom, P., Eisenberg, P., & Eisenberg, E. (2003, Spring/Summer). Reshaping early childhood programs to be more family responsive. *America's Family Support Magazine,* 36–38.

Braum, L., & Swap, S. (1987). *Building home school partnerships with America's changing families.* Boston: Wheelock College Center for Parenting Studies.

Buffin, L. (2001, January/February). Relationships in child care settings: Becoming fully human (or what matters most). *Child Care Information Exchange,* 16–18.

Coleman, M., & Wallinga, C. (1999/2000). Teacher training in family involvement: An interpersonal approach. *Childhood Education, 76*(2), 76–81.

Davies, D. (1991). Schools reaching out: Family, school, and community partnership for student success. *Phi Delta Kappan, 72*(5), 376–382.

Davis, C., & Yang, A. (2005). *Parents and teachers working together.* Turners Falls, MA: Northeast Foundation for Children.

Decker, C. A., & Decker, J. R. (2000). *Planning and administering early childhood programs* (7th ed.). Columbus: Charles E. Merrill [information on parent handbooks].

Eldridge, D. (2001). Parent involvement: It's worth the effort. *Young Children, 56*(4), 65–69.

Elkind, D. (1995, September). School and family in the postmodern world. *Phi Delta Kappan,* 8–14.

Hunt, D. E. (1987). *Beginning with ourselves in practice, theory, and human affairs.* Cambridge, MA: Brookline Books, Inc.

Kasting, A. (1994). Respect, responsibility and reciprocity: The 3 R's of parent involvement. *Childhood Education, 70*(3), 146–150.

Lueder, D. (1998). *Creating partnerships with parents: An educator's guide.* Lancaster, PA: Technomic Publishing.

Powell, D. (1991). How schools support families: Critical policy tensions. *The Elementary School Journal, 91,* 307–319.

Powers, J. (2005). *Parent-friendly early learning: Tips and strategies for working well with families.* St. Paul, MN: Redleaf Press.

Rosenthal, D., & Sawyers, J. (1996). Building successful home/school partnerships: Strategies for parent support and involvement. *Childhood Education, 72*(4), 194–200.

Stamp, L., & Groves, M. (1994). Strengthening the ethic of care: Planning and supporting family involvement. *Dimensions of Early Childhood, 22*(2), 5–9.

Stone, J. G. (1987). *Teacher–parent relationships.* Washington, DC: NAEYC.

U.S. Department of Education. (1996). *Reaching all families: Creating family-friendly schools.* Washington, DC: Author.

REFERENCES

Ames, C. (1995). *Teachers' school-to-home communications and parent involvement.* Report #28. East Lansing, MI: Michigan State Univ.

Baker, A., & Manfredi/Petitt, L. (2004). *Relationships, the heart of quality care: Creating community among adults in early care settings.* Washington, DC: NAEYC.

Bowman, B. (1995). The professional development challenge: Supporting young children and families. *Young Children, 51*(1), 30–34.

Brand, S. (1996). Making parent involvement a reality: Helping teachers develop partnerships with parents. *Young Children, 51*(2), 76–81.

Canter, L. (1989, January). How to speak so parents will listen. *Teaching K–8,* 34–36.

Carter, M. (1999). Developing meaningful relationships with families. *Child Care Information Exchange, 11/99,* 63–65.

Copeland, M. L., & McCreedy, B. (1997). Creating family-friendly policies—Are child care center policies in line with current family realities? *Child Care Information Exchange, 113,* 7–14.

Epstein, J. (1995, May). School/family/community partnerships: Caring for the children we share. *Phi Delta Kappan,* 701–712.

File, N. (2001). Family–professional partnerships: Practice that matches philosophy. *Young Children, 56*(4), 70–74.

Flake-Hobson, C., & Swick, K. J. (1979). Communication strategies for parents and teachers or how to say what you mean. *Dimensions, 7*(4), 112–115.

Fredericks, A. D. (1989, March). Step out to draw them in. *Teaching K–8,* 22–24.

Gamble, T., & Gamble, M. (1996). *Communication works* (5th ed.). New York: McGraw-Hill.

Gonzalez-Mena, J. (2000). *Multicultural issues in child care* (3rd ed.). Mountain View, CA: Mayfield.

Greenman, J. (1993). Places for childhoods include parents, too. *Child Care Information Exchange, 3/93,* 11–14.

Hoffman, E. (1997). *Starting small: Teaching tolerance in preschool and the early grades.* Montgomery, AL: Southern Poverty Law Center.

Jersild, A. T. (1955). *When teachers face themselves.* New York: Bureau of Publications, Teachers College, Columbia University.

Mehrabian, A. (1981). *Silent messages: Implicit communication of emotions and attitudes* (2nd ed.). Belmont, CA: Wadsworth.

Meservey, L. D. (1989, June). Handle with care: Strategies for retaining children in your program. *Child Care Information Exchange,* 21–24.

NAEYC. (1995). Professional preparation and family involvement. *Young Children, 50*(3), 9.

NAEYC. (2001). NAEYC standards for early childhood professional preparation for initial licensure programs. Available at http://www.naeyc.org.

———. (2003). NAEYC standards for early childhood professional preparation for associate degree programs. Available at http://www.naeyc.org.

Samovar, L., & Porter, R. (1995). *Communication between cultures.* Belmont, CA: Wadsworth.

Schon, D. (1987). *Educating the reflective practitioner.* San Francisco: Jossey-Bass.

Schorr, L. (1997). *Common purpose: Strengthening families and neighborhoods to rebuild America.* New York: Doubleday.

Vartuli, S. (2005). Beliefs: The heart of teaching. *Young Children 60*(5), 76–85.

Walker-Dalhouse, D., & Dalhouse, A. (2001). Parent–school relations: Communicating more effectively with African American parents. *Young Children,* 56(4), 75–80.

HELPFUL WEB SITES

http://www.naeyc.org
> Visit this site for more on the code of ethics and confidentiality.

http://www.ecrp.uiuc.edu
> An Internet journal on the development, care, and education of young children.

http://www.ed.gov
> The site of the U.S. Department of Education; here you can find much information about involving families in their children's education.

http://www.ncrel.org
> The site of the North Central Regional Educational Laboratory offers information about parent involvement.

Additional resources for this chapter can be found on the Online Companion to accompany this text at www.earlychilded.delmar.com. This supplemental material includes frequently asked questions; chapter outlines to be used as study guides; scenarios that both encourage large and small group discussions and provoke new thoughts and ideas; and chapter resources, including chapter summaries, interactive questions, Web links, and Web activities. In addition, forms from the text are available for download.

"Excellent communication skills. Poor choice of words."

SECTION III

METHODS FOR DEVELOPING PARTNERSHIPS

Now that we have examined the importance and challenges of working with families, it is time to consider the various methods teachers can use to develop communication and interaction with families.

There are a variety of techniques, and teachers should probably use a wide repertoire of methods to adapt to individual needs and personality preferences. Chapter 8 describes the process for establishing relationships with parents and children as they begin a program, helping them with separation difficulties. Chapter 9 discusses a number of informal techniques for communicating with families, such as newsletters, telephone calls, and bulletin boards. Chapter 10 takes teachers through steps in conducting effective parent conferences. Chapter 11 explores the topic of home visits. Chapter 12 considers involving families in the classroom. Chapter 13 describes several approaches to parent education. And Chapter 14 identifies ways that teachers and families work effectively together within the larger community. All of these separate topics are important facets to study as teachers develop their skills for communicating with families.

CHAPTER 8

At the Beginning with Parents and Children

OBJECTIVES

After reading this chapter, you should be able to:

1 Identify several steps helpful in establishing a relationship prior to the child's entrance into the classroom.
2 Discuss benefits associated with each step.
3 Discuss strategies associated with each step.
4 Describe the separation experience for children and parents, and discuss a teacher's role.

There is nothing more exciting and more touched with nervousness than children's first days in early education programs. Children face the challenge of leaving the security of parents and home and moving into the company of a group of peers, new routines and activities, and a relationship with a new adult. Families experience ambivalence of marking another milestone of development in their children's lives, insecurities regarding the decision they have made about the program, and the uncertainties of their own roles in helping their children move into an educational program. Teachers have the excitement of meeting new children and families and the challenge of making sure all the relationships get off on the right foot. Understanding the normal separation process and being able to support both parents and children through it is crucial for teachers in beginning the formation of trust and communication that will lay foundations for relationships. This chapter considers initial steps to take in establishing a partnership between home and school, and between parent, teacher, and child.

INITIAL CONTACT BETWEEN TEACHER, PARENT, AND CHILD

First impressions can have lasting significance. Early attitudes and behavior patterns will determine later limitations on a relationship or what direction it will take. Families and teachers who begin working together with particular expectations and understandings are likely to continue in that mode. Because it is often difficult to change patterns or behaviors once they have become habitual, it is important to involve teachers, parents, and children in a program of gradual orientation, information exchange, and increasing familiarity. No matter what children's ages, new school experiences are crucial steps for them. If these steps are facilitated by the adults around them, it is to the children's benefit, and therefore indirectly to the benefit of the adults as well. Between the time when parents first contact a school and the time when their child finally settles in is an important period when teachers have the opportunity to lay the foundations for successful family involvement. There are several purposes for an orientation process:

- To make a child's transition to school as easy and pleasant as possible.
- To demonstrate to families that they are welcome in the educational program and can learn to feel comfortable there.
- To help parents understand the school's goals and practices.
- To give teachers a chance to learn from parents about a child and the family situation.

Whether a child is entering a family child care home, an early childhood or Head Start center, a school that includes children with special needs, a new after-school care program, or a new elementary school classroom, the beginnings are still critical in establishing comfortable communication and patterns of partnership. In this chapter we will consider some ideas to involve families as Connie Martinez first meets Sylvia Ashley and Ricky. Although this describes the situation in a child care program for preschoolers, teachers who work with older or younger children will find principles they can modify to their situation. In any situation, time and family circumstances may dictate modification of these ideas, but teachers striving for effective relationships with parents and children will see them as a goal toward which to work.

Choosing a School

The first contact between families and a school or center is generally initiated by parents in their search for an appropriate facility for their child's care. (An obvious exception to this is when children are assigned to a particular school in a school district. Here parents often have no choice in the matter, and it is up to the school and teacher to give families appropriate welcome and information about the school and plans for the year so that parents can be pleased with an assignment in which they had no choice. However, with the NCLB legislation, parents in many more school districts and communities are finding themselves able to make choices.) The school, usually represented by the director or principal, has the dual responsibility of encouraging families to make the most appropriate educational choices for their children and sharing information about the school's philosophies and practices so parents can see if this particular school matches their needs. Margie Carter (1999) suggests that in initial phone calls or during tours of the center, the focus should be on the family and what they want for their child. Thus the initial conversations focus on relationships instead of taking care of pure business and lay the foundation for ongoing partnerships. Information concerning parental responsibilities and opportunities for participation should be included at this time as well.

In selecting a school or program for the early years, parents need to consider more than the usual consumer issues of convenience and cost. If this is their first experience in early childhood education, they may not yet be aware of the variations in educational goals and practices, licensing requirements, discipline practices, parental rights and involvement, and the like that exist in preschools within any community, as well as the variety of choices that may exist within their school system. Some child advocacy groups and schools offer parents a guide for questions and a checklist for observations to emphasize their key role in making this decision. Recent information, however, indicates that parents seem to make their choices less on the basis of these resources, and more on how parents' feelings about the program most closely match their own construct of what a good program for their child would look like (Zinzeleta & Little, 1997). In many cases parents feel panicky about finding care for their children in time to begin employment, and they are willing to assume the best rather than closely examining and evaluating situations. When they are driven by desperation or lack of knowledge or money, many parents are quick to accept the unacceptable. (The task of early education programs is to give families the information they need to make thoughtful decisions, and encourage them to see their responsibility in making them. See Figure 8-1.)

Programs also have a responsibility to try to understand families' needs and values. NAEYC has developed four brochures to help parents consider **developmentally appropriate programs**: *A Caring Place for Your Toddler* (#509); *A Good Preschool for Your Child* (#517); *A Good Kindergarten for Your Child* (#524); and *A Good Primary School for Your Child* (#579). Another good resource is *Child Care That Works* by E. and M. Cochran (1997). See also the Web sites listed at the end of the chapter.

In many programs parents are invited to observe a teacher in action with her present class before deciding whether to enroll their children. Such a practice sends two clear messages to parents: (1) the school respects their judgment and obligation to know exactly what arrangements they are making for their children; and (2) the school is proud of what it does and wants parents to see it for themselves. Families are justified in being suspicious of a center where such visiting is not encouraged or allowed.

It is preferable to enroll a child whose parents have carefully considered the issues important to them and their child, matched them with all the

SAMPLE GUIDE FOR PARENTS

THE STAFF	YES	NO
Are staff members friendly and enthusiastic?		
Do staff members seem to like and relate well to the children and to each other?		
Are staff members required to have special training in child care?		
Is there a staff in-service training program and other opportunities for continuous skill development?		
Are parent conferences held regularly?		
Do staff members welcome questions and inquiry?		

THE PROGRAM	YES	NO
Are teachers required to make daily lesson plans?		
Is the daily schedule posted?		
Is the program schedule balanced between active and quiet periods?		
Are there varieties of materials and equipment ready for use and accessible to children, both indoors and out?		
Do children have choices about activities?		
Do the activities foster the children's physical, social, intellectual, and emotional growth?		
Do the children know what to do?		
Do the children receive individual attention from the caregivers?		
Does the center have a policy on discipline? Do you agree with it?		
Are records kept about children and their development?		
Are snacks and meals nutritious and well-balanced, with menus posted?		
Are the parents linked to the daily life of the program?		

(continues)

(continued)

THE PHYSICAL SETTING   **YES**   **NO**

Are there comfortable, relaxed areas for
resting and naps?

Is the center bright, clean, comfortable?

Are the outdoor and indoor areas safe and
free from hazards?

Is there enough space for free, easy movement?

Does the setting allow for both group and
individual activities?

Does it provide possibilities for privacy?

Is there appropriate, clean equipment for
different age groups?

THE PHYSICAL SETTING   **YES**   **NO**

Quality care provides

- A caring, pleasant atmosphere.

- Care by an adequate number of well-
  trained, nurturing, and affectionate
  caregivers.

- A program that responds to each child as an
  individual.

- Experiences that facilitate exploring, skill
  development, and learning.

- Support for, communication with, and
  involvement of parents.

Consider what is best for your child. If you are not satisfied with
the care found, continue your search. You are the parent: The
choice is up to you.

—Adapted from Child Care Resources, Inc., Charlotte, N.C.

---

available options, and chosen a particular school on the basis of meeting needs,
rather than parents who made a hasty decision based on whether they have to
cross traffic to reach the parking lot. Too many decisions are based on cost
alone. Schools for young children have a responsibility to help families realize
the full extent of their decision-making role. Once parents choose a school,
their next contact moves beyond the director or principal as general spokesper-
son to meeting the specific teacher(s) with whom their child will begin.

FIGURE 8-1 The school's obligation is to give families the information they need to make thoughtful decisions about their child's education.

Let's look at the beginning for Sylvia Ashley and Ricky.

In Sylvia Ashley's case, social services had suggested the center for Ricky, and Sylvia went to look it over and talk to the director. As always, she had Ricky with her. "We're delighted that Ricky will be entering our school, Mrs. Ashley. Since he'll be entering our group of 3-year-olds, let me take you down to meet Connie Martinez, our lead teacher in that class. Then you two can find a convenient time to get further acquainted."

First Encounter—Teachers and Parents

The first conversation between parents and a teacher is best scheduled when parents can come without their child. Parents will be free to talk without concern for their child's response in a new situation, and a teacher can concentrate on helping parents become comfortable without her attention divided between adults and child.

Sylvia had told Connie Martinez that she had no one to leave Ricky with, so Connie was not surprised when Ricky walked in with his mother. Connie got two puzzles, a book, crayons, and blank paper and helped him settle in a corner distant enough that he could see his mother but not overhear the conversation. As

Connie thought about this later, she realized it was the first time she'd ever conducted the first conversation with the child present. It certainly was far from ideal, but she'd at least had some time to talk freely with this new mother.

This first meeting has several purposes. One is to permit a parent to share initial information about an entering child. Many schools ask families to fill in a questionnaire about their child's personal and social history. Parents may fill this out at home and bring it to the meeting. In practice, if teachers and parents talk their way through a completed questionnaire, parents often supply additional information in a more easily remembered way. Here are some sample questions teachers might like to ask parents:

- What are you most proud of about your child?
- What worries or concerns you about your child?
- What is your child's favorite place to play?
- What roles does your child frequently engage in during play?
- What activities do you most like to share with your child?
- Is there a favorite friend or relative your child might talk about, real or imaginary?
- What does your child do when he is upset, and how is he best comforted?
- Does your child have fears or worries that we should be aware of?
- Is there something that your child has just learned that is important to her?
- What would you like your child to get out of this year's program?
- Does your child have any medical conditions we should be aware of?

As parents talk, teachers can gain an impression of the relationship between parent and child, of how a child has reacted to other new situations, and of how parents feel about enrolling their child in the program (see Figure 8-2). This also establishes a precedent of cooperation, of sharing information, with families making important contributions and teachers listening. Teachers can also use this opportunity to acquire family resource information so they can plan for involving families in the classroom. When asking questions, teachers must let parents know how this information will be used and assure parents of the confidentiality of their communication.

Many ideas discussed in this initial conversation may be helpful in increasing a new child's comfort in the first days in school:

"I see here that you mentioned Ricky likes to sleep with a favorite teddy bear. Do you suppose you could bring that along to leave in

FIGURE 8-2 When teachers have specific information about children, they can help them get off to a happy start.

his cubby for nap time? It might feel good to have something so familiar. Pictures of you and his brother to put in his cubby might help, too."

This first meeting allows parents to ask specific questions about the classroom:

SAMPLE QUESTIONNAIRE

INFORMATION ON ROUTINES

Eating

As a rule, is your child's appetite excellent, good, fair, or poor?

Does your child eat alone or with the family?

List your child's favorite foods:

List foods that your child especially dislikes:

Sleeping

Approximate time your child goes to bed:

Approximate time your child wakes in morning:

Your child's attitude at bedtime:

Usual activities before your child goes to bed:

(continues)

(continued)

Elimination

At what age was training started for

Bowel control _____ Response to training

Bladder control _____ Response to training

What words does your child use when stating the need for elimination?

OTHER INFORMATION

What do you enjoy most about your child?

How does your child usually react to new situations?

What activities does your family enjoy most?

Has your child been separated from either parent for a long period? If so, how did your child react?

What things repeatedly cause conflict between parents and children in your family?

Is your child happy playing alone?

List the ages and genders of your child's most frequent playmates:

Your child's favorite activities:

"Yes, there are four other boys who have entered the classroom quite recently, so he won't be the only new one."

"Well, our morning snack is really a hot breakfast, served about 9:00 each day, so if he doesn't eat much in the early morning at home he won't have to wait too long."

Parents can help prepare their child for becoming comfortable in the classroom if they have accurate knowledge about what will happen and what to expect. The first meeting also allows parents and teachers an early chance to know each other on a one-to-one basis.

"You're going back to school—good for you! That's great. You'll certainly be busy, but I'll bet you'll find it's worth it when it's all over. I'm taking some classes at night, too, so we can complain about it together."

This is a good time to establish clearly what teachers and parents will call each other. If this subject is never discussed forthrightly, there is often awkwardness, with the result that neither calls the other anything:

> "Most of the parents call me Connie, though the children call me Miss Martinez. Then may I also call you Sylvia? Are you comfortable with that? I'm just more comfortable with first names."

During this time a teacher can inform parents about the rest of the orientation schedule, fix a time for the next visit, and discuss separation patterns that children and parents frequently experience. This establishes the precedent of a teacher casually informing and educating, as well as empathizing, with parents.

> "It's a good idea to get Ricky started a week or so before you have to start your classes. You know, we find a lot of our 3-year-olds take a couple of weeks or more to feel comfortable letting Mother leave. Please feel free to stay in the mornings as long as you can, but if he's upset when you leave, don't worry—we'll give him lots of special attention. I know it's hard for mothers too, but we'll help each other along."

By raising the issue of separation in advance, a teacher gives parents the opportunity to prepare themselves and their children for the transition. Many teachers find it helps to give parents a handout on separation to consider later at home. (See the sample in Figure 8-3.) Studies show that parents' verbal explanations are the most important influence in how well children adapt to a new situation (Powell, 1989).

In situations in which a school starts an entire new class of children at the same time, such as in kindergarten, elementary, or after-school child care situations, it works well to have an orientation meeting for all new parents to cover the common information all will need. A good video for such a group orientation for kindergarten parents is *Kindergarten, Here I Come!* by Educational Productions (2001). This lets a teacher offer information to the entire group and enables parents to meet each other right from the beginning. It can be reassuring to talk to other parents and find they are not alone in their concerns about leaving their children in a new environment (see Figure 8-4). Kines (1999) suggests such an initial meeting allows teachers to get parents of elementary-aged children on their side by talking about plans for the year and how the parents can get involved to support their children's learning. Because this meeting will not allow individual conversations about particular children, teachers can have a sign-up sheet for later calls. Also in elementary school situations, teachers can initiate friendly, personal contact with a letter that goes

We know that you want to help your child get off to a good start in beginning school. Young children often experience difficulties with separation from their significant adults in new situations. They may cry or cling or behave differently than you are used to. Be assured that this is a typical, normal response, and that these behaviors will slowly stop as children (and you) get more comfortable with the new situation. Some things you could do to support your child at this time are

- Accept and respect your child's temporary unhappiness. Say things like "I know you're feeling sad when Dad leaves, but you will have a good time, and soon you won't be so sad."
- Give yourselves enough time in the morning. Children often get anxious when rushed.
- Have pleasant conversation as you travel about some of the things your child enjoys about preschool.
- Remind your child of the predictability of your pickup arrangements, tying your return with an event, such as after naptime, and then arrive when you have said.
- Establish a pattern of what you will each do when you enter the classroom each day.
- Encourage your child to do as much as she can independently during the arrival process—for example, if your child is old enough, walking into the classroom herself.
- If you can stay for three or four minutes, help your child find an activity to focus on.
- After you have said you will go, make your goodbye prompt, affectionate, and positive. Don't ever be tempted to sneak away while your child is occupied.
- Have your child's teacher step in to help with goodbyes when you give the sign that you're ready to go.
- Avoid the temptation to pressure your child not to cry or to offer bribes for "good behavior." Learning to cope with sadness is important for your child.
- Let the teacher know if there are particular routines or objects that bring comfort to your child. The teacher will be helped by this knowledge.
- Understand that the process of learning to trust new people naturally takes time. The teacher will be glad to discuss your concerns with you—together you can make plans to meet your child's needs.

FIGURE 8-3 Many teachers find it helpful to give parents a handout on separation.

FIGURE 8-4 Teachers may hold group orientations for parents.

to all new families, or a telephone call if time permits. In any case the intent is to give welcoming information and a positive beginning to the relationship. Still, individual meetings between parents and teachers offer opportunities to gain specific information about a child, answer personal questions a parent might not raise in a group, and establish the parent–teacher relationship.

So this first brief meeting of parent and teacher establishes the patterns of relaxed communication, of mutual informing and asking, that are important for the working relationship to grow.

First Encounter—Teachers and Children

It is best if the first meeting between child and teacher can occur where the child is most comfortable—at home. Whenever a child has to get used to a new concept, such as school and new adults caring for her, she can adjust when fortified by the security of familiar people and surroundings. This first visit, scheduled at a family's convenience, may be brief—15 minutes or so—but the child will have a chance to briefly socialize and observe her parents doing so. One teacher likes to read a children's book to the child and then later have it available when the child visits the classroom as a tangible link to that first visit. Others bring photo albums of the classroom to create interest in coming to play there. Some leave a video for child and family to enjoy after the visit, and ask that it be returned at school. Others take pictures of the child and family to place in the child's cubby as a reminder of home and family. Any teacher who has experienced such an initial home visit will remember the

> **Home visits for first encounters are**
>
> - **At the invitation and convenience of the family.**
> - **Brief, social events.**
> - **Focused on the child–teacher interaction.**
> - **Used to bring or take materials to create a first home–school link.**
> - **Opportunities to begin building comfort and to learn about each other.**

comfort this gives children timidly entering a new classroom and recognizing an already familiar face. "You've been to my house." Children's feelings of security are enhanced by seeing that their parents and teachers are forming a relationship.

Parents, too, are reassured by watching teachers' sensitive approach when children are timid. When teachers speak quietly and get on children's eye level (being sensitive to cultures where eye-to-eye communication is not respectful), parents recognize that their children are being treated as special people. Parents pick up on that caring, feeling appreciative that someone has taken the time to help their child feel comfortable. (Home visits are discussed further in Chapter 11.)

The brief visit also offers a teacher a glimpse of the parent–child relationship and a child's home learning environment:

> Sylvia had been reluctant to have the teacher make a visit to their apartment, but when Connie Martinez explained it might help Ricky feel more comfortable with her (so far he wouldn't speak to this stranger), she agreed. Connie scheduled the brief visit for late afternoon, after learning Ricky's big brother would be home. And that did help. Terrence talked to the teacher and encouraged Ricky to show her their bedroom. Ricky smiled and waved good-bye when she left.

When home visits are absolutely not possible, teachers can write a letter to the family and include something special for the child, perhaps her photo. This can be a tangible tie for the child and this new person.

First Visit to a Classroom

During a home visit, a teacher can arrange a time for a parent and child to visit the classroom. It is best if a child can visit before first coming to the classroom

FIGURE 8-5 When children have the opportunity to visit the classroom with their parents, they can get comfortable enough to get excited about returning.

to stay (Blecher-Sass, 1997). This visit also will be brief—a chance for a child to see and become interested in a new environment (see Figure 8-5).

> Ricky and his mother came in midmorning, two days after the home visit. He said hello to Connie and let her show him around the room. He especially liked the big fire truck. When the other children came in from the playground, he clung to his mother but watched intently. He turned down the invitation to come to the table for juice, but joined his mother when she sat near Connie and drank juice. He nodded when Connie told him that next time he could stay longer and play with the fire truck.

It is sometimes overwhelming for a young child to enter a classroom full of other children busy with activities. For this reason it may be a good idea to schedule this visit when children from the classroom are outside, playing in a gym or other area with another teacher, or at the end of the day when fewer children are present. Then a child is free to be welcomed by the teacher she's met, shown that she will be a part of this classroom (having a cubby with her name and picture on it is a good idea; see Figure 8-6), and given a chance to investigate the toys and equipment. It may work well to have a visiting child join the group briefly for a snack or cup of juice. She can then enjoy the eating experience and have a chance to see other children without being called on to participate.

FIGURE 8-6 A cubby with a child's name and picture gives a sense of belonging.

Ideally the parent stays in the classroom during this visit, offering the child a secure base from which to move and sharing pleasure in new discoveries. Parental concerns may be allayed by observing the teacher and child interact and seeing how the classroom functions. This visit gives the parent specifics to discuss at home to continue to prepare the child for this new experience.

Introductory school visits are important. If necessary for the family's schedule, the visit could be at 7:00 a.m. or at 6:00 p.m. to allow the parent to stay throughout. This step is too important to skip. A visit is in the child's best interests, and ultimately in the family's, even if it is inconvenient.

If an entire class of entering children is new, teachers may schedule brief opportunities for a group of five or six children to come in for "tea parties" and a chance to look around the classroom. Breaking a class down offers teachers a chance to interact with each child while saving teacher time (see Figure 8-7).

Child's Entry into a Classroom

The groundwork is laid for a child's entry into a classroom. Teachers and parents need to remind themselves how much there is for a child to become accustomed to in a school experience: the "how's" of interacting with a large

FIGURE 8-7 It is helpful when the teacher has time to interact with individual children.

group of children; the new rules and practices of a classroom; leaving parents and becoming comfortable with another adult. (Teachers should let parents know that children facing all this may act out afterward in the secure environment of home.)

Because these adjustments can be exhausting for a child, it is helpful if his first days in a classroom are as abbreviated as possible, allowing for the family's schedule. For example, if a child is beginning a full-day child care program, it is helpful if he is picked up at the end of the morning for several days, then slowly extends the day to include lunch, nap, and then the afternoon. Even older children entering a new school situation may show signs of exhaustion and stress initially. Children entering a half-day program will benefit from attending for half the morning at first. A school that enters its whole class at one time can shorten the entire schedule for the first week or so, gradually extending from one hour to three. The people most inconvenienced during this **easing-in** period are parents, so it is important that they understand the rationale for this approach and its benefit for their children in building feelings of comfort and security (see Figure 8-8). Some centers offer a place where parents can have a cup of coffee during these shortened days, waiting and conversing with other parents. Other family members, such as grandparents or older siblings, may be able to assist during the easing-in process if parents' work schedules are inflexible.

FIGURE 8-8 There is much to get used to in this new school environment, such as waiting for a turn to wash hands.

Teachers should make every effort to accommodate family needs and pressures by modifying steps and timing, at the same time explaining the importance to the child of the visits and easing-in. Many parents will find the time, even if they didn't originally believe they could do so, or find another family member who can help during this period if parents are not free. At the same time, some children will be left "ready or not." For children whose parents cannot or will not stay, teachers should do what they can to help trust form. They may send preliminary notes or talk on the telephone. Teachers may suggest that the family bring transitional objects and pictures into the classroom. If teachers believe this process is important, they will convey this impression to families.

> After the teacher suggested it, Sylvia had decided to let Ricky stay for two mornings before she left him for the whole day. The first morning he cried hard as she left; Connie encouraged her to stay a little longer if she wanted, but she just hurried away, feeling a little sick herself. He was very quiet when she went back to get him before lunch, but after his nap he told her and Terrence a little about playing with the fire engine.
>
> The next morning he cried for about 10 minutes, but as she stood in the hall, she heard him stop. The third day she and Terrence went together to get him after his nap. Connie said he'd had a hard time falling asleep, but she'd rubbed his back until he drifted off. Sylvia was starting to think Ricky might be all right.

Parents as well as children need special attention during this transition time. A teacher's evident concern and specific comments do much to further

FIGURE 8-9 Parents and children both need special attention during beginning times.

a sense of partnership as she takes the time to communicate with families before and after school (see Figure 8-9).

> Every day when Sylvia came back to get Ricky, she looked eagerly for the teacher. Connie always tried to leave the children with her assistant briefly and come to tell her what Ricky had played with and how he seemed to feel.

Through the orientation process, no large amount of family time is spent; most of the visits are half an hour or less and can be worked into a parent's employment schedule. For a teacher this time can be scheduled into a normal teaching day with coverage from an assistant. The adults need to realize the priority of a child's growing security and try to fit in as many steps as practicable. In addition to a child's security, it is important to set patterns of teachers and parents working together in home–school transitions and discussing a child's needs. As they work together, parents and teachers will get to know each other and start to build trust that will help in the future—a good beginning for all.

> "You know," says Sylvia, "Ricky is going to get along all right in the school. I really like the teacher; she's helped me a lot to get used to things. I won't have to worry so much."

Transitions within Schools

Attention should also be paid to the new relationships and comfort that must be built when children move from one classroom to another within a preschool. Often schools offer helpful beginning orientations for children and families but neglect to recognize that change within the school should also be approached with sensitivity to the feelings involved in changing relationships. Often children or adults resist a change, and the resistance comes precisely because time and thought have not gone into a gradual transition. Appropriate transitions may include

- Advance notification to the current primary caregiver and family that change is approaching.

- A conference between the new primary caregiver and the family.

REFLECTIONS FOR JOURNAL ENTRIES

If you have had opportunities to work with families in any capacity, think about your first encounters. What seemed to work well as you got to know each other? What would you do differently next time?

- Current and new caregivers developing a schedule for the transition process, which may take a month or so, depending on the child's age and response.

- A visit to the child in the current classroom by the new caregiver.

- A visit by the child and the current caregiver to the new classroom.

- A gradual visitation schedule for the child to participate in the new classroom, then return to the current classroom.

- Gradual participation in routines of the new classroom: mealtime, naptime, and the like.

- Regular communication (telephone or face-to-face) among the parents and current and new caregivers about the child's response to transition process.

- A written report that details the process and reactions of all involved.

- Opportunities for children to maintain contact with beloved caregivers left behind (Baker and Manfredi/Pettit, 2004).

Attention to everyone concerned will allow relationships and communication to flourish.

DEALING WITH SEPARATION EXPERIENCES

The emotional responses to a new school experience may be heightened by the **separation anxiety** experienced by most children and parents. The mutual parent–child attachment, developed during the early years of a child's

FIGURE 8-10 Children may come in quietly and then begin to cry later in the morning.

life, means that both adult and child feel more secure in each other's presence. A removal from each other's presence causes concern and changes in behavior for both.

What behaviors are expected of children experiencing separation? Many children up to age 3 or so will cry and be sad when a parent leaves. Even older children may find the initial leaving difficult. Sometimes this sadness continues off and on for a good part of the day; some children continue this pattern of crying for weeks or, occasionally, months. A child may come in quietly in the morning, and then begin to cry later (see Figure 8-10). Such delayed reactions may occur days or even weeks later. Some children find times like mealtime or naptime particularly hard as they are reminded of home routines. Many children experiencing separation difficulties cling to a teacher and participate little. Separation problems are also demonstrated by an increase in dependence or disruptions and changed behavior patterns at home, such as resisting bedtime, out-of-bounds talk with parents, new and assertive ways of behaving, and "games" that play on parents' guilt. Some children demonstrate regressive behaviors, reverting to thumb sucking, wetting, or other earlier behaviors. And some children exhibit "very good" behaviors—no signs of upset, just controlled passivity. School-aged children may show their anxiety about a new situation by complaining of symptoms of "school phobia," including stomach upsets and headaches, as well as irritability and fatigue at home.

These behaviors are considered usual for a child experiencing separation, and the duration of the behaviors varies with each child. Although they require special considerations, the behaviors are not cause for alarm. Teachers need to be matter-of-fact in their expectation of these behaviors so they reassure parents of both their normalcy and temporary nature. Experiences, circumstances, and temperaments are different for each child. Children who have rarely been left by parents may react quite differently from those who have had lots of baby-sitters or group encounters. The child who approaches each new situation with zest and enthusiasm may leave parents without a backward glance, whereas the child who is slower to warm up in new situations may appear unhappy for quite some time. Most young children have this period of stressful adaptation to supplemental child care away from their parents. But once they understand that regular separation from parents does not imply their loss, the problematic behaviors subside.

Parents often have a difficult time with separation, too. This is a time of ambivalent feelings: satisfaction that their child is more independent; fear of becoming displaced in their child's affections; and sadness at the changing status in their relationship. Parents may feel concern that their child no longer needs them and jealous of the person she appears to need. They may be concerned about how their child is cared for in their absence and about this change being too disruptive to their child's life and their own, as evidence by upset behaviors (see Figure 8-11).

"Look, I thought it was going to work out fine at this center, but now I'm not so sure. Janie screams every morning when I leave and clings to my neck. I can hear those screams all day. I'm afraid of her changing; she's always been such a happy child. And I worry—wonder whether anybody's looking after her when she's so

FIGURE 8-11 It is just as hard for many parents to leave as it is for children to say good-bye.

upset. I miss her, too. But I'd hate to think I was one of those clinging mothers who can't let their kids go."

A parent may be struggling with more than her own separation feelings. If she's beginning a working situation, she may be feeling great pressure for her child to adjust to the care situation as quickly as possible. Getting her child adjusted is not an option; it has to work!

A teacher is in an important position to help parent and child deal with separation emotions and behaviors. The aim is for a teacher to remember that she is doing not just what works best, but what best strengthens a child. Teacher's attentions need to be directed to both parent and child, "for the way you treat the child affects the parents, and the way you treat the parents affects the child" (Balaban, 1985). Some basic strategies follow.

Prepare Parents for Separation Behaviors

Prepare parents in advance to accept separation behaviors and emotions as normal. Parents are more open about their concerns if they realize that a teacher is not judging their child or themselves negatively for experiencing separation anxieties.

Information about separation, such as the handout in Figure 8-3, should be a component of every orientation packet and interview. Discussing possible behaviors and feelings and helpful strategies ahead of time prepares parents for what may happen and how they can best support their child.

> "Most children Janie's age have a hard time at first saying good-bye to parents. We expect it. You're the most important person in her life, and it will take a while for her to realize she can be fine when you're gone. In fact, though they don't show it as freely as children, most parents find this a fairly major adjustment, too. I'll be here to help you both however I can. These are concerns we'll talk about each day."

Welcome Parents into a Classroom

Help parents feel welcome to stay in a classroom as long as this is helpful to a child. Some teachers have found it helpful to prepare a handout for parents suggesting some things they could do in the classroom during those first few days (see Figure 8-12). Both parents and children may benefit from not having a rushed good-bye in the morning, by slowly helping a child get interested in the classroom activities, and by having a parent see her child receive a teacher's attention. This approach will help a parent feel a part of her child's school world (see Figure 8-13).

Creating a cozy corner near the entrance (Stephens, 1996)—perhaps a loveseat and small table with a few curiosity items, like a music box, a rain

You're Welcome to Stay a While!

As you and your child get used to life in our classroom, feel free to stay if you can. Here are some things you could do:

- Help your child develop a morning routine of putting things in the cubby.

- Find the child's name tag, and move it to our "We're Here" board.

- Wash hands in the bathroom.

- Look around at each interest center to notice new materials.

- Go say good morning to our fish Henry.

- Choose a book and read to your child and any other child who wants to join you.

- Say goodbye and leave without lingering when you are ready—teachers will help your child say goodbye.

- Fee free to call or stop back and see us later in the day when you have time.

FIGURE 8-12 Some teachers prepare a handout for families suggesting some things they can do during the first days of school.

FIGURE 8-13 Coming in may get a little easier when parents have a few extra minutes to help their children slowly become involved in activities.

stick, minerals with magnifying glasses, or family photograph books—might help give parents and children a few pleasant moments together before departure.

> "Janie, maybe you'd like to show your mommy the puzzle you did yesterday."
>
> "We've got some nice, soft play dough on the table over there. Maybe that would be fun to do together for a few minutes."
>
> "Perhaps you'd like to find a book to read together before you say good-bye."

Parents look to teachers for cues about what their role should be in helping their children settle in. As teachers provide directions to families, parents will be able to act confidently with their children. Allowing a child to decide when parents should leave the room—"Shall Mom go now, or after our story time?"—may help a child experience self-confidence.

Teachers can help parents and children plan together for the next day's parting and move toward establishing a regular morning routine"

> "The two of you might like to decide before you come tomorrow whether she'll give you a hug at the door, or after she's put her things in her cubby."

Many classroom teachers help children develop the fun ritual of "pushing" their parents out the door; once again, the children feel a measure of control in the good-bye.

In general, teachers must let parents know they will follow their cues concerning their desire or ability to stay. But an alert teacher picks up on the times a child is ready to move away from her parent who is lingering on, perhaps due to her own needs. Here a teacher can help a parent leave:

> "Mrs. Smith, since Janie's starting to play, it might be a good time to tell her good-bye. You and I can watch her from outside, if you'd like."

Helping the parent create **parting rituals** may especially help those parents who linger on and seem determined not to leave in any clear fashion (Miller, 1995). As some teachers note, "It's almost as if they can't leave until they have seen the child get upset." This may indeed be so, though likely at an unconscious level. In these cases teachers should reassure parents of how important they are to their children—help the parent notice the child's delight when the parent returns at day's end. This is a place for empathy—understanding how much these parents may need comforting themselves.

It is important that teachers make decisions regarding the timing of actual separation in such cases, where a child's readiness precedes a parent's. When parents are feeling ambiguous and shaky, they may need or appreciate

FIGURE 8-14 Parents should feel free to stay as long as this is necessary and helpful to the child.
Courtesy ©1990, Washington Post Writers Group.

such help. However, when a parent is unable to respond to such a direct approach, it is probably an indication that the point of personal readiness for separation has not yet arrived, and teacher patience and support are necessary. It is also important for teachers not to become impatient with the process and arbitrarily set their own time limit. "Two weeks is long enough for any child or parent to get used to this!"

Should parents stay away? Some children don't seem to need their parents' presence at times of transition as much as others do, although they are usually quite agreeable to their presence in the room. However, there are also children who get so habituated to a particular pattern, like parents staying at school, that it becomes even harder for them when their parents finally do leave. Parents of these children might do well to concentrate efforts at home to prepare for the leave-taking. The best policy seems to be one that would allow parents to stay as long as is necessary and helpful to the child (see Figure 8-14).

An important concept for teachers and parents to consider is that parents must see their own anxiety as separate from that of their child's; in other words, the reactions of a parent may not be identical to a child's feelings, and it is important not to project those feelings onto a child. It can set up long-lasting problem patterns if a child learns to give a parent a demonstration of his reluctance to be left before a parent feels satisfied that she will be truly missed. A parent may be more able to deal with personal emotions with an awareness of whose problem it is.

Develop Children's Trust in Parents

An important step in a child's working through the separation process is to learn to trust that parents will reliably leave and then return. Teachers may need to help parents become aware of behaviors that can foster this sense of certainty (see Figure 8-15).

> **WHEN YOU LEAVE, MOTHER**
>   you don't need my permission.
> It's good for you and good for me
>   but tell me! Don't disappear.
> Better I scream my disapproval
>   than live in vague suspicion
>   that I'll find you gone again.
> For then I'd have to "guard" you,
>   afraid to leave your side to play.
> Don't disappear–tell me
>   that you're leaving,
>   and that you're coming back!
> In telling me, you're also teaching me
>   to feel all right one day,
> When I leave you . . . for short times,
>   and longer,
>   longer . . . times.

FIGURE 8-15 This could be a useful handout to remind parents of why to say good-bye.

Though it may be less painful at the time, it is not a good idea for parents to slip away unnoticed while a child is distracted. A child left in this way can't help but become a little dubious about a parent's trustworthiness. Teachers can help parents realize the need for a definite leave-taking. "Repeated good-byes strengthen children's beliefs that parents will come back" (Blecher-Sass, 1997).

"I know it bothers you when she cries as you leave; but it's really better for her in the long run to know she can rely on you to go and come just as you say you will. I'll help her say a quick good-bye to you."

In the same way, parents may not realize the importance of picking up a child at a predictable time. Clock time means little to children, and even a short time elapsing after a parent's expected arrival will seem like a very long time (see Figure 8-16). It is best for parents to equate their return with a scheduled event and absolutely keep to it, especially during this transition time.

"After you eat your snack, I'll be back to get you."
"Remember, Sally, Dad told us this morning that he'd come back to get you after snack. I know you're missing him. Come with us while we have our story, and then we'll be getting ready for snack."

FIGURE 8-16 It is important to a child's sense of security to be picked up on a predictable schedule.

Discuss the Separation Experience

It is helpful to discuss and validate the emotional responses to separation openly, with empathy. Such an approach frees both child and parent to realize that their feelings are recognized and accepted and can continue to be communicated. Keeping "stiff upper lips" is too costly in terms of emotional health.

> "I know you're sad when your Mom leaves, Janie. It's a little scary, too. But I'll be here to look after you until she gets back, and we can have a good time, too."
>
> "It will take a little while to get used to our classroom, but I'll help you, and so will your new friends."
>
> "Most parents have some pretty mixed feelings about their children starting off in school. It can be kind of sad and scary, I'm sure."

Small touches can demonstrate to parents and children a teacher's empathy: a midmorning phone call to let a parent know that her child who was screaming when she left is now playing happily with play dough; an extra minute to share the day's events fully with a returning parent; talking with a child throughout the day about what she'll have to show Daddy when he returns; taking dictation for a note the child would like to write to an absent parent. All of these can show children that teachers are there for them, that they can listen, understand, and help.

Teachers who understand separation anxiety and its manifestations will not become irritated or offended by the behaviors of children or parents. They will not take the tears or anxieties personally, as indications that their classrooms are not good places. They will not scold crying children, nor ignore the tears and sadness. They will enter empathetically into the child's experience, attempting to feel the fears that they feel. (See Waterland, 1995, for a sensitive reconstruction of school life at the beginning.) They will understand that time and support will solve most separation problems.

Special Attention to Parents and Children

Special attention to both parents and children is warranted at this time. Teachers may choose special children's books about separation and new experiences to read to children or lend to parents for home use (see Figure 8-17). They may stay close to children, holding their hands at transition times, holding them on their laps when they are sad, and talking with them often (see Figure 8-18). Teachers should talk about what will happen next in the classroom and where parents are now. They may hold monologue-type conversations, not pressuring children to respond. They may write notes from children's dictation to the absent parents; this helps ease the children's

Ahlberg, J. & A. *Starting School.*

———. *Peek-a-Boo!*

Albee, S. *I Don't Want to Go to School.*

Amoss, B. *The Very Worst Thing.*

Aseltine, L. *First Grade Can Wait.*

Baker, C. F. *My Mom Travels a Lot.*

Barkan, J. *Anna Marie's Blanket.*

Barkin, C., & James, E. *I'd Rather Stay Home.*

Berenstain, S. & J. *The Berenstain Bears Go Back to School.*

Berger, T. *A Friend Can Help.*

Bizen, B. *First Day in School.*

Blue, R. *I Am Here: Yo Estoy Aqui.*

Boelts, M. *Little Bunny's Preschool Countdown.*

Bram, E. *I Don't Want to Go to School.*

Brand, J., & Gladstone, N. *My Day Care Book.*

Breinburg, P. *Shawn Goes to School.*

Bunnett, R. *Friends at School.*

Burningham, J. *The Blanket.*

———. *The Friend.*

Calmenson, S. *The Kindergarten Book.*

Chalmers, M. *Be Good Harry.*

Civardi, A. *First Experiences: Going to School.*

Cohen, M. *The New Teacher.*

———. *See You Tomorrow, Charlie.*

———. *Will I Have a Friend?*

Coles, A. *Michael's First Day at School.*

Cooney, N. *The Blanket That Had to Go.*

Corey, D. *You Go Away.*

Crary, E. *Mommy Don't Go.*

DeGroat, D. *Brand-New Pencils, Brand-New Books.*

Delacre, L. *Time for School, Nathan!*

Eastman, P. *Are You My Mother?*

Elliott, D. *Grover Goes to School.*

Harris, R. *Don't Forget to Come Back.*

Henkes, K. *Owen.*

Hill, E. *Spot Goes to School.*

Hines, A. *Don't Worry, I'll Find You.*

Howe, J. *When You Go to Kindergarten.*

Hurwitz, J. *Rip-Roaring Russell.*

Johnson, D. *What Will Mommy Do When I'm at School?*

Kantrowitz, M. *Willy Bear.*

Lionni, L. *Little Blue and Little Yellow.*

Mannhein, G. *The Two Friends.*

Mayer, M. *Frog, Where Are You?*

Molnar, D., & Fenton, S. *Who Will Pick Me Up When I Fall?*

Moncure, J. *A New Boy in Kindergarten.*

Oh. J. *Mr. Monkey's Classroom*

Park, S. *Sumi's First Day of School Ever.*

Penn, A. *The Kissing Hand.*

Rogers, F. *Going to Day Care.*

Simon, N. *I'm Busy Too.*

Smath, J. *Elephant Goes to School.*

Soderstrom, M. *Maybe Tomorrow I'll Have a Good Time.*

Sperring, M. *Wanda's First Day.*

Stiles, N. *On My Very First School Day I Met…*

Sturges, P. *I Love School.*

Tompert, A. *Will You Come Back for Me?*

Warren, C. *Fred's First Day.*

Wells, R. *My Kindergarten.*

———. *Timothy Goes to School.*

Wild, M. *Tom Goes to Kindergarten.*

Wingest, S. *Tucker's Four-Carrot School Day.*

Wolde, B. *Betsy's First Day of Nursery School.*

For more titles, a good reference to consult in the library is *Books to Help Children Cope with Separation and Loss* by Joanne E. Bernstein (R. R. Bowker Co.).

FIGURE 8-17 Books about starting school and separation.

FIGURE 8-18 Teachers will stay close to children who are experiencing sadness.

feelings and shows that teachers can listen and help. They will encourage children to hold a transitional object from home or parent—holding Mom's scarf is reassurance that she will return. All of these techniques help children learn that teachers are there for them, and that sadness is accepted and can be channeled into work and play. They will make opportunities for parents to tape record brief messages to leave in the classroom for children to listen to, and encourage parents to bring family photos to school for a special book or to hang in the child's cubby.

Sometimes teachers are concerned that this special attention to a new child will shortchange the other children. It is useful to remember that individualizing responsive care for children means not always giving the same thing to all the children at the same time. The other children likely don't have such acute needs at this time. Further, they are learning valuable lessons about compassion, feelings, and adult trustworthiness. Teachers may call parents during the day with positive information to reassure them: "Jon has a new friend. He's been playing in the block corner with David all morning." They may take pictures of the child involved in activity and send them with a note describing the activity and naming the children playing with their child. Other teachers suggest giving parents a written outline of the day's activities on the first day they leave their children, so they can check the schedule and imagine what their children are doing. Gartrell (2000) suggests making a telephone call at the end of the first day for all teachers. Certainly in elementary or after-school situations, this could begin the relationships that so often are not established. All of these gestures indicate to parents that teachers care enough to make sure they are being included in these first adjustments. Teachers must try to empathize with some of the mixed feelings that parents have when their children begin first school experiences. A good resource to help here is the parents' viewpoint described in Hannigan, 1998.

REFLECTIONS FOR JOURNAL ENTRIES

Consider separation experiences you have had in your life. Recall, if you can, your first beginnings in a school setting or in staying away from home overnight. What feelings can you identify? How did you express these emotions? How did adults around you respond to your feelings? Now, if you are a parent, recall the first time you left a child in the care of another person. What were some of your concerns? Remembering personal experiences often increases teachers' ability to empathize.

Some teachers find that in order not to foster dependence, some of this special attention and support can be supplied by pairing a new child with a special friend, someone who has already adapted to the classroom and has a personality that would enjoy helping to nurture a new child. A new parent can be introduced to a parent who has weathered the stress of separation. But dependence is less of a concern than fostering feelings of comfort and confidence.

All beginnings are important. The long-term effects of establishing parent–teacher relationships with clear patterns of empathetic communication, as well as a child's successful adaptation, justify taking these careful steps.

SUMMARY

Ideally, good beginnings include the following:

1. A meeting with a school's administrator to consider what a parent is looking for in a preschool and how this matches a school's philosophy and practices.

2. An introductory conversation between a parent and an individual classroom teacher. Specific information about a child and classroom is exchanged. Further orientation plans are formed.

3. A brief home visit so a teacher and child can meet on a child's secure home base.

4. A brief visit of parent and child to a classroom, specifically planned for a time when a teacher is free to interact with the child.

5. An easing-in schedule so a child can slowly adjust to classroom life on less than a full-time basis.

6. Carefully planned transitions when children move to new classrooms within a school.

7. Teacher assistance to parent and child during peak separation stress.

When family schedules do not permit all these steps to be taken, teachers must remember the importance of finding ways to support children in a new situation and to begin the process of communication with their families.

STUDENT ACTIVITIES FOR FURTHER STUDY

1. With your classmates, role-play the following situations, with one of you being a teacher who is trying to get to know, support, and establish a relationship with a parent who is enrolling a child in your center:

   a. The parent says the child has never been left with anyone else in three years.

   b. The parent seems very reluctant to answer any questions about the child.

   c. The parent asks if she can stay until the child stops crying—"It may take a while"; the parent seems very tense.

   d. The parent says she really doesn't have time for the teacher to visit or have an extended conversation with the teacher, or allow the child to visit or "ease-in."

   e. The parent seems frightened of the teacher.

2. Role-play the following situations and have your "audience" discuss a teacher's role in helping both parent and child during separation stress:

   a. A teacher with a parent whose child is screaming and clinging to the parent's neck—the parent started a new job two days ago.

   b. A teacher with a parent whose child is screaming and clinging to the parent's neck—the parent starts a new job next week.

   c. A child says good-bye happily; the mother stands at the door looking very sad.

   d. Two hours after the parent left, the child begins to cry and says, "I want my Daddy."

   e. The parent begins to sneak out while the child is distracted with a toy.

3. Ask several parents how they chose their early childhood programs. Did they visit? Were there particular things they were looking for? What convinced them this was the place for their children?

4. Look at the information forms that parents fill in at your school and several others. Do the forms really allow the parents to begin to share their particular knowledge of their children? What additional questions might be helpful?

CASE STUDY

Isabella Rodriguez, age 4, is the only child of a single mother, Luz. They share an apartment with another family that also recently emigrated from the Dominican Republic. Luz is beginning a training program for data entry, which she hopes will lead to fulltime employment. Neither Luz nor Isabella speaks much English. Luz has enrolled her daughter in a family child care home in her neighborhood.

Isabella did not speak and hid her face when her mother went to the home to make the initial arrangements.

1. Put yourself in the position of the child care provider. What are some of the issues you need to be sensitive to in beginning relationships with Isabella and her mother?

2. What plans would you recommend to help Isabella adjust to your program?

3. How would you get the information about Isabella and her family situation that you would like to have as you begin work with her?

4. Imagine what some of Luz's concerns are as she begins to leave her daughter at the family child care home. How would you respond to these?

REVIEW QUESTIONS

1. Describe an ideal process of orientation to a center for a child and his parents.

2. Discuss why each step of the orientation process is beneficial and what strategies a teacher may consider with each step.

3. Identify several behaviors typically associated with separation problems in young children.

4. Discuss several teacher behaviors that help parents and children in adjusting to separation.

SUGGESTIONS FOR FURTHER READING

Balaban, N. (2006). *Everyday goodbyes: Starting school and early care/A guide to the separation process.* New York: Teachers College Press.

Briody, J. (2005). Separation through a parent's eyes. *Young Children,* 60(2): 110–111.

Briody, J., & McGarry, K. (2005). Using social stories to ease children's transitions. *Young Children,* 60(5): 38–42.

Daniel, J. (1995). New beginnings: Transitions for difficult children. *Young Children,* 50(3), 17–23.

Fine, P. (1999). Caregivers' corner: Successful separations for preschoolers. *Young Children,* 54(3), 58–60.

Gray, H. (2004). You go away and you come back. *Young Children,* 59(5): 100–107.

Harmon, C. (1996). In the beginning: Helping parents and children separate. *Young Children,* 51(4), 72.

Jervis, K. (Ed.) (1994). *Separation: Strategies for helping two to four year olds.* Washington, DC: NAEYC.

Kleckner, K. A., & Engel, R. E. (1988). A child begins school: Relieving anxiety with books. *Young Children, 43*(5), 14–18.

Montanari, E. (1993, March). Keeping families happy—communication is the key. *Child Care Information Exchange, 89,* 21–23.

Mundorf, N. K. (1994, November/December). Bye-bye's with fewer tears. *Early Childhood News,* 20–21.

Planta, R., & Krafft-Sayre, M. (1999). Parents' observations about their children's transitions to kindergarten. *Young Children, 54*(3), 47–52.

Viorst, J. (1986). *Necessary losses.* New York: Fawcett.

REFERENCES

Baker, A., & L. Manfredi/Petitt. (2004). *Relationships, the heart of quality care: Creating community among adults in early care settings.* Washington, D.C.: NAEYC.

Balaban, N. (1985). *Starting school: From separation to independence (a guide for early childhood teachers).* New York: Teachers College Press.

———. (1985). The name of the game is confidence: How to help kids recoup from separation anxiety. *Instructor, 95*(2), 108–112.

Blecher-Sass, H. (1997). Good-byes can build trust. *Young Children, 52*(2), 12–14.

Carter, M. (1999, November). Developing meaningful relationships with families. *Child Care Information Exchange,* 63–65.

Cochran, E., & Cochran, M. (1997). *Child care that works.* Boston: Houghton Mifflin Co.

Educational Productions. (2001). *Kindergarten, here I come!* [video]. Available from Educational Productions, 9000 SW Gemini Drive, Beaverton, OR 97008 (1-800-950-4949).

Gartrell, D. (2000). *What the kids said today: Using classroom conversations to become a better teacher.* St. Paul, MN: Redleaf Press.

Hannigan, I. (1998). *Off to school: A parent's-eye view of the kindergarten year.* Washington, DC: NAEYC.

Kines, B. (1999). Getting parents on your side. *Teachers K–8,* Sept. 1999, 41.

Miller, K. (1995, November). The parent who lingers. *Child Care Information Exchange,* 31–32.

Powell, D. R. (1989). *Families and early childhood programs.* Washington, DC: NAEYC.

Stephens, K. (1996, September/October). Smooth arrival routines. *First Teacher,* 8–9.

Waterland, L. (1995). *The bridge to school: Entering a new world.* Columbus, OH: Stenhouse Publishers.

Zinzeleta, E., & Little, N. (1997). How do parents really choose early childhood programs? *Young Children, 52*(7), 8–11.

HELPFUL WEB SITES

http://www.acei.org

The mission of the Association for Childhood Education International (ACEI) is to promote and support in the global community the optimal education and development of children, from birth through early adolescence, and to influence the professional growth of educators and the efforts of others who are committed to the needs of children in a changing society.

http://nccic.org

National Child Care Information Center. Here you will find many resources and links about child care, early education, and families.

http://www.nafcc.org

The focus of the National Association for Family Child Care is to provide technical assistance to family child care associations. This assistance is provided through developing leadership and professionalism, addressing issues of diversity, and promoting quality and professionalism through NAFCC's Family Child Care Association. This site has helpful information about good beginnings.

http://www.aap.org

The American Academy of Pediatrics is committed to the attainment of optimal physical, mental, and social health and well-being for all infants, children, adolescents, and young adults.

Many articles and tips for choosing child care can be found at the following sites:

http://www.ymcacrs.org

YMCA Child Care Resource Service.

http://www.childcaredirectory.com

Tips for choosing child care.

Additional resources for this chapter can be found on the Online Companion to accompany this text at www.earlychilded.delmar.com. This supplemental material includes frequently asked questions; chapter outlines to be used as study guides; scenarios that both encourage large and small group discussions and provoke new thoughts and ideas; and chapter resources, including chapter summaries, interactive questions, Web links, and Web activities. In addition, forms from the text are available for download.

CHAPTER 9

Informal Communication with Families

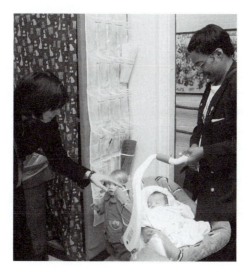

OBJECTIVES

After reading this chapter, you should able to

1 Identify 10 methods a teacher uses to convey information, interest, and support to families.

2 Discuss details for implementing each communication method.

KEY TERMS
daily news flash
literacy
    activities
one-way
communication
two-way
communication
transition times

Relationships that work are built on trust and open communication. Finding methods to communicate regularly with families is a challenge for teachers who already have many responsibilities within their classrooms. Obviously face-to-face conversations are most important in communication, and we will explore how to provide opportunities for these. But in addition, other strategies help keep information flowing both ways. This chapter examines a variety of methods of informal communication that teachers can utilize to build relationships with families.

COMMUNICATION METHODS

As teachers begin to work with parents and children, it is important to keep open communication lines. As previously discussed, the initiative for opening a dialogue should come from teachers. By approaching families, teachers demonstrate their willingness to adapt to individual differences in personality, preferences, and time constraints that may result in different responses to the same method. For example, a busy parent may barely glance at the parents' bulletin board while rushing by but enjoy reading a newsletter at home, whereas a quiet parent who does not usually talk much to the teachers may eagerly read everything offered on the bulletin board. For this reason teachers should utilize as many communication methods as they can. Most are not time-consuming; a few minutes a day may be sufficient to work on ideas for the next newsletter or bulletin board or to write several individual notes or make a few telephone calls. Most teachers probably do not take time to use a multitude of methods, feeling that one or two will get the message out. In actuality, many teachers are surprised when they learn that parents feel uninformed about the daily life of the classroom (Brand, 1996). It is important that teachers use a variety of methods, recognizing the variety of parental styles of getting information.

Communication strategies can be one-way or two-way (Berger, 1999). **One-way communication** from a class or school can inform families about events or plans or attempt to educate parents. This is the traditional method that many schools have used to communicate with families. This is important because parents need and want to know what is going on; but a real sense of partnership grows through **two-way communication** that encourages and facilitates true dialogue, with families actively reacting and responding. Devices can be incorporated into many communication methods that are normally one-way communication to expand them to two-way communication. In fact, expanding many ideas that have been traditionally used may make them interactive.

Teachers working in school settings have been influenced by traditional methods of communicating with families, those "ritualized and institutionalized" ideas: parent–teacher conferences scheduled for precisely 15 minutes and open house nights, when all parents are invited to the classroom at the same time, leaving no time for individual contact. Especially in school settings where teachers often do not have the luxury of daily contact, teachers must work to move beyond these encounters that yield few channels for communication. They must find their own ways of creating communication *between* school and families rather than continuing the tradition of sending messages *from* schools *to* families. The ideas in this chapter may help teachers from child care through elementary school.

Daily Conversations

No matter what other informal strategies teachers use as alternatives for establishing communication with parents, these should not replace personal contact. Nothing is as important as personal, face-to-face conversation for building relationships.

> Connie Martinez says, "I don't have time for too much else, but I do a lot of talking to parents every day."

FIGURE 9-1 When children are brought to school by bus, teachers have to work hard to maintain regular contact with families.

Frequent daily conversations when parents drop off and pick up their children are extremely important in building trust by fostering a sense of familiarity. A study of frequency of communication between parents and caregivers indicated that the highest frequency of communication occurs at the "transition point" when parents leave and pick up their child at a center. There is an obvious problem when children are brought by a carpool or bus; teachers in these situations have to work harder to maintain regular contact by telephone calls or notes (see Figure 9-1).

Important things happen during these brief exchanges. Parents want to know that their child is known and recognized as a person. To see a teacher greet their child personally by name is reassuring. Parents also want to be greeted by name themselves.

> "Good morning, Pete. You look ready to play today. I've put some of those new little cars that you like in the block corner. How are you this morning, Mrs. Lawrence? Pete's been telling me about his new bedroom—you must be pretty busy at home these days."

This can be a time for brief but substantive exchanges on child- and family-related issues. Studies indicate that these conversations may be the most

FIGURE 9-2 Daily opportunities for conversation help build relationships.

frequent form of parent involvement, although the substance of the conversations may not progress beyond social niceties (Powell, 1989). The topics discussed most frequently are child-related, including child–peer relations and child–caregiver relations. However, when communication is frequent, the diversity and number of topics discussed by parents and teachers increases, pointing to the need for frequent conversations to build relationships. With greater frequency, the number of family-related topics discussed increases. More than social conversation is needed; quality care demands that home and center coordinate their efforts and exchange information regularly. Extensive dialogue between parents and teachers is necessary for such coordination (see Figure 9-2).

But nothing happens if there is no contact. One study (Endsley & Minish, 1991, reported in Doherty-Derkowski, 1995) found that the average length of conversation between caregiver and parents at **transition times** was 12 seconds! Sixty-three percent of all "conversations" were greetings or other small talk with no real exchange of information. And in nearly half of the situations observed, the parent and caregiver did not even greet each other. Clearly this is no way to begin or to build a relationship.

The frequency and quality of these daily contacts depend primarily on factors in classroom routine and center policy that can be planned and regulated. Staffing patterns need to provide enough staff available to talk when parents arrive at the beginning and end of the day. Preparing materials before parents arrive, or saving cleanup for after parents depart, keeps a teacher's attention from being diverted away from the door as parents arrive. If teachers provide simple, open-ended materials that children can use with no adult assistance,

FIGURE 9-3 When teachers create the expectancy for conversation, parents usually respond.

neither parents nor teachers will have to devote full attention to the demands of children. When both members of a teaching team are in the classroom, making definite assignments for either child care or adult conversations clarifies expected behaviors for both teachers and parents. It is a good idea for the teachers in a team to take turns being responsible for conversations with parents, so parents develop relationships with both and do not feel they have no one to talk with in the absence of one teacher. (The obvious exception to this is primary caregiving arrangements for younger children; here the primary caregiver is usually the person who communicates regularly with the same families in her group.)

The atmosphere created by teachers and staff can either open or close opportunities for informal chats. The teacher who says, "Hello, how are you?" and turns to busy herself elsewhere indicates her unwillingness to prolong the contact. A teacher who asks a broad question that invites response—"Looks like you've had a busy day"—and stands by the parent, obviously ready to continue, creates an expectation of conversation (see Figure 9-3).

Some teachers complain they can never think of anything to say when a parent comes in. These teachers might consider what they most enjoy about a child and share these observations. It is difficult for most parents to resist a conversation that begins by focusing personally on their child. What else can teachers use to initiate conversation? Parents would love to hear about a favorite song, book, or activity; new things their child is interested in; whom their child plays with; or what the areas and materials in the classroom are called. Get started—other ideas will come.

Teachers striving for daily contact with all parents are helped to perceive their own patterns by keeping an informal tally (on a file card in a pocket or on a paper taped to the wall) briefly recording who was spoken to, for how long, and the topic of conversation. This often identifies a parent who was slipping in and out unnoticed or with whom the teacher never felt comfortable enough

FIGURE 9-4 A school policy requiring that parents accompany their children to the classroom facilitates daily contact with teachers.

to progress beyond the "How are you" stage. Once teachers have identified a deficiency, they can work on solving the communication gap.

One study indicates that almost 30% of child care parents do not enter a center when leaving their children for the day (Powell, 1989). A clear and firm center policy about parents accompanying their children to a classroom is needed, stressing to families both the need for safety and a child's emotional security, as well as the importance of making daily contact with a teacher (see Figure 9-4). The same study showed that as the frequency of communication between parents and teachers rises, communication attitudes become more positive. A policy that facilitates and supports this contact is beneficial.

One center posts a sign-in sheet on the parents' bulletin board just by the door. Rather than signing in just the time of their child's arrival, which most centers do, this sheet provides a space beside each child's name for parents to fill in the phone number at which they can be reached that day.

REFLECTIONS FOR JOURNAL ENTRIES

Consider your typical style of social interaction. Do you let others initiate conversation, or are you more likely to take the first step? Would you call yourself an extrovert or an introvert? Rate your level of comfort in unfamiliar social situations. Now reflect on what these patterns mean, related to the professional efforts you will have to make to set the expectation for regular communication with the families you work with. Where will you have to concentrate your efforts?

Sample Sign-In Sheet
Child's name
Arrival time
Brought by
Will be picked up by, and time
Contact phone number
Today's comments

Space in the last column allows for parents' regular comments. A device like this makes routine the concept that parents will come in each day. Many programs also add a pad for children to sign or mark themselves in—emphasizing beginning literacy as well as daily ritual. Classrooms that find parents are not coming in may also relocate the sign-in sheet so that parents have to come into the classroom.

Teachers may need to help sensitize families to the concept that conversations about children should not take place over children's heads as if they cannot understand the meaning or the fact that they are being discussed. By modeling such respect for children's feelings, teachers help families grow in their understanding of children's needs and emotions. Teachers also demonstrate a professional emphasis on confidentiality of conversations. It is appropriate to direct conversations that turn to specifics involving children or families to another time or place.

"I'd like to talk more about this with you—could we step outside for a minute?"

"This is important information that I'm not comfortable talking about right here—can we find a few minutes when you come back this afternoon to talk privately?"

Some teachers are afraid that by encouraging parents to talk, they will begin a flow of conversation that they will be unable to cut off, and the conversation will interfere with a teacher's accomplishing certain tasks and operating the classroom smoothly. In most situations this is not the case: Parents' own pressing demands limit their available time. In situations where parents completely accept an invitation to talk and spend long periods in a classroom, teachers should realize these parents are showing a need for companionship and feelings of belonging and try to find ways to meet this need. Teachers may suggest that parents join in an activity or find a way of linking one parent with another.

"I've enjoyed talking with you, but I must get busy mixing the paint now. If you can spend a little more time with us, I know the children in the block corner would enjoy having you play with them."

"Mrs. Jones, let me introduce Mrs. Brown. Your boys have been very busy building together this week; have you been hearing about these adventures at home?"

When parents ask teachers for lots of detailed information at a busy dismissal time, teachers may answer briefly, then set up an arrangement to give more information later by note or telephone. If these dismissal requests happen repeatedly, it may help the parent to become aware of classroom needs if teachers have children almost ready to leave when the parents arrive. If a teacher realizes that daily conversations are valuable, she is more likely to find creative ways of dealing with potential problems like this rather than cutting off all forms of communication.

Occasionally teachers can encourage parents to spend a few extra minutes in the classroom with their children and teachers by making a cup of coffee or juice available at the beginning or end of the day. No elaborate preparation is necessary for teachers or parents. Children can show things to parents or play as parents chat with teachers and other adults. Such an occasion offers a brief chance for everyone to relax together and is supportive for both parents and teachers. Chapter 12 will discuss opportunities for family members to become involved with visits and activities in children's classrooms. Every such involvement brings new opportunities for conversation between teachers and parents.

Teachers who work in most elementary schools may discover that a majority of their children arrive by bus or are dropped off in carpool lines. This does not allow daily conversations with families. Rather than assume that communication is impossible, these teachers must find other forms of communication, such as those discussed later in this chapter.

Although daily conversations are probably most important in the context of other plans for family involvement, they should not be seen as an end in themselves; other arrangements are needed to ensure the development of trust and full communication. Nevertheless, beginning steps toward openness are perceived in daily interaction.

Telephone Calls

For teachers who cannot be in daily contact with families, the telephone offers an opportunity for personal conversation. For teachers who have not had an opportunity to visit with parents or children before the first day of school, a telephone call may be a friendly overture to introduce the teacher to the family and express pleasure at having their child in the class (Barbour & Barbour, 2004). Sometimes teachers use phone calls to indicate concern if a child is absent for several days.

"Hello, Mrs. Rodriguez. I just wanted to let you know we've missed Tony at school. Has he been sick?"

FIGURE 9-5 Teachers of elementary school children have to find other forms of communication to replace daily conversations with families.

A most important use of the phone call is to share positive personal observations about a child. Imagine how a child's parents would respond when, tired after a long day at work, they receive a call telling how their child helped a new child in the classroom or said something insightful or funny. Knowing that past experience with schools leads parents to assume that there is a problem when they receive a phone call, teachers let the parent know immediately that everything is fine, and the call is to say hello and let them know something you think they would like to know (Schweikert, 1999). These are "no problem" telephone calls. They can be effective with families of children in elementary school as well (see Figure 9-5). However, it is not a good idea to initiate conversation on the telephone about problems that teachers and parents need to address. Without being able to see parents' facial expressions, it is difficult to gauge their full response. Such conversations are best handled face to face.

> "I thought you'd like to know that Lisa has been working so hard on the new climbing apparatus, and today she got to the top with no help at all! Was she pleased!"
>
> "I know you've been worried about Ricky's appetite, so I wanted to let you know I've been noticing him doing much better at lunch lately. Today he ate two helpings of macaroni and cheese."
>
> "It's really showing how you have been working with Ryan at home on his math skills. He got a perfect score on our multiplication test today."

Such phone calls take only a few minutes, but they let parents know of a teacher's interest in and knowledge of their child and go a long way in establishing positive teacher–parent relations. The telephone facilitates two-way communication.

Parents may be comfortable asking questions about progress or behavior they might not otherwise raise. Using the telephone is especially important to connect with parents who are not in frequent contact with the teacher, either because of work schedules or transportation arrangements. Communication opportunities can be further increased by the establishment of a telephone hour when parents can feel comfortable calling a teacher. One teacher chose an evening hour once a week; another chose a naptime hour when other staff were available to supervise her children (Swap, 1987). When the teacher has some control over when telephone calls will occur, they intrude less into her personal life. And when parents know about this regular opportunity, they will usually respect the appointed time.

Many schools around the country are making an innovative use of the telephone to increase interaction and communication between school and home. Each teacher records a one- to three-minute message at the end of the school day, summarizing learning assignments, stating homework assignments, and including suggestions to parents for home learning. Parents can call and hear the message at any time and can also leave a message for the teacher. This "transparent school" concept has been found to substantially increase numbers of parent contacts with the school. Students from the "frequent user" homes showed a significant increase in homework completion (Bauch, 1989).

Personal Notes

A teacher sending a personal note home with a child can also accomplish sharing positive, personal observations or anecdotes. Notes tend to be perceived as one-way communication, but a teacher may design them to invite response.

> "I wanted to let you know I've noticed Ricky is eating more at lunch lately. Have you also noticed an increase at home?"
>
> "Jonathan told me today that his Grandpa is his 'best buddy.' I thought Grandpa might like to know."
>
> "Tina scored the winning basket during our after-school game with the first graders. We were all thrilled."

Parents are always pleased to know that their child has accomplished some new skill and doubly pleased when the teacher takes the time to share the positive event with the parent. The parents' reinforcing comments to children after reading the note also help children perceive that parents and teachers are working together. A teacher once reported that her note about a preschooler's accomplishment was sent across the country to Grandma in California for display on the refrigerator. This is a lot of power in a few words to create positive family relationships. Some teachers use preprinted "Happy-Grams," filling in the blanks:

"Pete has been doing a good job at cleanup."

However, this type of note lacks a personal tone. All notes, e-mail messages, and letters should be personalized. The adults should be addressed by name and title or first names if the teacher is on a first-name basis with the family. Teachers should be sure they use the correct names, recognizing the different family structures of individual children. It is also better when teachers refer to children by name rather than "your child." Teachers can end the notes by writing their first and last names, or first name if that is the basis of the relationship (Lee & McDougal, 2000). Personal notes take only one or two minutes to write. If a teacher sends out two or three a day, each child in a classroom might take one home within a week or two.

Right Now

Pick up a pen, and write one or two specific sentences that a parent might enjoy receiving about her child.
Now look at the clock. Chances are it took you less than two minutes—time well spent!

Sometimes a note can accompany a sample of the child's work to explain or expand on the idea. For example, for parents who are new at appreciating the stages of art young children move through, it might lead to more productive conversation between parent and child if the teacher makes a comment:

"This is the first time Seth has made a closed scribble with his paint brush. That shows his small muscle coordination is really improving. He enjoyed the red paint today, as you can see!"

Notes back and forth may be exchanged in a notebook or file folder kept in each child's cubby or book bag. It is worth the effort to find a translator for a note sent to parents whose home language is not English. Personal notes of appreciation to parents who have shared materials, time, or ideas reinforce a teacher's expression of pleasure.

Electronic Communication

Now that many teachers and families have access to computers and e-mail, electronic communication offers another option for two-way communication. Some teachers send out daily classroom journals to their parent address

FIGURE 9-6 Electronic communication works well to reach parents busy at work in their offices.

list so that parents may read of events in their offices or homes. Others use e-mail to send reminders, an electronic newsletter, or personal notes. With the ease of a "reply" button, families can quickly respond. Because many parents are using computers in their offices, this allows easy access for asking teachers questions without playing telephone tag (see Figure 9-6).

Still other teachers have created their own Web sites and classroom pages. Through attractive links, teachers can present many aspects of classroom life and learning. Daily homework assignments can be posted here for parents to check (Huseth, 2001). For examples of teacher Web sites, see the end-of-chapter Web sites that can assist teachers in creating and maintaining their classroom links.

Although electronic communication offers additional options for communication with some families, teachers should also be aware of its limitations and cautions regarding its use. Some families do not have equipment or technological skills to access this information. Therefore, teachers should make sure that information offered electronically is also offered in a variety of other ways. Even some teachers are still intimidated by the world of computer technology. There also may be a sense of removal that could inhibit development of relationships. Nevertheless, for many families today, checking e-mail is so automatic that use of this method could ensure frequent contact.

In setting up Web sites, teachers must be mindful of privacy and protection concerns. Use of photographs and student names must be carefully monitored for permission and discussed with families. Even if photos or video are used only within the classroom and families, parents must give prior permission and be comfortable with the planned use. One teacher offers her time to take photos of individual children in action for their families' later enjoyment, asking the families to supply a disposable camera and returning it to them for developing when finished.

One teacher describes her experience in using her digital camera to help the children make slide shows on the computer for families to view during arrival and departure times (Gennarelli, 2004). Another speaks of text-messaging with an apprehensive mother of an infant to provide frequent reassurance through the day. Still another describes how a Virtual Pre-K becomes an interactive educational resource in English and Spanish that bridges classroom with hands-on home activities and community experiences (Narvaez, Feldman, and Theriot, 2006). Current technology allows teachers and families to create innovative ways of communicating.

Bulletin Boards

Bulletin boards offer another form of reaching out to parents. Powell found in his study of child care parents that those he characterized as "independent" had a low frequency of communication with staff and used nonstaff sources of information such as bulletin boards (Powell, 1978).

A bulletin board needs to be clearly visible in an area well traveled by parents, preferably just outside a classroom, so families make a clear connection between the information offered and the teacher as the source. Placing the board just outside the room also prevents congestion and confusion when parents stop to read the material. The board needs to be labeled for "Parents" or "Families" so parents realize this is information meant for them. Eye-catching materials, such as snapshots of children, classroom activities, and samples of work, invite closer attention. Using different colors of paper or fabric as backgrounds is a visual indication to families that there is a change in bulletin board offerings. One practical hint is to place several layers of paper on the board when creating the first board for the year; the next background is already in place when the current display is removed. It is helpful to enlarge articles for the bulletin board when photocopying because larger print is easier to read and is eye-catching.

The information offered by a bulletin board will be chosen by a teacher as she listens to parents' questions and comments or finds areas where they need resources or help (see Figure 9-7). Occasionally bulletin boards may offer guidelines on choosing books or toys; on childhood diseases and immunization needs; nutritious menus appealing to children; suggestions for movies, television, or local events; developmental information or solutions to family problems; or handouts or recent articles that prepare or follow up on a topic under discussion at a parents' meeting. The NAEYC publication *Family-Friendly Communication for Early Childhood Programs* (Diffily & Morrison, 1996) offers brief educational pieces that could be used for bulletin boards or newsletters. Topics include explanations of good early childhood education philosophy, explanations of typical classroom activities, literacy ideas, ideas for learning at home, positive guidance, tips for homework time, and other family/community issues.

(a)

(b)

FIGURE 9-7 Bulletin boards are another way of providing information for families.

Sometimes a sequence of bulletin boards can be planned—for example, one on how to choose good books for children, followed by one on library resources for parents and children. A third board on using books to help deal with childhood problems can be planned. Longer articles, recipes, or directions for making things can be copied and offered in a folder of "take-aways" (see Figure 9-8). The empty folder offers proof to a teacher that a bulletin board is used.

Bulletin boards can offer support to parents in the form of a wry cartoon or two, reminding parents that a teacher understands the childhood foibles confronting them. A bulletin board, or part of one, can be provided for parent contributions such as offers to baby-sit or exchange outgrown winter coats, or requests for carpool drivers. The bulletin board may be used for interactive communication if teachers ask or encourage parents to ask questions that demand others' answers.

If a teacher wants a bulletin board to be used, it is necessary to change it frequently; a board that stays the same for weeks teaches parents not to look at it. When a teacher puts new material out, it helps to emphasize it by a visual change—new pictures or background colors. (If a teacher has the dilemma of choosing to spend time on elaborate changes or new information, it is preferable to pick the latter and keep it neat, simple, and above all new.)

Many teachers who are influenced by the documentation that is an integral part of the Reggio Emilia approach now use their bulletin boards for daily communication about the meaningful work that children are involved in.

FIGURE 9-8 Longer articles can be offered in a folder of "take-aways."

They post pictures, sketches of constructions, recorded conversations, and children's art or writing, along with brief comments, captions, and progress notes. Not only does such documentation enable families to stay abreast of ongoing work, but it also provides opportunities for teachers to engage parents to consider appropriate learning activities and children's development. Design features that attract attention, such as bold titles, questions, or pointing arrows, are useful. See other ideas for design in Carter & Curtis (1996).

SAMPLE BULLETIN BOARD IDEAS

Developmental issues for a particular age in a classroom:

　　Toilet learning and separation for under 3s

　　Promoting imaginative play for preschoolers

　　Television for your school-aged child

　　Helping your child cope with bullies

Educational issues:

　　School readiness

　　Preschool literacy

(continues)

(continued)

How preschoolers learn math

Value of play

Whose homework is it?

Parenting issues:

   Discipline

   Healthful snacks

   Bedtime routines

Community issues:

   Family activity schedules at the library, YMCA, or children's museum

   Community resources for family support or health

   Educational opportunities

Adult issues:

   Tax tips for working families

   Support for single parents and families in transition

   Finding time for you and your family

If a center has enough room, a separate area for parents close to the main reception area can be provided with comfortable chairs, a coffeepot, and interesting periodicals. This is the area for storing resources available for parents to check out, such as parenting books, children's books and toys, videos the teacher has taken of the class, and so on. (If space is a problem, such materials can be stored in a rolling cabinet placed in a central spot during pickup and drop-off times.)

Having a space for parents is a concrete reminder that parents are welcome to stop, relax, and enjoy what the school has to offer.

Daily News Flash

"What about the parents who are in and out quickly?" wonders Dorothy Scott. "Is there any way of giving them classroom updates?"

There are a number of ways of connecting with parents who are too busy for conversation. A **daily news flash** is one method of letting parents know what's going on and information that teachers want parents to know (see Figure 9-9). In a prominent place outside the classroom door or near the main entrance for parents waiting in the carpool line is a large board—perhaps a chalkboard, a whiteboard, a bulletin board, or a corner of one—that briefly describes one thing children have done or talked about that day.

(a)

(b)

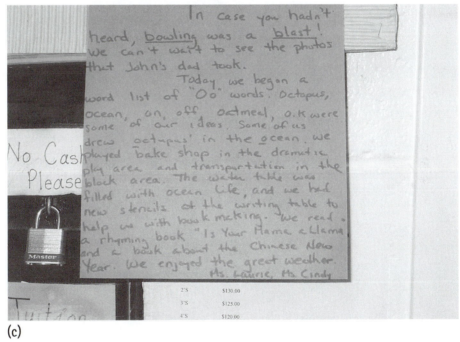

(c)

FIGURE 9-9 A daily news flash may be part of the bulletin board to catch families up on daily events.

"This morning we blew bubbles outside."

"We learned a new song today about squirrels."

"Tommy's mother had a new baby boy last night, so we talked a lot about babies."

"Today we talked about Rosa Parks."

"e started cursive writing today—ask your child for a demonstration."

Classroom daily news flashes are not earth-shaking, but they offer something tangible from the day that parents can pursue with their children. Most parents are grateful for these bits of news that make them feel a part of the day and able to connect with their children with a specific comment or question rather than the vague "What did you do today?"—likely to be answered unsatisfactorily with "Play."

Some centers post a board or memo pad for teachers to write personal reports on each child's day. This can be especially useful if there is a change in staff during the day, so that families have reports from all staff involved with their children.

Tommy: A busy morning, great block building; very sleepy after naptime.

Sarah: Quiet this morning; enjoyed talking with Jamie at lunch.

Seth: Sad for a short time after Dad left, then busy with play dough; hard time sleeping at naptime, so rested, then read a book.

LaTonya: Loved our new song "Alice the Camel"; discovered broccoli is all right!

Many programs use daily information sheets for individual children and families, with a section on top for parents to fill out at the beginning of the day to update staff about how the child is feeling, and a bottom section to tell families how the child's day went. It is important that there be space and opportunities to offer meaningful and specific information, rather than being a perfunctory checklist. Here is a sample:

Daily Sheet

Child's name _____   Date _____

Last night's sleep _____ hours

Awakened at _____

Breakfast _____   Mood _____

Special information today:

Comments/questions _____

Will be picked up by _____ at _____

Meals and snacks today _____

Appetite (circle one)   good   fair   poor   usual

Bathroom activity _____

(Note: This might be more specific for infant/toddlers, or for children in toilet learning phase.)

Naptime: Slept from _____ until _____

Activities enjoyed today _____

Particular events _____

Comments/questions _____

_____

_____

_____

All such efforts convince families that teachers are paying some personal attention to their children and that teachers are really trying to keep in touch. Many schools and programs have a message center with a pocket or mail slot for each family to receive daily reports, notes, or other communication.

Newsletters

Another communication technique involves sending regular newsletters to all families. Newsletters have four main objectives:

- To keep families informed about classroom activities and plans.
- To give parents insights into the educational purposes underlying classroom activities.
- To enhance children's and parents' abilities to communicate with each other.
- To reinforce and extend learning from school into the home.

Parents are often frustrated when attempting to learn directly from their children what has gone on in school, and newsletters can help solve this problem. The newsletter could describe events that have occurred since the last newsletter, upcoming activities and explorations and ways parents can help with them, or practical examples of how parents can reinforce learning at home.

> We had a exciting snack time last Thursday. The children watched in amazement while the popcorn popped—right out of the popper onto a clean sheet spread on the floor. The children enjoyed their snack of popcorn and milk. We are trying to emphasize healthful snacks now. If you would like to join us for

snack or have an idea that would be fun and healthful for snack, please share it with us.

I know some of you have been frustrated in trying to understand the newest songs your children have been singing this fall. Enclosed are some words so you can sing along. [Words added.]

With the holiday season approaching, we will be discussing families—how many people are in our families and the things families do together. If you have a family snapshot we could use for making a book together, we'd be grateful for you to share it.

We have begun working on word problems in our math. Please help your child focus on the logic. Your role might be to help her draw a picture to illustrate the words, such as "Hannah's apple is bigger than April's, but smaller than Daniel's. Who has the biggest apple?"

Dear Parents,

Here are some things we have done in the last two weeks to introduce the sense of smell to the children:

1. We made smell vials using cloves, peppermint, coffee, cinnamon, garlic, chili powder, vanilla, and perfume. We put each ingredient in a vial, poked holes in the lid, and covered them with nylon to keep the ingredients inside.

2. We roasted peanuts and used them in making peanut butter (2 cups roasted shelled peanuts, 2 tablespoons salad oil, salt). First we shelled the peanuts and put them in a meat grinder. This is much more fun for the children than a blender. Then we added the oil and salt.

3. One day we made collages out of magazine pictures of things that smell.

4. Another day we cooked play dough using oil of wintergreen. It sure smelled good!

5. We also learned "The Smelling Song." Tune: "Did You Ever See a Lassie?"

   Have you ever smelled a rosebud, a rosebud, a rosebud?
   Have you ever smelled a rosebud?
   Oh, how does it smell?

The children suggested substitutes by themselves and responded verbally after each verse. These are some basic understandings we were trying to teach:

1. We smell through our noses.

2. We learn about things by the way they smell.

3. Some things smell good; some things smell bad.

4. Animals find things by smelling.

5. Smelling some things warns us of danger.

This might be fun to carry on at home. Ask your child if he can close his eyes and identify foods in your kitchen or on the dinner table. Let us know how the game went.

Dear Parents,

You will likely have heard from your children that the end-of-grade tests will be held next week. We are trying to help the children relax about these, so please do your part at home. Don't talk about the tests too much, and reassure your child that the material on the test is all material that will be familiar. Make sure to get your child in bed early the nights before the tests, and see that there is lots of time for breakfast and an early arrival at school.

When the test results come back, we will explain them to you in a personal note.

Thanks for your support,

John Roberts

Newsletters need to be fairly short—one printed page is enough—so that parents do not set them aside unread, thinking they are too time-consuming. Newsletters sent regularly, monthly or biweekly, will not get too far behind on current activities. They need to be neat, attractive, and display great care for correct grammar and spelling. Have someone else check your correspondence for errors before distributing it to parents. A professional appearance is necessary when teachers are trying to have parents accept the importance of what they do.

Letters can be made visually interesting with bold headings, graphics, changed typeface, or content divided into sections and enclosed in boxes. Bullets can emphasize important points. Care with details indicates planning and effort on a teacher's part—further evidence of a teacher's concern. Teachers often complain that parents won't read their newsletters or notes anyway, so they question the effort put into preparing the materials. Although that may be true of some parents, the majority of families want to know about things that pertain to their children. Therefore, it is teachers' responsibility to inform parents, and "to do it in a way that is easy to read, reliable, and accurate" (Schweikert, 1999). Letters should be dated and signed so families know whom to speak with if they have questions.

It might be interesting for teachers to suggest a question families could ask their children to trigger the children's memories of classroom events:

Ask your child what we saw when we visited the dairy last week. Something special was being packaged!

Ask your second grader to explain to you how the earth moves. You may be surprised to see how much we have learned about space!

Sometimes dialogue or anecdotes from children and use of children's names capture parent interest:

We have some new toys we're enjoying. Maria and Lisa have been busy mothering the new dolls. Seth, Tony, and Matthew have been fighting fires with the new fire truck, and Justin and Isaac enjoy outside time when they can ride the new hot wheels.

Recognition of special parent involvement and contributions and announcements of family events may build feelings that the classroom sees itself as a link for connecting parents, and incidentally trigger more family involvement.

We especially enjoyed Mrs. Rodriguez's helping us build a piñata for the Christmas party.

We're all waiting, along with Pete, for the arrival of his new baby brother or sister. Fanny Lawrence will be taking a few months off from her teaching job after the baby arrives. Watch for the announcement of the arrival!

Although there is no substitute for the personal classroom news that each parent wants or the addition of simple explanatory comments for subtle education from a familiar teacher, busy teachers may occasionally find that they want to insert an article produced by another professional. Some of these are available commercially, as in the NAEYC publication *Family-Friendly Communication* mentioned earlier, or in the letters to families included in *The Creative Curriculum for Preschool* (Dodge, Colker, & Heroman, 2002).

To elicit two-way communication, teachers sometimes add a question for parent response and include the responses in the next newsletter:

Would you please share ideas with other parents about activities and places you and your child have recently enjoyed in the community on weekends? Drop them off in the newsletter box in the classroom, and we'll include these suggestions in our next letter.

Parents may be encouraged to run their own idea corner, with a parent editing this section. A regular feature for the newsletter could be a question and answer section, with parents encouraged to ask questions that teachers could answer for all. This might also be the section that is used for education and for reminders about community events.

Some teachers find that newsletters offer an opportunity for self-evaluation as they answer the questions asked by parents concerning what they have been doing and why. Others use a collection of the newsletters for the orientation of new parents because the pages present a summary of classroom activities throughout the year (see Figure 9-10).

Traveling Suitcase, Libraries, and Circulating Literacy Activities

Teachers can make contact with parents by sending home with a child a "traveling suitcase." On a rotating basis, each child has the privilege of overnight or weekend use of several items selected from the classroom. A child may choose a favorite book to have her parent read or a puzzle he has just mastered to show. Depending on a teacher's knowledge of the socioeconomic background of the families involved, one or more of the items might be to keep—a lump of cooked play dough, with a recipe for making more later; construction paper for use at home; or a teacher-made matching game. Some teachers include a class-made book with pictures and names of each child in the class; parents enjoy associating faces with the names they hear from their children and seeing the visual record of classroom daily life. It can extend home–school connections when teachers provide space at the back of the book for families to write a note back to the children (Gennarelli, 2004).

Most children are pleased to be able to show their parents something that has been enjoyed at school, and a child's enthusiasm often guarantees that the materials will be used and discussed. Children who have been taught that the "traveling suitcase" is a special privilege are also usually responsible about the care of these "school things." The bag can be used to exchange teacher and parent notes as well. A teacher may suggest "homework assignments" that parent and child can enjoy together. "Help your child find a picture of something big and of something little." "Help your child count out two crackers to bring—one for him and one to share with a friend."

Another teacher may use the suitcase to support a family **literacy activity** that is later shared at circle time; one teacher used "Traveling Polly," a stuffed parrot sent home with a notebook for parents to record Polly's adventures when she visited with their children at home. Read about a traveling doll named Heidi, and some of the stories families wrote about her visits, in Spicer (2000). As children dictate their stories to their parents and then hear their teachers read the stories aloud, both literacy and family connections are made. Kalata (1998) describes creating activity kits for families to use together with their children at home. These kits are stored in a "parent box" near an exit door where parents and children together can choose one of a large selection of activities to take home.

Offering parents the opportunity to borrow materials they can use with their children is further evidence of caring. A stock of paperback children's books, perhaps those no longer used in classrooms or homes, may be borrowed for use at home. Numerous classrooms are using a rotating system to encourage family literacy (Couse, 2003). Good children's books can be sent

MARCH NEWSLETTER

A TRIP

On Thursday, February 25, the class went for a nice walk to Dunwood Clinic. Mrs. Stallings showed us interesting areas of a doctor's office.

OUTSIDE ACTIVITY

Swimming has been a lot of fun for the class. It gives everyone a nice outing even if it has been cold. Thanks to Mrs. Huntley and Miss Jones for knowing when it was too cold to go.

CLASSROOM STUDY

For several weeks we have been studying community helpers. It is interesting to learn about firefighters, police, doctors, and others, and how important they are to us.

COMING SOON

In the following weeks the circus will be coming to town. We will be working with different areas of the circus. Animals, performers, and others will be recognized. This is always an exciting time for all.

UPCOMING EVENT

In March Mrs. Houser will come and talk to the class about good dental hygiene. We appreciate her coming in and spending time with us, especially discussing this important area of health.

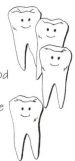

THANK YOU

Thanks to each of you, as parents, for taking the time to come to covered dish suppers, spending time in the classroom, and many other things that you do. With your help and support the year goes a lot smoother.

FIGURE 9-10 Samples of attractive and brief newsletters. (continues)

FROM THE TODDLERS
NewsletteR

WELCOME TO OUR ROOM!!!!
- ANGELICA
- LINDSEY
- RILEY

SELF-HELP SKILLS: We encourage our children to use self-help skills in daily routines because it boosts self-esteem by making them feel useful and independent. At lunch we encourage them to serve their own plates, pour their milk, and then clean up their spot at the table when finished eating. We also encourage them to take off their shoes and put them back on. We strive to help them become independent while at the same time giving them the loving and nurturing they so much need. We have experienced great success with this program. Please feel free to come in and observe us anytime.

THANK YOU TO OUR PARENTS!!!

Karen Forehand – Clothes, containers, and everything you do.

Alicia Andrews Tyler – Food for our hamsters.

Denise McAllister – Your help at lunchtime.

HAPPY FEBRUARY BIRTHDAYS
- Christopher Tyler
- Jasmine
- Ryan

VALENTINE'S DAY PARTY !!! Monday, February 14

Please feel free to let your children bring valentines to their friends. We will be making special mailboxes.

FIGURE 9-10 Continued

FIGURE 9-11 Family literacy is supported when books are sent home in a traveling suitcase.

home one at a time in a plastic bag. When the books are returned to school, another book is selected from the collection until all the children in the classroom have read the books, and then a new collection is begun. The excitement generated among the children about being able to take home a book that a friend has already enjoyed translates into real family interest. A family journal accompanying the book helps parents and teachers communicate about children's progress and pleasure in reading with families (Harding, 1996). Literacy benefits from this variation on the traveling suitcase (Brock & Dodd, 1994; see Figure 9-11). Parenting books can also be available on loan. In the same way children's toys can be available for loan to parents and children.

Another idea for circulating materials between home and school is to have classroom videos available for checkout (Greenwood, 1995). Teachers record classroom activities such as a cooking activity or story time, special visitors and events, and conversations. Children check out the videos to share at home with their families, with an attached comment sheet on which families can respond. Their comments are then shared with all the children back in the classroom. (Greenwood also comments that the videotapes may be used in other ways, such as for open houses, for parents who are sitting in the parent lounge, and to play over local-access cable stations.)

TRAVELING SUITCASE TO PROMOTE LITERACY

Suggestions:

- **A book about a bear, a stuffed bear, and a blank page for child and parent to write their own bear story.**

- **A book and a blank tape for a parent to use to record a story.**

- **A tracing of the child's foot that has been cut out of cardboard, and a list of things in the house. Parent and child measure and list the things that are longer, and those that are shorter, than the child's foot.**

- **A calendar with spaces for parent and child to write in special family dates and hang in the child's room.**

- **A collection of pads, markers, envelopes, and stickers for child and parent to write mail to send to family members.**

Another circulating form of communication could be letters sent home by teachers and school-aged children and answering letters from their parents (Manning, Manning, & Morrison, 1995). Teachers add a letter to all children's circulating notebooks each week about classroom learning activities. Then children add their own drawings and written letters, and parents respond. Not only does the growing notebook document the varied learning and writing progress during the year, it also gives children meaningful opportunities to develop their own communication skills and draws parents into seeing the real evidence of their children's learning.

All of these kinds of materials circulating between home and school both promote communication between classroom and family and suggest appropriate and enjoyable learning activities for parents to do with their children, thus involving them fully in the educational process.

Classroom Displays

Teachers who want to promote communication with families about the learning and development of their children use many opportunities to inform families about daily activities and their purposes. They hope that constant display of children's ideas, questions, and learning will "hook" parents into exploring important topics with their children and their children's teachers. So they regularly create displays that inform and communicate, such as these examples:

- An area to keep children's three-dimensional work with clay or small construction materials for parent viewing, with brief written explanations of the concepts and skills demonstrated.

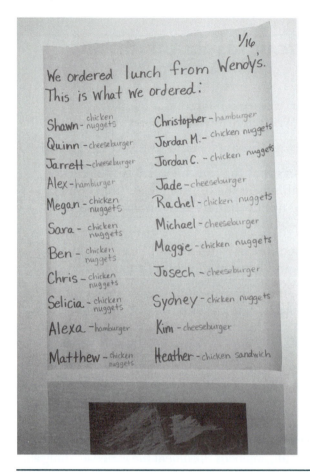

FIGURE 9-12 Posting charts of children's words, questions, and experiences keeps families informed and models uses of literacy for children.

- Posting of chart paper with individual children's answers to daily questions, written by teacher or beginning writers. Questions might be "Where is your favorite place?" "What do you want to do when you're older?" "What's the hardest thing for you to do?" Answers are intriguing to parents and could begin conversations about children's reasoning skills (see Figure 9-12).

- Pictures of individuals and groups at work, posted with brief explanations or children's words quoted.

- A list of what went on in an area during the week. Example: Our math activities this week:

   — Graphed our favorite crackers at snack time.

   — Counted to see how many cups we would need for lunch.

   — Measured feet to see who had the biggest and smallest.

— Weighed different kinds of seeds.

— Voted to choose our goldfish's name (Sparkles got 11 votes).

- Quotes of children's intriguing conversations and questions.
- Displays of children's favorite books, with quotes of children's comments.
- Displays of children's writing and drawing.

Suggestion Boxes

It is useful for teachers to devise several methods of obtaining feedback from parents about the classroom, their goals, and the methods of involving them in the program. Various tools can be designed for parent evaluation, from checklists, to fill-in-the-blank forms, to rating scales. For example, "Check which of the following have been useful to you this month: newsletter, bulletin board, daily flash, daily conversations." Parent interests can be surveyed—we'll talk more about this in Chapters 12 and 13. A suggestion box should be prominently located and its use encouraged. Some parents are reluctant to raise issues with teachers directly and may be more comfortable with the anonymity of forms or printed material. Other parents, less comfortable with literacy, may prefer to communicate through a designated parent representative for the classroom, who can then neutrally raise the issue. In whatever form, this is a demonstration of openness to parental input that teachers want to encourage (see Figure 9-13).

If teachers list the good ideas contributed by parents in newsletters, parents realize that their ideas have been read and appreciated. Newsletter references to the suggestions also provide a means of explaining when or how the suggestion will be acted on or why some things may not be possible.

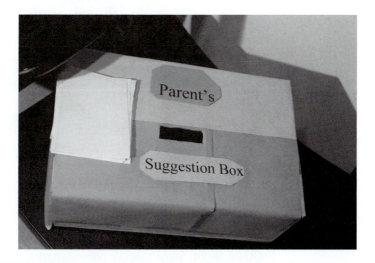

FIGURE 9-13 Suggestion boxes encourage families to give their input to teachers and schools.

SUMMARY

Remember that what is important in all of these methods is the attempt to keep families informed about events that are part of their children's daily lives and to communicate the teacher's willingness to enhance parent–child– teacher relationships (see Figure 9-14).

The ideas discussed in this chapter are not time-consuming, and most don't require a great deal of formal planning. Teachers who use newsletters and bulletin boards often keep a file of ideas, articles, and clippings for future use and save things from year to year. Moreover, these efforts convey to families that teachers are paying personal attention to their children and are really trying to keep in touch. Teachers should realize that these contacts provide vital, ongoing links between families and teacher that are irreplaceable for building knowledge of and comfort with one another and evidence for

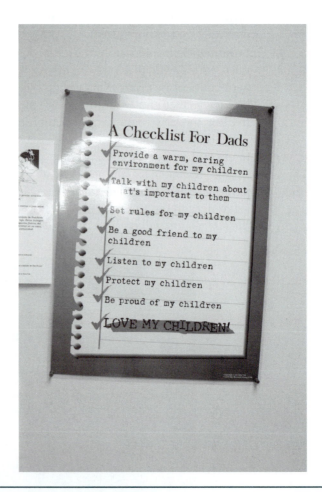

FIGURE 9-14 Some teacher communication is meant to support parent–child relationships.

families that their involvement is welcome. Communication is also enhanced when parents spend time in their children's classrooms, as we will discuss in Chapter 12.

To summarize, a parent–teacher partnership is strengthened as teachers utilize the following informal communication methods with parents:

1. Daily conversations.
2. Telephone calls.
3. Personal notes.
4. Electronic communication and use of technology.
5. Bulletin boards.
6. Daily news flashes.
7. Newsletters.
8. Traveling suitcases, libraries, and other circulating materials.
9. Classroom displays.
10. Parent suggestion boxes and other evaluation methods.

STUDENT ACTIVITIES FOR FURTHER STUDY

1. If you are in a classroom situation, keep a tally of the parents you speak to at drop-off and pickup times each day for a week. (A file card in your pocket can be used conveniently to jot down names.) Are there any families you are missing contact with? Do you know why? Are there any parents you have little conversation with beyond hello and good-bye? Do you know why? What circumstances create difficulties in finding time to talk in this particular classroom situation? Might any alternatives help solve the problem?

2. Observe the encounters as teachers and parents meet each other at drop-off and pickup times. What nonverbal clues of comfort or discomfort do you note? How do teachers use space to convey messages of welcome or distance? Are names used? What topics are discussed? What are children doing as parents and teachers talk?

3. Write and distribute a newsletter for your classroom. (Let families know what has happened recently and why it happened, or how the children reacted to it.)

4. Design a bulletin board with a theme that you feel would be helpful to a group of parents.

5. Plan a brief, personal note that you could write to each parent, sharing something positive about each child.

6. Talk with an elementary school teacher to learn what methods of communication are used.

CASE STUDY

Julia Morris is beginning a new school year and has set a goal of trying to improve her communication with the families of her kindergarten class. She has realized that 9 of the 18 children in her room will ride the bus, so she will rarely see their families. Three of the children will be dropped off by fathers on their way to work, so she will see only one parent out of each of those families, and often very briefly. The remaining six families will have regular contact as they bring their children into the classroom, though she knows that three of these families speak limited English. Last year Julia used a bulletin board as her primary method of communication.

1. Discuss some of the factors Julia needs to consider as she selects methods of communication with her kindergarten families.

2. What are the potential problems in limiting herself to the use of the bulletin board for communication this year?

3. Identify some communication methods that might be appropriate in Julia's situation.

4. What can Julia do to enhance communication with the families who speak little English?

REVIEW QUESTIONS

1. Identify 10 techniques teachers may use to convey information, interest, and support to families.

2. For each technique identified, discuss two ways to implement it.

SUGGESTIONS FOR FURTHER READING

Barbour, A. (1998/99). Home literacy bags promote family involvement. *Childhood Education, 75*(2), 71–75.

Boone, E., & Barclay, K. (1995). *Building a three-way partnership linking school, families, and community* (Chapter 4). New York: Scholastic Leadership Policy Research.

Cohen, L. (1997). How I developed my kindergarten book backpack program. *Young Children, 52*(2), 69–71.

Helm, J. (1994). Family theme bags: An innovative approach to family involvement in the school. *Young Children, 49*(4), 48–52.

Hurt, J. (2000). Create a parent place: Make the invitation for family involvement real. *Young Children, 55*(5), 88–92.

Mulcahey, C. (2002). Take-home art appreciation kits for kindergartners and their families. *Young Children, 57*(1), 80–88.

Teacher.Scholastic Many ways to reach parents. Available at http://teacher.scholastic.com.

REFERENCES

Barbour, C., & Barbour, N. (2004). *Families, schools, and communities: Building partnerships for educating children* (3rd ed., Chapter 9). Upper Saddle River, NJ: Prentice-Hall.

Bauch, J. (1989). The TransParent school model: New technology for parent involvement. *Educational Leadership, 47*(2), 32–34.

Berger, E. H. (1999). *Parents as partners in education* (5th ed.). St. Louis: C. V. Mosby.

Brand, S. (1996). Making parent involvement a reality: Helping teachers develop partnerships with parents. *Young Children, 51*(2), 76–81.

Brock, D. R., & Dodd, E. L. (1994). A family lending library: Promoting early literacy development. *Young Children, 49*(3), 16–21.

Carter, M., & Curtis, D. (1996). *Spreading the news: Sharing the stories of early childhood.* St. Paul, MN: Redleaf Press.

Couse, L. (2003). "MY book!" Building literacy into family involvement. *Young Children, 58*(3), 103.

Diffily, D., & Morrison, K. (Eds.). (1996). *Family-friendly communication for early childhood programs.* Washington, DC: NAEYC.

Dodge, D., Colker, L., & Heroman, C. (2002). *The creative curriculum for preschool* (4th ed.). Washington, DC: Teaching Strategies, Inc.

Doherty-Derkowski, G. (1995). *Quality matters: Excellence in early childhood programs.* Reading, MA: Addison-Wesley.

Gennarelli, C. (2004). Communicating with families: Children lead the way. *Young Children, 59*(1), 98–99.

Greenwood, D. (1995). Home–school communication via video. *Young Children, 50*(6), 66.

Harding, N. (1996). Family journals: The bridge for school to home and back again. *Young Children, 51*(2), 27–30.

Huseth, M. (2001). The school/home connection: Web site and e-mail improve teacher/parent communication. *Learning and Leading with Technology, 29*(6), 6–15.

Kalata, D. (1998). Parents! Let's play! *Young Children, 53*(5), 40–41.

Lee, J., & McDougal, O. (2000, Winter). Guidelines for writing notes to families of young children. *Focus on Pre-K and K, 13*(2), 4–6.

Manning, M., Manning, G., & Morrison, G. (1995). Letter-writing connections: A teacher, first-graders, and their parents. *Young Children, 50*(6), 34–38.

Narvaez, A., Feldman, J., and Theriot, C. (2006). Virtual Pre-K: Connecting home, school, and community. *Young Children, 61*(1), 52–53.

Powell, D. R. (1978). Personal relationship between parents and caregivers in day care settings. *American Journal of Orthopsychiatry, 48*(4), 680–689.

———. (1989). *Families and early childhood programs.* Washington, DC: NAEYC.

Schweikert, G. (1999, March). Remember me? I'm the other parent. *Child Care Information Exchange,* 14–17.

Spicer, T. (2000). Linking home and school—Meet a doll named Heidi. *Young Children, 55*(5), 86–7.

Swap, S. (1987). *Enhancing parent involvement in schools.* New York: Teachers College Press.

HELPFUL WEB SITES

http://www.fen.com

Family Education Network is the Web's leading source of educational content, resources, and shopping for parents, teachers, and kids. The site includes sections for parents and teachers, articles about parent–teacher communication, and advice from veteran teachers.

http://www.nea.org

The National Education Association connects school, families, and communities.

http://www.cpirc.org

The Colorado Parent Information and Resource Center Web site includes articles about parent–teacher communication.

http://www.4teachers.org

The online space for teachers integrating technology into the curriculum.

http://www.niost.org

National Institute on Out-of-School Time.

http://www.schoolnotes.com

Helps teachers create Web sites.

http://teacher.scholastic.com

This Web site has many resources for teachers, including information about ways to communicate effectively with families.

http://www.myschoolonline.com

MySchoolOnline is a Web site building and hosting solution for K–12 classes, schools, districts, and other educational organizations.

http://www.virtualpre-k.org

Virtual Pre-K is an early childhood resource for educators, child care providers, community members, and families that connects early learning from the classroom to the home and community.

Additional resources for this chapter can be found on the Online Companion to accompany this text at www.earlychilded.delmar.com. This supplemental material includes frequently asked questions; chapter outlines to be used as study guides; scenarios that both encourage large and small group discussions and provoke new thoughts and ideas; and chapter resources, including chapter summaries, interactive questions, Web links, and Web activities. In addition, forms from the text are available for download.

WHAT DEFINES A FAMILY?

Today, the world, the family, and the community are different than they were many years ago.

The changes that have occurred in the past century are profound. The family has been turned inside-out:, giving rise to single-parent homes, step children of second and even third marriages often blended together, women working outside the home, and children bearing children. Teachers must understand the different family contexts and respect their uniqueness while drawing the family into the child's educational world.

As America grows increasingly diverse, teachers need to prepare themselves to recognize, and appreciate diversity, using their knowledge and awareness to better work with families, the nature of which is constantly evolving.

Although the media reports that the family is a fatally wounded institution in today's world, the more traditional forms of the family are diminishing while other forms are rising. Read more about changes and challenges in contemporary families in Chapter 2.

The traditional form of the family may be diminishing while other forms are rising.

Permission from Jay and Catherine Gestwicki

Families may include people not related by blood and hereditary bonds, such as those created by adoption.

Due to divorce, many fathers spend only limited time with their visiting children.

Culture determines child-rearing practices, values, and parental behaviors. Read more about working with families of all cultures in Chapter 15.

Although numbers have declined in recent years, teenage mothers head many single-parent families.

A growing number of families include grandparents raising their children.

DIVERSITY OF EXPERIENCE

No one is ever likely to find another family that exactly duplicates the family in which they grew up. Families are created by the ideas, emotions, and experiences of unique individuals.

Their living places, foods, family traditions, and styles of communicating and living together are familiar and comfortable to those within the family and to no one else. Even families who share the same cultural, linguistic, and religious traditions will not be alike, because of the unique inner and outer views of the individuals involved. In contemporary society, with the myriad of cultures and lifestyles of people who live side-by-side, interacting within the same schools, workplaces, and communities, it is vital that this assumption and celebration of uniqueness be made explicit. Read about accepting and respecting diversity in Chapters 2 and 15.

Most family photos today do not include such an extended family close at hand.

There is no such thing as a single form of the American family, but all families have the same functions of nurturing the growth and development of the family members.

Families have their own rich traditions related to their religious or cultural backgrounds.

Culture determines the rules of behavior by which we give meaning to the world, including attitudes related to education.

TEACHER-FAMILY PARTNERSHIPS

A healthy relationship between teachers and family members is necessary for children's healthy development. Research has shown that a parent's or caregiver's level of involvement in a child's program or school is a major factor in a child's well-being and optimal development. Teachers have the responsibility of inviting and encouraging family involvement. They foster communication through a variety of methods, including regular conversations, conferences with families, family involvement in the classroom, and parent education meetings. Read more about this in Section III, particularly in Chapters 9, 10, 12, and 13.

Children benefit when their families are in regular communication with classroom teachers to share their knowledge and ideas.

Regular opportunities for parents and teachers to talk in conferences allow for mutual sharing of information and goal setting

A basic principle of parent education programs is that parents can often learn best from one another.

CHILDREN'S VIEW OF FAMILY

Family is the child's first experience of the world, and impacts his understanding of how people relate and live together. As children see that those around them respect their families, their own feelings of positive self-esteem are strengthened. In their classrooms and communities, children come to understand that families are alike in some ways and unique in others.

Through creative experiences, this perception of diversity is expressed.

In the textbook, you will find lists of children's literature to share with children to support the idea that a family is like no other family, and like all other families. Read more in Chapters 2 and 16.

Grandpa and I ride in his truck.

CHAPTER 10

Parent–Teacher Conferences

OBJECTIVES

After reading this chapter, you should be able to

1. Identify four reasons for holding regular parent–teacher conferences.
2. List eight factors that facilitate productive parent–teacher conferences.
3. List six pitfalls to avoid in parent–teacher conferences.

Besides regular informal contact and conversations, teachers need to provide opportunities for purposeful in-depth conversations with parents in conferences. Such structured meetings let both families and teachers discover additional information, assess their progress toward mutual and separate goals for children, and continue to develop their relationships. Such benefits do not occur without planning and preparation on the part of teachers and parents. Because these conversations cover a wider range of topics than the briefer daily encounters, teachers need to ready materials, questions, and observations to make good use of the time. Arrangements will also need to be made for parental time and participation. With preparation, practice, and care in communication, parent conferences need not be a matter for apprehension.

In this chapter we will examine techniques that can be part of a teacher's attempt to structure productive situations for the exchange of information and plans.

■ ■ ■ ■ IMPORTANCE OF REGULAR CONFERENCES

Casual conversations are extremely important, but the more formal arrangement of parent–teacher conferences offers additional opportunities for families and teachers to work as partners. Yet conferences are often not used by many schools or programs unless there are problems. The reasons for this include both fear and misunderstanding of the purposes of conferences.

The hearts of many parents and teachers may be filled with anxiety when it is time to schedule conferences. Part of this negative feeling may come from the fact that an infrequent parent–teacher conference may be virtually the only contact between them. Ideally a parent–teacher conference offers an opportunity for the free exchange of information, questions, and ideas, which can be accomplished best after a relationship is already established. Conferences can help a relationship grow, but they cannot function optimally if participants are not already comfortable with each other. All of the earlier contacts and communications are helpful prerequisites for a successful conference. Teachers should make it a goal to have some type of contact with every family before conference time. In some cases circumstances may prevent the formation of a prior relationship; however, this is no reason to avoid scheduling a conference to begin the communication process.

Unfortunately, many parents and teachers view conferences as a last step in dealing with negative behavior. If it is assumed that parents and teachers meet only when behavior is a problem, no one can anticipate such a meeting with pleasure. Parents' history of conflict or success in their own early school situations may lay the ground for this assumption. Some will recall negative experiences when their own parents were called in for conferences. In fact, most of this reluctance probably comes from the fact that for many years, in the school systems for elementary-aged children and beyond, the only parent–teacher contacts were infrequent conferences where virtual strangers came together rather defensively to clear up some difficulty.

Many school districts are now giving reports on student accomplishment during parent–teacher conferences. But because of the time pressure on teachers who may have to speak with parents of 25 or more students, these conferences often become purely perfunctory, one-way, mostly statistical reports, with little opportunity for real participation and offering of information and insights by parents. As early childhood education programs began to work with parents, teachers had little except these negative conference models to work from.

To be productive, it is important that conferences be seen as a routine and necessary component of the ongoing coordination of information and efforts in a teacher–family partnership.

"Oh sure, I understand how important it is for parents and teachers to talk," says Connie Martinez, "but I don't really see the need to get so formal as to have a conference. I talk to most of my parents every day. And these are, after all, preschoolers. It's not like we have to talk about reading and math test scores or anything. So why should I have conferences?"

"With everything I have to do," moans Frances Blake, a second grade teacher, "now they want me to sit down with every child's family? Where will I find the time for that? And half of them won't come anyway."

There are several reasons why holding regular parent–teacher conferences is important, regardless of a child's age.

To Provide a Developmental Overview of the Whole Child

Conferences provide an opportunity to examine the overall progress of a child in a detailed and organized way. In daily conversations, particular accomplishments or aspects of development may be discussed. This may be a new ability—such as climbing up the slide or learning to write his name—or a different behavior—such as a decrease in appetite at lunchtime or shyness around other children. Particular problems may catch the attention of a teacher or parent—a new tendency to cry when Mother leaves, or an increase in toileting accidents or temper outbursts; such matters are frequently discussed in daily exchanges. But a complete look at a child's development is not possible in these brief encounters.

In school settings it is too easy to concentrate solely on children's test results and academic progress, omitting consideration of other important aspects of the students' overall development, such as relationships with peers or physical development. Conferences provide opportunities for both parents and teachers to move beyond the daily specifics and limits of the prescribed curriculum to an objective examination of total development.

To Provide Time and Privacy

Conferences provide uninterrupted blocks of time and an atmosphere of privacy—two essentials for facilitating the sharing of information and the formulating of questions and plans (see Figure 10-1). Regardless of a teacher's commitment to talk with parents, the demands of caring for a group of young children may emphatically pull a teacher away from a conversation. She can't stand and discuss toilet training techniques at length while two children in the block corner are boisterously trying to knock down the tower of a third. And in elementary classrooms, bells control the set schedule.

Parents often postpone talking about their concerns because of their awareness of the demands for a teacher's time:

"I've been wanting to talk to Miss Briscoe about helping Pete get ready for the new baby," sighs Pete's mother. "But I hate to interrupt her—she's always got so much to do. I thought I'd go in

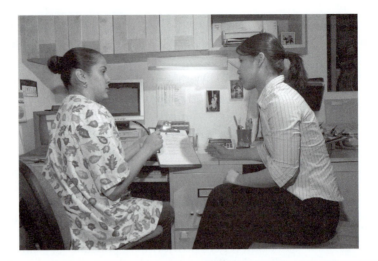

FIGURE 10-1 Conferences give teachers and parents time to talk away from the demands of the classroom and listening children.

a few minutes early this afternoon, but then a child upset some paint and another was crying when she got up from her nap, so it just didn't seem like a good time again."

"I'm concerned about Jason's complaints that the other kids are picking on him, but all the teacher had time to do was tell me his test scores and suggest he spend more time with math homework. The other parents were arriving for their conferences."

Knowing they have time for just talking is important for both parents and teachers.

Privacy is also needed to facilitate comfort in talking. Teachers who are trying to model sensitivity and respect for children's feelings usually prefer not to discuss them within their hearing or the hearing of other children. Although there are occasions when teachers feel it is appropriate to include a child in a parent–teacher conference, every conference should be considered separately, thinking of the individual child and the material for discussion. Many elementary-aged teachers plan to have students involved in parent–teacher conferences, although many others believe parents and teachers can talk more freely without the child present, feeling that a child's presence can seriously inhibit the parents' willingness to discuss family matters.

Parents are often understandably reluctant to ask for help with parenting issues or to discuss concerns where other adults might interrupt them. In the situation where teachers are seeing parents one after the other in their classrooms, they need to find a way to extend privacy for all. The privacy of a conference situation makes important discussion easier. It is vital that teachers make explicit their desire to keep family matters confidential.

While teachers attempt to include extended family members and others involved in the child's life in conversations to share and learn information, they do so only with the parents' permission. Both laws and professional ethics standards require that teachers always be completely mindful of confidentiality.

To Increase Mutual Knowledge

The unhurried flow of conversation in a conference setting allows an exchange of questions and information that brief contacts at the beginning or end of a classroom day simply cannot.

> "You know, it wasn't until after we'd gone through the developmental checklist and Mrs. Butler saw how well Sam compares with average 4-year-olds that she told me how worried she's always been that he'd be slow. It seems he resembles a cousin in her family who has a learning disability, and she was afraid Sam might have inherited the same problem. It really helped me understand why she's been asking so many questions about getting early academics started in the classroom, and doing so much at home. It was a relief for both of us to be able to talk about how well Sam does and to know what she really wanted to talk about was the best ways to stimulate learning in the preschool years."
>
> "It really helped me to have some time to talk with Hannah's dad. I've been concerned that she had no interest in reading independently because she just daydreams when we have our reading period. He told me that her grandmother has just died, and that she always read fairy tales to Hannah. I think now I have a way to reach her."

Misunderstandings and concerns can surface only in longer conference conversations, with time to reflect on what each other is saying. Conferences offer opportunities for clarification and deeper explanations of many issues. For teachers, conferences offer opportunities to get additional pieces of the puzzle. They often gain new information and insights from those who know children best and are aided in the endeavor to get to know children deeply.

To Formulate Goals

Conferences can provide an important basis for formulating future goals and working plans.

> "She decided, during our conversation, that maybe her teaching sessions with Sam at home weren't the best idea. I said that in the classroom I was trying to provide lots of books about dinosaurs,

---

FOUR REASONS FOR REGULAR CONFERENCES

- **To facilitate a balanced examination of all aspects of development.**

- **To provide uninterrupted time and privacy for conversation.**

- **To facilitate a free-flowing exchange of questions and information and to increase mutual knowledge and respect.**

- **To provide the opportunity to formulate and coordinate goals and plans.**

---

his current interest, and was trying to be available to read one to him each day. She thought she'd try something like that at home. We decided to get back together in three months and see whether this method was helping him enjoy books more."

Conference situations contribute to a sense of mutual knowledge and respect and enhance a parent–teacher partnership to a child's benefit.

■■■ GROUNDWORK FOR A SUCCESSFUL CONFERENCE

Such goals are not met without effort. There are important components to successful parent–teacher conferences.

Explain the Purpose of a Conference

Administrative policies and explanations help clarify the routine nature of parent–teacher conferences and the responsibilities of the participants. In both teacher job descriptions and parent handbooks, a statement about the purpose of regular conferences, an indication of when they will occur, such as November and May, and a description of probable content will make this procedure better understood. Offering examples of the topics that will be discussed and questions parents may want to ask helps to destroy any misconceptions about conferences. Parents who are informed during orientation when they enroll their children that conferences are part of a school's regular communication process do not immediately assume there is something wrong when asked to a conference, nor are they afraid to take the initiative when they want a conference.

Parent conferences are a routine part of our school life. A parent conference does not mean that your child is having a problem in the classroom. A parent conference is a time for parents and teachers to exchange thoughts and ideas, as well as a progress report from the team of teachers on all aspects of your child's learning and development. The teachers may ask you questions about how your child plays at home, any special friends, and so on. You will be able to ask the teachers about any aspect of his learning or development in or out of school and share any information that would help the teachers. Feel free to request a conference any time you would like one. We will schedule conferences in November and May. [Sample from hypothetical parent handbook.]

Plan for Uninterrupted Time

Carefully selecting conference times is important: Parents and teachers both have needs to be considered and must have a voice in choosing the time.

Teachers should first decide when they are most free to leave a classroom under the care of another teacher or assistant. In preschools naptime is often convenient. Other possibilities may be early morning, when children filter in slowly at different times, or late afternoon, as children's departure times are staggered and there are fewer for whom to care. Some teachers find they are available during outdoor play time, when other adults can supervise on the playground. In elementary schools sometimes whole days and evenings are set aside for conference times, enabling teachers to offer parents a range of choices for appointments.

With families where both parents work, it may be necessary to offer the option of evening or weekend hours. This may sound like a great inconvenience for a teacher, but being flexible enough to meet parents' needs indicates a real commitment to the idea of family involvement. It is desirable to have both parents from a two-parent family present so that questions and information are not dealt with secondhand. In too many cases mothers come to conferences alone (see Figure 10-2).

Specific invitations to fathers and accommodations to their schedules demonstrate that teachers value the participation of fathers and increase the probability that a conference will be fruitful. Any adults who have primary care for a child should be included; this may mean grandparents, stepparents, and other adults in the household. Teachers also need to be aware of cultural practices that may mean only fathers would speak on behalf of the family in a conference, and mothers would not be comfortable attending alone.

In team teaching situations it is rarely possible for both teachers to be free to join in the conference. It is a good idea for teachers to alternate responsibilities for conferences so that parents do not come to think of only one teacher as the one with current knowledge of the child. Members of the team should schedule time to discuss information to be shared, as well as what is learned during each conference. It is also important that conferences not be scheduled too tightly in rapid sequence. If parents see other parents waiting for their turn, neither they nor the teachers will likely settle into relaxed, productive conversation. In addition, teachers will not have time between meetings to jot down brief notes and reminders.

FIGURE 10-2 It is desirable to have both parents in a two-parent family present at a conference.

Having decided on available conference times, teachers may suggest to parents that they find a specific time convenient to their own schedules. These invitations can be made in person or by telephone. Merely posting a sign-up sheet eliminates the personal touch and tends to deemphasize the importance of a conference, as well as missing carpool parents. Personal contact also helps teachers find out if there are scheduling problems. When a sheet is posted, after a spoken invitation, it should make obvious the abundant choices of days and times, allowing for different working schedules, days off, giving employers advance warning for a long lunch hour, and the like. Teachers need to make it clear, from conversation as well as a sign-up sheet, that they are anxious to be as flexible as possible in accommodating the needs of parents. If teachers are clearly willing to adapt a schedule to parents' needs, they will find responsive parents.

A sign-up sheet might look like this:

NOTICE

It's time to get together to discuss your child's development. Please sign up for a time convenient to you. If you can't find one here, let's find one together.

Nap time 12:30–2:30 p.m.

Arrival time 8:00–9:00 a.m.

Departure time 3:30–5:00 p.m.

(continues)

(continued)

I can also arrange to be available from 6:00 to 7:30 p.m. on the following days: M–13, T–14, W–15, Th–16, M–20, T–21, W–22, Th–23.

> **Tommy**
>
> **Lisa**
>
> **Seth**
>
> **Jenny**
>
> **Isaac**
>
> **Akwanza**
>
> **Pete**
>
> **Ramon**
>
> **Matthew**
>
> **Hannah**
>
> **Emma**

Let's look at a sign-up sheet that is less of an invitation to a parent:

TIME TO SIGN UP FOR CONFERENCES

Any Monday, Wednesday, or Thursday between 4:00 and 5:00 p.m.

Do you see the problems here?

- For parents who cannot be off work between 4:00 and 5:00 p.m., it looks as if they have no other possibility, and the teacher doesn't much care to be either understanding or helpful.

- For busy parents it looks as if this conference may be scheduled almost any time, so there's no motivation to set an appointment now.

- It's too easy to walk by and leave blank a sheet of paper that doesn't seem specifically meant for you. It's much harder to ignore the message when your child's name is there with a space beside it.

As stated earlier, teachers should not depend on words on a sheet to make an invitation clear. When frustrated by parents' seeming indifference, teachers might consider these details.

Teachers and parents must remember that young children are sometimes upset by a change in the routine. Especially for very young children, it is valuable to schedule conferences for times when children can leave with their parents, rather than see the parents leave again without them.

Plan a Private Location

Planning a quiet, private location is important. In a center or school this may mean coordination among staff members for use of available space—staff room, conference room, empty classroom, or another arrangement. All that's really needed is two or three comfortable, adult-sized chairs, perhaps a table on which to spread papers or coffee cups, and a door that can be closed and posted with a sign—"Conference in Progress. Do Not Disturb." Teachers need to convey that the conversation will be strictly confidential.

The physical environment probably least helpful to the conference goals is a formal office, with the teacher sitting behind a desk; the separation of one participant from the other by a desk conveys avoidance. A desk can act as a barricade between parent and teacher; it implies that the person seated behind it is dominant. These are not the nonverbal messages teachers want to send as they try to establish a partnership with parents. Remember that parents will arrive at the conference feeling nervous and fearful. A relaxed setting can help put both them and the teacher at ease (see Figure 10-3).

FIGURE 10-3 A relaxed atmosphere sitting at a table, rather than behind a desk, creates an impression of partnership.

Plan Goals to Be Discussed

In preparation for a conference, teachers must set their goals and devise plans for meeting each goal. Because one goal for every conference is undoubtedly to share information for a developmental overview, teachers need to accumulate the resources they will use to guide this discussion. A simple developmental evaluation tool, which evaluates children's accomplishments in several areas including gross motor, fine motor, language, concepts, self-help skills, and social skills, can be used at the preschool level. Elementary teachers may have the outline of a district report card but must ensure that it addresses all areas of development.

The use of a developmental assessment tool in a conference with parents ensures that the conversation covers all aspects of development. The checklist also offers concrete examples of what is usually expected at broad stages of development, thereby educating parents as well as helping them to consider their children's behavior in an objective way (see Figure 10-4).

Other materials may be used to reinforce this developmental information visually and concretely for parents. Samples of art, collected over time, illustrate the refinement of small muscle skills, new concepts, or new stages in a child's art. Samples of writing or lists of books read may demonstrate emergent literary skills. Examples of daily work collected over time offer parents a perspective on progress. Snapshots of classroom activities may indicate

FIGURE 10-4 It may be helpful for teachers to use lesson plans and developmental checklists to illustrate information.

children's interests or interactions. Many teachers today, aware of developmentally appropriate practices, are maintaining portfolios on children over time to be able to assess their development and learning broadly, with natural methods, rather than by artificial test situations. A portfolio may include samples of work, anecdotal notes from observations, and checklists of observed skills and development. For an example of the contents in a portfolio, see Figure 10-5 (Nilsen, 2005). Sharing the portfolio at conference time provides real evidence to parents of the process of learning (SACUS, 1991). Sharing brief anecdotal records also helps to make the discussion of a changing child more vivid.

To say simply "Tony is doing well with the other children" conveys little a parent can learn from. Vague statements are not helpful to a parent and give the impression that a teacher has learned little specific information about a child.

To check "Yes" to three questions about social development on an evaluation scale offers more.

	YES	NO
A. Takes turns without objection.		
B. Can begin playing with other children without adult initiation.		
C. Plays with other children often.		

Sharing reports of actual incidents that reflect social growth is probably most meaningful.

"You know, each day I try to jot down things that may be interesting to look back on. Let me show you some notes about Tony that show how he's progressed this year in his relationships with other children. Here's one—September 30—the beginning of the year."

Tony was playing by himself in the block corner, pushing two trucks down a ramp he'd made. When David came over and wanted to play too, Tony grabbed the cars and held them tightly. When I went over and suggested they both could play, Tony lost interest and wandered over to the puzzle table.

Playing with other children and taking turns was pretty new and hard for all our children then. For some it's still pretty hard. But let me read you a later note, which suggests how Tony's doing in this area now. February 15. Tony began to build a gas station. He looked around, saw David, called him to come over. Said: You can help me build this gas station. David said: I know, let's build a fire station and I'll be the fire chief. Tony said: OK, and I'll drive the fire truck and make the siren go.

Portfolio Overview Sheet

Name _____ Birth Date _____

Separations and Adjustment Documentation	Recorder	Date	Self-Care Documentation	Recorder	Date

Physical Development Documentation	Recorder	Date	Social Development Documentation	Recorder	Date

Emotional Development Documentation	Recorder	Date	Speech and Language Documentation	Recorder	Date

Memory and Attention Span Documentation	Recorder	Date	Cognitive Development Documentation	Recorder	Date

Literacy Development Documentation	Recorder	Date	Creativity—Art and Blocks Documentation	Recorder	Date

Creative—Dramatic Play Documentation	Recorder	Date	Self-Identity Documentation	Recorder	Date

Group Interactions Documentation	Recorder	Date	Interactions with Adults Documentation	Recorder	Date

Other Documentation
_____
_____
_____

FIGURE 10-5 Portfolio checklist.

Reproduced with permission of author. Nilsen, B. (2005). Week by week: Plans for observing young children. 3rd Edition. Clifton Park, NY: Delmar/Thomson.

Teachers should present observations in such a way that parents will feel encouraged to comment on or react to them. Parents are not told precisely what an observation might imply about a child, but the data are presented for mutual discussion and consideration.

Anecdotal records are also useful in describing to parents, and not evaluating, aspects of behavior that are of concern. One of the best reasons for using such records in a conference is that they offer tangible evidence of how well teachers have paid attention to a particular child—important to every parent.

In addition to planning what to share, teachers should prepare a list of questions to ask so they will be sure to learn from a conference. One teacher's list follows:

Questions to ask:

Bedtime routine and time?
Which friends does he talk about at home?
What are favorite home activities?
Which parts of day are discussed at home?

Making a brief outline of the topics to be discussed is helpful to both teachers and parents. A teacher will not forget items of importance as the conversation continues. An initial sharing of the list of topics with parents and asking for their additions indicates to parents that they have more than a passive listening role to play, and may prevent them from beginning too quickly to discuss problems before a balanced overview is achieved. If there are delicate issues to be raised, teachers will want to particularly plan how they will talk about these subjects. A mental rehearsal of the conference plan will help teachers be more confident.

"Let me tell you some of the things I plan to cover today. We'll go through the school's developmental checklist, so you can see how Pete's doing in all areas of his development. I also wanted to tell you about some of his favorite classroom activities and friends. There are a couple of areas we're particularly working on—his participation at group time, and doing things for himself—so I'll tell you how that's going. Now let me add the questions you've brought in today. This will help us make sure we get it all covered."

Some teachers find it helpful to send home a form to parents to ask for specific things they want to talk about at the upcoming conferences. In this way the teacher learns of parents' concerns and can plan to discuss those issues and have available related materials. A sample conference letter appears in Figure 10-6.

The organization of anecdotal records and developmental assessments in preparation for a conference should take a small amount of time, since these are materials that should be part of a teacher's tools used for individualized goal setting and planning in the classroom curriculum. A last review and organization of the materials will help teachers see they are prepared; pencils

Parent–Teacher Conference Letter

Dear Parents,

As the day of our scheduled parent–teacher conference draws near, we need to collect our thoughts about your child so that our time can be put to good use. The following questionnaire is designed to assist me in covering all areas of concern to you and to me. Please take a few minutes to complete and return it to me *prior to* our conference. Remember, this is *not* an evaluation; it is a *sharing* of information about a child that we both care about.

Thank you for your cooperation.

1. My child communicates the following to me at home about school:

   a. Relationships with children and adults:

   b. Favorite activities and areas of play:

2. I see my child's areas of strength as:

3. I feel that my child needs to develop skills in:

4. I would like to discuss or have more information on:

Have you considered the whole child—social, emotional, physical, and intellectual?

What else have you been wondering lately?

FIGURE 10-6 Sample conference letter.
Reprinted with permission. Cathy Griffin, Dutch Neck Presbyterian Church, Princeton Junction, New Jersey.

and paper should be added for teachers and parents to use for any notes. Being confident in their preparation leaves teachers free to initiate the social interaction of a conference (see Figure 10-7)

Teachers may also suggest ways families can set goals and prepare for a conference. This may be accomplished in two ways. The first way is the letter or handout previously mentioned to stimulate parents' questions. Whatever

FIGURE 10-7 Being prepared for a conference is basic to helpful communication

FIGURE 10-8 It may be helpful for parents to observe their children at work with others in the classroom setting. What might teacher and parent be able to talk about after seeing this scene?

form this takes, the clear message is that parents can expect to talk about any issue or concern.

The second idea is to suggest that parents spend a brief period observing a classroom before a conference—perhaps joining a group for lunch before a naptime conference or coming into the classroom earlier before a late afternoon appointment (see Figure 10-8). Here again, a simple list with a few questions can guide parents in watching their children, the activities in which they are involved, their interaction with others, a teacher's methods, and so on. Such

---

Conference Preparation

1. _____ Time scheduled.
2. _____ Coverage in classroom arranged.
3. _____ Staff lounge reserved.
4. _____ Organization of anecdotal records and portfolio.
5. _____ Handout sent for parent preparation.
6. _____ Parent contacted for observation appointment.
7. _____ List of questions prepared.
8. _____ Outline of topics prepared.
9. _____ Plan for opening examples.
10. _____ Environment prepared—snacks, writing materials, privacy sign.

FIGURE 10-9 Checklist for teachers preparing for parent conference.

GROUNDWORK FOR A SUCCESSFUL CONFERENCE

1. Teacher and parent understanding of the purpose and their roles.

2. Planning for uninterrupted time, agreeable to teacher and parent.

3. A relaxed and private physical environment.

4. Planning of goals and organization of materials.

---

observation often stimulates immediate responses or questions, or it may allow parents to see some of the behaviors that a teacher will later discuss.

A class newsletter before conference time could well be devoted to reminding parents of actions they can take to help prepare for conferences. Suggestions might include setting their own goals for a conference, creating their own lists of questions and topics for discussion, and setting a time to observe in the classroom. Until teachers have prepared for and conducted many conferences, it is probably useful to use a checklist like the one in Figure 10-9 to ensure complete preparation.

STRATEGIES FOR A SUCCESSFUL CONFERENCE

Preparation for conferences has been discussed at length because setting attitudes and atmosphere conducive to full partner participation is vital. Now let's consider the conference itself.

Help Parents Feel at Ease

It is a teacher's responsibility to help parents become comfortable and at ease. Teachers are on familiar territory; parents are not. Unless parents are made to feel comfortable, their discomfort may be such a distraction that communication is hindered. A few minutes spent in casual conversation is time well spent. An offer of juice or coffee may be appreciated by a tired parent, as well as creating more social ease.

> "I appreciate your taking the time to come in today. Pete's been telling me about your camping trip plans. Sounds like you're going to cover a lot of territory!"

Although teachers need to recognize parents' likely fears when entering a conference situation, most teachers also feel some apprehension when approaching conferences. Certainly the advance preparation and thinking through of goals, questions, ways to phrase things, and possible conflicts will lessen this, as will experience. Getting to know parents as people will also make conferences less formidable. Awareness and acceptance of inevitable nervousness on the part of both teachers and parents will help teachers be sensitive to the emotional atmosphere.

Begin with a Positive Attitude

As teachers turn the conversation toward the child, they begin with a positive comment about the child. It is important to indicate to parents at the outset that you like and appreciate their child. Parents are more likely to accept later comments, even constructive criticism or concerns, if the conference begins with both adults obviously on the same side and with a teacher's clear indication that she has paid specific attention to a child and knows him well. A positive opening comment also removes any lingering concern a parent may have about the purpose of a conference.

> "I'm enjoying having Pete in my classroom. I think one of the things I most enjoy is his enthusiasm about everything! I wish you could have seen him this morning when he was talking about the plans for your trip—eyes sparkling and words just tumbling out!"

 REFLECTIONS FOR JOURNAL ENTRIES

Think about any experiences you have had with parent–teacher conferences. Perhaps your experiences have been as a parent, or as a teacher, or as a child hearing about a conference afterward. Identify some of the emotional responses you had about the conference. How do you think these earlier emotions and experiences affect your present attitude to holding conferences as a teacher?

Encourage Parent Participation

Although teachers clearly guide the conversation through the planned topics, they should be continually aware of the principle of partnership and try to draw a parent into participation at all times by frequently asking **open-ended questions**:

> "So he's achieved all of these self-help skills except for shoe tying, and we're working on that. What kinds of things do you see him doing for himself at home now?"
>
> "What kinds of things have you found that interest him for independent reading?"

The use of questions will help a parent expand on a statement so both teacher and parent can get a clearer picture:

> "When you say you're having problems with him at mealtime, could you tell me a bit more about some things that have been particularly troublesome at dinner recently?"
>
> "When you say you've been having a hard time interesting him in reading, can you tell me what kinds of things you've tried?"

Teachers who want to help parents assume the role of "expert" on their child use questions to guide parents toward thinking about possible courses of action instead of telling them what to do:

> "What are some of the things you've tried when he's begun playing with his food?"
>
> "What else have you thought might be causing him to lose interest in his meal?"
>
> "I wonder if reading could be tied in with his some of his other interests?"

They encourage parents to continue talking by **active listening**. This is the technique of giving sensitive attention and picking up a speaker's verbal and nonverbal messages, then reflecting back the total message empathetically for a speaker's verification (see Figure 10-10). Techniques involved in active listening include paraphrasing and reflecting.

Paraphrasing involves restating what another person has said in slightly different words. This is a useful method of checking whether the other's meaning has been understood, as well as eliciting more information.

> Parent: "We've always believed in eating with the children, but lately Pete's been giving us such problems that I'm tempted to give up."

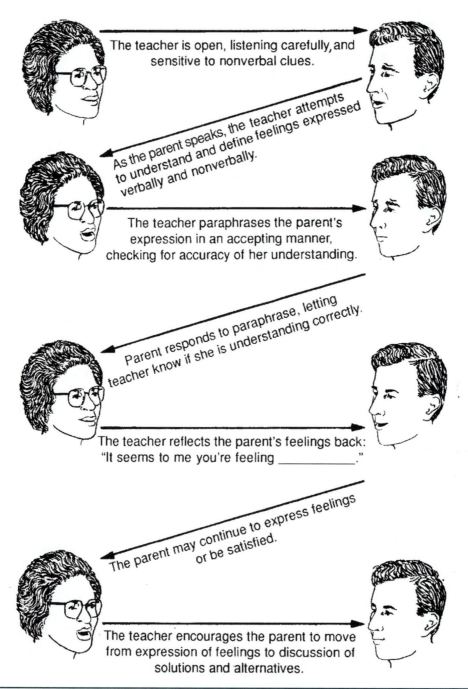

The teacher is open, listening carefully, and sensitive to nonverbal clues.

As the parent speaks, the teacher attempts to understand and define feelings expressed verbally and nonverbally.

The teacher paraphrases the parent's expression in an accepting manner, checking for accuracy of her understanding.

Parent responds to paraphrase, letting teacher know if she is understanding correctly.

The teacher reflects the parent's feelings back: "It seems to me you're feeling _____."

The parent may continue to express feelings or be satisfied.

The teacher encourages the parent to move from expression of feelings to discussion of solutions and alternatives.

FIGURE 10-10 Active listening involves reflecting and paraphrasing.

Teacher: "Mealtime with Pete has been unpleasant lately. It sounds to me like mealtime has become a time of day you really don't look forward to."

Parent: "Oh, it's been nagging to get him to eat, and fussing about his dawdling—it's awful!"

Reflecting offers feedback on the emotional meaning of a message. It is necessary for teachers to put themselves into the position of the other person, to be able to feel as he does, and to see the world as he is now seeing it. This involves accepting the feelings of a parent without judgment and reflecting the feelings back to him in a way that lets him know the teacher understands. When a teacher is not just quietly attentive but is responsive to the feelings behind the other person's words, active listening encourages fuller communication. As a teacher reflects her understanding of a parent's message, the parent is often stimulated to continue talking about a situation, allowing for a deeper understanding of feelings for both teacher and parent.

Teacher: "It really seems to concern you that he's not developing good mealtime habits."

Parent: "Well, you know, it does bother me. I guess because I used to be something of a food fusser and I remember some very unpleasant mealtimes as a child. I want to avoid it developing into a real problem with Pete, if I can."

Active listening has the advantages of sending a message of clear acceptance, defusing hostile behavior, and assisting in identifying real problems. (See Gordon, 1996, and Briggs, 1975, for a fuller study of active listening concepts.)

Throughout a conference teachers depend heavily on questions and reflective statements to indicate they have much to learn from a parent. Asking, not telling, is an important indication of partnership and respect for parents' opinions, as well as a good way to obtain information. Parents who sit through a conference and listen to a teacher talk are less likely to think about ideas that come through a one-way flow—or to come back for another conference.

TEN HINTS TO FACILITATE COMMUNICATION

1. **Stop talking. You cannot listen if you are talking.**

2. **Put the person talking at ease. Help the person feel free to talk.**

3. **Indicate your willingness to listen, nonverbally.**

4. **Remove distractions. Don't doodle or fidget.**

(continues)

(continued)

5. **Empathize with the person talking. See the other person's point of view.**

6. **Be patient. Allow plenty of time. Do not interrupt.**

7. **Hold your temper. You are the professional.**

8. **Go easy on argument and criticism, which would make the other clam up.**

9. **Ask questions. This shows you are listening and helps develop points.**

10. **Stop talking. This is both first and last because everything depends on it.**

Another communication technique that is useful to facilitate dialogue during conferences is the technique of **reframing**. Reframing is a strategy, borrowed from family therapists, that allows teachers and families to consider more hopeful stances regarding children's behaviors and abilities rather than evaluating them negatively and with pessimism. For example, when parents describe a child as "too active, out of control," a teacher may reframe that perspective to being "spirited." In this way, both teacher and parent can look at the child in a new way, working to channel that strong spirit rather than trying to break or stop it. This may help both teachers and families move away from focusing on deficits to appreciating strengths. Changing a mental perspective may not change behaviors, but it does change how adults approach a situation, especially if the behaviors have been labeled negatively in the past. More collaboration is likely when reframing puts both teachers and families on the same side as the child's allies (Rosenthal & Sawyers, 1996).

Summarize for Parents

There is much to talk about when parents and teachers get together. But teachers must be mindful of the time pressures on busy parents and keep a conference to the scheduled time. If more areas arise that need to be discussed, it is preferable to make a second appointment. Too much information at one time may be burdensome and not fully absorbed.

As a conference ends, it is again a teacher's responsibility to summarize the main points discussed, as well as any projected plans. It might be useful to offer a written copy of any assessment tool that the teacher discussed and to offer writing materials for the parent to make final notes. If the teacher also takes notes, this will make it easier to write the conference summary later. It is a good idea for both parent and teacher to leave the conference knowing each has a specific action to perform. Parents need to leave a conference feeling their time was well spent; a summary to reinforce the discussion is

FIGURE 10-11 Offering parents a written summary of any assessment information is helpful.

useful. Once again, it is especially appropriate to be positive about parents' efforts and contributions (see Figure 10-11).

> "Thank you for coming in today. I've certainly appreciated your sharing so much helpful information about Pete. As you've seen from our assessment, he's doing very well in every area. I'm particularly glad to know of your concern about mealtime so I can support your efforts here. Your plan of trying a time limit sounds good—do let me know how it goes."

These general strategies can help to achieve a successful conference:

STRATEGIES FOR A SUCCESSFUL CONFERENCE

1. Teacher taking initiative in putting parent at ease.

2. A positive beginning and ending.

3. Give-and-take in conversation, facilitated by a teacher's questions and reflective listening.

4. A summarizing of areas discussed and action to be taken.

▪▪▪▪ PITFALLS TO AVOID FOR A SUCCESSFUL CONFERENCE

In addition to paying attention to these strategies, teachers need to be aware of and avoid specific pitfalls.

Avoid Using Technical Terminology

When teachers explain developmental progress to parents, they must be careful not to use educational **jargon** or technical terms that are not easily understood and can create distance between the adults. Parents are not likely to listen to someone talking over their heads and are understandably reluctant to ask for clarification of terms.

NOT: "He functions well in the Piagetian sensorimotor stage!"

RATHER: "He is a very active explorer. Every time we offer him a new material, he examines it very carefully, from every angle."

NOT: "She did fairly well on her Denver."

RATHER: "We use this set of questions to see how the children are doing at their developmental level, and she did well, as you'll see."

NOT: "He scored in the 47th percentile."

RATHER: "He is doing about as well as most first graders in reading."

Avoid the Role of "Expert"

Teachers should be careful not to set themselves up as experts on any child. Such a stance prevents the growth of a working partnership; many parents feel shaky enough in the business of parenting without facing a teacher who seems to "know it all." Rather than peppering their comments with advice that focuses on "shoulds" and "musts," teachers need to avoid such authoritarian dogmatism. The implication that if one disagrees, one is wrong, will inhibit discussion.

To avoid the appearance of being a dogmatic expert, teachers need to be cautious about the phrases they use as they share knowledge. Many teachers say "lots of parents find" or "some of my parents have told me"; they find these phrases more easily accepted than "I think," which sounds too dominant. Teachers need to help parents realize that there are few absolutes in child development and guidance; some things work in one situation, others in another.

Certain areas of concern to a parent may be far beyond a teacher's scope of knowledge and competence. It is necessary for teachers to be straightforward in admitting this and to know when to refer a parent to an expert:

"I appreciate your concern about Billy's language. Let me give you the number of the people at Speech and Hearing. They can answer your questions far better than I can."

REFLECTIONS FOR JOURNAL ENTRIES

Imagine that you are a parent in a conference, and the teacher says to you, "Jennifer can't ever stand in line without causing trouble." What might be your response? How could the teacher have changed her language to avoid this response?

Now imagine being another parent, and this is what you hear: "Susan is very selfish. It's obvious she has never been taught to share. I think you should work on this." What is your immediate mental response, as a parent? How could this have been presented differently?

"You know, I'm not quite sure about those admission test score systems. Suppose I check with the school and let you know."

If teachers feel questions could be answered better by another, they may invite the administrator, psychologist, social worker, or co-teacher to join a discussion. Contrary to what some teachers believe, when they confess their limitations it tends not to demean them, but earns them respect in parents' eyes for their honesty.

Avoid Negative Evaluations

Knowing how closely parental self-esteem is tied to others' perceptions of their children, teachers must be sensitive to avoid the appearance of being critical or negative about a child's capabilities. Certain key words trigger defensive feelings in parents, and parents who feel defensive are unable to communicate and cooperate fully. Here are some words to avoid:

Problem—"I'm having a *problem* with Jimmy."

Behind—"Jimmy is *behind* in language."

Immature—"Jimmy is more *immature* than the rest of the class."

Never, can't—"Jimmy *never* finishes lunch with the others; Jimmy *can't* do most of our puzzles."

Slow—"Jimmy is *slow* at learning."

Failing—"Jimmy is failing all his spelling tests."

Remember the reframing discussed earlier? This is the place to consider the positive aspects of a situation rather than focusing on negatives or limitations.

Any labels, such as *hyperactive, learning disability,* or the like, should also be avoided. Many of these terms have been adopted and overused by the general public. Because teachers do not have clinical training, it is not appropriate for teachers to hypothesize diagnoses.

Labels—"Sometimes I wonder if Jimmy isn't *hyperactive*."

Comments that are objective observations rather than subjective characterizations are more helpful and more easily received:

NOT: "Jimmy doesn't like art" (subjective).

RATHER: "Jimmy usually chooses to play in blocks, building large buildings, and adding trucks and people to the scene. I have seen him choose to use art materials twice in the past two months" (objective).

NOT: "Jenny is not a very friendly child" (subjective).

RATHER: "Jenny usually plays by herself in the house corner. I have recently seen her leave the area twice if another child approaches" (objective).

When teachers merely describe specific behaviors, completely adhering to facts and forgoing the temptation to add their own interpretation of factual observations, parents are left to draw their own conclusions. This offers objective information without implying evaluation or criticism. Teachers have a responsibility to help parents think positively about their children, and negative judgments are simply not helpful. Any parent would react emotionally to hearing these. Parents need teachers who can help with realistic and constructive, not destructive, comments (see Figure 10-12).

"One of the things we're working on with Jimmy is . . ." A comment such as this does not imply negative evaluation, such as being behind or a problem, but states action that can be taken. Because behavior is complex, it would be impossible, as well as unproductive, to assign reasons or blame for a particular behavior.

FIGURE 10-12 Teachers need to offer information in an objective way without implying evaluation or criticism.

"That's the bad news. There isn't any good news."

FIGURE 10-13 This cartoon teacher was trapped in the pitfall of maintaining an extremely negative focus in the conference.
Courtesy Bob Vojtkol.

Do not say something like this: "Jimmy has been having so many temper tantrums because your husband has been out of town so much lately." The statement is not necessarily true, certainly not helpful, and so personal and pointed it could alienate a parent from a partnership. An observant teacher watches parents' body language to notice if there is an emotional reaction to what she has said. Some body messages to watch for include facial expression, tightening or withdrawal of the body, the degree of relaxation of hands and body posture, and change in position (see Figure 10-13).

Avoid Unprofessional Conversation

Teachers need to be sure a conversation remains professional, though warm, and centered on the adults' common concerns related to a child. Teachers must never discuss other children and parents in a conference with another; to do so would make parents question how confidential their own conversation is.

NOT: "You know, Mrs. Smith has been having an even worse time with Janie—she had a terrible tantrum the other day."

This might have been intended as a reassurance but is probably unsettling to the other parent who hears it.

> RATHER: "Many parents find that 4-year-olds can get quite out of bounds."

Teachers should not ask personal questions except when they are absolutely related to a concern being discussed about a child.

> NOT: "How do you spend your spare time on the weekends?"

> RATHER: "I've been wondering what time Jimmy goes to bed—he's been very sleepy in the midmorning."

> NOT: "Just how do you and your ex-husband get along?"

> RATHER: "Are there occasions I should know about when Sally will be in contact with her father?"

When parents turn a conversation to personal matters not directly related to their children, teachers need to make it clear that their only role is to listen supportively if the parent needs to talk—of course ensuring confidentiality—and to refer to more expert community resources if a parent seems interested.

> "I'm sorry to hear that you and Jimmy's father have been having some difficulties. If it helps you to talk about it, I'll be glad to listen. I can also suggest a couple of agencies that could be really helpful during such a difficult time."

It is inappropriate to cut this parent off completely; teachers are sometimes so oriented to children's problems that they do not realize that parents have their own exhausting problems that must be dealt with.

Sometimes, especially in a conference with two parents present, teachers can get caught in the middle of a family disagreement:

> "Mr. Jones, my husband and I just don't agree about disciplining Bobby. He spanks him whenever he misbehaves, but I don't believe in spanking kids. What would you say?"

There could only be future difficulty in working with this family if the teacher were to take sides. His answer needs to be helpful and neutral:

> "Discipline is a broad subject, and even many experts don't agree. I think families have to make up their minds and do what's right for them. If it would help, I can tell you some of the things we do in the classroom and why."

Teachers' awareness of their roles as professionals may help them avoid these pitfalls. Professional ethics also require that teachers not share personal family issues with other teachers except when necessary to understand children's behavior or situation. The information teachers learn about families must be protected both within the school and within the community. When teachers see parents away from school in public places, even quiet conversations can threaten confidentiality, with others nearby who could overhear.

Avoid Giving Advice

It is easy for teachers to make the error of giving unasked-for advice to parents; teachers may see a need and have a fairly good idea what could help. But advice from others is seldom effective; only when parents reach a personal conclusion do they become committed to action. Just because a parent mentions a problem, a teacher should not conclude that the parent is asking for a solution to that problem. A teacher is likely not to know the full complexity of the situation and may give inappropriate suggestions. A teacher should not tell the parent what to do at home, partly because the teacher will not be there to help in carrying out the action. Giving advice tends to distance a teacher from the parent. Parents might quietly listen to this advice while inwardly fuming:

> "Who does he think he is? A lot he knows about it anyway—this is my child, not his."

Giving advice may usurp the parent's right to decide and may also detract from parents' feelings of competence and self-worth. Giving advice may also be dangerous; when the "expert's" suggestions don't work, the expert gets the blame and future mistrust. A more effective teacher role may be to help parents move through several steps in problem solving and discovering options that they may follow.

STEPS IN FINDING SOLUTIONS

1. Identify the problem, including agreeing that there *is* a problem.

2. Identify options for responding to the situation. Multiple solutions can be generated by parent and professional brainstorming together, with neither's suggestions being ignored or put down. Teachers will have to set the stage for openness and encourage parent participation.

3. Discuss the advantages and disadvantages of each option.

4. Teachers and parents should choose a solution to try first.

5. Discuss a plan to help implement the idea.

6. Agree to meet again to evaluate how the option is working.

Teachers should remember that time spent helping parents find their own best solution is time well spent in enhancing parental competence and avoiding disrupting a relationship or partnership. It's easy to fall into the trap of giving advice to parents when they ask for it—probably because it's a good feeling to know you have the answer someone else needs! The best way to avoid such a pitfall is to make several suggestions and turn the thinking process back to the parent:

"Some of the things we've tried in the classroom for that are . . ."
    "Let me pass along some ideas that have worked for other parents. . . . Do any of those sound like something that could work for you?"

It's appropriate to help parents understand that in guidance there is seldom one right answer. Parents should be encouraged to come up with their own plans, which they are more likely to carry out than a plan handed to them. If teachers remember that one of their goals is to enhance not only parenting skills but also parental self-esteem, they will realize how important it is to be speculative in offering suggestions, not dogmatic in giving advice. "If I were you, I'd . . ." is definitely not the most helpful phrase because it implies such an absolute and sure position.

Avoid Rushing into Solutions

Another easy error for either parent or teacher is to feel that all problems must be solved and conclusions reached during a designated conference period. Changing behaviors and understanding is a process that takes time and cannot be artificially rushed to fit into a brief conference. It is better to suggest the need for time:

"All right, both of us will try to watch and see when these outbursts occur. Maybe then we can work out some appropriate response. Let's plan to get back together and talk again next month."

It is also a mistake to assume that parents and teachers will always be able to agree and work together, and that a conference is a failure if the teacher is unable to "convert" a parent to her understanding. Different experiences, personalities, value systems, and needs influence how readily each can agree with the other's viewpoint. A successful conference is one in which there is an exchange and acceptance of various insights, including those that conflict.

■■■ DIFFICULT CONFERENCES

What about the conference situations when teachers have to communicate difficult things to parents, such as a concern about development or a worrisome behavior? No matter how trusting the parent–teacher relationship is, communicating about difficulties stretches teacher abilities and parent emotions. It is vital that teachers do considerable planning—reviewing notes and documentation, listing strategies and "what-ifs," perhaps even role-playing with a director or coworker to try responses to different parental reactions (Manning & Schindler, 1997). It may be useful for teachers to consider the analogy of throwing a ball, which may be accomplished simply without a great deal of thought or planning, as opposed to throwing an egg covered with oil. The ball could be considered the typical, casual communication passing between teacher and parent, and the slippery egg could symbolize the communication about matters that have significant consequences for children and their parents. In throwing a slippery egg, the thrower is much slower to deliver the object; the egg is thrown with much more care, with careful preparation and observation of the catcher's readiness and ability to successfully receive the egg. Planning for delivering difficult information must be done with as much care as for throwing slippery eggs (Leading Edge, NAEYC, 1998).

During the conference, teachers need to focus on identifying the concern they share with the parent for the child. It is important that teachers already have laid some groundwork in previous conversations; the concern should not come as a complete surprise to the parent. Teachers must empathize with the emotional responses of a parent hearing difficult news:

> "It makes you extremely angry to hear that Bobby may not yet be ready for kindergarten. I imagine there's some disappointment for you, too?"
>
> "I know it can be hard to hear unwelcome news. Is there anything I can do to help make the disappointment easier for you?"
>
> "I want to help you find the best plan for Bobby. My biggest concern, as I know yours is, is to have a classroom experience next year that will contribute to his growth."

It is vital for teachers to say that they are not being critical, but just reporting what they have seen, citing specific classroom incidents and behaviors and what has been tried so far. It is important for teachers to emphasize how what they are seeing is affecting the child. No matter how gentle the teacher is in broaching the matter, anger is a likely response, perhaps masked as hostility or blame. If parents have trouble accepting information, it is not uncommon for them to employ the defense mechanisms of projection—"If only you could teach better he wouldn't have this problem"—or denial—"Don't you dare tell me my son has a problem." If parents become verbally abusive or irrational in anger, it is impossible to communicate effectively. At that point a teacher's task is to defuse the anger so that communication can begin. To do this, it is crucial that the teacher not become defensive or angry in return. Retaliating verbally, arguing, and

FIGURE 10-14 Teachers must demonstrate an acceptance of parents' different viewpoints and opinions.

retreating from the parents' anger are not helpful responses. A teacher needs to remain calm, speaking softly and slowly. Active listening will allow parents to see their own words and feelings from the other's point of view. Teachers must demonstrate an acceptance of the parents' right to their opinions (see Figure 10-14).

Handling an expression of hostility this way will help a teacher work with a parent on the areas of disagreement instead of losing the issues in personal attacks or emotional responses. (Specific examples of how to work with hostility will be discussed further in Chapter 17.)

Teachers must respect the time it takes parents to process the knowledge and implications of difficult communication about a child. If, in spite of teacher efforts, parents choose to ignore the communication, teachers must realize that "that is their right" (Manning & Schindler, 1997). In the future parents may be able to follow through on recommendations or agree to referral to a specialist.

Sometimes parents need to hear concerns and recommendations several times before they are able to act on them. Sometimes denial for at least a while is a healthy coping strategy, enabling the parent not to become overwhelmed by pain. It is also important that teachers not become overwhelmed by guilt, disappointment, or frustration with parents who do not immediately respond and act on their children's behalf. Teachers must remain available to continue supporting and documenting the concern. Even if parents deny, teachers are not absolved of the responsibility to support and care for the child and family. Teachers also must realize that there will inevitably be unhappy endings.

PITFALLS TO AVOID FOR SUCCESSFUL CONFERENCES

1. **Overly technical terminology or jargon.**

2. **Playing the role of an "expert."**

3. **Negative or destructive evaluations about a child's capabilities.**

4. **Unprofessional conversation: about others, too personal, or taking sides.**

5. **Giving advice—either invited or not.**

6. **Trying to solve all problems on the spot, or trying to force agreement.**

CONFERENCE EVALUATION

Soon after a conference is over, it is a good idea to summarize the information gained and plans made (see Figure 10-15).

> 2/1/06. Conference with Pete's mother. (Stepfather unable to come due to work schedule.) She is concerned about Pete playing with food at meals.
>
> Topics discussed: LAP assessment. Preparation for new sibling due 5/2. Pete's readiness for kindergarten. Mother's concern about Pete playing with food at meals.
>
> Plan: 1. Share information with co-teacher.
>
> 2. Observe Pete at lunch—move seat near mine.
>
> 3. Talk with mother again in two months.

See the parent conference report form on page 351.

It is also useful for a teacher's professional growth to evaluate her own participation in the conference by asking herself questions such as these:

- How well did I listen?
- How well did I facilitate parents' participation?
- Did I offer enough specifics?
- Was I positive in beginning and ending the conference?
- How comfortable were we in the conversation?

FIGURE 10-15 Teachers should summarize the information gained and plans made during a conference in the child's record.

With experience, teachers grow in their ability to facilitate an effective conference.

It is appropriate for a preschool teacher to hold conferences to discuss developmental progress and goals at least every six months because change occurs so rapidly at this time. For the needs of particular families and children, conferences may be held more frequently at the request of either parent or teacher. In elementary schools it is also ideal to hold twice-a-year conferences.

Remember that nonattendance at a conference does not necessarily indicate disinterest in the child or the school. Instead it may reflect different cultural or socioeconomic values, extreme pressures, or the stress of family or work demands. A teacher's response to nonattendance should be to review the possible explanations for nonattendance, see if different scheduling or educational actions will help, persist in invitations and efforts, and understand that other methods of reaching a parent will have to be used in the meantime.

PARENT CONFERENCE REPORT FORM

Name of child: _____

Person giving conference: _____ Date _____

Parent present: _____ Age of child: _____

Reason for conference: _____

_____

Items to be reported to the parent: _____

_____

Parent comments: _____

_____

_____

Teacher's summary: _____

_____

_____

_____

Signed (Teacher): _____

Signed (Parent): _____

TIPS FOR SUCCESSFUL CONFERENCES

1. Prepare carefully.

2. Ensure privacy.

3. Provide an informal setting.

4. Be mindful of parents' time.

5. Establish rapport.

6. Begin on a positive note.

(continues)

(continued)

7. **Encourage the parents to talk.**

8. **Listen attentively.**

9. **Develop an attitude of mutual cooperation.**

10. **Delay making suggestions yourself.**

11. **Encourage suggestions from the parents.**

12. **Summarize points covered.**

13. **Make plans together for future actions.**

14. **End on a note of continuing cooperation.**

15. **Make notes about the conference after the parents leave.**

SUMMARY

Parent–teacher conferences provide the time and opportunity for parents and teachers to consider together all aspects of a child's overall development, including any particular interests, needs, or problems that may concern either parents or teachers. Such an opportunity will help further a sense of working together with shared information and common goals.

A teacher has the responsibility for setting the tone of a partnership in such a conversation by informing parents of the purpose for conferences, preparing parents for their participatory role in a conversation, guiding a conversation, and encouraging more parent participation by the use of questions and active listening.

Being sensitive to the dynamics of interpersonal relations in general, and more specifically to parental reactions, will help a teacher avoid communication errors that can block real understanding or inhibit the growth of a relationship. Careful planning and evaluation of conferences will help teachers grow in the skills necessary for effective parent–teacher conferences.

STUDENT ACTIVITIES FOR FURTHER STUDY

1. With your classmates, set up a role-playing situation in which one of you is a teacher, one a parent. Remember to concentrate on facilitating a dialogue in the conversation by the teacher's questions and active listening. Your "audience" can help you evaluate and suggest other possibilities. Try these situations and any others you have encountered:

   a. A mother asks how to prepare her 3-year-old for a new baby.

   b. A teacher is concerned about coordinating toilet learning efforts.

   c. A mother comments that her 4-year-old son is being very "bad" lately.

   d. A teacher is concerned about a recent increase in a child's aggressive behavior.

    e. A father is concerned about his son who is in your classroom; he feels he is not as advanced at 4 as his older brother was.

    f. A mother asks you what to do about her toddler biting.

    g. A parent is worried about his 7-year-old son giving in to playground bullies.

    h. A teacher wants to find ways to help a first grade English language learner develop confidence in the classroom.

2. With a partner, brainstorm many possible teacher responses to these comments and questions from parents. Then decide which is most appropriate, and why:

    a. I honestly don't know how you do it—kids this age drive me crazy.

    b. What I want to know is, when are the kids in your classroom going to do some real work, not just this playing?

    c. Do you think my Sarah is slow? She doesn't seem to me to be talking right.

    d. Well, I don't agree with your soft approach—I say when kids are bad, they should be spanked.

    e. I don't know if I should tell you this, but my husband has left us, and I don't think he's coming back.

    f. What's the best way to get a child to go to bed?

    g. What should I do about my second grader and his obsession with videogames?

    h. I certainly don't want my first grader held back because of some test score.

3. After reading the following record, develop an outline for sharing this information with parents during a conference:

> Judy is 3 years and 6 months old and is much smaller than the other children in her classroom. She speaks indistinctly, often not more than two words at a time. She plays by herself most of the time and in fact seems to shrink back when other children or most adults approach her. She has well-developed fine motor skills and is extremely creative when she paints.
>
> Despite the well-developed fine motor skills, her self-help skills lag behind, and she often asks for assistance in the bathroom and in simple dressing tasks. She enjoys music and often sits for long periods listening to records with earphones.

CASE STUDY Amelia Jackson is a 5-year-old in a kindergarten classroom. Amelia lives with her mother and grandmother and sees her father every other weekend. Now that it is January, her teacher, Christine Richardson, is becoming concerned about Amelia's solitary play behavior and developmental level. Amelia can identify only two colors and the letters that begin her first and last names. Her mother was unavailable during the last conference period, but Christine feels it is time they spent some time discussing Amelia's development. The teacher has many questions that she would like to ask the mother.

1. What are some of the reasons that Amelia's mother may have been unavailable during the last conference period? What could Miss Richardson do to make it more likely that the mother would be able to meet for a conversation?

2. As the teacher prepares for this conference, what are some issues she needs to take into account?

3. Suggest a first sentence or two that might help set a positive tone for the conference.

4. Describe several potential pitfalls that this teacher needs to be careful to avoid.

5. What would you see as a hoped-for result of this conference?

REVIEW QUESTIONS

1. Identify three of four reasons for holding regular parent–teacher conferences.

2. List five of eight factors that facilitate productive parent–teacher conferences.

3. List four of six pitfalls to avoid in parent–teacher conferences.

SUGGESTIONS FOR FURTHER READING

Abbott, C. F., & Gold, S. (1991). Conferring with parents when you're concerned that their child needs special services. *Young Children, 46*(4), 10–14.

Adams, L. (1999/2000). Conferring with Amanda's Mom. *Childhood Education, 76*(2), 106–7.

Cesarone, B. (2000). Parent–teacher conferences. *Childhood Education, 76*(3): 180–185.

Child Care Information Exchange. (1997). Beginnings workshop. *Child Care Information Exchange,* 116. The entire journal deals with conferences, including conferences with parents of infants and school-aged children and cross-cultural conferences.

Fay, J. (1995). *How to handle difficult parents: Teacher conferences.* Golden, CO: Love and Logic Press.

Flannery, M. (2004). Turning the tables: In a twist on the traditional parent–teacher conference, teachers are inviting somebody else to run the show—their students. *NEA Today, 23*(3), 36–42.

Galinsky, E. (1988). Parents and teacher caregivers: Sources of tension, sources of support. *Young Children, 43*(3), 4–11.

Hauser-Cram, P. (1986). Backing away helpfully: Some roles teachers shouldn't fill. *Beginnings, 3*(1), 18–20.

Koch, P., & McDonough, M. (1999). Improving parent–teacher conferences through collaborative conversations. *Young Children, 54*(2), 11–15.

Lawler, S. (1991). *Parent–teacher conferencing in early childhood education.* Washington, DC: National Education Association.

McLoughlin, C. (1987). *Parent–teacher conferencing.* Springfield, Il: Thomas.

Murphy, D. (1997). Parent and teacher plan for the child. *Young Children, 52*(4), 32–36.

Nielson, L., & Finkelstein, J. (1993). A new approach to parent conferences. *Teaching PreK-8, 24*(1), 90–92.

Quiroz, B., Greenfield, P., & Altchech, M. (1999). Bridging cultures with a parent–teacher conference. *Educational Leadership, 56*(7), 68–70.

Rotter, J. C. (1987). *Parent–teacher conferencing. What research says to the teacher.* Washington, DC: National Education Association.

Seligman, M. (2000). *Conducting effective conferences with parents of children with disabilities: A guide for teachers.* New York: Guilford Press.

Stephens, K. (1996). Aiding families with referrals. In K. Paciorek, & J. Munro (Eds.), *Early childhood education 96/97.* Guilford, CT: Dushkin.

Stevens, B., & Tollafield, A. (2003). Classroom practice: Creating comfortable and productive parent/teacher conferences. *Phi Delta Kappan, 84*(7), 521–531.

Studer, J. R. (1993/1994, Winter). Listen so that parents will speak. *Childhood Education, 70*(2), 74–76.

Taylor, J. (1999). Child-led parent/school conferences: In second grade? *Young Children, 54,* 78–82.

Young, M. E. (1992). *Counseling methods and techniques: An eclectic approach.* New York: Merrill.

REFERENCES

Briggs, D. C. (1975). *Your child's self-esteem.* Garden City, NY: Doubleday.

Gordon, T. (1996). *Parent effectiveness training.* New York: Wyden.

Leading Edge. (1998). Washington, DC: NAEYC.

Manning, D., & Schindler, P. (1997). Communicating with parents when their children have difficulties. *Young Children, 52*(5), 27–33.

Nilsen, B. (2005). *Week by week: Plans for observing and recording young children* (3rd ed.). Albany, NY: Delmar.

Rosenthal, D., & Sawyers, J. (1996, Summer). Building successful home/school partnerships: Strategies for parent support and involvement. *Childhood Education,* 194–199.

Southern Association on Children under Six (SACUS). (1991). *The portfolio and its use: Developmentally appropriate assessment of young children.* Little Rock, AR: SACUS.

HELPFUL WEB SITES

All of these Web sites contain helpful tips for both teachers and parents in conferences.

http://www.cpirc.org
> Colorado Parent Information and Resource Center.

http://www.NEA.org
> The Web site of the National Education Association has much information for teachers and parents.

http://atozteacherstuff.com
> This teacher-created Web site helps teachers find online resources.

http://www.teachervision.fen.com
> The Web site for Teacher Vision has several components, including the Family Education Network (FEN).

Additional resources for this chapter can be found on the Online Companion to accompany this text at www.earlychilded.delmar.com. This supplemental material includes frequently asked questions; chapter outlines to be used as study guides; scenarios that both encourage large and small group discussions and provoke new thoughts and ideas; and chapter resources, including chapter summaries, interactive questions, Web links, and Web activities. In addition, forms from the text are available for download.

CHAPTER 11

Home Visits with Parents and Children

OBJECTIVES

After reading this chapter, you should be able to

1. Discuss several purposes for home visits.
2. Discuss points to consider in undertaking home visits.
3. Describe advantages and disadvantages of home visits.
4. Identify the general purpose and techniques of home-based programs.

Perhaps one of the least used methods of working with families is that of teachers making visits to the family's home. This is not really surprising: Home visits place both teachers and families in unusual positions, making all participants initially wary. Home is the place of family privacy, and everyone is concerned lest this privacy be violated. In full-day schools and programs, it is difficult to arrange the time for staff to make visits, especially to families who are themselves busy with work and family responsibilities.

Nevertheless, when teachers have found their way around these obstacles, they have discovered that there are benefits for all concerned. Children's feelings of self-worth are reinforced as they can take the initiative in entertaining the teacher; parents are reassured about the teacher's real commitment to working with the family; and teachers learn even more about children's lives. In this chapter we concentrate on the occasional home visits made by a classroom teacher as part of the effort to build parent–teacher–child relationships. Varying aspects of home visitation programs, or home-based educational programs, are also described. (See Chapter 8 for a discussion of the initial home visit as part of the orientation process.)

■■■ PURPOSES OF A HOME VISIT

Many students who read this text may never be involved in home visits. Indeed, the only early childhood organizations where home visits are a routine part of the teacher–family partnership are Head Start and Early Head Start. Some Title 1 prekindergarten programs also incorporate home visits. Few elementary teachers do home visits. If this is the case, why read about home visits? The reason is that home visits keep coming up as an appropriate way to create partnerships with families, and therefore it is important to consider the benefits.

A home visit often presents scheduling difficulties for both teachers and families and is therefore one of the components of a family involvement program that is most frequently left out. However, a home visit adds a dimension that is not possible via other methods.

The prospect of a home visit may be frightening for a teacher who has not yet discovered how rewarding this encounter can be for everyone. John Roberts is frank in expressing some of his reservations to his coworker:

> "This whole thing makes me nervous. I'm not all that familiar with the Rodriguezes; the father never drops Tony off, and his mother doesn't talk much. I have a feeling they're pretty old-fashioned. And I never go over to the side of town where they live. I'm always afraid I'll get lost, and hardly anybody speaks English over there. Who knows what I could get into when I knock on their door!"

The Rodriguez family has their own reaction when the note about the home visit first comes home:

> "What does Tony's teacher want to come here for?" wonders Mr. Rodriguez. "Has he got some problem, do you think?"
>
> Mrs. Rodriguez replies, "He said not, but I don't know. You've got to try to be home from work when he comes—my English is too bad for him. I wish we had some better chairs in the living room; I don't know what he'll think."

It is only natural that both participants have these concerns. A home visit takes teachers out of the familiar classroom world for which they are trained and directly into the diverse worlds in which the children live. Some teacher concerns may include

- A lack of confidence in communicating with parents in their own homes.
- Concern about cultural and language differences.
- Concern about perceived conflicts in family values.
- Child-rearing practices they may encounter.
- Worry over personal safety (Boone & Barclay, 1995).

Parent concerns may be

- Worry about their function.
- Concern about whether the home and family "measure up" to a teacher's standards.
- Concern whether the home visit will become intrusive, with the teacher telling them what to do in their own homes and taking too much of their scarce time.

"The biggest concern that most parents have is that the teacher will *judge* them. They worry that the teacher will not approve of their housekeeping, their furniture, or the toys they have for their children" (Boone & Barclay, 1995).

With such apprehensions on both sides, it is easy to overlook the reasons for the visit. But the reasons can be seen in this parent's comment after a home visit:

> Please continue doing this. It really makes a child feel important and special. It also continues my feeling about her school as a "family away from home" and further reinforces the tie between family at home and the "family feeling" at school. (Fox-Barnett & Meyer, 1992, p. 50)

The most important aspect of a home visit, as this parent expresses, is the strong evidence that a teacher cares enough to move beyond the territorial confines of classroom to reach out to a child and his family (see Figure 11-1).

> The visit of John Roberts to the Rodriguez family corroborates the value for both parents and teachers. After the visit is over, Mrs. Rodriguez comments to her husband, "Well, that was nice. He really does like Tony, doesn't he, and he's not a bit stuck up like I thought he was. Maybe I will go into the classroom to do some Spanish cooking with the children, like he said." Her husband agreed. "I'm glad to have had a chance to meet him, since I never get to go to school. He must be a good teacher to go to such trouble."

One teacher said she had thought of home visits as just another means of talking with parents that was probably not as effective as a conference at school because one cannot talk as well in front of a child at home. But from the reactions of children and parents after her first visits, she realized what should have been obvious all along: that the home visit should be chiefly for the child, and that what should be conveyed to the parents is that the teacher likes and is interested in their child, and therefore would like to see his toys, his pets, and where he lives or to meet other members of his family (Bromberg, 1968).

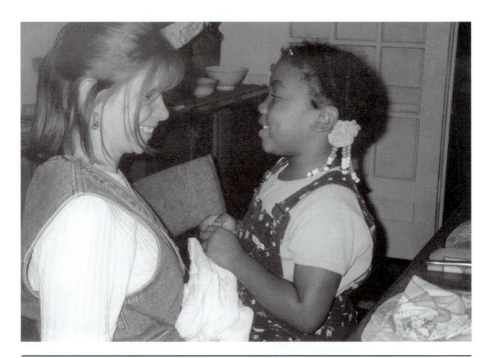

FIGURE 11-1 Teachers indicate their willingness to reach out to families with home visits.

The only purpose for a child-centered home visit is for teacher and child to spend some time together in the child's home. There is no "hidden agenda" of parent education or evaluation; child-centered visits just make children and parents feel good about themselves, and they communicate in an informal way beyond institutional barriers. Home visits help create for teacher and child a shared context that allows the teacher to more quickly understand a child. "In the best visits, a child enjoys her favorite adults laughing and talking together, modeling the art of relationship building, and encircling her with relaxed, shared, loving care" (Baker & Manfredi/Petitt, 2004, p. 152).

Parents at home can communicate more comfortably in their own territory. They often gain the sense that "school is a more approachable place should they need contact or help in the future" (Fox-Barnett & Meyer, 1992). Questions and worries are easier to bring up. It is difficult for parents to be adversaries of teachers when they show such interest and concern.

For a parent who finds it difficult to get to school because of job or family responsibilities, a home visit offers the only opportunity for face-to-face contact with a teacher. A home visit allows this parent the chance to feel involved in the educational process and offers a reassuring look at teacher and child interacting.

To continue to ally themselves with families as they indicate their interest and caring for a child is the primary purpose for classroom teachers to make home visits. Their efforts to make a visit and their warm concentration on a child during a visit help to create a sense of partnership with parents. Once teachers get beyond their initial discomfort, the shared concern for the child opens the way for the relationship among the adults to grow.

Of course, a home visit is important to teachers also in providing first-hand information about a child's physical environment. Information about a home setting and family can be learned by the teacher's observations; a data sheet filled out at a school usually does not convey this information and its implications. Because the home environment is where children learn probably more than in school, it is important for teachers to understand that part of a child's life; exposure to the cultural contexts and practices of individual family life helps teachers respect the importance of the culture and its influence on the child. Learning about the "whole child" includes learning about every family member who is important to that child. Entering a child's world helps a teacher understand why he behaves as he does in a classroom. When teachers have a "feel" for what parents are doing with their children at home and why they are doing it, their own efforts can complement and supplement the home efforts. Carol Hillman says she gains a sense of the parent–child relationship during home visits as she notices whether parents allow their children to take her to their rooms by themselves (Hillman, 1988).

John Roberts's experience points out these benefits for teachers:

"I haven't taught many Mexican children. I've been worried about Tony's shyness in the classroom. After I visited his family at home, I realized that their expectations for a preschooler are that he not take the initiative when speaking with an adult. He really does have beautiful manners—I saw that when he was with his parents; it's not really shyness, just the respect he's been taught. I also discovered that only Spanish is spoken at home, which helps me realize some of his language needs in the classroom. It was fun to see Tony at home—he was obviously very proud to see me there. All this week since, at school, he's been coming to me more."

Because home visits allow teachers to learn about the children they teach and to continue to develop comfortable relationships with parents, it is important for both teachers in a classroom team to be involved, if at all feasible (see Figure 11-2). Teachers may also feel more comfortable if they visit in teams of two.

For children, home visits offer opportunities to feel very special, with teacher's and parents' attention focused on them individually. Seeing a teacher in his home helps build greater feelings of trust and intimacy for a child as well (see Figure 11-3).

FIGURE 11-2 It is preferable for both members of the teaching team to be able to make a home visit.

(a)

(b)

FIGURE 11-3 Only by seeing children in their home environments, with familiar toys and family, can teachers begin to understand children, and children become comfortable with the teacher.

◼◼◼◼ UNDERTAKING HOME VISITS

Although home visits can be beneficial for children, teachers, and parents, they are not accomplished without effort and planning. Here are some points to consider.

Explain the Purpose in Advance

Families need to receive a clear explanation of the child-centered purpose of a home visit in advance. Although the parent handbook and orientation discussion should do this, a reminding note from a teacher before a visit is reassuring. Such explanations may decrease the threatening aspects of a home visit, especially with families who are accustomed to official visitors evaluating or judging their home, financial matters, and functions of family members.

> The reason for this visit is to help the child and parents to get to know the teachers away from the child care center. It also helps to establish a relationship that is both open and friendly. Teachers' visits are mainly social; if you have concerns about your child or the child care center we will be glad to discuss these at another time when your child is not present. [Sample from hypothetical parent handbook.]

Arrange Time with Parents

A teacher needs to make clear arrangements regarding the date and time of a visit at the parents' convenience by sending a note home with a child and following up with a telephone call. An unexpected visit does not permit families to feel at ease and in charge of the situation. Some families like to make a visit a social occasion and prepare refreshments and tidy their house. To be caught off guard does not facilitate a relaxed atmosphere.

> Mrs. Rodriguez reported to her husband, "This is the day Tony's teacher is coming to visit at 5:30. Can you be sure to be home from work by then? He called and said I should say a time when we'd both be here, so I said 5:30. He said he won't stay long, but I made some pan dulce. This is nice of him to come. Tony's excited."

Behave Like a Guest

Despite the fact that teachers take the initiative to set up a visit, they are still the guests in another's home. Actually, this puts them in a desirable position of having to follow another's lead. This aspect of a family involvement program gives parents the clear advantage in feeling comfortable, even though both

ESSENTIALS FOR TEACHERS MAKING HOME VISITS

1. **Make the purpose clear.**

2. **Arrange a time convenient with the family.**

3. **Behave as a guest, accepting the family's hospitality.**

4. **Be on time.**

5. **Expect distractions.**

families and teachers probably experience some discomfort when faced with the unfamiliar. This is a new role for the classroom teacher who is used to being in control.

As visitors, teachers graciously accept family offers, whether this includes sitting on a sagging chair from which the family cats have been hastily removed or sampling an unfamiliar food. There should be no indication, word, or expression of surprise or disdain for the family's environment or lifestyle. They are not there to evaluate, but to indicate support. One of the most essential ingredients for a successful home visit is flexibility on the part of the teachers, an ability to accept variations in family behavior and conditions that are different from what they have experienced themselves.

One suggestion is for a teacher to see herself as taking on a "neighbor" persona; visualize a continuum with "novice" at the far right, "expert" at the far left, and "neighbor" somewhere between these two points (Boone & Barclay, 1995).

A teacher's way of dressing may be important; a style of dressing that is either too casual (old jeans) or too fancy (a new designer suit) may indicate presuppositions about the family's lifestyle and make all participants uncomfortable.

Teachers should begin the visit in a friendly, relaxed way:

> "I see you have quite a vegetable plot out front, Mr. Rodriguez. Who's the gardener in the family?"

Let parents share whatever family mementos or anecdotes they'd like, but avoid leading conversation into personal issues themselves:

> "Oh, I'd love to see your pictures of Tony and his big sister."

Listen respectfully to both children and parents.

> "Tony, I do want to see your kitten. Let me just finish looking at these pictures with your Mom."

In short, teachers use all their social skills of tact, sensitivity, and interest to help both themselves and family participants feel at ease with one another and accomplish the overall goal of enhancing a parent–teacher–child relationship.

Be on Time

Teachers need to be sensitive to the demands on a family's time. Teachers must be careful to arrive and leave on time, allowing enough time to find unfamiliar locations. Scheduled visits should be canceled only when absolutely necessary because the family will likely have made advance preparations. A visit should last from 15 to 30 minutes—certainly not much longer unless the family has invited them for a particular social event.

Expect Distractions

Teachers must remember that they have left the institution in which they somewhat control the environment. When they are in a private home, controlled by the family, it is the teacher who must adapt to the distractions that normal households offer. "It is the parents' phone that rings . . . , the parent's friend who drops in unexpectedly, and the parent who decides whether the television is to be on or off and whether the dog is to be in or out" (Powell, 1990). When the baby cries or the child being visited scrapes his leg, teachers need to adjust to distractions with grace.

■■■ POSTVISIT RESPONSIBILITIES

After a home visit a teacher should do several things to build on what has been accomplished.

Thank-You Note

Send a thank-you note to the family for allowing a home visit to take place. By including positive comments on some aspect of the home environment and comments directed particularly to the child, a teacher further indicates his interest in and appreciation of a family.

> Dear Mr. and Mrs. Rodriguez and family,
>
> Thank you for making time in your busy schedule for me to visit you at your home on Thursday. I enjoyed the chance to see Tony at home and to see some of his favorite things. Tony, your kitten is very pretty, and you are doing a good job of looking after him.
>
> Thank you also for those delicious pan dulce, Mrs. Rodriguez. I hope you can come soon to the classroom and cook with our children.
>
> Sincerely,
>
> John Roberts

Follow Up

In the weeks and months that follow, a teacher must continue to be in touch with the family about the information learned and issues discussed during a home visit. For example, if a teacher discovered ways that parents can act as classroom resources, a teacher should make an arrangement promptly.

> "Mr. Rodriguez, when I visited your home and talked about your garden, we said it would be fun for you to visit the classroom with some of the ripe vegetables. Could you come one day next week? We're talking about harvest season."

Evaluation

A teacher needs to evaluate the home visit to learn how effective it was in strengthening the parent–teacher–child relationship, and how his own participation helped meet this goal. A statement summarizing the teacher's learning should be added to the child's file, to document the home visit and to help the teacher record the information that will be useful in future assessment and planning for the child.

> 3/9
>
> Visit to Rodriguez family. 392 So. Main St.
>
> Present: Mr. and Mrs. Rodriguez, Tony, sister Sandra, age 8.
>
> Learned home language is Spanish only. Tony very well behaved and quiet.
>
> Resource ideas: Mrs. Rodriguez enjoys Spanish cooking; Mr. Rodriguez gardens.

◼◼◼ ADVANTAGES OF HOME VISITS

Home visits provide positive impetus to a family–teacher relationship. Realistically, there can be advantages and disadvantages to this method. Let's first examine the advantages.

Increase in Trust

Parents and children usually feel more comfortable and secure in their familiar home environment. In most other aspects of the relationship a teacher has the advantage as the professional person, of knowing what to do and how to do it. During a home visit parents can take more initiative in furthering the relationship. A child who sees his teacher welcomed as a guest into his home gets positive feelings about his parents' acceptance of his teacher. A sense of trust is increased among parents, teachers, and children.

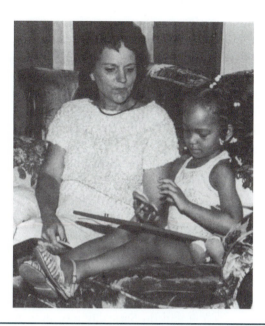

FIGURE 11-4 Children see their teachers welcomed into their homes and get positive feelings about their parents' acceptance of the teacher.

Firsthand Insights

A teacher gains not only the rewarding experience of feeling accepted by a family, but also the firsthand insights afforded by a chance to see parents and child interact in their home environment (see Figure 11-4). Home visits can thus enhance and extend the classroom experience as a teacher uses his knowledge to modify skills and plans to match individual children's interests and learning styles, and utilizes family resources learned about during his visits. Teachers may also increase their sensitivity to cultural diversity and discover ways of responding to the varied backgrounds of children.

Increased Learning for Children

Another advantage of home visits is that children of all ages may receive benefits to their ability to learn when teachers know well how to frame experiences that are familiar, and parents understand how they can support their children's learning (Kyle & McIntyre, 2000).

■■■■ DISADVANTAGES OF HOME VISITS

Although the advantages are more important, there are definite disadvantages to home visits that need to be overcome.

Additional Time Involved

Time is no doubt the greatest disadvantage. Not only do home visits take time, but it is often difficult to schedule a visit during a teacher's normal daytime working hours, especially in a full-day school or program. (In a part-day or part-week program, a teacher can often use some of his planning and preparation time for visits, when a child is at home.) In a full-day program, even if coverage for a teacher in the classroom can be arranged, parents are often at work and the child at school. School administrators may offer compensation time to teachers who use some of their own time off.

Both teachers and parents must be convinced that they will gain from a visit before they will give up time after work or during evenings, days off, or weekends to schedule a visit. A teacher's explanations and persistence as he tries to schedule a convenient visit should show parents how valuable a teacher perceives this activity to be.

As a parent, the author has been impressed by elementary school teachers' evident caring for her children, to care enough to visit in the late afternoon and on Saturday morning. As a teacher, the author's most productive visit came at 9:30 a.m. before both parents went off to late morning jobs. The visit came after weeks of trying to find a convenient time. After this visit, they consented to visit in the Head Start classroom for the first time; their little daughter blossomed.

Scheduling time is a definite disadvantage, but one that is worth overcoming. Expense needs to be considered too; it seems fair for teachers to be paid mileage and overtime for home visits.

Children Misbehaving

Another possible disadvantage is that during this exciting, unfamiliar event children may become overly excited and act out-of-bounds. Then comes the question "Who is in charge?" This can be an uncomfortable position for both parents and teachers. Teachers will be understandably reluctant to intervene in the parents' home, and parents may hesitate lest they show themselves in a negative light.

Advance preparation and explanation for children may help prevent some of this. Teachers familiar with particular personality characteristics of a child may anticipate this possibility and discuss strategies with parents in advance. Teachers may have to be flexible enough to cut the visit short if it proves too stressful for child, parents, or teacher.

Possible Negative Feelings

An obstacle to overcome for a successful home visit is the negative presuppositions of each participant. Many families feel suspicious and threatened by an "official" visit, and it takes sensitive, open efforts by schools and teachers to

FIGURE 11-5 Families may be apprehensive about home visits, so teachers must avoid any appearance of being judgmental.

educate parents and remove these fears. After the experience of a visit much of this concern should be allayed, so teachers must take care to do nothing during a visit that appears to be official scrutiny or to be judgmental (see Figure 11-5). Teachers' care to focus on the positive is necessary.

Teachers must honestly scrutinize their own attitudes and prejudices. In making home visits they frequently find themselves in neighborhoods and lifestyles quite removed from what they are accustomed to, and they must become aware of their biases. When faced directly, personal biases are less destructive than those not admitted, which will manifest themselves in behavior.

By focusing their attention on the children and parents' concern for their children, teachers can find positive things in a home situation rather than focusing on aspects that are different from their experiences. There is no question that emotional responses are complex, but teachers who are conscious of these dynamics of the relationship are more likely to be effective.

Home visits offer

- To families, evidence of the teachers' interest and caring for their children, and an opportunity to play a more comfortable and dominant role in the home setting.

- To teachers, another chance to reach out to families, and opportunities to experience the children's home environments and relationships firsthand.

- To children, a chance to build a deeper personal relationship with the teacher in a comfortable home setting.

■■■ HOME-BASED EDUCATIONAL AND SUPPORT PROGRAMS

This text assumes that most teachers are part of traditional, school-based learning situations and that they consider home visits to be one of a number of methods that build parent–teacher working relationships. It is interesting to note that home visitation programs have developed over the last 30 or more years that focus specifically on teachers educating parents and children in the home.

The goal of most **home-based programs** has been to help families become better teachers of their children and improve the quality of life for individual families. Typically home-based programs serve families who are isolated physically or culturally or who would have problems attending a center. Frequently disadvantaged families are involved in home-based programs; Head Start began its Home Start Component in 1972, and the well-known intervention programs of the 1960s and 1970s referred to in Chapter 4 (pages 135–138) served primarily families considered at risk because of socioeconomic conditions.

Early Head Start programs, funded in 1995 to serve low-income families of infants and toddlers, has both home-based and center-based programs, as well as a combination of the two. Programs serving children with disabilities also use home visits frequently; there has been recent attention to visits to families of infants and toddlers with special needs (Powell, 1990). Some recently established family support and resource programs offer home visits as one of the available options for parent contact.

Family support and resource programs often offer services to families at all socioeconomic levels, thus moving home visitation away from purely economically at-risk families. Some of the most significant models of home visiting in recent family support efforts include Parents as Teachers, the Home Instruction Program for Preschool Youngsters (HIPPY), Healthy Start (Hawaii), Healthy Families America, and the Comprehensive Child Development Program. One survey found over 4,500 home visiting programs nationally, typically operating through schools, health departments, and mental health agencies (Powell, 1990). Schorr suggests that visiting the homes of families with newborns may be the most promising tool "at the prevention end of the spectrum" (Schorr, 1997). In her book she describes numerous current efforts to revive home visiting in the United States. The primary goals of most home visiting programs are mostly preventive: to prevent preterm or low birth weight infants; to promote healthy child development or school readiness; and to prevent child abuse. A study done by the David and Lucille Packard Foundation (Culross, Gomby, & Behrman, 1999) estimated that 550,000 children nationally are enrolled in home visiting programs for pregnant women and families with young children.

These various programs all send individuals into the homes of young children, seeking to improve the lives of young children by encouraging changes in attitudes, knowledge, and behavior of parents. They all offer social support, practical assistance, and education to some degree. Programs differ in specific goals, level of services, staffing, and the population served. Some begin during pregnancy, others later. Programs may work with families from two to five years and may schedule weekly or monthly visits. The study found that there was also variability in the benefits received across the various models; because home visiting programs do not all have the same components, they cannot be expected to produce the same effects.

Various policy and program design decisions determine the content of the home visit. Some programs focus primarily on the child, whereas others include attention to parent and family functioning. If the home visitors concentrate their efforts on working with parents rather than children, they often teach parents how to use everyday caregiving or household situations as opportunities to stimulate learning (see Figure 11-6). When a teacher works with a child, it is a way of modeling appropriate teaching behavior to parents who are present and involved. All home-based programs assume that parents are the most important teachers of their children during the early years, and the skills they are taught have a long-term impact on all children in a family. Parents are expected to add the responsibilities of learners, and then teachers, to their roles as parents and family members. In multiple-focus programs, the assumption is that "pressing factors operating in the environment or parent often interfere with the parent's ability to attend to the child and to other

FIGURE 11-6 Home visitors encourage parents to use household objects and activities to stimulate learning.

information and suggestions of the home visitor" (Powell, 1990). Thus it is thought that resources that support family functioning may ultimately free parents to be more available to their children.

The home visits in these programs require different skills and techniques in addition to those necessary for working with children. In these programs home visitors are parent educators. The importance of a strong interpersonal tie between parent and home visitor is emphasized in most programs. In several programs successful home visitors are trained paraprofessionals. This has several advantages, including the economic factor: It is less expensive to use paraprofessionals.

Another advantage to the use of trained paraprofessionals is that residents of the same community may be used. A resident of the community may already have established rapport with a family, understand the values and attitudes of the area, and be able to use the home language. One program evaluation suggested that the home visitor's role is critical and recommended that home visitors need extensive training and close supervision to function optimally (Culross, Gomby, & Behrman, 1999).

What is taught in each home-based program varies with the goals, but in most programs time and activities are used to build trust and communication between parents and the home visitor, to improve parent–child interaction and learning situations, and to improve home and family life.

Parents who feel isolated and burdened with the demands of young children respond to visitors who treat them with concerned interest. The Home Start guide lists criteria for selection of home visitors that include the abilities to listen with empathy and sensitivity, to relate effectively to many different people, and to adapt one's personality to meet varying needs. Home visitors spend time at each visit talking informally about whatever concerns parents wish to discuss, as well as having sociable chats.

Home visitors are also observant of family needs and spend time helping parents discover resources and methods of improving home practices, such as nutritional information and classes, financial planning, or recreational opportunities in the community. But the majority of time is spent in helping parents become sensitive to the development, characteristics, and needs of their children and in teaching and demonstrating activities and techniques that parents can use with their children at home. Sometimes home visitors bring toys and books and demonstrate how these can be used to stimulate communication and creative play. Often these are left as "gifts," with their use encouraged between visits. Home visitors develop activities or help parents improvise toys from the home environment. Home visitors will individualize activities according to the circumstances, often including ideas for younger children and ideas that other family members can also carry out. They may encourage parents to find their own ways of stimulating learning—perhaps by having a child participate in a household task such as washing dishes or folding laundry, or undertaking a routine caregiving situation with an infant in such a way as to create a learning game.

The following are some of the well-documented home visitation programs:

1. DARCEE, from the George Peabody College in Tennessee, developed home visitation techniques and activities for mothers of preschoolers, hoping to provide mothers with the coping skills and assurance they need to be their child's sole preschool teacher (Gray et al., 1983).

2. The Verbal Interaction Project by Levenstein, based on the idea that parents can be taught to stimulate their children's intellectual development through verbal interaction about specific toys and books brought by the "toy demonstrator," as these home visitors are called (Levenstein, 1971). The Verbal Interaction Project evolved into the Mother–Child Home Program, and today it exists as the Parent–Child Home Program, a home-based literacy and parenting program. The Parent–Child Home Program has a national center that assists communities in replicating its programs. Information about the national center for the Parent–Child Home Program can be gathered by visiting http://www.parent-child.org.

3. The Ypsilanti-Carnegie Infant Education Project and the Wisconsin Portage Project, which work with parents of particular children (infants and handicapped preschoolers) (Lambie, Bond, & Weikart, 1980; Shearer et al., 1976).

4. Home Start Projects, added in 1972 to extend the operations of the center-based Head Start programs by making the home the base and helping parents become the teachers of their children (Scott and Thompson, 1973 and Scott et al., 1976). Early Head Start in many communities is using home-based programs, with home visitors typically making two to four visits a month to families with infants and toddlers (Love et al., 2003).

More recent family support and education programs have been evaluated in a comprehensive study by Future of Children. These include Parents as Teachers, the Home Instruction Program for Preschool Youngsters (HIPPY), Healthy Start, Healthy Families America, and the Comprehensive Child Development program. One finding was that benefits of the various programs were difficult to evaluate and compare; there was no clear pattern of results. Most seemed to produce some benefits in parenting practices, attitudes, and knowledge, although these were often self-reported. Benefits for children were less obvious and usually occurred to only some of the participating children, in fairly small statistics. "No home visiting model produces impressive or consistent benefits in child development or child health" (Culross, Gomby, & Behrman, 1999, p. 23).

Another finding was that, in all the programs, the frequency of the visits was less than had been designed, suggesting that families were either not willing or not able to take as much service as had been intended. The researchers speculated that at least four visits or three to six months are required before change can occur. The researchers state that the existing data do not permit conclusions about which families are best suited to which home visiting model, or about the advantages of home visiting versus some other service delivery system. The research suggests that home visiting programs will not produce benefits across the whole population of families with young children, and it questions whether universal home visiting would lead to broad benefits. Rather the researchers suggest that change is necessary to improve the home visiting services that are currently in place, and that new service strategies should be tried.

The recommendations of the study include the following:

- Existing home visiting programs should try to improve the implementation and quality of their services by ongoing assessment of their functioning and improving training requirements and support for staff.

- Expectations of programs should be more modest, thus adding other service strategies.

Such findings seem to corroborate the statement of Powell (1990), who comments that the full potential of home visits as an effective method of working with young children and parents has yet to be realized.

SUMMARY

Home visits offer evidence of a teacher's interest in and caring about the parents' child, as well as an opportunity for families to play a more comfortable and dominant role in their home setting. For teachers this is another chance to reach out to families and an opportunity to experience a child's home environment and relationships firsthand. For children it is a chance to build a deeper personal relationship with a teacher in a secure home setting. Much has been learned from the home-based educational programs, and any community deciding to investigate or institute such a program has abundant resource information from which to draw. Some of the references and Web sites at the end of this chapter can help a student who wishes to investigate these programs further.

STUDENT ACTIVITIES FOR FURTHER STUDY

1. Role-play, then discuss the dynamics in, the following situations a teacher might encounter during a home visit:

   a. A mother is fearful lest her husband be awakened from sleep—he's a third-shift worker.

   b. A child begins to "show off"; the mother is embarrassed.

   c. A mother begins talking negatively about her child's behavior as her child sits in the same room.

   d. A mother appears shy—virtually inarticulate.

   e. The parents keep watching a television program after a teacher sits down.

    f. The parents seem ill at ease—they keep asking if their child is doing anything bad.

    g. The mother speaks no English at all, and the father speaks not much.

2. Discover whether there is any kind of home-based program in your community. If so, try to arrange to accompany a home visitor.

3. Discover whether there is a Head Start or other preschool program in your community where teachers make regular home visits. If so, try to arrange to visit along with a teacher.

4. Investigate whether any elementary teachers or schools in your community conduct home visits. If not, try to discover why not.

CASE STUDIES

I. You live in a community that is considering a number of ways to support families to prepare their children for school success. One of the suggestions being explored is a home-based literacy program, with trained home visitors who work with families during biweekly visits. In preparing your comments to support this plan, consider some of these questions:

1. What would be important criteria for selection and training of the home visitors?

2. How might a home-based program offer benefits that a center-based program might not?

3. What information should be given to families to help them understand what the program is (and what it is not)?

II. You are a kindergarten teacher working in a school that encourages teachers to do home visits to the children and their families, though it does not make time in the schedule for them. You have decided you want to do home visits before school starts this year. Your principal says you can use some of the teacher workdays in August for this purpose. You know that several of the families do not speak English.

1. How will you arrange these visits to families you have not yet met? What forms of communication will you use, and how will you explain your purpose?

2. What will you need to think about in planning these visits? How will you prepare?

3. What will you do to be able to visit the families who do not speak English? What community resources might help you with this issue?

REVIEW QUESTIONS

1. Identify several purposes for teachers making home visits.

2. Discuss several points to consider in undertaking home visits.

3. Name one advantage and one disadvantage of a home visit.

4. Identify the general purposes and techniques of home-based programs.

SUGGESTIONS FOR FURTHER READING

Epstein, A., Larner, M. and Halpern, R. (1995). *A guide to developing community-based family support programs.* Ypsilanti, MI: High/Scope Press.

Gomby, S., Larson, S., Lewit, E., & Berhman, R. (1993). Home visiting: Analysis and recommendations. *The Future of Children, 3*(3).

Goodson, B. D., & Hess, R. (1975). *Parents as teachers of young children: An evaluative review of some contemporary concepts and programs.* Stanford, CA: Stanford University Press.

Gorter-Reu, M., & Anderson, J. (1998). Home, kits, home visits, and more! *Young Children, 53*(3), 71–74.

Gray, S. W., et al. (1983). The early training project 1962–80. In Consortium for Longitudinal Studies (Ed.), *As the twig is bent: Lasting effects of preschool programs.* Hillsdale, NJ: Erlbaum.

"Home visiting with families with infants and toddlers." (1997). *Zero to Three, 17*(4).

Johnston, L., & Mermin, J. (1994). Easing children's entry to school: Home visits help. *Young Children, 49*(5), 62–68.

Karnes, M. B., & Zehrbach, R. (1977). Educational intervention at home. In M. C. Day & R. Parker (Eds.), *Preschool in action: Explaining early childhood programs.* Boston: Allyn & Bacon.

Klass, C. (1996). *Home visiting: Promoting healthy parent and child development.* Baltimore, MD: Paul H. Brookes Publ. Co.

Meyer, T. (1990). Home visits: A child-centered approach to an old concept. *Day Care and Early Education, 17*(3), 18–21.

Packer, A., Hoffman, S., Bozler, B., & Bear, N. (1976). Home learning activities for children. In I. Gordon & W. Breivogel (Eds.), *Building effective home–school relationships.* Boston, MA: Allyn and Bacon.

Paulsell, D., et al. (2000). *Leading the way: Characteristics and early experiences of selected Early Head Start programs. Executive summary, vols. I, II, and III.* Prepared by Mathematica Policy Research, Inc. Available online at http://www2.acf.dhhs.gov/programs/hsb/index.htm.

Wasik, B., & Bryant, D. (2000). *Home visiting: Procedures for helping families* (2nd ed.). Mountain View, CA: Sage Pubs.

Weiss, H. (1993). Home visits: Necessary but not sufficient. *The Future of Children, 3*(3).

REFERENCES

Baker, A. and Manfredi/Petitt, L. (2004). *Relationships, the heart of quality care: Creating community among adults in early care settings.* Washington, DC: NAEYC.

Boone, E., & Barclay, K. (1995). *Building a three-way partnership: Linking school, families, and community.* New York: Scholastic Leadership Policy Research.

Bromberg, S. (1968). A beginning teacher works with parents. *Young Children, 24*(2), 75–80.

Culross, P., Gomby, D., & Behrman, R. (1999). Home visiting: Recent program evaluations—Analysis and recommendations. *Future of Children, 9*(1). Available online at http://www.futureofchildren.org.

Fox-Barnett, M., & Meyer, T. (1992). The teacher's playing at my house this week! *Young Children, 47*(5), 45–50.

Gordon, J. J., & Breivogel, W. F. (Eds.). (1976). *Building effective home–school relationships.* Boston: Allyn & Bacon.

Gray, S. W., et al. (1983). The early training project 1962–80. In Consortium for Longitudinal Studies (Ed.), *As the twig is bent: Lasting effects of preschool programs.* Hillsdale, NJ: Erlbaum.

Hillman, C. (1988). *Teaching four-year-olds.* Bloomington, IN: Phi Delta Kappan.

Kyle, D., & McIntyre, E. (2000). Family visits benefit teachers and families—and students most of all. Available at http://www.cal.org/crede/pubs/.

Lambie, D. Z., Bond, J. T., & Weikart, D. (1980). *Home teaching with mothers and infants.* Ypsilanti, MI: High/Scope Educational Research Foundation.

Levenstein, P. (1971). The mother child home program. In M. C. Day & R. Parker (Eds.), *Preschool in action: Explaining early childhood programs.* Boston: Allyn & Bacon.

Love, J., Harrison, L., Sagi-Schwartz, A., et al. (2003). " Child care quality matters: How conclusions may vary with context." *Child Development, 74*(4), 1021–1033.

Powell, D. R. (1990). Home visiting in the early years: Policy and program design decisions. *Young Children, 45*(6), 65–73.

Schorr, L. (1997). *Common purposes: Strengthening families and neighborhoods to rebuild America.* New York: Doubleday.

Scott, R., & Thompson, H. (1973). Home Starts I and II. *Today's Education, 62*(2), 32–34.

Scott, R., Wagner, G., & Casinger, J. (1976). *Home Start idea books.* Darien, CT: Early Years Press.

Shearer, D., et al. (1976). *Portage guide to early education.* Portage, WI: Cooperative Educational Service Agency 12.

U.S. Dept. of Health, Education, and Welfare (Office of Child Development). (1985). *A guide for planning and operating home-based program option.* Washington, DC: U.S. Govt. Printing Office.

U.S. Dept. of Health, Education, and Welfare. (1985). *Home start and other programs for parents and children.* Washington, DC: U.S. Govt. Printing Office.

HELPFUL WEB SITES

http://www.parent-child.org

The Parent–Child Home Program (formerly the Verbal Interaction Project, one of the first home-based visitation programs) is committed to helping families challenged by poverty, low levels of education, language barriers, and other obstacles to educational success guide their children to school success by stimulating parent–child verbal interaction and developing critical language and literacy skills.

http://www.patnc.org

Parents as Teachers (PAT) is an international early childhood parent education and family support program serving families throughout pregnancy until their children enter kindergarten, usually at age 5. The program is designed to enhance child development and school achievement through parent education accessible to all families. It is a universal access model that utilizes home visits.

www.ehsnrc.org

 The Web site for Early Head Start.

www.headstartinfo.org

 The Head Start Publications Center Web site, which offers publications related to home-based programs.

www.hippyusa.org

 The Web site for Home Instruction Program for Preschool Youngsters (HIPPY) has much information on its services for families delivered by home visits.

www.perpetualpreschool.com

 This Web site offers home visit ideas and opportunities for teachers to discuss common issues.

www.inspiringteachers.com

 The Web site for this teacher-created organization, dedicated to empowering teachers and improving student success, has articles about home visits.

http://www.portageproject.org

 The Portage Project is committed to creating and enhancing quality programs that promote the development and education of all children through services, materials, and advocacy. This is one of the original home-based programs.

Additional resources for this chapter can be found on the Online Companion to accompany this text at www.earlychilded.delmar.com. This supplemental material includes frequently asked questions; chapter outlines to be used as study guides; scenarios that both encourage large and small group discussions and provoke new thoughts and ideas; and chapter resources, including chapter summaries, interactive questions, Web links, and Web activities. In addition, forms from the text are available for download.

CHAPTER 12

Families in the Classroom

OBJECTIVES

After reading this chapter, you should be able to

1 Discuss several advantages and potential problems of working with parents in a classroom.

2 Identify methods of encouraging family visitations.

3 Discuss methods to facilitate parent observation.

4 Describe methods of utilizing families as resources in a classroom.

KEY TERMS
latchkey child care
parent cooperative nursery schools
resource file

One traditional way families have been involved in their children's education has been as volunteers in the classroom. The parent cooperative preschools that began in the first decades of the 20th century believed that including parents in nursery school classrooms would educate them as parents and would extend the learning experiences available to their children. Certainly bringing families into the classroom does this, as well as giving them opportunities to understand the program through firsthand observation. But in too many cases parent participation in classrooms has deteriorated into assignments of unattractive tasks, rather than seeing their participation as another method of developing communication and working partnerships.

There are many roles parents can play within the preschool and elementary school classroom, from observer to teacher. This chapter examines these roles and considers ways teachers can make their participation enjoyable for everyone, including their children. Planning, preparation of all participants, and positive attitudes will help teachers draw families into the educational process of their children.

▓▓■ ADVANTAGES AND POTENTIAL PROBLEMS

There is a lively discussion going on in the teacher's lounge. Jane Briscoe has just announced she has a parent coming in to play the guitar at group time. MiLan Ha says nothing; she's never had a parent in, but Anne Morgan has told Jane she's just asking for trouble.

"It's a disaster when a parent comes in; the whole routine gets turned upside down, and worst of all, I guarantee you the parent's child will act up dreadfully."

Connie Martinez agrees. "One of my parents came in last year and brought a cake and balloons for everybody on her daughter's birthday. When the birthday girl's balloon broke, she burst into tears and her mother slapped her. I was furious, but what could I do? Now I just ask them to have parties at home."

Jane looks thoughtful and a little worried, too.

There is no question that bringing families into a classroom adds responsibilities for teachers as they cope with various aspects of behavior and reactions of both children and visitors. Teachers often object to having parents in the classroom for reasons both professional and personal.

Involving parents in a classroom for any reason demands extra time and effort from a teacher because there are plans to make and fit into the routine. The best use of parents' time and skills must be determined, and both children and parents must be prepared for their roles in the unusual event.

Jane Briscoe admits it took several conversations with Mr. Butler to learn about his guitar-playing skill, and then more to convince him that the children would enjoy having him come and that he would know what to do when he got there! She's also had to reschedule the visit twice to fit around his working schedule and has spent considerable time helping Sam understand his dad will be coming for a visit, but that Sam will be staying at school and not leaving when his dad goes back to work.

Teachers often have professional reservations about parents' functioning in a classroom. Teachers may be convinced that parents who do not have a professional teachers' education will behave inappropriately with children, especially with their own children, and therefore put teachers in the awkward position of observing unsuitable adult actions in their own classrooms. Some teachers still mistakenly believe that they alone should be the resource for learning in the classroom, rather than valuing the potential contributions of others—this despite all the evidence that children's learning is enhanced by their families' involvement.

> Connie Martinez sighs. "I could have predicted that child was going to get overexcited with that whole birthday party hoopla. What I didn't know was that her mother would react so angrily. I was embarrassed not only for that child, but also that the other children saw that happen in my classroom."

Teachers may be concerned that parents will behave unprofessionally in other ways, such as discussing children with others outside the classroom or making inappropriate remarks to other children.

Another concern of teachers results from their knowledge of young children's reactions when adjusting to changed routines. Some teachers who perceive a child's overexcitement or distress when a parent leaves the classroom after a special event feel the experience is too disruptive to be beneficial.

> "Look, it's a nice idea, but in practice it's too upsetting. Children can't understand why their parents can't stay the whole time, and it undoes a lot of adjustment."

Teachers may also have personal qualms about parents being on hand to observe their actions for an extended period. Whether it is true or not, many teachers feel that they are constantly watched and evaluated when parents are present and therefore feel uncomfortable throughout a visit, feeling the need to perform.

MiLan says, "Frankly, I don't need the additional stress of having a parent watch me through the whole morning."

Considering these objections, are there reasons for including parents in the classroom that outweigh the disadvantages? There certainly are great benefits for parents, children, and teachers.

For parents, spending time in a classroom is the best way to understand what is going on in a program or school (see Figure 12-1). Parents have often equated school with purely cognitive learning and are sometimes surprised and dismayed to learn that early childhood classrooms do not emphasize overtly academic learning. Parents of children in primary school may not realize how much teaching methods and curriculum have changed since their own school days. Seeing what is actually happening gives them more respect for the developmentally appropriate learning that is taking place.

> Mr. Butler, the guitar-playing father, helps explain this. "It was good to see what they do at their group time. Those kids are really learning to listen, to take turns talking and participating. Then they had their snack. Several children were responsible for getting the tables set, and they did it just right. And they poured their own juice, and not a drop spilled. Then they all tried these vegetables in a dip; at home Sam would never have touched the stuff, but there with his friends he did."

FIGURE 12-1 For parents, spending time in a classroom is the best way to understand what is going on in a program.

>   And Mrs. Murphy says after a visit to her first grader's classroom, "I realized the difference between what writing meant when I was in school and what it means in Kathleen's classroom We used to spend hours practicing forming letters, one after another, across the page. Kathleen spends time writing in her journal every day. She makes lots of mistakes in spelling, and the letters aren't very neat, but she is learning how to express her ideas. It's amazing."

Such firsthand knowledge provides a ready basis for discussion with teachers and leads to parental support of classroom practices and the teacher.

In a classroom parents can see how their children are functioning with peers and other adults. They can also observe typical behaviors and skills for a cross section of children the same age, increasing their understanding of typical child development and education. This observation may also enable parents to see firsthand the kinds of problem behaviors that teachers may want to discuss later:

>   "You know, it's kind of reassuring to find out that most 2-year-olds grab things from each other. I'd been thinking mine was particularly aggressive."

>   "Now I can talk with the teacher about how I should help her with her writing—all that misspelling bothers me."

FIGURE 12-2 Most parents enjoy getting to know their children's friends.

Being in a classroom also gives parents a feeling of satisfaction as they contribute to a program, are welcomed by a teacher, and are recognized as important adults by their child and his or her friends—a real ego boost. Most parents enjoy getting to know their children's friends (Figure 12-2).

"I'd never play my guitar for a group of adults, but the kids loved it, I must say."

"Every time I come, I really can see how my listening to children read one on one is helping them as well as the teacher."

Children also feel special and important when their parents are in a classroom (see Figure 12-3):

"That's my Daddy," beams Sam as his dad leads the singing with his guitar.

"My Mom helps out in our classroom sometimes," says Kathleen.

Such good feelings probably have a more lasting impact than the transitory distress for a young child caused by a parent saying good-bye twice in one morning. Children's feelings of security increase as they see parents and teachers working together cooperatively, each respecting the other's contribution. Children see how important education is to their parents when parents support it with their presence. Children also benefit as parents gain in understanding the process of learning and children's interaction skills.

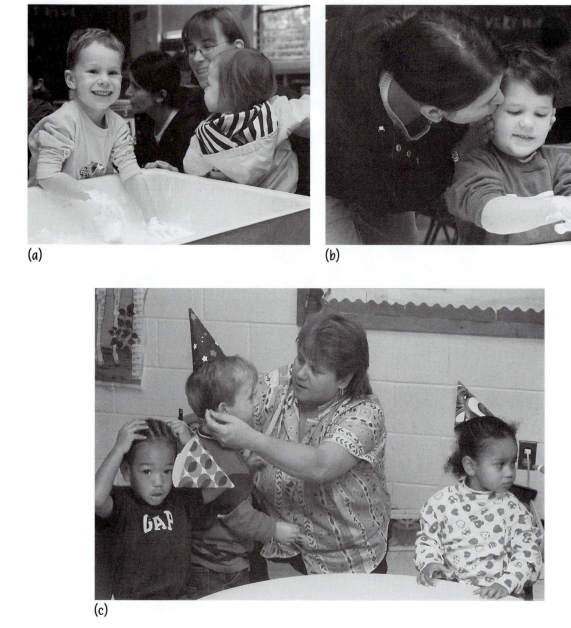

FIGURE 12-3 Children feel special and important when their parents are in the classroom.

Teachers as well as children gain through the expanded opportunities for learning that other adults bring into a classroom. Parents' skills, knowledge, interests, and talents add up to lots of possible resources for curriculum learning and more than expanded opportunities: Countless recent studies underline the vital importance of family involvement in children's classrooms at all levels. Around the country elementary schools are trying their best to bring family and community partners into the classroom for meaningful work: to read to children

FIGURE 12-4 When parents go along to help, a special trip is possible.

and be part of other literacy efforts, to tutor children, to work with children on special projects, or just to be a lunch buddy. Everyone, from the principal to the PTA, is joined in the recognition that family involvement far beyond the "room mother" (Newquist, 1997) enhances teachers' instructional efforts.

> "I really like to give them as much music as I can, but I don't have a musical bone in my body. There's no substitute for having a real instrument in the classroom. From me they get a lot of records."
>
> "I really appreciate Mrs. Murphy coming in to have children read to her individually. There's just never enough time in the day for me to get to every child who needs my help."

Having an extra pair of hands in a group of children often allows activities that just aren't possible without enough adults (see Figure 12-4). In primary classrooms parent volunteers provide individual support and instruction.

Classroom visitation by parents gives teachers another chance to see parent–child interaction and parental attitudes:

> "It's interesting to me to see Sam and his dad together. Mr. Butler is very comfortable in the nurturing role."
>
> "Kathleen really strives to do her best work when her mother is visiting."

Teachers perceive family involvement in a classroom as evidence of support of their efforts as parents gain empathy toward a teacher and the problems of teaching a group of children. It is professionally and personally rewarding to deepen a parent–teacher partnership through such cooperative efforts:

> "I really enjoyed having Mr. Butler with us, and I appreciated his interest in sharing some time with us. It makes me feel like I'm

not the only one who cares what goes on in this classroom. You know, when he went home, he shook his head and said he didn't see how I do it, all day, every day."

Mrs. Murphy said to me, "I wish more parents would come to volunteer in the classroom. Then I don't think we'd hear so many complaints about the teachers and schools."

It is true there are potential problems when parents are involved in a classroom. Teachers may have professional concerns about the possible reactions of children and parents in a classroom, or they may have personal concerns about performing before an adult audience. And extra time and effort are needed on the part of teachers and parents to plan ahead for the event. However, the following advantages make it worth the effort:

- Parents gain firsthand experience of a program and of their child's reactions in a classroom, as well as feelings of satisfaction from making a contribution.

- Children feel special when their parents are involved, feel secure with the tangible evidence of parents and teachers cooperating, realize the value their parents place on education, and gain directly as parental understanding and skills increase.

- Teachers gain resources to extend learning opportunities, observe parent–child interaction, and feel supported as parents participate and empathize with them (see Figure 12-5).

FIGURE 12-5 In primary classrooms, parent volunteers provide individual support and encouragement in learning new skills.

■■■ GETTING FAMILIES INVOLVED

There are many different ways to involve parents in early childhood class-rooms. Nonworking parents can be regular volunteers assisting teachers in **parent cooperative nursery schools**, Head Start programs, or other programs set up to educate both parents and children. When parents regularly assume auxiliary teaching roles, it is advisable to prepare them for this experience with a training program. Then issues of teaching philosophy and goals, children's behavior and learning styles, and appropriate adult guidance and interactive techniques can be explored so parents entering a classroom clearly understand their expected roles. A training program may include classroom visits, workshops, orientation discussions, handbooks, and guided observation.

Many other parents, particularly those who work and whose children are in schools or child care programs, may visit a classroom infrequently for planned social events and opportunities to observe, or as an extra resource. There are a number of ways teachers can facilitate family involvement in the classroom.

Exploring Resources and Needs

Before establishing any plan to bring parents into a classroom, teachers need to gather information about the families to discover which family members can be involved, interests and experiences that can be shared, and time resources (see Figure 12-6). Some of this information can be gathered informally as teachers learn about families during initial interviews, home visits, and casual conversations with parents and children. Other information may be gathered more formally by the use of questionnaires and application forms to acquire written responses to specific questions.

FIGURE 12-6 A father's musical instrument may add a resource to the classroom.

FIGURE 12-7 An older sibling can visit the playground to play with children.

A brief background questionnaire may ask parents about the following:

1. *The names and ages of other children and family members in the home,* to learn whether grandparents or teenaged siblings are available to come in occasionally (see Figure 12-7), or if young children keep a parent too busy to visit.

REFLECTIONS FOR JOURNAL ENTRIES

If you are a parent, have you had experiences visiting your child's classroom in a child care program or school? What insights did this visit give you about your child, the teacher, and the classroom? What circumstances made you feel comfortable or not, welcome or not? If you are not a parent, ask these questions of a friend or family member who is.

2. *Occupations,* to learn a little about working hours and days off (to see if there is available time) and jobs that are of interest to children or that offer interesting field trip possibilities, that can provide scrap materials and expertise for classroom use, or that can help out other parents (see Figure 12-8).

3. *Interests and hobbies, pets, travel, and cultural or religious backgrounds.*

FIGURE 12-8 Visiting a parent at work (in this case a restaurant that makes pasta) can make an interesting trip.

Butler, Bill and Joan (divorced).

Other child: Lisa—4 (in center).

Bill: Salesman, Angel Stone, 8:00–5:00; can be flexible in morning sometimes; usually out of town Wednesday and Thursday.

Joan: Secretary, South West Telephone; 8:30–5:00, Monday–Friday; access to old computer sheets, discarded telephones.

Interests: Joan—tennis, needlepoint, Chinese cooking; Bill—plays guitar, golf.

Possibilities: Bill—play guitar —Chanukah celebration (December; Bill is Jewish); Joan—ask for paper—stir-fry vegetables (spring).

Note: No social for parents on Wednesday or Thursday.

Weaver, Bob and Jane.

No other children.

Jane: homemaker.

Bob: production in furniture factory, 7:30–4:30, Monday–Friday.

(continues)

(continued)

Other: Grandparents in neighborhood, retired. Grandmother likes to cook.

Interests: Jane—gardening, sewing; Bob—volunteer fireman.

Possibilities: Jane—help with planting (spring)—cloth scraps—free most days (field trips); Bob—wood scraps—bring fire truck or uniform, late afternoon.

Grandparents—invite grandmother to cook with us.

Ashley, Sylvia.

Terrence—9.

Sylvia: job training program, 9:00–4:00, for next nine months.

Possibilities: Invite for late afternoon time.

Come in to read informally with children.

Invite Terrence to throw ball with children on playground.

A wealth of resources is obtained by these few questions. As teachers accumulate information, it is a good idea to organize it into a **resource file**, with a card or page for each family. This file can be easily updated as new information is accumulated. Tentative plans for using these resources throughout the year can be noted, along with times parents are free to come to school.

Some teachers ask parents at the beginning of the year to sign up in their areas of interest, while making it clear that this is an option to welcome families who are willing and able to visit. Parents certainly do not need teachers to make them feel guilty if they choose not to participate in this way. Options might include

- Going along on field trips.
- Being a guest reader.
- Helping in the classroom with special projects, such as woodworking or cooking.
- Working with individual children who might need particular assistance and tutoring.
- Preparing classroom materials at home, such as cutting out collage pieces.
- Coming into the classroom to talk about their work.
- Bringing in a pet. (adapted from DeSteno, 2000)

Encourage Informal Visits

How do teachers get parents into a classroom? At first casual, unstructured visits are often best because parents feel no pressure to perform a role and no demands on their time. If allowed to get comfortable in a classroom, they will enjoy interacting with the children, other parents, and teachers.

Reserve Time

One morning or afternoon every week or so open for visiting creates a welcoming atmosphere. Parents are encouraged to spend an extra few minutes while dropping off or picking up their children—or more if they can stay—to join in or observe some activities and perhaps have a drink or snack prepared by the children. Parents enjoy coming to a school to briefly participate in their children's work. Such a regular occurrence demystifies for children the idea of having parents in a classroom and allows parents to stay occasionally as their schedules permit. These visitations require little effort on a teacher's part beyond the usual setting up of activity choices that require little supervision or assistance so teachers are free to move about. The casual nature of such visits means that only a few parents at a time are in a classroom, thereby avoiding overcrowding that may be too stimulating for children. There is also less chance of children feeling left out if their own parents are not there because play activities go on as usual, and many other parents are absent as well. The clear message of just sharing an ordinary day is relaxing as well as reassuring to parents that the classroom is always open for their viewing.

Birthday Celebrations

Most schools for young children have a special way of celebrating children's birthdays. Inviting parents to be present for the celebration can make it even more special (see Figure 12-9). This may mean having the celebration at a time suited to a parent's schedule. Most parents enjoy an event that centers on their child. When classrooms have specific guidelines for celebrations, parents will not be drawn to compete in parties or make decisions deemed unsuitable for the group of children.

Because particular foods may not be acceptable to all families, many programs move the celebration away from a focus on food such as cake or ice cream. For families whose religious beliefs preclude birthday celebrations, many classrooms have moved away from the party idea toward acknowledging the importance of meaningful events in the child's life. For example, one teacher asked parents to help prepare a "growing" display, showing pictures of the child at various ages, perhaps adding toys or clothes that had been used as the child grew. It seems appropriate for a birthday to be a celebration of the child's life, including the people and things that are important. In this spirit all families could join in a developmentally appropriate celebration.

FIGURE 12-9 Parents may enjoy visiting for parties and special events.

Personal Invitations

Some teachers include a "Family of the Week" component in their classroom plans. Specific, personal invitations made to an individual family may include siblings and other family members. The child whose family comes is host for the day, getting chairs for parents and siblings, serving them drinks and snacks, showing them around the room, discussing the art and writing on the walls, and so on. Families are asked to share something about their lives with all the children, whether it's talking about jobs or other interests, or something that the family enjoys doing together. When each family is invited in turn, most will make a special effort to come as their child is honored. Some schools call these "family days" and ask families to schedule them early in the school year. Not only is this a useful way to draw parents into classroom life, but it is also a concrete model of demonstrating multicultural diversity and the uniqueness of all families.

Lunch Invitations

Families can be invited for lunch in their children's classrooms or cafeterias. Most schools do not require much advance notice to set an extra place for lunch; this offers another chance for a social visit and a special treat for a child. Having Mom, Dad, or Grandpa just theirs for lunch, away from other siblings, may be fun. Parents get an opportunity to see firsthand how teachers help children develop appropriate table behavior and self-help and conversational skills, and encourage tasting a variety of foods. In elementary school, parents enjoy the opportunity to eat along with their children's friends, and then may have a few minutes to join in classroom activities.

Special Occasions

Whether a family tea party, early morning coffee, or a picnic lunch, most families try to respond to invitations made to a whole group. With various family structures, it creates problems or discomfort when invitations are made to "fathers only" or "mothers only." Parents with particular work schedules may be unable to accept, and children who do not have the specified parent in their lives will feel left out (Hasson, 1996; Lewis, 1996). Even when well-meaning teachers say, "That's all right. You can bring Uncle Joe or your Grandpa," children still feel that this is only second best if the day is named so specifically for fathers.

In planning to include all families with sensitivity to potential barriers that would prevent or limit attendance at particular events, teachers should consider what they know about the children and families in their classrooms (Kieff & Wellhousen, 2000). They should consider the following:

- *Family structures:* Who are the primary caregivers for the children? Should teachers remember to include divorced parents, grandparents, blended families, foster parents, same-sex parents, family members with disabilities, and teenaged parents?

- *Family cultures:* What do you know about your children's family religious backgrounds, holiday celebrations, dietary restrictions, languages spoken, and views on child rearing and education?

- *Family lifestyles:* What do you know about the daily challenges and routines affecting each family, such as employment hours, transportation, caring for elderly or disabled family members, unemployment, income and education level, reading ability, access to telephones and computers, and **latchkey child care**?

When teachers become sensitive to the reasons why many families may not be able to participate easily or comfortably in typical classroom involvement activities, they may change traditional ways of trying to involve families in classrooms. "Doughnuts with Dad" or "Muffins with Mom," long mainstays of inviting parents into classrooms for snack (and not incidentally working on literacy skills) for preschool and primary teachers, may need to give way to invitations for Lunch for Special Adults. See Figures 12-10 and 12-11 for a family involvement planning worksheet and checklist for possible modifications. If teachers use such tools they are less likely to offend or create barriers to family involvement in classroom activities.

Walking Report Cards

Walking report cards (Anderson, 2000) provide opportunities for family members to walk with a child through a series of classroom centers and activities.

Family Involvement Planning Worksheet

Name of activity/event: _____

Proposed date and time: _____

Location: _____

Targeted participants: _____

Consider the following descriptors to identify family-related factors that could create barriers and prevent or limit the participation of families. After identifying possible barriers, adapt the activity or event to include all families.

Family Structures

Consider who are the primary caregivers for the children. Consider the presence of younger and older siblings living at home:

❑ Divorced parents   ❑ Split families   ❑ Same-sex parents

❑ Single parent   ❑ Foster parents   ❑ Family member with disability

❑ Grandparent(s)   ❑ Legal guardian   ❑ Teen parents

❑ Blended family   ❑ Widowed parent   ❑ Other _____

Possible barriers include _____

Family Lifestyles

Consider the daily challenges or routines affecting the children and each family:

Possible barriers include _____

Family Cultures

Consider the cultural aspects of each family; avoid stereotypes:

❑ Religous backgrounds   ❑ Nonverbal communication styles

❑ Holiday celebrations   Eye contact

❑ Dietary restrictions   Gestures

❑ Views on child rearing   Touching

❑ Languages   Proximity during conversations

                                  ❑ Other _____

Possible barriers include _____

How the activity or event can be adapted to include all families represented in the class or school: _____
_____
_____

FIGURE 12-10 Family involvement planning worksheet.

Common Barriers and Possible Modifications Checklist

Barriers	Modifications
Time	❑ Breakfast meetings
	❑ Weekend events
	❑ One event scheduled over a number of days
	❑ Open invitations
Transportation	❑ School bus or van
	❑ Carpool arranged by teacher or parent volunteer
	❑ Buddy system among families
Child care	❑ School-provided child care
	❑ Child care provided by parent organization
	❑ Buddy system among families
Decorations/celebrations	❑ Artwork created by children in the art center
	❑ Artwork generated during a theme/project study
Curriculum	❑ Opportunities for children to make multiple gifts and cards and to pick their recipients
	❑ Family members share expertise and culture
	❑ Bias-free curriculum
Food	❑ Multiple menus available
	❑ Buffets
	❑ Picnics
Printed material	❑ Translate copies
	❑ Make audiotapes
	❑ Make telephone calls
	❑ Use voice mail or e-mail
Special guest	❑ Guest not specified by role
	❑ A pal or friend
	❑ Open invitations to extended family members or a noncustodial parent
Expense	❑ Support provided by community businesses underwriting the event or materials needed
Misunderstanding the role as parent volunteer in the classroom	❑ Volunteer training sessions
	❑ Specific routines created
	❑ Recorded or printed instructions
Misunderstanding the parental role in home-extension learning activities	❑ Specific routines created for home-extension learning activities
	❑ Parent workshops to explain activities
	❑ Demonstration tapes
	❑ Demonstrations during home visits
Discomfort in school situations	❑ Alternative home visits or neighborhood meetings
	❑ Buddy systems among families
	❑ Small group meetings

FIGURE 12-11 Common barriers and possible modifications checklist.

Adults can then observe the child's performance in various activities. Teachers select specific materials and tasks to set out that will highlight children's developing abilities.

Some teachers add the walking report card to portfolio assessments and regular parent–teacher conferences as additional methods of sharing information with families. Teachers say that families enjoy the opportunity to see their children in action. Walking report card visits work well with older preschool and primary-aged children.

Drop In and Read (DIAR), See Our Successes (SOS), and Other Invitations

Many elementary teachers are establishing regular family involvement events to help showcase children's work and accomplishments. For example, DIAR days are when family members are invited to drop in and read with children and have their children read to them. SOS (See Our Successes) events are to enjoy displays of writing or math or see children's long-term projects. (Any creative teacher could invent an appropriate acronym.) When teachers schedule such events for several days at different times, families are more likely to be able to participate. Sometimes such an event could be combined with a potluck supper, providing social opportunities as well as meeting teacher goals of informing families. When children are involved in inviting their families, many parents will make an effort to please their children.

Zoo Day

A "zoo" day when families are asked to bring pets provides a good situation for getting parents to share and volunteer their resources (see Figure 12-12).

FIGURE 12-12 A pet from home may be interesting to all children.

Parents often find their own ways of becoming involved in classroom life when allowed to take the initiative. One center reports that when parents come to take their children out of a classroom for appointments or a special lunch, they come back in time for the toothbrushing ritual or to read stories to their own children and some friends before helping a teacher settle everyone for naps—satisfying for everyone. Informal occasions such as these may be the only times some parents come to the classroom. (See additional notes about social occasions in Chapter 13). Other parents may get involved in additional ways; see Figure 12-13 for a list that a center offers to stimulate family thinking about the variety of contributions they can make to the classroom or program.

Volunteer Opportunities

- Answer phones—any help would be appreciated, even a couple of hours a week. This would free the staff to work on lesson plans and so on.

- Rock the babies—it's good for them and you!

- Read stories—the staff would love to have some new faces (and voices) to read to the children. If you're a good storyteller, please come and share your life experiences or childhood remembrances.

- Watch children during naptime (from 1:00 to 3:00 p.m.). Teachers need a break and could use the time to work on lesson plans or future projects.

- Assist with center events—go on field trips, help with staff appreciation week, and so forth. Our field trips are FUN! Some of the latest ones have been to Discovery Place, the Nature Museum, the circus, the opera, and the like.

- Give career miniworkshops—come in for an hour and tell the children about your job, show them the tools you use, and so on. The older children are very interested in what grown-ups do all day!

- Sponsor a field trip to your workplace—this does not have to be difficult. Children can come in the center vans and tour your workplace. This kind of field trip is a real adventure for them.

- Provide some assistance with typing/computer service. The center always has a need for newsletters, meeting notices, and so on.

FIGURE 12-13 Help parents to see that there are many ways they can be involved. (continues)

- Donate toys or clothes—playground toys are especially needed.
- Bring "store-bought" treats for the children (state regulations do not permit home-baked goodies). Watermelon and ice cream are especially popular with this crowd.
- Help with cutting out materials and/or decorating bulletin boards.
- Repair furniture, equipment, or toys.
- Sew doll clothes or costumes.

FIGURE 12-13 Continued

REFLECTIONS FOR JOURNAL ENTRIES

Think about any experiences you have had with families visiting in classrooms. How comfortable did the families seem? Did any problems arise? How have these experiences affected your willingness to consider finding more ways to involve families? If you have not had classroom experience, ask a teacher you know.

Encourage Parent Observations

Parents who are comfortable in a classroom may accept an invitation to spend a short period observing. This is beneficial for all parents, particularly for parents with special concerns about their children or questions about a program, in anticipation of an extended conversation at a later conference.

Observation periods are most productive when parents and children are prepared for their roles. Teachers may explain to children that parents will be coming "so they can see all the fun things and work we do in the classroom." Children can also be told that the visiting grown-ups will probably want to sit at one side and not play or talk for a time. (It is ideal to have an observation booth or window where visitors can observe undetected. But not many schools boast such an opportunity, so both parents and children will have to accustom themselves to the others' presence.)

Both parents and teachers should be aware that children may act differently in the presence of parents. It is helpful to discuss this openly and to suggest that parents observe on several occasions to accustom their children to the practice. Parents should also feel comfortable leaving if their children are having difficulty with their presence. Teachers can reassure parents that such behavior is normal and that the parents can try coming again later.

Observing outdoor play is a good first step for both children and parents. Outdoor play may offer more natural opportunities for children to play freely without feeling they're being watched. Parents who seem hesitant about the observer's role may also be more comfortable outdoors. In elementary class-rooms parents can sit apart, watching children and teachers busy with their normal routines and assigned tasks.

Many parents feel uncertain about their role as an observer and may feel more secure when given both verbal and written guidelines for helpful class-room behaviors and points for observation. The following is a sample form that may be used:

WELCOME TO OUR CLASSROOM

The children will be delighted to see you and may need a gentle reminder that you've come to see them at work and play. A crowd could make it difficult for you to observe or jot down questions.

1. Observe your child and as many others as you can. This can be a learning experience about

   - Your child and how he relates to other children and the classroom activities.

   - What children the same age as your child are like.

   - How the teacher guides each child.

2. Observe your child and several others. Notice how they

   - Respond to other children.

   - Use language.

   - Choose activities, and how long they stay with each activity.

   - Solve problems and obtain assistance.

3. Observe your child's particular interests and interactions.

4. Observe the teacher in a variety of activities. Notice how the teacher

   - Relates to each child.

   - Handles difficult situations.

   - Prevents problems and guides behavior.

5. Write down any impressions, surprises, suggestions, or questions you would like to discuss later.

A parent with particular concerns should be given individual guidelines. Parents who observe on several occasions will appreciate having an observation booklet with specific points on each page.

Parents as Classroom Resources

As teachers get to know the families they work with, they become aware of parents' wealth of experience that can be used to deepen children's understanding of the world around them. Parents should be invited into classroom experiences to involve and include them, not merely to exploit them as an extra pair of hands to complete chores in the classroom. Parents are resources in a variety of ways. Parents' competence, creativity, and knowledge should be respected so they will be involved in tasks that are worth doing and from which they can gain a sense of accomplishment and make real contributions. The learning opportunities when parents work with individuals or small groups are innumerable.

Parents may be invited to find a time convenient for them to visit a classroom and share an experience. When appropriate, children may also be able to visit a parent at work or at home.

Jobs

Many parents' jobs are interesting to children when demonstrated along with the "tools of the trade." Visitors may be a dental hygienist with a giant set of teeth and toothbrush, a truck driver complete with a truck, a hair stylist, or a carpenter with tools. Even parents who have more ordinary jobs sometimes work in places that make wonderful field trips. A tall glass office building with an exciting elevator ride up to see the view, a company next to a construction site, a shopping mall, a neighborhood store, or a bus terminal all may have a cheery parent to greet the children as they explore the different places people work.

Elementary school teachers can incorporate such learning experiences into their plans for social studies units or to extend literacy and math curricula.

Hobbies

Parents with particular interests and hobbies may offer fascinating substance to a curriculum. A guitar player, an avid camper with backpack and pup tent, a gardener, a cook, an aerobic dancer, a cyclist, a rock hound, or a carpenter all have enthusiasm and skills to share with the children. A parent who enjoys using a video camera may record children busy at play—fun for the children to see replayed and interesting for parents to view later at a parent meeting. Most adults, even if initially hesitant, enjoy themselves thoroughly as children respond with zest to the new activities. Sometimes hobbies that appear to be strictly for adults create interesting situations as children relate to them in

FIGURE 12-14 Many parents will enjoy sharing their interests with children.

their own way; one parent who shared tapes of his favorite classical music was delighted to watch children spontaneously improvise movement and dance (see Figure 12-14). Such interests expand the curriculum in elementary and preschool classrooms.

Cultures

Multicultural experiences are promoted within good early childhood classrooms. Children need to learn respect and value for the unique differences among people. Families may help a teacher offer firsthand experiences for children in exploring customs, foods, or celebrations of a variety of cultural or religious traditions. Activities like the following can be woven into a classroom curriculum to enrich and stimulate learning for children:

- Chanukah songs, games, and foods from a Jewish parent.

- A Chinese parent demonstrating use of a wok and chopsticks.

- Spanish children's songs taught by a Puerto Rican parent.

- The sharing of some family treasures by a Vietnamese parent.

- An African American parent explaining the traditions of Kwanzaa celebrations.

- A Native American parent sharing a craft artifact.

- Mementos brought back from a vacation trip.

More important, inviting families to share aspects of their lives and cultures lets teachers demonstrate respect for the diverse family backgrounds in a classroom. Both children and their parents receive a self-esteem boost when they share a representation of their own lives. All children benefit as they learn to enjoy and accept the aspects of uniqueness and universality in multi-cultural experiences. We'll talk more about this in Chapter 15.

Extended Family

Knowing the makeup of each family will help teachers find resources beyond the parents. A retired grandmother who enjoys reading stories to children, a teenaged brother who can help with ball-throwing on the playground, a baby who can be brought to visit for a bath or feeding, and other family members can provide additional experiences.

Time

One resource provided by many parents is time. A parent coming into the classroom is helpful when an extra pair of hands is needed. Walks or field trips, classroom parties, or more complicated projects become possible when teachers can count on additional assistance from parents. Many classrooms today are encouraging family presence as an important component of literacy experiences (Otto & Johnson, 1996). (See Figure 12-15.) When parents come into the classroom to read to large or small groups of children, they model the pleasurable and useful aspects of literacy.

FIGURE 12-15 When parents come into the classroom to read, they model the pleasurable and useful aspects of literacy.

FIGURE 12-16 Parents may enjoy sharing an everyday experience, such as making a cake.

Sometimes parents are more comfortable offering to share time instead of demonstrating a talent. As parents interact with children, they are often drawn into an activity they have done as parents—supervising cooking experiences, carving a jack-o'lantern, or playing a game (see Figure 12-16). The parents' presence alone offers a learning experience for children as they see, for example, men nurturing and doing classroom tasks such as pouring juice or cleaning tables, roles more commonly associated with mothers. It is also important that parents' time not be wasted. Teachers need to have materials ready for their use and be efficient in explaining classroom routines and activities so that parents do not feel they are just waiting for something to happen.

Sometimes parents would rather use at-home time to support classroom activities. Parents can launder and mend dress-up clothes and toys, use personal computers to type newsletters, make phone calls to remind other parents of meetings, or prepare simple classroom games.

Materials

Families who are unavailable to come into a classroom may still provide resources in the form of materials to be used in classroom activities. Scraps and throwaways from jobs (computer paper, Styrofoam packing bits, spools from a cotton mill), scraps and discards from home (kitchen utensils, dress-up clothes, magazines, fabric pieces), and recycled or natural materials that can be used for collections to sort or math manipulatives all make a contribution that allows both parents and teachers to feel a sense of cooperation. Some teachers regularly post a list of "Treasures Wanted" via a newsletter or bulletin board, like this example:

CONTRIBUTIONS FROM HOME

Throughout the year we can always use

- **Writing supplies—envelopes, paper, postcards, small notepads, and any sizes of paper, including computer paper.**
- **Appliance boxes and cardboard boxes of all sizes.**
- **Yogurt containers for paint.**
- **Discarded clothing for dress-up.**
- **Small appliances to take apart.**
- **Wood for the workbench.**
- **Fabric, yarn, and large needles for sewing.**
- **Ideas for local field trips.**
- **Collections of buttons, nuts and bolts, or other small objects.**

Parents outside a classroom will feel involved as they prepare materials for classroom use. Tracing and cutting out pieces for teacher-made games is something a homebound parent can feel important in doing.

In some communities it is possible for parents to host an "open house" for their children's classmates. The children may visit a child's home for a snack or a picnic lunch.

Special Skills

Families may have skills or knowledge that can be drawn on as resources beyond the classroom to support a center or to offer to other parents. Architects, builders, or landscape designers can contribute to playground design; accountants or businesspeople can help with budgets, insurance, and tax matters; medical personnel can set up first aid kits and procedures; particularly handy parents can repair toys as needed; "bargain hunter" parents can aid the person who purchases for a center, answering such questions as "Where can we get the best deal on sand?" Knowledgeable parents are possible resources for parent meetings or workshops: A high school counselor can lead a discussion of communication techniques; parents who have successfully negotiated divorce and remarriage can share insights on stepparenting; an accountant can discuss tax tips for working parents; a parent with older children can advise on the intricacies of the school system and understanding tests.

THE TEACHER'S ROLE

As teachers invite families to participate in classroom learning activities, they need to concentrate on their skills for working with adults. Teachers need to be able to relax and enjoy the contributions of others to their classrooms without feeling threatened by any attention transferred from themselves to a visiting adult.

As more specific information is given to parents, they will feel more comfortable knowing what is expected of them. Parents should know what time frame to plan on and that it is acceptable to leave or stay as their schedules allow. It is helpful to confirm all arrangements in writing so that parents have a concrete reminder of an event to fit into their schedules:

Dear Mr. Butler,

We are looking forward to your visit to our classroom next Friday, February 2, at 9:15 a.m. The children will have snack at 9:45, so that will give you about half an hour to sing songs with us. We'll probably have some favorites to request, too! Please feel free to stay and have snack with us, if you're able. See you next week.

Sincerely,

Jane Briscoe

Dear Mrs. Murphy,

I appreciate your offer to help in our classroom on Thursdays this semester. The children have individual reading time from 9:00 to 9:30 a.m. This would be the best time for you to be able to read with individuals. I will have a list on my desk each morning of children who would benefit by having you listen to them read.

This is such an important support to their learning, and they will enjoy the time alone with you. We look forward to seeing you next Thursday, and hope you will feel free to stay as long as you are able to participate in our day.

Sincerely,

John Roberts

Teachers should immediately greet parents coming into a classroom and make them feel welcome, pointing out an area to sit or begin their preparations. Parents appreciate knowing beforehand exactly what they will be expected to do, not vague suggestions that they "join in." For example, if the parent is helping with a cooking experience, demonstrate how to help prepare children for participation: washing hands, rolling up sleeves, putting on a smock. The teacher might demonstrate how to show children the recipe to follow and how to involve the children in measuring and stirring. After working with one child, the teacher can stand back and let the parent take over, still being available if needed. Even if parents are just coming to share time in the classroom, they will be more comfortable if teachers help them get started.

> "Our children love for someone to read to them. If you just sit in that chair in the book corner, I'm sure you'll have children joining you before long. There are two small chairs there, too, to limit the number of children to two. Usually they'll move on to something else when they see the chairs are filled. There'll be about half an hour before we clean up for snack."

If parents are coming to help out on field trips, they should be given specific duties. Teachers should give parents a list of the children they are expected to keep track of, and make sure the children wear name tags and know whose parent they are with. Parents should have all guidelines for behavior explained to them before setting out. Information is the key to parent comfort and helpfulness. See the additional specific suggestions for involving parents in the classroom and out in DiNatale (2002; see Figure 12-17).

When parents come into the classroom frequently, it may be helpful to have specific work cards that indicate which part of the room to be responsible for, suggestions of questions or comments to facilitate learning, clean-up responsibilities, and so on. See Figure 12-18 for sample work cards.

Teachers should watch parents for signs of discomfort or indications of how much they want teachers to help them out in uncertain situations. When teachers prepare parents for potentially disruptive situations that could occur, especially if their own children are involved, parents are more likely to feel comfortable at school. Teachers help children of visiting parents understand that Mom or Dad will be helping all the children and will have special things to do today. This helps to clarify the visiting parent's role for the child. Occasionally a child of invited parents reacts by showing off or clinging and being possessive of his parents' attention. It is a good idea to warn parents ahead of time that this may happen and that a teacher is prepared for it and won't mind. Parents should also be reassured that a teacher will step in if necessary to remind a child of classroom rules so that parents will not feel the full burden of guidance is theirs and perhaps react inappropriately because of embarrassment. In the classroom, teachers should enforce classroom rules. This understanding helps clarify adult responsibilities.

> "It's so special when parents come in that sometimes we get some unusual behaviors. No problem. If Sam forgets our rules, I'll just remind him."

FIGURE 12-17 This father has been made comfortable to participate with children in the block corner.

Block Area

Thanks for helping in the block area today.

—Limit to four children.

—Sit in the small chair.

—Enjoy conversation about the buildings.

—Good questions are open-ended: Tell me about your building.
                                      What do people do in your building?
                                      What is your building called?

—If children argue, ask if they can work the problem out.

—Children are responsible for returning blocks to shelves—encourage effort.

Art Area

Thanks for helping in the art area today.

—Set out four chairs to limit participation.

—All children put on smocks.

—Children use displayed materials freely and independently.

—Children may use any other materials from art shelf.

—When children ask for assistance, demonstrate and see if you can encourage them to try again.

FIGURE 12-18 Sample work cards. (continues)

—When children ask you to make them something, tell them you'd rather watch them make it.

—Sometimes children busy at work do not have time for conversation.

—Respond as they initiate conversation, and use comments to describe their work, such as "Wow, you glued so many pieces," or "You certainly used a lot of green in your painting."

—Children may continue using materials, making several creations, as long as no one else is waiting for a turn.

—Ask if they would like to write their name on their work or if would they like your help.

—Remind children of where to place work for drying, and of hand washing and hanging up smocks when finished.

Reading Buddies

Thanks for coming in to be a Reading Buddy today.

—Find the red folder with names of children scheduled for reading buddies today.

—Find the first child (all children wear name tags).

—Invite the child to come to Quiet Corner to read with you.

—Ask the child whether he or she would like to read to you first, or have you read to them; let the child choose a book.

—When finished reading, converse about the story.

—Switch roles, with you being the listener this time.

—When children get stuck on a word, supply it for them.

—Move down the list of reading buddies. Enjoy.

FIGURE 12-18 Continued

FIGURE 12-19 Displaying photos of this father's classroom visit on the bulletin board may encourage other parents to visit.

The unusual event may cause a young child to get upset when his parent leaves, even though separation is not normally a problem. A teacher needs to comfort him and to reassure the parent that the classroom visit was still a great idea even though there were a few tears at the end. The positive feelings for both child and parent far outweigh any brief distress.

Parents like feeling that they're making a valuable contribution to a classroom. Many parents will try to find the time for a visit if they feel truly needed and wanted. A note of appreciation from the teacher and children afterward, pictures of the event displayed on a bulletin board, a mention of the event as a classroom highlight in the next newsletter—all these convey to parents that their time was well spent (see Figure 12-19).

SUMMARY

Families may become involved in the classroom as

1. Casual visitors, to participate in classroom activities, meals, or celebrations.

2. Observers, to extend their knowledge of children's functioning in a classroom.

3. Resources, to extend and enrich opportunities for the children.

STUDENT ACTIVITIES FOR FURTHER STUDY

1. If you are working or interning in a classroom, gather information about parents—family composition, jobs and details of what is involved, hobbies and interests, and religious and ethnic backgrounds. Find out whether families have access to any materials that are useful in your classroom or have particular periods of time free. Organize this information into a resource file. (If you are not presently in a preschool classroom, use the fictional family information described in Chapter 2 to make a sample resource file.)

2. Use your resource file to

   a. Make a hypothetical plan for how you will use your resource knowledge to invite families into the classroom for particular activities, events, and curriculum topics throughout the year.

   b. Invite three different parents into your classroom, if possible.

Remember it will be your role to prepare parents and children for what to expect; play hostess in making parents feel comfortable in the room, and guide children's behavior. Use this as an opportunity to observe parents and children in the classroom and the effect of the visit on each.

CASE STUDY

Read the following letter to parents and answer the questions that follow.

Dear Parents:
There will be a special Mother's Luncheon on Wednesday, December 8. It will be held in our kindergarten classroom from

12:30 to 2:00 p.m. The cafeteria will serve barbecued pork at $5.00 a plate. We are asking moms to donate baked items for dessert. The kindergarten class will entertain after lunch, singing Christmas songs from around the world. Please plan to attend.

1. As you put yourself in the place of parents receiving this letter, what is your initial response to this invitation?

2. As a single mother who works both a full-time and a part-time job and has trouble making ends meet, what is your response?

3. As the custodial father of a child whose biological mother lives in another state and whose stepmother travels out of town frequently in her work, what is your response?

4. As a Middle Eastern, Muslim immigrant family who speak little English, what is your response to this letter?

5. Considering the barriers you just identified, how might this invitation be changed to be more inclusive?

REVIEW QUESTIONS

1. Describe at least one advantage for children, parents, and teachers when teachers work with families in the classroom, and any one of three disadvantages.

2. List at least two methods of encouraging parental visits to the classroom.

3. Describe at least one method to facilitate parental observation in a classroom.

4. Discuss at least two ways families can be used as resources in a classroom.

SUGGESTIONS FOR FURTHER READING

Berger, E. (1995). Reaching for the stars: Families and schools working together. *Early Childhood Journal, 23,* 119–123.

Cavaretta, J. (1998). Parents are a school's best friend. *Educational Leadership, 55*(8), 12–15.

Christenson, S., & Sheridan, S. (2001). *Schools and families: Creating essential connections for learning.* New York: Guilford Press.

Coleman, M. (1997). Families and schools: In search of common ground. *Young Children, 52*(5), 14–221.

Comer, J., & Haynes, M. (1991). Parent involvement in schools: An ecological approach. *Elementary School Journal, 91*(3), 271–278.

Craven, H. (2004). Using parent volunteers in the classroom. Available online at http://www.inspiringteachers.com; see the Web site information at chapter end.

Epstein, J. (2001). *School, family, and community partnerships: Preparing educators and improving schools.* Philadelphia: Westview Press.

Epstein, J., Sanders, M., Salinas, K., Simon, B., Jansorn, N., & VanVoorhis, F. (1997). *School, family, and community partnerships: Your handbook for action.* Thousand Oaks, CA: Corwin/Sage Publications.

Fisher, B. (1998). *Joyful learning: A whole language kindergarten* (rev. ed.). Portsmouth, NH: Heinemann.

Gorham, P., & Nason, P. (1997). Why make teachers' work more visible to parents? *Young Children, 52*(5), 22–26.

Horsfall, J. (1999). Welcoming volunteers to your child care center. *Young Children, 54*(6), 35–36.

McBride, S. L. (1999). Research in review: Family-centered practices. *Young Children, 54*(3), 62–68.

Powell, D. (1998). Research in review: Reweaving parents into the fabric of early childhood programs. *Young Children, 53*(5), 60–67.

Rosenthal, D., & Sawyers, J. (1996). Building successful home–school partnerships: Strategies for parent support and involvement. *Childhood Education, 72*(4), 194–2000.

St. John, E., Griffith, A., & Allen-Hayes, L. (1997). *Families in schools: A chorus of voices in restructuring.* Waltham, MA: Heinemann.

Topping, K. (2001). *Thinking, reading, writing: A practical guide to paired learning with peers, parents, and volunteers.* New York: Continuum International Publishing Group.

Vopat, J. (1998). *Beyond bake sales: The resource guide for family involvement.* New York: Stenhouse Publishers.

Webb, N. (1997). Working with parents from cradle to preschool: A university collaborates with an urban public school. *Young Children, 52*(4), 15–19.

Workman, S., & Gage, J. (1997). Family–school partnerships: A family strengths approach. *Young Children, 52*(4), 10–14.

REFERENCES

Anderson, G. (2000). A "walking" report card in preschool. *Focus on Pre-K and K, 13*(2), 1–3.

DeSteno, N. (2000). Parent involvement in the classroom: The fine line. *Young Children, 55*(3), 13–17.

Hasson, J. (1996) Grandparent's day: What to do for children who don't have a grandparent. *Young Children, 51*(3), 28–29.

DiNatale, L. (2002). Developing high-quality family involvement programs in early childhood settings. *Young Children, 57*(5), 90–95.

Kieff, J., & Wellhousen, K. (2000). Planning family involvement in early childhood programs. *Young Children, 55*(3), 18–25.

Lewis, E. (1996). What mother? What father? *Young Children, 51*(3), 27.

Newquist, C. (1997). Room mothers and a whole lot more. *Education World.* Available online at http://www.educationworld.com/a_admin/admin002.shtml.

Otto, B., & Johnson, L. (1996, February). Parents in your classroom: A valuable literacy link. *Teaching K–8,* 56–57.

HELPFUL WEB SITES

http://www.cpirc.org

The Colorado Parent Information and Resource Center (CPIRC) has been created to help families and schools work better together to ensure that children succeed in school.

http://www.napehq.org

The mission of the National Partners in Education is to provide leadership in the formation and growth of effective partnerships that ensure success for all students.

http://www.ncpie.org

National Coalition for Parent Involvement in Education (NCPIE). NCPIE is a coalition of major education, community, public service, and advocacy organizations working to create meaningful family–school partnerships in every school in America.

http://www.naesp.org

The mission of the National Association of Elementary School Principals is to lead in the advocacy and support for elementary and middle-level principals and other education leaders in their commitment to all children.

http://www.education-world.com

http://www.inspiringteachers.com

This teacher-created Web site is dedicated to empowering teachers and improving student success.

http://www.teachersnetwork.org

This is the Web site for this nationwide, nonprofit educational organization designed to connect teachers.

http://www.teachernet.gov.uk

The educational site for teachers and school managers.

Additional resources for this chapter can be found on the Online Companion to accompany this text at www.earlychilded.delmar.com. This supplemental material includes frequently asked questions; chapter outlines to be used as study guides; scenarios that both encourage large and small group discussions and provoke new thoughts and ideas; and chapter resources, including chapter summaries, interactive questions, Web links, and Web activities. In addition, forms from the text are available for download.

CHAPTER 13

Parent Education

OBJECTIVES

After reading this chapter, you should be able to

1. Discuss a rationale for parent education.
2. Identify several assumptions regarding parent education and corresponding implications for planning programs.
3. Describe ways in which parents can function as advisers.

KEY TERMS
democratic models
I-messages

A traditional way of trying to reach families in the school systems has been to hold occasional meetings. Generally the meetings are designed to give information to large groups of parents. Frequently parents will attend one of these meetings to discover what the meetings are about; but the large group aspects are usually unappealing, so future attendance may be less likely. This is unfortunate because it continues the distance between home and school and fails to give parents assistance that may be truly helpful. Until children come with complete instruction booklets or the education system becomes less complex, parents will continue to need information and ideas to support their child rearing and involvement in their children's learning. Many parental needs for support, social contact, and increased information may be satisfied in meetings.

This chapter explores how schools and programs can offer more than that traditional meeting, so that families may be more likely to participate. In addition, parents may be involved in the decision-making aspects of a program. Teachers need to consider this facet of working with families.

Anne Morgan and Dorothy Scott do a lot of things differently in their classrooms, but they agree on one idea: Neither of them wants to attend the center's parents' meeting next week. Dorothy sounds quite cynical about it: "Look, I've been going to parents' meetings for 13 years, and it's always the same thing. A handful of parents show up—always the same ones, the ones who are already doing a pretty good job and don't need to hear the guest speaker anyway. I'm just getting tired of the whole thing."

Anne is also disappointed with the results of the last meeting she attended. "If there's one thing the parents need to understand, it's the terrible effect of television on their children. So after they listened to the man we invited to speak on that topic, do you think I noticed any difference in what my children tell me they've watched? It doesn't seem worth the effort."

Even their director seems less than certain of the value of the parents' meetings she continues to arrange. "It does seem there must be something else we could do to attract more families."

These comments are frequently expressed teacher attitudes toward the attempts at parent education they have encountered. It would be interesting to hear the reactions of families involved in the experiences and of parents who stayed home rather than attend such meetings; in all probability, additional negative responses would be heard.

Traditional parent education consists of various methods for giving to parents information deemed necessary by a professional. The traditional approach stresses information and training that is directly related to parent–child interaction or school success. The model is that of a competent professional dispensing facts to a less competent parent. This one-way model implies a passive audience and a need to overcome a deficit in parental knowledge. Such a stance increases parental self-doubt; it is not surprising that parents frequently engage in these educational approaches with minimal enthusiasm or maximal avoidance! Such a parent education program can make parents feel powerless and dependent on the advice of professionals. Research on learned helplessness reports that experiences and expectations of failure decrease the ability to learn and take the initiative and increase the tendency to turn to others for assistance. The more parents are treated as if they are not capable, the less they will try to do for themselves. The system through which they are educated is itself an important part of any parent education program. The usefulness of many informational programs is hindered by procedures that point to the authority of professionals and the incompetence of parents.

In considering models that may be more effective, we need to examine attitudes and practices that support and strengthen parents' sense of competence.

■■■ WHAT IS PARENT EDUCATION?

Although some programs refer to all efforts at parent involvement as *parent education*, the term is usually used to refer to specific attempts to offer knowledge and support to parents in hopes of increasing parenting effectiveness. Parent education has taken many forms, for different purposes, with varying results.

Consider the following contrasts: Some programs focus on family–community relations, while others teach parents how to stimulate a child's cognitive development. Some programs prescribe specific skills and styles for relating to young children, while other programs help parents determine what is best for them. Some programs are designed primarily to disseminate child development information to parents; others attempt to foster supportive relationships among program participants. Some programs are highly structured, while others let parents select activities they wish to pursue. In some programs the staff serve as child development experts; other programs adhere to a self-help model with staff in nondirective facilitator roles.

There also are important differences in the use of professionals, assistants or volunteers, program length (weeks versus years), and program setting (group versus home-based). Programs are operated by schools, hospitals, health centers, child care centers, mental health agencies, churches, libraries, colleges and universities, and organizations that have parent education as their sole mission. Those served include first-time parents, expectant parents, future parents, teenage parents, single parents, parents of handicapped children, and grandparents (Powell, 1986). (See Figure 13-1 A and B)

This listing of diversity could go on. Some of the divergent opinions involve differences in interpretation of the same phenomena; others seem to address different reference points. Parent education is a complex phenomenon. Its history and development have been and continue to be marked by major shifts in purposes, contents, and approaches.

In the past decade or so a major direction for programs for parents has been the development of family support programs (Kagan, 1995). This broad approach to parent education focuses on all of family life and emphasizes developing support systems for families. The changing terminology increasingly used today indicates the change in emphasis and structure; besides *parent education*, terms include

- Parent empowerment.
- Family education.
- Family life education.
- Parent support.
- Family support. (Kagan, 1995)

A goal is to help families prevent problems and optimize their functioning, motivated by the belief that families receiving support are empowered to

(a)

(b)

FIGURE 13-1 Parent education must meet the needs of various family structures, including grandparents, single parents, and teenage parents.

act on their own behalf. Other principles embraced by family support programs include these:

- A recognition of the need to work with the entire family and community.
- A commitment to regarding the family as an active participant in planning and implementing the program.
- An acknowledgment of the importance of nourishing cultural diversity.
- A focus on strength-based needs assessment and programming. (Dunst & Trivette, 1994)

The Family Resource Coalition promotes family empowerment programs and offers information about local funding methods and organization models. (For more information on the FRC, see Chapter 4.)

Auerbach defines *parent education* as "intervention to help parents function more effectively in their parental role" (Auerbach, 1968). Swick expands this to "any effort to increase the development and learning of parents in carrying out the diverse roles they perform," including the personal dimensions of marital roles and relationships and personal needs as adults (Swick, 1985).

Perhaps the main functions of a parent education curriculum are (1) to stimulate parents to examine their relationship with their children more closely and (2) to encourage interaction among parents and between parents and program staff (Powell, 1986). Although the education of parents is primarily for the benefit of the children, the parents' own development can also be enhanced in the process of interacting with other adults.

The term *education* is part of the problem because it connotes the formal study of facts associated with a narrowly cognitive academic world. In reality the subject of parent–child relations and education is not usually so much concerned with facts and knowledge as it is with concepts, attitudes, and ideas. The content of any educational program may be less important than the methods of bringing families together to widen their horizons and sensitize them to feelings in a parent–child relationship.

A vital realization for teachers is that it is families, not teachers, who raise children, and that teachers can play crucial roles in supporting families to be optimally effective in supporting children's development and learning. Teachers become involved in family education so that every professional opportunity is taken to help parents develop their skills as children's first teachers and nurturers, with children ultimately benefiting.

A broader consideration of parent education implies a dynamic learning process in which families are active participants, growing out of parents' interests and needs, and in which parents participate as individuals. Research-based information increasingly suggests that the ways in which parents see their parenting roles and interact with their children directly influence how young children learn to think, talk, solve problems, and feel about themselves

---

FOCUS OF PARENT EDUCATION

Parent education focuses on

- Educational experiences to give parents new knowledge and understanding.

- Support for parenting roles.

- Support for marital roles.

- Support for self-awareness and personal growth.

- Support for adult roles and relationships within the community.

- Opportunities to question habitual ways of thinking and acting.

- Help to develop new methods (where needed) in relationships with children.

and others. As teachers of their children, parents need the same awareness and skills that teachers have so they can feel the same confidence in their ability to guide children to the fullest extent. Therefore, parent education needs to offer a broad variety of services designed to complement families' responsibilities and knowledge and to increase their understanding of children and their educational needs and their competence in caring for them.

Samples of Predesigned Parent Education Programs

Several popular program models have been developed for widespread use and have been used primarily with middle-class parents. These include Parent Effectiveness Training (PET), Systematic Training for Effective Parenting (STEP), Active Parenting Today, the AVANCE parenting education curriculum, and the curricula from the Center for the Improvement of Child Caring (see Figure 13-2).

Parent Effectiveness Training (PET)

Thomas Gordon developed a course and wrote a book with this title. The method focuses primarily on helping parents develop communication skills that allow them to act as counselors to children regarding their behavior and feelings and resolve conflicts between parents and children. Parents are taught techniques such as active listening, **I-messages**, and no-lose methods of conflict resolution. Although the principles of communication are adaptable for use with children of any age, many of the examples used in the curriculum are of communication with elementary-age children. Studies of attitudes and behaviors of parents who have attended PET sessions indicate

FIGURE 13-2 Parents generally enjoy the opportunity to share their experiences with other parents.

increases in understanding of children and in positive interactions with children and cohesion in the family, along with decreases in the frequency of family conflicts. Note also that similar training for teachers is given in Teacher Effectiveness Training. (For more information about PET methods see Gordon, 2000, and the Web site at chapter end.)

Systematic Training for Effective Parenting (STEP)

This program offers a structured curriculum in cassettes, parent manuals, and a leadership manual, supplying material for nine parent group sessions, based on the child management principles of Alfred Adler and Rudolf Dreikurs. Communication methods and nonpunitive discipline techniques such as natural and logical consequences are emphasized, along with skills for developing responsibility, decision making, and family problem solving. More recently programs for using STEP methods for parents of children under 6 and for parents of teenagers have been developed (Dinkmeyer et al., 1997b; Dinkmeyer et al., 1998). (For more information about STEP methods, see Dinkmeyer et al, 1997a.)

Active Parenting Today (APT)

Active Parenting Today, now over 20 years old, offers a number of parenting programs based on the use of videotapes and workbooks in structured sessions with trained leaders. The program claims to "emerge from the concepts of psychologists such as Alfred Adler, Rudolf Dreikurs, and Carl Rogers, and goes beyond groundbreaking programs like PET and STEP to make parenting education easier to teach—and more compelling to learn—than ever before" (APT Newsletter). Concepts emphasized include "freedom within limits" and "democratic family units," with ideas for family council meetings. Tested techniques such as I-messages, active listening, and natural and logical consequences are illustrated in the video vignettes, along with basic understandings of causes of misbehavior, formation of self-esteem, and helpful praise and encouragement in developing responsibility. Numerous video-based parent education programs are recently available from Active Parenting. These include Active Parenting of Teens; Active Teaching; Parents on Board: Building Academic Success through Parent Involvement; 1, 2, 3, 4 Parents!; Cooperative Parenting and Divorce; and Spanish language versions of the major programs. For more information on Active Parenting Today and its video programs, contact Active Parenting Publishing, 810 Franklin Court, Suite B, Marietta, GA 30067 (800-825-0060) and at its Web address (listed at the end of this chapter).

Such programs that appeal widely to middle-class parents may be quite unappealing for lower-income parents or parents from cultural backgrounds that may not value **democratic models** and open expression of feelings. This is not to suggest that the information and ideas proposed by these predesigned education programs would not benefit all parents. Even the best information may not be helpful if the model conflicts with a family's cultural values and experiences. Rather, teachers and administrators should consider carefully the methods and style of instruction to ensure that parents are learning in styles and circumstances that match their cultural values and experiences and their comfort levels (Fine & Lee, 2000).

AVANCE Parenting Education

The AVANCE Parenting Education Curriculum was developed in that agency's work with parents from poor, predominantly Hispanic neighborhoods. Established in San Antonio in 1973, AVANCE has become a model as one of the first family support and education programs in the United States, and one of the first comprehensive, community-based programs to target at-risk and Latino populations. In working with the parents of infants and young children, AVANCE offers parenting education, social support, adult basic and higher education, early childhood education and youth programs, and personal development (Cohen, 1994). The parenting curriculum includes an intensive nine-month set of parenting classes (27 lessons divided into 11 units.) Topics include an overview of parenting, prenatal care, infant needs, physical needs of young children, childhood illnesses, nutrition and the young child, children's behavior, cognitive and language development, emotional needs, social needs, self-awareness, and goal setting. The curriculum, now available for sale and replication in other communities, suggests that although it was designed for high-risk Hispanic families, it is also effective in African American communities and Native American communities. Descriptions of AVANCE successful work in the community are found in both Clinton (1996) and Schorr (1997). For more information, contact Family Support and Education Program, Hasbro National Family Resource Center, Mercedes Perez de Colon, 301 S. Frio, Suite 310, San Antonio TX 78207, (210) 270-4630.

Center for the Improvement of Child Caring

This organization is a private, nonprofit group that sees its role as being a major organizer of the Effective Parent movement. Two of the programs they have developed are designed specifically for minority parents. Effective Black Parenting is described as a "culturally relevant skill-building program for raising proud and confident African American children." A step-by-step curriculum leads participants through 15 three-hour sessions teaching parenting skills that respect African American patterns of communication and recognize the roots of the extended black family. African proverbs guide the topics, and role-playing of home situations is used. Los Ninos Bien Educados is a parent education program developed specifically for Spanish-speaking and Latino-origin parents, dealing specifically with traditions and customs in child rearing and with adjustments being made as families acculturate to life in the United

States. These programs are available through the Center for the Improvement of Child Caring, 11331 Ventura Blvd, Suite 103, Studio City CA 91604-3147, (818) 980-0903, or at its Web site, listed at the chapter end.

It is often tempting for teachers to use formats or activities planned by others. Using a ready-made manual or suggestions sometimes seems more efficient and removes the additional responsibilities of planning and preparing activities. There are a number of resources available; see Wilson (1993) and Vopat (1998) for examples of such resources. However, the great danger is not matching ideas or activities to the particular group of families with whom a teacher or administrator is working at a particular time. Although time-consuming, the only way to plan activities that are truly meaningful is to work with the knowledge of a unique group. Resources may be useful to provide ideas that teachers can adapt rather than simply adopting them.

Powell states that there have been major changes in the content and procedures of parent education programs in current times, with a new interest in

- Matching programs with the intended parent populations.
- Changing relations between program staff and participants.
- Paying attention to the social context of parent functioning. (Powell, 1989)

It is worthwhile to note these as important current issues in parent education to be examined now.

Matching Programs to Parent Characteristics

We have noted that parent education methods often used with groups of middle-class families do not necessarily transfer to low-income parents. For example, group discussion methods may have limited appeal with these groups. Planned programs must recognize and respond to the needs and wishes of the individual participants. This suggests an active role for parents in determining content and method of learning.

Changing Relationships between Professionals and Families

There is an increasing trend toward equal relationships between program staff and parent participants. Principals, directors, or teachers do not always play dominant roles or make all decisions. Professionals who work with parents take on a collaborative partnership role rather than a professional-as-expert role. This puts staff into the role of facilitator of goals and activities that are jointly determined by parents and staff. Such an understanding focuses more on adult education within the relationship than on purely parent education, assuming that parents and teachers educate each other. Parents build on their strengths as individuals.

Attention to the Social Context of Parenting

Increasingly it is recognized that social networks and support are important for parents in their parenting role. Families who receive adequate social support are more capable of supporting themselves. Traditional parent education programs rely on disseminating information to parents to affect behavior, but the parent support approach assumes that social ties will positively assist parent functioning (see Figure 13-3). Professionals who work with families in groups facilitate the group members' ability to share ideas and experiences and to support one another.

Parent education involves making available to all parents the necessary support and attitudes that

1. Encourage them to use and depend on what they know.
2. Encourage them to share their experience with other parents.
3. Support what they are doing.
4. Expose them to new ideas they have not considered.

These ideas eliminate the connotation that parent education is associated only with deficit models of parenting and emphasize the need to support and help *all* parents.

In recent years the number of programs working to help families in aspects of their lives has greatly increased. Nevertheless, the value of parent education programs continues to be questioned by policy makers and funders,

FIGURE 13-3 The social ties formed with other parents at parent education programs may be as important as the information.

who seem to believe that parenting is instinctive and only problem families need outside advice or help. Questions about effectiveness are raised by the wide variety of program types. What methods are most effective, and what are the desired outcomes? Assuming that the goal of parent education is to facilitate positive additions to parent–child relationships and to children's functioning, evaluating whether such a goal is met is difficult to research. One reason why attempts to assess the effects of parent education yield inconclusive results is that many questions related to parent education imply a concern with long-term results of the increased knowledge, status, and altered behavior. Most methods used to study the effects preclude the wait for such long-term answers. It is also difficult to correlate the results of one program to another.

Most studies of parent education programs have focused on children and found strong short-term effects. Effects on families have been studied less frequently but yield evidence of some immediate positive effects on interaction and attitudes. Family support types of programs have studied effects of parent involvement on families' socioeconomic and life circumstances and found positive correlations (Powell, 1994).

Assumptions Underlying Parent Education

A philosophy of parent education that involves parents actively in a dynamic situation makes these assumptions:

1. Parents can learn. Parenting behaviors are not determined by the unfolding of instinctive reactions but are learned behaviors that can be acquired or improved with effort. The more parents know about child development and the effects of parent–child interaction, the more they examine what they do and why they do it, and the more skillful they become in displaying appropriate behaviors.

2. Parenting is an area in which a knowledge base exists pertaining to effective types of parent behavior. Studies and research have indicated specific parental attitudes and actions that result in specific responses from children. It is important to state here that there is no unanimous agreement about what knowledge should be taught in any parent education program; however, the knowledge base is there for whatever areas need to be addressed.

3. Knowledge alone is not sufficient to develop parenting competence. That is, all major efforts at parenting education deal in some way with emotions and attitudes. Feelings about family and parent–child dynamics run deep. Parents are sometimes fooled by the myth that parenting is always joyful and delightful; they need to accept their own emotional responses of anxiety, frustration, and hostility. Attitudes about power, authority, reciprocity, and related issues are often more influential than

facts. Parent education must provide a vehicle for dealing with both facts and feelings.

4. All parents, no matter how well-educated, well-adjusted, or fortunate in their social and economic arrangements, need help with learning how to cope with the parenting role. This need is intensified by current changes in living styles for some, as well as at particular stages of the family's life cycle for all.

5. Parents want to learn. Parents care about their children and will participate when they believe they are helping their children or are doing something that makes them better parents. It follows that if parents do not participate in available education programs, they are not yet convinced of a program's value to their children or to themselves. Also, specific stresses in parents' lives must be alleviated to enable parents to involve themselves in learning and change.

6. Parents learn best when the subject matter is closely related to them and their children. All parents have unique experiences in the relationships and circumstances of their lives and need to make specific applications of new ideas to their situations. This places the basic responsibility for growth and change within each parent as each identifies particular needs and motivations. No person or agency outside the parent can decide what that parent needs.

7. Parents can often learn best from one another. A negative expression of this idea is that parents are adults who don't want to be told anything by a stranger, even an expert; parents also frequently resist being told things by experts they do know. Learning from the common experiences of other adults who are perceived as peers can be meaningful because parents remind each other of what they already know and increase their feelings of self-worth as they empathize and understand.

8. Parents learn in their own way. Basic educational principles point out individual differences in pace, style, and patterns of learning. A dynamic program offers flexible approaches that allow parents to proceed as they feel comfortable, to concentrate on what they find significant, and to participate actively to the extent that they are able. Professionals who work in parent education must understand principles of adult learning. (see Figure 13-4).

REFLECTIONS FOR JOURNAL ENTRIES

As an adult, have you been involved in educational experiences that did not recognize these principles of adult learning? What was your reaction when treated without respect for your own needs or particular interests in learning? How can those experiences help you plan meaningful, respectful parent education?

FIGURE 13-4 Professionals who work in parent education must understand principles of adult learning.

Some of the more typical problems that parent education programs have to address can be prevented or resolved with more attention to the implications of these assumptions. These problems include

1. Initial recruitment problems or lack of interest. Attention to program content and format, program time, transportation, child care, and other support services can all help here.

2. Conflict in views and values. Collaborative discussion and planning can help turn differences in ideas and attitudes into stimulating situations that can cause parents to examine their own positions more deeply.

3. Group management problems. Administrators and teachers have to learn skills necessary to work with adults. Part of the training should be a change from the professional stance of domination to group process techniques.

Recently the Family Resource Coalition has responded to the interest in new theories and techniques in parent education by offering summer institutes to train professionals. The training explores group process, peer support theory, dealing with diversity, curriculum and program models, and the role of the professional in social support networks. For information about the summer training institutes, contact the Family Resource Coalition (discussed in Chapter 4).

■■■ IMPLEMENTING A PARENT EDUCATION PROGRAM

Families must be actively involved in planning the educational programs in which they will participate. A collaborative effort in which teachers and parents function as partners in needs assessment differs from the traditional approach of a professional making these decisions alone. There are numerous ways to facilitate this (see Figure 13-5).

Initial Parent Involvement

Parents may come together first for purely social occasions such as potluck suppers, brown bag lunches, or parents' breakfasts. As comfort levels increase and relationships grow, the general discussion among the parents may narrow to particular interests and concerns. Teachers can help parents structure a program evolved directly from the discovery of common needs and questions. Teachers are then acting not as "experts" but as resources as families define their own needs. It is a natural progression for parents to become involved because they already feel welcomed as a member of the group of parents.

Remembering that family education may be broader than merely focusing on children's issues, programs may bring parents together first to learn skills in which they have indicated interest—see some of the choices on the interest survey here, such as using the Internet or financial planning and investments. As the monthly meetings become popular, interest may cycle back to parenting topics (Carter, 1999).

To involve parents directly in planning education efforts, structure a meeting soon after the school year starts, specifically to generate and discuss

FIGURE 13-5 Families must be actively involved in planning the educational programs in which they will participate.

ideas that parents are interested in pursuing. At this initial meeting parents can take an active role if staff members ask one or two parents to help plan and lead the first discussion.

Answering an assessment questionnaire or survey is one way of receiving input from parents on their interests and needs for future parent programs. A sample survey might look like this:

PARENT EDUCATION INTEREST SURVEY

As we plan our parents' meetings for this year, your ideas are needed. Let us know if you would like to learn more about the following topics.

1. Rate the following topics:

	Interest:		
	Great	Slight	None

Discipline for self-control

Using the Internet

Sibling rivalry

Nutrition and children

Financial planning and investments

Understanding No Child Left Behind legislation and what it means to you

Getting ready for school

Choosing good books and toys

Sex education

Normal development

Preserving family stories

Being an only parent

Television and its effects on children

Language development: what's normal and what's not

Cooking fast suppers in a wok

Resources in the community: where to get help

When to call the doctor

Avoiding your child's "I need" trap

(continues)

(continued)

> **How to make your child responsible**
> **for his or her own homework**
>
> **Please add topics of interest to you:** _____
>
> _____
>
> 2. **Circle the day that fits your schedule: M T W Th F**
>
> 3. **Indicate the time of day that is best:**
>
>   **Lunch hour**
>
>   **Right after work**
>
>   **Evening—7 or 7:30**
>
> **Thank you for your help. Watch for coming notices.**

The disadvantage to using a survey form is that some parents may have difficulty with the reading and writing aspects of it and may not bother to return it. If the survey is also posted on the parent bulletin board, parents may stop and respond in the school. The form lacks the personal involvement of individuals in a discussion, but at least a survey conveys the message that parents' ideas are needed and wanted and can yield a lot of helpful planning information. Parents will pay attention to subsequent announcements of meetings that they have helped to plan.

Teachers are often tempted to plan programs based on what they believe parents need to learn. But unless parents are motivated by a current need to gain particular knowledge or skills, they may reject plans imposed by teachers, no matter how important the ideas are. Parent education programs have a greater likelihood of effecting change if they are sensitive to and design activities around the basic assumptions and beliefs parents hold regarding child rearing and education. Reports of successful parent education efforts (Luethy, 1991; Rose, 1990) point out that in each case the curriculum is not preset and prescribed, but follows the interests and needs identified by families. That is, programs should start where the parents presently are, rather than where teachers think parents should be. Only parents can accurately define this starting place by expressing their needs and interests. They can also keep the program responsive to differences of culture and class.

Selecting the Style of a Meeting

Group size and style of meeting must be considered when providing for parents' comfort and an opportunity to talk with other parents. Studies find that the most important variable in parent attendance and participation in meetings is group size; smaller groups create feelings of closeness, community, and ownership of the endeavor. Other studies indicate that meetings involving families

FIGURE 13-6 Bringing together a small group of parents with children of similar ages or grade levels facilitates the sharing of information and concerns.

of just one class are preferable to whole school meetings; bringing together a dozen or so parents with children of similar ages or grade levels facilitates the sharing of experiences and concerns (see Figure 13-6). The advantage to large group meetings is that a timid parent can listen without feeling pressure to participate; the disadvantage is that individual needs are often not met because not all parents will have the opportunity to ask questions related to their particular situations or gain the satisfaction of sharing with other parents.

Because parents learn from each other as well as from professionals, the style of a meeting should encourage such interaction. Greater changes may occur in parents' behavior and attitudes following discussions within a group of parents than following lectures. Powell refers to the importance of what he calls "kitchen talk," the informal conversation that occurs in the breaks of more formal planned education efforts, as both desirable and worthwhile (Powell, 1989). This requires a reconceptualization of the roles of supervisors, teachers, and parents in parent education, emphasizing the importance of parents speaking to each other and putting professionals in the role of consultants, supporting instead of instructing. In some instances of successful parent education, nonprofessionals function well as group leaders. When parents identify a need that requires an expert, teachers can help locate and invite suitable resources.

The Teacher's Role in Setting the Style of a Meeting

A teacher's role in a parent discussion group is first to provide a structure that helps establish a warm atmosphere of informality and friendly sharing, and then to function as a facilitator of group discussion. Such a leader displays

- Acceptance, support, and encouragement for all parents in a group to express themselves.

Sample Plan for a Meeting to Satisfy Parent's Needs for Participation and Social Interaction

1. Welcome and introductions—round robin to talk with at least three people, then introduce the last person you speak with.

2. Discussion of purpose of evening: to answer parents' questions and concerns about the No Child Left Behind Legislation; overview of activities.

3. Break into groups of four to five members with chart paper and a marker. Appoint one member to record the group's questions, comments, and concerns. Allow 15 minutes for this discussion—more if needed.

4. One member from each group presents the main points of their discussion and posts their questions.

5. The facilitator (the director of the parent information and resource center located behind the school) will summarize the questions and lead a discussion that provides relevant information.

6. Time for further questions and discussion.

7. Break for refreshments and informal conversation.

8. Tour of the parental information and resource center, and closing.

Notice how this plan allows informal parental interaction and participation, as well as providing information to address parental concerns and letting parents explore the resources that can continue to support them.

- Objectivity, to avoid taking sides in most discussions.
- Tact, to protect each parent's right to discuss in a nonthreatening environment.
- Alertness to both verbal and nonverbal responses of group members, using that feedback to guide a discussion and maintain group morale.

It is possible for teachers or administrators to function this way only when they have relinquished the attitude that only they know about children. Such an attitude shows clearly in their interaction with parents and inhibits the formation of any informal group discussions. Heavy utilization of media or lecture techniques does not allow parents to participate, whereas group discussions or small group work formats do.

Icebreaker Activities

1. Ask participants to find someone who

   • Has the same number of children.

   • Has the same birthday month.

   • Was born in the same hospital.

   • Has the same middle name.

   • Has the same favorite food.

   • Has the same favorite TV show.

2. Pair up participants to share the stories of how they were given their names. They can use this information to introduce their partners to the group.

3. Ask participants to find a partner to share their worst memories of school. When the group reconvenes, ask for a few volunteers to tell their partners' stories. When the laughter dies down, names can be shared.

4. Create small groups, and give them chart paper and markers. Ask them to create a group drawing incorporating characteristics of their least favorite teachers. Group members must all contribute ideas to whoever volunteers to draw or represent them.

Teachers can structure the initial meeting of parents to ease interpersonal communication. Name tags, with reminders of whose parent this is, help parents make initial connections.

Icebreaker games or activities may start a conversation. It is important to remember, however, that teachers are now dealing with adults, not children, so a teacher must learn techniques that are appropriate for adults. Most adults would feel discomfort at being asked to participate in children's songs until the group had moved to a level of familiarity with each other. More ideas for icebreakers can be found in West (1996) and Newstrom and Scannell (1997).

Teachers can demonstrate the philosophy that parents' meetings are another way of working with the whole family by involving children in making refreshments or decorations during a classroom day, by asking children to leave a picture or note for their parent to find, or asking parents to make a picture at the meeting to leave in a child's cubby for the next morning (see Figure 13-7). Margie Carter (1999) describes a parent meeting at a preschool where children wrote the letters to entice their parents to come to the meeting. The teachers worked with the children to identify what they wanted their

FIGURE 13-7 When parents come to the Open House meeting, children can leave notes for their parents, asking them to do a favorite activity or assignment.

families to discover when they came to the classroom. They created letters and drawings with instructions from each child on how they wanted their families to spend their time at the meeting. When the families arrived for the meeting, they were given their children's messages and sent off to follow the directions for exploration. The activities led to valuable discussion about the children's learning and curriculum. Teachers took photos and notes, and parents wrote their own letters back to leave for the children, along with the paintings and block buildings they had created.

The prior existence of a social network of friends and relatives correlates with a lower level of attendance at regular group sessions and special events for parents (Powell, 1983). In other words, parents without reciprocal ties with other adults are more eager for the support and interaction with adults in parent education settings. This may be especially true for single parents. The opportunities for social interaction and new relationships provide incentives for some parents to become involved in such a parent education group.

Selecting a Time for a Meeting

Other stresses and concerns of daily life may prevent some parents from involving themselves in parent education activities. Teachers need to be conscious of any accommodations they can make to help alleviate some of these problems.

Meetings may be more convenient if parents help select the dates and times. Sometimes parents' attendance is precluded by child care demands; providing child care may allow a family to attend. This is why many successful parent education efforts of full-day programs occur during the lunch hour or late afternoon, while children are still in their classrooms. Transportation difficulties may keep parents from participating; parent committees can set up carpools or arrange meetings in more central locations, or parents may come to school on the bus with their children for a morning meeting. Some programs that are located close to parents' worksites, such as employer-sponsored child care, take the parent education program right into the office building during lunch hour (Luethy, 1991). Such assistance lets parents become involved and is evidence that teachers understand some of their problems.

Traditionally, parent meetings for elementary schools have been held in the evening. For working parents, evening meetings are often difficult to attend; after a long day at the job, then taking children home to prepare supper and getting through the evening routine, going back to school becomes quite unattractive. Many schools find success in providing an evening meal—a covered dish supper or a spaghetti dinner—when parents come to pick up their children.

One school's favorite dinner is undemanding and involves the children in preparation during the day, heightening their anticipation of the pleasant social occasion. The menu is simple: baked potatoes with toppings and tossed salad. The preschoolers expend enormous amounts of energy scrubbing the potatoes in the water table during morning work time before the potatoes are taken to the kitchen for final touches and baking, while other children prepare some of the vegetables for salad. No one has to work too hard, and there is a real sense of community for the event. Parents, children, and teachers relax together after a workday, enjoying a social occasion without parents having to worry about hurrying home with tired, hungry children. The children can play or do homework supervised in another room while parents continue a more serious discussion. Parents and children can still get home early in the evening after a pleasant and productive time for all. (See Figure 13-8 for a listing of books that might provide useful resources for teachers and parents planning discussions of particular topics.)

Schools centrally located to parents' workplaces find that asking parents to "brown bag" it occasionally for a lunch meeting brings parents together while children are busy at school. Such meetings recognize the many demands on parents' nonworking time.

Busy, weary parents are more likely to attend meetings where the time frame, announced in advance, will not be much more than an hour and will begin and end promptly. It is helpful to announce meetings well in advance (a month, minimum), with weekly, then daily, reminders. Coordinating plans and arrangements takes time, so staff should assume parents are not able to come on short notice. Attention to physical comfort, with adult-sized chairs,

---

Books about Topics That Teachers and Parents May Enjoy Discussing

Ames, L. (1991). *Raising good kids: A development approach to discipline.* Rosemont, NY: Modern Learning Press.

Brazelton, T. (1994). *Touchpoints: Your child's emotional and behavioral development.* Cambridge, MA: Perseus.

————. (2001). *Touchpoints 3 to 6: Your child's emotional and behavioral development.* Cambridge, MA: Perseus.

Calderone, M., & Ramey, J. (1983). *Talking with your child about sex.* New York: Ballantine Books.

Cantor, J. & Stoughton, C. (Eds.). (2000). *Media violence alert: Informing parents about the number one health threat in America today.* (Parent Education Series # 1). Toronto, ONT: Dreamcatcher Press.

Carlsson-Paige, N., & Levin, D. (1990). *Who's calling the shots?* Philadelphia: New Society Publishers.

Elkind, D. (1988). *The hurried child.* Reading, MA: Addison-Wesley.

Faber, A., & Mazlisch, E. (1998). *Siblings without rivalry: How to help your children live together so you can live, too.* New York: Avon Books.

Ginott, H. (1976). *Between parent and child.* New York: Avon Books.

Gordon, T. (1996). *Parent effectiveness training.* New York: Berkley.

Kurcinka, M. (2000). *Kids, parents, and power struggles: Winning for a lifetime.* New York: HarperCollins.

Levin, D. (1998). *Remote control childhood? Combating the hazards of media culture.* Washington, DC: NAEYC.

Mackenzie, M. (1998). *Setting limits: How to raise responsible, independent children by providing clear boundaries.* Rocklin, CA: Prima Publishing.

Rubin, T. (1990). *Child potential.* New York: Continuum Press.

Shore, R. (1997). *Rethinking the brain: New insights into early development.* New York: Families and Work Institute.

White, B. (1996). *A new parent's guide to the first three years.* Upper Saddle River, NJ: Prentice Hall.

FIGURE 13-8 Books to help teachers and parents planning discussion.

refreshments, and a relaxed, uncrowded atmosphere, creates optimal conditions for concentrating on a discussion (see Figure 13-9).

As parent education discussion groups evolve, the participants will more strictly define their purposes and goals. It is important to the ongoing success of such programs that parents and teachers occasionally evaluate whether activities are meeting the intended goals. Remember that the effectiveness of any parent education program is measured not by how many people come (the "bodies in the building" assessment) but by the effect the program has in changing attitudes and behaviors and increasing parental competence. An evaluation should center on how a program works for those who attend and what additional steps can be taken to include others.

For teachers like Anne Morgan and Dorothy Scott, who have been part of a traditional professional-giving-information type of parent education

FIGURE 13-9 Comfortable chairs and a relaxed atmosphere create optimal conditions for participating in a discussion.

program, it may require determined effort to accept the concept of parents choosing, guiding, and actively participating in a discussion. But such forms of education give strength and power to parents as they gain confidence in their own ideas and abilities.

PARENTS AS DECISION MAKERS

Some programs and schools involve parents as advisers and policy makers. Parent membership on parent councils or policy boards brings them into decision-making positions that may affect their children and the communities they represent. The exact roles of decision makers may vary according to the regulations of the school or agency involved (see Figure 13-10).

Federally funded programs, such as Head Start and Title 1, have federal guidelines and local regulations to govern parental roles on advisory councils that have 50% parent membership. These roles are active, with the power to decide on budget matters, curriculum, and hiring. Parent cooperative schools generally allow their parent boards to make all policy decisions.

Many school districts have now established parent advisory or decision-making councils for each school site. Variously called Parent Advisory Councils (PACS), Site-Based Councils, School Improvement Councils (SICS), and Local School Councils (LSCS), these bodies usually include parents with teachers and staff to serve on the council (Henry, 1996).

Other parent councils in some public and private educational settings may function as purely advisory bodies, with decision-making powers vested in professional personnel. A parent advisory council can be a first link to successful communication and collaboration between staff and parents. As the staff works with the parents on the parent advisory council, there is less

FIGURE 13-10 Parents are involved as decision makers in some schools.

impression of "experts" advising or controlling the situation. The difficulty may be that the parents who are invited to participate may not fully represent the diversity of parents in the school or may be volunteers who may feel most comfortable in the school setting. Schools must try to include all voices represented in the school community.

Many parents are eager to have a voice in their children's schools. Effectively involving parents in cooperative decision making can benefit everyone. Children benefit as programs shape their offerings to fit community character and need. Parents assuming leadership roles develop skills that benefit themselves and their communities and increase their confidence in their abilities to shape their children's lives. They also may demonstrate more support for a school as they perceive a closer connection between its functioning and their own goals. Parents who feel they have a vehicle to voice their concerns will not withdraw or resort to negative methods of making themselves heard. As parents learn more about how a school functions and why, they learn more about children's needs. Directors and teachers benefit by the expansion of their viewpoints with the addition of parents' perspectives. They also may find their efforts are strengthened with the addition of parent understanding, advocacy, and support.

In poorly planned parent advisory situations, a variety of problems may surface:

- Conflicts about how to conduct the organizational process.
- Power struggles between parents vying for control of a group.

- Confusion about the responsibilities of group members.
- Disagreements over institutional philosophies and goals.

When an organization develops a trusting relationship among its members and helps develop group communication and planning skills, parents participating in the decision-making process develop important relationships between home and school. Specific guidelines for, and clear understandings of, parent action are most helpful. For example, rather than vague phrases like "the director will decide in conjunction with the parents," a more specific statement is desirable, like "the director will screen job candidates and present three choices, without recommendation, for final selection by the parent council." The real advantages of involving parents as decision makers should encourage professionals to find methods that avoid conflict and misunderstanding.

SUMMARY

Each early childhood education program and school has its particular characteristics, goals, and client populations, and each school must consider how it brings parents together for education, support, and advisory purposes in the total effort of parent involvement. The following assumptions must be made if a philosophy of parent education is to involve parents actively:

1. Parents can learn.
2. A specific body of knowledge exists that can help parents become more effective.
3. Knowledge alone is not enough. Attitudes and feelings must be dealt with.
4. All parents need education and help.
5. Parents want to learn.
6. Parents learn best when the subject matter is closely related to their particular circumstances.
7. Parents can often learn best from one another.
8. Parents will learn at their own paces, in their own ways.

Teachers can structure meetings with parents in ways that facilitate family participation, where parents will define for teachers their individual needs and wants. Meeting times should be decided according to when parents are available.

STUDENT ACTIVITIES FOR FURTHER STUDY

1. Attend a parent meeting at your own, or any other, school. Notice efforts made to promote social comfort and interaction; physical arrangements and services, such as child care, seating, and refreshments; planned activity, amounts of interaction, and parents' response to it. Find out how and when the meeting was publicized. Discuss your findings with your classmates.

2. If you are working or interning in a school, devise a survey form to assess parents' interest and needs for making future program plans. After you obtain the responses, analyze the information and then devise several plans that match parents' expressed needs and wants. If you are not currently in a classroom situation, work in pairs to devise a questionnaire, then answer it as each of the hypothetical families in Chapter 1 might. Analyze the information and devise several education plans that match those needs and wants.

   For the parents' meeting:

   • List the purpose of the meeting.
   • List the instructional strategies you will be using and the materials and equipment you will need.
   • Describe the room arrangement you will use.
   • List the tentative schedule, with approximate times for the events.
   • List five questions you would expect parents to discuss about this topic.
   • List five questions you might use to stimulate discussion about this topic.

3. Plan a simple ice-breaking social activity for the beginning of a meeting.

   Discuss this with your classmates.

4. Contact several schools in your area, including a Head Start or other federally funded program if one exists in your community. Find out whether parents participate in any advisory capacity.

CASE STUDY

The faculty at Jackson Early Childhood Center has always had one required parent meeting each year, held on an evening in January. For the last two years fewer than one-third of the families were represented in attendance, even though they know it is expected of them. The teachers have been discouraged by this lack of response. One outspoken parent told her teacher recently that she did not plan to attend again because the meeting was a waste of her time.

1. What would be the most helpful response to this parent? The least helpful response?

2. How could this parent's response be useful to the faculty and administrator as they plan this year's parent education meeting?

3. What are some questions the faculty should be asking as they try to change the situation?

4. Brainstorm a list of strategies that might help in the planning process.

REVIEW QUESTIONS

1. Discuss a rationale for parent education.

2. Identify five of eight assumptions regarding parent education.

3. For each assumption, describe a corresponding implication for planning parent education programs.

4. Describe how parents may act as advisers in a program.

SUGGESTIONS FOR FURTHER READING

Anastasiow, N. (1988). Should parenting education be mandatory? *Topics in Early Childhood: Special Education, 8*(1), 60–72.

Burningham, L., & Dever, M. (2005). An interactive model for fostering family literacy. *Young Children, 60*(5), 87–93.

Campbell, D., & Palm, G. (2003). *Group parent education: Promoting parent learning and support.* Thousand Oaks, CA: Sage Publications.

Carter, N. (1996). *See how we grow: A report on the status of parenting education in the U.S.* Philadelphia, PA: Pew Charitable Trust. Available online at http:www.npen.org.

Cataldo, C. Z. (1987). *Parent education for early childhood.* New York: Teachers College Press.

Foster, S. M. (1994). Successful parent meetings. *Young Children, 50*(1), 78–80.

Goetz, K. (Ed.). (1992). *Programs to strengthen families: A resource guide* (3rd ed.). Chicago: Family Resource Coalition.

Mass, Y. and Cohan, K. (2006). "Home connections to learning: Supporting parents as teachers." *Young Children, 61*(1), 54–55.

Powell, D. (Ed.). (1988). *Parent education as early childhood intervention.* Norwood, NJ: Ablex.

Rockwell, B., & Kniepkamp, J. (2003). *Partnering with parents: Easy programs to involve parents in the early learning process.* Beltsville, MD: Gryphon House Press.

Sheridan, S., & Christenson, S. (Eds.). (2001). *Schools and families: Creating essential connections for learning.* New York: Guilford Press.

Smith, L., & Wells, W. (1997). *Urban parent education: Dilemmas and resolutions. (Qualitative Studies on Schools and Schooling.)* Cresskill, NJ: Hampton Press.

Vopat, J. (1994). *The parent project: A workshop approach to parent involvement.* New York: Stenhouse Pubs.

Webb, N. (1997). Working with parents from cradle to preschool: A university collaborates with an urban public school. *Young Children, 52*(4), 15–19.

Wetzel, L. (1990). *Parents of young children: A parent education curriculum.* St. Paul, MN: Toys and Things Press.

Wlodkowski, R. J. (1985). *Enhancing adult motivation to learn.* San Francisco: Jossey-Bass.

REFERENCES

Auerbach, A. B. (1968). *Parents learn through discussion: Principles and practices of parent group education.* New York: John Wiley and Sons.

Carter, M. (1999, November). Developing meaningful relationships with families. *Child Care Information Exchange,* 63–65.

Clinton, H. (1996). *It takes a village and other lessons children teach us.* New York: Simon and Schuster.

Cohen, D. (1994, October 19). Teach their parents well: A family outreach program helps Hispanic moms—and dads—learn how to become effective advocates for their children. *Education Week,* On assignment.

Dinkmeyer, D., et al. (1997a). *The parents' handbook: Systematic training for effective parenting.* Circle Pines, MN: American Guidance Systems.

———. (1997b). *Parenting young children: Systematic training for effective parenting (STEP) of children under 6.* Circle Pines, MN: American Guidance Systems.

———. (1998). *Parenting teenagers: Systematic training for effective parenting of teenagers.* Circle Pines, MN: American Guidance Systems.

Dunst, C., & Trivette, C. (1994). Aims and principles of family support programs. In C. Dunst, C. Trivette, & A. Deal (Eds.), *Supporting and strengthening families: Volume 1—Methods, strategies, and practices.* Cambridge, MA: Brookline Books.

Fine, M., & Lee, S. (2000). *Handbook of diversity in parent education: The changing faces of parenting and parent education.* New York: Academic Press.

Gordon, T. (2000). *Parent effectiveness training: The proven program for raising responsible children.* New York: Random House.

Henry, M. (1996). *Parent–school collaboration.* Albany, NY: State University of New York Press.

Kagan, S. (1995, May). The changing face of parent education. *ERIC Digest.*

Luethy, G. (1991). An example of parent education at the work site. *Young Children, 46*(4), 62–63.

Newstrom, J., & Scannell, E. (1997). *The big book of presentation games: Wake-em-up tricks, icebreakers, and other fun stuff.* New York: McGraw Hill.

Powell, D. R. (1983). Individual differences in participation in a parent–child support program. In I. E. Sigel & L. M. Laosa (Eds.), *Changing families.* New York: Plenum Press.

———. (1986). Parent education and support programs. *Young Children, 41*(3), 47–52.

———. (1989). *Families and early childhood programs.* Washington, DC: NAEYC.

———. (1994). Evaluating family support programs: Are we making progress? In S. Kagan & B. Weissbourd (Eds.), *Putting families first: America's family support movement and the challenge of change.* San Francisco: Jossey-Bass.

Rose, B. (1990, Winter). Early childhood family education. *Day Care and Early Education,* 27–29.

Schorr, L. (1997). *Common purpose: Strengthening families and neighborhoods to rebuild America.* New York: Doubleday.

Swick, K. (1985). Critical issues in parent education. *Dimensions, 14*(1), 4–7.

Vopat, J. (1998). *More than bake sales: The resource guide to family involvement in education.* New York: Stenhouse Publishers.

West, E. (1996). *201 icebreakers: Group mixers, warm-ups, energizers, and playful activities.* New York: McGraw Hill.

Wilson, G. B. (1993). *Activities for parent groups* (rev. ed.). Atlanta, GA: Humanics, Ltd.

HELPFUL WEB SITES

http://www.gordontraining.com

Parent Effectiveness Training. Their mission is to provide people worldwide with the communication and conflict resolution skills necessary for creating effective and lasting relationships in the workplace, in families, and in schools.

http://www.ciccparenting.org

Center for the Improvement of Child Care. CICC is a private, nonprofit community service, training, and research corporation, and a major supporter and participant in a nationwide effective parenting movement to improve the overall quality of child rearing and child caring in the United States.

http://www.activeparenting.com

Active Parenting Today. Using this program, you will provide parents with the skills that will help them develop cooperation, responsibility, and self-esteem in their children. They'll also learn positive discipline techniques so they can avoid those all-too-familiar power struggles.

http://www.fen.com

Family Education Network is the Web's leading source of educational content, resources, and shopping for parents, teachers, and kids.

http://www.ncea.com

The mission of the National Community Education Association is to provide leadership to those who build learning communities in response to individual and community needs.

http://www.aap.org

The mission of the American Academy of Pediatrics is to attain optimal physical, mental, and social health and well-being for all infants, children, adolescents, and young adults. Information on this site could be useful for designing parent meetings on a variety of topics.

http://www.famlit.org

The National Center for Family Literacy's mission is to create educational and economic opportunities for the most at-risk children and parents.

http://www.parenteducationnetwork.ca

The Web site for the Parent Education Network has information about online skills courses and workshops for parents, referrals, and community linkages.

Additional resources for this chapter can be found on the Online Companion to accompany this text at www.earlychilded.delmar.com. This supplemental material includes frequently asked questions; chapter outlines to be used as study guides; scenarios that both encourage large and small group discussions and provoke new thoughts and ideas; and chapter resources, including chapter summaries, interactive questions, Web links, and Web activities. In addition, forms from the text are available for download.

CHAPTER 14

It Takes a Village: Teachers, Families, and Communities

OBJECTIVES

After reading this chapter, you should be able to

1 Discuss corporate involvement in family, education, and child care issues.
2 Describe current legislative initiatives that shape policy affecting families, schools, and children.
3 Discuss community linkages that support families and children.
4 Identify and discuss advocacy roles for teachers and families.
5 Identify three ways the community can provide resources for teachers and children.

As communities reel from the impact of troubled families that are themselves crumbling with change and stress, the attention of the nation and its individual communities is drawn to the realization that healthy families are essential to every community. Furthermore, it becomes obvious that it is in the best interests of everyone within the community to support families to be effective in their child-rearing functions. When families, isolated and struggling, are left on their own to do what they can without the support of the larger community, the community bears the brunt of the family's failure. The entire village that it takes to raise a child, which we have heard so much about in recent years, has come to the certain knowledge that the vision that supports children, families, and the institutions that serve families is a vision that impacts us all.

In this chapter we examine the ways that the community at large affects schools and early childhood programs and the families they serve, and the ways that teachers and families may function as advocates for child and family issues within the community. Together teachers and families have the power to turn community attention to supports that will mutually benefit them and the children they care for.

Children live in many worlds. Home and family, schools and early education programs, the neighborhood, and the community beyond shape their lives. Just as every family is unique, so too is each community.

Children exist in the context of community, depending on a multitude of adults who touch their lives directly through relationships and indirectly through the decisions they make that affect children and families. In the words of former First Lady, now Senator, Hilary Rodham Clinton:

> Adults police their streets, monitor the quality of their food, air, and water, produce the programs that appear on their televisions, run the businesses that employ their parents, and write the laws that protect them. Each of us plays a part in every child's life. It takes a village to raise a child.
>
> I chose that old African proverb to title this book because it offers a timeless reminder that children will thrive only if their families thrive and if the whole of society cares enough to provide for them (Clinton, 1996).

In the best of circumstances the many worlds of children are complementary and reinforcing, and each world is supported by the other, forming a circle of protection around children. As we have seen in earlier discussions, when teachers and families create real partnerships, their spheres of influence overlap and a "caring community forms around students and begins its work" (Epstein, 1995). However, the claim has been made that there has been an erosion of **social capital** over past decades, both within the family and in the larger community. In the family *social capital* refers to the presence and availability of adults and opportunities for a range of parent–child communication about social and personal matters. In the community *social capital* includes norms of social control, organizations for youth sponsored by adults, and a variety of informal social relations between adults and children that allow adults to support children in ways they might not seek from their parents (Coleman, 1987). Many today believe that the erosion of community is fundamental to contemporary unrest and breakdown. "Without a sense of community . . . people lose the conviction they can improve the quality of their lives through their own efforts" (Schorr, 1997). Cornell University professor Urie Bronfenbrenner considers the development of children in all of their contexts: at home and in school, in neighborhoods and communities, and in the larger context of influences such as the health care system, the media, and the economy. He notes the silent crisis of contemporary society: "The present state of children and families in the United States represents the greatest domestic problem our nation has faced since the founding of the Republic. It is sapping our very roots" (Clinton, 1996).

As society has increasingly centered on advancing one's individual interests, there has been less attention paid to a sense of community responsibility for raising other peoples' children (see Figure 14-1). Specific government actions during the past two decades have removed visible support from some agencies within the community and left individual families to care for themselves as best they could. Most of this government withdrawal has been done under the stance of noninterference in responsibilities that are stated to belong rightfully to families; in reality, families are often left without necessary community supports and resources. During this same period the numbers of children and families living beneath the poverty line have increased dramatically. However, at the same time that the rhetoric of individualism and government removal seems to be withdrawing community attention from the family, other interests within the community bring attention back to the family and its needs.

Where America Stands

Among industrialized countries, the United States ranks

1st	in gross domestic product.
1st	in the number of millionaires and billionaires.
1st	in health technology.
1st	in military technology.
1st	in military exports.
1st	in defense spending.
10th	in eighth grade science scores.
16th	in living standards among the poorest one-fifth of children.
17th	in rates of low-birthweight births.
18th	in the income gap between rich and poor children.
18th	in infant mortality.
21st	in eighth grade math scores.
Last	in protecting our children against gun violence.

According to the Centers for Disease Control and Prevention, U.S. children under age 15 are

12	times more likely to die from gunfire
16	times more likely to be murdered by a gun
11	times more likely to commit suicide with a gun
9	times more likely to die in a firearm accident

than children in 25 other industrialized countries *combined.*

FIGURE 14-1 There are real community concerns about the standings of American children.

An examination of society's ills brings renewed awareness of the problems that arise when parenting roles are ineffective and the family unit is weakened. The community is left to face problems:

- High school dropout rates with the results of illiteracy and underprepared workers.

- Resulting high unemployment rates and increasing numbers of citizens living in poverty.

- Increasing numbers of adolescent and unmarried girls becoming mothers.

- Violence in both families and schools as anger and isolation cause painful eruptions.

- Higher crime rates and drug addictions that accompany hopelessness and poverty.

- Family breakdowns and stress for adults and children that accompany changed family structures.

- Different working patterns of parents that take away already small reserves of family time.

Considering how to deal with the primary causes of these problems has focused community attention on examining family situations and needs. Interest in child and family policy has been "accelerated by the timely collision of research, demographics, corporate concern, and presidential platforming" (Kagan, 1989). These phenomena were still driving community attention as we entered a new century. Society depends on parents

> . . . to have the moral sense, the beliefs, and the capacity to
> assume their responsibilities. But as we give heavy weight to
> relying on parents to carry out their obligations, we must also
> be aware that *individual parents cannot meet their responsibilities
> in our complex twenty-first century world without support
> from outside.* Collectively, we must make sure that the societal
> structures that can support families, and that can strengthen
> communities, are in place (Schorr, 1997).

The ideas of Urie Bronfenbrenner's ecological systems theory (1979) portray the child developing within the context of the system of relationships that forms his or her environment. He describes a series of connected and interrelated social systems:

- The microsystem, which includes the relationships and interactions a child has with immediate surroundings. Structures in the microsystem include family, school or child care program, church, and neighborhood.

- The mesosystem, which provides the connections between the structures of the child's microsystem. Examples of this would be the connection between the child's teacher and family or between the child's church and neighborhood.

- The exosystem, which describes the larger social system in which the child does not function directly; but the structures in this layer impact the child's development by interacting with some structure within the microsystem. For example, the schedules of the parent's workplace or availability of community-based family resources may have a positive or negative impact on the child.

- The macrosystem, which describes the surrounding cultural values, customs, and laws that affect the structures within which the family functions. For example, if the belief of the culture is that parents are solely responsible for child rearing, the culture is less likely to provide resources for families.

Bronfenbrenner's Propositions

Proposition 1   In order to develop—intellectually, emotionally, socially, and morally—a child requires participation in progressively more complex reciprocal activity, on a regular basis over an extended period in the child's life, with one or more persons with whom the child develops a strong mutual, irrational, emotional attachment, and who is committed to the child's well-being and development, preferably for life.

Proposition 2   The establishment of patterns of progressive interpersonal interaction under conditions of strong mutual attachment enhances the young child's responsiveness to other features of the immediate physical, social, and symbolic environment that invite exploration, manipulation, elaboration, and imagination. Such activities, in turn, also accelerate the child's psychological growth.

Proposition 3   The establishment and maintenance of patterns of progressively more complex interaction and emotional attachment between caregiver and child depend in substantial degree on the availability and involvement of another adult, a third party who assists, encourages, spells off, gives status to, and expresses admiration and affection for the person caring for and engaging in joint activity with the child.

Proposition 4   The effective functioning of child-rearing processes in the family and other child settings requires establishing ongoing patterns of exchange of information, two-way communication, mutual accommodation, and mutual trust between the principal settings in which children and their parents live their lives. These settings are the home, child care programs, the school, and the parents' place of work.

Proposition 5   The effective functioning of child-rearing processes in the family and other child settings requires public policies and practices that provide place, time, stability, status, recognition, belief systems, customs, and actions in support of child-rearing activities not only on the part of parents, caregivers, teachers, and other professional personnel, but also relatives, friends, neighbors, coworkers, communities, and the major economic, social, and political institutions of the entire society.

FIGURE 14-2

Extract from Bronfenbrenner, U. (1990). Discovering what families do. In Rebuilding the Nest: A new commitment to the American family. *Family Service America. Available on the Web site of the International Child and Youth Care Network: http://www.cyc-net.org.*

These ideas suggest the importance of examining the interconnections among the ideas and structures that surround the child and family. Bronfenbrenner's principles show clearly the connections between values and decisions of the larger community and their effect on children and families. Carefully read his ideas in Figure 14-2. Notice especially the support for teacher–family connections in propositions 3 and 4 and the importance of community and society described in proposition 5.

Families and schools exist within larger communities. Research makes it clear that "the capacity of families to do their child-rearing job is powerfully dependent on the health of their communities" (Schorr, 1997). The decisions and actions taken by those communities impinge on the functioning of the family and the school. In turn, actions of families and teachers can influence the community. A vital role for teachers and parents to consider together is their opportunity to be advocates for social conditions, legislation, and support for optimal functioning for families and schools. Consider first some of the actions being taken within the community that have impact on families and schools.

■■■ CORPORATE INVOLVEMENT

The business community has to deal with its employees as family members. Now that well over half of all mothers are in the workforce along with fathers, employers are facing conflicts that arise when their employees are trying to fill the roles of parent and worker at the same time. Concern about child care may interfere with an employee's productivity, as in the case of parents of latchkey children worrying through the work hours remaining after 3:00 p.m.—the hour at which telephone companies report their highest volume of calls, when children call their parents to let them know they are home from school. Parents may have to be absent from work when child care arrangements fall through, when a baby-sitter doesn't come, or when a child is sick and can't go to school. Almost daily, many working parents have events, conferences, or meetings for which they have to decide whether to be responsible to their employers or their children and the schools. Good employees may be lost because of the lack of helpful parental leave policies. In fact, research has shown the business world that attention and assistance to parents' child care needs pays off in recruitment, retention, productivity, absenteeism patterns, and morale of employees (Galinsky et al., 2001, 1991).

A study by the Du Pont Company, one of the first to institute work–family programs such as job sharing and subsidized and emergency child care, confirmed that these practices are good for business, making the workforce more committed and engaged (Clinton, 1996). A White House event in 1995 honored 21 large companies in the American Business Collaboration for Quality Dependent Care for spending millions and initiating workplace policies that support parents and families: Allstate, AT&T, Chevron, Citibank, Hewlett-Packard, Johnson & Johnson, Mobil, Texaco, and Xerox were among those honored. Policies are varied and adapt to parents' needs: Eastman Kodak provides backup child care services in employees' homes when regular child care arrangements fall through; IBM allows some employees flexibility to work at home and also sponsors child care programs. Corporate America is rising to the challenge of supporting its workers' families.

Between 1978 and 1988 there was an increase of 2,000% in the number of companies participating in some type of employer-assisted child care, to about 5,400 companies. By 1990 half of all U.S. families reported having some employer benefit or policy that helped them manage child care and other family responsibilities (Olsen, 1997). Those numbers continue to rise today. About 7% of employers offer on-site child care centers, while far more offer referral services to help employees find child care. Still others allow employees to designate pretax dollars for child care. In addition, employers offer a variety of programs to assist families, including sick care referral services, flexible scheduling, job sharing, and subsidized payments of child care.

The Conference Board, an international business research and information network, has a Work and Family Information Center, formed in 1983. This is a national clearinghouse of information designed to meet the needs of the business community, government agencies, and other organizations concerned with changes in work and family relationships. The center is concerned with the reciprocal impact of work and family interaction—how today's families are affected by what happens in the workplace and how the workplace is influenced by the special needs and resources that family members bring to their jobs. Seminars are held around the country to influence the thinking of business leaders as they consider their relationship to the families of their employees (see Figure 14-3). The center assists corporate leaders

FIGURE 14-3 With corporate support, employees can volunteer time to work in community classrooms.

with individualized consultations, conferences on issues of family concern, information services, and research. For more information, contact the Work and Family Information Center, The Conference Board, 845 Third Ave., New York, NY 10022, or see the Web site at chapter end.

Another organization that works on issues related to work and family life is the Families and Work Institute. Established as a nonprofit organization in 1989, the institute's focus is to address the changing nature of work and family life. As it identifies emerging issues, the organization engages in policy and worksite research and provides data to inform decision making on the changing workforce, changing family, and changing community. Numerous publications are available—see the suggestions for reading at the end of this chapter. More information can be obtained from the Families and Work Institute, 330 Seventh Ave., 14th Floor, New York, NY 10001, and the Web site at chapter end.

The increased awareness of child care, need for educational improvements, and other family needs have brought corporate leaders into discussion and collaboration with other community organizations in efforts to improve services offered to families. Many communities have included corporate leaders in their child advocacy organizations and school systems. In Charlotte, North Carolina, for example, top executives from 20 of the city's largest corporations have become Corporate Champions, cooperating with the local resource and referral agency on funding to explore child care issues and upgrade available child care quality. Corporate Champions in Fort Worth, Texas, have not only contributed funds (to support grants for child care centers, scholarships for providers working toward accreditation, and resource and referral services), but have also pledged the involvement of a high-level executive (Children's Defense Fund, 1998). Involvement of business executives in Cincinnati with the city's school system has resulted in dramatic improvements in school administration and in the quality of instruction. With awareness comes policy, such as the urging of many local Chambers of Commerce to all local businesses to implement policies that release parents for necessary conferences with their children's schools and for volunteering in the school system. As they become involved in ways to ease the stress of family care for their workers, employers are educating themselves about community school and child care needs and becoming collaborators in the private sector.

LEGISLATIVE INITIATIVES

The public sector is also increasingly aware of children's and family issues. In the early 1980s the Reagan administration established policies that opposed government regulation of child care at any level. By the end of the same decade, Congress had finally passed and funded a first-ever comprehensive federal system for supporting child care to address issues of affordability, availability, and quality.

Now reauthorized, the Child Care and Development Block Grants now provide over $4 billion a year in federal funds to states; the states supply additional funds, including some of the funds allotted under TANF. The block grants offer a great deal of flexibility for states to determine how funds should be spent within the broad constraints of improving child care affordability, quality, and availability. The CCDBG provide money to states to

- Provide child care assistance to low- and moderate-income families.
- Recruit family child care providers.
- Develop local resource and referral programs to help link families to child care services.
- Train providers.
- Expand the supply of child care.

Other political initiatives and media campaigns (I am Your Child, 1997; the White House Conference on Child Care, 1997; the president's State of the Union Address, 1998) have directed national attention to the needs of working families and the child care community. For the first time the needs of children have been discussed in weekly newsmagazines and in television specials.

With members of Congress responding to their constituents by introducing a number of bills to increase federal funds to help families with the cost and quality of child care and to provide incentives for businesses to become involved in child care, hope for additional legislative support is high in the early childhood education community. Teachers and parents can get up-to-date information about current legislative issues from the National Association for the Education of Young Children via *Young Children* or the associations's Web site (listed at the end of this chapter).

Temporary Assistance for Needy Families

In August 1996 the Personal Opportunity and Work Opportunity Reconciliation Act changed welfare by eliminating the guarantee of cash assistance to needy families with children, and by requiring work in exchange for time-limited assistance. Temporary Assistance for Needy Families (TANF) replaced the 60-year-old guarantee of the Aid to Families with Dependent Children (AFDC) program. TANF is funded by block grants to the states, which have enormous flexibility to design their own programs. The requirements for work are rigid, and there are lifetime limits for receiving the funds—60 months in most states, with shorter times in others; many states dictate periods of ineligibility after two years.

Bonuses are paid to states on the basis of numbers removed from the welfare system and reductions of out-of-wedlock births. Although welfare caseloads across the nation have decreased more than 40% since the change, there is concern that the well-being of children and families is suffering. Children's Defense Fund notes that by mid-1997 states reported that only 15% of closed cases were due to increased family income. (The average monthly amount paid to families by TANF funds is $351: Children's Defense Fund, 2004.) Most of those losing welfare support were not gaining the remuneration from work that could support a family; former welfare recipients who find jobs typically earn wages below the poverty level (Children's Defense Fund, 2004). More than a third of the homeless Americans in urban areas who sought shelter in 25 U.S. cities were families with children (National Coalition for the Homeless, 2001). With over 20% of children in this country living below the poverty level, the TANF legislation may have created additional risks for children and families in the segment of the population that has the least access to good jobs and the supports that make work possible. The late Senator Daniel Patrick Moynihan called the 1996 repeal of the federal welfare guarantee "the largest gamble in social policy made in the twentieth century" (Schorr, 1997). The political parties have spouted rhetoric about "cleaning up welfare waste." But along with those possible changes, they have made enormous changes in the lives of many children and families. With TANF work requirements, many single parent–headed families have very little time to spend with family or school communication. Teachers will have to monitor the progress and effects on families of this legislation over time; certainly a major effect already has been to push the need for child care and after-school care to new limits as more parents move into the work force (Branch et al., 2001).

Family Medical Leave Act

As we saw in Chapter 3, America lags behind most industrialized nations in parental leave policies for care of children after birth in their earliest months. While most European nations offer 6 to 12 months of paid parental leave with provisions also available for fathers, the United States is the only Western country where an employer does not provide paid leave for mothers and fathers. In the late 1980s the Family and Medical Leave Act was discussed by legislators, with sponsorship by over 100 members of the House and at least 20 senators. In 1990 Congress passed the proposal, which could generate up to 12 weeks of unpaid leave to care for an elderly parent, sick spouse, newborn, or newly adopted child; but President Bush vetoed the bill, stating he believed it would hurt the economy. The bill was finally signed into law in 1993; since then at least 26 million employees have taken advantage of its provisions. Unfortunately the bill covers only employers with 50 or more employees, and the economic status of most families creates financial hardship if they go for long periods without salary. Studies show that two-thirds of the employees who needed a family or medical leave but didn't take one said they could not afford to take time off without pay. Passage of the Family and Medical Leave Act was a first step in indicating awareness of some community responsibility to support families in times of change. Currently there is a move to support extension of the act to cover all employers with 25 or more employees; the law does not presently apply to 41 million private employers, or nearly 43% of U.S. workers. Some states are funding or exploring methods to make family leave affordable by using unemployment insurance or temporary disability insurance (Hutter, 2000).

No Child Left Behind Act

The No Child Left Behind Act, signed into law by President George W. Bush in 2002, represented the federal government's most dramatic move to involve itself in education. In an attempt to reform public education, the legislation is stated to be designed to

- Gain stronger accountability from schools and school systems for educational results.
- Provide more freedom for states and communities.
- Encourage the use of proven educational methods.
- Offer more choices for parents.

The legislation requires standardized tests nearly every year and demands that schools give parents an annual report card that shows how well students in each school performed, with statistics broken out by race, gender, and disability. The law allows parents to choose another public school if their child attends a school that needs improvement or is unsafe. In Chapter 4 we read about this legislation's provisions to involve families in their children's education; this is certainly a positive feature.

Although the Department of Education states that the results of the 2004 National Assessment of Educational Progress (NAEP) Long-Term Trends in Academic Progress, or nation's report card, indicate real progress in reading achievement for children of all races and family backgrounds (Proof No Child Left Behind is working, 2005), support and approval of the legislation is mixed. Many educators and professional organizations express concern about the narrow focus on test results; they urge a broader approach to considering achievement of both children and schools. Some states and professional associations have sued the government to gain freedom from the demands of the legislation, citing lack of funding support to carry out its requirements. Several senators and congressional representatives have recently proposed changes in the legislation to broaden its focus. While most families and educators agree on a need for both quality and accountability in the public schools, the agreement on methods is not unanimous. This is a situation that will need careful monitoring by both families and those involved in education (see Figure 14-4).

In addition to these large federal actions, presently most states are involved in funding some kinds of preschool education and family support services. (See the discussion of some examples in Chapter 4. Be sure to learn what your state is currently doing or considering.)

It seems that this is a time of increasing community attention at the legislative level to child care, education, and family issues. At local, state, and national levels, economic and child care policies affect the quality of life that parents and teachers can provide for children.

FIGURE 14-4 The No Child Left Behind legislation requires frequent use of standardized tests in elementary schools to assess school achievement.

LINKAGES WITHIN THE COMMUNITY

In these times of enormous social problems and limited funding resources, many agencies within the community have found it productive to form linkages to support each other's services. "We can get more bang for our buck if we collaborate and cooperate. . . . You're seeing more and more multiple-funded things that cross over and fertilize each other" (Washington, Johnson, & McCracken, 1995). Collaborations come in all shapes and sizes. Both public and private funding collaborations and alliances result from common community concerns. "They can be a tool to increase accessibility for families, to consolidate or upgrade services, or to arrange new services that would be impossible to provide otherwise" (Washington, Johnson, & McCracken, 1995). For example, library systems may work with schools and child care centers and health departments that run child health clinics in efforts to get parents involved in reading to young children. High schools, Planned Parenthood, health departments, and other civic organizations may unite their efforts to combat adolescent pregnancy. Connections strengthen attempts while preventing wasteful duplication of services. Such linkages also heighten overall community awareness of the problems as citizens and professionals from diverse backgrounds come together to discuss common concerns.

The 1994 Report of the Carnegie Corporation on Meeting the Needs of Young Children—*Starting Points*—states that broad-based community supports and services are necessary. "The old ways of providing services and supports must be reassessed, and broad, integrated approaches must be found to ensure that every family with a newborn is linked to a source of health care, child care, and parenting support" (Carnegie Corporation, 1996).

In her important book on efforts to strengthen families and communities, Lisbeth Schorr (1997) describes many individual collaborative programs, noting seven attributes of highly effective programs:

1. Successful programs are comprehensive, flexible, responsive, and persevering.

2. Successful programs see children in the context of their families.

3. Successful programs deal with families as parts of neighborhoods and communities.

4. Successful programs have a long-term, preventive orientation, have a clear mission, and continue to evolve over time.

5. Successful programs are well managed by competent and committed individuals with clearly identifiable skills.

6. Staffs of successful programs are trained and supported to provide high-quality, responsive services.

7. Successful programs operate in settings that encourage practitioners to build strong relationships based on mutual trust and respect. (Schorr, 1997)

Kagan (1994) notes that the forging of coalitions to address specific problems has successfully united those working within government and advocates in the private sector. Marian Wright Edelman of the Children's Defense Fund states the need for this collaboration:

No single person, institution, or government agency can meet all of our children's and families' needs. But each of us, taking one or more of those needs, can together weave the seamless web of family and community and private sector support children need. We must work together and resist the political either/or-ism and organizational turf-ism that plague so much policy development, advocacy, service, and organizing today. Good parenting and good community, employer, and governmental supports for parents are inextricably intertwined. (Children's Defense Fund, 1998)

Teachers may play an important role in helping link families with community agencies that can provide needed services. Every teacher should know what community resources exist for parent referral. It is also important to know how to use the Internet to access information about national organizations that might be supportive. A file of pamphlets and referral information can be accumulated and kept at the center for reference by all staff. If you do not already have such a file, now is a great time to begin to explore and accumulate information about your community resources. Frequently families learn of sources of help only through teachers (see Figure 14-5).

SAMPLE OF TEACHER'S COMMUNITY RESOURCE FILE

Pamphlets and contact information from

- United Way agencies, such as family counseling and health services.

- Agencies that work with families in crisis: abuse, domestic violence, housing, food and clothing resources, bereavement.

- Organizations that support families with specific concerns: divorce, teenagers, drug and alcohol abuse, single parents, adoptive families.

- Groups to support new parents.

- Groups that meet family recreational needs.

- Service programs such as Big Brothers and Sisters and Children's Law.

- Child care resource and referral agencies.

- Developmental screening resources.

- Educational options within the community.

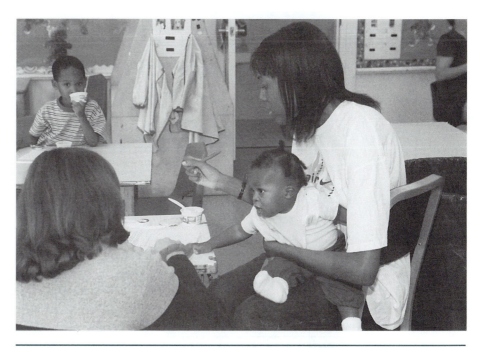

FIGURE 14-5 Parents can learn about community resources from teachers.

A spirit of volunteerism may spring to life from raised awareness. In some communities civic organizations and businesses have "adopted" schools, linking volunteers with a specific school or center. Senior citizens find helpful roles as "foster grandparents," giving individual attention to children in early childhood classrooms. "Mentor mothers" pair experienced volunteers with new adolescent mothers. Families and schools alike may reap benefits from such volunteer efforts.

The family resource and support movement discussed in Chapter 4 is a graphic example of the power generated by community agencies forming linkages. Frequently such programs link to other community services rather than providing the services directly. Such an arrangement is far more cost-effective, encouraging the optimal use of available resources. A community-established "umbrella" organization can encourage linkages at the administrative level. Networking and providing coordinating mechanisms accomplish this. Thus conflict and fragmentation in the field are reduced while training, funding streams, regulating mechanisms, and information are coordinated.

Child care resource and referral agencies across the country offer ways for professionals and families to procure resources and information. They represent avenues for local networking and planning. Most are supported by a combination of funding from city, county, and state budgets, business and United Way contributions, and federal dependent care funds (Bellm, 1991; see Figure 14-6). In both large and small ways, decisions made in business,

FIGURE 14-6 Child care resource and referral agencies help link families with quality child care.

government, and social and medical service agencies affect the quality of life for families and the ways schools can meet family needs.

THE ROLE OF ADVOCATE

Because of their positions, teachers and families have the capacity and obligation to influence, both by separate and united action, community segments that are making decisions that affect their lives. As those who best know and care about the needs of developing children, parents and teachers are uniquely suited to be **advocates** working to convince the community of what actions must be taken on their behalf.

Teachers and Parents as Advocates

As people who see firsthand the everyday issues facing children, their families, and the child care and educational community at large, teachers must become advocates within the community. This is a relatively new role for many teachers, who have often concentrated efforts on direct education and care of children, sometimes convinced that "no amount of advocacy would render change" (Kagan, 1989) or unsure of how to be an advocate. Other teachers have not acted, perhaps absorbing society's low evaluation of teachers, demonstrated by low wages and status, in their earliest career years. But as Kagan states, it is now essential to become advocates because "the policy train has left the station, and if we want to influence its direction, we are forced to get on board" (Kagan, 1989). As those who best understand what is developmentally appropriate and supportive of families' needs and interests, teachers must become articulate proponents of what should be by

- Demonstrating the vital importance of early care and education to the community.
- Using influence to persuade local power brokers that early care and education must be near the top of the community's agenda.
- Functioning as community experts in early care and education to define what needs to be done and influence policy making on a communitywide basis. (Crompton, 1997)

As teachers advocate for improved conditions for children and their families, they also advocate for their own profession and improving conditions for early childhood education personnel.

In exactly the same way, teachers of older children also see the impact of family and community conditions and of the emphases in educational institutions on children and healthy development. In the current climate of legislated school reform, teachers have strong opinions about how these situations are affecting excellence in education. To remain silent in the face of clear conflicts with good practice would be to ignore the importance of teachers speaking out as advocates.

Where does a teacher/advocate start?

Become Visible

Perhaps the most important starting place is to realize that our image and definition of an educational professional must change. It is no longer possible for teachers and administrators to concentrate solely on the functioning of single classrooms or schools. Advocates must become involved in the community, caring about and participating in a variety of social and civic concerns rather than simply on their own issues. Becoming recognized as a positive force in the community helps educators gain credibility beyond their sphere of influence. Teachers can start small, joining local neighborhood groups that work to improve the quality of life in the community. Through their participation teachers will be recognized as valuable group members; then their communication about the needs of children and families will be listened to.

REFLECTIONS FOR JOURNAL ENTRIES

What educational issue in your school, program, or community do you feel passionately about? What have you done about it up to this point? Why have you not done more? What else could you do? What supports and information would you need as you become involved in advocating for this issue?

Be Informed

Community policies are developing rapidly and continually. Teachers need to keep informed about problems, issues, and proposals at local levels and beyond and to know how these issues and proposals affect education, child care, and family support.

There are many ways to become informed: newspaper or television reports about legislative and corporate discussion and action; bulletins and statements from professional and advocacy organizations; local hearings; Internet searches; staff meetings; discussion with colleagues; and classes and workshops. Two helpful current publications are *The State of America's Children*—the annual yearbook published by the Children's Defense Fund— and *Issues and Advocacy in Early Education* by Jensen and Chevalier (see the suggestions for further reading at the end of this chapter). The important thing is to demonstrate professional willingness to stay abreast and learn what is going on.

Tell the Story

Many people who are not directly involved with education or young families have no firsthand knowledge of problems and concerns. For example, most citizens probably could not accurately answer questions on why early childhood education programs are important, what types of programs are offered

---

WHAT DOES AN ADVOCATE DO?

- Become visible.
- Become informed.
- Tell the story.
- Adapt and replicate.
- Join professional organizations.
- Connect with the community power structure.
- Contact representatives.
- Vote.
- Persist.

---

in the community, the length of waiting lists, average salaries and turnover rates of local child care workers, the average cost of infant care, or the like. Even many parents may not understand differences in state licensing requirements, legal adult–child ratios, or staff training requirements. Despite the publication of brain development research confirming the vital importance of the earliest years, many adults still do not recognize the urgency of providing environments at home and elsewhere that nurture optimal development or how the factors just listed affect program quality. Many citizens likewise have no current knowledge of how the latest legislation is affecting schools and children. Teachers who have this information can perform an important service in helping others learn the magnitude of the problems and needs. Teachers have the stories to illustrate the information—to give it meaning—and passion in demonstrating the contrasts between what could be and what is (Crompton, 1997). Personal conversations, newsletters, and letters to the editor are all important in raising community awareness of the issues. Carter and Curtis (1997) offer creative suggestions for making the community aware of quality. Making methods obvious and outcomes clear helps the community understand what the vision is, how far from the vision the community is, and the action plan needed to reach the vision. Here parents can join teachers in their efforts (see Figure 14-7).

The National Association for the Education of Young Children sponsors the annual Week of the Young Child in communities across the country in April to call attention to the critical significance of the years between birth and age 8. Individual community activities focus on advocacy and information activities. NAEYC has also recently published an excellent book that discusses specific actions for advocates (Robinson & Stark, 2002).

FIGURE 14-7 Teachers can join with parents in planning advocacy efforts.

Adapt and Replicate

Every community is unique in its organization, specific population, and problems. Yet some programs and ideas have worked well in communities around the country. Rather than try to reinvent the wheel, advocates should become familiar with these successful endeavors. The purpose of learning about successful programs is not to simply reproduce them but rather to build on previous experiences, adapt them to the unique community, and improve on the original model. Not every program will work in all contexts and climates of support; it is important to take advantage of the information that already exists about what programs are most effective at various stages of community organization.

As community leaders meet to synthesize their visions and their efforts, agreement about particular directions for a particular community will inform necessary adaptations. See the discussion of successful community programs in Clinton (1996) and Schorr (1997).

Join Professional Organizations

Teachers become empowered as they unite with others to learn, support one another, define professional goals and standards, and wield political power. Increasingly the National Association for the Education of Young Children (NAEYC) is recognized as the professional organization that unites those from various occupations working in the early childhood education field. With a membership of over 100,000, the organization has an annual national conference attended by over 20,000 individuals, with hundreds of workshops offering current research and practical knowledge. State and local liaison groups offer teachers frequent opportunities to meet others concerned with children and families, share ideas and concerns, and network with professionals to build a united front within the community. The professional organization's publication *Young Children* is one way for teachers to become informed. The columns "Policy Alert" and "Washington Update" provide current information and calls for professional action.

Recent statements of standards by the organization have helped teachers and administrators define and evaluate appropriate curricula and services within centers. Standards for training and behavior of professionals have been delineated. These actions have helped child caregivers and early childhood teachers to see themselves as part of a profession that is taking steps to prove its value to the community. In fact, the code of ethical conduct adopted by the NAEYC governing board in 1989 and revised in 2005 includes a section on specific ideals and principles of teachers' ethical responsibilities to community and society that says, in part,

> Our responsibilities to the community are to provide programs
> that meet the diverse needs of families, to cooperate with
> agencies and professions that share responsibility for children, to
> assist families in gaining access to those agencies and
> professionals, and to assist in the development of community
> programs that are needed but not currently available. . . . Because
> of our specialized expertise in early childhood development and
> education and because the larger society shares responsibility for
> the welfare and protection of children, we acknowledge a
> collective obligation to advocate for the best interests of young
> children within early childhood programs and in the larger
> community and to serve as a voice for young children everywhere.
> (NAEYC, 2005)

The political power of a large professional organization can yield results. In addition, NAEYC is a powerful philosophical leader for early childhood education professionals and the larger community. In *A Call for Excellence in Early Childhood Education*, adopted in July 2000, these statements are made by the organization:

- Our nation can and must do better to create opportunities that help all children and families succeed. The time for action is now.
- All communities are accountable for the quality of early childhood programs provided to all children, backed by the local, state, and federal funding needed to deliver quality programs and services.
- Making this vision of excellence a reality will require commitment from and a partnership among the federal, state, and local governments, business and labor, private institutions, and the public. As we stand at the beginning of a new millennium, we must join forces to advocate and implement the policies at the appropriate federal, state, and local levels that will lead to excellence in early childhood education programs (NAEYC, 2000).

For more information about this professional organization, contact NAEYC, 1509 16th St N.W., Washington, DC 20036-1426.

There are many other organizations in which membership may be an important part of a teacher's role as advocate. The Children's Defense Fund (CDF) is a private organization supported by foundations, corporate grants, and individual donations to provide a voice for the children of America, educate the nation about children's needs, and encourage prevention of problems. Its staff members include specialists in health, child care, education, child welfare, mental health, child development, adolescent pregnancy prevention, homelessness, and employment. CDF gathers and disseminates data on key issues affecting children; monitors development and implementation of federal and state policies; provides information, technical assistance, and support to a network of state and local child advocates; pursues an annual legislative agenda in the U.S. Congress, and litigates selected cases of major importance. CDF is a national organization with a main office in Washington, D.C., that monitors the effects of changes in national and local social policies and helps people and organizations who are concerned with what happens to children. CDF has state offices in Minnesota and Ohio, as well as local project offices, and works on cooperative projects with groups in many states. For more information, write to The Children's Defense Fund, 25 E. St. N.W., Washington, DC 20001.

The Black Child Development Institute and the Family Resource Coalition, referred to in Chapter 4, are other organizations that can help teachers and parents feel united in their community efforts.

> ## NAEYC'S Five Ways to Become a "Children's Champion"
>
> - **Speak out on behalf of children.**
> - **Improve the life of one child beyond your own family.**
> - **Hold public officials accountable for a national commitment in actions as well as words.**
> - **Encourage organizations to commit to children and families.**
> - **Urge others to become children's champions.**
>
> —*From Young Children, 51(5), 56.*

Many communities have local advocacy organizations for child and family issues; teachers should find out if their local community has one. There is strength in numbers. Parents can be encouraged to join these and other organizations. A number of Web sites listed at the end of this chapter have complete listings of organizations for parents. As parents and teachers gain confidence in their ability to speak and influence others, they may find themselves able to link with other community representatives and committees: the local school board, the dropout prevention task force, the council on adolescent pregnancy—whatever opportunities the community offers.

Connect with the Community Power Structure

Before advocates can go into the community looking for support for education and children's issues, they need to identify three things:

1. Who's out there? Identifying the prominent stakeholders in the community who carry clout will help advocates know who can impact policy and programs.

2. Who among them are known personally? In reaching out to community leaders, it makes sense to first advocate with leaders who are already known or acquainted with early childhood issues.

3. Who are the "significant others"? To make a difference in community issues, advocates will have to form relationships with all who are important in the community decisions. Advocates have to identify them, learn their points of view, and determine how best to communicate positively with them.

Figure 14-8 illustrates this process of identifying the community power structure as a step to connecting with the individuals with whom communication must be opened and collaborative efforts must be joined.

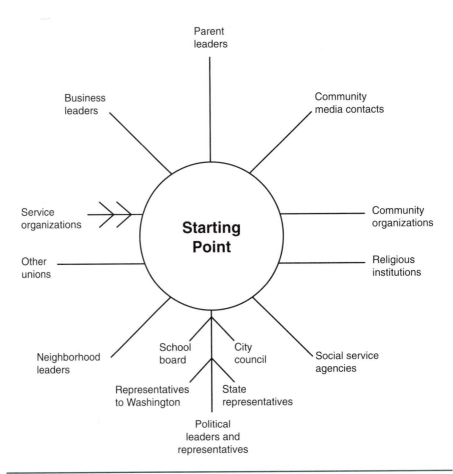

FIGURE 14-8 Teachers have to learn who can support advocacy efforts.

Contact Representatives

As concerned citizens, as professionals employed in specific capacities, and as members of professional organizations, teachers and parents need to contact their legislative representatives and state their positions, along with the specific reasons for their beliefs. Legislators can be influenced as they hear from even small numbers of constituents who speak with passion regarding specific community needs.

Vote

Advocates must follow up on their interests by learning what responsive actions businesses, government officials, and others who can shape policy have taken. With the power of purchase choices or voting decisions, teachers and parents can express their approval or disapproval of officials' actions. As private citizens, families and teachers can support leaders who favor family and early education issues. In analyzing successful efforts to improve conditions for early childhood professionals in New York, Marx and Granger highlight

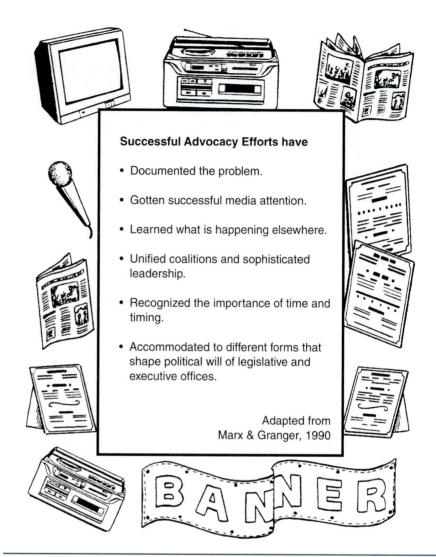

Successful Advocacy Efforts have

- Documented the problem.

- Gotten successful media attention.

- Learned what is happening elsewhere.

- Unified coalitions and sophisticated leadership.

- Recognized the importance of time and timing.

- Accommodated to different forms that shape political will of legislative and executive offices.

Adapted from
Marx & Granger, 1990

FIGURE 14-9 Tips for successful advocacy efforts.

lessons for others who want to succeed in their advocacy efforts in other communities (Marx & Granger, 1990; see Figure 14-9). The NAEYC publication *Grassroots Success!* (Washington, Johnson, & McCracken, 1995) documents specific successful programs of collaboration with various communities; read it for inspiration and ideas for your own community.

COMMUNITY AS AN EDUCATIONAL RESOURCE

Schools and centers exist within particular communities, and each community has much to offer as a resource to teachers planning curricula for children in their classrooms. Teachers need to assess what the community can provide. Resources may be categorized as natural resources, people resources, and material resources.

(a) (b)

FIGURE 14-10 Every community has interesting places for children to visit.

Natural Resources

Within reach of most schools, teachers may find businesses, shopping areas, transportation systems and depots, construction sites, police and fire stations, parks and recreation areas, churches, zoos, museums, and residential streets. Each one of these offers countless learning experiences. It is a useful exercise for teachers to review the areas within 10 minutes' walking distance of their centers to discover all the places that might be intriguing from a child's point of view (see Figure 14-10). There might be, for example, a service station where children could watch cars being elevated and serviced, a bakery with a large oven for many loaves of bread, a grocery store where children could watch delivery trucks being unloaded before purchasing cooking ingredients to take back to the center, or an enormous construction crane working on a tall office building. Alert teachers use these natural community resources to design curricula outside and inside the classroom. Elementary teachers will find opportunities for real-life social studies within their communities as children investigate, document, and report on various aspects of community life.

People Resources

Every neighborhood has its own socioeconomic, racial, and cultural composition. Teachers who familiarize themselves with the customs and lifestyles of the people in the community surrounding their center may find richness and diversity to share with the children (see Figure 14-11). Parents themselves may be the link to assist teachers in learning the community's people resources as they disclose aspects of their home lives. For example, teachers may find neighbors experienced in ethnic cooking or traditional music who could share their interests with the children. Many community service agencies have representatives prepared to explain the agency to children, such as a firefighter with boots, hat, and truck (see Figure 14-12). Teachers who

FIGURE 14-11 People from the community may enrich classroom activities and offer positive role models.

FIGURE 14-12 A firefighter visiting the school is an example of using community resources.

notice the people in neighborhoods surrounding their centers may discover others who would have interest in spending time with young children: a retired grandfather who enjoys showing the children how to hammer nails in a woodworking activity, or tutors who enjoy sharing skills with children (see Figure 14-13). People resources of all types can enrich a school (see Figure 14-14). (For more about parent resources, see Chapter 12.)

Teachers and parents should also remember that children can learn how to be resources for their own communities. No child is too young to learn valuable lessons of making contributions to others and feeling responsible as a member of a community. Preschoolers can collect materials for less advantaged families, visit older people in nursing homes, or participate in neighborhood

FIGURE 14-13 "Foster grandparents" are making a contribution in child care programs in many communities.

FIGURE 14-14 High school students may be resources for after-school tutoring.

FIGURE 14-15 School-aged children may become involved in cleaning up their community.

cleanup efforts. School-aged children can learn about issues in their communities and help plan projects to benefit others. The mutual benefit of people resources in each community should be explored (see Figure 14-15).

Material Resources

Teachers who make community connections can find their classrooms recipients of many objects children can use. Fast-food chains may donate cups and napkins and props for dramatic play. Lumber stores may provide scraps for woodworking. The telephone company may offer old telephone sets, more inviting for their realism. Large packing cases from the local appliance or furniture store can be transformed into storage or play spaces. A decorating shop's wallpaper sample books can be used in dozens of ways by creative teachers. Teachers should make lists of all community businesses and then brainstorm all possible material resources. Most businesspeople like to feel they can make a contribution.

Families are often helpful connections in identifying and obtaining material resources. Some communities have established central recycling centers where businesses can donate disposables or other materials that can find many uses in early education classrooms.

All of these community connections can enrich curriculum offerings, as well as convey evidence of community interest and support for teachers and families.

The modern world often seems too busy to allow a sense of connectedness. As teachers and families work together as partners, they are in fact forming their own community that can reach out to and support the world around them. As members of the community, teachers and families can

- Involve themselves fully within the surrounding community.
- Work together for improvements in the community that benefit both families and schools.
- Learn about, tell each other about, and use community resources.
- Understand that the community itself may provide learning resources for schools.
- Build a sense of community within a school.

SUMMARY

There are three ways community agencies and actions affect families and schools:

1. Corporate involvement.
2. Legislative policies.
3. Linkages within the community.

Teachers and parents can work within their communities to support their best interests. Eight courses of action are open to them:

1. Become visible.
2. Be informed.
3. Tell the story.
4. Adapt and replicate.
5. Join professional organizations.
6. Connect with the community power structure.
7. Contact representatives.
8. Vote.

Teachers who have learned about local agencies and organizations can help parents make connections with community resources to support their families. They can also make community connections to use natural, people, and material resources to enrich curriculum offerings.

STUDENT ACTIVITIES FOR FURTHER STUDY

1. Obtain several copies of *Young Children* from your local college library or an NAEYC member. Examine the table of contents to find articles of interest for teachers of young children. Read the Washington Update and Public Policy Report columns. Discuss the current issues with your classmates.

2. Get information from your local or state NAEYC affiliate about program plans for the year and any legislative initiatives in your community that need your support.

3. Discover if your community has a child advocacy group or an organization to coordinate services for families. Invite a representative to visit your class.

4. Create a community resource file. Obtain current pamphlets and referral information from the community agencies that offer services for families with various needs—economic, social, special medical and educational, recreation, and so on. Your instructor may make assignments for individual class members to report to other students about specific agencies within your community.

CASE STUDY

As a teacher of young children, you learn that proposed legislation in your state for a universal prekindergarten program is not in the best interest of developmentally appropriate practice in early childhood education programs. The impact of this legislation is a concern to you. As a new advocate, you are unsure how to proceed.

1. How might you get families together to help them understand this issue?

   Are there others in the community who should be involved in an advocacy effort?

2. What resources might you use to get information and data to support your case?

3. What steps could be taken to lobby for the rights of children and best practice?

4. What could your school do to get support and help?

5. Identify three or four first actions in your campaign.

REVIEW QUESTIONS

1. Discuss ways that corporations are becoming involved in family, education, and child care issues.

2. Describe current legislative initiatives that shape policies affecting families, education, and child care.

3. Discuss what happens within community linkages.

4. Identify and discuss eight advocacy roles for teachers and parents.

5. Identify three ways the community can provide resources for teachers, families, and children.

SUGGESTIONS FOR FURTHER READING

Child care initiatives across the country. (1997, January/February). *Child Care Bulletin, 3.*

Children's Defense Fund. (2005). *The state of America's children yearbook 2005.* Washington, DC: Author.

Dombro, A., O'Donnell, N., Galinsky, E., Gilkeson, S., & Farber, A. (1996). *Community mobilization: Strategies to support young children and their families.* New York: Families and Work Institute.

Edwards, P. A., & Jones Young, L. S. (1992, May). Beyond parents: Family, community, and school involvement. *Phi Delta Kappan,* 721–780.

Jensen, M. A., & Chevalier, Z. W. (1990). *Issues and advocacy in early education.* Needham Heights, MA: Allyn and Bacon.

Kagan, S. (1991). *United we stand: Collaboration for child care and early education services.* New York: Teachers College Press.

Keresty, B., O'Leary, S., & Wortley, D. (1998). *You can make a difference: A teacher's guide to political action.* Westport, CT: Heinemann.

Nelson, D. (2000). Connections count: An alternative framework for understanding and strengthening America's vulnerable families. *Young Children,* 55(6), 39–42.

O'Donnell, N., & Galinsky, E. (2000). *The seven lessons of early childhood public engagement.* New York: Families and Work Institute.

O'Donnell, N., & McJunker, C. (2001). *Ten tips for getting and keeping business involved: An illustrated guide for early childhood leaders.* New York: Families and Work Institute.

O'Hanlon, E. and Griffin, A. (2004). "Parent advocacy: Two approaches to change, one goal." *Leadership Development in the Infant-Family Field,* 25(2), 27–31.

Skolnick, A. (2001). *A time of transition: Work, family, and community in the information age.* New York: Families and Work Institute.

Westheimer, M. (2002). *Parents becoming leaders: Getting involved on behalf of children.* New York: Families and Work Institute.

REFERENCES

Bellm, D. (1991). Child care resources and referral agencies. *Eric Digest,* 1991.

Branch, S., et al. (2001, January/February). Child care for families leaving temporary assistance for needy families. 34 *Clearinghouse Review* 527. Available online at http://www.welfarelaw.org/childcare

Bronfenbrenner, U. (1979). *Two Worlds of childhood: US and USSR.* New York: Pocket Books.

Carnegie Corporation. (1996). Starting points: Executive summary of the report of the Carnegie Corporation of New York task force on meeting the needs of young children. In K. Paciorek & J. Munro (Eds.), *Early Childhood Education 96/97.* Guilford, CT: Dushkin Publishing Group.

Carter, M., & Curtis, D. (1997). *Spreading the news: Sharing the stories of early childhood education.* St. Paul, MN: Redleaf Press.

Children's Defense Fund (1998). *The state of America's children: Yearbook 1998.* Wasington, DC: Author.

———. (2004). *The state of America's children: Yearbook 2004.* Washington, DC: Author.

———. (2005). *The state of America's children: Yearbook 2005.* Washington, DC: Author.

Clinton, H. (1996). *It takes a village and other lessons children teach us.* New York: Simon and Schuster.

Coleman, J. S. (1987). Families and schools. *Educational Researcher, 16,* 32–38.

Crompton, D. (1997). Community leadership. In S. Kagan & B. Bowman (Eds.), *Leadership in early care and education.* Washington, DC: NAEYC.

Epstein, J. (1995, May). School/family/community partnerships: Caring for the children we share. *Phi Delta Kappan,* 701–712.

Galinsky, E., Friedman, D., & Hernandez, C. (1991). *The corporate reference guide of work–family programs.* New York: Families and Work Institute.

Galinsky, E., Kim, S., & Bond, J. (2001). *Feeling overworked: When work becomes too much.* New York: Families and Work Institute.

Hutter, S. (2000). Precious time. *Working Mother, 55*(2), 46–48, 108.

Kagan, S. (1989, May). Dealing with our ambivalence about advocacy. *Child Care Information Exchange, 61,* 31-34.

———. (1994). Families and children: Who is responsible? *Childhood Education, 71*(1), 4–8.

Marx, E., & Granger, R. C. (1990). Analysis of salary enhancement efforts in New York. *Young Children, 45*(4), 53–59.

NAEYC. (2000). *A call for excellence in early childhood education.* Washington, DC: NAEYC. Available online at http://www.naeyc.org.

———. (2005). Code of ethics (revised). Available online at http://www.naeyc.org.

National Coalition for the Homeless. (2001). *NCH fact sheet #7.* Available online at http://www.nationalhomeless.org.

Olsen, D. (1997, October 23). The advancing nanny state: Why the government should stay out of child care. *Cato Policy Analysis, 285.*

Proof No Child Left Behind is working. (2005, July 14). Press release on www.ed.gov.

Robinson, A., & Stark, D. (2002). *Advocates in action: Making a difference for young children.* Washington, DC: NAEYC.

Schorr, L. (1997). *Common purpose: Strengthening families and neighborhoods to rebuild America.* New York: Doubleday.

Washington, V., Johnson, V., & McCracken, J. B. (1995). *Grassroots success! Preparing schools and families for each other.* Washington, DC: NAEYC.

HELPFUL WEB SITES

http://www.conference-board.org

The Conference Board creates and disseminates knowledge about management and the marketplace to help businesses strengthen their performance and better serve society.

http://www.familiesandwork.org

The Families and Work Institute is a nonprofit center for research that provides data to inform decision making about the changing workforce, changing family, and changing community. The Web site has information about their publications, including the National Study of the Changing Work Force (2002) conducted every five years.

http://www.workfamily.com

> Work & Family Connection helps employers create a workplace that is both supportive and effective for a workforce with important personal responsibilities.

http://www.childadvocacy.org

> National Association for Child Advocates (NACA) is a nationwide network of child advocacy organizations working at the increasingly critical level of America's statehouses, county commissions, and city councils. NACA serves as the forum where child advocacy leaders from across the country convene to share ideas and exchange information, formulate joint efforts and coordinate strategies, sharpen their skills, and increase the impact of the child advocacy movement. NACA establishes links between state and local child advocates and national experts and provides a clearinghouse of information about issues affecting children and effective advocacy.

http://www.cwla.org

> Child Welfare League of America is the nation's oldest and largest membership-based child welfare organization and is committed to engaging people everywhere in promoting the well-being of children, youth, and their families and protecting every child from harm.

http://www.childadvocate.net

> Child Advocates serves the needs of children, families, and professionals while addressing mental health, medical, educational, legal, and legislative issues.

http://www.4children.org

> Action Alliance for Children exists to inform, educate, and persuade a statewide constituency of people who work with and on behalf of children by providing the most reliable information about current issues, trends, and public policies that affect children and families. AAC is a resource for policy makers, children's service providers and advocates, and the media.

http://www.childrensdefense.org

> The mission of the Children's Defense Fund is to Leave No Child Behind® and to ensure every child a Healthy Start, a Head Start, a Fair Start, a Safe Start, and a Moral Start in life and successful passage to adulthood with the help of caring families and communities. There is much information at this site about community issues to support family needs.

http://www.projectappleseed.org

> The National Campaign for Public School Improvement. Project Appleseed provides parents with the information and resources necessary to become committed to school improvement.

http://www.csos.jhu.edu

> Center on Families, Communities, Schools, and Children's Learning, Johns Hopkins University. The Center for Social Organization of

Schools (CSOS) was established in 1966 as an educational research and development center at Johns Hopkins University to study how changes in the social organization of schools can make them more effective for all students in promoting academic achievement, development of potential, and eventual career success.

http://www.naeyc.org

The National Association for the Education of Young Children (NAEYC) exists to lead and consolidate the efforts of individuals and groups working to achieve healthy development and constructive education for all young children. This site offers information about events in federal and state policy.

http://www.togetherwecan.org

TWC's Mission Leaders across America are endeavoring to work together toward a shared vision for their communities and improved results for their children and families. The mission of Together We Can is to strengthen and sustain the capacity of community efforts and state initiatives to move toward that shared vision.

Additional resources for this chapter can be found on the Online Companion to accompany this text at www.earlychilded.delmar.com. This supplemental material includes frequently asked questions; chapter outlines to be used as study guides; scenarios that both encourage large and small group discussions and provoke new thoughts and ideas; and chapter resources, including chapter summaries, interactive questions, Web links, and Web activities. In addition, forms from the text are available for download.

No use debating environmental versus genetic causes. Either way, it's your fault.

SECTION IV
MAKING A PARTNERSHIP WORK

In this section we consider the challenges of going beyond a general consideration of communication strategies to particularize communication with individual families. Every family's situation is unique, so teachers have to individualize their strategies and styles to fit different circumstances. In addition, families who have particular needs because of life events create special challenges. Other challenges result from attitudes and behaviors that teachers may find particularly troublesome. Even if teachers are committed to the concept of working with parents as partners, the complexity of working with diverse personalities, backgrounds, and situations frequently offers real challenges. Though it may be tempting to abandon the effort, teachers have to persevere with professional skills. It is sometimes helpful to learn how other programs structure their family involvement and communication. This section continues to consider the absolute necessity of teachers going beyond merely perfunctory gestures to ensure that partnership works.

Chapter 15 explores methods teachers can use to welcome families of diverse backgrounds into partnership. Chapter 16 considers the particular circumstances of families experiencing divorce, of families with children who have special developmental needs, of families with infants, of families who have experienced abuse or neglect or family violence, and of adoptive families. Chapter 17 discusses attitudes that create unique challenges, as well as behaviors that are frequent causes of tension. Chapter 18 describes several programs and how they include parents.

CHAPTER 15

Working with Families from Diverse Backgrounds

KEY TERMS
colorblindedness
culture
culturally
  assaultive
dominant
  culture

OBJECTIVES
After reading this chapter, you should be able to

1 Discuss a rationale for recognizing the importance of culture and working with families from diverse backgrounds, identifying benefits for children, parents, and teachers.

2 Describe several specific strategies for teachers welcoming all families.

3 Identify methods of resolving cultural conflicts.

4 Discuss common cultural issues that arise in classrooms.

Teachers working in schools and programs today frequently find that the families with whom they work exemplify the diversity typical at this time in most parts of the world. Families can come with as many configurations, colors, and cultural and class orientations, and communicate in as many languages, as there are children in a classroom. Many Western nations' cities report that students in the same school may speak close to 60 different languages and that foreign-owned companies in most cities number several hundred. A report from the U.S. Census Bureau states that in 1994, nearly one in seven people spoke a language other than English at home (Tabors, 1997). Twenty-eight percent of Head Start children speak a home language other than English. By 2010 more than 30% of all school-age children will come from American homes in which the primary language is not English. Presently one in four Americans is a member of a cultural minority, and the latest census numbers show that number is rising. By the end of the 20th century students of color comprised one-third of the school population;

by 2020 this percentage will be nearly half. Less than half of the school population in California and Texas is white. Students of color comprise at least half of the school population in the largest 20 cities in America. About 20% of children live below the poverty line (Gollnick & Chinn, 2005) A recent study by the U.S. Department of Labor projected that by 2050, 75% of this country's workforce will be people of color, and by that time the U.S. population will include 82 million people who arrived in this country after 1991 or were born of parents who did. This will include two out of every five people in America. In 1997 an analysis of census data indicated that the number of children who were either immigrants or the American-born offspring of immigrants had nearly doubled since 1990, making them the fastest-growing segment of the U.S. population under the age of 18. Canada and Australia experienced similar increases in diverse populations. Rather than the "melting pot," a phrase that has been used to describe America, a better metaphor might be a complex tapestry full of variations, colors, and backgrounds.

These statistics make clear what classroom teachers already know: They must be prepared to live in a diverse society, welcoming and working with families from very different backgrounds. In this chapter we explore how teachers can work with families of diverse cultural experiences, respecting their uniqueness, supporting them in partnership, and providing continuity in their children's educational experiences.

■■■ A RATIONALE FOR TEACHER ATTENTION TO DIVERSITY

Consider the children enrolled in Dorothy Scott's classroom this fall. Of the 15, 5 live with their biological mothers and fathers, although two of these couples are not married. Two live with single, divorced mothers; one lives with his single, divorced father. Two live with one parent and a stepparent; one of these children was born in Asia and adopted by the mother and her first husband. One lives with her grandparents. One lives with a never-married mother, and another with two mothers. One moves midweek between the homes and care of his divorced parents. The last child lives with foster parents, the third home he has known in four years. Of these families, nearly all the parents work, many in factory jobs, several in downtown offices, three in professional positions. Parental education levels range from several who have not completed high school to others with college and graduate degrees. One parent receives funds from TANF and food stamps; two others receive government assistance with medical and child care needs. Eight are children of color, including African American, Hispanic, a family recently arrived from a Caribbean island, and a child adopted from Vietnam. Three of the families do not speak English in their homes. Six of the families own their homes; three others rent a house, five rent apartments, and one lives with other relatives. Two of the children regularly fly long distances to visit grandparents and parents who live apart; six of them ride the bus to the center with their parents who do not own cars.

Dorothy Scott says that, in her mind, they're all children, and she never notices what color they are or what their families do. "They're all the same to me. I treat them all alike. Of course, some of these parents do a much better job of raising their children than others, and the ones who need the most help don't do a thing to get it."

What such a statement fails to recognize is that to treat all families as if they are the same is both unrealistic and disrespectful. It is unrealistic because it does not take into consideration what cultural values and experiences mean to people and how profoundly **culture** influences their approach to life. And it is disrespectful because individuals deserve recognition and acceptance of their unique identities. When teachers do not take the time to learn about the circumstances and experiences that shape each family, they effectively put up barriers to healthy identity formation for children and effective partnerships with their parents. Furthermore, they do not follow the guidelines of the NAEYC position statement on developmentally appropriate practice:

> Increasingly, programs serve children and families from diverse cultural and linguistic backgrounds, requiring that all programs demonstrate understanding of and responsiveness to cultural and linguistic diversity. Because culture and language are critical components of children's development, practices cannot be developmentally appropriate unless they are responsive to cultural and linguistic diversity (NAEYC, in Bredekamp & Copple, 1997).

Developmentally appropriate practices result from the process of professionals making decisions about the well-being and education of children based on at least three important kinds of information or knowledge:

1. What is known about child development and learning.

2. What is known about the strengths, interests, and needs of each individual child.

FIGURE 15-1 Knowing about children's social and cultural contexts ensures that learning experiences are meaningful, relevant, and respectful for children and their families.

3. Knowledge of the social and cultural contexts in which children live to ensure that learning experiences are meaningful, relevant, and respectful for the participating children and their families (NAEYC, in Bredekamp & Copple, 1997; see Figure 15-1).

NAEYC has also published a position statement called *Responding to Linguistic and Cultural Diversity: Recommendations for Effective Early Childhood Education* (NAEYC, 1996). Here are some of its key points:

1. Actively involve families in the early learning program.

2. Help all families realize the cognitive advantages of a child knowing more than one language, and provide them with strategies to support, maintain, and preserve home language learning.

3. Convince families that their homes' cultural values and norms are honored.

4. Ensure that children remain cognitively, linguistically, and emotionally connected to their home languages and cultures.

5. Encourage home language and literacy development, knowing that this contributes to children's ability to acquire English language proficiency.

6. Help develop essential concepts in the children's first language and within cultural contexts that they understand.

7. Support and preserve home language usage.

8. Develop and provide alternative, creative strategies to promote all children's participation and learning.

9. Give children many ways of showing what they know and can do.

10. Provide professional preparation and development in the areas of culture, language, and diversity.

What do we mean by *culture*? Culture is "in its broadest sense a set of rules for behavior by which we organize and give meaning to the world" (Phillips, 1988). Culture refers to the values, beliefs, behaviors, language and styles of communication, traits, artifacts, and products shared by and associated with a group of people. It is a way of "perceiving, believing, evaluating, and behaving. It provides the blueprint that determines the way we think, feel, and behave in society. . . . Culturally determined norms guide our language, behavior, emotions, and thinking in different situations; they are the do's and don'ts of appropriate behavior" (Gollnick & Chinn, 2005). Culture becomes the lens through which we see and judge the world; it defines what we know, how we behave, and what we believe (Swiniarski, Breiborde, & Murphy, 1999). Culture is passed on through the first social relationships of the family and through all the additional environmental influences that are channeled through that family's place in the world.

Issues that are determined by culture include the definition of family structure and the hierarchy of authority within the family; the rites of passage that define milestones in the life cycle; the roles available to individuals; the history, traditions, and kinship patterns that determine which events and people are sources of pride; the foods that are eaten; awareness and habits of using time and space, including orientations to punctuality and speed in completing tasks; feelings about group or personal property; religious and political beliefs, including restrictions on the topics that can be discussed; practices of health and hygiene, including ideas about treatment and causes of illness; orientations toward independence and interdependence; and discipline and rearing of children (Garcia & McLaughlin, 1995). Culture influences specific behaviors and attitudes related to education such as these:

- The role modeling of parents as learners themselves.
- Educational resources of the home and the uses made of them.
- The willingness and ability of parents to participate in their children's school experiences.
- The nature and extent of parental expectations and demands.
- The value placed on education and on children's learning efforts.
- Attitudes toward the teacher's profession.

Culturally determined actions, behaviors, and ways of dealing with people don't have to be thought about; they are automatic. Clearly teachers must recognize the complexity of cultural influences on both the development and learning of the children with whom they work and on the patterns of communication they are striving to develop with families. These concepts encompass, yet move far beyond, the obvious awareness of racial, ethnic, and linguistic diversity.

There is much to be gained when teachers recognize and learn more about individual family cultural patterns and customs.

For Individual Children

"'**Colorblindedness**' ignores what we know about children's development of identity and attitudes as well as the realities of racism in the daily lives of people of color" (Jones & Derman-Sparks, 1992). Although not racist in the conventional sense, this attitude masks an uncritical way of thinking that accepts the existing status quo. Supporting equality is not the same thing as insisting on sameness. To profess colorblindedness is to "dismiss one of the most salient features of a child's identity, and does not allow for it in curriculum or instruction" (Ladson-Billings, 1994). (See Figure 15-2.) So too does failure to talk about the other differences that children perceive, such as differences in family structure, in socioeconomic status, and in customary ways of behaving.

As young children develop a sense of who they are and who their families are in relation to others, they become aware of culture and of the response of others to their cultural beliefs and images. Cultural identity is achieved by age 5 (Lynch & Hanson, 1992). Children need to absorb positive attitudes toward that cultural identity from the world around them. These attitudes need to be affirmations of their personal identity, clear messages from the larger

COMPARISON OF VALUES FROM DOMINANT AND NONDOMINANT CULTURAL PERSPECTIVES

Anglo-American	Other Ethnocultural Groups
Mastery over nature	Harmony with nature
Personal control over environment	Fate
Doing/activity	Being
Time dominates	Personal interaction dominates
Human equality	Hierarchy/rank/status
Individualism/privacy	Group welfare
Youth	Elders
Competition	Cooperation
Future orientation	Past or present orientation
Informality	Formality
Directness/openness/honesty	Indirectness/ritual/face
Practicality/efficiency	Idealism
Materialism	Spiritualism/detachment

—*From Schilling and Brannon in Randall-David, 1989*

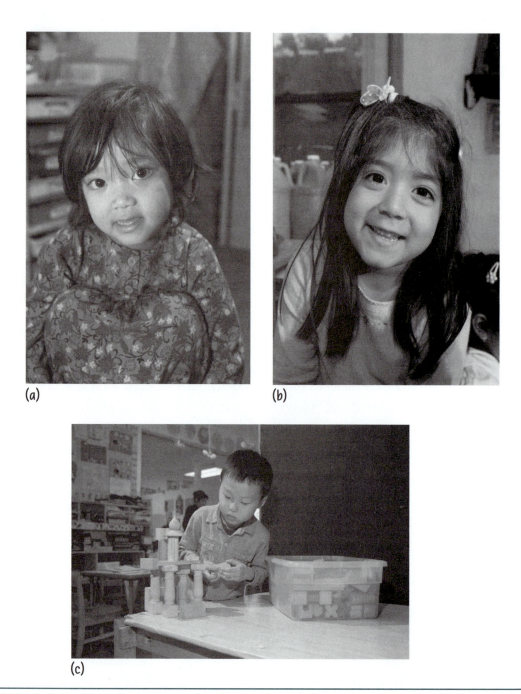

(a)

(b)

(c)

FIGURE 15-2 Healthy self-identity results when children of all backgrounds find acceptance in their environment.

society that who they are, and who their families are, is accepted and respected by others. When children find that the images of person and family with whom they identify are either responded to negatively or are oddly missing from the social images surrounding them, positive self-identity suffers. Teachers and families who are concerned with healthy formation of identity in young children must ensure that children of all backgrounds find evidence of social acceptance of the cultural norms with which they identify. It is important that teachers recognize the value of the individual child's culture, and not perceive culturally different as culturally deficient, feeling they must replace the norms of the family with those with which the teachers are more culturally comfortable. The norms of the family are those with which individual children form their sense of identity and connection.

It is also not healthy for children of the **dominant culture** when recognition of diversity is absent. Children who can find only images of themselves and their families in the dominant social institutions are at risk of developing a falsely superior identity. This will diminish those whose cultural identity is devalued or omitted by the explicit or implicit policies or structure of the schools.

How can this experience become real to you? Imagine that you are learning to read using the primer that most adults used in first grade several decades ago. You would be exposed every day to the adventures of a white middle-class family. Father went off to work dressed in a business suit in an appropriate automobile. Mother was also well dressed and was busy caring for her well-appointed home and three blond and blue-eyed children. Dick, Jane, and Sally led the life that suburban children lead, with their varieties of toys, pets, and activities. But if your own life experiences suggested different family structures, different places to live and ways of living, and events with people who dressed and looked differently, the implicit message received during that year of daily reading would be that this was the desirable, the norm, and that your cultural experience was somehow deficient. Although Dick, Jane, and Sally have fortunately disappeared, there are still too many occasions when children of all backgrounds are not given the clear message that their unique cultural circumstances are recognized and accepted. One of the easiest ways to do this is to reach out to families, encourage full participation, and offer a variety of ways to become involved.

Individual children can also be taught and assessed most appropriately when their individual cultural context and its impact on their development are appreciated. If teachers operate in cultural myopia, they may not recognize the culturally different strengths and abilities of an individual child and may, in fact, interpret as problems or delays behaviors that are quite typical within the child's cultural context. Cultural differences can cause teachers to misunderstand children and incorrectly plan their educational experiences.

As families from the cultural minority communicate about their children, they may help teachers understand the children's developmental history and avoid inaccurate assessments or cultural biases in the observers or testing instruments (Kendall, 1996).

For All Children

The statistics presented in the beginning of this chapter make it evident that adults must prepare children to live comfortably in a world filled with diversity. Exposing young children to cultural differences and modeling appreciation and acceptance of the diversity enables children to grow up without developing the kind of prejudices and biases that are largely the result of fear and lack of experience. When differences are not acknowledged, talked about, explained, and seen as positive, children sometimes find them frightening and respond to them negatively. Thus bias has roots in children's early experiences. When adults provide an environment that allows children to explore differences and supports them in discovering similarities as well as respecting differences in others' lives, children are more likely to respond positively to diversity (see Figure 15-3). When the true variety of experiences of the families within classrooms is recognized and voiced, curriculum and learning experiences can become richer. Utilizing the firsthand experiences that families provide allows children to experience variation in culture, not just learn about it passively.

When teachers do not incorporate children's cultural experiences into classroom life, all children miss opportunities to promote both their social and cognitive growth (Chang, 1993).

For Partnerships with Families

Families transmit their culture to their children. Each culture's values and beliefs underlie parenting practices and ways of living and influence children's learning and communication styles. Culture determines how parents perceive their roles in relation to their children and in relation to society. Culture

FIGURE 15-3 Children respond positively to diversity in an environment where they can comfortably explore both differences and similarities.

determines families' age-related expectations of children and their expectations of a school; their ways of showing affection and disciplining their children; and their attitudes about independence, cleanliness, attendance, achievement, desirable socialization of children, expression of feelings, and hundreds of other beliefs that are unconsciously absorbed within the individual culture.

Cultural attitudes also determine how parents view teachers' roles and their relationship to the teacher. Culture influences some of the factors that can become sources of irritation in teachers. For example, many teachers interpret lack of punctuality as a sign of indifference or hostility; it may also indicate a different orientation toward time in the family's culture. Other cultural orientation regarding gender roles may mean that some parents are uncomfortable with a female teacher or with a teacher's expectation of communicating with mothers in a culture where fathers communicate for the family (Kendall, 1996). (See Figure 15-4.)

When teachers and families who do not move in the same cultural framework meet, it is a jarring experience from both perspectives. Janet Gonzalez-Mena, in her important book on multicultural issues in child care (2000), describes what many do when faced with cultural differences:

> Because my way seems right, even normal, I tend to judge others based on my own perspective. I may consider them exotic or

FIGURE 15-4 Teachers and parents who come from different cultural backgrounds are likely to have different views on child rearing and expectations of school.

interesting, or I may consider them weird. But being a polite person who tries to get along with others, I do what I can not to notice. Because my way is normal to me, it seems rude to make an issue of the fact that someone else is not normal. And because I have a whole society behind me giving me the message that "my people" are the standard by which everyone else is judged, I can afford to keep on ignoring what I choose to.

But can I? What does this attitude do to me? It shields me from reality. It gives me a slanted perspective, a narrow view. I miss out on a lot because of my perspective. . . . What does it do to those who are not "my people" if I continue in this narrow, slanted perspective, ignoring what I consider "not normal"? . . .

Imagine the harm I can do both to "my people" and those whose differences I ignore when I carry out my job with this

---

CULTURE AND CHILD REARING

Culture influences

- **Age-related expectations of children.**
- **Concern over children acquiring skills by a particular age.**
- **Sleep patterns and bedtime routines.**
- **Children's roles and responsibilities in the family.**
- **Toilet learning.**
- **Diet and mealtime behavior.**
- **Discipline and guidance.**
- **How parents talk to children and children to parents.**
- **How parents show affection.**
- **Importance of gender identity and traditional sex roles.**
- **Dress and hair care.**
- **Ideas about illness and use of medicine.**
- **Use of supplemental child care.**
- **Acceptance of, meaning of, and response to emotion.**
- **Children's attachment to adults and separation from adults.**

—Adapted from York, 2003.

biased attitude. . . . What does it do to people who are different from me to have those differences defined as abnormal? What does it do to people who are different from me to have those differences ignored? (Gonzales-Mena, 2000)

By ignoring the differences in behavior, communication style, and beliefs created by culture, teachers run the risk of creating real conflicts and barriers to effective partnership with families. The potential barriers to communication arising from culture are real and must be recognized:

- Families may have few basic communication skills in English.

- Families may not be familiar with school systems, including knowing whom to approach about what or how to arrange appointments.

- Families may have had little experience of being consulted regarding their children's education.

- Families may have become accustomed to superficial conversation, to smiling and passing on, when interpreters are rarely available.

- Families may be anxious regarding approaching figures of authority or disclosing personal information.

- Families may find written communication daunting.

- Families may have expectations of education and ways of supporting children at home that are different from the school's. (Bastiani, 1997)

It is far too easy for teachers who are of one culture to assume that children of another culture are culturally deprived and that their families need to be taught how to better accomplish tasks of parenting. There is a genuine challenge to teachers to improve their sensitivity to cultural and individual differences and increase communication across cultural divisions. This process is hard work and takes time and effort. Nevertheless, the best schools and programs continue to press for communication across cultural differences, to avoid eroding or conflicting with parental responsibility and value systems. True partnerships with families come when teachers genuinely attempt to learn and understand the ideas that are central to each family's experience.

For Teacher Growth

The past experiences of every teacher are unique, and each teacher is a product of her or his own culture. Working within educational institutions, teachers of whatever culture are generally proponents of the predominant values espoused by the schools—typically the values of the white middle class. These include concepts supporting equality of all; a basic belief in the goodness of humanity; an orientation toward achievement, action, work, and progress; an emphasis on the individual and rights of privacy; an orientation toward direct communication and assertiveness; and an orientation to the future, change, and progress, with an emphasis on efficient use of time (Lynch & Hanson,

1992). It is too easy for teachers to feel that ideas and values beyond these of the mainstream society are somehow wrong or inferior.

Nevertheless, professional experiences offer individual teachers the opportunity to reach beyond their limited cultural experiences, learning to understand and value diversity. "But I'm not prejudiced!" you may protest. The attitudes that we all learned beginning in childhood deserve honest examination; such examination offers teachers a chance for increased self-awareness and change. And by genuinely trying to explore the ideas, values, and customs that are meaningful to the families with whom they work, teachers are granted real opportunities for personal growth.

▢▢▢ STRATEGIES FOR TEACHERS

To create an atmosphere in classrooms and schools that conveys welcome and acceptance of diversity, teachers and administrators can do many specific things. Some of these are discussed here.

Examine Personal Attitudes

Teachers must begin with genuine examinations of their attitudes and assumptions about children and families of diverse configurations and ethnic and class backgrounds. They must explore the stereotypes they have learned that are racist and ethnocentric, and find ways to change what they believe about themselves and others, about the way families are supposed to look and behave. This can be both difficult and painful, but it is a necessary prerequisite for successfully conveying an attitude of acceptance. Phillips suggests that teachers might begin these explorations "by discussing the stereotypes we know and hold, by looking at where stereotypes come from and what purpose they serve, and by identifying ways to confront each other about our divisiveness" (Phillips, 1988). Only through this process can teachers reach the point of genuine openness to others.

There will be times when teachers experience personal discomfort when facing particular ideas and behaviors of others. It is vital that teachers work with this feeling, identifying what it is that makes them uncomfortable and being clear about their own values and goals that guide them. Accepting others' rights to hold different beliefs does not mean teachers have to let go of their own values. Teachers must accept that there will be different perspectives, and these may be equally valid to the people who hold them.

Many teachers have found it helpful to develop a support group among colleagues who are interested in doing this kind of self-reflective work. Working with trusted peers can encourage a more honest examination and discussion of values, beliefs, and the accompanying inherent biases and prejudices (Cronin et al., 1998). Support groups can also be valuable to teachers who are seeking ideas on how to reach out to families to become more inclusive of all cultures.

REFLECTIONS FOR JOURNAL ENTRIES

What do you recall of your first experience in perceiving differences among people? Where were you and what were the circumstances? What emotion can you identify as part of that experience? What did you do when you noticed the difference? If you spoke with an adult, do you remember the response? Consider how these events affected your view of diversity.

Learn about Other Cultures

When dealing with families whose culture is different from their own, teachers must educate themselves about the values, practices, and communication methods that are comfortable to the others. How does this education take place? Reading books and articles may help; see the list of suggestions in this chapter and at the end of Chapter 1.

Teachers should also realize that cultural heritage is learned and is not innately based on the culture into which an individual is born. That is, individuals of a particular ethnic background whose families have lived for several generations in America may now have a culture that is an adaptation of the earlier culture. Culture is a dynamic system that changes continuously, so written generalities must be viewed as tentative guides at best. Perhaps the best resources for learning are families themselves. Through careful observation of parent–child interaction and learning how parents care for their children (see Figure 15-5), teachers will learn much about how messages are transmitted verbally and nonverbally and about what is important to the family. Intercultural communication shows real differences in the proximity of people when communicating, in facial expressions and eye contact, and in the desirability of touching another. (See Dodd, 1997; Samovar & Porter, 2002; Brown, 1991; and Brislin, 1993, for specifics about intercultural communication and culturally influenced behavior.) It is vital for teachers to realize that the general cultural characteristics associated with particular cultural or ethnic backgrounds are meant to be helpful guidelines and are *not* to be interpreted as limited stereotypes. They must recognize that uniqueness and individual patterns are always present. Showing a genuine desire to learn respectfully will help families become comfortable with demonstrating and discussing their family systems and style with the teacher.

Establish an Environment That Welcomes

When each family first crosses the classroom or school threshold, they should find evidence that their presence is recognized and accepted. Enrollment forms may be a first place to begin to learn about families and to convey the message that diversity in family styles is expected. Rather than having blanks

FIGURE 15-5 Teachers will learn much about cultural patterns of child rearing through observing parent–child interaction.

for "mother," "father," and "siblings," schools might change this to "adults in the home" and "children in the home" and "family living out of the child's home." There should be spaces to indicate which language is primary at home, as well as other languages used there. Enrollment forms and information booklets should be printed in as many languages as possible; families are often happy to help with translating the information if it has not already been done, and the school's invitation to do so indicates genuine intentions of including all. Individual teachers may already have visited the family in their home setting and have learned something about the family's neighborhood, work, and living conditions. Often teachers take a snapshot of the family, or ask for a family picture to add to their family picture board—a sure way of including every family.

Teachers should use initial visits and survey forms to obtain information that will help both the child and family feel comfortable in the new setting and assist the teacher in working more effectively with the child. Learning what language is spoken in the home allows the teacher to obtain the services of an interpreter for the first conversations with child and parent or to post a welcoming greeting in the family's native language. If the teacher does not know how to add this, parents will often willingly write it if they feel their help would be welcome.

The classroom can appear "culturally safe" to both parent and child when materials, pictures, books, and room design reflect family and home ex-

> ## Culturally Welcoming Programs
>
> - **Examine all printed materials to be sure they are inclusive of all family structures.**
> - **Translate all printed materials, notices, and signs.**
> - **Provide interpreters.**
> - **Post "welcomes" in languages represented in the program.**
> - **Use family pictures in the environment.**
> - **Display items and artifacts that are familiar to all families.**
> - **Collect and use music and books from different cultures.**
> - **Allow families ways of sharing their culture in the program.**
> - **Bring families together for comfortable social events.**
> - **Share teachers' and staff's culture.**
> - **Welcome the larger community.**
> - **Participate in collective and meaningful social action.**

periences. Utensils and clothing in the home living center can reflect the items children might see in use in their own homes; a wok, a garlic braid, or a string of dried chilies for pretend cooking; a pair of work coveralls for dress-up; and woven baskets for decor could reflect varied meanings from different homes. Parents can be asked to contribute culturally specific materials, such as empty food containers or hair care products. Dolls that represent the various racial and ethnic traditions of the classroom and community show awareness of differences. Photographs and posters that depict the ethnic heritage, social classes, and family configurations representative of all children in the classroom convey acceptance.

Displaying books that depict particular cultures or represent traditional literature and stories also conveys welcome. All of these additions to the environment help both children and their parents feel secure and accepted.

Asking families to contribute songs, tapes, musical instruments, and recordings representative of their culture's music can help build the diversity of the classroom listening library. Exposing young children to different tonal patterns and rhythms can enhance their musical experiences and build positive acceptance of a wide variety of music forms.

Teachers can plan family get-togethers scheduled for times that are convenient for all parents to attend. A potluck dinner where each family brings a favorite food helps parents meet their children's friends and families and welcomes everyone into the program (see Figure 15-6).

FIGURE 15-6 Mealtime is a cultural experience.

Open the Door for Communication about Culture

Teachers need to send clear and constant messages that they are interested in learning how a family wants to have their culture represented and supported in the classroom. Remember that we are using the term *culture* here in its broadest sense to indicate the uniqueness of each family in its ideas, attitudes, and values. Some teachers seem to feel that if they are working with a homogeneous collection of white families who have lived in this country for generations, they do not have to concern themselves with culture. But every family is still individual in its beliefs and attitudes, parenting methods, celebrations, and ordinary lifestyle. Teachers need to elicit from parents their wishes with regard to their children's care and education, as well as their ideas about how family experiences can enrich the classroom curriculum.

How do teachers open the door for such communication? Many teachers survey their parents at the beginning of the school year, either through conversation, written questionnaires, or both methods. They ask families about their goals for their children and what they want their children to accomplish at school during the year. They elicit detailed information about family caregiving practices, such as toilet learning, discipline, and so on. They attempt to learn as much as they can about family activities and experiences. They ask families what holidays the families celebrate in their homes and how the school can support such celebrations without lessening the families' primary importance. They ask families if they would be willing to share some holiday traditions and practices or other parts of their family life in the classroom. They also ask what holidays the families do not celebrate and in which they would prefer their children not be included. They find out information about home languages, places the families have lived, and experiences the

FIGURE 15-7 An example of a cultural conflict could be the caregiver allowing the toddler to feed herself when that was not the custom at home.

children have had (see Figure 15-7). And with all this they let parents know that their primary desire is to use this knowledge to preserve and enhance the families' culture, to support parents and their beliefs as the primary influence on the children's lives. They empower families with the knowledge that they can play an active role in helping the school better address the aspects of their cultural heritage that are meaningful to families, rather than smolder resentfully in silence while the institution imposes ideas and activities with which they disagree.

One important area of sensitivity for teachers is not to make any assumptions about a family's cultural background, priorities, or resources based on limited knowledge. For example, one teacher asked a parent if she would come in to explain Kwanzaa customs to the children, assuming that the family would celebrate that holiday important to many African American families simply because the family was black. Another parent, whose great-grandparents had been immigrants from Japan, recounted the story of the teacher who had asked if she could bring "a kimono or something to show the children." The mother firmly declined, saying she had no such items. Fortunately the teacher was wise enough to ask the parent what she could share with the children. The mother, a nurse in a coronary surgery unit, visited to help the children understand what

FIGURE 15-8 Opening the dialogue about cultural background sends messages of acceptance.

keeps hearts healthy. Jumping to conclusions that arise from stereotyped assumptions about a family's culture can be avoided when teachers take the time to form relationships that lead to real knowledge of families.

When teachers open dialogue about the issues that are meaningful to families, parents feel freer to ask questions, to talk about conflicts they perceive. As teachers work to see the parents' point of view, they model acceptance of differences (see Figure 15-8).

■■■ NEGOTIATING WITH CULTURAL CONFLICT

It is inevitable and predictable that when teachers and parents from diverse cultural settings come together, conflict and differences will appear. Culture determines that both families and teachers have strong viewpoints about what is good and necessary for children's development. All the most basic acts of daily care and nurturing—feeding, sleeping, toilet learning, comforting, playing—reflect the cultural values of both parents and caregivers, and their expectations will likely not match. Although differences are inevitable, "what is not necessarily inevitable is that one cultural view remains dominant over the other" (Chang, 1993). Gonzalez-Mena (1992) identifies four possible outcomes to cultural conflicts. Three of them involve activity and change to resolve the conflict.

The first possibility is that the conflict is resolved through understanding and negotiation, with both sides seeing the other's perspective and finding a compromise. An example here might be the familiar situation where the parent objects to seeing her child messy and dirty, and the early educator provides many classroom opportunities for sensory exploration with water, sand, and paint. As the teacher communicates with the parent about why cleanliness is so important to this parent, she learns that this family equates sending children to school clean and well-dressed with the parent's respect for education and with the family maintaining decent standards within the community. The teacher is also able to help the parent learn something about good early childhood practice and the importance of sensory experience in early learning. The teacher agrees that she will change the child's clothes or cover them well during messy play. The parent agrees to allow the child to do messy play as long as the clothes are protected. Both parties feel they are right (and the other is unnecessarily worried about something that doesn't seem very important), but they feel that the compromise is satisfactory.

The second possibility is that the situation could be resolved when the caregiver learns a new perspective from the parent and subsequently changes her actions. The example Gonzalez-Mena offers is of a caregiver who is convinced that the best place for babies to sleep is in a crib in a quiet nap room; this seems to provide optimal rest for most infants. But a baby from a family who is used to sleeping in the midst of an active household is unable to sleep. When the parents express dismay that their child will be isolated and alone in his crib, the caregiver discovers their point of view and works with the licensing consultant to accommodate parental requests and infant needs. The caregiver changes her actions because she recognizes and accepts the cultural difference.

A third possibility is to resolve the situation through parent education. Parents gain knowledge and learn ideas that might be different from their traditional cultural ideas, but they come to see that the new ideas will provide optimal developmental environments for their children. This requires thoughtful, respectful sensitivity on the part of the caregiver, to be very sure that the education relates to ideas that seem essential for children's development, not merely to help the family conform to some arbitrary standard of what is "normal." Gonzalez-Mena's example regards the conflict between parents of infants whose cultural beliefs are that babies should not be left free on the floor to play with toys but instead should be held and involved with human interaction. Rather than stopping floor freedom, the teacher helps the family understand the importance of physical freedom for muscle development and cognitive stimulation. When parents understand this importance, they are more open to learning how they can keep their children safe while they play on the floor. The teacher displays cultural sensitivity to the parents' concerns but finds the developmental issue important enough to pursue.

The last, and indeed fairly common, possibility in cultural conflicts is that there may be no resolution of the conflict. The worst-case scenario here is for neither family nor teacher to perceive or accept the other's perspective and for both to persist in their separate beliefs and practices. Children caught in the middle of such separation may be confused and uncomfortable when the practices in the school setting "are so very different from those at home that they represent an alien culture to them" (Phillips, 1988). The term **culturally assaultive** has been used to refer to such negative experiences because the family's culture is in fact under attack.

A better outcome would be for both families and teachers to gain an understanding of the other's ideas, which are treated with respect and sensitivity but without changing the strong beliefs. The achievement is for parent and teacher to learn to cope with the differences, each in a way that is acceptable to the individual. With sensitivity, communication, and working at problem solving, teachers and families may find ways of reconciling cultural differences, or at least becoming sensitive to separate perspectives.

REFLECTIONS FOR JOURNAL ENTRIES

Can you recall a situation in which you have been involved in a cultural conflict regarding child rearing, whether in your professional or personal life? What was the conflict? How was it resolved or not resolved? What insights does this give you about culturally determined differences of opinion?

▚▚■ COMMON CULTURAL ISSUES THAT ARISE IN CLASSROOMS

Linguistic Diversity

Communication with both families and children is challenged when the primary language of a family is different from the teacher's and that used in the classroom. A vital attitude for teachers is to consider a "nondeficit perspective in relation to linguistic diversity" (Rosegrant, 1992). That is, it is not so much that the child and parent are limited in English but that they are proficient in their primary language while learning a second language. Rather than seeing linguistically different children as less capable, less intelligent, and educationally delayed and their parents as less able to successfully raise their children,

FIGURE 15-9 Teachers must find ways to communicate across language differences.

teachers must understand that abilities in languages other than English demonstrate competencies that will slowly apply to learning English as a second language and also to learning the new cultural and social values associated with the classroom culture. "Only recently has attention been paid to what can be lost where the language and culture of the child's home are not reinforced in the early care setting" (Chang, 1993). It is not a matter of giving up one language and culture in favor of adopting another, but adding other skills and experiences to those that already exist and are important in the lives of children and their families (see Figure 15-9).

CULTURAL DILEMMAS

When faced with cultural dilemmas, teachers should

- Analyze the situation. What is the child's experience at home? What is my belief about this? Is the child's welfare at stake?

- Do not blame the child or the family.

- Get information. What does this behavior mean to the parents? What do parents do in this situation, and why?

- Realize the child can't cope with being caught between two cultural expectations.

- Respond to the child and parents as individuals.

- Keep talking and trying to find common ground.

FIGURE 15-10 Learning greeting words in families' native languages is a welcoming action.

Here are some specific things teachers can do to show respect and to facilitate communication:

- Learn greeting words in the families' native languages. These can also be posted on the wall so that other teachers and families in the classroom can use them: "Hello to Eleni and her family is 'Kalimera.' Good-bye is 'Yia sou.'" (See Figure 15-10.)

- Provide written materials in the families' native languages. Help with translation can often be obtained from others in the community, such as university faculty or students, English as second language programs, churches associated with particular cultures, school system personnel, representatives from foreign-owned businesses, international clubs, or bilingual members of the same nationality. Explore your community resources to help find individuals who can help with translating materials or interpreting conversations. There are also two useful Web sites that offer free translation services from English to a number of languages: Spanish, Italian, French, German, Chinese, and many others. These are http://www.freetranslation.com and http://www.babelfish.altavista.com.

- Encourage the families to bring family members who can speak English to conferences, meetings, and classroom activities. If there are other

Getting to Know Your Students

Instructions: Please fill out as much as you can. Do not feel you must answer every question. These questions are meant to make your child's experience in our classroom more enjoyable:

1. Child's name:

2. Father's name:

3. Father's country of origin:

4. Mother's name:

5. Mother's country of origin:

6. What name do you use for your child?

7. How did you decide to give your child this name?

8. Does this name have a particular meaning or translation?

9. Where was your child born?

10. Where else has your child lived and when?

11. How long has your family lived in [name of community]?

12. What language or languages do you use to talk to your child?

    Father:

    Mother:

13. Do you speak any other languages?

    Father:

    Mother:

14. Who else does your child spend time with besides you? (Please include sisters and brothers, aunts and uncles, cousins, grandparents, family friends, and child care providers.)

    Name   Relation to child   Age   Language used with child

(continues)

(continued)

15. If English is *not* your home language, please estimate how many English words your child knows (circle one):

Fewer than 10   0 to 50   50 to 100   More than 100

16. Do you belong to a particular religious group?

17. List the foods that your child likes to eat:

18. List the foods that your child does *not* like to eat:

19. What does your child usually eat with? (circle one)

Fingers   Chopsticks   Fork and spoon

20. How does your child let you know he or she needs to use the toilet?

Please complete the following sentences:

21. When my child is with a group of children, I would expect my child to

22. When my child needs help from an adult, I would expect my child to

23. If my child is misbehaving in class, I would expect the teacher to

24. If my child is unhappy in class, I would expect the teacher to

25. The most important thing my child can learn in class this year would be

26. Is there any other information you would like to give us about your family or your child?

parents who also speak the same language, be sure the parents meet. These other parents may be able to support the new families and also act as a bridge for involving them in the school.

- Encourage parents to use their primary languages with their children at home. Children will quickly pick up the second language in the classroom, and it is vital not to disturb the parent–child relationship and the language in which they are primarily communicating. Teachers must acknowledge that there are functions of language beyond exchange of information. "Every language embodies both the historical experience of a particular cultural group and the conscious effort by that group to transmit its cultural values" (Teaching Tolerance, 1997). In addition, both

FIGURE 15-11 English language learners need special support as they learn a second language.

teachers and parents need to realize that interacting and working with children in their native languages at home will help the children at school. The language principles learned in one language will help children transfer these to a second language. When parents are encouraged to "practice more English at home," the quality of their interaction with their children may be limited. This hurts self-esteem and social competence and ultimately affects the children's abilities to do well in school (Wolfe, 1992). (See Figure 15-11.)

- Label objects and pictures in the classroom with all the languages represented in the room. Parents will be happy to supply the words. This will allow the teachers and all the children to enjoy learning new words in each others' languages.

- Make a photograph book or picture sequence that represents the daily life and routines in the classroom. Pictures tell the story when words are not understood. Another strategy is to make a video of the children during the day. Parents can interpret the actions even if they do not understand the language.

- Create many opportunities for two-way communication, particularly with face-to-face contact, such as home visits, conversations at the door, potluck dinners, conferences, and classroom open houses. In this way the teacher's real attempts to include the families with primary language differences may be seen more clearly—and gestures and body language can help the communication process.

- Make a collection of take-home children's books in the children's primary languages. This will encourage families to reinforce their native languages as well as read to their children (Rosegrant, 1992).

- Invite family members to teach songs or tell stories in their native languages in the classroom. This will welcome parents' contributions and give a positive message about diversity to all children.

- Be sensitive to not assuming developmental delays or personality difficulties in children when behavior may be limited by the children's language understanding in the classroom, as well as by cultural differences. An example is a child who does not make eye contact with a teacher because of cultural teachings about respectful communication. Help children by demonstration, gestures, and support as they become involved in play activities. Also be sensitive to overlooking needs for special attention that can be masked by assuming that the problem is lack of understanding or failure to assess children in ways that consider their cultural background. An example is a hard-of-hearing child who is assumed to be nonresponsive because of the language difference.

Holidays

Because of religious traditions or cultural backgrounds, many families in schools may celebrate their holidays in their own way, may celebrate holidays that are unfamiliar to mainstream society, or may not wish their children to participate in celebrations that are traditional in many schools and centers. Examples are a family that celebrates Buddha's birthday or Chanukah; one that has never heard of Halloween or feels it is contrary to their religious views; one that wants only the religious aspects of Christmas recognized; one that is offended by the teacher's creation of a dragon to celebrate Chinese New Year as though it were merely a tourist attraction; or one that does not want their child to participate in a Christmas story pageant.

Teachers need to be sensitive to the cultural diversity within their classrooms and must think long and hard about building much of their curriculum around holidays that may not be celebrated or valued by the families in their classroom. Exploring the issue with families and colleagues can help teachers gain different perspectives and develop new ideas for celebrations.

There is a point of view that suggests that early childhood programs may be inappropriate places to celebrate holidays (Neugebauer, 1990). This approach points out that

1. It is extremely difficult to give holidays meaning that is developmentally appropriate for young children. "Most holidays are based on abstract concepts that are beyond their comprehension" (Neugebauer, 1990).

2. Holidays challenge inclusiveness because of decisions about whether to include holidays that represent all the family traditions in a center, or what to do if many other traditions are not represented in a center, or what to do when all families do not agree on the celebration or method of celebration of a particular holiday.

3. Many holidays are overdone in any case, with great emphasis on commercialization, leading to uncomfortable situations of competition and pressure on families of limited economic means, as well as trivialization of deeper feelings that families may hold. These are certainly points worth considering.

In the *Anti-Bias Curriculum* (1989), Derman-Sparks presents useful guidelines for thinking about the holiday question:

• Make sure that the holiday activities included in classrooms are related to children's lives. If not, such activities take time away from other meaningful curricula.

• Holiday activities should be connected to peoples' daily lives and beliefs—to the specific families and teachers in the classroom. If holidays are meaningful to real people in children's lives, children can happily participate as "guests" in holiday activities that are not part of their culture. The participants whose holiday it is can share their feelings and memories about the importance of the holiday, as well as information.

• Encourage children and families to talk about family traditions of holiday celebration, even of holidays that the teacher discovers are shared by the group. This increases children's awareness of diversity even when the main holiday is the same. For example, a conversation about the favorite dishes of the family's traditional holiday dinner or how each family uniquely celebrates birthdays is both enjoyable and illustrative of different approaches to celebrations.

• The holidays of every group that is represented in the classroom should be honored, with their agreement and active participation. Participation prevents the holiday celebration from becoming just a "tourist" experience, where the holiday is seen as exotic rather than regular. The participation of all concerned also allows the particular differences in the way individual families within a culture celebrate the same holiday to be respected and demonstrated. When holidays are celebrated without any connection to real people in the children's lives, or without anyone in the classroom having ever participated in this holiday before, the danger is that the holiday celebration may deteriorate into a rather trivial and superficial experience that actually works against developing respect for diversity. There is much more to Cinco de Mayo than eating tacos!

• Families whose beliefs do not permit their children to participate in particular holiday celebrations should be included in planning satisfactory alternatives for the children within the classroom. Teachers must guard against feeling sorry that these children are being deprived of some experience that the teacher believes is important. Such an attitude implies that the only desirable cultural beliefs are those tied in with celebration of that holiday—a truly ethnocentric error. By becoming knowledgeable about particular family beliefs and traditions, teachers can help support children in making the explanations to their peers.

"Henry's family doesn't celebrate Halloween, so that's why he decided he didn't want to help carve the jack-o'-lantern. He's going to help me wash and bake the pumpkin seeds for our harvest snack. Who would like to help us?"

- Think and rethink every classroom practice to be sure that everyone's traditions and beliefs are represented throughout the curriculum.

There is a thorough discussion of holiday practices in *Celebrate: An Anti-Bias Guide to Enjoying Holidays in Early Childhood Programs* (Bisson, 1997).

Classroom Curriculum

An obvious way to draw families of diverse backgrounds into their children's early education programs is by inviting them to enrich the classroom curriculum with their ideas and presence. Some parents are reluctant to come into the classroom, fearful that this will identify their child as being "different." Teachers need to be able to articulate the benefits for all children and families in becoming comfortable with their differences and similarities. What are some of the ways in which the cultural diversity of individual families can enrich the classroom? A first essential is obviously for teachers to learn about their children's families through the kinds of methods discussed earlier. Again, when teachers clearly open the door by indicating recognition and appreciation for individual family experiences, parents will likely become comfortable enough to offer ideas of importance to them. Teachers can avoid making assumptions about particular ethnic or religious backgrounds by allowing families to decide which aspects of their family life they will share.

It is vital that teachers include *all* families in enriching the curriculum, not merely the ones who present more obvious cultural differences. Parents from sociological groups that have not traditionally been involved in their children's schools or are called only when their children have problems may require particularly persistent invitations. The basic principle that teachers are trying to demonstrate is that all families are unique and special and have their own rich experience to share with others. Teachers can invite parents to

- Talk about what makes their family unique—what they enjoy doing together. Children enjoy the storytelling of family members, including grandparents. Stories about individual family experiences help children begin to understand diversity.

- Bring records and cassettes, photos, art, and artifacts of their home cultures into the classroom to share and discuss. Everybody has something they treasure that has meaning to the family.

- Share their experiences with traditional celebrations, literature, dance, and religious ceremonies by activities, discussion, and display. Because these are important to the child and family, other children will gain an

FIGURE 15-12 The class visits a family's Italian restaurant to watch pasta being made.

appreciation of the depth and breadth of human experience, finding similarities with their own experience as well as appreciating the differences.

- Cook and share recipes with the children (see Figure 15-12). A cookbook of favorite recipes from each family could be compiled. When culturally diverse foods are shared regularly, children may learn new food experiences, see how foods relate across cultures, and feel comfortable sharing their own family traditions with others without fear of stereotyping. Parents can help explain religious or cultural food restrictions followed by children in the group.

- Share maps and travel experiences with the children to enliven social studies learning.

- Help identify community resources that may help teachers plan field trips or invite visitors who can increase multicultural experiences for the classroom. (Swick, Boutte, & Van Scoy, 1995, March)

- Help teachers evaluate curriculum materials and activities to be sure no stereotypical influences creep in and to make sure all children and families are fairly represented (see Figure 15-13). Conversations about curriculum will help make sure that individual needs are being recognized.

- Help teachers interpret areas of similarity and differences to children.

Learning about diversity takes thoughtful processing after experiences. As teachers and parents work with children, they can gradually help them sort

FIGURE 15-13 Parents help the teacher create and evaluate the curriculum materials and activities as the children explore Native American culture.

out the experiences that join us together in humanity. Read more about families in the classroom in Chapter 12.

WHAT DOES WORKING WITH DIVERSITY LOOK LIKE?

It can be helpful to consider examples of programs that are attempting to work respectfully with culturally and linguistically diverse families. Two summaries follow.

Buen Dia Family School

In the heart of San Francisco's Mission District in a narrow townhouse is Buen Dia Family School, offering a full- and part-day developmentally based preschool program for about 40 families with children ages 2 years, 9 months, through 6 years. Yvonne Gavre, the director who was one of the founders of the program in the late 1970s, envisioned a familylike program that could meet the needs she felt children really wanted when they were cared for away from home: a small, "cozy" program where they could be intimately involved with activities that were important to them and where adults could help them feel important.

A visitor immediately feels the homelike atmosphere when entering. There are a couple of large playrooms in front and a large kitchen for eating, working, and displaying in back. The kitchen door opens to the backyard play area, which boasts the rarity of a couple of city trees. A downstairs area is arranged for play and more formal drama presentations (one of the two visiting artists-in-residence is a performance artist, and several parents are involved in theater and film). The director's office upstairs shows evidence of children coming in to play, read, and visit. Because some of the children are present only for morning or afternoon hours, there are never more than 24 children in the school at a time, adding to the homelike atmosphere. Each teacher has her own small group of children who come together for snack and small group conversation or activity once in the morning and once in the afternoon.

Another guiding idea was that anyone living in contemporary California should be able to speak both Spanish and English, so today Buen Dia is a bilingual program, serving a cross section of families with diverse ethnic, cultural, and religious backgrounds. A statement from the parent handbook illustrates the school's emphasis on a multicultural/antibias approach:

> We, as teachers, are constantly questioning and revising our own perceptions while developing and implementing an antibias approach in our manner of interacting with children as well as in our basic developmentally based curriculum. We all believe in the value of fairness, self-esteem, and respect for individual differences. A curriculum that emphasizes these is especially critical in a city like San Francisco with its rich ethnic diversity and where 53% of families (according to the SFUSD) are nontraditional.
>
> Our program integrates not only materials and activities that are sensitive to the uniqueness of each child and family but also includes a conscious way of being, talking, and acting according to the needs of each. We try to make the children feel good and comfortable about themselves, their culture, and their families. . . . Throughout the year we celebrate every holiday possible in nonreligious ways and encourage parents to participate in any way they want.

This underlying theme of uniqueness and acceptance of family and individuals is visible everywhere at Buen Dia. Early in the year the children bring their "Personality Bags," filled with their own special things, to share at group time. A newsletter has explained the concept and purposes of the activity to the parents; one of the purposes is to give the parent and child a time to talk together about "what makes each of them special." Parents sign up on the parent bulletin board for a time and day for their child to share with the group. In the following weeks children create a "Me Book—Un Libro sobre Mi!" On various pages children list their school friends, make their fingerprints, and glue a string that is as tall as they are. Each child creates an audiotape of his or her own stories. Some of these can be acted out at group time each day, with the child acting as "director." Staff have found this activity to be not only a valuable language experience but also a way for children to work on a theme throughout the year in safe surroundings. A book of some favorite stories is published at year-end.

A corner in the front playroom is devoted to pictures of "Our Families— Nuestra Familias." A glance indicates the true diversity of cultural background and family structure. Not only are there single-parent families, but there are also two-parent families with different- and same-gender parents, as well as families where adopted children are of different racial backgrounds than their parents. The director speaks of the school's support of the gay and lesbian families who have been part of the school's population since the beginning:

> "We've almost had to throw out all the books that attempt to
> explain families and babies and come up with our own words. We
> talk about 'home' daddies and mommies and 'seed' daddies and
> mommies, when the inevitable discussion arises about 'he doesn't
> have a daddy' or 'her mommy looks different from her.'"

A look in the display area tells of parents' involvement in the curriculum. Nahoa's father has just been in to talk about farmworkers and has left behind some pictures labeled "Farmworkers from a Presentation by Nahoa's Dad, Jesus." Another corner has a section on study of Native Americans, including a clay representation of a Navajo pueblo, a listing of the children who include Native American as part of their heritage, and the story of another father's visit to discuss kachina dolls. Such parent participation is encouraged, not required; but many parents are eager to help extend the children's perceptions and experiences of others. As a result, the children have celebrated Buddha's birthday, Jewish holidays, Dia de Los Muertos, and Kwanzaa. Every year is a bit different, depending on the interests and background of parents. The director remarks that they are careful not to assume that parents will necessarily want to celebrate a particular cultural holiday, and they ask each family what they would like to do.

Parents and children visit the center to decide if they wish to be placed on the waiting list; children are admitted with attention to male/female ratio and cultural diversity. At this initial visit the program's philosophy is explained, and it is suggested to parents that if they are looking for academic emphasis this is probably not the school for them. Many families have fees subsidized or are assisted by scholarship or alternative payment plans. (Buen Dia is a non-profit, tax-exempt corporation, receiving funds from the Child Development Block Grants of San Francisco, as well as foundation grants.) Parents sign a work incentive agreement, agreeing to work for the center for 25 hours each year in lieu of a fee. Families who do not wish to or are unable to work pay the fee. Possible activities include driving on field trips, participating in monthly cleanup days, buying food, making repairs, writing grant proposals, sewing, organizing the recycling center, working on fundraisers, and the like. Some parents follow their interests or professions for the volunteer work; a father who is an arborist is involved with sprucing up the playground, and an Academy Award–winning filmmaker mother is making a video about the school.

At the beginning of the school year there is a big open house, with teachers planning activities for parents to experience what their children do. Throughout the year there are many small meetings, usually held from 4:30 to 5:30 or 5:00 to 6:00 p.m., with parents choosing the kinds of topics they want to talk about: transitions into school, siblings, and so on. There are three big social events each year. Newsletters are sent out monthly, bringing parents up to date on past and coming events and mentioning specific parent involvement. A newsletter at the beginning of the year introduces the staff of Buen Dia—themselves a diverse lot—with teachers from Colombia, Peru, and France and of various ethnic and language backgrounds, with varied travel and work experiences. Each teacher particularly communicates with the parents of the children in his or her small group daily.

Buen Dia does not have to advertise. Parents choose this center because of the atmosphere of extended family. Parents and staff talk on weekends, are invited to bar mitzvahs, and stay involved with the school even after their children have moved on to elementary school and beyond. Some middle school "alumni" come in to work in the afternoons. Buen Dia, with its emphasis on the value and uniqueness of individuals and families, creates a supportive atmosphere for its small group of families.

Wu Yee and Generations Child Care Centers

Lisa Lee, the director of Wu Yee Centers, also in San Francisco, explains the symbolic significance of red eggs and ginger:

> "When a Chinese baby is born, there is a monthlong celebration, a 'coming out' party. Friends and family, anyone whose life touches the child's, are given eggs dyed red to signify joy and ginger root to be sliced and eaten. Ginger is the toughest root, signifying the strength and importance of the family that will hold the child secure as he or she grows."

An indication of the position of trust that Wu Yee Child Care Centers hold with their Chinese families is that the staff members are included in the celebration: Red eggs are sent for the children in the classroom and ginger root for the teachers. They have become part of the network of those who will play major roles in the lives of the new baby and the family.

Wu Yee operates three different centers in and near Chinatown, serving three distinct populations, mostly recent Asian immigrant families. The newest center, in the infamous Tenderloin area, serves mainly refugee families from Southeast Asia and five different language and ethnic groups (Laos, Thailand, Cambodia, Vietnam, and Hmong). A unique feature of this program is a home-based infant care program, staffed by a MSW and five paraprofessionals, one from each community. Most of the families in this program are considered environmentally at risk, having endured the trauma of refugee life and now living in a 16-block area that has 40,000 children, no schools or playground, and serious substance abuse problems. The mental health component supports both families and the child care center staff as they learn how to interact with each other through their cultural differences and varying perspectives.

Wu Yee Center, in the heart of Chinatown, serves primarily first-generation Chinese immigrant families. Generations, a multicultural, bilingual child care center, features an intergenerational preschool program that is the result of a joint venture between Wu Yee and On Lok, an agency that provides long-term care for frail older adults. The same building houses single-room occupancy residences and an adult day health care program for older adults who require nursing home care, and an onsite child care program for the staff of On Lok and eligible neighborhood children.

Both partners in Generations share the underlying philosophy that it is important to provide opportunities for the children and the elderly to interact and develop positive relationships that enrich their lives. Opportunities are planned for children to see the seniors both formally and informally. They visit the seniors daily in their living room, where the older adults tell stories or play freely with the children. They have a weekly "Breakfast Club" in the seniors' common dining area. There are periods when the children join the seniors in the day health center for exercises or singing. There are joint project times, such as art and cooking. Birthdays are celebrated together. A common garden bears the fruit of both elders' and youngsters' efforts. Generations values the involvement of the children's families and the community. Indeed, as the children have learned more about the needs of their older friends, they have involved their families in discussions about older people, death, and other important concerns.

For the first few days after a new child enters the program, one or both parents are asked to remain with the child and to participate in the intergenerational activities. Parents are invited to special sessions and celebrations, but because their time is committed to work or learning language, there is no expectation that they will regularly participate in classroom activities. Bringing items from home often includes parents, and grandparents may come in to offer an extra pair of hands.

Wu Yee is committed to the concept of supporting families by offering them a range of services that will meet parents' needs as defined by the parents themselves. Because each center serves a distinctive population, the array of parent activities varies from center to center. With immigrant families, many of the needs involve opportunities to learn about how this country works so parents can become culturally competent. Parents want to understand American traditions such as Santa Claus and Halloween, so a gingerbread-making workshop might be planned for December. Language is a need, so English classes are offered; parents might bring in a form they received in the mail but did not understand, and they might help each other. They want to understand the American school system and learn both how to help their children succeed in it and how to approach the school system when they need to advocate for their children.

Because of language limitations, many parents have been restricted within the boundaries of Chinatown, so some of the plans include trips to help them learn how to use the public transportation system and find places in the city to take their children. Monthly meetings are held with potluck meals and child care. Parents may get together for flower-arranging or jewelry-making workshops. When there are many languages, activities where parents can "do" may be most successful. Because most of the families are nuclear families, fathers are involved as much as their work hours will allow. Parents are involved in every level of decision making and are also asked to cook for special occasions.

Every attempt is made to validate the languages and cultures of the families in the center. Parents are encouraged to speak their native languages with children at home. Parents are reminded that the children will always have opportunities to learn English, but they must retain their families' personal values in the surrounding culture. The center staff recognizes that there are true cultural clashes when Asian parents and their children enter the world of the child care center. There are real differences between the American emphasis on teaching problem-solving skills and independent decision making and the way many Asian children have been expected to rely on adults for even basic decisions about such needs as food and clothing. Staff are sensitive to validating the strength of the immigrant mothers, who have often not had this strength acknowledged before. In many cases this means directors and teachers give up some of their power so the parents will feel strong. Lisa Lee comments that because education is greatly valued in Asian cultures, teachers are treated with great respect. When parents feel strong enough to voice a complaint to a teacher, this means they have moved beyond their cultural constraint to become assertive for their children; teachers have had to work hard to promote this idea as an attitude they will need to succeed in this country.

Wu Yee is one of 30 centers that are part of the Parent Services Project (PSP), begun in the Bay Area in 1980 and now serving families in California, Florida, and Georgia. PSP transforms child care programs into family care programs by offering a spectrum of parent support services in a "seamless" system that strengthens the entire family. Services may include parent respite, sick child care, family outings, parenting education, adults-only social activities, stress reduction workshops, skill-building classes, and leadership and training opportunities. Parents are seen as having strengths and assets—not as part of a problem or as something that needs to be fixed. The activities are seen as part of a process to create a sense of community and to diminish the stress, isolation, and loneliness of parenting. Parents become decision-making partners, choosing which parts of the services they want at any time.

Parent Services Project is grounded in the following beliefs:

1. Preventing mental, physical, and emotional stress on parents and children is the most humane and cost-effective way to build strong families today and healthy, productive citizens tomorrow.

2. One of the best ways to ensure the health and well-being of children is to ensure the health and well-being of their parents.

3. Social support networks are a crucial element in the happiness, health, and productivity of people.

Ethel Seiderman, executive director of PSP, believes that parents care and want to be involved in their children's development but are often overwhelmed by the obstacles they face. The program is a "stress buffer," and results of a three-year study on PSP indicate that PSP seems to have had a more direct effect on stress than expected. In addition, parenting classes and social support seem to alter many authoritarian child-rearing practices. Presently funded by several foundations, this pioneer in the family resources movement has proven itself not only cost-effective but an important leader in the area of changing the concept of child care to family care. (You can learn more about the Parent Services project at its Web site, listed at chapter end.)

For more examples of schools working effectively to include diverse families, see Teaching Tolerance (1997).

SUMMARY

Because culture has influenced us all in so many ways and without our awareness, working with parents of diverse backgrounds presents major challenges for teachers. Becoming sensitive to personal experiences and feelings is an important beginning point for teachers. Learning about individual cultural values, behaviors, and communication styles through reading, conversation, and observation is important. Teachers must identify and use strategies to welcome each family fully into the school environment (see Figure 15-14). Cultural conflicts can often be resolved through sensitivity, communication, and/or education.

Common issues that teachers face include dealing with linguistic diversity, deciding how to honor family feelings about holiday celebrations, and finding ways to enrich classroom experiences with the diversity of family experiences. Classroom teachers can get additional free information by visiting the Web sites and resources listed at the end of this chapter.

FIGURE 15-14 Parents and teachers worked together to create this mural that welcomes all community residents to the school.

STUDENT ACTIVITIES FOR FURTHER STUDY

1. Evaluate the forms and written materials of a school to see how welcoming they appear to be of diverse family experiences.

2. Discover the resources available in your community to assist teachers working with parents with primary languages other than English. Investigate churches, university programs, international centers, and so on.

3. Talk with teachers in early childhood programs and schools to learn how they make their decisions about holiday celebrations. Consider whether what you learn indicates a real respect for families of diverse backgrounds.

4. Devise a questionnaire that could be used with families to learn more of their ideas about child rearing and home practices. Consider also questions that could help a teacher get insights from families about holidays and celebrations.

CASE STUDY

One of the families in Stephanie Briggs's Head Start classroom this year is an immigrant family from Sudan. She is having a difficult time getting the parents to communicate with her about their child, who is often ill and seems fearful, with eyes always cast down. She brought up this dilemma in her early childhood class at the college one evening and was dismayed when several of her classmates also described families that were creating challenges in their classrooms: a family with two mothers and child adopted from China, as well as several Latino families who speak little English and seem overprotective of their children.

Their instructor asked them to defer the discussion until next week and come prepared to identify potential problems and solutions.

1. What might be several causes of tension in working with the families described?

2. What are some of the issues these teachers must consider personally?

3. What are ways that Stephanie and her fellow students might suggest to reach out to these families, creating culturally safe environments?

4. Identify two or three starting points for working with each of these families.

REVIEW QUESTIONS

1. Discuss a rationale for working with families of diverse backgrounds. What are some of the benefits for individual children? For the group of children? For families? For teachers?

2. What are some specific things teachers can do to ensure that all families feel welcome?

3. Identify and discuss the four possible outcomes in resolving cultural conflicts.

4. Discuss several common cultural issues that arise in classrooms, as well as possible teacher actions.

SUGGESTIONS FOR FURTHER READING

Ball, J., & Pence, A. (1999). Beyond developmentally appropriate practice: Developing community and culturally appropriate practice. *Young Children, 54*(2), 46–50.

Bowman, B. (1994). The challenge of diversity. *Phi Delta Kappan, 76*(3), 218–225.

Bradley, J. and Kibera, P. (2006). "Closing the gap: Culture and the promotion of inclusion in child care." *Young Children, 61*(1), 34–40.

Bromer, J. (1999). Cultural variations in child care: Values and actions. *Young Children, 54*(6), 72–78.

Chavkin, N. (Ed.). (1993). *Families and schools in a pluralistic society.* Albany, NY: State University of New York Press.

Church, E. B. (1992, November/December). Celebrating families celebrating together. *Scholastic Pre-K Today,* 44–46.

Clay, J. (2004). Creating safe, just places to learn for children of lesbian and gay parents. *Young Children, 59*(6), 34–38.

Copple, C. (Ed.). (2003) *A world of difference: Readings on teaching young children in a diverse society.* Washington, DC: NAEYC.

Davies, D. (1997). Crossing boundaries: How to create successful partnerships with families and communities. *Early Childhood Education Journal, 25*(1).

Delpit, L. (1995). *Other peoples' children: Cultural conflict in the classroom.* New York: The New Press.

Diamond, K., Okagaki, L., & Kontos, S. (2000). Responding to cultural and linguistic differences in the beliefs and practices of families with young children. *Young Children* 55(3), 74–80.

Duarte, G., & Rafanello, D. (2001). The migrant child: A special place in the field. *Young Children, 56(2),* 26–33.

Elswood, R. (1999). Really including diversity in early childhood classrooms. *Young Children, 54(4),* 62–66.

Espinosa, L. (1995). Hispanic parent involvement in early childhood programs. *ERIC Digest.* Urbana, IL: ERIC Clearinghouse on Elementary and Early Childhood Education.

Garcia, E. (1997, March). The education of Hispanics in early childhood: Of roots and wings. *Young Children, 52(3),* 5–14.

Gay, G. (2000). *Culturally responsive teaching: Theory, research, and practice.* New York: Teachers College Press.

Hildebrand, V., Phenice, L., Gray, M., & Hines, R. (1999). *Knowing and serving diverse families* (2nd ed.). Columbus, OH: Merrill (Prentice Hall).

Hilliard, A., Derman-Sparks, L., & Phillips, C. (1997). *Teaching/learning anti-racism: A developmental approach.* New York: Teachers College Press.

Huntsinger, C., Huntsinger, P., Ching, W., & Lee, C. (2000). Understanding cultural contexts fosters sensitive caregiving of Chinese American children. *Young Children, 55(6),* 7–15.

Kabagarama, D. (1997). *Breaking the ice: A guide to understanding people from other cultures.* Boston, MA: Allyn and Bacon.

Kaufman, H. (2001). Skills for working with all families. *Young Children, 56(4),* 81–83.

Klein, H. (1995). Urban Appalachian children in northern schools: A study in diversity. *Young Children, 50(3),* 10–16.

Klein, M., & Chen, D. (2001). *Working with children from culturally diverse backgrounds.* Clifton Park, NY: Delmar/Thomson Learning.

Lakey, J. (1997). Teachers and parents define diversity in an Oregon preschool cooperative—Democracy at work. *Young Children, 52(4),* 20–28.

Lee, F. (1995). Asian parents as partners. *Young Children, 50(3),* 4–9.

Locke, D. (1998). *Increasing multicultural understanding.* Thousand Oaks, CA: Sage Publications.

Lundgren, D., & Morrison, J. (2003). Involving Spanish-speaking families in early education programs. *Young Children, 58(3),* 88–95.

Manfredi/Petitt, L. (1994). Multicultural sensitivity: It's more than skin deep! *Young Children, 50(1),* 72–73.

McLeod, B. (1996). *School reform and student diversity: Exemplary schooling for language minority students.* Washington, DC: The George Washington University, National Clearinghouse for Bilingual Education.

Morrison, J., & Rodgers, L. (1996). Being responsive to the needs of children from dual heritage backgrounds. *Young Children, 52(1),* 29–33.

Okagaki, L., & Diamond, K. (2000). Research in review. Responding to cultural and linguistic differences in the beliefs and practices of families with young children. *Young Children, 55*(3), 74–80.

Ordonez-Jasis, R. and Ortiz, R. (2006). Reading their worlds: Working with diverse families to enhance children's early literacy development. *Young Children, 61*(1), 42–47.

Pryor, C. (2001). New immigrants and refugees in American schools: Multiple voices. *Childhood Education, 77*(5), 275–283.

Riojas-Cortez, M., Flores, B., & Clark, E. (2003). Los ninos aprenden en casa: Valuing and connecting home cultural knowledge with an early childhood program. *Young Children, 58*(6), 78–83.

Russell, C. (1998). *Racial and ethnic diversity: Asians, blacks, Hispanics, Native Americans, and whites* (2nd ed.). New York: Strategist.

Ryan, S., & Grieshaber, S. (2004). It's more than child development: Critical theories, research, and teaching young children. *Young Children, 59*(6), 44–52.

Swick, K., Boutte, G., & Van Scoy, I. (1995/1996). Families and schools building multicultural values together. *Childhood Education, 72*(2), 75–79.

Swick, K., & Graves, S. (1993). *Empowering at-risk families during the early childhood years.* Washington, DC: National Education Association.

Sturm, C. (1997). Creating parent–teacher dialogue: Intercultural communication in child care. *Young Children, 52*(5), 34–38.

Thomson, B. J. (1993). *Words can hurt you: Beginning a program of anti-bias education* [especially Chapters 2, 7, and 9]. Reading, MA: Addison-Wesley.

Valdes, G. (1996). *Con respeto: Bridging the distance between culturally diverse families and schools.* New York: Teachers College Press.

Walker-Dalhouse, D., & Dalhouse, A. D. (2001). Parent–school relations: Communicating more effectively with African American parents. *Young Children, 56*(4), 75–80.

Wardle, F. (2001). Supporting multiracial and multiethnic children and their families. *Young Children, 56*(6), 38–39.

Wong, F. (1991). When learning a second language means losing a first. *Early Childhood Research Quarterly, 6*(3), 323–346.

REFERENCES

Bastiani, J. (1997). *Home–school work in multicultural settings.* London: David Fulton, Publishers.

Bisson, J. (1997). *Celebrate: An anti-bias guide to enjoying holidays in early childhood programs.* Mt. Rainier, MD: Gryphon House.

Bredekamp, S., & Copple, C. (Eds.). (1997). *Developmentally appropriate practice in early childhood programs* (rev. ed.). Washington, DC: NAEYC.

Brislin, R. W. (1993). *Understanding culture's influence on behavior.* New York: Harcourt Brace.

Brown, D. H. (1991). *Breaking the language barrier.* Yarmouth, ME: Intercultural Press.

Chang, H. N. (1993). *Affirming children's roots: Cultural and linguistic diversity in early care and education.* San Francisco: California Tomorrow.

Cronin, S., Derman-Sparks, L., Henry, S., Olatuji, C., & Yard, S. (1998). *Future vision, present work: Learning from the culturally relevant anti-bias leadership project.* St. Paul, MN: Redleaf Press.

Derman-Sparks, L. (1989). *Anti-bias curriculum: Tools for empowering young children.* Washington, DC: NAEYC.

Dodd, C. H. (1997). *Dynamics of intercultural communication* (5th ed.). Dubuque, IA: Wm. C. Brown Publishers.

Garcia, E., & McLaughlin, B., with Spodek, B., & Saracho, O. (1995). *Meeting the challenge of linguistic and cultural diversity in early childhood education. Yearbook in Early Childhood Education, Vol. 6.* New York: Teachers College Press.

Gollnick, D., & Chinn, P. (2005). *Multicultural education in a pluralistic society* (7th ed.). Upper Saddle River, NJ: Prentice Hall.

Gonzalez-Mena, J. (1992). Taking a culturally sensitive approach in infant–toddler programs. *Young Children, 47*(2), 4–9.

———. (2000). *Multicultural issues in child care* (3rd ed.). Mountain View, CA: Mayfield.

Jones, E., & Derman-Sparks, L. (1992). Meeting the challenge of diversity. *Young Children, 47*(2), 12–18.

Kendall, F. (1996). *Diversity in the classroom: New approaches to the education of young children* (2nd ed.). New York: Teachers College Press.

Ladson-Billings, G. (1994). *The dreamkeepers: Successful teachers of African American children.* San Francisco: Jossey-Bass.

Lynch, E., & Hanson, M. (1992). *Developing cross-cultural competence: A guide for working with young children and their families* (2nd ed.). Baltimore, MD: Paul H. Brookes.

NAEYC. (1996). Position statement: Responding to linguistic and cultural diversity. *Young Children, 52*(2), 4–12.

Neugebauer, B. (1990, August). Going one step further—no traditional holidays. *Child Care Information Exchange, 42.*

Phillips, C. B. (1988). Nurturing diversity for today's children and tomorrow's leaders. *Young Children, 43*(2), 42–47.

Randall-David, E. (1989). *Strategies for working with culturally diverse communities.* Washington, DC: Maternal and Child Health Bureau.

Rosegrant, T. (1992). Reaching potentials in a multilingual classroom: Opportunities and challenges. In *Reaching Potentials: Appropriate Curriculum and Assessment for Young Children, 1.* Washington, DC: NAEYC.

Samovar, L. A., & Porter, R. E. (Eds.). (2002). *Intercultural communication: A reader* (10th ed.). Belmont, CA: Wadsworth.

Swick, K., Boutte, G. & Van Scoy, J. (March, 1995). Family involvement in early multicultural learning. *ERIC Digest.*

Swiniarski, L., Breiborde, M., & Murphy, J. (1999). *Educating the global village: Including the young child in the world.* Upper Saddle River, NJ: Prentice Hall.

Tabors, P. (1997). *One child, two languages: A guide for preschool educators of children learning English as a second language.* Baltimore, MD: Paul H. Brookes.

Teaching Tolerance. (1997). *Starting small: Teaching tolerance in preschool and the early grades.* Montgomery, AL: Southern Poverty Law Center.

Wolfe, L. (1992). Reaching potentials through bilingual education. In *Reaching Potentials: Appropriate Curriculum and Assessment for Young Children, 1.* Washington, DC: NAEYC.

York, S. (2003). *Roots and wings: Affirming culture in early childhood programs* (rev. ed.). St. Paul, MN: Redleaf Press.

HELPFUL WEB SITES

http://www.tolerance.org

Teaching Tolerance, Southern Poverty Law Center. Free resources for teachers on developing accepting classrooms.

http://www.clas.uiuc.edu

Early Childhood Research Institute on Culturally & Linguistically Appropriate Services (CLAS). The CLAS Institute identifies, evaluates, and promotes effective and appropriate early intervention practices and preschool practices that are sensitive and respectful to children and families from culturally and linguistically diverse backgrounds.

http://www.nabe.org

The National Association for Bilingual Education (NABE) is a dynamic nonprofit professional organization at the national level, devoted to representing both the interests of language minority students and the bilingual education professionals who serve them.

http://www.ncela.gwu.edu

NCELA, the National Clearinghouse for English Language Acquisition and Language Instruction Educational Programs (formerly NCBE, the National Clearinghouse for Bilingual Education), is funded by the U.S. Department of Education's Office of English Language Acquisition, Language Enhancement, and Academic Achievement for Limited English Proficient Students (OELA, formerly OBEMLA) to collect, analyze, and disseminate information relating to the effective education of linguistically and culturally diverse learners in the United States.

http://www.cal.org

The Center for Applied Linguistics (CAL) aims to promote and improve the teaching and learning of languages, identify and solve problems related to language and culture, and serve as a resource for information about language and culture.

http://www.ed.gov/offices/OELA

The Office of English Language Acquisition (OELA), Language Enhancement, and Academic Achievement for Limited English Proficient Students (formerly OBEMLA) provides national leadership in promoting high-quality education for the nation's population of English language learners (ELLs). Traditionally this population has been known as limited English proficient students (LEPs). OELA's mission is to include various elements of school reform in programs designed to assist the language minority agenda. These include an emphasis on high academic standards, school accountability, professional development, family literacy, early reading, and partnerships between parents and the communities.

http://www.nbcdi.org

The National Black Child Development Institute's mission is to improve and protect the lives of children.

http://www.nameorg.org

The National Association for Multicultural Education works to foster the understanding of unique cultural and ethnic heritage and promotes the development of culturally responsible and responsive curricula.

http://www.ecehispanic.org

The National Task Force on Early Childhood for Hispanics works to enhance educational achievement and opportunities for children of Hispanic descent and to influence educational policy.

http://www.parentservices.org

The Parent Services Project, described in this chapter, has the mission to promote the health and well-being of children, families, and communities by developing and expanding quality family support and parent involvement services in early care and education settings.

Additional resources for this chapter can be found on the Online Companion to accompany this text at www.earlychilded.delmar.com. This supplemental material includes frequently asked questions; chapter outlines to be used as study guides; scenarios that both encourage large and small group discussions and provoke new thoughts and ideas; and chapter resources, including chapter summaries, interactive questions, Web links, and Web activities. In addition, forms from the text are available for download.

CHAPTER 16

Working with Families in Particular Circumstances

OBJECTIVES

After reading this chapter, you should be able to

1. Describe behaviors in children and parents associated with the stress of divorce and remarriage and discuss ways teachers can be helpful.

2. Describe possible emotional responses of parents of children with special needs or disabilities, and discuss ways teachers can work effectively with them.

3. Describe typical responses of parents of infants and discuss ways teachers can work effectively with them.

4. Discuss factors that create an abusive situation, indicators that suggest abuse or neglect, and teachers' responsibilities in working with these families.

5. Identify ways that classroom teachers can support adoptive families.

Every family's situation is unique in its history, emotions, and demands. As such, there is no neat package of services or supports that meets the needs of every family at every time. Teachers find themselves working with families who have specific needs at particular times.

This chapter examines several of these circumstances and discusses helpful teacher responses. One frequent occurrence in contemporary society is the dissolution of existing family structures due to divorce. At this critical time, both children and parents need help in making the necessary emotional adjustments. Remarriage and the formation of stepfamilies is another stressful period when sensitive classroom teachers can help. Families who are providing for the special developmental or learning needs of children whose development is not typical face continual stress and emotional adjustment. Parents who are adjusting to the demands of an infant and to leaving their little ones in the care of others also have unique needs. Teachers must also be aware of their responsibilities to children and parents when abuse or neglect, substance abuse, or violence is a family pattern. And families created by adoption have their own unique situations. This list is by no means complete; there are unique concerns seen in families headed by adolescent parents and in homeless families, to mention just a few other circumstances in our world today. Teachers are in a position to help them all.

■■■ WORKING WITH FAMILIES UNDERGOING CHANGE DUE TO DIVORCE

> Dorothy Scott has recently noticed some disturbing behaviors in one of the children in her classroom. He has been quite out of bounds, almost defiantly breaking the group rules and striking out aggressively at other children. She's also bothered by the quiet sadness she sees in him at other times. She knows his parents' divorce is now final and wonders what she might do to help the family during this time of change.

The family that concerns her is not alone. Mr. Rogers, of the well-known children's television show, once said, "If someone told me 20 years ago that I was going to produce a whole week on divorce, I never would have believed them." The norm of lasting marriages has been shaken. The rate of divorce in American marriages rose steeply in the 1970s and reached a plateau in the 1980s that shows no sign of decreasing. Currently nearly one out of two marriages is expected to end in divorce (see Figure 16-1). Two-thirds of divorces involve children; over 1 million American children experience the divorce of their parents each year. Because about 50% of all divorces occur in the first seven years of marriage, the children involved in divorce are often quite young. Five out of six men and three out of four women remarry after divorce, often creating stepfamilies. Currently stepfamilies make up nearly 20% of all two-parent families with children under age 18 (Heatherington and Kelly, 2002.) Moving into the 21st century, some researchers predict that more

FIGURE 16-1 Divorce affects about half of all American families.

children will soon be living in second marriages or in single-parent families than in first marriages.

Such large numbers have led to the societal acceptance of divorce; divorced people are no longer as stigmatized or considered deviant, partly because "no-fault" divorce laws refrain from naming a wrongdoer. Though the societal stigma may be reduced, the pain experienced by children and their parents is not. In addition to real pain and disruption, common ideas about the functioning of a "broken home" may still work to the detriment of many families undergoing this transition. Perhaps the most positive way to view the divorced family is as a bifocal or binuclear family. In such circumstances children may have two homes and two major centers of decision making and activity. An important first step for teachers working with such families is to be informed about the facts concerning divorce and to examine their own attitudes and expectations in order to avoid stereotyping.

There are many myths concerning divorce and its effects, particularly on the children involved. Several researchers have in fact tracked and studied divorced families for long periods after the divorce (Heatherington & Kelly, 2002, Wallerstein & Blakeslee, 1989). In fact, a recent publication followed the effects on children through 25 years of their lives that followed their parents' divorce (Wallerstein, Lewis, & Blakeslee, 2000). Such studies contain many interesting implications for those in positions of support to families experiencing divorce.

Divorce, the second most stressful experience for families after death, is a critical experience for the entire family, affecting each member differently. To some degree all family members experience abandonment, trauma, rejection, loss of income, a lower standard of living, and change in many other areas of their lives. Adults, however, usually also experience relief to be finished with a difficult situation. No children in a recent study reported they were relieved that their parents were getting divorced, even if the parents were "often in violent conflict with each other" (Clarke-Stewart, 1989). Children do not consider divorce a relief or a remedy. In Wallerstein's latest work (2000), she challenges one of the myths about families: that if parents are happier, children will be happier also. She says bluntly, "Children don't care if parents sleep in separate beds, as long as the family is together. . . . The central moral dilemma of divorce is that in many families what may benefit the parents may not benefit the children." Whatever findings show—and they often show contradictory results of divorce—most researchers find evidence that "divorce often leads to a partial or complete collapse in an adult's ability to parent for months and sometimes years after the breakup. Caught up in rebuilding their own lives, mothers and fathers are preoccupied with a thousand and one concerns, which can blind them to the needs of their children" (Wallerstein, 2000). As Heatherington (with Kelly, 2002) puts it, "Divorce destroys the reassuring rhythms and structures of family life, especially those that give a child's life order and predictability." The divorced family is not a version of the two-parent family minus one parent. It is a different kind of family, and the entire family system is strained.

"For adults, divorce brings *a* world to an end; for young children, whose lives are focused in the family, it seems to bring *the* world to an end" (Heatherington & Kelly, 2002). This is a time of bereavement for everyone in a family; the family they knew is gone. One parent usually leaves the home and is less available to a child, and sometimes siblings may leave as well. There are no proven guidelines for noncustodial or nonresidential parents. This is an unfamiliar parenting experience for those who move out and see their children on visits.

A mother's working pattern may increase, and a family's living standard is likely to change with increasing economic stress. Although three-quarters of divorcing mothers have child support agreements, only about half receive the full amount ordered; one-quarter receive funds irregularly or less than ordered; and still another quarter receive no support at all. Recent studies have shown that in many states a woman and her children suffer a drastic drop in income; this drop not only creates a new impoverished class but is demoralizing as well.

Each family member grieves in different ways peculiar to their roles and ages. The stages of grief are similar to the Kubler-Ross model for dealing with loss through death; anger and then bargaining to find a happy way out follow initial denial. Depression follows as ultimate realizations are made. The final stage is acceptance of the loss. It is important to be aware of patterns, but not to expect all children and parents to react similarly to divorce due to individual personalities, genders, experiences, and outside supports, as well as varying ages and developmental levels in children. See Figure 16-2 to consider all the losses that family members experience.

The second myth about divorce explored by Wallerstein in her 25-year study is that the divorce triggers a temporary crisis with the most harmful effects in adjusting to loss at the time of the breakup. Instead, in her studies of adults, she points out that children who grow up in postdivorce families experience not only one loss, that of the intact family, but a series of losses as

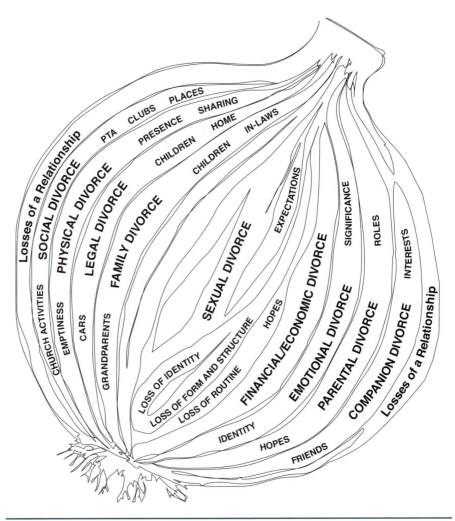

FIGURE 16-2 The "divorce onion": Families undergo many kinds of changes with divorce.

people come and go. "Divorce is a life-transforming experience. After divorce, childhood is different. Adolescence is different. Adulthood—with the decision to marry or not, and have children or not—is different." Wallerstein indicates that what may be the solution for the parents' troubles may indeed be the cause of the children's troubles—a disturbing idea for those who would like to both advocate for children and safeguard adults' rights to pursue personal happiness.

Although Wallerstein's conclusions have concerned many who work with divorcing families, it is nevertheless important to realize that there may be irreconcilable differences between parents' and children's needs. Divorce may offer adults new opportunities for personal growth and a better life, as well as bring stress and confusion to their children.

Wallerstein claims that divorce is almost always more devastating for children than for their parents, and that the effects of divorce are often long-lasting. The conventional wisdom has been that the divorcing family goes through the stress of adjustment in about two years. But longitudinal studies indicate that children's fundamental attitudes about society and about themselves can be forever changed by divorce and by related events experienced in the years afterward: "We have not fully appreciated how divorce continues to shape the lives of young people after they reach *full adulthood*" (Wallerstein, Lewis, & Blakeslee, 2000). Twenty-five years after divorce many children, now adults, feel less protected, less cared for, and less certain about their future than children who grew up in reasonably good, intact families. What they saw and experienced at the time of family breakup becomes part of their inner world. For example, violence witnessed at that time may dominate their relationships 10–15 years later. It is important, then, that the adults who are intimately involved with children realize what a critical point this is for their development.

Children are in particularly vulnerable positions at the time of divorce. As Wallerstein puts it, "In what other life crises are children used as bullets?" (Wallerstein and Blakeslee, 1989):

> In most crisis situations, such as an earthquake, flood, or fire,
> parents instinctively reach out and grab hold of their children,
> bringing them to safety first. In the crisis of divorce, however,
> mothers and fathers put children on hold, attending to adult
> problems first (Wallerstein & Blakeslee, 1989).

The mother and father may resolve this life crisis and move on to the next chapter. For children, divorce is not a chapter, but a long continuum of life experiences.

Children react with a variety of behaviors, related to their dependent position in a family and age level of intellectual development. In general, preschool children are the most frightened and show the most dramatic symptoms with separation and divorce (see Figure 16-3). Their self-concept seems

FIGURE 16-3 Preschool children are generally the most frightened and show the most dramatic symptoms when their parents' marriages break up.

to be particularly affected, with an increased sense of powerlessness. Their view of predictability, dependability, and order in the world is disrupted. In their anxiety to be sure their needs are met, preschool children may show an increase in dependence, whining, demanding, and disobedient behaviors. In their fear of abandonment, they may have trouble sleeping or being left by adults. Other noted behaviors are regression to immature behavior; separation anxiety and intense attachment to one parent; and guilt, shame, and anxiety about loss of love and bodily harm. Young children often express the denial stage of grief in rhythmic behavior, such as bouncing, hitting, banging, or kicking: Children seem to keep moving so they don't feel the pain. Symptoms of emotional stress may take the form of nightmares, temper tantrums, bed-wetting, and unusual fears. In their play, preschool children may be less imaginative, exhibiting less associative and cooperative play and more unoccupied and onlooker play. More aggression is frequently noted. Preschool children, because of the egocentric nature of their thinking, often feel responsible for the divorce and behave "better than good," fearing to lose the remaining parent's love through more "bad" behavior. Sometimes the exact opposite behavior is seen as a child literally tries to test every limit to see what it takes to lose the other parent. Even infants show behavioral changes such as sleeping and feeding irregularities, clinginess, and lack of trust as they react to tension felt at home. But in the long run, preschoolers may adjust well. They have spent less time in a family riddled with conflict; their experience in the family unit is less; and the parents themselves are younger and more able to recover easily.

Wallerstein (with Blakeslee, 2003) suggests the most helpful thing for adults to do to help preschoolers is to deal with the child's central fear of being abandoned. They can stress that the child is not losing his parents and siblings, and that he is not at all responsible for the divorce.

School-aged children may show great sadness and despair, fears and phobias, anger, loneliness, shaken identity, and an inability to focus attention on school-related tasks. The growing ability to understand the feelings and perspectives of others allows them to be sympathetic and concerned for their parents. They may feel conflict in their loyalties to each parent. Other behaviors of school-aged children may include nervousness, withdrawal and moodiness, absent-mindedness, poor grades, physical complaints, and acting-out behaviors (see Figure 16-4). Often unhealthy patterns of fantasy or anger are seen when children rarely see their fathers.

The helpful behaviors that Wallerstein identifies for these youngsters try to encourage his staying tuned in to life at school. This age can benefit as parents cultivate a sense of a postdivorce family, setting up recreational plans for

FIGURE 16-4 School-aged children may show loneliness and withdrawal.

the child and his siblings and friends. By not overreacting to angry outbursts and providing structure, kindness, and rules, teachers can help children get through it. And help is important: In Wallerstein's study children in this age group were still functioning poorly 10 and 25 years after the divorce.

Although this is concerning, it is also important to keep our perspective about this; Heatherington estimates that 20 to 25% of children from divorced families have problems, contrasted with 10% of children from nondivorced families who have problems. This is twice the risk, but 75 to 80% of children from divorced families don't have problems related to the divorce (Heatherington, 1990).

There are also differential effects seen in the impact of divorce according to gender. In general, girls seem to have fewer behavioral changes than do boys, although they may show increases in depression. These differences may be related to differences in expression of emotion and communication. In Heatherington's research (with Kelly, 2002), it is noted that "divorce is particularly challenging for women with young sons, who may get caught up in a series of escalating hostile exchanges that feed the child's anger and the woman's sense of being an incompetent parent." Gender differences also seem related to living arrangements.

Preadolescent boys generally have more difficulty adjusting to life in a family where the mother is the single parent. Children who live with the same-sex parent are generally happier and more socially competent than those living with the opposite-sex parent. Because the majority of custody arrangements place girls with their mothers, this may be a factor in the different reactions of girls and boys. However, it is interesting to note that girls who live with their mother and a stepfather do not do so well, perhaps indicating that their positive adjustment in earlier situations is related to the amount of time spent with the custodial parent. Although father custody is increasing, it still involves only a small fraction of children. Only one in three divorced fathers sees his children once a week or more, and noncustodial father involvement with children tends to decline over time. (Heatherington found that two years after a divorce, only one-quarter of noncustodial fathers were still seeing their children once a week or more; and by the sixth year, one-quarter of the children in the study saw their fathers once a year or less.) This may put boys at the disadvantage of little father contact. Studies show that boys are more likely than girls to benefit from being in stepfamilies, again suggesting the presence of a same-sex adult. However, more recent studies have found that gender differences in response to divorce are less pronounced and consistent than was previously believed (Heatherington and Kelly, 2002).

Children react best when open conflict between parents is limited and when children can maintain good relationships with each parent individually. The major danger to children is the conflict between parents during and after the divorce. The quality of the mother–child relationship is the single most important factor in determining how children feel about themselves in the postdivorce decade and how well they function. A critical factor in children's adjustment is how effectively the custodial parent functions (Coontz, 1997). Other factors predictive of positive outcomes include the parents' flexibility and adaptability in redefining roles; availability of social support for family members; and provisions for a secure and predictable environment.

Parents, at the same time, have their own difficulties. They often feel a double sense of failure for not living up to the American dream of happily-ever-after and for their unsuccessful efforts to make a marriage work. This decreases their confidence, self-image, and feelings of competence while increasing feelings of anger, guilt, terror, and helplessness. Some of these feelings directly relate to their children as they worry that they have endangered them by their actions. In most cases there is disorganization of the household; even meeting rudimentary needs seems overwhelming when an exhausted and anxious parent takes on more roles. Parents display a diminished capacity to parent in almost all dimensions, and children feel this most deeply in their heightened state of need. Frequently unavailable to the child, parents at this time exert less consistent and effective discipline, communicate less well, may be less nurturing, and make fewer demands for mature behavior. "In the first couple of years after the divorce, children have less regular bedtimes and mealtimes, eat together as a family less, hear fewer bedtime stories, and are more often late for school" (Clarke-Stewart, 1989). In many instances conditions in a postdivorce family are more stressful and less supportive than conditions in failing marriages.

Wallerstein and Blakeslee (2003) point out that parents and children have different tasks to work on during and after a divorce. Adult tasks include ending the marriage; mourning the loss; reclaiming oneself; resolving passions; venturing forth again; rebuilding; and helping the children. Children's tasks are understanding the divorce; strategic withdrawal; dealing with loss; dealing with anger; working out guilt; accepting permanence; and taking chances on love.

Factors That Contribute to Children's Adjustment after Divorce

- **Mental health of parents.**

- **Quality of parent–child relationships.**

- **Degree of open anger versus cooperation between parents.**

- **Age, temperament, and flexibility of child.**

- **Extent to which parents are willing to have the same routines for the child in each home.**

—*From Wallerstein, Lewis, & Blakeslee, 2000.*

Working with Children in the Classroom

A family overwhelmed by its own turmoil is greatly helped by the understanding and support of teachers and others outside the family. A teacher can help a child within the classroom and provide information and supportive guidance to parents in a variety of ways.

Maintain a Structured Environment

Children whose lives are in a state of transition are helped by the maintenance of a relatively structured and predictable environment. Knowing that this environment is not likely provided at home just now, teachers should work to ensure that it is provided at school. Some certainty is provided when a child's classroom world is unshaken. Keeping familiar activities and a scheduled routine will lessen some of the negative effects of a stressful home environment. As a child perceives that his basic physical and emotional needs are being met, he may come to feel personally safe. Part of an environment's stability is demonstrated by consistent expectations. Teachers who firmly and gently maintain limits enhance a child's sense of certainty during this uncertain time:

> "I know you're sad today, but we do need to pick up our toys
> before we can have a snack. Shall I help you, or do you think you
> can do it by yourself?"

Sometimes teachers feel so sorry for children and what they are experiencing that they are tempted to be lax on maintaining limits. They may feel that they will help the child by lifting the burden of limits and expectations. Although this is definitely a time for being understanding, it is also a time for gently providing consistent limits.

Encourage Expression of Feelings

Teachers' knowledge of specific areas where these children need attention comes from observing and listening to them in the school setting, rather than making assumptions about problems. Because all children have unique responses to the situation, depending on their temperament, support systems, and other factors, it would be unproductive for teachers to assume that all will need the same help or have similar difficulties. A teacher can guide children to work through feelings by opening up an area for discussion and understanding and accepting a child's reactions (see Figure 16-5).

> "It can be pretty scary not to have both your daddy and your
> mommy living in your house together anymore."
>> "Sometimes children get pretty mad at their mommy and
> daddy when they change a lot of things in their family."

FIGURE 16-5 Being able to talk about their fears and feelings helps children.

> "You're going to your Dad's for Thanksgiving? Sometimes it's hard to do new things, but I'll bet you'll have fun."

Teachers who use active listening skills (discussed in Chapter 10) to listen empathetically can help children release many pent-up feelings. This may be particularly important for school-aged children, who are often reluctant to discuss some of their sadness with either parents or peers. Some elementary schools around the country have had success with establishing support groups for children who are going through divorce to meet and discuss their problems (Beekman, 1986).

Teachers can also provide classroom activities and materials that offer acceptable opportunities to work through feelings: Clay, water and sand play, paint, family figures and props for dramatic play, and books about various family styles may help younger children. Older children may prefer to write in journals or listen to music. Several dozen children's books about divorce have been published recently; a list of books for preschool children and beginning readers is included in Figure 16-6.

Privacy and additional opportunities to be alone may help some children, especially school-aged children. Teachers may offer concrete evidence that a child is loved through touch, hugs, and smiles; but they must be careful to discern whether a child might welcome such contact, and also take care that a child does not become too dependent on them.

Teachers may discover that some young children need additional help in understanding a family's changed situation; repeated, clear explanations of information supplied by the family may be appropriate. Teachers must remind parents that they need information to be able to help a child, not because they are curious. Parents will be more comfortable sharing information when teachers have previously established a caring relationship.

Divorce

Ballard, Robin. *Gracie.*

Baum, Louis. *One More Time.*

Bienenfeld, F. *My Mom and Dad Are Getting a Divorce.*

Brown, Laurene K., & Brown, Marc. *Dinosaurs Divorce.*

Caines, J. *Daddy.*

Carney, K. *Together We'll Get through This.*

Forrai, M. *A Look at Divorce.*

Gardner, R. *The Boys' and Girls' Book about Divorce.*

Girard, Linda. *At Daddy's on Saturdays.*

Goff, Beth. *Where Is Daddy? The Story of a Divorce.*

Haughton, E. *Rainy Day.*

Hazen, Barbara. *Two Homes to Live In: A Child's-Eye View of Divorce.*

Kimball, G. *How to Survive Your Parents' Divorce: Kids' Advice to Kids.*

Lach, M., Loughridge, S., & Fassler, D. *My Kind of Family: A Book for Kids in Single-Parent Homes.*

Lansky, V. *It's Not Your Fault KokoBear: A Read-Together Book for Parents and Young Children during Divorce.*

LeShan, E. *What's Going to Happen to Me?*

Lindsay, Jeanne Warren. *Do I Have a Daddy: A Story about a Single-Parent Child.*

MacGregor, C. *The Divorce Helpbook for Kids.*

Mayle, P. *Divorce Can Happen to the Nicest People.*

———. *Why Are We Getting a Divorce?*

McCoy, J. *Two Old Potatoes and Me.*

McGinnis, L. *If Daddy Only Knew Me.*

Nightingale, L. *My Parents Still Love Me Even Though They're Getting a Divorce: An Interactive Tale for Children.*

Prestine, J. S. *Mom and Dad Break Up.*

Rodell, S. *Dear Fred.*

Rogers, F. *Let's Talk about It: Divorce.*

Sanford, D. *Please Come Home: A Child's Book about Divorce.*

Schindel, J. *Dear Daddy.*

Sharmat, M. *Sometimes Mama and Papa Fight.*

Simon, Norma. *I Wish I Had My Father.*

Spellman, C. *Mama and Daddy Bear's Divorce.*

Stern, Z. & Stern, E. *Divorce Is Not the End of the World: Zoe's and Evan's Coping Guide for Kids.*

Stinson, Kathy. *Mom and Dad Don't Live Together Any More.*

Thomas, P. *My Family's Changing.*

Vigna, Judith. *Mommy and Me by Ourselves Again.*

Weninger, B. *Good-bye Daddy!*

Willner-Pardo, G. *What I'll Remember When I'm a Grownup.*

Winchester, K., et al. *What in the World Do You Do When Your Parents Divorce? A Survival Guide for Kids.*

Wyeth, S. *Ginger Brown: Too Many Houses.*

Stepfamilies

Ballard, R. *When I Am a Sister.*

Bender, E. *Search for a Fawn.*

Berman, C. *What Am I Doing in a Stepfamily?*

Bowdish, L. *Living with My Stepfather Is Like Living with a Moose.*

Bunting, E. *The Memory String.*

Cook, J. *Room for a Stepdaddy.*

Helmering, D. *I Have Two Families.*

Herman, G. *Just Like Mike.*

Hoffman, M. *Boundless Grace: Sequel to Amazing Grace.*

Holub, J. *Cinderdog and the Wicked Stepcat.*

FIGURE 16–6 Books for children about divorce and stepfamilies. (continues)

Jukes, M. *Like Jake and Me.*

Marshall, L. *What Is a Step?*

Monroe, R. *I Have a New Family Now: Understanding Blended Families.*

Park, B. *My Mother Got Married and Other Disasters.*

Parks, C. *The Beautiful Duckling.*

Rogers, F. *Let's Talk about It—Stepfamilies.*

Schwab, L. *My Dad Is Getting Married Again.*

Seuling, B. *What Kind of Family Is This? A Book about Stepfamilies.*

Taylor, L. *My Whole Family.*

Venable, L. *The Not So Wicked Stepmother: A Book for Children and Adults.*

Vigna, J. *She's Not My Real Mother.*

——. *Daddy's New Baby.*

Weitzman, E. *Let's Talk about Living in a Blended Family.*

Wilson, J. *The Suitcase Kid.*

Zornes, J. *Patchwork Family.*

FIGURE 16-6 Continued

"Mrs. Butler, I know this is a confusing time for all of you. We find it helps children get used to changes if they get facts they can understand. If you let me know how you've explained the situation to her, I can reinforce it when she brings it up."

Encourage Acceptance

Teachers can guide children in accepting their changed family structure. In words and actions, teachers demonstrate their respect for each family, stressing how unique each family is. Books or pictures that show only traditional family groupings are not helpful. Teachers want to avoid activities for an entire group that make some children feel uncomfortable, such as making Father's Day cards or gifts. If this is just one of several choices planned for activity time, children can choose whether to participate. As a teacher becomes knowledgeable about family patterns, adjustments will need to be made.

Be Aware of Group Reactions

Teachers may find that other children in a group express or experience anxiety about their own parents divorcing or leaving. It is best to remind children that all families are different; that when grown-ups have problems, they still love and look after their children; and that they need to tell their parents what they're worried about.

Working with Parents

As teachers become aware of parents' probable emotional reactions, they will be more able to understand some puzzling behaviors.

"Honestly, I don't understand the woman. Every time I ask how Danny has been at home, like if he's having trouble sleeping there, too, she changes the subject. Doesn't she even care that her own son seems upset?"

Because of their feelings of guilt and isolation, parents may be evasive or hostile when asked innocent questions about a child's daily routine. Often parents are so preoccupied with their own concerns that they are unavailable to teachers as well as to their children. Teachers must remind themselves frequently that this does not mean they are disinterested.

When teachers are aware of parents' emotional state, they are less likely to become angry at parents' behavior and seeming indifference to their children's problems.

Reassure Parents

Teachers who empathize and demonstrate their caring are in a position to encourage parents in helpful actions with their children. Teachers can remind parents that an open and honest discussion of adults' and children's feelings will help, as will clear statements of the facts of divorce and a new living situation. Teachers can reassure parents about the amount of time needed for families to adjust; giving information regarding the grief process and positive outcomes may help alleviate parental guilt.

Teachers can provide books about divorce for both children and adults, such as those in Figure 16-7. Having a lending library of such books readily available in a center is useful.

Keep Requests Light

Teachers must be especially conscious of any requests they make. Asking stressed single parents to "Bring two dozen cookies tomorrow" or "Send a new package of crayons" may be overwhelming in light of the new strains on both time and budget.

Be Aware of Legal Agreements

Teachers should know the legal and informal agreements between parents regarding their children's care. It is important that teachers release children only to people who are authorized to take them. Joint custody is the newest family form, agreed to by parents and courts to soften children's loss. The District of Columbia and at least 14 states have adopted tougher laws in favor of joint custody.

There are two types of joint custody. The most common form is joint legal custody, in which parents share legal rights to make major decisions for children about education, religious upbringing, medical care, sports participation,

Ahrons, C. *The Good Divorce: Keeping Your Family Together When Your Marriage Comes Apart.*

Atlas, S. L. *Single Parenting: A Practical Resource Guide.*

BelGeddes, J. *How to Parent Alone—A Guide for Single Parents.*

Benedek, E., & Brown, C. *How to Help Your Child Overcome Your Divorce.*

Berman, C. *Making It as a Stepparent.*

Beyer, R. & Winchester K. *Speaking of Divorce: How to Talk with Your Kids and Help Them Cope.*

Bienenfeld, F. *Helping Your Child Succeed after Divorce.*

Blau, M. *Ten Keys to Successful Co-Parenting.*

Burns, C. *Stepmotherhood: How to Survive without Feeling Frustrated, Left Out, or Wicked (rev. ed.).*

Clapp, G. *Divorce and New Beginnings: A Complete Guide to Recovery, Solo Parenting, Co-Parenting and Stepfamilies.*

Coleman, W. *What Children Need to Know When Parents Get Divorced.*

Corcoran, R. *Joint Custody with a Jerk: Raising a Child with an Uncooperative Ex.*

Dodson, F. *How to Single Parent.*

Einstein, E. *The Stepfamily: Living, Loving, Learning.*

Fischer, B. *Rebuilding: When Your Relationship Ends.*

Francke, L. *Growing Up Divorced.*

Galper, M. *Co-Parenting: A Source Book for the Separated or Divorced Family.*

Garrity, C. *Caught in the Middle: Protecting the Children of High-Conflict Divorce.*

Gold, L. *Between Love and Hate: A Guide to Civilized Divorce.*

Gould, D. *The Divorce Decisions Workbook: A Planning and Action Guide.*

Grollman, E. *Talking about Divorce: A Dialogue between Parent and Child.*

Hart, A. *Helping Children Survive Divorce.*

Hill, G. *Divorced Father: Coping with Problems and Creating Solutions.*

Kennedy, M., & King, J. S. *The Single Parent Family: Living Happily in a Changing World.*

Klein, C. *The Single Parent Experience.*

Krementz, J. *How It Feels When Parents Divorce.*

LeShan, E. *What's Going to Happen to Me?*

Mayer, G. *The Divorced Dad Dilemma.*

Noble, J. & W. *How to Live with Other Peoples' Children.*

Prestine, J. S. *Helping Children Understand Divorce: A Practical Resource Guide for Mom and Dad.*

Salk, L. *What Every Child Would Like Parents to Know about Divorce.*

Schneider, M., et al. *Difficult Questions Kids Ask and Are Too Afraid to Ask about Divorce.*

Sinberg, J. *Divorce Is a Grown-up Problem: A Book about Divorce for Young Children and Their Parents.*

Teyber, E. *Helping Children Cope with Divorce (revised and updated).*

Visher, E. J. *How to Win as a Stepfamily.*

Wallerstein, J. *What about the Kids? Raising Your Children Before, During, and After Divorce.*

Weyburne, D. *What to Tell Your Kids about Your Divorce.*

FIGURE 16-7 Books to suggest for parents about divorce and remarriage.

and other lifestyle issues. More unusual is joint physical custody, in which both parents have substantial and significant time with their children, with time not always split 50–50. Sometimes children divide time between parents' houses by day, week, or month; occasionally children remain in one place while parents move in and out. Papers regarding the legal agreements should be on file in the school office so that school personnel know who can pick children up, give permission for medical treatment, and so on.

Although there is still debate about how well such arrangements work for children and families (Wallerstein, Lewis, & Blakeslee, 2000), sharing parenting responsibilities reflects the growing interchangeability of men's and women's roles in the workplace and in family life. Wallerstein warns that joint custody arrangements that involve children going back and forth at frequent intervals are particularly harmful to children in high-conflict families, and that children crossing the "battleground between warring parents show serious symptoms that affect their physical and mental health." Teachers need to be sure they are relating equally to both parents in a joint custody arrangement, rather than unconsciously giving more attention or information to one. For example, both parents in a joint custody arrangement may be contacted to arrange for joint or separate parent–teacher conferences. Both parents should be invited to class parties; it is up to parents to decide if either or both will attend.

Know Available Community Resources

Teachers should refer parents to community resources that can help families in times of stress. It is important that teachers remember their professional expertise is in working with children. However caring and concerned they may be about family situations, their only role here is to provide emotional support, information, and an accepting, listening ear. When parents need professional counseling to work out their problems, teachers should refer them to appropriate community agencies. Many communities have family and children's service agencies with qualified family therapists and counselors. United Way agencies may offer this information; teachers should be familiar with the appropriate agencies for referral in their own communities.

REFLECTIONS FOR JOURNAL ENTRIES

Consider any personal experiences you have had regarding divorce and stepfamilies. Identify the emotional responses of the individuals involved and how those emotions affected their behavior. Reflect on experiences you have had working with people experiencing emotional pain. How did you feel as you worked with them? What are you conscious of needing to work on to best support families experiencing divorce or remarriage?

Teachers also may refer parents to agencies that help families in economic distress, being particularly aware of state and federal resources to suggest. During the divorce and after, family finances may be a severe source of stress.

Another helpful referral is to organizations that provide support and social opportunities for isolated parents and children. One example is Parents Without Partners, an international organization of more than 200,000 full- or part-time single parents and their children, offering single-parent education and support. Many churches offer similar programs. (For more information about Parents Without Partners, see the organization's Web site.) Parents may also be interested in discovering if their community offers an organization of Big Brothers and Big Sisters that provides opportunities for children of single parents to form relationships with interested adults to supplement possible missing relationships in a family.

Teachers should be knowledgeable about their specific community resources and have information ready for referral if the opportunity arises. In working with families undergoing divorce, teachers need to be conscious of their own attitudes, values, and emotional reactions. These personal aspects can influence a teacher's ability to function well with parents and children and may cause a teacher to expect more problem behaviors than are really present. Truly helpful teachers do not get caught up in assigning blame or evaluating families negatively. Teachers should remind themselves that everybody is doing the best he or she can. Crisis is difficult, but it presents opportunities for change and growth.

Working with Stepfamilies

A teacher notices that whenever Pete Lawrence's stepbrothers visit for the weekend, the Monday after is a disaster. Pete is frequently whining and demanding, and his mother always looks frazzled and exhausted. And when Pete was asked to draw his family last week, he drew his mother and sister, then his stepfather, then his "other" father, and then lost interest in the project. She doesn't know if she should be concerned with this behavior.

About 250,000 families are "recycled" every year—created after the breakup of old families and the remarriage of one or both of the parents; from one-third to one-half of these new families have children from either or both former marriages. Most of the remarriages occur within two to three years of the end of the first marriage, when children are still coping with the pain and loss of that first family. About 40% of all families with children under 18 will become stepfamilies before the children turn 18. Such family structures can be complex: The number of possible relationships is multiplied, and the stepfamily is highly influenced by another adult or family, thus having less control over their family life. As one modern writer expressed it, "Today's stepfamily consists of you, me, your kids, my kids, our kids, your ex'es, my ex'es, even our ex'es new mates, and all the kin of these various folks. Stepfamilies give a new meaning to the concept of complex family relationships" (Delia Ephron in Hildebrand et al., 2000). This complexity is the source of both the positive and negative aspects of a "blended" family (see Figure 16-8). The very term *blended* may be part of the problem: It suggests that, as in a melting pot, individual differences will disappear along with the existence of the previous family history—clearly impossible and undesirable. (*Blended families* are families that have been created by the coming together of previously existing families or parts of them; an example would be a mother and her two children from a previous marriage becoming part of a new **blended family** when the mother marries a widowed father who has three children.)

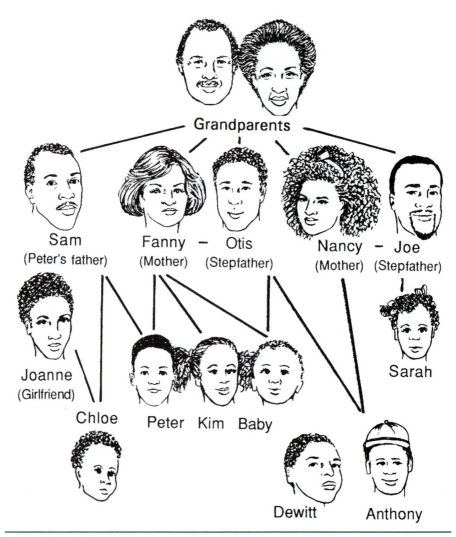

FIGURE 16-8 Stepfamilies offer children a complex assortment of relationships.

One major difficulty is that parents often feel ambiguity in their roles, unsure of when to step in or to stand back. Here the only cultural role models offered are distinctly negative—everybody remembers Cinderella's very unattractive stepmother! Being a good stepparent is different from being a good biological parent, and there really is no model for this. Parents often want to make up for the upset in the original family by instantly creating a close-knit, happy family. The stakes are higher the second time around. For everyone it becomes more important to succeed.

> All children come to second marriages shaped by the earlier
> marriage and burdened by its failure. Children of divorce are
> more eager to be loved and more frightened of being rejected and
> pushed outside (Wallerstein & Blakeslee, 1989).

However, second marriages that include children from a first marriage are more prone to divorce; 60% of these end in divorce. Differences in child-rearing beliefs and methods, friction, conflicts with other parents, and children testing the entire situation result in a good amount of stress. In Wallerstein's studies half the children had experienced at least two divorces of their mothers or fathers within a 10-year period.

Teachers may need to remind stepparents and themselves that there are also positive aspects for the children involved: They have multiple role models and an extended kin network; they may have happy parents, additional siblings, and a higher standard of living; and a new family may offer experience with conflict resolution and flexibility.

In working with stepfamilies teachers can provide similar kinds of emotional support and information as they offer to adults and children undergoing the transition of divorce. It is helpful to reassure parents that adjustment takes time, usually years, and to provide children with a secure, stable classroom environment.

Many communities may have a local organization of the Stepfamily Association of America to offer information and support to these families. (Information can be obtained from the Web site listed at the end of this chapter.)

Teachers need to be sensitive to family name differences. If John Smith is the stepfather of Billy Jones, he may not appreciate being called "Mr. Jones." Again, teachers need to learn the legalities in each family situation, including who has the right to pick up children or give permission for their care.

Teachers can help a child adjust by accepting the multitude of family styles represented in a classroom. Attention to language and the message it conveys to children is important; what does it imply to talk about "real" parents? (Coleman, Ganong, & Henry, 1984). Teachers should not put stepchildren in awkward positions by promoting activities that cause confusion. "Mothers' tea parties" or "fathers' breakfasts" can cause problems about who gets the invitation. Designating "family" events might remove this awkwardness. (If teachers are concerned that fathers will be left out, they can make this clear through personal conversations.) If children are making holiday gifts for mothers, encourage stepchildren and others in diverse family structures to provide gifts for as many people as they'd like!

It is worth noting parenthetically that many of the children's reactions and teacher's strategies would be similar for children experiencing the stress of loss of a parent through death, or even temporarily through hospitalization or imprisonment. There are obvious differences in each situation, but sensitivity to supporting children and their families at these times of crisis is necessary. See the ideas and other excellent resources in Goldman (1996), Greenberg (1996), and Hopkins (2002). Divorce and remarriage are dealt with more extensively here because of the statistics showing that most classroom teachers will likely encounter those phenomena more frequently.

■■■■ WORKING WITH PARENTS OF CHILDREN WITH SPECIAL NEEDS

> Sylvia Rodriguez presently attends the Cerebral Palsy Kindergarten in the mornings, but her mother has asked the child care program if she can go there in the afternoons if Mrs. Rodriguez begins to work full-time. The teacher in the afternoon program is concerned about this because she has not worked with a physically disabled child before.

Since 1974 Head Start has been mandated by Congress to have 10% of its children be those who have disabilities (Community Services Act, PL 96-644). With the passing of the Education for All Handicapped Children Act of 1975 (PL 94-142), which directed that all children aged 3 through 18 must be given free and appropriate education in the least restrictive setting, many teachers besides those trained in special education have children with special needs included in their classrooms with typically developing children. Working with these children presents new challenges and opportunities for all, and working with their families raises particular issues.

The same laws directed educators to involve parents in the development and implementation of Individualized Educational Plans (IEPs) for their children. The Education for the Handicapped Act Amendments of 1986 (PL 99-457) lowered the age for intervention to birth and provided emphatically for significant involvement of and focus on families as essential collaborative members of the intervention team. PL 101-576, the Individuals with Disabilities Education Act, commonly referred to as IDEA, reauthorized the Education for All Handicapped Children Act in 1990 and emphasized the concept of the family as expert in creating the Individualized Family Service Plan—IFSP. "The IFSP effectively redefines the service recipient as being the family (rather than the child alone), requires explicit judgments about the family's service needs, and reconstitutes the decision-making team by mandating family representation" (Krauss, 1991, in Smith et al., 1995). The more recent legislation, the amendments of 1997, PL 105-17, and the reauthorization of 2004 PL108-446, are continuing to strengthen and clarify the intent of involving families fully in the education and decisions regarding their children with disabilities.

The stated purposes of the laws are

- To enhance the development of infants and toddlers with special needs and to minimize the risk of developmental delays.

- To reduce educational costs by minimizing the need for special education and related services after these infants and toddlers reach school age.

- To minimize the likelihood of institutionalizing the disabled and maximize their potential for independent living.

- To enhance the capacity of families to meet the special needs of their infants and toddlers with disabilities.

PL 105-17 requires a written Individualized Family Service Plan (IFSP) that addresses not only the needs of the infant but also the strengths and needs of the family related to enhancing the development of their child. Going beyond the IEP model, where goals were often based on professionals' perceptions of the family's needs, the IFSP approach challenges professionals to develop practices that allow families to assess their own needs and encourage collaborative goal setting (see Figure 16-9). In the IDEA amendments

FIGURE 16-9 Current legislation includes families in assessing their own needs and encourages collaborative goal setting.

there is discussion of the importance of strengthening the role of parents to ensure that families have meaningful opportunities to participate in the education of their children at school and at home. The Individualized Family Service Plan requires

1. A multidisciplinary assessment of the unique strengths and needs of the infant or toddler and identification of the services appropriate to meet such needs.

2. A family-directed assessment of the resources, priorities, and concerns of the family, and identification of the supports and services necessary to enhance the family's capacity to meet the developmental needs of the infant or toddler.

3. A written individualized family service plan developed by a multidisciplinary team, including the parents (PL 105-17, Section 636). The reauthorization of the IDEA law from 2004 builds on the educational reforms of the NCLB Act, making public education accessible and excellent for all children with disabilities.

Working with families of children with special needs offers particular challenges to teachers. Because it is now common for children with special needs to be included in most schools and classrooms, all teachers should prepare for working with this special group of families. It is beyond the scope of this textbook to examine in detail the kinds of exceptionalities—physical, emotional, and cognitive—that teachers might encounter. Rather, that information will be learned in specific courses and reading about children with special needs. Our focus here is on understanding the common emotional reactions, anxieties, and problems that their families face so that teachers realize how best to communicate with and support these families.

Emotional Reactions

Parents of children with developmental challenges undergo an adjustment process that is lifelong; its emotional stages resemble the process of grieving (see Figure 16-10). The shock of learning that one's child has a disability is frequently followed by feelings of guilt, of somehow being responsible. Many parents experience feelings of denial that may take the form of searching from one professional to another, always looking for a more optimistic opinion or magical solution. Sometimes denial takes the form of projecting blame onto others or attempting to hide the disability. Anger often follows before acceptance finally takes place. These feelings are often recycled as stages that were previously experienced reappear and influence behavior. This may happen in response to particular events in the lives of children or their families, such as beginning a new school year or when a sibling is born (Gargiulo & Graves, 1991). This sadness that is part of the life of families of children with special needs has been called *chronic sorrow*. But the recognition of

FIGURE 16-10 Parents of children with disabilities undergo a lifelong adjustment process.

the presence of this grief does not mean the family is maladjusted in some way (Heward, 1996). Rather, the "grief cycle" suggested by Anderegg, Vergason, and Smith (1992) identifies three stages: confronting, adjusting, and adapting.

Although most parents of children with special needs entering school have probably been aware of their child's situation since birth, entering a classroom with children who do not have similar problems may be another reminder that the condition will always exist, necessitating constant adjustment and adaptation. Other emotions frequently experienced by parents of children with developmental challenges are frustration, guilt, ambivalence, and a desire to overprotect.

For many parents, the realization that their child has a disability is a blow to their sense of self-worth. They are in difficult parenting situations with many unknowns and may feel less than capable. See Figure 16-11 for a mother's words that describe the unknowns, as well as the growth experiences, of parenting a child with a disability.

Most parents of children with special needs live with increased amounts of stress in their lives, caused by

- The increasing amount of time and energy spent parenting their children, often with no respite.

- The economic strain of medical expenses, therapy, and treatment.

- The strain of living with complex emotions and shattered dreams.

- The isolation that results as families either anticipate or experience social rejection, pity, or ridicule.

Welcome to Holland

I am often asked to describe the experience of raising a child with a disability—to try to help people who have not shared that unique experience to understand it, and to imagine how it would feel. It's like this. . . .

When you're going to have a baby, it's like planning a fabulous vacation trip to Italy. You buy a bunch of guide books and make your wonderful plans. The Coliseum. The Michelangelo David. The gondolas in Venice. You may learn some handy phrases in Italian. It's all very exciting.

After months of eager anticipation, the day finally arrives. You pack your bags and off you go. Several hours later, the plane lands. The stewardess comes in and says, "Welcome to Holland."

"*Holland?!?*" you say. "What do you mean Holland?? I signed up for Italy! I'm supposed to be in Italy. All my life I've dreamed of going to Italy."

But there's been a change in the flight plan. They've landed in Holland and there you must stay.

The important thing is that they haven't taken you to a horrible, disgusting, filthy place, full of pestilence, famine, and disease. It's just a different place.

So you must go out and buy new guide books. And you must learn a whole new language. And you will meet a whole new group of people you would never have met.

It's just a *different* place. It's slower-paced than Italy, less flashy than Italy. But after you've been there for a while and you catch your breath, you look around . . . and you begin to notice that Holland has windmills . . . and Holland has tulips. Holland even has Rembrandts.

But everyone you know is busy coming and going from Italy . . . and they're all bragging about what a wonderful time they had there. And for the rest of your life, you will say "Yes, that's where I was supposed to go. That's what I had planned."

And the pain of that will never, ever, ever go away . . . because the loss of that is a very, very significant loss.

But . . . if you spend your life mourning the fact that you didn't get to Italy, you may never be free to enjoy the very special, the very lovely things . . . about Holland.

FIGURE 16-11 A mother of a child with a disability describes her parenting experience.

- The stress of the parent-to-parent relationship, particularly endangered by the amount of time and energy spent on the child with special needs.
- Managing the needs and responses of siblings without disabilities.

Parents of a child with special needs find themselves trying to maintain the family's integrity as a group with its own developmental tasks while providing for the distinctive needs of their child.

No parent is ever prepared for a child with special needs. There are no role models or guidelines to assist parents in modifying their child-rearing practices to match their child's special needs. Parenting is a task that can make people feel shaky under the best of circumstances; parents of children with disabilities often feel most insecure in their position.

Parental reactions can best be understood by hearing them in the words of a parent of a child with a disability talking to a group of professionals:

> It's a strange life, because I don't consider myself an unhappy person, and I'm doing okay, but there's a part of every parent who has a child who is damaged which is in perpetual mourning. . . . What happens to a family when you have a handicapped child? I think that really it is a myth that tragedy brings families together. It does not. We grieve very, very privately, and men and women grieve differently. . . . There is a certain animosity that is just there between parents and professionals that will always be there because you have these intervention programs . . . but you can't make our kids better. And when push comes to shove, that's what we really want. . . .
>
> The bottom line is, he can't be fixed. And that always makes a parent sad. And as a professional that's something you have to understand. . . . As a professional you should keep in a part of you the idea "I don't know what it's like, I have not been in this parent's shoes." And make yourself a little less judgmental. But there is this anger that we parents have because we're in the know, but you're writing out the IEPs [Individual Educational Plans], and you're making the judgments, and you're the one who's determining things. . . . There is a free-floating anger that has to do, very simply, with our children not being whole, and there's nothing really that you can do about that. . . . So sometimes when parents are aggressive and upsetting, I don't think you should take it personally. . . . I never had so many people (helping me). . . . And I can remember feeling that I didn't like it, that this was a real intrusion on my life and who I was as a mother . . . (but still) I really needed help. I need a great deal of help. . . . People who are in your profession have chosen it, and it is a profession that gives you a lot of self-esteem and a lot of good feelings. . . . *The parents have not chosen this.* No parent would choose to have a child that is anything less than normal and whole. And so while we both want the best for our child, the best program, we also have to realize that we're coming from different places. You're coming from a place that gives you a lot of self-esteem. A parent of a handicapped child does not have that self-esteem (Kupfer, 1984).

When teachers increase their awareness of these particular emotional reactions and tasks, insensitive responses can be avoided.

Parent Relations with Professionals, Teachers, and Others

Many families of children with disabilities already have an established history of relationships with professionals by the time they encounter a classroom teacher. Families of children with special needs learn to allow professionals into their lives to provide the help and knowledge they need. These families also have learned how to enter a professional's world to equip themselves to better help their child.

Some of these earlier experiences with professionals may not have been positive. Parents of children with special needs relate stories of being shuttled from one professional to another, finding a confusing lack of integration between these professional evaluations. Sometimes they feel they have only been partially informed of the findings and prognosis and have not been given complete knowledge of the available resources.

The emphasis on the team approach mandated by PL105-17 means that parents and various early intervention professionals must now function interdependently and collaboratively. "Families are being viewed as competent decision makers who must be allowed to choose their level of involvement with an early intervention program according to their values, resources, strengths, needs, and supports" (McGonigel & Garland, 1990). This stance may help parents become less suspicious and hostile when interacting with professionals, including teachers.

A partnership between parents of a child with special needs and a teacher is crucial to the child's optimal functioning. Only when teachers interact with these families do they gain valuable information about the children's developmental, medical, social, and emotional history. In addition, teachers can help parents obtain the skills and information necessary for directly working with their children at home. Continuity between home and school is crucial for the optimal development of a child with a disability; efforts to learn and coordinate similar techniques that can be used throughout a child's life are important.

How can a teacher work effectively with these families? Several ideas are important.

Treat Parents as Individuals

Parents of children with special needs want most to be treated as individuals. They want not to be categorized, but to be treated with dignity. Teachers who know and respond to parents as individuals show such respect. In fact, parents of children with special needs are more like the parents of typically developing children than they are different. They will appreciate being accepted as individuals and as parents rather than as some kind of curiosity.

Teachers who examine their own attitudes toward children with special needs and their parents will avoid treating them as stereotypes. Recall that the culture of the individual family will influence a number of attitudes about the disability, including the meaning of the disability (Klein & Chen, 2001), the family's attitudes about professionals and about seeking and receiving assistance, and their attitudes about children, family roles, and interactions. All of these culturally determined attitudes influence an individual family's level of acceptance of the disability and their willingness to participate in their child's care plan.

Focus on the Present and Future

Teachers must be aware of families' tendencies to project blame and feel guilty for their children's problems. Teachers should avoid discussing the past or the source of a child's disability, and focus conversations and plans on the present and future—what actions can best help a child and parent now and in the future (see Figure 16-12). Focusing on the present will help families appreciate children's progress and abilities rather than dwelling on disabilities.

Clarify Information

Teachers may have to reinterpret or reinforce earlier communication from other professionals. Parents who are uncomfortable with medical or educational terminology may ask a teacher to clarify the information. Teachers should remember that their function is to clarify, not comment on, the diagnosis.

Teachers working with children included or mainstreamed into their classrooms need to communicate regularly with other members of the professional team who are planning the overall care and methods of treatment.

FIGURE 16-12 Teachers should help parents focus on the present.

By speaking in plain, everyday language, teachers can help demystify the professional jargon for families. Teachers can also help families as they transition from preschool to kindergarten (Fenlon, 2005). Planning the steps for this transition allows preschool and kindergarten teams to support the family through the transition. Parents of children with disabilities often have questions about how their children's special services will be provided and whether they will have the same kind of support systems they had with the preschool.

Be Hopefully Realistic

Families value teachers' realistic approaches. It is only natural to want to comfort parents with optimism, but raising false expectations is unacceptable. Teachers should offer hope whenever possible and help parents rejoice in small successes (see Figure 16-13). Specific and frequent reporting to families

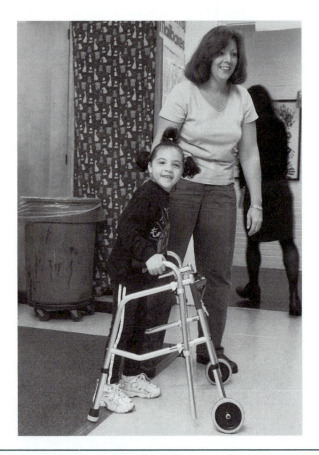

FIGURE 16-13 Teachers should help families see children's small successes and rejoice with them.

is helpful here. Teachers should be as positive as possible, striving for realistic optimism (Heward, 1996). The schools in Reggio Emilia in northern Italy have become famous for their many excellent practices. One is for the positive way they have included children with disabilities in their classrooms. They are called "children with special rights" (Smith, 1998), signifying not a position of helplessness, but rather a position deserving extra support. Surely this is an example of both hopeful and realistic viewpoints.

Help Families Let Go

Families must undertake the process of letting go, especially difficult when complicated by a desire to overprotect their children, a frequent reaction due to feelings of guilt. Teachers can have an important role in supporting parents as they try to strengthen their children to function independently. Separation and letting go are always hard, but in this case parents may experience real conflict as they perceive children's real or imagined dependence.

> "I know it must feel almost cruel to have her walk into the classroom on her own—it's such hard work for her. But the light of accomplishment on her face is worth it to see, isn't it? Good for you!"

As teachers help children develop self-help skills in the classroom and encourage children's responsibility in classroom tasks, they support children's feelings of confidence in new abilities, strengthening children's willingness to venture forth on their own. (Incidentally, in classrooms with older children who may feel particular sympathy for the peer with disabilities, teachers must also help others avoid doing too much for the individual who is striving to do for herself.)

Increase Family Involvement in the Classroom

Recognizing that parents of children with special needs often feel impotent, teachers should provide opportunities for families to contribute meaningfully in the process of helping their children. Opportunities to observe and participate in a classroom help parents feel included, as well as providing firsthand knowledge of their children's functioning and a teacher's methods of working with them. As teachers help families devise and follow through on plans for home training, parents are able to function more effectively with their children.

Teachers must also remember that there already are many burdens and expectations on these parents, so they must feel free to become involved in ways that fit into their lives. Teachers should open the door of obvious welcome and let families choose best ways to respond. In the schools in Reggio

Emilia previously mentioned, teachers try to help parents find some projects to help with so that they can feel they are contributing to the well-being of their children and the other children.

> We want the child with special rights to become part of the classroom routines, and for their parents to see their child in a more positive and capable way and to watch the child participating with others in exciting and interesting projects. Our hope is to avoid negative comparisons and to pay attention to the particular gifts and contributions of each individual. We like the parents of children with special rights to spend time at the center so they can see how their children are making friends; and we also encourage a network among parents of special children. It is good for these parents to find mutual support and to see other viewpoints (Soncini, in Smith, 1998).

Know Available Community Resources

Teachers must be familiar with all community resources that can be helpful to families of children with special needs. Parents who don't know where to turn for assistance will need teachers' knowledge for referrals. See the Web site addresses at chapter end for helpful sources of information and support for families and others who care for children with disabilities.

Help Reestablish Self-Confidence

Recognizing the social and emotional isolation of many families with disabled children, teachers should make particular efforts to help them establish social linkages with the outside world. Introducing and involving them in work or discussion projects with other families, and arranging for other parents to take the initiative in approaching them, are methods for helping these parents reestablish self-confidence in relating to others. (See Figure 16-14 for suggestions of books that may help families of children with special needs to realize the common threads of their experiences.)

Many families of children with special needs have found that involving themselves in advocacy efforts on behalf of their own and other children with disabilities is a way of feeling more powerful and able to impact the community and educational systems. Many local agencies that support children with special needs and their families find that parent support groups help parents see they are not alone. They also allow them to share and work with others with similar concerns.

Teachers who recognize the emotional reactions and needs of parents of children with special needs are best able to support and strengthen these families' abilities to function optimally for their children.

Baker, B. & Brightman, A. (1997). *Steps to Independence: Teaching Everyday Skills to Children with Special Needs* (3rd ed.). Baltimore, MD: Paul H. Brookes Publishing Co.

Capper, L. (1996). *That's My Child: Strategies for Parents of Children with Disabilities,* Washington, DC: Child Welfare League of America.

Cutler, B. (1993). *You, Your Child, and "Special" Education: A Guide to Making the System Work.* Baltimore, MD: Paul H. Brookes.

Gill B. (1998). *Changed by a Child: Companion Notes for Parents of a Child with a Disability.* New York: Doubleday.

Klein, S. (2001). *You Will Dream New Dreams: Inspiring Personal Stories by Parents of Children with Disabilities.* New York: Kensington Publishing Corporation.

Lavin, J. (2001). *Special Kids Need Special Parents: A Resource for Parents of Children with Special Needs.* New York: Berkley Publishing Group.

Marsh, J., Ed. (1995). *From the Heart: On Being the Mother of a Child with Special Needs.* Bethesda, MD: Woodbine.

Meyer, D., Ed. (1995). *Uncommon Fathers: Reflections on Raising a Child with Disabilities.* Bethesda, MD: Woodbine.

Miller, N. (1998). *Everybody's Different: Understanding and Changing Our Reactions to Disabilities.* Baltimore, MD: Paul H. Brookes.

Miller, N. (1994). *Nobody's Perfect: Living and Growing with Children Who Have Special Needs.* Baltimore, MD: Paul H. Brookes.

Pover, P., & Dell Orto, A. (2003). *The Resilient Family: Living with Your Childs Illness or Disability.* Notre Dame, IN: Sorin Books.

Pueschel, S., Bernier, J., & Weidenman, L. (1988, 2nd ed. 1995). *The Special Child: A Source Book for Parents of Children with Developmental Disabilities.* Baltimore, MD: Paul H. Brookes.

Simons, R. (1987). *After the Tears: Parents Talk about Raising a Child with a Disability.* New York: Harcourt Brace Jovanovich.

Sullivan, T. (1996). *Special Parent, Special Child: Parents and Children with Disabilities Share Their Trials, Triumphs, and Hard-Won Wisdom.* New York: Putnam Publishing Group.

York, R. (2001). *Touching the halo: An emotional and spiritual journey of parenting a child with disabilities.* New York: Writers Showcase Press.

FIGURE 16-14 Books to offer to families of children with special needs.

WORKING WITH FAMILIES OF INFANTS

Another group of families with particular needs requiring consideration consists of families of infants.

> "Honestly, that Mrs. Black! Doesn't she think I know anything at all? You should see the list of instructions she left with the baby this morning—how much to feed, when to feed, what to do if she doesn't finish it all, what it might mean when she cries. I'd be furious if it wasn't so funny."

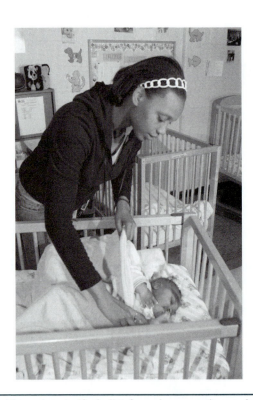

FIGURE 16–15 More than half of all infants have mothers who are back at work before their first birthday, leaving them in the care of others.

There are often strained feelings between the caregivers of babies and their parents. The inherent tension that exists between the individualized focus of parents on the well-being of their child and the generalized focus of the program on the well-being of all children is exacerbated by the particular aspects of parental development that are at work in the parents of infants. Teachers who are working with families of infants need to consider the particular emotional responses characteristic of the first stages of parenting. Caregivers also must remind themselves how new is the phenomenon of many mothers having to leave their babies early in the children's lives. In 1950 it was so rare to have mothers of babies working that the Labor Department did not keep statistics on it! Currently about 35% of mothers have returned to work by the time their babies are two months old. More than half are back at work by the infants' first birthdays (see Figure 16-15).

Reactions of Parents of Infants

The important process of attachment in the first two years of a baby's life is mutual: Adults are becoming attached to their babies, just as babies are becoming attached to the adults who care for them. Attachment is an enduring process that is both cognitive and emotional and is supported by interaction and information involving the senses. When baby and parent are attached, not only do they care for each other deeply, but they also feel more secure and comfortable in each other's presence. This feeling of a special close relationship with the baby is crucial to the beginning parent–child relationship and the optimal development of the baby. But this is also the cause for parents' possessive feelings toward their babies. They do not want to be away from them for too long and are convinced that their babies are not safe with anyone else. This is the reason that, for example, mothers leave long, explicit lists of directions that a caregiver may find insulting to her intelligence, or demand exactly detailed accounts of every minute of the babies' days away from them. It may help caregivers if they can respect parental anxiety as flowing positively from the attachment process. It is important to realize that parents are always anxious about putting their infants into substitute care. There are usually other emotions involved, too. Most new parents feel guilty, or at best ambivalent, about leaving their babies for someone else to care for, fearing that the babies might not continue to love them if someone else is caring for them.

Attachment leads adults to engage in what Dr. Berry Brazelton calls "gatekeeping"—strategies to keep rival adults distant from the adored infant. Caregivers and parents all want to do well for the child, but it can end up as a contest of who is best able to nurture or know the child. This is a sign that strong bonds are forming with the child; although it can create stress, it is a good sign. This happens within families, as well as with outside caregivers.

> Within the family, gatekeeping may look like Mother saying to father, "Don't lay him down like that. He likes to be on his tummy. Here, I'll do it."
>
> With the caregiver, a gatekeeping mother might say, "Well, she doesn't have any trouble sleeping at home on the weekends when I settle her down."
>
> A gatekeeping caregiver might say, "If you'd just burp her like I do, halfway through her feeding, you'd see that she won't spit up."

Any infant caregiver knows that you don't have to be related to become strongly attached to babies, so it is not surprising that tension between parents and teachers in an infant room may be present (see Figure 16-16). What both parent and caregiver need to understand is that warm, attentive caregiving is necessary to support the development of attachment, and it is that caregiving that should be the focus, not how much is supplied by whom. Both parents and caregivers will be more comfortable with strong child–caregiver attachments if they understand that children can love many people. The child–caregiver relationship will not diminish the connection with parents, which cannot be duplicated in its duration and intensity (Baker and Manfredi/Petitt, 2004).

Another factor to consider is that new parents are often anxious and tentative as they approach the unfamiliar tasks and decisions of caring for an

FIGURE 16-16 When all the adults caring for a baby are strongly attached, tension and rivalry may develop.

infant. Very rapidly they have experienced pregnancy, birth, and parenting, and integrating these experiences is an important **developmental task** for parents. Often they are unsure of how they measure up to the expected standards in their new role. The confident behaviors of a very experienced caregiver may increase the parents' feelings of incompetence by contrast.

Many life adjustments are necessitated by adding a baby to a household:

- New demands on time and money.
- Disruptions in the marital relationship and the smooth-running household and careers.
- Physical exhaustion from attending to a baby's needs 24 hours a day.
- Stress of returning to work outside the home.

The parent of an infant is often emotionally and physically stretched with the stress of the new lifestyle and roles.

> The growth spurt associated with the first year of parenting is probably the most intense, compact, and pressurized period of growth in a young adult life (Joffe & Viertel, 1984).

Brazelton feels that many new parents are in deep emotional trouble due to having to share their babies with others too soon in the development of the parenting relationship. He predicts two possible courses of action for these young parents. One is to protect themselves from forming attachments because it will hurt too much to care; the second is to grieve. Grieving, he claims, may be manifested by blaming, anger, guilt, or helplessness, which may lead to the distortions in behavior that infant room staff see. Child care

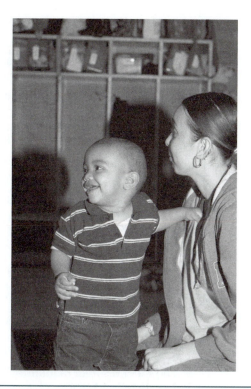

FIGURE 16-17 The relationship between infant and parent needs to be supported by the staff.

providers, then, have a special responsibility to help new parents so they will have an opportunity to move into attachment (see Figure 16-17).

> I would press for one more set of stipulations on day care for infants: that the care include nurturing of mothers. Unless a mother is included in the planning for her baby, she will feel shoved out and useless at a time when it is critical that she continue to feel important to him. If she is left out, she is likely to grieve about losing him and may begin to detach at an unconscious level in order to defend herself from her feelings about having to share him. This will make her raw and competitive with his caregivers (Brazelton, 1992).

Adolescent Mothers of Infants

The emotional reactions and changes in life roles are different, but equally momentous, in adolescent mothers. Just imagine the complexity of dealing with the added role of becoming a responsible parent when still reeling from the identity issues of adolescence. The developmental tasks of adolescence and parenthood "can easily conflict with each other, meaning that a teenage mother often will compromise one role or fail at both" (Lowenthal & Lowenthal, 1997).

The usual self-absorption of adolescence means that it may be difficult for these mothers to distinguish the baby's needs from their own. Their expectations of typical child development are often unrealistic, as is their expectation of what the baby can offer them. It is difficult for many adolescent mothers to be patient and nurturing with their children because they need nurturing themselves. Adolescent mothers have to cope with changed relationships with their own parents. Conflict is often increased by their need to rely on their parents for help with the infant's care and for help with their own financial and emotional needs while they need to establish a separate identity as an individual and a parent. There may be strained feelings between the adolescent and her parents related to the early pregnancy. Often adolescent mothers are emotionally isolated: They are separated from the lives and interests of their peers who are not parents, yet perhaps still living in the high school world after leaving their infants at the child care center. The majority of adolescent mothers today do not marry the fathers of their infants. Depending on the relationships they have with the fathers of their children, these mothers may also be trying to establish relationships of parenting with other people, who may or may not be willing to accept such responsibility.

The sheer number of identity issues precipitated by the arrival of the baby may mean that an adolescent parent is emotionally unavailable to the child care provider, who may be seen as yet another interfering adult. While needing assistance and information to care for the baby, a young mother may resist attempts of caregivers to communicate with her, wanting to prove her independence and entry into the adult role of parent. Some adolescent mothers find it easier to withdraw from their responsibility and are too willing to become dependent on the provider (or their parents), allowing them to take too much responsibility for the infant's care. Either alternative is not likely to be healthy for the formation of an attachment between the adolescent parent and infant, nor for the growth of positive parenting skills. Caregivers who work with young adolescent mothers will be challenged to find the right combination of caring and professional support for optimal development of this young family (De Jong, 2003).

Teacher Relationships with Families of Infants

Recognizing the emotional responses and needs of new parents, caregivers can do several things to form effective partnerships with these parents. Generally it is developmentally appropriate to "focus on the mother–child as a unit" (Daniel, 1998).

Support the Attachment Process

Competition over the children can be transferred into concern for the parents' degree of attachment to their children. Teachers can make sure that infant room practices facilitate the attachment process. The function of good

FIGURE 16-18 Parents should feel welcome to drop in whenever they can.

infant child care is to support a family's developmental needs, and attachment is the primary need of both infants and parents. Caregivers should be given specialized knowledge about the attachment process and should celebrate the attachment between children and parents (see Bowlby, 1988; Karen, 1994).

Parents should feel welcome to drop in whenever they can (see Figure 16-18). Many parents of infants will come and feed their babies during lunch hours or other free times during a day if they feel welcomed. Mothers who want to nurse or offer a bottle should be provided with comfortable chairs and as much privacy for one-on-one time with their babies as they would like. No matter what a caregiver's personal feelings about breast- or bottle-feeding, the caregiver's positive attitudes can be very important in supporting a mother's ability to continue to nurse even while her infant is in child care (Morris, 1995). This is not an intrusion into an infant room routine, but an important time for parent and baby. The physical environment makes a statement of welcome; creating a parent corner right in the baby room, with soft chairs and an array of helpful books and pamphlets, conveys a warm message that parents are welcome to stay. It is also very important that caregivers and administrators offer clear welcoming messages to fathers in the infant room, rather than ignoring them or including them in only a special and artificial role, rather than in the natural role of a parent learning attachment roles and behaviors (Meyerhoff, 1994).

If parents feel that routines and regulations are not separating them from their babies, they will feel less possessive in their relationships with a caregiver and reassured that their babies' care is satisfactory.

Standardize Informational Procedures

An important responsibility is to enable families to share their information and so build their feelings of competence in parenting. When parents can share specific knowledge of their infants, they can help create an individualized care plan. Procedures for passing information back and forth between parent and caregiver must be standardized and clear. Many programs keep a written record of daily occurrences such as feedings, naps, diaper changes, activities, and behavior, as well as recording developmental progress. They offer parents additional forms and a chance to record information that can help a caregiver, such as the last feeding time, amount of sleep, unusual behavior, or home routine. Keeping this individual form conveniently located—on top of a baby's cubby, perhaps—makes its use routine for all adults. When parents are convinced that an infant room staff wants to share with them fully and that the information they offer as parents is important to their baby's day, feelings of anxiety and rivalry often decrease (see Figure 16-19).

Remain Objective

Caregivers of infants need to be conscious of their own feelings toward the infants in their care. This relationship is warm and nurturing on a caregiver's part, but brief—probably lasting only through the months of infancy. What these babies most need from a caregiver is support warmly offered to a total

All About Me

My name is _____

I like to be called _____

My birthday is _____

My parents names are _____

In case of emergency call _____

_____

I like to sleep on my side, tummy, back. (Circle one.)

I hame/haven't a special blanket.

I have/haven't a pacifier.

I like to eat every _____ hours.

I am allergic to _____

I am afraid of _____

When I cry it helps me if you _____

_____

My favorite thing to do is _____

_____

I want you to know _____

_____

_____

FIGURE 16-19 Sample information sheet for families to complete.

family unit as baby and parents work through the process of attachment. The family is at the center of things, with child care being just one satellite of the services the family has chosen to use. There is no place in this relationship for caregivers who disapprove of the decisions parents have made or who think how much better a job they do for a baby than his own anxious, inexperienced parents. Parents are the primary people in an infant's life. With connotations of rivalry among adults, a baby will suffer. It is important for caregivers to examine their feelings about authority so they can become sensitive to ways of sharing power without abdicating their role. Loving caregivers realize that the best way they can help an infant is to support his parents' growth.

Introduce New Parenting Techniques

Teachers of infants should offer information and ideas to new parents. During their infants' first year, first-time parents are most open to learning basic parenting behaviors that have a lasting effect on themselves and their children. As their relationship develops, teachers should have frequent conversations in which it is appropriate to introduce ideas and answer questions subtly (see Figure 16-20). At the same time teachers must guard against overt behaviors that suggest parental incompetence contrasted with professional expert knowledge. A teacher in an infant room educates gently—as a friend.

> "Wow, we should really have a celebration today. When I noticed how hard it was for her to say good-bye to you this morning, I realized this was the first time she's done that. That crying when you leave is a good sign that she loves you very much, that all your hard work these past few months has paid off and she's become attached to you. This is a very special day."

FIGURE 16-20 Teachers can introduce new parenting ideas subtly.

Sometimes the meaningful communication can be done lightly by "talking through the baby."

> "Tell Mom how you like it when she wraps you up so securely."
> "It does make you feel good to see Mommy come back, doesn't it?
> See how she gets all your best smiles!"

Pamphlets, books, articles, and parenting magazines should be made available for parents who prefer to get their information through printed matter.

As teachers educate, they should also be sensitive to the fact that ideas about parenting are born from cultural contexts, and some practices they would like to introduce may be quite alien or even unacceptable to parents from other cultures (Gonzalez-Mena, 1995). It is important for teachers to hear parents' viewpoints as well as learn their child-rearing philosophies, rather than focus solely on information they want to impart. Teachers who are open to communicating with culturally diverse families will come to understand that best practices are not universal, but are influenced by the family's cultural beliefs. "Our ideas about child rearing are an amalgam of personal experience from watching our own parents, thoughts about how things might be improved upon from the past, and culturally driven directives that guide acceptable behavior in a particular culture" (Small, 1998). For an example of this, see the interesting discussion of differences in beliefs about infant sleep habits in Bhavnagri and Gonzalez-Mena (1997) and the more detailed discussions of ethnopediatrics in Small (1998).

As an increasing number of infants are cared for by other adults outside their homes, these teachers will have important opportunities to support families and act as resources at this crucial point in their lives. Indeed, by establishing the pattern of sharing care, rather than handing a child over to the professionals to be educated, infant caregivers can begin the precedent of reducing the distance and formality often found in school encounters.

■■■ WORKING WITH FAMILIES WHEN ABUSE OCCURS

> Every time Dorothy Scott reads an article in the paper about child abuse and neglect, she shudders. "What kind of parents could do a thing like that?" she wonders. "Thank goodness we'll never have that problem in our school—not with our kind of parents."

Many teachers believe that in their communities, with their particular populations, they will never have to face this problem. But this is simply not so. Child abuse occurs in every segment of society, among families who are just like everyone else. In fact, it is likely that one in four teachers experienced abuse themselves as children or know someone well who is a survivor of abuse.

Although reporting of cases seems to have improved in recent years due to more public information and awareness, it is still difficult to quote reliable statistics on occurrences of abuse and neglect. The most recent statistics on abuse and neglect indicate a continuing trend to decrease over the past 10 years.

Reports of abuse or neglect were made on more than 2.9 million children and substantiated on over 906,000 children nationally in 2003, a decrease from more than 13 children in every 1,000 in 1990 to over 12 in 1,000 in 2003. Experts believe that real figures are probably at least three times greater. Of these cases about 60% of the children are victims of neglect, about 20% are victims of physical abuse, 10% have suffered sexual abuse, 5% emotional abuse—certainly the most difficult to prove—and the remainder a combination. In the case of neglect and physical abuse, more than 80% of the children were abused by their parents or unmarried partners of their parents.

Experts are not yet in agreement whether children who are not abused themselves but are in homes where family violence occurs should be considered maltreated (Edelson, 2001), although many child protection agencies already treat childhood exposure to domestic violence as a form of maltreatment that should be reported, investigated, and result in state intervention. Certainly in many children, exposure to domestic violence is associated with behavioral, emotional, and cognitive problems that may last at least into young adulthood. Thus teachers should be aware that many children exposed to domestic violence will themselves need sensitive responsiveness (see Figure 16-21).

FIGURE 16-21 Schools can raise awareness of the effects on children of domestic violence.

It is indeed inevitable that classroom teachers will encounter abuse and neglect and their effects on families. Teachers must understand the dynamics of abusive or violent families and the indicators that suggest a problem may exist, as well as the legal obligations and possibilities for helping a child and her family. Perhaps even more important, teachers must be aware of their own emotional responses to the idea of abuse so they will be able to act in professional and helpful ways with the children and families involved, rather than merely react with personal emotion. Of the reports of suspected abuse and neglect, professionals made more than half, with a majority of these reports made by educators and child care personnel. It is vital that early educators perceive that they have several roles in relation to child abuse. These roles include a role of primary prevention—both by modeling positive child guidance and enhancing the development of positive self-esteem in children and by supporting parents in developing positive parenting skills. Caregivers play a role in secondary prevention when they identify suspected child abuse and report it to the appropriate child protection agency for investigation. They also play a tertiary role in child abuse prevention as they support both children and parents when child abuse has been confirmed (Pimento & Kernested, 1996).

REFLECTIONS FOR JOURNAL ENTRIES

Child abuse is an emotionally charged topic. When you hear those words, what is your initial emotional response? What thoughts and images occur to you?

List some words that come to mind when you think of a parent abusing a child—let them flow freely from your mind and pen. Now look at what you have written down; consider how these feelings and attitudes will support or hinder your work with abusive families. What will you need to do to be able to perform at your professional best?

The Child Abuse Prevention and Treatment Act of 1974 defines abuse and neglect as "the physical or mental injury, sexual abuse, negligent treatment, or maltreatment of a child under the age of 18 by a person who is responsible for the child's welfare, under circumstances which indicate that the child's health or welfare is harmed or threatened thereby." The act was most recently amended under PL 104-235 in 1996. Most child abuse is perpetrated by family members.

Physical abuse includes the deliberate hurting and inflicting of injuries on children, often becoming more severe over time. Emotional abuse is more difficult to prove, lacking the more obvious evidence of physical injury. Emotional abuse includes all acts of omission or commission that result in an absence of a nurturing environment for a child, resulting in damage to a child's sense of self. It should be obvious that emotional abuse will also accompany any other form of abuse or neglect because the explicit and implicit message is always of the child's lack of worth. Sexual abuse may include any involvement of children in sexual activities for the gratification of the offender, including sexual contact and exploitation of children for pornographic purposes. Neglect occurs when adults do not provide for the physical, emotional, and social needs that are necessary for healthy growth and development.

NAEYC has issued a position statement on prevention of child abuse in early childhood programs and the responsibilities of early childhood professionals to prevent child abuse (NAEYC, 1997). Adults who are entrusted with the care of children are responsible for their well-being. When this well-being is at risk, the law enables others to intervene on a child's behalf. In this discussion we focus on the professional's role in working with families to prevent, report, and change patterns of abuse.

What forces cause parents to abuse their children? "Child abuse is always a misuse of power—a person with greater physical, cognitive, and/or emotional power and authority controls a child in a way that does not contribute to the child's growth and development" (Pimento & Kernested, 1996). Child abuse is a complex subject; many different factors or components in the environment may come together and interact. These include social, educational, cultural, economic, religious, family, and individual circumstances and ideas. Specifically, these factors may include

- The examples of adult control absorbed in their own childhoods.
- The cultural messages of the individual community about the responsibilities and styles of "good parents."
- The lack of child development knowledge and skills.
- Religious teaching that children are inherently evil and must be broken in spirit.
- The isolation of a family that has moved too many times to develop supports.
- A rigid and demanding personality in a parent or a difficult child.

> Abuse is insidious and continues in the fabric of families for generations—abused children become abusive adults or the victims of other abusers later in their lives. Abuse is an infection coloring the feelings and attitudes of families, and it destroys normal relationships for the entire family (Barbour & Barbour, 2004).

Although it is true that many children who were abused become abusive parents themselves, it is also true that many children who were abused can, with conscious effort, support, and education, become excellent parents who move beyond abuse and offer positive examples of nonviolent guidance to their own children (see Figure 16-22).

Precipitating Circumstances

In most cases the personality potentials for both parent and child are present, but a crisis event is needed before a parent loses control and abuse occurs.

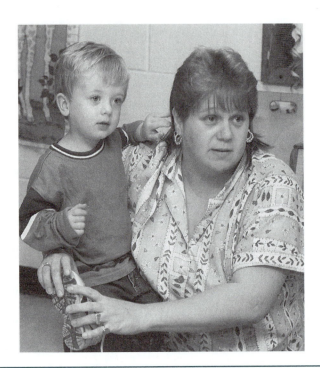

FIGURE 16-22 Parents who were themselves abused can break the cycle of abuse with education and support.

Often a family undergoes too much change too fast, with no time to recover before being hit by a new crisis. The crisis may be *economic*—loss of a job, financial problems; it may be *personal*—desertion by a spouse or other marital problems, death of a family member or other transitional events; it may be the *perception* that a child needs extraordinarily strong discipline; it may be *environmental*—a move, substance abuse, inadequate housing, the washing machine breaking down. Whatever it is, however remote from the child, this event is the last straw, and a parent loses control. Because these are circumstances that know no socioeconomic or cultural barrier, abusive situations are found in every stratum of society.

Indicators of Abuse and Neglect

Physical Abuse

There are four general groups of injuries that may result from physical abuse (Ayoub et al., in Pimento & Kernested, 1996). These include injuries to the skin and soft undertissues, including bruises, abrasions, bites, and burns; injuries to the skeletal system from direct blows or from shaking or squeezing; injuries to the head and central nervous system from being shaken or choked; or internal injuries from being punched, kicked, or thrown. Teachers might see signs like the following.

Physical Indicators of Physical Abuse

- Unexplained bruises or welts, especially in places where a child's physical activity cannot account for them: on the face, throat, upper arms, buttocks, thighs, backs of knees, or lower back.
- Bilateral marks or those with unusual patterns that suggest the use of an instrument (belt buckle or electrical cord).
- Unexplained small burns as might be made by match or cigarette, especially on palms, soles of feet, abdomen, or buttocks.
- Immersion burns, producing marks like socks or gloves on feet or hands, or a doughnut-shaped burn on buttocks.
- Rope burns.
- Infected burns, indicating a delay in treatment.

Behavioral Indicators of Physical Abuse

- Wearing inappropriate clothing to cover physical indicators.
- Inappropriate, excessive fear of parent or caretaker.
- Unbelievable, inconsistent explanations for injuries.
- Unusual shyness and wariness of physical contact.
- Extremes of behavior—withdrawal, aggression, regression, depression.
- (Infant) lies unusually still while surveying surroundings.

Sexual Abuse

Physical Indicators of Sexual Abuse

- Stained or bloody underwear.
- Difficulty sitting or walking.
- Frequent unexplained sore throats or yeast or urinary infections.
- Somatic complaints, including pain and irritation of genitals.
- Sexually transmitted diseases or pregnancy.

Behavioral Indicators of Sexual Abuse

- Disclosure.
- Regressive behavior, such as thumb sucking, wetting, fear of dark.
- Disturbed sleep patterns and recurring nightmares.
- Unusual or age-inappropriate interest in sexual matters.
- Avoidance of undressing or wearing extra layers of clothing.
- Sudden decrease in school performance or truancy.
- Promiscuity or seductive behavior.

Emotional Abuse

Physical Indicators of Emotional Abuse

- Eating disorders—obesity or anorexia.
- Speech disorders—stuttering or stammering.
- Developmental delays in speech or motor skills.
- Weight or height substantially below norm.
- Nervous disorders—rashes, hives, tics, stomachaches.
- (Infants) flat or bald spots on head.

Behavioral Indicators of Emotional Abuse

- Habit disorders—biting, rocking, head banging.
- Cruel behaviors—taking apparent pleasure in hurting animals, children, adults.
- Age-inappropriate behaviors—wetting or soiling.
- Behavioral extremes—listless/excitable, overly compliant/defiant.

Neglect

Physical Indicators of Neglect

- Poor hygiene, including lice, scabies, severe diaper rash, body odor.
- Squinting.
- Clothing unsuitable for weather, or missing key items of clothing.
- Untreated injury or illness.
- Lack of immunizations.
- Height and weight significantly below age norms.

Behavioral Indicators of Neglect

- Unusual school attendance and absenteeism.
- Chronic hunger, tiredness, lethargy.
- Begging for food.
- Report of no caretaker at home.

Abuse and neglect may include any or all of these indicators and are not limited to these.

The Teacher's Role

When a teacher suspects abuse or neglect in a family situation, several courses of action are indicated. Information gathering and clarifying should occur

---

Questions Teachers Can Ask Themselves

- Does the child have a low threshold for frustration, crying over tiny difficulties?

- Does the child's mood shift abruptly without apparent reason?

- Do the parents appear to be hiding something? Do they deny or minimize any observable injuries or give explanations that do not seem plausible?

- Does the child appear withdrawn or depressed or have difficulty making friends?

- Does the child threaten or bully to get his way? Is the child timid, passive, or fearful with peers?

- Is the child apprehensive about going home? Does the child express a wish that you were his parent?

- Does the child appear sleepy or lethargic at school?

- Does child frequently have stomachaches or headaches?

- Does the child seem preoccupied or startle easily?

—*Adapted from Kearney, 1999.*

---

continually as teachers try to determine if there is cause for concern. Teachers can ask for explanations of injuries or appearances, neutrally inquiring, "What happened to your knee?" or "What did the doctor say about the bruises?" so that the child or parent may explain the situation without being put on the defensive. Parental responses may either confirm teacher suspicions or resolve the question. The director or principal should have an opportunity to observe the concerning injury or behavior.

Document Evidence

When teachers become aware of possible abuse and neglect, they must document what they see. Such records indicate patterns for teachers and administrators and may determine their next actions. Documentation is to substantiate any suspicions with recorded evidence and is useful to an investigator. Many schools or programs will have their own forms for such documentation. Otherwise, simple, objective descriptions are all that is required, including the child's full name, the date when the information was recorded, and the date when the observation occurred. Include also the verbatim conversations held with the child or the parent. If concerns are removed after clarification with the family, documentation may be the only step to take at this time.

> November 18. Two large bruises, on each upper arm, including distinct finger marks.
> December 3. Bright red welts on backs of legs. Child reports father was very angry previous night.

Report to Proper Agencies

Laws in all states and provinces mandate teachers to report cases of suspected abuse and similarly obligate child care workers in most areas. Teachers should check their local regulations for current laws and the appropriate protective agency to which to report. In addition to the mandate of law, the NAEYC Code of Ethical Conduct (1998) clearly states obligations for early childhood professionals. Under the section regarding ethical responsibilities to children, the following principles are directly related:

> P-1.5 We shall be familiar with the symptoms of child abuse, including physical, sexual, verbal, and emotional abuse, and neglect. We shall know and follow state laws and community procedures that protect children against abuse and neglect.

> P-1.6 When we have reasonable cause to suspect child abuse or neglect, we shall report it to the appropriate community agency and follow up to ensure that appropriate action has been taken. When appropriate, parents or guardians will be informed that the referral has been made.

> P-1.7 When another person tells us of a suspicion that a child is being abused or neglected, we shall assist that person in taking appropriate action to protect the child.

> P-1.8 When a child protective agency fails to provide adequate protection for abused or neglected children, we acknowledge a collective ethical responsibility to work toward improvement of these services.

In reporting, the burden of proof is not on teachers, but on the protective services agency to whom teachers must report; if a report of suspected abuse or neglect is made in good faith (contrasted with the malicious intention of a parent who is trying to discredit another in a custody battle, for example), the reporting adult is protected from liability.

There are instances of teachers and schools who try to ignore the problems they suspect or see in families, perhaps fearing reprisals or parents' anger if they involve themselves in "family matters." Teachers need to accept their responsibility as perhaps the only people who know what is going on with some children and their families and as the only outside advocates a child might have. Teachers need to realize their own legal and moral responsibilities even if they discover their school's policies discourage such active advocacy roles. The Code of Ethics makes it absolutely clear that early childhood professionals have a definite responsibility to act to protect children, and that this responsibility takes precedence over other responsibilities to employers or families (P1.1, Code of Ethics):

> Above all, we shall not harm children. We shall not participate in practices that are disrespectful, degrading, dangerous, exploitative, intimidating, psychologically damaging, or physically harmful to children. **This principle has precedence over all others in this Code.**

When reports are made, they should include the child's and parents' full names and addresses; the child's age, sex, and birth date; the name and address of the person making the report; and the name, address, and telephone number of the child care center. Professionals should realize that less attention is usually paid to anonymous reports, according to some overworked caseworkers.

Examine Personal Attitudes

Teachers need to examine their own attitudes to be able to work with these families. Many teachers feel great anger toward parents who hurt their small children or expose them to adult violence. It is important to recognize the existence of this anger and to work especially hard to get to know parents and the circumstances of their parenting in order to develop true empathy for their situations. It is more appropriate for teachers to release some of their negative feelings in conversation with colleagues, rather than with parents, because parents are themselves in need of nurturing and acceptance, not expressions of anger. It is important to remember, however, that confidential material or statements that have not yet been confirmed must be treated with utmost care and professional responsibility for privacy. A family's reputation could be damaged by thoughtless comments or casual display of papers.

Create an Atmosphere of Trust and Healing

Teachers' concern and caring for children in these troubled families enable them to support children through difficult times. It helps these children to know teachers care for them, are dependable and trustworthy, and are concerned enough to help them and their parents. Such an atmosphere of trust may free children to confide their problems and allow them to feel confident in the ability of other adults to help them and their parents. Children need allies in the classroom who can help them express their anger safely (Caughey, 1991). Play is a vehicle that helps build trust as teachers accept the children's self-expression. These children do not need to hear condemnation of their angry feelings or of their parents, who are the most important people in their lives no matter how troubled at this time.

Teachers can also comfort themselves in the knowledge that they are providing an important model for children, helping them to realize that not all adults are abusive. All of this is true whether the children have been abused themselves or have witnessed abuse and violence directed toward someone they love. Children who have been exposed to violence or neglect have experienced a world in which important adults have not guaranteed their safety and well-being. Coming daily to a classroom with different adults who provide a safe and predictable environment can help them experience security. Classroom teachers need to realize the importance of unvarying routines and gentle limits in helping these children to make sense of their world and make the classroom an emotionally safe place. Teachers need to be careful to alert these children to any changes in the class schedule, discussing any new or different procedures and preparing them for the presence of new people in the classroom. Teachers should maintain calm and cheerful voices.

Just as young children are particularly vulnerable to the effects of abuse and neglect, even to the alteration of brain development, so too are they capable of **resilience** and healing in supportive environments. They need the support and reassurance of caring adults and tools and activities to allow them to transform their memories of fear and helplessness, choosing symbolic ways to control the ways the adults in their memories act and talk. Healing activities may include imaginative play, art and creative activities, or literary experiences. A number of children's books can help children identify with others' pain and hope for the future. See the list of book suggestions in Figure 16-23. The adult's role is not to be that of a play or art therapist; the children are themselves capable of processing their own grief, anger, and fears in a supportive environment.

Teachers can support children's progress in self-healing activities by posing open-ended questions such as these:

"What happens next?"

"I wonder what the baby would like to happen differently?"

"What makes your dolly happy?"

Healing activities are not used to get information for reports. Rather, they are opportunities for children to process painful memories and experiences in a supportive and caring classroom environment.

Helpful Behaviors for Teachers Who Become Aware of Abuse

- Remain calm and reassuring.
- Listen without judgment, paying close attention.
- Speak with children privately, positioning yourself at eye level.
- Take the child seriously.
- Allow the child to have feelings.
- Reassure the child that the abuse is not the child's fault.
- Refrain from using "why" questions.
- Do not condemn the abuser.
- Assure the child that he or she is not alone.
- Tell the truth, and don't make promises you cannot keep.
- Inform the child of process that must be followed to help keep him or her safe.
- Let the child know you are going to help.

—*Adapted from Austin, 2000.*

Refer Families to Support Groups

Many communities offer agencies and groups to support families under stress. If teachers know these community resources, they can refer parents on a preventive basis or reassure them after a court's referral. Many agencies, such as the Family Center in Charlotte, North Carolina, offer support to families in the form of therapy, a 24-hour stress telephone line staffed by trained volunteers, and reparenting education for parents who have abused. One method found to be effective is to give families a "parent aide"—a parent, trained in counseling skills, who makes home visits and models positive and appropriate ways to interact with children.

In recent years courts have tended to be less punitive with parents and have concentrated on efforts to help families learn alternative methods of discipline and appropriate expectations. Teachers can wholeheartedly support such efforts. There are benefits for an entire family when families learn new methods of parenting.

Support for these efforts can also come from families who have experienced similar problems. Many communities have a local group of the national

Parents Anonymous organization, whose members are formerly abusive parents who meet to encourage each other in their attempts to change their behavior. For more information about this organization, see the Web address at the end of this chapter.

Working with Substance-Abusing Families and Their Children

Related to the topic of abuse and neglect is the topic of substance abuse in the adults of a family. In fact, an estimated 40–80% of the families who become child protective services cases have problems with alcohol or drugs (Child Welfare League of America, 2004). Children in homes where substances are abused are three times as likely to be abused and four times as likely to be neglected as in homes without substance abuse. When parents are addicted to alcohol or other drugs, it means that " . . . their primary relationship is with their drug, not their child. Their lives become organized around getting their drug, not caring for their children" (Rice & Sanoff, 1998). When parents abuse drugs and alcohol, their children are in an emotionally neglectful environment and are at risk for physical neglect and abuse (Thompson, 1998).

Early childhood professionals can help these families. For parents trying to recover from addiction, it is important that caregivers understand the nature of addiction and the lifetime recovery process. While other professionals will work with the parents on the specifics of their addiction, caregivers can also be involved in a caring, therapeutic type of relationship, nurturing the parent because of concern for the child. When they suspect substance abuse may be a family problem, caregivers must turn to supervisors and other community resources, recognizing the limits of their roles and expertise. Caregivers can learn about referral sources for substance abuse treatment programs in the community and post information about Alcoholics Anonymous and other recovery meeting groups.

With the children of these families, teachers can make a difference in providing an emotionally safe environment that children can learn to trust. They help when they provide daily routines, consistency, and firm boundaries in a world where children can count on little and may have taken on too much responsibility for themselves (Thompson, 1998). Teachers can provide materials and opportunities for therapeutic play, as in art expression and sensitive dramatic play. They can acknowledge children's feelings so children learn to express the emotions they have kept pent up. They may read books about children in families with substance abuse and other sensitive issues, perhaps helping children to tell their own stories to an understanding adult (see Figure 16-23). These books are appropriate for reading privately with a child affected by the abuse or violence. Above all, teachers must recognize the need to support the whole family during a difficult journey. The reality is that child abuse and neglect, family violence, and substance abuse are problems many teachers will encounter. The best scenario is for teachers to be able to recognize signs of distress

Al-Anon Family Group. *What's Drunk Mama?*

Bass, E., et al. *I Like You to Make Jokes with Me, but I Don't Want You to Touch Me.*

Behm, B. *Tears of Joy.*

Boyd, C., & Cooper, F. *Daddy, Daddy, Be There.*

Bernstein, S. *A Family That Fights.*

Carrick, C. *Banana Beer.*

Cavaciuti. *Someone Hurt Me.*

Clifton, L. *One of the Problems of Everett Anderson.*

Davis, D. *Something Is Wrong at My House.*

DiGiovanni, K. *My House Is Different.*

Girard, L. *My Body Is Private.*

Havelin, K. *Child Abuse: Why Do My Parents Hit Me?*

Hornbum, T. *Hear My Roar: A Story of Family Violence.*

Jessie. *Please Tell! A Child's Story about Sexual Abuse.*

Katz, I., et al. *Sarah.*

Kehoe, P. *Something Happened and I'm Scared to Tell: A Book for Young Victims of Abuse.*

Klassen, H. *I Don't Want to Go to Justin's House Any More.*

Kleven, S. *The Right Touch: A Read Aloud Story to Help Prevent Child Sexual Abuse.*

McAndrew, L. *Little Flower: A Story for Children.*

Otto, M. *Never, No Matter What.*

Paris, S. *Mommy and Daddy Are Fighting.*

Porett, J. *When I Was Little Like You.*

Sanford, D. *I Know the World's Worst Secret: A Child's Book about Living with an Alcoholic Parent.*

Spelman, C. *Your Body Belongs to You.*

Stanek, M. *Don't Hurt Me Mama.*

Vigna, J. *I Wish Daddy Didn't Drink So Much.*

———. *My Big Sister Takes Drugs.*

Williams, C. *The True Colors of Caitlynne Jackson.*

Winn, C., & Walsh, D. *Clover's Secret.*

FIGURE 16-23 Books to read with children about abuse, substance abuse, and violence in the family.

and problems, to know their legal and moral obligations and their community resources, and to support families through the agonizing process of evaluation and reconstruction. Building a caring relationship with families is the best gift a teacher can give to an abused child.

▌▌▌ WORKING WITH ADOPTIVE FAMILIES

As we have discussed throughout this book, every family is unique in its situation, history, and structure. Adoptive families are created by legal agreement, not by biological ties. Parents frequently receive little notice that a child is available for adoption, often after long waiting periods and even longer preceding periods of attempting to conceive a child. Adoptive families are diverse in many ways (Hunt, 2003). Adoptive families are often multiracial, with the rate of transracial adoption doubling in recent years to more than 15% in 2000. International adoption has seen enormous growth in the same period, with more than 20,000 in 2002 (see Figure 16-24). Single-parent adoption is on the rise as well, accounting for one-third of all adoptions in 2000, and many

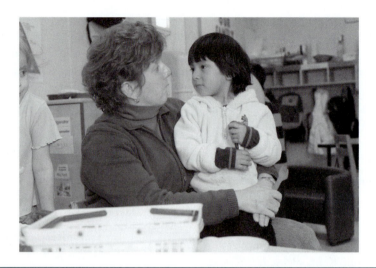

FIGURE 16-24 International adoptions create many new families.

gay and lesbian adoptions are included in that number. Adoptions from foster care have risen, often initiated by black or Latino parents, as well as by parents who are not affluent. And stepchild adoptions are common across racial groups and socioeconomic classes. Sometimes older children who are adopted into families have already experienced difficulties such as death of parents, abuse, neglect, abandonment, or leaving a home or country. Such circumstances create adjustment difficulties for children and their adoptive parents. Although a minority of families in a classroom, these families deserve sensitive and supportive responses from classroom teachers.

What are some things that classroom teachers can do?

Know the Facts

Teachers and administrators need to support parents in the information they have given to their children. "Thinkers and leaders in the field of adoption teach that the more openness and education there is about adoption issues, the better off everyone will be" (Greenberg, 2001). Programs generally need to explain that they are as open with children about adoption as about the myriad other different situations that children live in and may have questions about. Nevertheless, they must be sensitive to information that individual families consider private.

Admission information forms need to have a place to include adoption information about this child or other siblings that may be adopted. Teachers must also be sure to find out whether the child knows this, how questions have been answered at home, and whether people in the community are aware of information that the child is not aware of. Greenberg suggests making the comment, "I'd love to hear how you've been telling Annie her adoption story." This is obviously a sensitive area that some parents may be reluctant to answer; teachers must explain to parents their need for information to be sure they are supporting children's comfort and also not lying to children.

"Adopted children should know they are adopted. . . . They need to know as much of their history as is appropriate for their development, told in a way that is respectful of them, of their genetic parents, and of their adoptive parents" (Munsch, 1992). Teachers may have had personal experience with adoption through their own family backgrounds, and may need to focus on their own comfort level before helping children explain their circumstances to other children and adults. There are myths and fears about adoption, and teachers need to be sure they are doing nothing to increase these fears.

Include Adoption in the Curriculum

When topics such as babies, family trees, types of families, and family resemblance arise in the early childhood classroom, teachers need to include adoption as a concept for children to understand whether or not there are adopted children in the classroom. The school's task is to normalize children's thinking about the many different kinds of families that exist by promoting discussion and activities that allow children to experience the diversity in family structure and appearance. Children's books (see Figure 16-25) about adoption can help children understand that all children deserve parents who can look after them, and that there are both joy and pain in adoption. Modern books focus on honest, sensitive approaches that look at both children's and adults' feelings.

Teachers should be aware that some adopted children will not necessarily have photos of themselves as babies, and plan accordingly when using family materials in curricula. The once common assignment in elementary schools of creating family trees or interviewing grandparents for information about family heritage can give way to choices for all students such as "Circles of Caring" as a more flexible way of tracing family relationships (Hunt, 2003). This activity accommodates variety in all families, not just adoptive families, by putting the child's name in the center of the page, rather than the traditional format that assumes one father and one mother in each generation. This allows the tree to connect all the important people to the child, allowing room for diverse family formats, including birth parents (or not).

Some parents whose children are adopted from other countries or cultures may welcome the opportunity to include their children's native cultures in classroom activities. These experiences expand children's thinking about the complex subject of families.

Talking to Families

Heightening their awareness of parental feelings regarding adoption may help teachers prevent insensitive communication. These parents cannot have their relationship to their children affirmed by appearance: "Your son is certainly the image of his dad." Instead their relationship must be affirmed in less

Banish, R., & Jordan-Wong, J. *A Forever Family.*

Bunin, Catherine and Sherry. *Is That Your Sister?*

Burwash, L. *All about Me: Adopted and Special; An Interactive Tool for Parents and Children.*

Cole, J. *How I Was Adopted: Samantha's Story.*

Cosby, E. *A Is for Adopted.*

Curtis, J. L. *Tell Me Again: About the Night I was Born.*

D'Antonio, N. *Our Baby from China: An Adoption Story.*

Girard, L. *Adoption Is for Always.*

———. *We Adopted You, Benjamin Koo.*

Kasza, K. *A Mother for Choco.*

Katz, K. *Over the Moon: An Adoption Tale.*

Keller, H. *Horace.*

Koehler, P. *The Day We Met You.*

Kroll, V. *Beginnings: How Families Come to Be.*

Lewis, R. *I Love You Like Crazycakes.*

Lifton, B. *Tell Me a Real Adoption Story.*

Livingston, C. *Why Was I Adopted?*

London, J. *A Koala for Katie: An Adoption Story.*

McCutcheon, J. *Happy Adoption Day.*

Miller, K. *Did My First Mother Love Me?*

Mora, P. *Pablo's Tree.*

Nystrom, C. *Mario's Big Question.*

Peacock, C. *Mommy Far, Mommy Near: An Adoption Story.*

Rogers, F. *Adoption.*

Schwartz, P. *Carolyn's Story: A Book about an Adopted Girl.*

Sobol, H. *We Don't Look Like Our Mom and Dad.*

Stanley, D. *The Mulberry Bird: An Adoption Story.*

Stinson, K. *Steven's Baseball Mitt: A Book about Being Adopted.*

Turner, A. *Through the Moon and Stars and Night Skies.*

Wright, Susan. *Real Sisters.*

See also Miles, Susan G. *Adoption Literature for Children and Young Adults: An Annotated Bibliography.* New York: Greenwood Press, 1991.

FIGURE 16-25 Books for children about adoption.

concrete ways: "The baby really watches you." "Your son really enjoys spending time with you."

Talking about "real" parents is insulting to adoptive families who *are* real parents. Instead, where necessary, teachers can refer to "birth" or "biological" parents and "forever" parents, all of whom are real.

Many adoptive families have limited information about their children's backgrounds or their lives before adoption. Teachers should make it clear that they welcome any information parents can give them, but that they are focusing on helping the child and family in the current adjustment. Parents may understandably feel sad or even guilty that there are gaps in their knowledge of the child. In many of the adjustments that occur in families after adoption, parents may feel frightened, worried, angry, and stressed in the new situation. Teachers can help best by providing a supportive listening ear.

As newly adoptive parents are getting to know their children day by day, teachers can assist by sharing objective observations and specific information about what the child is like while under their care. Often newly adopted children may show great problems with separation. Having already, perhaps, experienced the loss of significant adults, they may understandably be less than trusting when they see their new adults depart. Families are often very reluctant to cause their children additional pain and will need teacher support through the difficult adjustment process. Help parents understand that their predictable leaving and return will eventually help the children learn to trust again. Both parents and children will need particular attention while working on this task.

Talking with Children

Teachers should be emotionally and cognitively prepared to answer questions from children who have not been adopted as well as from adopted children. Children might wonder

- Why do families give up their children?
- Will it happen to me?
- Will it happen again?
- Why don't I look like my parents?
- What was so bad about me that my mother didn't want me?
- Why didn't her real mother want her?
- Why is his skin a different color than his mom and dad?

Knowing that questions can create doubt about self and identity for adopted children if not answered helpfully, teachers can be very supportive here, talking acceptingly and matter-of-factly about these issues. Phrases and responses that teachers might use include these:

- "Being adopted means Lena had another mother before, but her first mommy couldn't take care of her, so Mrs. Peters is Lena's mommy now."
- "Children need to have families who can look after them."
- "Real parents are the ones who feed you and put you to bed and take you places and live with you while you grow up" (Munsch, 1992).
- "Grown-ups sometimes aren't able to take care of their babies, so they make a plan to find a family to love and take care of the baby."

Offer Resources

Knowledgeable teachers can assist family adjustment by providing books (see Figure 16-26), information about support groups, and opportunities to meet with mental health professionals experienced with adoption issues. The Web sites listed at the end of the chapter may provide additional information for teachers and families.

Anderson, R. *Second Choice: Growing Up Adopted.*

Bartholdt, E. *Family Bonds: Adoption and the Politics of Parenting.*

Berg, Barbara. *Nothing to Cry About.*

Brodzinsky, D., Schecter, M., & Henig, R. *Being Adopted: The Lifelong Search for Self.*

Canape, C. Adoption: *Parenthood without Pregnancy.*

Chase, M. *Waiting for Baby.*

Gilman, L. *The Adoption Resource Book.*

Hormann, E. *After the Adoption.*

Jewett, C. *Adopting the Older Child.*

Keck, G., & Kupecky, R. *Adopting the Hurt Child: Hope for Families with Special Needs.*

Melina, L. *Making Sense of Adoption: A Parent's Guide.*

Melina, L., & Rosia, S. *The Open Adoption Experience.*

Plumez, J. *Successful Adoption.*

Siegel, S. *Parenting Your Adopted Child.*

Tukas, M. *To Love a Child: A Complete Guide to Adoption.*

Watkins, M. *Talking with Young Children about Adoption.*

Wirth, E., & Worden, J. *How to Adopt a Child from Another Country.*

FIGURE 16-26 Books to suggest to families about adoption.

SUMMARY

Some families with particular circumstances include parents experiencing separation, divorce, and remarriage; parents of children with special needs; parents of infants; abusive or neglectful parents; and parents who adopt. Teachers working with families in these circumstances will be challenged to develop new sensitivities in understanding the dynamics and emotional responses of both parents and children in each situation. Teachers must also incorporate necessary classroom behaviors that can help children, as well as skills and knowledge to support parents. In such professional growth teachers will be able to help the families who need them most.

STUDENT ACTIVITIES FOR FURTHER STUDY

1. Investigate and gather referral information and brochures on any agencies that exist in your community to

   • Assist or support parents and children undergoing separation and divorce, such as counseling services, Parents Without Partners, Big Brothers and Big Sisters, and the like.

   • Assist parents and their children with special needs, or help in the identification and early intervention process.

   • Offer support to new parents.

   • Assist, treat, and support families in abusive or violent situations.

   • Support adoptive families.

   If there are many such agencies, it is useful for each class member to visit one to gather information and report back to the class.

2. Find the state law that defines the legal responsibilities for professionals and paraprofessionals in schools and child care programs in your state regarding reporting abuse and neglect. Learn about your local reporting agency. It is helpful to invite a representative of that agency to visit your class.

3. Investigate your library resources for parents and children with special needs. Compile a list of these to have available for parents.

4. If children with special needs are included in classrooms in your community, plan a visit to these classrooms or to any specialized schools. Learn what their parent involvement policies and practices are.

5. Role-play and discuss the following situations:

   a. You are concerned by a 6-year-old's aggression and regression in your classroom. The father moved out of the home two months ago. You want to discuss the child's behavior with his mother.

   b. A mother wants to tell you all about how terribly she and the children were treated by her ex-husband.

   c. A child in a recent divorce situation seems totally withdrawn and sad. Your conversation with the child?

   d. A child tells you, "He's not my real daddy, he just married my mother. I hate him." Your response?

   e. A child tells you, "My daddy hit my mommy hard. He scares me when he's so mean to us." Your response?

   f. A child has been observed in explicit sexual activity (not exploration). You want to discuss this with the parent.

   g. A mother of a child with cerebral palsy says, "The doctors say she'll never walk or talk right, but she seems so much better in your class. What do you think?" Your response?

   h. A mother of an infant says, "My mother visited this weekend and says for me not to pick the baby up so much, just to let him cry, so you shouldn't either." Your response?

   i. A mother of a 5-year-old who was adopted as an infant requests that you not mention the adoption to other children and parents in the classroom. Your response?

CASE STUDY

In question 5 under Student Activities for Further Study, you will find nine scenarios based on families who are experiencing the situations discussed in this chapter. Choose several, and for each consider the following questions:

1. What are the primary emotions that seem to be at work in the individuals described in the scenario?

2. What are several helpful teacher responses in this scenario? Consider also any that would be less helpful, and identify reasons why.

3. Identify classroom activities and materials that teachers should consider providing for children from these families.

1. List several behaviors in both children and parents associated with the stress of divorce or remarriage.

2. Discuss three ways teachers can help children experiencing divorce or remarriage.

3. Discuss three ways teachers can help parents experiencing divorce or re-marriage.

4. Identify three possible emotional responses of parents of children with special needs.

5. Describe four ways teachers can work effectively with parents of children with special needs.

6. Discuss typical responses of families of infants.

7. Identify three helpful behaviors for teachers of infants.

8. List two factors that can create abusive situations.

9. List any six indicators of abuse and neglect.

10. Identify three responsibilities of teachers in situations involving abuse and neglect.

11. Describe ways teachers can support adoptive families.

Divorce and Remarriage

Carlile, C. (1991, Summer). Children of divorce: How teachers can help ease the pain. *Childhood Education*, 232–234.

Children and divorce. (1994). *The Future of Children, 4*(1).

Frieman, B. (1993). Separation and divorce: Children want their parents to know: Meeting the emotional needs of preschool and primary school children. *Young Children, 48*(6), 58–63.

Miller, P., Ryan, P., & Morrison, W. (1999). Practical strategies for helping children of divorce in today's classroom. *Childhood Education, 75*(5), 285–289.

Procidano, M. E., & Fisher, C. B. (Eds.) (1993). *Contemporary families: A handbook for school professionals.* New York: Teachers College Press.

Sammons, W., & Lewis, J. (2000). What schools are doing to help the children of divorce. *Young Children, 55*(5), 64–65.

Simons, R., & Associates. (1996). *Understanding differences between divorced and intact families: Stress, interaction, and child outcome.* Thousand Oaks, CA: Sage, 1996.

Smilansky, S. (1992). *Children of divorce: The roles of family and school.* Rockville, MD: BJE Press.

Parents of Children with Special Needs

Diamond, K. E. (1994, Spring). Parents who have a child with a disability. *Childhood Education,* 168–170.

Gartner, A., Lipsky, D., & Turnbull, A. (1990). *Supporting families with a child with a disability.* Baltimore: Paul H. Brookes.

Graves, S., & Gargiulo, R. (1989). Parents and early childhood professionals as program partners: Meeting the needs of the preschool exceptional child. *Dimensions, 18*(1), 23–24.

Griffel, G. (1991). Walking on a tightrope: Parents shouldn't have to walk it alone. *Young Children, 46*(3), 40–42.

Leff, P. T., & Walizer, E. (1992). *Building the healing partnership: Parents, professionals, and children with chronic illnesses and disabilities.* Cambridge, MA: Brookline Books.

Robinson, M. (1992, November/December). Parenting a child with special needs. *Child Care Information Exchange,* 31–34.

Shea, T., & Bauer, A. (1993). *Parents and teachers of children with exceptionalities.* Needham Heights, MA: Allyn & Bacon.

Singer, G., & Powers, L. (Eds.). (1993). *Families, disabilities, and empowerment: Active coping skills and strategies for family intervention.* Baltimore: Paul H. Brookes.

Turnbull, A. P., & Turnbull, H. R. III. (2000). *Families, professionals and exceptionality: A special partnership* (4th ed.). Columbus, OH: Merrill.

Working with Parents of Infants

Bernhardt, J. (2000). A primary caregiving system for infants and toddlers: Best for everyone involved. *Young Children, 55*(2), 74–80.

Brazelton, T. B. (1984). Cementing family relationships through child care. In L. L. Dittmann (Ed.), *The infants we care for* (rev. ed.). Washington, DC: NAEYC.

Dombro, A. and Lerner, C. (2006). "Sharing the care of infants and toddlers." *Young Children, 61*(1), 29–33.

Galinsky, E. (1982). Understanding ourselves and parents. In R. Lurie & R. Neugebauer (Eds.), *Caring for infants and toddlers: What works, what doesn't, 2.* Redmond, WA: Child Care Information Exchange.

Gonzalez-Mena, J., & Peshotan Bhavnagri, N. (2000). Diversity and infant/toddler caregiving. *Young Children, 55*(5), 31–35.

Greenberg, P. (1991). *Character development: Encouraging self-esteem and self-discipline in infants, toddlers, and two-year-olds.* Washington, DC: NAEYC.

Hamilton, C., & Howes, C. (1992). A comparison of young children's relationships with mothers and teachers. In R. Planta (Ed.), *Beyond the parent: The role of other adults in children's lives.* San Francisco: Jossey-Bass.

Lurie, R., & Newman, K. (1982). A healthy tension: Parent and group infant-toddler care. In R. Lurie & R. Neugebauer (Eds.), *Caring for infants and toddlers: What works, what doesn't, 2.* Redmond, WA: Child Care Information Exchange.

Raikes, H. (1996). A secure base for babies: Applying attachment concepts to the infant care setting. *Young Children, 51*(5), 59–67.

Rosenheim, M., & Testa, M. (Eds.). (1992). *Early parenthood and coming of age in the 1990s.* Brunswick, NJ: Rutgers University Press.

Small, M. (1998). *Our babies, ourselves: How biology and culture shape the way we parent.* New York: Anchor Books.

Warren, R. (1998). Letter from child care provider to mother on baby's first day. *Young Children, 53*(1), 27.

Wieder, S., (1989). Mediating successful parenting: Guidelines for practitioners. *Zero to Three, X*(1), 21–22.

Working with Abusive or Violent Parents

Bear, T., Schenk, S., & Buckner, L. (1993). Supporting victims of child abuse. *Educational Leadership, 50*(4), 42–47.

Brodkin, A. (1998, March). Helping a child of an alcoholic. *Scholastic Early Childhood Today,* 18–19.

Brohl, K. (1996). *Working with traumatized children: A handbook for healing.* Washington, DC: Child Welfare League.

Domestic violence and children. (1999). *The Future of Children, 9*(3). (The entire journal is devoted to this topic.)

Good, L. (1996). When a child has been sexually abused: Several resources for parents and early childhood professionals. *Young Children, 51*(5), 84–85.

Gootman, M. (1993). Reaching and teaching abused children. *Childhood Education, 70*(1), 15–19.

Greenberg, R. (1999/2000). Substance abuse in families: Educational issues. *Childhood Education, 76*(2), 66–69.

Gunsberg, A. (1989). Empowering young abused and neglected children through contingency play. *Childhood Education, 66*(1), 8–10.

Koplow, L. (1996). *Unsmiling faces: How preschools can heal.* New York: Teachers College Press.

Mikkelson, E. (1997). Responding to allegations of sexual abuse in child care and early childhood education. *Young Children 52*(3), 47–51.

Miller, K. (1996). *The crisis manual for early childhood teachers: How to handle the really difficult problems.* Beltsville, MD: Gryphon House.

NAEYC. (1998). What would you do? Real-life ethical problems early childhood professionals face. *Young Children, 53*(4), 52–54.

Nunnelley, J., & Fields, T. (1999). Anger, dismay, guilt, anxiety—The realities and roles in reporting child abuse. *Young Children 54*(5), 74–79.

Oehlberg, B. (1996). *Making it better: Activities for children living in a stressful world.* St. Paul, MN: Redleaf Press.

Protecting children from abuse and neglect. (1998). *The Future of Children, 8*(1). (The entire journal is devoted to this topic.)

Smith, G. H., Coles, C. D., Poulsen, M., & Coles, C. K. (1995). *Children, families and substance abuse: Challenges for changing educational and social outcomes.* Baltimore, MD: Paul H. Brookes.

Thompson, S. (1998). Working with children of substance-abusing parents. *Young Children, 53*(1), 34–37.

Wallach, L (1993). Helping children cope with violence. *Young Children, 48*(4), 4–11.

Working with Adoptive Families

Brodkin, A. M. (1992, November/December). You don't look like your mom! *Scholastic Pre–K Today,* 18–19.

FAIR. (2002). *Adoption and the schools: Resources for parents and teachers.* Palo Alto CA: FAIR. Order information online at www.fairfamilies.org.

Institute for Adoption Information. (2002). *An educator's guide to adoption.* Bennington, VT: Author. Order information online at www.adoptioninformationinstitute.org.

Kaatz, K. (2000). Talking to teachers about adoption. *Adoption Today, 3*(1).

Stroud, J. E., Stroud, J. C., & Staly, L. (1997). Understanding and supporting adoptive families. *Early Childhood Education Journal, 24*(4), 229–234.

REFERENCES ## Divorce and Remarriage

Beekman, N. (1986). Helping children cope with divorce: The school counselor's role. Available online at http://www.ericdigestsorg.

Clarke-Stewart, A. (1989, January). Single-parent families: How bad for the children? *NEA Today,* 60–64.

Coleman, M., Ganong, L. H., & Henry, J. (1984). What teachers should know about stepfamilies. *Childhood Education, 60*(5), 306–309.

Coontz, S. (1997). *The way we really are: Coming to terms with America's changing families.* New York: Basic Books.

Goldman, L. (1996). We can help children grieve: A child-oriented model for memorializing. *Young Children, 51*(6), 69–73.

Greenberg, J. (1996). Seeing children through tragedy: My mother died today— When is she coming back? *Young Children, 51*(6), 76–77.

Heatherington, E. M. (1990). Coping with family transitions: Winners, losers, and survivors. In *Annual Progress in Child Psychiatry and Child Development.* New York: Brunner/Mazel.

Heatherington, M., Bridges, M., & Insabella, G. (1998, February). What matters? What does not? Five perspectives on the association between marital transitions and children's adjustment. *American Psychologist,* 167–184.

Heatherington, M., & Kelly, J. (2002). *For better or worse: Divorce reconsidered.* New York: W. W. Norton.

Hildebrand, V., Phenice, L., Gray, M., & Hines R. (2000). *Knowing and serving diverse families* (2nd ed.). Upper Saddle River, NJ: Prentice-Hall.

Hopkins, A. (2002). Children and grief: The role of the early childhood educator. *Young Children, 57*(1), 40–47.

Visher, E. B., & Visher, J. S. (1979). *Stepfamilies: A guide to working with stepparents and stepchildren.* New York: Brunner/Mizel.

Wallerstein, J. S., & Blakeslee, S. (1989). *Second chances: Men, women, and children: A decade after divorce.* New York: Ticknor and Fields.

———. (2003). *What about the kids? Raising your children before, during, and after divorce.* New York: Hyperion Press.

Wallerstein, J., Lewis, J., & Blakeslee, S. (2000). *The unexpected legacy of divorce: A twenty-five year landmark study.* New York: Hyperion Press.

Parents of Children with Special Needs

Anderegg, M., Vergason, G., & Smith, M. (1992). A visual representation of the grief cycle for use by teachers with families children with disabilities. *Remedial and Special Education, 13*(2), 17–23.

Fenlon, A. (2005). Collaborative steps: Paving the way to kindergarten for young children with disabilities. *Young Children, 60*(2), 32–37.

Gargiulo, R. M., & Graves, S. B. (1991, Spring). Parental feelings: The forgotten component when working with parents of handicapped preschool children. *Childhood Education,* 176–178.

Heward, W. (1996). *Exceptional children: An introduction of special education* (5th ed.). Englewood Cliffs, NJ: Prentice-Hall.

Kupfer, F. (1984). Severely and/or multiply disabled children. *Equals in this partnership: Parents of disabled and at-risk infants and toddlers speak to professionals.* Washington, DC: National Center for Clinical Infant Programs.

Klein, M. D., & Chen, D. (2001). *Working with children from culturally diverse backgrounds.* Albany, NY: Delmar.

McGonigel, M. J., & Garland, C. W. (1990). The individualized family service plan and the early intervention team: Team and family issues and recommended practices. In K. L. Freiberg (Ed.), *Educating exceptional children* (5th ed.). Guilford, CT: The Dushkin Publishing Group.

Smith, C. (1998). Children with "special rights" in the preprimary schools and infant–toddler centers of Reggio Emilia. In *The hundred languages of children: The Reggio Emilia approach—Advanced reflections* (2nd ed.). Greenwich, CT: Ablex Publishing Corp.

Smith, T., Polloway, E., Patton, J., & Dowdy, C. (1995). *Teaching children with special needs in inclusive settings.* Boston: Allyn & Bacon.

Working with Parents of Infants

Baker, A., & Manfredi/Pettit, L. (2004). *Relationships, the heart of quality care: Creating community among adults in early care settings.* Washington, DC: NAEYC.

Daniel, J. (1998). A modern mother's place is wherever her children are: Facilitating infant and toddler mothers' transitions in child care. *Young Children, 53*(6), 4–12.

Bhavnagri, N., & Gonzales-Mena, J. (1997). The cultural context of infant caregiving. *Childhood Education, 74*(1), 2–8.

Bowlby, J. (1988). *A secure base: Parent–child attachment and healthy human development.* New York: Basic Books.

Brazelton, T. (1992). *On becoming a family: The growth of attachment before and after birth.* New York: Delacorte.

De Jong, L. (2003). Using Erikson to work more effectively with teenage parents. *Young Children, 58*(2), 87–95.

Gonzalez-Mena, J. (1995). Cultural sensitivity in routine caregiving tasks. In P. Mangione (Ed.), *Infant/toddler caregiving: A guide to culturally sensitive care.* Sacramento, CA: Far West Laboratory and California Department of Education.

Joffe, S., & Viertel, J. (1984). *Becoming parents: Preparing for the emotional changes of first-time parenthood.* New York: Atheneum Books.

Karen, R. (1994). *Becoming attached: Unfolding the mystery of the infant–mother bond and its impact on later life.* New York: Warner Books.

Lowenthal, B., & Lowenthal, R. (1997). Teenage parenting: Challenges, interventions, and programs. *Childhood Education, 74*(1), 29–32.

Meyerhoff, M. (1994). Of baseball and babies: Are you unconsciously discouraging father involvement in infant care? *Young Children, 49*(4), 17–19.

Morris, S. L. (1995). Supporting the breastfeeding relationship during child care: Why is it important? *Young Children, 50*(2), 59–62.

Working with Abusive Parents

Austin, J. S. (2000). When a child discloses sexual abuse: Immediate and appropriate teacher responses. *Childhood Education, 77*(1), 1–5

Barbour, C., Barbour, N., & Scully, P. (2004). *Families, schools, and communities: Building partnerships for educating children.* Upper Saddle River, NJ: Prentice-Hall.

Barthel, J. (1991). *For children's sake. The promise of family preservation.* New York: The Edna McConnell Clark Foundation.

Caughey, C. (1991). Becoming the child's ally—observations in a classroom for children who have been abused. *Young Children, 46*(4), 22–28.

Child Welfare League. (2004). *Parental substance abuse: A major factor in child abuse and neglect.* New York: Child Welfare League.

Edelson, J. (2001). Should childhood exposure to adult domestic violence be defined as child maltreatment under the law? *University of Minnesota School of Social Work.*

Helfer, R. (1975). *The diagnostic process and treatment programs.* U.S. Dept. of Health, Education, and Welfare. Washington, DC: U.S. Govt. Printing Office.

Kearney, M. (1999). The role of teachers in helping children of domestic violence. *Childhood Education, 75*(5), 290–296.

"NAEYC position statement on the prevention of child abuse in early childhood programs and the responsibilities of early childhood professionals to prevent child abuse." (1997). *Young Children, 52*(3), 42–46.

Pimento, B., & Kernested, D. (1996). *Healthy foundations in child care.* Toronto, Ontario: Nelson Canada.

Rice, K., & Sanoff, M. (1998). Growing strong together: Helping mothers and their children affected by substance abuse. *Young Children 53*(1), 28–33.

Thompson, S. (1998). Working with children of substance-abusing parents. *Young Children, 53*(1), 34–37.

Tower, C. (1993). *Understanding child abuse and neglect* (2nd ed.). Boston, MA: Allyn & Bacon.

Working with Adoptive Families

Greenberg, J. (2001). She is so my real mom! Helping children understand adoption as one form of family diversity. *Young Children, 56*(2), 90–91.

Hunt, E. (2003). Out of the shadows. *Teaching Tolerance, 24*, 38–43.

Munsch, A. B. (1992, November). Understanding and meeting the needs of adopted children and families. *Child Care Information Exchange*, 47–51.

HELPFUL WEB SITES

Divorce

http://www.aacap.org

American Academy of Child and Adolescent Psychiatry. This site offers concise and up-to-date information about issues that affect children, teenagers, and their families.

http://www.kidsturn.org

For children of divorced parents, a nonprofit organization to help kids and parents through divorce.

http://www.divorcetransitions.com

Divorce Transitions is a divorce information and support community for those anticipating, experiencing, or recovering from separation and divorce.

http://www.abanet.org

Parent Education and Custody Effectiveness (P.E.A.C.E.) is sponsored by the American Bar Association, Family Law Section. The P.E.A.C.E. Program is an educational program designed to provide information to parents about the divorce and separation process, hoping this will result in improved parent–child relationships after divorce and a reduction in the number of contested custody, visitation, and support disputes that now face our courts.

http://www.dadsdivorce.com

Dads Divorce is dedicated to helping divorced and divorcing fathers maximize their role in their children's lives.

http://www.divorceabc.com

Children of separation and divorce. The National Family Resiliency Center (formerly Children of Separation and Divorce Center) (NFRC) is committed to helping children and adults preserve a sense of family, foster healthy relationships, and constructively adjust to change, especially during times of separation, divorce, and other family transitions.

http://www.parentswithoutpartners.org

This website explains the resources offered by the international organization that focuses on single parents and their children.

Stepfamilies

http://www.stepfamily.org

Stepfamily Foundation's mission is to assist you to make the family, as it is now, work.

http://www.saafamilies.org

Stepfamily Association of America is a national, nonprofit membership organization dedicated to successful stepfamily living. This Web site provides educational information and resources for anyone interested in stepfamilies and their issues.

http://www.stepfamilyinfo.org

Stepfamily information. This nonprofit, research-based educational site exists to help co-parents (bioparents and stepparents) build high-nurturance relationships and families. It promotes avoiding or healing five remarriage and divorce hazards by growing awareness and knowledge.

Families of Children with Special Needs

http://www.modimes.org

March of Dimes Birth Defects Foundation researchers, volunteers, educators, outreach workers, and advocates work together to give all babies a fighting chance against the threats to their health.

http://www.cec.sped.org

The worldwide mission of the Council for Exceptional Children (CEC) is to improve educational outcomes for individuals with exceptionalities.

http://www.specialchild.com

Special Child: for parents and caregivers of children with special needs.

http://www.familyvoices.org

Family Voices: families and friends speaking on behalf of children with special health care needs; for parents and caregivers of children with special needs.

http://www.brightfutures.org

> Bright Futures is a national initiative to promote and improve the health and well-being of infants, children, and adolescents. Bright Futures is dedicated to the principle that every child deserves to be healthy and that optimal health involves a trusting relationship between the health professional, the child, the family, and the community as partners in health practice.

http://www.fcsn.org

> Federation for Children with Special Needs (FCSN) is a center for parents and parent organizations to work together on behalf of children with special needs and their families. FCSN is a coalition of parent groups representing children with a variety of disabilities, offering a variety of services to parents, parent groups, and others who are concerned with children with special needs.

http://www.pacer.org

> The mission of the Parent Advocacy Coalition for Education Rights (PACER) Center is to expand opportunities and enhance the quality of life of children and young adults with disabilities and their families, based on the concept of parents helping parents.

http://www.specialedlaw.net

> Special Education Law Resources for Parents and Teachers (SpecialEdLaw.net) is a multidisciplinary Internet resource for parents of special needs children, as well as attorneys, special education administrators, teachers, psychologists, and others with a need for information relating to special education law.

Families with Infants

http://www.rie.org

> Resources for Infant Educators (RIE), Magda Gerber's organization, is a nonprofit group that has developed and is teaching a unique philosophy and methodology in working with infants. The RIE approach, based on respect, helps raise authentic infants who are competent, confident, curious, attentive, exploring, cooperative, secure, peaceful, focused, self-initiating, resourceful, involved, cheerful, aware, interested, and inner-directed.

http://www.touchpoints.org

> Dr. Berry Brazelton's organization, Touchpoints Center (BTC), offers training at the Child Development Unit, Children's Hospital, Boston. BTC training, based on the work of Dr. T. Berry Brazelton, combines relationship building and child development into a framework that professionals can use to enhance their work with families.

http://www.babytalk.org

> The mission of Baby Talk, sponsored by Kindermusik, is to encourage parents to nurture their very young children (ages 0–3 years). Using a

method of anticipatory guidance, Baby TALK provides information and services to parents to equip them for challenges and to help them enjoy their children's development.

Abuse and Neglect

http://nccach.acf.hhs.gov

> The National Clearinghouse on Child Abuse and Neglect Information, sponsored by the Administration for Children and Families under the Department of Health and Human Services, is a national resource for professionals and others seeking information about child abuse and neglect and child welfare.

http://www.preventchildabuse.org

> Prevent Child Abuse (PCA) America has led the way in building awareness, providing education, and inspiring hope to everyone involved in the effort to prevent the abuse and neglect of our nation's children.

http://www.childrensinstitute.org

> Children's Institute International (CII) is a private, nonprofit organization dedicated to protecting, preserving, and strengthening the family through child abuse prevention and treatment services for high-need, low-resource families, as well as through professional training, research, and advocacy.

http://www.healthyfamiliesamerica.org

> Healthy Families America (HFA), a national program of Prevent Child Abuse America, has three goals: to promote positive parenting; to encourage child health and development; and to prevent child abuse and neglect.

www.nccafv.org

> The National Council on Child Abuse and Family Violence provides information for public awareness and education.

http://www.ispcan.org

> The mission of the International Society for Prevention of Child Abuse and Neglect is to support individuals and organizations working to protect children from abuse and neglect worldwide.

http://endabuse.org

> The mission of the Family Violence Prevention Fund is to prevent violence against women and children within the home and community and to help those whose lives have been touched by violence.

http://www.parentsanonymous.org

> The mission of Parents Anonymous is to seek to prevent child abuse by offering programs where parents and children learn new behaviors and create positive changes in their lives.

Adoptive Families

http://www.iafonline.org

> International Adoptive Families (IAF) is an adoptive parent group devoted to empowerment of those touched by international adoption. The organization is a gathering of people looking to build families by adopting the world's orphans. IAF's membership is open to anyone interested in furthering these efforts through adoption, education, financial contributions, or moral support.

http://www.adoptioninstitute.org

> The Evan B. Donaldson Adoption Institute is a national organization devoted to improving adoption policy and practice, and providing resources for eductors.

http://naic.acf.hhs.gov

> The Web site of the National Adoption Information Clearinghouse, from Children's Bureau, Administration on Children, Youth, and Families,. contains information to connect professionals and concerned citizens with research and statistics to create permanent families.

http://www.adoptioninformationinstitute.org

> This organization's mission is to enhance the understanding of adoption by educating the public, including educators, about adoption.

Additional resources for this chapter can be found on the Online Companion to accompany this text at www.earlychilded.delmar.com. This supplemental material includes frequently asked questions; chapter outlines to be used as study guides; scenarios that both encourage large and small group discussions and provoke new thoughts and ideas; and chapter resources, including chapter summaries, interactive questions, Web links, and Web activities. In addition, forms from the text are available for download.

CHAPTER 17

Working to Resolve Troublesome Attitudes and Behaviors

OBJECTIVES

After reading this chapter, you should be able to

1. Discuss reasons for hostile reactions and considerations in dealing with them.
2. Discuss reasons for apparent indifference and considerations in overcoming it.
3. Discuss overinvolvement of parents and ways of handling it.
4. Discuss several frequent causes of parent–teacher tension and ways of dealing with them.

KEY TERMS
empathic
I-messages
pedagogical
    issues
readiness
sandwiching

Human nature being what it is, teachers occasionally find themselves working with families whose attitudes and behaviors are difficult to deal with, no matter how positive the teacher's attempts have been. Stress or personality may cause some parents to display responses that range from belligerence to indifference, and either extreme is quite daunting to work with. In addition, any classroom teacher can tell you that particular situations with parents arise regularly enough to become sources of chronic irritation. Such encounters may be so discouraging or threatening that teachers retreat from future efforts to work with families. But when this happens, children's well-being will suffer, so it is important that teachers develop skills and strategies to help counter the negatives.

   In this chapter we will consider reasons for parents' behaviors and strategies for handling them. This does not suggest that there are magical solutions to these difficulties. Rather, there are teacher and program responses that may get the teacher through the immediate encounter, and policies or procedures that may prevent recurrences. Perhaps most important is the teacher belief that partnership with families is important enough to keep on trying.

As professionals, teachers have the responsibility to keep working toward effective relationships with parents, even under difficult conditions. Perhaps the most difficult circumstances arise when teachers and families view a situation quite differently. These differences may center on **pedagogical issues**. Examples of pedagogical issues might be

- Families who refuse to let their children be tested, despite evidence to warrant it, or who refuse special educational services.
- Families who want to push academic work before a teacher believes the children are ready.
- Families who disagree about methods used to discipline their children.
- Families who insist that teachers prohibit their sons from playing dress-up.

Parent–teacher differences may also center on parent behaviors that conflict with teachers' responsibilities for the whole group. These might include

- Families who urge their children to "fight back" knowing it is against school rules.
- Families who gossip or make unfavorable comments about other children in the group.

Other predicaments for teachers sometimes arise from parent behaviors perceived to put children at risk. Examples of this might be

- A child using foul language that has evidently been heard at home.
- An immature child for whom a teacher has concerns about parental "smother-love" and overprotection.
- A perfectionist parent who makes a child do and redo homework until the child is in tears.
- A parent who has failed to show up for several appointments with a teacher to discuss a child's inattention and declining achievement in school.

Yet another predicament that often faces teachers is the need to communicate negative information to a parent about a child's behavior, development, or progress at school. This might be that

- A child is not ready for the next grade and retention is recommended.
- A child is extremely aggressive toward other children.

These situations and causes of strained communication may sound familiar to most teachers. Both teachers and families feel extremely uncomfortable coming together to discuss issues such as these. But all of them demand getting past the feelings of discomfort so that real communication and problem solving can take place.

How does a teacher proceed? In general, as a teacher contemplates such situations, it is important to

- Analyze a situation critically from both teacher's and parents' viewpoints.

- Define the issue clearly.

- Break a problem into its component parts to see how each person perceives a situation.

- Attempt to find mutually acceptable solutions.

In some cases there may be no solution to the vast differences in perspective or emotional response of teacher and parent; but in others a careful analysis of the dynamics and facts of a situation may help the parties find common ground on which to work together. Teachers must realize that dealing with attitudes and values is a long, slow process. There are no instant solutions or successes. An understanding of human growth and development, not just child development, is necessary for a teacher working with a variety of adults at different stages of their unique lives. It is too easy for teachers to force parents into a lose–lose situation where any outcome is a loss. If parents become defensive and feel that teachers are criticizing them, both teachers and parents will suffer from the breakdown in communication. If families feel they are being forced into compliance and acceptance of the teacher's viewpoint, they may become silenced, and teachers will lose the valuable perspective of the parents' knowledge. Careful analysis of the conflict from the perspectives of all participants may help teachers move toward professional actions and mutually acceptable solutions—more of a win–win situation.

See the Critical Analysis form printed at the end of the chapter for a tool that teachers could use to consider predicaments in teacher–parent relationships.

HOSTILITY

In a recent conference the parent angrily burst out at the teacher. "My son has never had this problem before with his other teacher. If you ask me, there's something wrong with a teacher who can't get a child to obey her. Don't tell me he needs limits! I think your principal should watch *you* more carefully!"

As a teacher responds to this attack, it is important to consider several points.

Hostility as a Mask

Teachers need to realize that not everything that seems like hostility is really so. Sometimes parents are motivated by genuine concern for their children, and questioning the practices or evaluation of another is a form of healthy self-assertion. The intensity of concern may be expressed in voices that sound angry. Individuals who are not used to being assertive may go too far and appear aggressive instead. Sometimes parents who feel powerless attempt to grab power inappropriately.

Another emotion that may be masked by hostility is the grief parents feel when realizing that their child has a developmental problem or disability (see Chapter 16). When teachers realize that parents may be overwhelmed and extremely upset by teachers' reports or interpretations, they will realize that parents' defensive reactions are more a method of coping with anxiety and less an attempt to stop the process of getting help for their children.

Also, parents who feel inadequate or guilty about their effectiveness as parents may strongly resist teachers' comments. It is essential that a teacher think about a parent's emotional position before automatically labeling a response as hostile.

True hostility appears as an individual reacts with anger when dealing with a person seen to be in authority. A hostile person is defensive and suspicious, assumes that others have unfriendly intentions, and therefore feels impelled to strike the first blow. Such hostile reactions often indicate a carryover of childhood attitudes or earlier experiences with authority.

Hostility Inhibits Communication

When parents are verbally abusive or irrationally angry, it is impossible to communicate effectively. It is a teacher's task to defuse the anger so that communication can begin (Jaksec, 2004).

Remain Calm

To be able to work through the parent's anger, it is vital that a teacher remain calm in every way. Teachers need to avoid being caught up in parents' strong emotions, while making an effort to understand what is behind the feelings. Being attacked by an angry parent triggers emotional responses in teachers, including feelings of frustration, fear, helplessness, and anger (Boone & Barclay, 1995). Although actual physical danger from angry parents is rare, the verbal abuse is itself unsettling for a teacher to receive. Nevertheless, the teacher's response is critical. It is important that the teacher remain as outwardly calm and unemotional as possible, even though internally emotions may be churning.

Emotional behavior may be escalated if teachers do not attempt to control their own outward responses. The louder and more vehement a parent's voice, the more softly and slowly a teacher should speak, being careful that her body language remains open and positive—avoiding, for example, the crossed arms or lack of eye contact that suggest being closed to the parent's position. It helps teachers remain calm when they don't interpret the parents' approach as a personal attack, but as a code for expressing emotions that spring from the parenting role. It is very important that teachers not become defensive or argumentative and not retaliate verbally as in the following negative example:

> "Look, don't you talk to me about my teaching. If you were doing a halfway decent job with parenting I wouldn't be having these problems in my classroom."

Defensive behavior suggests that the attacker is right and tends to escalate the tension. Responding to a parent's emotion with a teacher's emotion can only lead to an explosive situation (see Figure 17-1). Nevertheless, a teacher must continue to maintain composure by trying to perceive a situation from a parent's perspective and identify with the emotional responses of a parent.

Learning to support parents nonjudgmentally, without losing emotional control, is crucial. Professionals do not have the right to lose control with parents. By taking on the role of teacher, they commit themselves to working constructively with those who need assistance.

Remaining calm is not an easy task. Teachers are just ordinary human beings, with limits to remaining calm in the face of persistent inappropriate

FIGURE 17-1 If teachers remain calm in the face of parents' strong emotions, they may prevent the hostility from escalating.

behavior, no matter how hard they try to understand or tolerate it. Neverthe-less, if they lose control and treat parents with disrespect, they cannot expect that parents will be respectful of them or that anything constructive will be accomplished.

Acknowledge and Accept the Anger

The first step in working with an angry reaction is to accept it. An expressed feeling is real, no matter how distorted the perception of facts that caused the feeling. Accepting someone else and her feelings does not mean giving up one's own perspective; it simply means being more sensitive to that of the other (see Figure 17-2). By taking a parent's perspective, a teacher is able to show genuine concern and is more likely to respond appropriately. As a teacher reflects an understanding of a parent's point of view, a parent realizes that her feelings are recognized:

> "You're really very upset by my comments about Roger's behavior, aren't you?"

The teacher has listened carefully to the concern; asked herself, "What is she feeling?" and tried to define the emotion being expressed; then reflected that understanding back to the parent to see if she is right. Such feedback acknowledges the parent's anger and may eliminate a parent's need to show more anger because the teacher clearly has picked up on the message. The teacher's reflective comment may elicit a response from the parent that can clarify a concern in terms of specific details:

> "You bet I'm upset, and I'll tell you, I don't think it's fair to be talking about making him keep rules after all that kid has had on

FIGURE 17-2 Accepting the parent's feelings does not mean giving up the teacher's own perspective, but rather being sensitive to the parent.

him. With his dad being so strict with him and then leaving last year, he's had enough to get used to without you being strict, too."

When active listening does not evoke an opportunity to hear the reasons behind the anger, a teacher should continue to reflect back her **empathic** perception of a parent's response:

Parent: "Of course I'm upset—anybody would be, to hear a teacher say such things about their child."
    Teacher: "It really troubles you to hear the kind of comments I made."
    Parent: "It certainly does. It's just not fair—what do you know about it anyway?"
    Teacher: "I know there's a lot about Roger I don't know, and I'm counting on you to help me understand. What can you tell me that would help me?" and so on.

It is necessary for a teacher to analyze her own emotional responses, determining whether this has become a power struggle and why she feels so strongly about an issue. Are facts involved, or only emotional responses?

Teachers, being human, sometimes overlook details or simply make mistakes in dealing with certain situations. This may become a source of hostility or anger in parents. Teachers need to be prepared to admit the mistake or responsibility openly and honestly to parents, empathize with their frustration and anger, and then share a plan to ensure this will not occur again. Such honesty can mitigate the hostility:

"I don't blame you for feeling so upset with me. This was my mistake, and I'm sorry for it. I'd feel angry too, if it had happened to my child. Here is what I plan to do so this doesn't happen again."

Adhere to Facts

As a conversation proceeds, teachers must be careful that any disagreeing statements concern facts and issues, not personalities. In discussing different viewpoints, participants should use descriptive statements, not evaluative ones. It is easier to deal with descriptions rather than labels. By being objective and factual in the statements made to families, and by having written observations that support the statements, teachers will sound less judgmental or accusing:

NOT: "Roger is a very undisciplined, out-of-bounds child."

RATHER: "I'm noticing that it's hard for Roger to follow the rule about hitting others. This week when he was angry with Eddie on three different occasions, he hit him. Do you notice hitting at home?

NOT: "Jennifer is very careless in her work."

RATHER: "If you look at these assignments Jennifer handed in last week, you will see the errors I circled. I have seen her do this work correctly on other occasions. What have you noticed about her making errors?"

Parents would be more likely to respond to each of the second statements with information and suggestions, whereas the first statements would likely produce defensive, angry reactions. When teachers take care to use words that describe behaviors without adding their own interpretation, they are more likely to engage the parents in dialogue that moves toward problem solving, rather than alienating the listener.

Express Concerns Constructively

Teachers need to remember that angry outbursts may be triggered if they approach parents with problems so directly that the parents' only recourse is to attack back in order to protect themselves. It is effective to use more palatable methods, such as **sandwiching** the meat of a problem between two slices of positive, supportive statements regarding a parent's interest and concern:

"I appreciate how deeply concerned you are for Roger. There's no more important thing for a child than to know his parents care. I'm concerned about his ability to develop some self-control, and I feel sure this is an area that we can work on to come up with some things that might help him."

Using the communication technique of **I-messages** to express concerns allows teachers to express their feelings constructively and so indirectly encourage parents to do so as well. An I-message has three basic parts:

1. "When . . ."—a statement of the behavior that troubles a teacher,.

2. "I feel . . ."—a statement of the feeling about the behavior or its consequences,.

3. "Because . . ."—a statement of the reason for the concern. (For more about I-messages, see Gordon, 2000.)

So an I-message sounds something like these examples:

"When Roger hits other children, I feel frustrated because I'm not able to help him understand our rule about everybody being safe here."

"When Roger forgets our rules, I feel very concerned about his level of self-control."

"When you refuse to discuss these problems, I get upset because the problems seem urgent to me."

Some of the potential explosiveness is removed when feelings are expressed in I-messages rather than "you-judgments" that focus blame squarely on the other:

> "You're just not helping this situation."
>
> "You're refusing to admit there's a problem."
>
> "You always take Roger's side and refuse to listen to what's really happening."

Respect Families' Concerns

It is important that angry parents know their concerns are taken seriously. These problems are important to a parent and must not be minimized by a teacher. One way to indicate respect for parents' problems is to write down every complaint, allowing them to truly vent their feelings. (see Figure 17-3). When they slow down, teachers can ask if anything else is bothering them, so their list of complaints is exhausted. If teachers then read back the list, using the parents' own words, it suggests that the teachers truly value the concerns. Teachers can next ask for any suggestions that parents have for solutions to the problems, and write these down as well. This conveys a valuing of the parents' input, although the teacher is not necessarily committing to follow these suggestions. These actions say that the concerns are important and the parents are being listened to. It is also valuable to state that educators don't have all the answers and need all the help they can get.

FIGURE 17-3 One way to indicate respect for parents' concerns is for teachers to write down every complaint.

Express Teacher Emotions Constructively

If these earlier steps are not successful in stemming the flow of the parent's anger, it is appropriate for teachers to express their own emotional responses to the verbal attacks. It is entirely appropriate for teachers to state something like this:

> "I am feeling disturbed by the tone of voice you are using as we speak."
> "I am bothered that you are not giving me a chance to explain my perspective."

The example of a teacher discussing her emotions calmly may help parents calm down.

It is also important that a teacher not retreat from the anger by suggesting, "You'd better talk to the director," or "I won't talk to you unless you stop shouting at me." The potential for communication and learning more about a problem is available here and now. As teachers help parents express feelings and perceptions, they both have an opportunity to see the issues from a different perspective.

REFLECTIONS FOR JOURNAL ENTRIES

What experiences have you already had in dealing with people who became angry and aggressive with you? How did you handle it? How did you feel after the encounter? What does this suggest you will have to consider when put in a professional position of dealing with a hostile parent?

Reschedule the Meeting

On those occasions when all attempts to reduce the amount of anger and facilitate communication fail, it may be wise to schedule another meeting. "No one benefits from an extended angry outburst: not the teacher, not the child, not even the parent. To accept abuse will not remedy the situation, and it is terribly emotionally draining on the teacher" (Boone & Barclay, 1995).

> "I don't think we can accomplish anything more today. Could we meet again next Wednesday at this time? Maybe some new ideas will occur to us in the meantime."

It can be useful to invite a colleague or supervisor to sit in on the next conference because some participant at every conference needs to be free of emotional responses and have skills to help the other participants deal with their emotions quickly and fully (see Figure 17-4). Checking out a situation with a

FIGURE 17-4 It may useful to invite a colleague or supervisor to sit in on another meeting to help facilitate the discussion.

colleague may also help a teacher see it from a different perspective. If the teacher and parent can come up with a plan for responding to their mutual problem, it is important to schedule another meeting promptly to attempt to follow up on the original conversation as an indication of the teacher's sincere desire to work with the parent.

Anger is a powerful emotion—destructive if allowed to rage unleashed but potentially a strong motivation to examine a situation and work together for understanding and change (see Figure 17-5).

INDIFFERENCE

Connie Martinez is concerned about a different kind of behavior. There are a couple of parents in her classroom that she simply can't reach. They seem apathetic, uncaring about their children's needs or the teacher's attempts to involve them in any way.

"Hard-to-reach" families include those "whose physical, social, or psychological distance from the school place extra barriers in the school's or family's path, and make communication and interaction even more difficult than usual" (Epstein, in Boone & Barclay, 1995). These families may include single parents; less educated parents; very young or very old parents; language minority parents; parents with low incomes; the homeless; families new to the community; parents with personal problems such as alcoholism, drug abuse, or mental illness; and parents preoccupied with careers.

There are several possible reasons behind apparent indifference. One may be that the overwhelming pressure in families' lives prevents them from

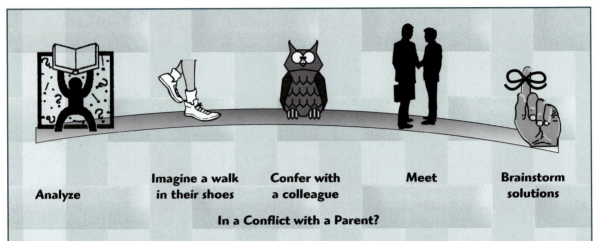

Analyze   **Imagine a walk**   **Confer with**   **Meet**   **Brainstorm**
                   in their shoes   **a colleague**   **solutions**

In a Conflict with a Parent?

Five Steps to Take . . .

Analyze

1. Analyze your own feelings. Why do you feel so strongly about this issue? Are you emotionally involved? Has this become a power struggle? Are factors other than the child's best interest entering into your thinking about the conflict? If so, what are they?

Imagine a walk in their shoes

2. Put yourself in the parents' shoes. What are they thinking and why might they look at the situation the way they do? Assuming that they have their child's best interests in mind, why are they behaving as they are?

Confer with a colleague

3. Check out your perceptions. Find a friend or colleague whom you respect but who often sees things differently from you. Describe the situation as objectively as you can. Can your colleague give you any insight into why you and the parent are at odds?

Meet

4. Arrange to meet with the parent. Make all preconference communications as friendly and unthreatening as possible. Do not get drawn into playing out the dispute before you meet. If you are very angry, have someone else look at your notes before you send them or role-play with a colleague what you will say.

Brainstorm solutions

5. Avoid coming to the conference with a prearranged solution. Learn more about the parents' point of view. Try to be non-judgmental. Negotiate. Try to come up with a solution that meets the child's needs. Try to agree at least on the next step.

NEXT STEPS . . .

- Congratulate yourself if it went well and you learned something new about the child or the family.
- If it did not go well, ask to meet with a third party or supervisor.
- Stay cool, try to remain objective, and don't take it personally. KEEP THE CHILD'S BEST INTEREST AS THE PRIMARY FOCUS FOR DECISIONS.

FIGURE 17-5 Five steps for working through conflicts.

focusing much attention on their child, as much as they care for him. Too many concerns about basic physical needs may crowd in. A parent who worries that her resources will not stretch to cover both food for the rest of the month and the electric bill has little emotional energy left to care about higher emotional or social needs.

Pressure in families' lives can come from the opposite end of the socioeconomic spectrum—from having two sets of career demands and the problems of meshing two schedules, relocating households when told to, and continuing to push up the ladder of success. Sometimes there is little time or energy left for personal relationships or development. Such parents are often more than willing to entrust child care and education to the professionals and to withdraw to more obviously gainful career pursuits.

Parents who feel particularly uncomfortable due to differences in social class or cultural backgrounds may withdraw from a situation and appear indifferent. Noninvolvement or indifference may indicate an attempt to disguise illiteracy or other problems (Boutte et al., 1992). Some families, including families of some cultural minorities, may have a high regard for teachers and education but feel that education is a one-way street and that they have nothing to offer. Some child care parents may see teachers simply as employees in a low-status occupation and feel there is no need for their involvement in a "baby-sitting" arrangement.

Still other families who seem indifferent may be adults who missed childhood, who are themselves products of abnormal parenting. Such parents spend their grown-up years attempting to have their own lost needs met by their children, and by doing so raise children whose own needs are never met.

Whatever the reason for families' lack of interest or involvement, most teachers don't like not being able to reach them. As is human nature, teachers who feel unsuccessful in reaching particular parents often withdraw from them, thereby increasing the distance between them. It is common for teachers to shift the blame from themselves to parents:

"Well, I'm sure I don't know what's the matter with them—
goodness knows I've tried."

"What kind of parents are they anyway—not even caring
about their own child enough to come in for a conference."

These responses do not improve a situation. It is more helpful to adopt an attitude that parents are not unreachable, but that teachers have not yet found ways to reach them. Teachers must not interpret inaccessibility personally. Rejection is something teachers must learn to manage. A positive way to look at rejection is that it is an opportunity to reconsider methods or redirect energies. The key is not to give up but to consider other ways of getting through, reminding oneself of specifics about this particular parent.

Teachers must assess the reasons for families' unavailability and consider various ideas to overcome it. It is vital that teachers not fall into the trap of making stereotypic judgments about the involvement or abilities of families, particularly those who are disadvantaged socioeconomically. Such stereotypes would prevent teachers from truly reaching out to involve all families.

Personal and Economic Pressures

For families overwhelmed by economic and personal pressures, there is little probability of their becoming involved or less "indifferent" to their children's needs as long as these external pressures exist. The most positive action for a teacher is to be an advocate for these families, referring them to appropriate agencies for assistance. Such concern and help will lay the basis for trust in a relationship that may develop as these parents' other concerns are lessened.

Career Interests

For parents busy with their own career interests, teachers may emphasize particular techniques to reach them—newsletters or e-mail that can be read at their convenience, or perhaps occasional bag lunches with their children issuing the invitation, planned with plenty of advance notice. Opportunities to talk with other upwardly mobile families may be appreciated as a source of support.

Cultural Differences

With families who may remain distant because of discomfort with social or cultural differences, teachers must be warm, friendly, and casual in their contacts. It may be important to consciously simplify speech styles and vocabulary.

Other families from similar backgrounds who are more comfortable in a school setting can be helpful in making contact with these parents and personally inviting and accompanying them to informal events. Casual social activities or hands-on workshops (making toys for their children or materials for the classroom) provide less threatening experiences and give a sense of being important in their child's education.

Through genuine indications that a teacher needs and values family participation, parents who feel they have nothing to offer may see that education is not as formidable or as unimportant as they had believed. Persistence can pay off here.

Emotional Pressures

Perhaps the greatest challenge to teachers comes in attempting to reach parents who are less sensitive to their child's and a teacher's needs because of their own overwhelming emotional needs. This can be any parent at any particular time of her life. Teachers must realize that their expectations for these families to understand and be involved are often unrealistic.

A truly helpful stance is to be prepared to accept these parents as they are and to offer them not what we need in the way of their involvement in our programs or what their child needs in parenting, but what the parents need themselves to grow (Rundall & Smith, 1982).

What they need is nurturing. These parents need to be accepted for what they are, encouraged for whatever they have done, reinforced for any strength and efforts, and helped to feel understood. As teachers slowly establish a climate of trust with these parents, they should recognize that this relationship may help lessen parents' neediness.

In conversation teachers can focus the discussion on the parents and their concerns and interests. Where possible teachers should provide services for parents—a cup of coffee when they're looking tired, an opportunity to trade outgrown clothes with another family—as an indication that teachers care for parents and understand their needs. In fact, teachers are creating a dependent relationship—not for the professional's needs but as a way to assist a parent in establishing a trust relationship. Once a parent exhibits trust in the relationship, a teacher can gradually begin to set limits and make requests that would have been too frightening before the relationship was secure. It may be a long and trying struggle; but by responding to parents' needs, teachers may be able to reach parents who are "unreachable" in ways teachers had first expected to involve them.

There is an important consideration for teachers about parental under-involvement. Some have expressed a current concern that families want teachers and schools to just fix all students' needs and problems, leaving it all to them and not giving their own support and efforts in collaboration. This is a line that teachers and schools must draw, realizing what their roles are and making it clear that they will not go it alone. Parents must assume their full responsibilities.

▮▮▮ OVERINVOLVEMENT

To teachers struggling to get families involved in a program or even indicate an interest in their children's welfare, the predicament of overinvolvement might seem a lesser problem. But a parent who is too involved in a school situation may hinder his child's move toward independence or do the wrong thing at the wrong time, disrupting his child and the class. A phenomenon that many teachers note today is the many parents who are totally involved in their children's lives—hovering over them, anxious to see that their children achieve and develop as quickly as possible, and ready to tackle any obstacle they perceive on their children's behalf. They often refuse to believe their children are not the brightest and best, and insist on overprotecting or demanding special privileges for them. They are sometimes the parents who "know it all" and are full of recommendations or criticisms. Certainly they don't want to hear a teacher's observations of their children. Sometimes these parents just get in the way of orderly classroom procedures as they linger to talk indefinitely despite a teacher's need to care for the children or set up activities. How does a teacher respond to these behaviors?

Understanding a parent's behavior is a first step to tolerating or dealing with it. A teacher must get to know a particular parent to assess the individual situation and motivation.

Reluctance to Separate

Many parents are overwhelmed because of their own reluctance to separate from their young children. Being uncomfortable with separation is a natural experience in the developmental stages of parenthood, but a positive resolution of the conflicting feelings is important for both child and parent.

These parents may need particular reassurance that their child is being well cared for. Regular and specific reporting of information helps, as will personal notes and phone calls to share anecdotes about the child. This communication reassures parents that individual attention is paid to their child and that they are not losing contact with him.

Empathizing frankly with a parent's feelings can bring separation into the open:

> "I know there must be a lot of mixed feelings about seeing her grow up— rejoicing at all the new things, sadness at the idea of the little one left behind. It must seem to you sometimes like you're not as close as you once were. But it's just different, isn't it? Believe me, you're still the most important person in her world. Why, just the other day . . ."

Teachers should encourage parents to share their feelings and thoughts. Such communication allows teachers to reassure and subtly remind parents of a growing child's needs:

> "Hard as it is for you, the most loving thing a parent can do is to allow the child some room to move on, feeling stronger about being able to function without you. She needs to know you have enough confidence in her that she can be all right, for a while, without your presence."

When presented with the idea that it is for their child's welfare, many parents try harder to let go.

Unmet Personal Needs

A parent who is overinvolved because of unmet personal, social, or emotional needs benefits when a teacher responds with genuine appreciation and praise for his efforts. It is counterproductive to try to stop this involvement because it is so important for a parent's emotional health, as well as potentially helpful to a school or program.

When a parent's overinvolvement in a classroom becomes a problem to a child and teacher, his efforts can be redirected to other areas that are less disruptive—another classroom, working to involve other parents, or preparing materials. The particular strengths of families should be identified and utilized fully, always with sincere appreciation for the value of their contribution. Positive ways to contribute may be found—an extra pair of hands at lunchtime in the infant room, a cozy lap for an upset toddler, gathering the dress-up clothes that need mending, reading with a child who needs extra help, or calling other families to remind them about an upcoming meeting. Such efforts are not disruptive to a child's independent functioning and allow a parent to feel important to a school.

Insecurities

For a parent who "knows it all" and wants to share that knowledge, a teacher may need to indicate frequently that she considers a parent to be the real expert on his particular child. Sometimes a parent acts this way out of insecurities caused by real or imagined perceptions of a teacher's competence and dominance in a situation. When a teacher emphasizes partnership and defers to a parent's knowledge of his child, parental feelings of unimportance may diminish:

> "You know, parents really know their own children best. I need to know all I can about Johnny, and I appreciate you sharing your knowledge. What can you tell me about his projects at home?"

Sometimes a parent's information can be acknowledged and shared with others:

> "That's a good tip about those children's books. Could you write that down so I can add it to next month's newsletter? I think a lot of parents would like to know."

Teachers have to realize and acknowledge that in many cases parents really are more knowledgeable than they are. As a parent's knowledge and contribution can be directed in positive channels, her urge to criticize and complain may diminish.

When the "know it all" parent is unable to hear a teacher's points, a teacher must exercise skills of assertiveness and state her position clearly without belittling a parent's ideas or antagonizing and hurting. Teachers who recognize the complexity of human behavior know that a situation may be perceived in a variety of ways, and it is healthful to air all perspectives. This realization often prevents becoming too aggressive in presenting one's views. Assertiveness in a discussion may be helpful; aggressiveness will likely be destructive.

If reluctant to accept the validity of another's viewpoint for information, a parent may be more susceptible to information conveyed by less personal means. Making pertinent articles available to parents allows them to absorb the ideas and make them their own; an exposure to new ideas is accomplished without the resistance that can be inherent in personal discussions.

Lingering to Talk

For a parent who lingers on indefinitely to talk, a teacher should draw clear limits while still making the parent feel welcome. After a few minute of talk, when other responsibilities press, the teacher can say, "I enjoy talking with you, but right now I need to get over to those children at the water table. We'd love to have you stay if you have a few extra minutes. Perhaps you'd like to sit near the book corner—there's always someone looking for a story to be read." This reassures a parent that his presence is welcomed and provides a chance for him to be useful in classroom life. If he is uneasy about leaving his child, it allows him to observe a teacher and see how busy she really is. If such patterns continue, a teacher may need to say frankly,

> "I really want to talk with you, Mr. Jones. It's important to me to hear from you. But arrival time is so busy I'm not able to give you my full attention. Let's see if we can find some time to talk that's less hectic for me. I can be free at naptime or at my break this afternoon at 3:30."

Specific guidelines help a parent realize the many facets of a teacher's responsibility.

In addition to these troubling attitudes and behaviors, several situations frequently arise in schools and programs and cause irritation for the staff involved. Let's consider some ways schools can deal with these situations.

■■■■ FREQUENT CAUSES OF TENSION BETWEEN PARENTS AND TEACHERS

Late Parents

Among recurrent problems that annoy teachers is the frequent late arrival of parents picking up their children. At the end of a long and tiring day, this becomes a final insult for hardworking teachers and is a cause of resentment and relationship breakdowns. If teachers confront parents at the time of lateness, there is potential for explosive responses on both sides.

This is one situation that is probably best handled by administrators rather than by teachers themselves. It is important to stress timely pickups in the parents' handbook and in orientation information. Some programs ask parents to sign a contract agreeing that because staying with children after school closing times is a personal service to the family, late fees will be paid directly to the teachers who use personal time to stay and care for children. Other programs find that a late fee must be more than modest because some parents find it worthwhile to pay a small fee and have extra time. A substantial fee, such as $5.00 for every five minutes, often eliminates the problem. With parents who are habitually late, some directors find it necessary to ask parents to make contingency plans or provide lists of people who can be called to pick up children when parents are late. Termination warnings and follow-through may be a final step. It is important for late policies to be strict, clearly communicated, and consistently administered by those in charge, leaving teachers and children free of the emotional issue.

Releasing Children to Adults Who Are "Under the Influence" or Noncustodial Parents

A very uncomfortable and potentially dangerous situation arises when teachers are asked to release children under their care to adults they suspect to be impaired by drugs or alcohol, or to an adult who does not have legal custody of the child.

The best protection against such occurrences is to have written policies that are discussed at the time of enrollment. Complete information about people permitted to pick up children should be on file with a verifying signature, and parents should understand that any changes must be made in writing, with a signature that can be compared. Identities should be confirmed with picture identification. Teachers should not hesitate to delay the departure to confirm the legitimacy of any person's claim. Certified copies of court orders regarding custody should be made available for the center's files; verbal requests of one parent to prohibit access of another parent are not valid without a court document. Teachers should not be put in a position of having the responsibility to decide which parent has legal custody without such a document. If asked to release children to noncustodial parents, teachers should try to reach the custodial parent, and law enforcement if necessary, to protect all the children in the teacher's care as well as herself.

If a teacher feels that the adult picking up a child is not in a condition to be driving, he can call other authorized adults, call law enforcement officials, or pay for a cab (a requirement for reimbursement can be part of a parent contract [Cohen, 1993]). In either case the concern is to protect children under teacher care.

Lack of Respect

Many teachers complain that parents fail to treat them with respect. Especially in the child care environment, some parents seem to feel that teachers are merely employed lackeys and deserve no particular esteem at best—or at worst, downright contemptuous rudeness. Rather than the former belief that teachers were doing important and worthwhile work, when parents more often valued their efforts and opinions, many parents today seem to display lack of courtesy to teachers. Unfortunately, their children often echo this attitude. Such a lack of civility colors all communication between home and school. What can teachers do about this problem? (NEA, 1999).

It is important that teachers themselves realize the significance of the work they do with children and families. Their demeanor and attitudes best convey to others how deserving of respect they are. Succumbing to others' disrespectful behaviors would be an unfortunate loss for society and education.

It is vital that teachers continue to treat others with respect, no matter how rude or demanding they are. This example may go a long way toward helping parents and children see more appropriate models of interaction.

Sick Children

Another frequent cause of home–school friction is parents' disregard for policies that exclude sick children. It is, of course, understandable that families are sometimes overwhelmed by the difficulty of finding substitute care for sick children when parents feel that they must be at work themselves. Nevertheless, teachers cannot be expected to allow sick children into their classrooms, knowing the danger of the spread of infections and the special needs of children who don't feel well enough to participate in the usual routine. Clearly stated policies may help with this problem. Parent handbooks and orientation information should state specific conditions that demand exclusion from the classroom, as well as expected parent responses when they are called to pick up sick children. It is probably useful to require parents to file plans and names of providers for sick child care during the application process. Many parents would not consider this eventuality until a time of crisis unless directed to do so at the outset.

Teachers can and should empathize with parents who are torn between their child's and employer's needs, while gently focusing on the sick child's needs and holding firm to policies:

> "I know how hard it is to have to be at work when you wish you
> could be home looking after Jessica. I also know how difficult it is
> to find someone who will agree to look after a sick child. I wish we
> could help you, but our policy on her staying home for at least 24
> hours after a fever is there to protect Jessica—she just won't feel
> up to being here, and her health is extra vulnerable, too."

It is important not to interpret parents' actions in bringing sick children to the center or reluctance to leave work to come and get a sick child as poor parenting or a sign of indifference. It is more likely desperation at the role conflicts of parent and worker. As center staff discover community resources that can assist parents needing care for sick children, directors can post the information and notify parents.

Care of sick children of working parents has become a community issue. Some companies and communities have created linkages between medical facilities and personnel and the child care community to ease the problem (Jacobs, 1992).

End-of-Day Problems

When parents, children, and teachers come together at the end of the day, problems can be created by the transition and magnified by fatigue. Children sometimes test and evade parents, almost as if challenging them to take charge again. Parents sometimes demand information and answers from teachers, again appearing to challenge how the day has actually gone. From their side, teachers may have reports of negative behavior they feel are necessary to make. Fragile relationships can be stretched at this time.

What can teachers do to make the end of the day less stressful for everyone? Part of the solution may lie in preparation for the transition. Quiet activities such as reading books or working puzzles should fill the last period of the day. This way both teachers and children can have a calm period at the end of the day. While children are quietly occupied, teachers can be free to do some of the closing chores so they are not feeling rushed in hectic cleanup when parents arrive. Teachers can post summaries of the classroom or individual children's day so that parents can get some answers to their questions by reading the notice board or individual daily sheets when they enter. If teachers help children gather their belongings or get partly dressed for departure, this helps parents and children move toward home going.

The end of the day is probably not the best time to discuss behavior problems. Parents who are continually given negative reports about their children at pickup time are not being helped to feel positively about either their children or the teachers. Teachers need to avoid the temptation to give daily reports of negative behaviors when everyone is tired and least likely to be receptive to sensitive discussion. A better strategy is to arrange a later sit-down discussion:

> "Mrs. Alexander, I think it would be useful for you and me to have a chance to talk away from the classroom. I know you've had questions about Roger, and there are some things I'd like to share, too. Can we find a time this week? Perhaps if you'd come in 20 minutes or so before your usual time, I could arrange for Miss Phillips to be in the classroom."

Such a conversation is likely to be more productive than an at-the-door confrontation between harried parents and teachers.

Parents Who Ask for Special Treatment

Teachers are frequently annoyed by parents' requests for services or attention for their children that go beyond typical classroom practices.

> "Jane's father asked if we can let her stay in today when the other children go out to the playground, since she's just getting over her cold."
>
> "Jeremy's grandmother wants him not to take a nap today because they want him to sleep in the car when they leave for their trip. Now how am I supposed to do that—he'll bother everybody else."
>
> "Another toy from home—her Mom says she just wanted to let her bring it, even though she knows it's against our rules."

Rather than simply being irritated and refusing the requests arbitrarily, teachers may need to remember that early childhood programs are there to provide support services for families, and families have a right to define some of the individual services they need. Teachers should consider how a requested service might be provided rather than immediately refusing. Could Jane stay in with another class? Could Jeremy spend some time with books in the director's office? A cooperative stance may find a solution satisfactory for everyone.

Requests that have no solution need to be explained to families so they understand the problems their requests make for the center. When policies have been clearly communicated in parent handbooks before the request, teachers can refer to the policy as they state the decision, rather than making it a personal teacher decision. Existing policies mean that parents and children come to understand that teachers' treatment is even-handed, not open to favoritism, yet applied with sensitivity to individuals.

> "We'll keep her toy in her cubby so it will be safe. She can show it to her friends at group time, and then we'll put it back. I know you'd both be sad if it got lost or broken. Remember our policy about toys from home."

But it is most important to remember that families do have individual, unique needs, and arbitrary refusal of all special requests does not recognize this.

Disagreement over Readiness

A current issue that is emotionally charged for the parents and teachers involved is the issue of **readiness** for children moving on, usually into elementary school situations.

> "I can't believe it. We've been planning all along for Tammy to start kindergarten this fall—her birthday is in August, well before

the cutoff date. And at last I was planning to go back to my job full-time—both my boss and I have been counting on it. Then the teacher calls me in for a conference and tells me she's not 'ready,' all because they gave her some test and she couldn't tell the difference between upper- and lowercase letters. Letters, for Pete's sake. She's as smart as can be, and she gets along just fine with other kids. I can't believe they can do this to us.

More and more families are getting the kind of news that Tammy's mother just received. As school programs need to demonstrate improved quality and accountability, there is a growing tendency to use standardized test results to dictate placement decisions. School systems nationwide are using various types of tests to assess children prior to or after the kindergarten year. Unfortunately this often leads to practices that are inappropriate considering the age and developmental level of the children involved. Testing narrows the curriculum as teachers try to prepare children to succeed on tests. Many important early childhood skills are not easily measured by standardized tests, so social, emotional, and physical development and learning are not given equal importance in decisions about readiness. Standardized group and individual testing is inappropriate for young children, who often don't have good test-taking skills, such as sitting still, being quiet, and following a series of directions, often to write or make particular marks. Young children are growing and learning so rapidly that there is great potential for obtaining inaccurate test results and thus mislabeling children. Children who are English language learners are especially at risk for misassessment with testing in the early years.

The best information about readiness comes from systematic observations by trained teachers, along with information from parents, who know their children better than anyone else and should be active participants in the assessment process. What this means is that teachers as well as parents should work against practices that exclude children's own parents from providing meaningful input into decisions that affect families and the educational future and self-esteem of children. Together they can become advocates of developmentally appropriate practices that are not potentially harmful for young children.

If teachers find themselves working in situations that use arbitrary (and often proven invalid) test results to decide readiness, they must realize that parents will find the decisions painful and disruptive to the family's plans and image of the child. Discussions of the findings must be careful and specific so that parents carry away no misunderstandings about future prognoses for learning.

Teachers can give families specific information and guidelines about what is developmentally appropriate and what is not, perhaps helping them become advocates to work for change in community school practices. Teachers can convey support for the parents' perceptions of their child, always indicating that parents are the real experts on their children. If this sounds as if the recommendation is that the teacher should sympathize with the parent who is left out of the decision-making process and forced to accept the school's view of readiness, that is correct. Teachers should not lend support to practices that are developmentally inappropriate for children and families.

On the other hand, many of today's parents are focused on their children's academic achievements, often demanding excessively early instruction or methods. This situation demands continual education on how children best learn and appropriate experiences. Workshops, discussions, speakers, and offering reading materials may help. When teachers find themselves in disagreement with parents' perceptions of children's abilities and developmental levels, it will be wise to bring in a third party to observe the child and join the conversation. Another perspective may help both parent and teacher approach the situation from a fresh viewpoint.

SUMMARY

Teachers may encounter troublesome behaviors and attitudes that are personally annoying and professionally discouraging. In each case a teacher's first step should be to attempt to identify the feelings or circumstances that might be the cause. A stance that is directed toward solutions rather than accusations is important. Meeting these needs constructively will eliminate some of the destructive reactions, including teacher frustration.

A teacher who makes genuine efforts to understand and solve problems, but still finds situations that seem to have no solution, should remember that he or she is not alone. Any teacher has had similar experiences that sometimes linger in memory long after forgetting more positive experiences. It is important to learn as much as possible from these negative experiences and to keep on trying!

Many teachers find that recording their feelings, perceptions, and experiences in working with parents is a valuable tool for their own growth. Informal notes or journal entries document concerns, needs, and progress, and pinpoint areas that need attention. Such personal notes, meant purely for a teacher's use, provide both an emotional release and evidence that her efforts are effective.

Critical Analysis Form for Predicaments in Teacher–Parent Relationships

Parent's Perspective

How does the parent describe the problem?

How does the parent seem to feel about the problem?

What do you think the parent expects the teacher to do about the problem?

If the teacher did this, what might be the result?

(continues)

(continued)

Teacher's Perspective

How does the teacher describe the problem?

How does the teacher feel about the problem?

What does the teacher expect the parent to do about the problem?

If the parent did this, what might be the result?

Child's Perspective

How might the child see the problem?

How does the child feel about the problem?

If the problem is not resolved, how might this affect the child?

If the problem is resolved, how would that affect the child?

Overall Perspective

What is known about the problem?

What knowledge is applicable?

What principles of ethical behavior are involved?

What are possible solutions?

STUDENT ACTIVITIES FOR FURTHER STUDY

Role-play, and then discuss with your classmates, the following situations where teachers are faced with hostile reactions:

1. "I refuse to talk to you any more. You're just plain wrong about Sarah— she's a very bright child."

2. "How dare you ask me so many questions about my child? It's none of your business."

3. "I want to talk to your principal. If you were doing your job properly, there would not be a problem with Melvin. She should know how incompetent you are."

4. "If you ask me, you want me to do your job for you. You can't handle him in the classroom, so you want me to get tough with him at home."

5. "As long as I'm the one paying the bill for child care, I want things done as I ask. I insist that you get busy and teach Barbara to read this year before she goes to kindergarten. Are you saying I don't know what's best for my own child?"

6. "What is this stuff about readiness? I know my own child. I say she's ready for kindergarten, and I don't care what your test results say."

CASE STUDY

Rhoda Williams, a single mother of two children who are kindergarten and first grade students in your after-school program, has been late twice this week already. You also know that she was late earlier this month and has not paid those late fees. Just now you received a call that she was delayed leaving her office and will not likely arrive until 6:30 p.m. Your center closes at 6, and you have a social engagement some distance away at 7 p.m.

1. Use the Critical Analysis form to consider your responses and possible solutions to this chronic problem.

2. Consider the issue from the parent's viewpoint. What might some of her emotional responses and behaviors be?

3. Consider the issue from the children's viewpoint. How might they be reacting emotionally?

4. From the teacher's viewpoint, what are your feelings and concerns?

5. Identify some possible solutions to this predicament.

REVIEW QUESTIONS

1. Discuss possible reasons for apparently hostile responses.

2. Describe three considerations for teachers dealing with hostile reactions.

3. Discuss three possible reasons for apparent indifference; for each, identify a consideration for teachers' overcoming indifference.

4. Discuss three possible reasons for overinvolvement; for each, identify ways of working with these parents.

5. Describe considerations for dealing with several causes of parent–teacher tension.

SUGGESTIONS FOR FURTHER READING

Canter, L. (2002). *Parents on your side: A teacher's guide to creating positive relationships with parents* (2nd ed.). Los Angeles, CA: Canter and Associates.

Galinsky, E. (1988). Parents and teacher–caregivers: Sources of tension, sources of support. *Young Children, 43*(3), 4–11.

———. (1990). Why are some parent/teacher partnerships clouded with difficulties? *Young Children, 45*(5), 2–3, 38–39.

Gonzalez-Mena, J., & Stonehouse, A. (2003, July/August). High-maintenance parent or parent partner? Working with a parent's concern. *Child Care Information Exchange,* 16–18.

Jaksec, C. (2003). *The confrontational parent: A practical guide for school leaders.* Larchmont, NY: Eye on Education.

Kagan, S. (1999). Cracking the readiness mystique. *Young Children, 54*(5), 2–3.

Katz, L. G. (1992). Readiness: Children and their schools. *The ERIC Review, 2*(1), 2–6.

Katz, L. (1996). Building resilience: Helping your child cope with frustrations at school. *Instructor, 106*(3), 95–98.

Macfarlane, E. (1998). Reaching reluctant parents. *Education Digest, 67*(7).

Manning, D., & Schwindler, O. (1997). Communicating with parents when their children have difficulties. *Young Children, 52*(5), 27–33.

McEwan, E. (1998). *How to deal with parents who are angry, troubled, afraid, or just plain crazy.* Thousand Oaks, CA: Corwin Press.

Morgan, E. L. (1988, January). Prickly problems #1: The late parent. *Child Care Information Exchange, 59,* 16.

———. (1989). Talking with parents when concerns come up. *Young Children, 44*(2), 52–56.

NAEYC Ethics Panel. (1998). Using NAEYC's Code of Ethics to negotiate professional problems. What should a teacher do when a parent defines academically rigorous education differently than she does? *Young Children, 53*(6), 56–57.

———. (1998). Using NAEYC's Code of Ethics: What happens when school/parent relationships aren't good. *Young Children, 53*(6), 75.

Powers, J. (2005). *Parent-friendly early learning.* St. Paul, MN: Redleaf Press.

Rudney, G. (2005). *Every teacher's guide to working with parents.* Thousand Oaks, CA: Corwin Press, a division of Sage.

Whitaker, T., & Fiore, D. (2000). *Dealing with difficult parents, and with parents in difficult situations.* Larchmont, NY: Eye on Education.

Willis, S. (1995). When parents object to classroom practice. *Education Update, 37*(1), 1, 6, 8.

REFERENCES

Boone, E., & Barclay, K. (1995). *Building a three-way partnership: Linking school, families, and community.* New York: Scholastic Leadership Policy Research.

Boutte, G. S., Keepler, D. L., Tyler, V. S., & Terry, B. Z. (1992). Effective techniques for involving difficult parents. *Young Children, 47*(3), 19–22.

Cohen, A. (1993, March). Releasing a child to an adult under the influence or a noncustodial adult. *Child Care Information Exchange,* 15–16.

Gordon, T. (2000). *Parent effectiveness training: The proven program for raising responsible children.* New York: Random House (Three Rivers Press).

Graue, E. (2001). Research in review: What's going on in the children's garden? Kindergarten today. *Young Children, 56*(3), 67–73.

Jacobs, G. (1992, November). The search for sick-child care. *Working Mother,* 80–85.

Jaksek, C. (2004). *The difficult parent: An educator's guide to handling aggressive behavior.* Thousand Oaks, CA: Corwin Press, a division of Sage.

NEA. (1999). What do you do when parents show no respect for school employees? Tips for teachers. *NEA Today, 18*(3), 29–30.

Rundall, R. D., & Smith, S. L. (1982). Working with difficult parents. In Brigham Young University Press (Ed.), *How to involve parents in early childhood education.* Provo, UT: Brigham Young University Press.

**HELPFUL
WEB SITES**

http://www.croton.com/allpie
>   Alliance for Parent Involvement in Education is a nonprofit organization that assists and encourages parental involvement in education, wherever that education takes place: in public school, in private school, or at home.

http://www.acresolution.org [or http://www.crenet.org: Conflict Resolution Education network]
>   Association for Conflict Resolution is a professional organization dedicated to enhancing the practice and public understanding of conflict resolution.

http://www.ericeece.org
>   ERIC EECE Clearinghouse on Elementary and Early Childhood Education.

http://www.parentsoup.com
>   Contains articles about parent–teacher relationships.

Additional resources for this chapter can be found on the Online Companion to accompany this text at www.earlychilded.delmar.com. This supplemental material includes frequently asked questions; chapter outlines to be used as study guides; scenarios that both encourage large and small group discussions and provoke new thoughts and ideas; and chapter resources, including chapter summaries, interactive questions, Web links, and Web activities. In addition, forms from the text are available for download.

CHAPTER 18

Looking at Parent Involvement Programs That Work

OBJECTIVES
After reading this chapter, you should be able to

1 Understand the ways various early education programs function to involve families in their programs.

This text has offered a rationale for working as partners with families in early education and has considered numerous strategies and practices that may open and enhance the communication process. It remains for teachers and families to create their own family involvement programs, to respond in the ways that seem most appropriate to the particular needs of their populations.

Some of you may already know of some good programs for children and their families that exist around the country. Schools and child care programs vary a good deal in how they look and function, depending on the needs of the populations they serve, amount of funding and staff available, philosophy, and goals. Each school must create its own patterns that work well for the staff and families concerned. As schools consider ideas to try, it may be useful to look at some programs that work effectively with children and families.

■■■ LAKEWOOD PRESCHOOL COOPERATIVE, CHARLOTTE, NORTH CAROLINA

Within view of the towering office buildings of prosperous downtown Charlotte, North Carolina, a small, neighborhood preschool program works to support a culturally diverse group of families. In a neighborhood where the average household income is below the poverty level even though at least three-quarters of the families have at least one adult working full-time, and over half of the adults have not earned a high school diploma, the beautiful new building created by Habitat for Humanity volunteers stands as a sign of community commitment to supporting families. Lakewood Preschool Cooperative is a part-day preschool for children up to age 5, and it includes a family education program for residents of the Lakewood community. *Cooperative* is included in the name because the program is designed as a cooperative effort among parents, children, staff, neighbors, and volunteers to address the educational, emotional, physical, and social needs of the preschool children in this underserved community. Indeed, volunteers from churches and businesses have been instrumental in the establishment and ongoing operations of the school; as the director takes visitors on tours, she points out the donations, which range from appliances to cleaning materials, from a brand new 15-passenger van to the time given by employees of a local building supply store who put together the playground equipment. There are no fees; the program is funded by scholarships that come from grants, individuals, local churches and foundations, and businesses (see Figure 18-1).

The children in the preschool reflect the racial and linguistic diversity of the community, which is home to African American, Laotian, and Vietnamese families; for half of Lakewood's children English is a second language. This diversity makes it especially challenging to meet the stated goals of the Lakewood Preschool Cooperative:

1. To prepare the children for successful entry and performance in the public school system.

2. To provide a forum in which families can receive the information, resources, and opportunities necessary to find solutions to common problems.

3. To support the children and their families as they advance through the public school system.

As a member of an Alliance of Part-Day Preschools in Charlotte that all include strong parent cooperative components, Lakewood works from a philosophy that recognizes parents as the first and foremost teachers of their children. The idea is that family support programs provide emotional sustenance, information, and instrumental assistance to families within a context of empowerment (Dunlap, 1996). Common goals of such programs include enhancement of parents' child-rearing capacities, empowerment of parents as advocates for change, and brokerage of resources (Dunlap, 1997). Resources

(a)

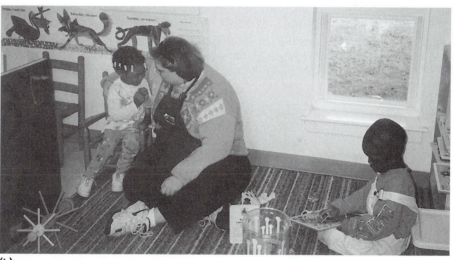

(b)

FIGURE 18-1 Lakewood serves children from families of diverse backgrounds, including African American, Vietnamese, and Laotian.
Courtesy Lakewood Preschool Cooperative.

may help parents reach their own goals, especially with respect to education, self-sufficiency, and citizenship Preschools.

When families enroll their children in the preschool, they sign a family agreement. Stated clearly as a contract, the preschool cooperative agrees to provide a quality, developmentally appropriate early childhood program (the **High/Scope model** is used) and a family support program that includes classes, workshops, and support sessions, and to assist in the transition from preschool to public school. In turn, families must agree to six separate contract items. (The program recognizes that a variety of important adults may function as caregivers in children's lives, including grandparents and other members of the extended family, and so is careful to use the terminology "family agreement.")

First, they must agree to bring their children to school every day at 8:30 a.m. and pick them up at 12:00 p.m. (or be available to connect with the van driver during home pickup and drop-off.) For adults who have lived in the culture of poverty, which tends to develop behaviors of dependence and little tendency to plan for the future, this is an important responsibility, signifying their active role in providing for their children's education and in being role models themselves for responsibility.

A second agreement is to participate in a daily at-home activity with their children. Although this is not assigned as formal "homework," parents are asked to spend 15 minutes every day with each individual child, free of television or other distractions. They are asked to plan what they will do during this time, with abundant suggestions made by the director and teachers. "Activity bags" are sent home every Friday. The director states clearly that there is a conscious effort not to institutionalize this family time as an assignment, but rather to help parents see the importance of their interaction with their youngsters. A recent activity was sending home colored construction paper and asking parents and children to find things in (donated) magazines of that color, then cut them out and paste them on the construction paper to bring back to school. When teachers make their initial home visits, they take along a "homework" box to leave, containing items such as crayons, scissors, glue, construction paper, and sticker books. Children frequently use these materials at home when older brothers and sisters are doing homework and bring the work back to the preschool to show.

A third item in the agreement is to take a turn monthly as a parent assistant in the classroom (at least two hours) or to support other work in the program (see Figure 18-2). Family members may accompany children on field trips, assist with food service and cleanup, read to children individually in their own language, or tend to administrative tasks such as filing or helping to maintain the building—raking leaves, planting gardens, or the like.

The fourth component that families agree to participate in is the weekly family support class. Held in an attractive parent room at the center one morning each week, families agree that one adult who is important in the life of the child from each family will participate. Because of various working schedules and family structures, the director admits she never knows who will attend—sometimes a father, other times a grandmother. Topics for the sessions are determined by parent completion of a checklist of possible topics; when parents identify a topic that is of special importance to them, they may check it several times (see Figure 18-3). Possibilities include the following:

- Topics related to children: What can I do about crying, whining, or screaming? What can I do about fears? What can I do about fighting with siblings? What can I do when my ideas about raising a child are

FIGURE 18-2 Parents are responsible for spending at least two hours each month assisting in the classroom.
Courtesy Lakewood Preschool Cooperative.

FIGURE 18-3 Regular family support meetings discuss topics of interest to parents.
Courtesy Lakewood Preschool Cooperative.

different from those of another family member (a very popular topic)? Why should I listen to children's feelings? What are some cheap and fun things to do with my children?

- Health issues: How do I know when to take my child to the doctor?
- Fitness and exercise.
- Life skills: Managing money or organizing your life.
- Seeking solutions: Whom can you trust? Do you have a support system? What resources are in my community to help families?
- School success: Is watching TV harmful to my child's school performance? How to talk to your child's teacher or principal about problems.

As the adults come together, the director functions as the family educator. She comments that there are no guidelines for facilitating a group that combines members from four distinct cultural groups (Caucasian, African American, Hmong, and Vietnamese) and in which some participants have limited English skills or experience in sharing personal stories and ideas in groups.

One enormously nutrition successful series recently was taught by the local 4-H program. Participants were randomly assigned to groups to work together on recipe preparation, with the common activity helping to bridge cultural and language gaps (see Figure 18-4).

As a result of trying to find community resources to help meet all the interests identified by the survey, a list of individuals and agencies in the

FIGURE 18-4 It is challenging to facilitate discussion among participants from different cultural and linguistic backgrounds.

Courtesy Lakewood Preschool Cooperative.

community who may be called upon to run education sessions has been compiled. The director also notes the sensitive need to walk a fine line between making assumptions about skills based on spoken language or experiences, and saying too much and appearing condescending to those who may not express but clearly understand. An example of this was provided by a recent class activity of writing thank-you notes after the holiday season.

Several different groups had provided gifts of clothing and toys for the children. At this meeting the director wanted to raise the issue of writing to thank the donors. Realizing that writing such a note might be a new experience for many of the adults, she facilitated the composition of a letter, with appropriate blanks for children's names and mention of the specific toy or item of clothing for personalization. She hinted that some might like to use these ideas and others might prefer to use their own words. With the help of a "buddy" system (some who were more proficient in English were able to help others), at morning's end everyone was satisfied to have written their own five letters of thanks.

This example wonderfully illustrates the idea that through involvement with the family component of this preschool, adults acquire **cultural capital**— comfort and familiarity with the customs and demands of the culture in which they live or to which they want to adapt. Over time, cultural capital is translated to human capital or economic gain as participants become more easily able to function within the mainstream culture instead of remaining isolated in the culture of poverty. This process of empowerment ultimately strengthens families and neighborhoods.

The program recognizes the real difficulties parents of limited resources have in fulfilling some of their responsibilities. Therefore, the program supports parents by offering transportation to the parenting classes in the children's van, or arranging for the local Mobile Solution van to call on the center so parents may schedule their children's immunizations conveniently; nevertheless, the responsibility belongs to the parents.

Collaborating with the early childhood club at a nearby community college, the parent group helped run a sale of lightly used toys, books, and clothing before Christmas (see Figure 18-5). In this way residents of the neighborhood and their friends could provide Christmas gifts for their children at very low prices. With the proceeds, the family support group could plan an expensive outing to the zoo in a distant town for their children and families—true empowerment.

Still another requirement of the family agreement is "to welcome the director and teachers into my home for conversation about my child." Home visits are made by the teaching team before school starts in the fall, and again in January and at year-end. The first visit is a time to get acquainted, allowing children to meet their teachers at home where they are most comfortable, and teachers to gain firsthand insights into the culture and lifestyle of the home. The later two visits are to report children's progress, sharing assessment results and plans with parents. Teachers share the results of COR

FIGURE 18-5 The parent group helped sponsor a sale for Christmas toys.
Courtesy Lakewood Preschool Cooperative.

(Child Observation Record)—the High/Scope tool to assess children's developmental progress in the High/Scope key experiences. As discussed in earlier chapters, home visits are an instrumental part of the teacher attitude that they are working with families, not just children. Communication becomes easier with these agreed contacts. Another communication method involves sending materials and messages back and forth between school to home in plastic bags.

Another stipulation of the family contract is the agreement to abide by the policies of the Family Handbook, a clearly designed booklet that outlines educational policy and such typical items as health and clothing requirements, birthday celebrations, and opportunities for parents to volunteer.

One final stated component is that families who do not abide by the policies they have agreed to will be called for a conference with the director, at which time a plan will be developed to correct the situation. If the problem remains after one month, the child's participation in the program will be terminated. Lakewood wants their families to understand the seriousness of their participation.

With English being a learning experience for so many of the families, the preschool program and the family support class both emphasize literacy. In a monthly Share-a-Book program the parents are introduced to a book during

FIGURE 18-6 The Share-a-Book program helps families understand how to support their children's literacy development.
Courtesy Lakewood Preschool Cooperative.

their class (see Figure 18-6). The director reads the book to the parent group, talking about the illustrations, the words and rhythms of the language, the techniques she is using in sharing the book, and whether the book would translate well into the families' other languages. The books are already familiar to the children from classroom readings, so when the parents bring the book home to read to them, they can participate comfortably. Parenting magazines and books are available for parents to check out, as well as a lending library of children's books. Donated magazines are available for parents to help themselves.

Lakewood celebrates family success stories. A recent newsletter to the community told the story of Angel, who could only say her name when she enrolled in the preschool a year ago. Her parents had begun a new life by immigrating to the United States from Vietnam four years earlier, and when Angel started school they immediately began to attend the family support class. They were encouraged to enroll in English classes at the local college, and Angel's mother was also studying for her citizenship test, coming frequently to the parent classroom to study.

One year later Angel is an active preschool participant—singing all the songs and listening to all the stories—and is now fluent in English, often interpreting for her younger brother who began at the preschool this year. From elaborate pictures, she has progressed to writing letters and words—all in English. Her mother was quoted as saying, "Before my kids come here, we don't know English, and it look like we don't know anything. Now my children

FIGURE 18-7 Parents and children learn English through activity and interaction.
Courtesy Lakewood Preschool Cooperative.

talk English good; they singing English and they feel happy now. Thank you to Karen and all the teachers in the preschool." A family moves on, and their children flourish—thanks to the support for the whole family (see Figure 18-7).

Such a story suggests the subjective success of the program. Lakewood, though, is involved in additional efforts to create objective data about the program's effects. There is limited research nationally on whether family support programs make measurable differences when combined with quality preschool education. A local university is compiling abundant information that may provide such data when synthesized. A Family Assessment Scale will measure the status of families on factors that include overall environment, overall social support, overall family characteristics and interactions, overall child well-being, program participation, and community connections. Each month the teachers participate by completing a monthly contact sheet; this documents the number of days children were absent or late, the number of days parents attended classes or volunteered, and all parent–teacher contacts.

For more information about the Family Assessment Scale, contact Kathryn M. Dunlap Ph.D. ACSW, School of Social Work, UNC-Charlotte, 460 J. Fretwell, Charlotte, NC 28223-0001.

Confident, creative preschoolers and parents becoming comfortable in their relationship with educational institutions, with parenting skills, and with the resources to support their participation in the community are evidence enough to show that Lakewood Preschool Cooperative is working with families in ways that will have lasting effects.

■■■ FAMILY RESOURCE CENTER, FORT MYERS, FLORIDA

The name states clearly the intent with which this small center on the campus of Florida Gulf Coast University in Fort Myers was created. Planners of this newest member of the state university system in Florida were intentional about providing a resource to serve the campus families, primarily students of the university busy at their studies and work. Of the 40 infants, toddlers, and preschoolers enrolled in the program, approximately 75% are from families of university students, another 15% are drawn from families of faculty and staff, and the remaining 10% come from the community. Five positions are contracted with Lee County Head Start, again with priority given to student parents. One of ten Educational Research Centers for Child Development in Florida's state university system, the center is a model for quality in the surrounding counties, nurturing connections with the community as teachers visit the center to observe or to borrow teacher resources.

Receiving NAEYC accreditation only one year after opening in 1998, the center also serves as a learning and research environment for university students and faculty. Student interns, student assistants, and students volunteering through the service learning program contribute to the family feel by providing low ratios and opportunities for individual interaction. The family atmosphere is enhanced with just three classrooms: one for infants from six weeks through 18 months, where infants each have a primary caregiver; a toddler room for children aged 18 months through 3 years; and a preschool classroom for 3-, 4-, and 5-year-olds.

The idea of partnership is explicit in the vision statement, adopted by the center staff and families in January 1999: ". . . a place where a partnership between family and school creates an optimally safe, nurturing, and diverse learning environment, which all children deserve." See Figure 18-8 for the center's mission statement and goals; later in this overview we will discuss the process of communication of staff and parents that created these documents.

Among the theoretical influences on the director working to implement the philosophy of family involvement in the center is the model of school/family/community partnerships drawn from the work of Joyce Epstein. (See again the discussion of the Epstein model of six types of family involvement in Chapter 4 and in Epstein et al., 1997, in the references.) Although use of the Epstein model has been primarily directed to school settings for older children, it is instructive to realize that the six kinds of involvement are what help make the Family Center an example of productive efforts to create partnerships.

> The mission of the Family Resource Center is
> - To promote the social, emotional, moral, cognitive, language, and physical development of each child by
>   - Providing support and resources for families.
>   - Forming and enhancing nurturing relationships between each child and teacher where each child is cherished for his or her own unique qualities.
>   - Creating rich developmentally and culturally appropriate curriculum.
> - To build partnerships with families through mutual respect, open communication, and opportunities for active participation.
> - To facilitate interactions between and among families.
> - To model, convey, and promote high-quality developmentally and culturally appropriate practices in early care and education to families, professionals, and the community at large.
> - To create a nurturing and responsive environment that provides resources and supports the personal and professional growth of the Center staff.

FIGURE 18-8 Mission and goals of the Family Resource Center.
Adopted by center staff and parents, 1999.

In the Epstein model, the first type of involvement is directed to supporting families with their parenting and child-rearing skills. Reciprocally, this type of involvement also helps schools to understand the unique families they serve. Until budget constraints meant insufficient funds, the center had a half-time position for a family and community liaison professional. This permitted numerous family education classes, which have had to be decreased while remaining staff members find time to take over some of these responsibilities. For example, the head toddler teacher recently facilitated a discussion group for toddler parents.

In addition, because of the contract with Head Start, at least four parent activities are held each year. The Head Start contracted families also receive the traditional home visits. The center's excellent Web site offers information to support parent education. There are several articles written by the director and staff, listings of books available for loan in the resource library housed in the multipurpose room, and links to other helpful Web sites for parents for information and local resources. The resource library was funded through a grant and includes both print materials and audiovisual resources.

FIGURE 18-9 Parents are able to learn new ideas and strategies by observing skilled professionals interacting with their children.
Courtesy Family Resource Center.

An accessible table in the entry area is supplied with magazines about parenting and ideas for family activities. Parents are encouraged to visit in the classrooms at any time except the quiet time after lunch, and many do because of the proximity of the center to the university classroom buildings. Thus parents are able to learn new ideas and strategies by observing skilled professionals interacting with their children. Such visits also promote conversations that help professionals learn about each family. (See Figure 18-9.)

The second type of involvement in the Epstein model is communication. Many opportunities for communication have been created at the center. When parents enter, they must log in on the computer on the front desk before they accompany their children to the classrooms. Often individual notes and general messages are posted there. Technology enhances communication in other ways. The attractive Web site includes much information for families, including the Family Handbook, with detailed information; the Policies and Procedures manual; an online tour; a short video showing the children and staff busy at activities in the center; and other essential information. Parents are given daily sheets detailing the activities of the children's day, and an e-mail copy is sent to parents who might not have access to this firsthand information, such as divorced parents. There are family folders in each classroom for parents to check each day; these contain the daily sheets and any personal communication from the teacher. Parents are also encouraged to leave their instructions and comments for the day in writing for later referral. Pagers are available to families at no charge and must, in fact, be carried by parents of infants so they can be contacted immediately when necessary. Each classroom has a separate

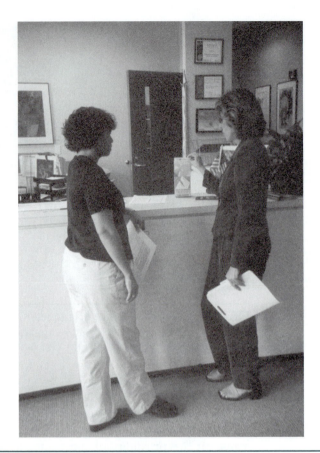

FIGURE 18-10 Staff and parents strive for regular communication.
Courtesy Family Resource Center.

telephone number, and parents are encouraged to call when they would like. Parents create and produce the newsletter; currently faculty and student parents are collaborating on this effort. (See Figures 18-10 and 18-11.)

Parent–teacher conferences are held twice each year, except in the infant room where, as the director smiles, "They are having conferences every day as they discuss milestones and activities." Teachers keep portfolios of the children's work, discussing them monthly with the children as they consider progress and special memories. These portfolios are shared with families at the conferences. Parents are asked to complete a survey with opportunities to describe things that they most appreciate about the day-to-day care and education their children receive, as well as to make recommendations for future practices. Staff discuss these surveys at a retreat as they set goals for the coming year.

And most important, there is a good deal of talk. The friendly, informal atmosphere promotes a sense of community. A faculty father pauses in the university's cafe to share an anecdote from home with the director, and the director responds with her observation of his child from just that morning. Parents are reminded about confidentiality, and there is a sense of respect for all families.

FIGURE 18-11 Technology enhances communication between parents and staff.
Courtesy Family Resource Center.

Epstein's third type of family involvement is volunteering. When parents complete the application for the waiting list at the Family Resource Center, they check off this statement: "I understand that parent participation is essential at the Family Resource Center. If my child is enrolled in the center, I will agree to become actively involved in some manner. My participation will be discussed upon my child's enrollment." Parents have choices of action groups that include fundraising, working on the newsletter or Web site, designing education and recreation programs, and working on policies and projects. In addition, the center has a leadership team composed of two parents from each classroom, along with a teacher representative and the director. A representative from the leadership team is selected to represent the group on the board of directors. The leadership team and action groups plan events and projects and work with the director to support the center in various ways.

The volunteer parent participation shows! The outdoor wall of the center that faces the playground is currently adorned with a marvelous painted mural of the environment of Southwest Florida, complete with the kinds of vegetation and animals seen by the children daily. (See Figure 18-12.) A Head Start parent, also a talented artist, is creating the mural as part of her volunteer service learning. Parents and grandparents participate regularly in the classroom, often coming to accompany children on walks or join in activities with special visitors, such as the fire department puppet show. When children will be singing at a tree lighting ceremony, parents meet them on campus to help walk the children there safely. Families contribute many items to the center, including extra

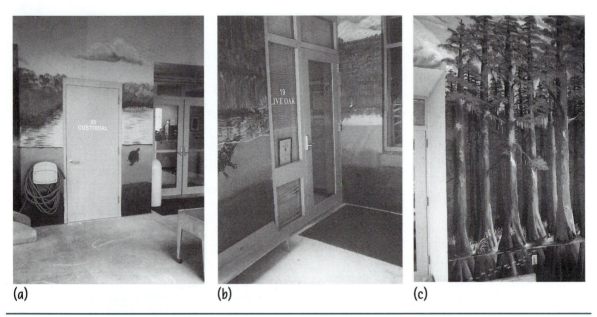

(a) (b) (c)

FIGURE 18-12 A parent created the outdoor mural of the environment of Southwest Florida.
Courtesy Family Resource Center.

clothing, books, and financial gifts to purchase classroom materials. Families share their family traditions and customs in the classroom. As the director describes it, "Every family makes its unique contribution. When nothing is set specifically, their contributions come from the heart."

Epstein describes the fourth type of family involvement as learning at home, where families work with their children on learning activities. Classroom teachers suggest home activities for the Head Start families. As the center compiles volunteer hours, they also tabulate these hours spent in home activities. Last year the five parents involved in the Head Start contract accrued close to 500 hours spent in activities at home with their children. As families visit the classrooms, they learn strategies and activities they can use at home with their children.

The fifth type of family involvement from Epstein is decision making. As previously mentioned, families are involved in the leadership team, action groups, and board of directors. In addition, a representative from the Family Resource Center attends the Lee County Head Start Policy Council. The mission/vision/goals statement was the product of full collaboration of parents and staff. Look again at the mission statement in Figure 18-8. Notice the wording of the second point under the first bullet. The director tells the story of how staff had worked separately on their mission statement and then met with families to continue to refine the ideas and language. As the group struggled over the word that should follow the phrase "where each child is," one mother suddenly exclaimed, "*Cherished!* It has to be cherished. That so exactly describes what happens between the teachers and children." And *cherished* it was. An important insight from the parent enhanced the overall decision-making process.

Finally, the sixth type of family involvement from the Epstein model is collaboration with the community—in this case, the community involves the university as well as the community beyond. The contract with Head Start has enriched the population of the center, and its services have added opportunities for all the children. The community has been tapped for fund-raising as well as for programs about police and fire safety. Community grants have provided the lending resources and other supports. The center collaborates with the local child care resource and referral agency in family tuition subsidies as well as staff training.

As standards for quality show, it is not possible to provide excellent programs for young children without creating partnerships with their families. Using the Epstein model of the six various types of family involvement, it is clear that one of the reasons the Family Resource Center offers an excellent environment for growing children is the attention to creating partnerships with their families. Although any program would obviously be enhanced by the presence of a professional specifically focused on family and community liaison, as was the case when this program began, the reality is that usually the center staff must do the work of creating partnerships. The vision and clear mission statement of the Family Resource Center guide them to creating the kind of place where families can thrive.

GORHAM HOUSE PRESCHOOL, GORHAM, MAINE

Employer-sponsored onsite child care is one of the family supports most desired by working parents. It is estimated that currently over 8,000 workplaces have onsite centers, a huge increase over the 204 that existed in 1982. Many of these employer-sponsored programs are large, serving hundreds of children and families in sites such as military bases and *Fortune* 500 companies. Others are smaller, preserving the sense of family that many parents want. Gorham House Preschool in Gorham, Maine, is one such program.

Located within the Gorham House nursing home and retirement community, the preschool is an integral part of life within the residence. The program is licensed for 15 3- to 5-year-old children, and children of staff members and others from the community are cared for in an NAEYC-accredited program. The unique location gives the children opportunities for onsite intergenerational experiences with the elderly residents. That, combined with a developmentally appropriate program, makes the Gorham House Preschool a very attractive choice for families in this small Maine town.

The preschool is housed in an attractive room just off the main corridor on the first floor of the modern building, with staff offices, kitchen, and dining room just down the hall. A large room used as a sitting area is also shared with the children when their activities need more space. The playground out front

FIGURE 18-13 When teachers share pictures, they help families enjoy the events in which their children have participated.
Courtesy Gorham House Preschool.

is easily viewed from residents' rooms and employee offices. The children's activities add vibrancy to the lives of all the adults in the community; the receptionist calls out to greet the children walking along the corridor to take the elevator up to the second floor Alzheimer's unit and join the residents for their regular 10:30 chance to sing and play together.

Parents accompany their children into the classroom, located just off the parking lot. The teachers have prepared a book of photographs of last week's visit by firefighters and fire truck and have left it right by the parents' sign-in area (Figure 18-13). Together parents and children enjoy reliving the event, as children excitedly point themselves out wearing the fire hat or sitting behind the wheel in the fire truck. The teacher joins in the relaxed conversation, and an easy transition into the classroom is effected. A mother reminds her son of another morning ritual, his signing in, which he does by turning his picture over in the pocket labeled with his name. Finally she leaves, with her child going over to the low window labeled the "Waving Window" for a last view of Mom going to work (Figure 18-14).

FIGURE 18-14 The "Waving Window" is a popular spot for children to say a last good-bye.
Courtesy Gorham House Preschool.

Communication between the two teachers and parents is valued at Gorham House Preschool. In addition to conversations at the beginning and ending of the day, parents are encouraged to telephone for longer conversations between 2:00 and 3:00 p.m. when most children are napping and teachers are freer to chat. The Family Handbook suggests that talking then will allow parents and teachers to discuss issues regarding children privately rather than in the children's presence. Parents are also given staff home telephone numbers and encouraged to call in the evening; the teacher/director comments that this has never been abused. A statement in the handbook emphasizes the confidential nature of any communication with families and the importance of all concerns and questions.

A white board is posted beside the door for parents to read as they help their children gather belongings. Daily events and interests listed there keep parents up to date. In addition, individual daily reports are sent home each day. A monthly newsletter and calendar help families know what is coming.

Conferences are held twice a year. The fall conference is voluntary, allowing families to focus on how children are adjusting and share any issues parents or teachers may feel need to be addressed. The second conference later in the year is structured around sharing work samples in children's portfolios for more formal assessment.

How does all this communication support the needs of individual children? The office manager at Gorham House, the parent of a recently enrolled 3-year-old, shared a story about how the close proximity of working parents to the preschool allowed teacher and parent to work closely on the child's adjustment.

> "Allyssa was having a tough time last week for some reason. Maybe she's had too many changes all at once. But with me being here, it made such a difference. For one thing, Sue just came right down to my office to discuss what was going on with Allyssa, asking what I thought was going on, how we were handling it at home. If she had been someplace away from where I work, I might have got a call from the teacher, but we were right into dealing with it right away. What Sue did, she suggested that Allyssa paint a picture and bring it right down the hall to my office. And that really seemed to help her, knowing that I was right down the hall."

Not only did this help Allyssa, but as the mother told the story, her relief at the support she and her daughter were receiving during their adjustment was obvious. She went on, "I love being able to peek in at her or watch her on the playground when she doesn't even know I'm looking. That way, I really get to see her as she is, without her being conscious of me watching. The other day, I just peeked in the door, and got a quick thumbs-up from the teacher, and then I felt great going back to work, knowing that she was doing fine."

One way children's beginnings are supported is by the director and family making individual decisions about timing for increasing the number of days they stay. All children are required to make at least one visit to Gorham House Preschool with their parent remaining with them during the visit to explore together. Home visits are offered but not required. Teachers support parents to stay as long as they need to and encourage up-front good-byes, believing that trust is important in the separation process.

The employee mother also reported her gratitude that the senior management of Gorham House was so supportive of parents interacting with the program, going on field trips and coming in for lunch or activities. Other employer supports for this child care situation include deducting child care costs directly from the paycheck, as well as a 25 percent discount for the cost of child care. The employer subsidizes the operation of the program by not charging for rent, utilities, and the like. Employers providing onsite child care centers nationwide report greater satisfaction and productivity of employees, producing less turnover and absenteeism, and more loyalty to the employers. When parents feel that their family needs are recognized, employers reap benefits as well as find it easy to recruit employees.

Another comment from the parent regarding the intergenerational program at Gorham House concerned the benefits to her older child, who has already gone through the onsite program:

> "I honestly believe that the experiences with the older people helped make her kinder, less judgmental. She is comfortable around all kinds of people, whether they need walkers or other equipment, look somewhat different, or whatever. I love having my child near me at work, but I also love her having these experiences in her daily life."

Every morning the children from the preschool join a group of "grand-friends" to sing and play. Many of the older people don't participate much, but they watch the children with evident pleasure. When the children arrive and depart, they go around the circle of their elders, greeting them and shaking hands. The groups of young and old are happy to be together. At least one pizza party is held each month, as well as other lunch functions through the year. Grandfriends are available to be with children who do not nap. The intergenerational aspects of the program offer enrichment for all.

The director has made a conscious decision not to put too many demands on family events for participation, feeling that working families need to protect their time at home with their children. There are three social events each year. The first, on the first Friday in September, is required of all families. This is a back-to-school barbecue, held on the playground, with the Gorham House cooks providing all the food. The purpose is for families to make friends with other families. Because many of the families have older siblings who are "graduates" of the program, this is a real coming together of the community. A second event is a Christmas party at which the children perform, parents have a cookie swap, and Santa Claus visits. And the final family activity of the year is a "growing-away" celebration in June for the children who are going on to other experiences. Here there is a candle ceremony, with nice things said about each child, then a chance to make a wish and blow out the candle.

The Family Handbook given to all families clarifies information to help make relationships clear and comfortable. In addition to philosophy and goals, parents are given information on operating hours (7:00 a.m.–5:30 p.m. Monday through Friday) and days off; late pickup policy ($1.00 per minute past 5:30 p.m.); outdoor play (need for appropriate clothing); toys from home (discouraged for good reasons and kept in cubbies if brought); absences (if parent does not call by 10 a.m., teachers will call parent to determine cause of absence); guidelines for healthful lunches (packed by parents); birthday parties (healthful snacks if parents wish to celebrate at school, mailed invitations to out-of-school parties); sick policies; and pre-enrollment guidance. In large letters the handbook states, "PARENTS ARE WELCOME AT ALL TIMES AT PRESCHOOL!"

This small employer-supported preschool program meets the needs of children and families beautifully and recognizes the importance of home and school connections for the well-being of children and their parents.

REFLECTIONS FOR JOURNAL ENTRIES

As you think about these programs and others you have experience with, what elements support positive teacher interaction, no matter what the structure, curriculum, or administration of the educational program? In other words, what attitudes and philosophy can you make part of your own practice, wherever you teach?

■■■ LINCOLN NURSERY SCHOOL, LINCOLN, MASSACHUSETTS

As discussed in Chapter 4, some of the earliest efforts to involve families in early childhood education were found within the parent cooperative preschool movement. The nursery school established more than 60 years ago in Lincoln, Massachusetts, continues to demonstrate how the philosophy and practices of a cooperative preschool benefit children and their parents alike. The mission statement from the family handbook makes explicit the school's central belief (see Figure 18-15):

> Lincoln Nursery School's mission is to provide a meaningful and stimulating first school experience for children by forming a cooperative partnership between committed, caring teachers and involved, loving parents. We strive to create an amiable environment, in which open communication and mutual respect for one another are highly valued, and children, families, and teachers feel at ease. We foster a sense of community and cooperative spirit from which children learn by example. We promote self-esteem, self-expression, and self-confidence in a safe and nurturing environment, enabling children to grow socially in friendships with children and adults (p. 2).

Such a statement describes an environment that appeals to those who strive for family collaboration. But how does this statement translate into practice, and what are the benefits for children and their families?

Lincoln is a small town within an hour's drive of Boston. Many of the young families in the community move to town as part of today's mobile society, following work opportunities, far from the support of extended family. Within the preschool, parents and children alike find a new kind of extended family, as members of a close and supportive community. The school offers a

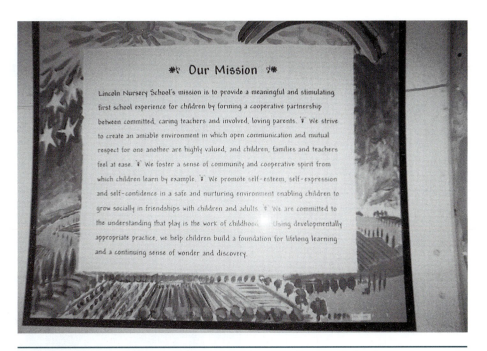

FIGURE 18-15 The mission statement of Lincoln Nursery School.

Courtesy Lincoln Nursery School.

half-day program, as well as extended days, for about 60 children, ages 2 through 5. Parents describe their involvement in the cooperative as a "two-way street: giving to the community and getting so much from it, for themselves and their children."

The school environment conveys the welcome of a warm neighborhood. A staff member greets each arriving parent and child at the gate to the playground (see Figure 18-16). In good weather some classes begin directly on the playground, while parents and siblings may linger to visit for a short time. The school's main entrance leads directly into a parent room, through which all arrivals pass—bright with large windows that overlook the playground and allow a glimpse beyond into the classrooms. Within the parent room, there are tables and chairs for parents to sit and chat, toys to occupy younger siblings, a mailbox for each family, and a large parent education board. Clearly this is a spot that parents can feel is their own. Every classroom has notes and pictures of activities for families to enjoy, as well as family pictures.

Parents are present in more than pictures, however; they are deeply involved in the workings of the school. In keeping with the philosophy of cooperative education, parents are involved in all aspects of the school: policy making, helping in the classroom, maintaining the school's facilities, providing feedback to the staff, fund-raising, and attending social events. Each family at the school is represented by a parent serving either on the board of directors—21 families out of 51 are represented—or on a standing committee. All families

FIGURE 18-16 Teachers greet every child and parent at the gate.
Courtesy Lincoln Nursery School.

who enroll their children make a basic commitment: to involve themselves in school administration and school maintenance and help in their child's classroom regularly.

As children enter the classrooms, they see their teachers and assistant teachers, as well as a parent helper each day. A parent from each family helps in the classroom approximately once every three weeks. No substitutions of nannies or even grandparents are allowed, although the school also has a backup parent helper system, where another parent steps in if the scheduled parent can't make it because of an emergency. (Each parent is scheduled for this backup system about three times a year, knowing the days they must be available far in advance.) Recognizing that every family has its own situation, some with two working parents and others with a parent at home full-time, the school tries to help parents balance their other responsibilities with their commitments to the school. Room parents consult with families as they create the schedule for the year. A member of the parent liaison committee helps parents find child care alternatives for younger siblings during parent help days. It is often easy to arrange a child care "swap" with another LNS family (see Figure 18-17).

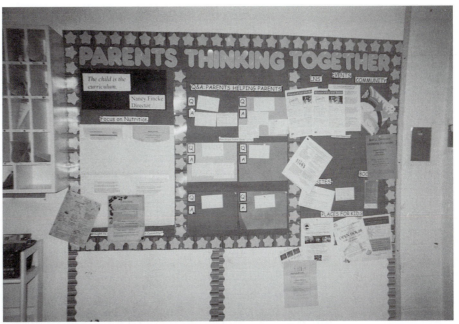

(a)

(b)

FIGURE 18-17 The parent room has a mailbox for each family and an informative parent board.
Courtesy Lincoln Nursery School.

Parents begin learning about their roles as a parent helper in a parent orientation with the teacher for their classroom group. They are eager to learn the mechanics of how they function in the classroom team, and are given important beginning information. They are told that their most important task is to play with the children, although they also are responsible for snack preparation, classroom cleanup, and generally assisting the teachers. They may also arrange to provide enrichment activities based on their own talents and interests. As the school year gets under way, there is a required workshop for parents to explore more specifics of the learning process. Parents learn appropriate language to use with children, how to observe ongoing activities, and how to support children's growing independence. Through role-plays representing typical scenarios involving children with such issues as turn taking and conflicts, parents practice their own growing skills.

One parent described this classroom participation as a parent helper as a "gift, to be able to participate, to have this unique opportunity to participate in my child's education." She went on to explain that her participation helps blur the line between home and school, so that now she can really talk with her children about life in the classroom. Another benefit, from the parent's point of view, is getting to know her children's friends, away from their parents, and have the children come to know her as an interesting person, "not just a Mom. Children develop a level of comfort with other adults, so it seems like one great big family, knowing each other in and out of school." Children learn to feel safe with many adults as helpful resources; parents express feeling safe as well, with many opportunities to build trust in the teachers and the director.

The director sees that the parents' classroom experiences make them more confident in their parenting, feeling supported in the decisions they make. These classroom contacts, as well as the work with parent peers in decision making, give parents the support they need at this stage in their lives with young children, when many parents feel lonely and isolated. Evidence of the way parents support each other is found on the parent bulletin board, where a question and answer section titled "Parents Helping Parents" allows parents to reach out to others for help in considering some of their parenting concerns (see Figure 18-18). Recent questions posted and receiving answers included these: "I am having a tough time getting my child out the door in the morning. Does anyone have advice?" "How can I support my child in making good friends?" "How can we expand our ways of greeting children besides simply noticing appearances? Any ideas?"

When teachers first begin to work in the cooperative setting, it can often feel overwhelming and exhausting. Everything they do is on display for the whole world to see. On the inevitable days when they make mistakes, parents are right there watching. But such opportunities to recover and move on give parents an important learning model to apply in their own situations. The collaboration benefits all participants.

Each classroom has a room parent, who serves as the primary liaison between the teacher, other parents, and the board. This individual arranges the

FIGURE 18-18 Parents ask questions and supply responses to others.
Courtesy Lincoln Nursery School.

schedule for parent helper and backup parent help days, welcomes new families, organizes feedback sessions and potluck dinners, and generally maximizes communication for all parents in the class. If any difficulties arise with parental participation in the classroom, the room parent works to solve them.

Another family commitment is to volunteer for one Saturday shift, either morning or afternoon, to work on maintenance-related projects in the fall or spring parent workdays, involving painting, cleaning, carpentry, and other maintenance tasks. Opportunities to complete jobs at home or at other times of the year may help parents who cannot attend workdays. This commitment is taken seriously, with a substantial fine for families that do not meet their obligation. A recent parent work project was to help erect the equipment on the newly designed playground (see Figure 18-19).

As mentioned earlier, each family also has a responsibility to participate in the administration of the school, either on the board of directors or on a parent committee. Recognizing that families have varied backgrounds and situations, the available jobs have wide-ranging time commitments. For example, the board of directors—composed of the officers and some committee chairs (enrollment, maintenance, fund-raising, staff search, welcoming/orientation, alumni relations, and room parents)—meets monthly. The steering committee, composed of president of the board, vice presidents of operations and programs, and treasurer, along with the director, meets biweekly and acts as a liaison between the staff and families to facilitate issues within the school. Other

FIGURE 18-19 A recent parent project was helping install the equipment on the redesigned playground.
Courtesy Lincoln Nursery School.

committees that may require less time include children's literature/parent resource center, refreshments, parent education, long-range planning, staff appreciation, manuals and forms, gardening, and social coordinator. Individuals may apply for particular tasks: supplies purchaser, legal adviser, seamstress, photographer, information management, class photo coordinator, design consultant, financial adviser, and assistant to the secretary. Each position and its time requirements are described fully in the comprehensive parent handbook.

A parent described her involvement with the board as an excellent way to enter the community and to make herself known within the school community (see Figure 18-20). "It gives us the potential for growth, being asked to do things we have never done before, or using our talents from earlier employment." She describes the example of a graphic designer who used her talents to design the school stationery and change the appearance of the enrollment package, as well as the parent who learned new skills as head of the maintenance committee.

The director describes the complex collaboration of all the parents as a kind of organic process. "You get a group of people together and see what issues bubble up." It is not easy to agree with everything that everyone else is doing, or to be fair to the wishes and viewpoints of parents who become so passionately involved with ideas involving their children. In a cooperative environment parents come to feel that they can effect a change, and they

FIGURE 18-20 Working with other parents on committees gives parents new experiences and support.
Courtesy Lincoln Nursery School.

often become quite emotional in arguing their points of view. The board strives to make sure everyone believes they have been heard, even though finding a balance may become a challenge. Another challenge is to make parents aware of confidentiality for children and families; parents are instructed not to engage in inappropriate "parking lot conversations" about what is going on in the classroom. Real ownership of responsibilities and privileges does not make for simple decision making but does demonstrate the true principles of the partnership in a cooperative preschool.

Even though parents participate regularly in their children's classrooms, they still have formal conferences with the teachers twice a year. Parent conferences are held in the fall and the spring. School is closed on those days, but child care is provided for children and their siblings while parents are in their conferences. During the fall conference teachers learn more about children from their parents and share preliminary observations within the school environment. At the spring conference teachers share a complete developmental assessment, given parents a written summary of the developmental profile and placing a copy in the child's record.

Answer to Questions, the parent handbook, is a complete description of all parent responsibilities, as well as the general philosophy and workings of the school. Parents can read detailed comments under headings such as these:

- Parent commitment: classroom parent helper and bringing snacks those days; backup parent helper; maintenance workday; serving on committee or board; supporting fund-raising activities; attending orientation meeting, class development discussions, and a variety of other events throughout the year; completing annual program evaluation.

- Teacher–parent communication: two parent conferences; class development discussions; and telephone tree.
- What happens when you enroll in LNS: steps in enrollment process.
- What happens before school starts: a home visit by the teacher; a lemonade party at the school; an orientation for parents; a class play date scheduled by the room parent.
- What happens when you bring your child to school: supplies and clothing requirements; tips for arriving and leaving.
- What happens when school is dismissed; pickup methods and responsibilities.
- What happens when you participate in extended day: signing up; lunch.
- What happens when you parent help: schedule; responsibilities and school rules; suggestions for interaction.
- What happens when you are the backup parent helper.
- When to call the school: sickness; lateness arriving or picking up; informing the school about the family situation.

Such a complete information guide helps parents learn how best to support the school and participate comfortably.

What is the net effect of such intensive family involvement? Parents who have had children go on to the public schools speak of the education they have received in how to be involved partners in their children's education, noting that parents who came from the cooperative nursery school continue to participate in their children's primary classrooms and communicate closely with the teachers. One mother speaks of feeling a loss—sadness at not being asked to be involved in the same way in her child's life in elementary school. "Here at LNS everything regarding our children is our business. In the public school, I get to be told academically what is going on, but my role is not made clear to me." Surely the model of the cooperative preschool demonstrates both parents' desire to be involved in their children's education, and the benefits to all when they collaborate with early childhood education professionals. Lifelong patterns of partnership with teachers are being set.

SUMMARY

From these accounts of four different programs, it is evident that there are multiple methods of working with families. The common thread is the philosophy that families deserve support and respect as they undertake the massive and vital tasks of parenting, and that teachers can work most effectively with children when they work closely with families. Each center has worked to find the particular methods that best suit its program and its specific goals, needs, and perception of the needs of the families served. There are some things that work well; in general, methods of working to ensure the fullest communication possible are important. The challenge is always there as teachers and schools continue to reach out to the families they serve.

STUDENT ACTIVITIES FOR FURTHER STUDY

1. Visit a local child care program or preschool half-day program. Arrange to interview the director, a teacher, and a parent about their perceptions of how the parent–teacher relationship has been developed and how each participant feels about the degree of communication established. Learn what methods of communication exist and how parents become involved in the program. How do your findings compare with the descriptions of the four programs in the chapter? Visit a local elementary school. Find out what methods of communication exist and how families are involved in the schools. How does this compare with the preschool or child care program?

2. Draw a chart with a column for each of the four programs described. Summarize the information given in the descriptions under the headings Philosophy of Working with Parents; Orientation Procedures; Communication Methods; Parent Involvement in the Program; and Parents as Decision Makers. What similarities do you discover? What differences?

3. Draw up a similar chart for the school where you are involved as a student, or where you work, and for the schools you visited in Question 1. What similarities do you find with the chart of the four programs from the chapter? What differences?

CASE STUDY

After reading the descriptions of the early childhood programs in this chapter, consider the following questions:

1. What factors seem to create an atmosphere that welcomes all families?

2. What practices foster regular communication in a variety of forms?

3. How is respect for individual families and circumstances conveyed?

4. Name three or four specific practices that you would like to incorporate into a program in which you are involved.

REVIEW QUESTIONS

1. Using the chart you drew in question 2 of the Student Activities for Further Study, compare and contrast the four programs regarding the ways each involves parents in the programs and in relationships with classroom teachers.

2. List those components and philosophies the four programs have in common.

SUGGESTIONS FOR FURTHER READING

Note: Due to the nature of this chapter, the information was gained firsthand by interviews and by reading handouts from each center. Students may be interested in reading descriptions of several other types of programs, including the ways they involve parents. Such descriptions may be found in Driscoll, A. (1995). *Cases in early childhood education: Stories of programs and practices.* Needham Heights, MA: Allyn & Bacon.

REFERENCES

Dunlap, K. (1996). Supporting and empowering families through cooperative preschool education. *Social Work and Education, 18*(4), 210–220.

———. (1997). Family empowerment: One outcome of cooperative preschool education. *Child Welfare, 76*(4), 501–518.

Epstein, J., Coates, L., Salinas, K., Sanders, M., & Simon, B. (1997). *School, family, and community partnerships: Your handbook for action.* Thousand Oaks, CA: Corwin.

HELPFUL WEB SITES

http://www.lakewoodpreschool.com
    This is the Web site for Lakewood Preschool Cooperative.
http://family.fgcu.edu.
    This is the Web site for the Family Resource Center.
http://www.mainecare.com/gorhamhouse/commons/preschool
    This is the Web site for Gorham House preschool.
http://www.lincolnnurseryschool.org
    This is the Web site for the Lincoln Nursery School.

Additional resources for this chapter can be found on the Online Companion to accompany this text at www.earlychilded.delmar.com. This supplemental material includes frequently asked questions; chapter outlines to be used as study guides; scenarios that both encourage large and small group discussions and provoke new thoughts and ideas; and chapter resources, including chapter summaries, interactive questions, Web links, and Web activities. In addition, forms from the text are available for download.

APPENDIX

Resource Directory

Please note that the mailing addresses and telephone numbers for national organizations may change frequently. The Web addresses, which are found at the end of the relevant chapters, are more likely to remain constant. Also, when looking for particular organizations that you do not find here, use an Internet search engine, such as google.com or yahoo.com, and type in the name of the organization or general category of resource. The Web site will usually also give current mail contact information.

Abuse and Neglect

International Society for the Prevention of Child Abuse and Neglect 245 W. Roosevelt Rd., Building 6, Suite 39, West Chicago, IL 60185; (630)876-6913

National Clearing House on Child Abuse and Neglect Information Children's Bureau, Administration on Children, Youth, and Families, 370 L'Enfant Promenade SW, Washington, DC 20447; (800)394-3366

Parents Anonymous, Inc. 675 W. Foothill Blvd., Suite 220 Claremont, CA 91711; (909)621-6184

Prevent Child Abuse America 200 S. Michigan Ave. 13th Floor Chicago, IL 60604; (312)663-3520

Advocacy Organizations

Action Alliance for Children 1201 Martin Luther King Jr. Way Oakland, CA 94612; (510)444-7136

Child Care Action Campaign 330 Seventh Ave. New York, NY 10001; (212)239-0138

Children Now 1212 Broadway, 5th Floor Oakland, CA 94612; (510)763-1974

The Children's Defense Fund 25 E. St. NW Washington, DC 20001; (202)628-8787

Child Welfare League of America 40 First St. NW, 3rd Floor Washington, DC 20001; (202)638-2952

National Association of Child Advocates 1522 K St. NW, Suite 600 Washington, DC 20005; (202)289-0777

Community/Work/Family Links

Families and Work Institute 267 Fifth Ave., Floor 2, New York, NY 10016

Work and Family Information Center The Conference Board 845 Third Ave. New York, NY 10022; (212)339-0345

Family Diversity

Intercultural Development Research Association 5835 Callaghan, Suite 350 San Antonio, TX 78228; (210)444-1710

National Adoption Information Clearinghouse Children's Bureau, Administration on Children, Youth, and Families, 370 L'Enfant Promenade SW Washington, DC 20447; (888)251-0075

National Association for Bilingual Education 1030 15th St. NW Washington, DC 20002; (202)898-1829

653

Parents without Partners 1650 S. Dixie Highway, Ste 510 Boca Raton, FL 33432; (561)391–8833

Stepfamily Association of America 650 J St., Suite 205 Lincoln, NE 68508; (800)735-0239

Families of Children with Special Needs

Council for Exceptional Children 1110 N. Glebe Rd., Suite 300 Arlington, VA 22201; (888)CEC-SPED

Federation for Children with Special Needs 1135 Tremont St., Suite 420 Boston, MA 02120; (617)236-7210

National Information Center for Children and Youth with Disabilities 1155 15th St. NW, Suite 1002, P.O. Box 1492 Washington, DC 20013; (800)695-0285

Family Support

Family Support America, formerly Family Resource Coalition 205 West Randolph St., Suite 222, Chicago, IL 60606; (312)338-0900

National Council on Family Relations 3989 Central Ave. NE, Suite 550 Minneapolis, MN 55421; (888)781-9931

For and about Fathers

American Coalition for Fathers & Children 1718 M St. NW, Suite 187 Washington, DC 20036; (800)978-DADS

The Fatherhood Project c/o Families and Work Institute 267 Fifth Ave., Floor 2, New York, NY 10016; (212)465-2044

National Center for Fathering PO # 413888, Kansas City, MO 64141; (800)93-DADS

National Fatherhood Initiative 101 Lake Forest Blvd., Suite 360 Gaithersburg, Maryland 20877; (301)948-0599

Organizations for Parents

National Parenting Association 1841 Broadway, Room 808, New York, NY 10023; (212)315-2333

National Partnership for Women and Families 1875 Connecticut Ave. NW, Suite 710 Washington, DC 20009; (202)986-2600

Parent Education

Active Parenting Today 1955 Vaughn Rd. NW, Suite 108, Kennesaw, GA 30144; (800)825-0060

AVANCE Family Support and Education Programs Hasbro National Family Resource Center Mercedes Perez de Colon 301 S. Frio, Suite 310 San Antonio, TX 78207; (210)270-4630

Center for Improvement of Child Caring 11331 Ventura Blvd., Suite 103 Studio City, CA 91604; (818)980-0903

Parents as Teachers National Center, Inc. 2228 Ball Drive, St. Louis MO 63146

Parent Effectiveness Training Gordon Training International 531 Stevens Ave. West Solana Beach, CA 92075; (800)628-1197

Parent/Teacher Involvement

Alliance for Parental Involvement in Education P.O. Box 59 East Chatham, NY 12060; (518)392-6900

Center on Families, Communities, Schools and Children's Learning The Johns Hopkins University 3505 N. Charles St. Baltimore, MD 21218

The Home and School Institute 1500 Massachusetts Ave. NW Washington, DC 20005; (202)466-3633

National Coalition for Parent Involvement in Education 3929 Old Lee Highway, Suite 91-A Fairfax, VA 22030; (703)359-8973

National Parent Teacher Association (PTA) 1090 Vermont Ave. NW, Suite 1200, Washington, DC 20005; (202)289-6790

Professional Early Childhood Organizations

National Association for the Education of Young Children 1509 16th St. NW Washington, DC 20036; (800)424-2460

National Black Child Development Institute 1023 15th Ave. NW Washington, DC 20002; (202)833-2220

GLOSSARY

A

active listening Technique of sensitively picking up on a speaker's verbal and nonverbal messages and reflecting back the total message for the speaker's verification.

advocate One who defends or espouses a cause.

affect Demonstration of feelings.

androgynous Having the characteristics of both sexes.

assertive/democratic With the weight of predictable authority. See also *authoritative*.

attachment The strong, affectionate, mutual tie formed in the first two years following birth and enduring over time.

authentic Genuine, real.

authoritarian Requiring complete obedience to authority.

authoritative See *assertive/democratic*.

B

blended family A family created by the coming together of previously existing families or parts of them.

C

Code of Ethics Statement adopted by the National Association for the Education of Young Children (NAEYC) in 1989, revised in 2005, to provide guidelines for ethical behavior of professionals.

collaborative Working with one another.

colorblindedness Professed unawareness of skin color of others.

cultural capital Comfort and familiarity with customs and demands of one's culture.

cultural mores Customs and beliefs associated with a particular culture.

culturally assaultive Behaviors that attack the culture of another by ignoring, failing to accept and respect, demeaning, or attacking the behaviors and beliefs of another.

culture The various understandings, traditions, and guidance of the groups to which we all belong; the ways of living developed by a social group and transmitted to succeeding generations; the social backgrounds that imbue children with particular forms of knowledge, values, and expectations for behavior.

D

daily news flash Brief written news of the day posted for families.

deficit model Working from the perspective of being inadequate or inferior.

democratic models Models in which power is shared.

demographics The statistical data of a human population.

dendritic Branching process of neurons or brain cells.

developmental tasks Appropriate accomplishments at specific stages of development.

developmentally appropriate programs Programs that base their decisions about curriculum, care, routines, and guidance on knowledge about development of individual children and the needs of their families.

diversity State of being varied, as by family structure, race, religion, socioeconomic class, primary language, ethnic background, and so on.

dominant culture The culture that is most influential in a society, both numerically and by power of ideas and behaviors.

dysfunctional Impaired in function.

E

easing-in A schedule of gradually increasing the amount of time a child spends in a classroom so the child does not spend a full period at the beginning.

ecology Interaction between the individual and the environment.

empathic Identifying with feelings of another.

empathize To identify with or experience the feelings of another individual.

empowerment Enabling, strengthening.

expertise Special skill or knowledge in a particular field.

extended family Kinship group consisting of parents, their children, and close relatives.

F

family-centered Focusing on children and parents as a unit, with the parents becoming active in their children's development—not teaching parents and children in separate and distinct programs.

G

gatekeeping Keeping others away from the child, either physically or by subtle interference.

H

High/Scope Model Early childhood curriculum based on principle of children as active learners who plan, carry out, and reflect on learning choices during free choice periods, and small group teacher-led experiences to help children focus on key experiences.

home-based programs Programs in which a family's home is the primary location for delivery of services to the child and/or the parents.

I

I-messages Verbal expression of an individual's emotional response to a specific situation.

intervention Process of interfering with particular circumstances so as to change them.

J

jargon Vocabulary peculiar to a particular profession or group.

L

latchkey child care Children caring for themselves, at home, after school.

literacy activities Activities that promote development of oral communication skills and understanding of print communication.

M

mandate An authoritative order or command; something that must be done.

microsystem Small part of a system that forms a unified whole; related to children, bounds of a child's world, such as home, school, Grandma's house, or the like.

N

nuclear family A social unit composed of parents and children.

nurturing Encouraging, supporting, caring, nourishing.

O

one-way communication Communication sent from school to inform families without expectation of response.

open-ended questions With no fixed answer; unrestricted.

P

paraphrasing Restating in slightly different words what another has said.

parent cooperative nursery schools Nursery schools in which parents participate along with paid professionals, or are involved in decision making and maintenance of the school.

partiality Tendency to favor one person over another.

parting ritual Expected behaviors and activities repeated each day when saying good-bye.

pedagogical issues Issues related to teaching.

permissive Having a low level of demands or expectations for children's behavior; tolerating behavior outside of bounds; a hands-off style of interaction.

professionalism Display of professional character, spirit, or methods.

R

rationality Thinking based on reason.

readiness Characteristics, skills, and dispositions that make a successful student; particularly used when talking about moving into kindergarten.

reflecting Giving back to a speaker words that convey the listener's impression of the speaker's meaning.

reframing Shifting from a negative perspective to a perspective that recognizes strengths by choosing different words and frames of reference.

resilience Ability to spring back, adjust, or adapt to stress, misfortune, or change.

resource file File of information about each family and ways they can be potential resources for a classroom.

S

sandwiching Presenting an issue of concern with positive statements preceding and following the concern.

separation anxiety Feelings of sadness and discomfort experienced by children and adults when apart from one another. Separation anxiety is most common in children under 4 years.

social capital Available resources provided by efforts, knowledge, and relationships of people.

spontaneity Acting from natural impulses.

T

TANF Temporary Aid to Needy Families—the welfare reform legislation passed in 1996.

Touchpoints model Model developed by T. Berry Brazelton to support families at key points of disruption during their children's development.

turf Area of familiarity over which one asserts authority.

two-way communication Communication designed to elicit dialogue between home and school.

INDEX